ndy 12/97

S

TANZANIA ON TUESDAY

TANZANIA ON TUESDAY

Writing by American Women Abroad

Edited by
Kathleen Coskran & C. W. Truesdale

A New Rivers Abroad Book

NEW RIVERS PRESS

S

The publication of *Tanzania on Tuesday* has been made possible by a generous grant from the Metropolitan Regional Arts Council (from an appropriation from the Minnesota Legislature).

Additional support has been provided by the Elmer and Eleanor J. Andersen Foundation, General Mills, Liberty State Bank, the McKnight Foundation, the Minnesota State Arts Board (through an appropriation from the Minnesota Legislature), the Star Tribune/Cowles Media Company, the Tennant Company Foundation, the United Arts Council, and the contributing members of New Rivers Press. New Rivers Press also wishes to acknowledge the Minnesota Non-Profits Assistance Fund for its invaluable support.

Tanzania on Tuesday has been manufactured in the United States of America for New Rivers Press, 420 North 5th Street, Suite 910, Minneapolis, MN 55401 in a first edition of 3000 copies.

Acknowledgments

Andrea Wright Alemazkoor's "Iran: Private Perceptions" was originally published in somewhat different form and as a serial in the Laredo *Morning Times*.

Melanie Braverman's "The Memory of Unusual Things" was originally published in the "Place, Displacement, Travel" issue of *Five Fingers Review* (#10).

Ruth Moon Kempher's "Four *Viuda* Stories" are excerpted from *The Loca Viuda*, first published by Rose Shell Press.

Geraldine Kennedy's "A Grain of Sand" is excerpted from *Harmattan: A Journey Across the Sahara*, published by Clover Park Press (Copyright 1994 by Geraldine Kennedy). Used by permission of the author.

Margaret Todd Maitland's "The Dome of Creation" was originally published in the *Hungry Mind Review*.

Anita Mathias's "Kalighat" was published in *New Letters*, Volume 59, Number 2, in 1993.

Karen L. McDermott's "Margaret" was originally published in the Geneva *Post*.

Judy Ray's "Shiva Was the First Dancer" is drawn from three chapters in her memoir, *Jaipur Sketchbook: Impressions of India*, Chariton Review Press, 1991.

Gretchen Scherer's "Lounge Girls" was published in a slightly different version in *Hurricane Alice*, Spring 1995.

Susan M. Tiberghien's "Red Geraniums" previously appeared in *The Dickinson Magazine* and in *Offshoots, Writing in Geneva*.

Catherine Watson's "Tibet: The Search for Shangri-La" was originally published in the Minneapolis *Star Tribune*.

Contents

ASIA

Introduction

TANZANIA ON TUESDAY is the second of three anthologies of women's travel writing that New Rivers has been publishing since 1991 when *The House on Via Gombito* was brought out. The third anthology will be published in the spring of 1998.

The House on Via Gombito is the most successful anthology New Rivers has ever published and was more widely reviewed than any single New Rivers Press book up to that time. It was reprinted in 1992 and will be soon reprinted again.

In my introduction to that first volume, I said that:

> The idea for this anthology came about a long time ago at the Loeb Student Center (at the annual bookfair) in New York City. . . .
> One afternoon, a young woman came up to my table carrying a large black portfolio full of interesting drawings and a few essays she had published accompanied by her own art work. She identified herself as Michelle Anderson. I was struck immediately by the quality of her work and the degree of craftsmanship it displayed. But what really fascinated me were the stories about her wanderings in Africa she began to tell me. I asked her to leave some stuff with me and come back the next day.
> Much as I liked her art work, I was intrigued and excited by her story and by its potentialities. She began telling me how she had gone to Europe and Asia on her own when she was barely twenty and had spent two or three years moving from place to place as her spirit led her. She had lived, she told me, on an island off the coast of Kenya and had explored among the veiled Muslim women there the mysterious world of African magic and ritual. I knew that some day I would try to get her to write out those stories for me and that I would publish them in one form or another.
> It was then that the idea for a travel anthology began to form in the shadows of my mind—a natural one for me, since I love traveling (when I can afford it) and the perspectives it has always given me on my own country.

Tanzania on Tuesday grew directly out of the success of *The House on Via Gombito* and from our knowledge that a great deal of very good contemporary writing by American women on travel existed beyond what we were able to include in that first volume. In fact, the response to a call for manuscript submissions to the projected second anthology in the series was so great and of such high quality that the co-editors decided that New Rivers would do a third such anthology as soon as possible after *Tanzania on Tuesday*.

Some of the authors in this new anthology appeared in *The House on Via Gombito*, but most of them did not and are new to us. Some of them are very well known, but many are not and a few have never been published at all in this country. In this respect, *Tanzania on Tuesday* is typical of all the anthologies that New Rivers publishes and is entirely consistent with our long-standing mission. (Rhianon Payne, whose three little and extremely funny pieces on traveling in England appeared in *The House on Via Gombito*, told me afterwards that this was the first writing she had published anywhere. Another piece of hers—on working in Japan—will be included in the 1998 anthology.)

～

The motives that drive American women to travel and sometimes even to live abroad are as complicated and individual as the women themselves. What these women have in common, however, is—though ultimately less important than the individuality that characterizes all of this writing—still of some significance. In all of these pieces, there is a sense of encountering a strange, unfamiliar culture on a one-to-one basis that at once characterizes these writers and the culture(s) they are exploring and discovering.

Tanzania on Tuesday is a testament to American women—the broadness of their interests, their imaginations, and their willingness, often, to endure hardship and even suffering in pursuit of these journeys of discovery.

At first glance, the title piece by Jeanne D'Haem ("*Tanzania on Tuesday*") is merely an account of a vacation trip she took (as a Peace Corps Volunteer in Ethiopia) from Nairobi, Kenya, to the famous Ngorongoro Gorge in Tanzania—a place she never gets to in her essay, though she told me recently that she and her companions did actually visit it on that trip. For D'Haem, the journey itself is what mattered and the bizarre, surrealist things that happened to her on the way—like playing the black market money game in Nairobi, or almost being overrun by a huge herd of wildebeest, or her and her companion, hitchhiking their way across Kenya and Tanzania and being picked up by a pair of famous English archæologists named Leakey that neither of them had heard of. Like most of the first-rate writers I know of, she brings that journey into a region I have never visited so vividly alive and immediate that I feel I have been there myself—in her company. This is something I have seldom experienced on any of the many TV nature programs that cover the same region.

Similarly, Lavonne Mueller—a playwright from Iowa—describes in rich detail a trip to India she made in connection with the production of her play on Nehru. It is not only a fascinating description of the intricacies of getting a play produced over there and the public reaction to it, but a detailed account of the India she encountered in Bombay and New Delhi. Like D'Haem, what makes her writing so interesting is that combination of a very strong character with the sometimes but not always alien culture of another country. Here is Mueller's description of street life in Bombay:

> I go shopping in the late afternoon. I pass men fixing betal leaf cones, women dusting the steps of a sweets shop with dirty rags. Street photographers display their smiling victims on a sandwich board. An old astrologer with his cards carefully placed before him on a blanket tugs at my skirt. A Muhammedan barber smiles at me, his razor and scissors on a small crate, his profession clearly written in red Hindustani letters. Everywhere are

leather handbags, jeweled elephants, colorful silks, Tibetan brassware, bracelets of agate. Vendors hawk their wares with slow natural movements, stepping calmly over stagnant drains, rotten grain, fresh cow-dung, and urine. I am persistently followed until I have a dragon's tail of beggars following me. I am warned not to give money or I will be mobbed and suffocated. To escape, I hail a rickshaw; the old driver sweats in the sun as he pedals to keep me and the rickshaw from bouncing out of control. His skin is like dried banana peels.

For some of these writers the experiences described were acutely disturbing—but for very different reasons. Nancy Raeburn, for instance (who supplied us with two splendid chapters from her later New Rivers book, *Mykonos*, in *The House on Via Gombito*) describes her return to that Greek island some eleven years after she had lived and worked there for a year as a painter. She had expected a happy, even triumphant, return only to discover that changes brought on by the increasing tourist traffic overwhelmed the place she remembered so vividly. Most of the people she had known were dead or dying and most of the little villages had been overrun by tourists and attractions designed to loosen them from their money.

In "Rita's House," Anne Panning describes her sojourn for two years as a teacher in the Phillipines and the house she rented there whose owner, Rita, was forever intruding on her privacy and eventually taking over the whole place:

> Then one morning I woke up to the sound of my own pump handle squeaking back and forth. Jumping out of bed, I peered out, and saw Rita back behind my house, rinsing little Ryan's little ragged T-shirts and hanging them on the rusty line. She filled up all the rusty lines and the banana leaves with their clothes, and began to do this regularly. Then it was the food stand in front of my house. Her house. It started out with a small wooden table where she lay bags of fried corn, Skyflakes crackers, hard green guavas, garlic peanuts locked in tiny brown sacks, stalks of fresh sugarcane, and Stork menthol candies. This soon drew a crowd, and hordes of children emerged, leaned their elbows on the table, deciding, then hung around all afternoon. Then their mothers came, and smoked, gawked at me, looked in my windows, laughed at my height, said I was fat. Then the grandmothers. I felt encroached upon; the store was growing. Rita banged around in my yard at the crack of dawn, and stayed until dark. When she started cooking bloody-bloody and ox tongue for the rice farmers passing by, I knew I was in trouble. No more quiet. No more alone.

Joan K. Peters, in "Foreign Exchange," describes a similarly harrowing and unpleasant experience—a "vacation" trek in Nepal into the Himalayas for which she hired her own guide and porters. Her essay turns out to be not so much about the gorgeous mountains and the views she had of them as it is about her own horrible difficulties with the group of men she had hired for the trip. And Catherine Watson, travel editor of the Minneapolis *Star Tribune*, describes in "Tibet: The Search for Shangri-La" an equally harrowing trip she took with a tour group through the same mountains into Tibet. (She started off her trip ill from dysentery and then altitude sickness.) But in the end, she achieves, if not the mystical experience many travelers to that ancient civilization expect to have, something fairly close to it:

My mother had died, and in the emptiness that followed, all I wanted was to be far away from home.
Travel has curative powers for me, and I turned to it as a healing drug.
I craved a place so distant and so difficult that it would take full concentration to survive the present moment, with nothing left for the future or the past.
I chose Tibet. I wanted escape and epiphany; I got dust and distraction. In the end, they were almost the same, and I was grateful.

Watson goes on to present us not only with a sense of what Tibet is like today, but something of the history of that remote land before and after the Dali Lhama fled from the Chinese invaders many years ago.

Cheri Register's "My Pseudonymous Life" also presents us with a great deal of contemporary history of the feminist movement in Sweden. "Between 1968 and 1982," she says, "I made seven trips to Sweden, varying in length from three weeks to six months." She got to know many of these women very well in the course of time—long enough in some cases that—like the characters in a novel—we can see them mature, age, and come near death. This is particularly true of Karin Westman Berg, "the mother of women's studies" in Sweden, in whose apartment she stayed (and vividly describes). By the end of the piece, this extraordinary woman has grown old and diseased and no longer recognizes anyone. Register's essay is shot through with the immediacy of her Swedish visits and the poignancy and sadness of her deep impressions of that country and its people:

"Karin would probably be happy to see you," Barbro said, "even if she doesn't know who you are." It was not Alzheimer's but a form of senile dementia that didn't affect her mood. "We bring her along sometimes to lectures and introduce her as the mother of women's studies and everyone applauds. She seems to like that, but we have to be careful that she doesn't wander away." She still lived in her apartment, alone except for a nursing assistant who came in to help her dress and fix meals. "See her for your own sake," Barbro urged, but my phone calls to Karin's sister, now her guardian, went unanswered. I considered taking the elevator up and simply ringing the doorbell of the apartment, hoping I might stir a memory that had not yet hardened over. We never made it up the hill. . . . As the subway passed Ostermalmstorg Station, I pointed out Siri Derkert's wall etching, where the name of Karin Westman Berg is preserved beside Sappho, Virginia Woolf, and Simone de Beauvoir.

～

I trust that these quotations and discussions of some of the writers included in *Tanzania on Tuesday* will give the reader a taste for the richness, variety—and poignancy—of all that has been included here. My co-editor Kathleen Coskran and I hope—in the words I ended my introduction to *The House on Via Gombito* with—"you will enjoy this immense collective journey as much as we have putting it all together. For us this has been a real trip, an adventure of discovery in itself."

Preface

A YOUNG WOMAN graduate student in a class at the University of Minnesota held up a copy of that morning's *Minnesota Daily*. The front page article told the incredible story of a young guy bicycling across Central America. I had read the story and had been impressed with his accomplishment—the hardships he'd endured, the adventures he'd encountered, the stamina and courage he'd found in often trying situations.

"I was with him," the graduate student said.

"You mean you know him?" I said.

"Yes, I know him," she said impatiently. "I biked with him."

"Here in Minnesota?"

"No! In Central America. On this trip." She waved the paper at me.

In the long interview in the *Daily*, the young adventurer made no mention of a companion, never used the pronoun *we*, never admitted that a woman had ridden with him, all day, every day.

That singular male perspective is true of much of the travel writing that predated *The House on Via Gombito*, New Rivers's first anthology of the writing of North American women abroad. The great travel narratives, the odysseys, the fiction in exotic settings, were in the voices of men, with the assumption that the women were left home nesting. With Conrad on the river, Stevenson on his donkey, Lawrence in the desert, Theroux on the train, there is no trace of women, other than "native" women. The writer is on the move, pulled by the seduction of the exotic and the expectation of adventure that will test his true mettle. He is also alone. Not just unaccompanied, but without significant human encounters. He describes the "natives" but doesn't make human connections; his role may have a tinge of the anthropological, but it seldom probes deeper.

Writers who love to travel often suggest a distinction between the traveler and the tourist, elevating the true traveler to the loftier position. The tourist skims the surface of countries and capitals, flits from the Acropolis to the Eiffel Tower to Mount Fuji in fifteen days, but the traveler moves slowly, with respect and understanding for people and places; the traveler is an artist, the tourist, a voyeur.

Tanzania on Tuesday suggests a third category: she who lives and works abroad. Many of the heroines of these narratives are Peace Corps Volunteers, nurses, writers, waitresses, scholars, teachers. The original title of two of the pieces in this collection was "Lost in Translation," one set in China, the other in the Netherlands, by writers who knew nothing of each other. The coincidence of that title speaks to the focus on communication and relationships in these pieces. These heroines are neither traveler nor tourist, but North American women living and working abroad, struggling to understand and to make themselves understood across the invisible barrier of language and culture. I say invisible, because the obviousness of the difference can make us feel we understand it, can lead us to stereotypes. These writers have lived beyond the stereotype and know the challenge of continually being aware that their lives abroad lack nuance because of all that slides through the cracks of language and culture.

So, these stories are not travel narratives so much as encounters with the exotic, with the other, with the person who is not like us. The great contribution of *Tanzania on Tuesday* is the exploration of relationships in a woman's voice. There is adventure aplenty—the title story is a prime example—but many of these stories and essays focus on the transformation that occurs when we connect with a person whose life experience is profoundly different from ours. At the end of Nancy Kelly's moving story, "*Sal Si Puedes*," the narrator suggests that her Panamanian friend come to the States with her until the violent demonstrations stop, until things blow over.

> "Until things blow over?" I see the flash of color come to her cheeks as she draws her mouth into a tight line. . . . "You *norteamericanos* think it's so easy. When things get bad you think we should all go and live in your country where it's so much better."

In this collection we discover that twentieth-century North American women, whoever they are, travel from these affluent shores with an unconscious assumption of comfort and plenty. Even those who consciously refrain from participating in the commercial extremes carry the complexity and jangle of American culture with them. Women who can eat anything and sleep anywhere are transformed by the relationships they forge in China, Indonesia, South Africa, and Turkey.

The exotic has the pull of easy entertainment: show up and something you're not expecting will happen. Travel provides a classic escape route, but these writers discover that what you're running from always finds you. What is revealed so powerfully here is the collective experience and intelligence of forty-seven North American women abroad. They go to India, Wales, China, Italy, Morocco to see the world, but what they see the most clearly at the end of the journey is themselves.

Many are about coming home, about finding some essential part of themselves in the place they or their mothers left as young women. Anita Witt in "Home/*Heimat*" writes of her annual visit to her mother in Germany and the pull of "loyalty to opposite shores."

> Sometimes I feel as if my life in the United States had been like swimming easily on the surface of a river, but in Germany I am pulled here and there by deep and invisible currents. Is this what it means to be home, to see people who have known my parents, who tell me stories of my childhood, who speak that familiar dialect? . . .

These stories are more likely to grapple with the essential connections of life than with the mountains climbed and the deserts crossed. Linda Lappin, in perhaps the most sensuous piece in the collection, discovers the ability simply to be present to life in "A Quiet Life in the Country." The narrators in these stories and essays are present in luxurious detail and their connections to place and people run wide and deep. Here is not the lone cyclist battling the elements, but the alert sojourner, looking for connections and continually being surprised by them. Rather than a collection of narratives about life in China, life in Italy, life in India, *Tanzania on Tuesday* is a collection of stories about life. Choose any of these pieces to lose yourself to the seductive allure of travel. All the exotic detail and suspense of the unknown is there, but you'll also find yourself nodding sagely with these wonderful writers and murmuring, "Yes, that's how life is."

AFRICA

A Grain of Sand

THE ONLY TIES now were those among the five of us. We rode for several hours out of Zinder without speaking. Contained in our island *camion*, the great roaring truck of the desert, we savored our independence. We felt vital, whole, strong. We had done it, were doing it. We were crossing the great Sahara Desert because we wanted to. We had come so far with the help of many others to be sure. But at that moment, on the top of the *camion*, over the infamous, indeterminate *piste*, we felt the great power of having done it ourselves and we relished it.

This was the *piste*, seen and felt, but ever eluding definition. It seemed to be anything as long as it was less than a road. It varied from bone-rattling rocks to frighteningly soft sand. At best it bore the imprint of tires of previous travelers— a lifeline stretching to infinity, before and behind. But when the marks in the dust have been blown off by the wind, the *piste* is a wish, a hope, is nothing.

∼

The other passengers were two men; one an Arab the color of sand, the other black, but Arabic-speaking. Both were turbaned and barefooted. The dark one, never without his worn brown overcoat, was the driver's assistant, the "greaser," as they were called. Whenever the *camion* began to slow down he was over the side, running along to see to any problem. When a wheel spun in sand, it was he who dashed forward to shovel a slope in which to wedge an iron grate.

These grates hung from both sides of the *camion*. Each was about two feet wide and ten feet long, heavy enough to support the weight of the vehicle while providing traction. The greaser laid several grates in a row. Once the tire caught hold of one grate and passed over it, he picked it up, ran in front of the slowly moving *camion*, and threw it down again to extend the track. Where the earth was soft for a long distance and the driver could not find a space firm enough to stop, the greaser collected driven-over grates, ran to catch up with the *camion*, and hung the grates on their racks while the *camion* continued to move slowly ahead. The other passenger, although he did not handle the iron grates, shared in other chores and in the maintenance of the vehicle.

The *camion* lumbered on, guided by the watchful driver. We knew about the danger of soft spots. They could appear anywhere along the ever-changing and uncharted *piste*. A slight miscalculation or mishandling could overturn the truck. Decisions had to be quick, maneuvers deft. Both the driver and the greaser respected the perils of the desert.

1

It did occur to me that we ought to have been frightened by the looks of these tough, leathered truckers. At home, in a similar situation, we could have easily expected to be propositioned and embarrassed by a lot of macho posturing. But at home there would not have been a similar situation. We would never have felt as free and as safe. Despite their rough looks, the men on the *camion* were restrained and gentle, facing serious and frustrating work with patience and quiet voices. We didn't understand a lot of what they said, nor did we know what they thought of us. But they treated us as equal adults, and we countered by taking care of ourselves.

∼

The bubble of invincibility which had enveloped us on our bumpy perch at the top of the world thinned with the falling sun and burst on a rising wind. Pat tied the hood of her yellow sweatshirt tightly under her chin. I rewrapped my turban to leave only my eyes exposed. We divided the blankets and snuggled down below the sides of the load. The wind would curl over our little cavity, we thought, and we would weather the chill.

Instead, the temperature dropped even more. The wind swelled without a pause. We huddled together and stacked the blankets over us. It was not enough. The *camion* seemed to be moving faster. The wind whipped from every side and from beneath, through the cargo. My feet grew numb. The tarp hardened to the angular shapes under it, its texture rough and abrasive. Night fell. We raced onward. The speed of the truck and the bombardment of wind and sand took our breath away.

Why did the driver not stop? Didn't he know what was happening to us? Didn't he care? When would we eat? It was madness to charge on headlong like this. The world swirled out of control as we burrowed under the blankets, unable to talk, unable to move, unable to see.

The *camion* stopped, abruptly, mercifully. It was over. We had not been catapulted off the edge of the earth after all. We staggered into the *campement* at Tanout, dragging our stiffened selves, blankets and baskets. The shelter was basic, iron beds, mud walls, crumbling whitewash. It didn't matter. After a drink of water and a little food, we slept, as we were, unchanged, unwashed, soundly, where the wind could not reach us.

In the morning sun we warmed ourselves slowly. The old *gardien* brought a pitcher of washing water and hot coffee. Eighty cents each for the bed and breakfast. Gruber was the first on top of the truck. The rest of us made a few trips, hauling and arranging things—just for the fun of going up and down.

A crowd of children danced about. Beggars, the blind and crippled, reached out for alms. Through it all Gruber did not budge. She was securing her territory, not giving anyone a chance to do her out of it. I finally realized what was happening, but not until the *camion* was about to pull away and I found myself the last one standing on the ground, left to ride in the cab.

The cab was stuffy and confining, boring after riding on top. But the windshield made it possible to look directly toward the horizon. I could follow the gas gauge or watch the speedometer. Now and then I converted kilometers-per-hour to miles-per-hour in my head. I chatted a little with the driver in French, though it meant shouting to be heard over the roar of the vehicle. Throughout the day we moved steadily at thirty-five to forty-five kilometers per hour (twenty-two to twenty-eight miles per hour).

The route from Zinder to Agadez was well known and regularly traveled, as flat and constant and fascinating a landscape as any three-hundred miles can be. This is the great wonder of the desert. At first it appears empty, fixed, lifeless. Nothing more. Hour after rumbling hour the horizon holds firm. We will never reach that line at the edge of the earth that is as far away as it has been. But closer there are rocks that we do reach and pass. And twisted acacia, brittle bushes of wild thyme and mint. Scattered across the land, these seem of no consequence to us, but the desert people know them and how to feed them to their animals or cook them in their tea.

At one particularly long stretch I sat back in the cab and allowed a lovely lake mirage full play. Only my mind knew it was a mirage. My eyes saw glistening water, the hint of a forest on its far right bank and a black post the size of a road marker on the left. When I tired of staring at this rippling scene out of that window, I closed my eyes to wipe it away and started anew to fix my attention to a place on the other side of the truck.

It only took a moment for the water to sparkle on the horizon. This time the background took the shape of clouds instead of trees, but the black post was unquestionably a black post. With the mirage shifted to the left, the post now stood at its right.

I watched that post for perhaps half an hour until the bottom of it appeared wider than the top. I even imagined that it moved. It did move! A teen-aged boy, wrapped and turbaned in blue-black cloth, walked steadily on until his path met ours.

He brought a skin of goat's milk to trade for a bag of salt. With an exchange of friendly greetings and gentle joking, he and the driver completed the trade. We drove off and the boy turned to walk in the direction from which he had come. In all the time I watched him on the horizon, he was alone. There was no camp, no animal, no other person in sight.

~

Our colors atop the *camion* announced our coming. At the Tuareg camps, the women and children, unrestrained in their curiosity, climbed the sides of the truck, peered and laughed. We looked them over in return and commented openly in English.

"Look at her hands and neck. They're blue from the dye of their cloth."

"Just like the magazine said."

They admired our jewelry, pointed to a ring or watch and asked for it. The women touched our hair, freely talking about us in their language as we did about them in ours.

"What a great face!"

"They do have marvelous fine bones."

We smiled broadly at each other. Later we would be advised that it was important to smile and laugh a lot when dealing with the Tuareg. But we did it then because we couldn't resist.

"I don't see any fat ones."

"Hey, what is she doing!" Darlene cried as a young woman pulled at her arm, nodding and grinning with approval.

"She likes you."

"I think she wants to take you."

"What do you think we can get if we trade Darlene?"

"At least a camel."

Darlene didn't think any of this was funny.

"I knew it was a mistake to ride up here," she said as she shrank back into our canvas pit. She never voluntarily rode on top again.

~

One might expect hours and days of such a journey to be tedious, but the opposite is the case. A dun-colored fluttering in the distance becomes a herd of bounding gazelle. I watch a line far to the left grow to a caravan as we gain on it. The camels bob and sway against the western horizon. We run parallel for a few minutes before leaving the caravan to its pace and time. I later learn that a pack camel in caravan travels at about two miles per hour. The lumbering *camion*, by comparison, travels ten times as fast—a blinding speed.

The sweep of sun itself is compelling, passing over the earth from gray dawn to rose to gold to blinding white to apricot to burnt orange to beige of evening. The earth, the rocks, the thorny shrubs lie low and monotonous, gradations of a mass, prostrate under the power of the sun. Thus, neither the light nor the land can be called the name of one shade, moving as they do in endless mutation from one to another.

In the morning, before the world had passed from rose to gold, we discovered a wreck by the side of the road. An oil tanker had broken from its cab and overturned. It was a clean break, no oil spill, no fire, no mangled metal. We saw nothing in this bare, flat space to account for the force that had jackknifed and flipped it. Such was the treachery of soft sand.

By and by we came to the wells of Takoukout, *l'eau douce* (sweet water) of Eliki and Tchin-Garargen, *l'eau bonne* (good water) of Tadelaka, Aderbissinat, and Timboulaga. The Michelin map told us which wells had sweet water, good water, or water that was not potable. Those that had been improved by the French had concrete rims and a pump. Water could be drawn out of them most of the year. They attracted many more people and animals than could have been supported by hand-dug wells subject to long periodic dry seasons.

The French wells changed the patterns of migration and the ecology of fragile scrub grasslands around them. Some wells welcomed travelers, some marked the seasonal camps of the Tuareg, others nurtured small settlements. In every case, the place was the well, and the name of the place was the name of the well.

At one especially fine well, walled with a broad concrete platform, we counted more than a hundred head of blue-black longhorn cattle drinking from a concrete trough. A score of white goats nudged for places among them. Our driver sat for a while on the rim of the well visiting with the owner of the animals.

What did they talk about? The price of goats? The water level? The five white women staring at them from the *camion*? They smiled amiably and nodded, neither of them ever looking at a watch.

The sun moved to gold, warmed us, and reddened our faces, feet, and hands. We passed around the *crème* and eye drops. With Gruber having had her turn at the top of the truck, we rotated without much to-do. Despite a steep rise in the temperature, we kept on the many layers of clothes which protected us against sunburn and dehydration. Throughout the day the wind never rested. It varied from gentle to forceful but never stopped, never let us forget the experience of two nights ago. And so the monochromatic pallet of the desert was punctuated by Victoria's red blanket poncho, Pat's yellow sweatshirt, Gruber's blue and gold Mandingo robe, Darlene's orange scarf, and the flutter of dazzling white, pink and blue turbans.

~

This is where it begins, I thought, as the sandy haze enveloped us on the second day atop M. Joyce's *camion*. The Harmattan rose out of the desert with a force that carried sand and dust more than a thousand miles south to the Atlantic. This was the season—the months of winter—of Harmattan. Days of unrelenting wind, of unabated discomfort. The noise of wind and *camion* grew oppressive. We could not read, or write, or have a conversation. We tried to protect ourselves with a low tent made by tying a blanket to the guy wires. The tent helped to shield us from blown sand, but it was only about two feet high, and, in addition to turning the little pocket underneath into an oven, it required us to lie flat and still so as not to dislodge it. I felt so confined and uncomfortable under the tent, I preferred to take my chances outside, with the wind.

As I settled myself in the open, a sudden dust-devil churned a spout of sand into my face, straight into my eyes, nostrils, mouth, and hair. I spit out what I could and lowered my head to try to shake it out of my hair so that it would not blow back. Impossible. My eyes closed and filled with water. I felt my way back under the tent.

The little pocket of air in which we huddled grew stale and heavy. There was something in my eye. I couldn't pinpoint it. The whole eye and the underside of the lid were sharply painful. As luck would have it, Victoria was next to me in the tent—Victoria, who froze at the thought of pain and was repulsed by any bodily wounds or imperfections. Nevertheless, she agreed to look at my eye, but could not see well enough in the dim light under the blanket. I tried to lie very still, to avoid moving my eye, to not touch. It did not get better. I needed to sit upright, if not to directly relieve my eye, at least to give myself a sense of greater control. This meant going down into the cab.

At the first lull in the wind, we instituted the system we had devised for communicating with the driver. Soon after leaving Zinder, we had discovered that shouting or pounding on the roof of the cab was ineffective. Any racket we could make was lost in the rumbling of the *camion* and carried off in the wind. The only way to get the driver's attention was to catch his eye. While the truck roared ahead into the wind, I climbed out onto the baggage at the front and hung head-down so my arms reached to the side window of the cab. It was my method, and I did it even now because Victoria and Gruber were afraid. They did, however, hold my feet.

I took Pat's place in the cab. In the rear view mirror I saw that a large grain of sand was embedded in my left eye, in the exact center of the pupil. This one white speck, implanted as if on target in the center of the blackest part of the eye, now loomed larger than all the rest of the desert.

We reached Agadez late in the day. The driver cruised the streets slowly, so that by the time we pulled up at M. Joyce's store, quite a crowd had formed.

"Can you believe this!"

"Where did they all come from?"

The people smiled and cheered as we alighted, greatly amused by our arrival. They approved of Victoria's blue eyes and the bright colors of our clothing.

"Hang on to your stuff."

"Is this how Tecumseh felt when they put him on display in London?" Pat wryly observed through her green tinted glasses. But she continued to smile, as we all did.

There were murmurs and nods of astonishment when we carried our own baggage. The people congratulated the driver, who beamed as if he were the father of the bride.

By this time my left eye was swollen shut. I worried about communicating. The bulk of translation had fallen to me, and I simply did not hear French well enough. Lip reading and eye contact would be impaired with only one useful eye. All of this was on my mind as we met the edge of evening in front of M. Joyce's store.

The young woman who managed the store turned out to be M. Joyce's daughter. With her help, word of our arrival was sent to the priest, who, her father had assured us, had guest rooms we might use. We paid the driver as arranged, ten dollars each in West African francs.

The *camion* drove off, the store closed. As night fell, the crowd dispersed until we were left nearly alone, sitting on our heap of belongings, growing cold.

With a flash of headlights and dust across the square, a small open jeep sped to a stop before us. A fiftyish man of stocky build and wiry gray hair stomped out. He paced back and forth between the jeep and us, and again around the jeep and around us. He gruffly mumbled in a harsh-sounding French something about a mistake. A terrible mistake, and what was he to do?

"There are no rooms," he said.

"But M. Joyce told us! Here is his letter to you," I protested.

"*Ach!*" He brushed the letter away. He did not need letters.

It was always hard for me to communicate in French with someone who was impatient. And as the priest paced about, muttering and angry, I found it even harder to understand him, or to respond quickly enough.

Victoria sat very still on the edge of her suitcase, staring straight ahead, rocking ever so slightly, as she did when she was very tired.

"Do you speak English?" I tried. No answer.

Two days of being jostled on the truck and battered by the wind had drained even the reserve of excitement we were usually able to draw upon when coming to a new place.

I explained to the others what I thought I had understood him to say. We were too weary to be upset. Even Darlene rallied and put aside hysteria to discuss this latest predicament in a quiet voice.

The priest scratched his head and paced in frustration.

"*Sprechen sie Deutsch?*" he sputtered, his eyes darting from one of us to the other.

What was that? We were caught off guard.

"*Sprechen sie Deutsch?*" he asked again.

"*Ja, ja,*" popped up Pat with awakened enthusiasm. But after realizing how misleading her enthusiasm might be, she added "a little."

From then on he spoke only to Pat, though never looking directly at her or at any of us. He used an impossible mix of hard-edged French and lightning-fast German, disregarding the fact that she hardly understood him. It was just the way he talked.

"There is a terrible mistake. I don't know what's to be done," he said, throwing up his arms and turning to his jeep.

"No, no, don't let him go!" Gruber hopped about excitedly.

"*Monsieur, monsieur*, wait! Somebody tell him about Jerrie's eye. Look, look," she shouted over the sound of the unmuffled Jeep, pulling him toward me and pointing to the inflamed, swollen-shut left lid. The word for eye was not easy for us to say in French, and the more excited Gruber got, the less clear was her pronunciation.

"*Sic hat etwas in die augen!*" Pat blurted out.

"What did she say?" asked Darlene.

"Beats me."

The priest glared at her.

"Oh God, I hope I said it right." Pat planted herself firmly in the path of the priest. "I said," she explained without flinching, "'she has something in her eye.' At least I hope I said that."

He looked closer and nodded that he got the idea. He would keep us for the night, and we would go to a doctor.

"But it is only for this one night," making the point sternly with his finger in the air.

"What about the doctor?" Gruber continued.

"*Demain, mademoiselles*," he said.

"When, when," Gruber persisted.

"Tomorrow morning," he assured her.

"OK you guys, you heard him, tomorrow morning," she repeated.

With the wave of his arm, we picked up our things and moved toward his vehicle like robots. There were too many things. Too many of us. He'll realize that. We should split up, I thought, make two trips. But my thought was slow and never made it to words. He meant us all to go at once. So, sitting on each other, standing, holding onto suitcases slung over the side, and altogether clinging to that jeep for our lives, we raced through the dusty night of Agadez to . . . to wherever it was we were going.

We sped through town and out the other side a short distance to a cluster of low buildings. We called it a mission, but the priest insisted it was not. He opened the door to a small dark room and said he would return.

He drove away, taking the light and noise of his jeep with him. We were left enveloped in sudden darkness and welcome silence.

Even in the dark, we could sense the room had not been used in a long time. The essence of dust that pervaded the stale air warned us to move carefully so as to not stir it. With Gruber's flashlight we saw a small room divided in half by a post and rail partition about three feet high which ran from the far wall about three-fourths of the way across the room. On the near side of the rail was a low narrow bed, strung with a sagging wire spring and no mattress. A small bedside table stood near the door.

Pat and Darlene pulled back a part of an old gate that leaned against another narrow steel bed. This one had a pad, too thin to be called a mattress. They tried to be careful, but every move stirred more dust. In no time the room became hazy. They took the pad off the second bed so that someone could have it on the floor.

"I think Jer ought to get a bed tonight," Gruber said. "She's the one with the problem."

Even though our material lives were, for the greatest part, quite the same and equally spare, there was always opportunity to jockey for small advantage on the margin. Gruber had followed each of the other's movements and spoke up to avert what she anticipated would be selfish positions. I appreciated her looking after me.

"Thanks," I answered. "I don't want a bed. Those springs make me seasick."

It was true. My eye ached and my ears rang from the day-long howling of the wind. I longed to sleep on something firm and unmoving. I dragged a straw mat to an empty spot between the bed Darlene would use and the door and slowly unfolded my blankets. In the yellow glow of the flashlight, I watched the others arrange themselves. We were hungry. But were we more hungry than tired? That was the question. Everyone seemed to move so slowly, even to think slowly.

"Shh. Do you guys hear anything?"

We listened.

"I can't tell if it's anything more than the wind."

"Should we open the door?"

"Are you kidding!"

The knock was gentle, but clear and repeated. As Pat went to answer it, Gruber focused her light on the opening. A small dark man holding a large box tentatively stepped inside.

"With the compliments of M. Joyce," he said, handing the box to Pat and leaving.

We were stunned. The box contained oranges, pâté, canned foods, cartons of English cookies, a long *baguette* of fresh bread, and two bottles of red wine.

"How really thoughtful," Victoria managed to say as we examined our gift.

Within minutes there was another knock at the door. This time a single thud pushed it open. The priest stood with a lantern and a steaming bowl of food. He handed the bowl to Pat, who was about to protest that it was far too much for her when he swept his arm out to indicate the food was for all of us.

"Do you think that's all we're going to get?" asked Darlene, as if the priest were not standing a few feet from her.

"*Merci*," Pat remembered to tell him, ignoring Darlene. Then she repeated herself in German until it finally sounded sincere.

"*Oui, merci*," the rest of us added.

The priest continued to stand in the doorway after we had run out of thanks and nods. How could we talk to him, catch his darting eyes? His French was too difficult for us. It was up to Pat.

He handed her a small bottle, nodded toward my eye, and rattled on in German. Pat had a bookish knowledge of German, which she hadn't used in years. She was lost.

"I think it's weird the way he's so brusque," noted Darlene.

"He looks so uncomfortable."

"Oh man, you guys, we're the weird ones. Five of us, dropping in from nowhere."

"What's in the bottle?" I asked.

"Eyedrops."

"I know that," I sighed. "What kind of eyedrops?"

"Aw, come on, Jer, what difference does it make?"

"I just like to know what I'm using." It was not a protest, only words to assure myself that I was awake and not dreaming. I managed to get a few drops into my eye, and many more down my cheek.

"*Merci beaucoup, monsieur.*" I did not know what to call this priest in French, since he acted so unlike a traditional "father." He did not seem to care what we called him, but abruptly took his eyedrops, wished us good sleep, and left.

"What's the food?"

"Seems to be a stew. I think I see some big chunks, like potatoes," Pat reported. She was guessing. She looked closely and stirred the bowl. The kerosene lantern provided barely a flicker of light.

"Would you believe a lamp could be so dim?"

It was not a question, just another groggy sigh, much like inquiring about the taste of the food, or the contents of the bottle.

"I don't see any meat, but it tastes a little like ham or bacon."

"Pass it over here."

"What I'd give for a pressure lamp!"

"There's some rice in it, too."

"That's not rice, it's couscous."

And so it went, each of us setting forth an expert opinion, like the blindfolded wise women called upon to identify the elephant, each on precious little evidence.

"I swear, I can't see a thing." My space by the door was farthest from the lamp. When the bowl came to me, a little sauce ran off the spoon and down the outside of the bowl.

"Oh damn." I blamed that one on impaired depth perception. But really, I was just tired. And hungry. But more tired than hungry. I allowed myself only a few sips of orange sweetened water to wash down two APCs to cut the pain of my eye. I did not want to think of searching for a toilet before morning.

The conversation drifted on, becoming more sparse, less coherent. I don't know when it ceased, or who put out the lantern. I closed my good eye as Gruber prepared a place on the floor, curled in the corner with her beloved pack as a pillow. Victoria lay straight on her back on the thin bed pad. Carolyn's wool blanket, in which I wrapped myself, protected my legs from the concrete floor. The wind shifted. The draft from under the door stopped.

～

I awoke confused about where I was, but did not move or open my eyes. The blanket cocoon in which I'd gone to sleep was still wrapped tight. I concentrated on the sounds in the room to orient me. I knew them well. The voices. The flopping of Darlene's slippers as she shuffled about.

Our room at Lott Carey appeared whole in my mind.

Too dry and cold for there.

The sound of a little water poured into a basin.

The Buffet Hôtel?

No mosquitoes. Without them it could not be Ouagadougou.

I should open my eyes. Too hard. Must wait.

Pat began, or was she in the midst of telling a story. I listened carefully.

"I was so intrigued by his German and his mysterious manner," she said, "I had to find out more about him and what he's doing here."

She had gone out to find the priest before anyone else was awake. He took breakfast at a small table outdoors behind his room. She had spent part of the night preparing for the meeting, dusting off the back rooms of her memory in search of what she had once known of German.

He had been more kindly disposed to Pat, knowing she spoke his language. He offered coffee and hot milk and spoke of the old days. It was a vague remembrance, of a time "before the war" without dates or names. For Pat, as for all of us born in the forties, "the war" was World War II. Before that, we had heard from our parents, was the Depression, and before that the Dark Ages of our parents' childhood. Their childhood was also his, and it was of that time he told, of the blissful distant time when he was young and the world was whole and German.

He was born in Alsace, that place we casually hyphenated with Lorraine and knew to be contested and traded repeatedly over the centuries between France and Germany. He corrected Pat when she used the combined name. For him it was quite specifically and solely Alsace. As to whether it was French or German, he was not as sure.

"We had both been staring out over our coffee cups into the desert," Pat continued, "when I realized that he would begin to repeat himself and glance at me as if to say 'now where was I?' or 'who are you?'"

Someone poured more water. Darlene picked up her restless pace. I knew where I was—on the concrete floor of a dusty room in Agadez. Why were my knees warm while the rest of me felt so cold? I couldn't open my eyes. I wanted to sleep and be warm. Instead, I was stiff and cold. I concentrated on Pat's story.

Alsace went to France in 1919, Pat reminded us, before the priest was grown, but well after his language and identity were clearly and immutably German. With the political change, he became an alien in his own land. Later there was an occupation by the German enemy, who were his ancient cousins returned to restore their language and their power. It confused this boy, growing up not sure who he was. Years of hiding and testing his identity, of surviving by not revealing anything which might compromise him took their toll.

He came to his middle age with a studied craftiness metamorphosed to a sad and frightening disorientation. His eyes darted in search of friend or foe. But now he could not tell one from the other, could not trust himself to distinguish, could not trust.

How much of this was his telling and how much Pat's interpretation, we did not know. It was an intriguing story, and everything she said rang true enough to be an "explanation" of his odd manner.

"Do you think he was a Nazi?"

"How did he get to be a priest, if that's what he really is?"

"How long has he been in Agadez?"

"I don't know any of that," Pat admitted. "As soon as I asked how long he'd been here, he said 'a while' and ended the discussion."

"Just like that?"

"That was it." She sighed. "Just when I thought he was a little more relaxed, he shut up completely, stuck this pot of tea in my hands and waved me away."

My right eye slowly opened to a hot shaft of light cutting across the room from the little window. The left would not budge. It had oozed in the night and now was sealed shut and adhered to a stiff blotch on my sleeve. I carefully pried it free and lightly touched it with my finger. It was swollen and encrusted.

"Let's go, Markos," Pat pulled at my shoes, "last call for breakfast."

I propped up on one elbow. The beam of sun passing over my legs saturated the dark gray wool blanket and explained my warm knees. The rest of me shivered in the shadows, and I did not want to move.

"How's your eye?" Darlene inquired.

"How does it look?" I asked.

"Red. Swollen," interrupted Gruber. "Does it hurt?"

"Sure."

"Gee, maybe you won't be able to go on."

Darlene said it. The thought had just occurred to her. The rest of us had understood that possibility for nearly a day.

"And then there were four," Pat added, taking advantage of the opportunity Darlene had opened.

It was not an idea I wanted to become established. I ate what was left of the bread from M. Joyce's surprise package—a quarter of a loaf spread with jam, now so dry it crunched when I bit it.

"Gee, Jer, you're really a sight." Darlene had her way with words.

"Hey, you guys, I don't think it's fair to pick on Jerrie." Gruber stepped in again to my defense. "Think of all the good she's done for us. All those times she has to translate. That's a big responsibility."

"Oh stop! I'm not dead yet."

My right eye watched Victoria methodically washing herself. She had filled a basin from a pitcher of water. While the rest of us felt and looked as if we had been in the desert for two days, Victoria's skin gleamed fresh and rosy. Her fair hair, dampened and combed down, began to spring into its soft curls.

"You better get moving," Pat said. "The priest will take you to a doctor this morning."

"Do you know what kind of a doctor it is?" I asked.

"French. He has a clinic," she replied.

Has anybody found the bathroom yet?" I asked, unwinding my blankets.

"It's a flush and run, out back."

I rewrapped my turban and reached for my dark glasses.

"It's just around the building, not across town," Pat commented.

"I don't want to scare anyone."

When I returned, there was less than half a cup of water left in the pitcher. The price of Victoria's cleanliness. I rinsed my eye, brushed my teeth and carefully wrapped the turban across my face.

～

The priest drove like a madman. We heard the jeep well before it screeched to a stop at our door. It had no muffler and made a great racket even over the wind. I got in behind Pat and, squinting through swirling sand, held on as we careened through a maze of nameless narrow streets.

On the outskirts of town, the long low earthen French clinic rose out of the haze on a knoll above the road. We ascended a series of wind-swept terraces, making our way among others who waited. Dozens of patients filled the broad steps and landings, waiting to be touched by healing hands.

How could they stand it? I'd had enough of the damn wind that scratched my skin, tore at my clothes, stole my breath, and blew a grain of sand in my eye.

Yet they waited. A leg wrapped in a wooden splint, a spastic cough, an open sore, faces that neither smiled nor scowled. Only an infant squealed its misery and was put quiet at a breast. The young men leaned against a low wall, the old squatted beside their baskets. The women stood or sat, as ever with their perfectly straight backs, their heads up. They wrapped themselves and their young against the wind but did not cower from it.

I walked on through an illusion bathed in dusty rose haze, two-dimensional and filtered through the tearing of one eye. Apparitions lined the terraces, weightless sentinels, their edges blurred. So many people exposed to the dust-stirring tempest that engulfed us. So many poised with patience in this surreal still life. Was I an apparition, too?

I hesitated, rewrapping my turban, clutching the *lapa* around my shoulders to break the wind.

Seen through only one eye, the world was flat. I stumbled along not sure how deep the steps were, or how far it was across a terrace.

"Pat," I shouted, "I've only got a piece of sand in my eye."

"Sure, sure. And you don't really want to cross the desert, do you?" Pat turned me forward.

A film of bleached dust, like rose-colored snowfall, covered everything. Flies harassed without mercy and drank at every eye, nostril, and mouth. Those who could see stared at us. How could any place on earth be so desolate?

"Shouldn't we at least wait our turn?" I held back.

Pat was as uncomfortable as I about going to the front of the line. Risking the wrath of the priest, she told him in German that we would not mind waiting.

Even as she said it, I knew I would mind. I would mind very much being lashed for hours by the sand-ladened air. I would mind.

Her words and our feelings were of as much consequence as the wind. The priest stormed forward, ignoring everyone. He charged up toward the clinic, leaving us to make our way through the crowd of waiting patients. I clung to Pat, whose two eyes guided us.

Before we reached the second level, the priest returned with the French doctor. Wind whipped at his khaki shirt and deepened the furrows in his face. Our introduction was brief, wordless, a nod of the head, a quick handshake.

The doctor led us up to the clinic, to an inner room which was cold but miraculously quiet. How I was growing to hate the wind!

The doctor was a small thin man, fortyish, a major in the army. His manner was curt, expressionless, but not unkind. He moved with his head down, not catching anyone's eye. His angular gestures had an air of formality about them. Was that the military influence, or uncertainty? We had enough time to ask a lot of questions to ourselves. Why was he in Agadez? Was it a punishment, a reflection of his competence, or merely an unlucky draw of duty?

"*Voilà, mademoiselle.*" He held open my eye so I could see it in a mirror.

There was no speck of sand. It had washed away in the night, leaving the pupil black and smooth. I was deeply embarrassed. I had taken his time away from those who were truly sick for a nonexistent speck. I wanted to run.

Instead, he took more time to give me a bottle of eyedrops, instructions to stay out of the wind, and to assure me that the swelling would go down in a day. It was not the importance of my ailment, but my self that merited this attention. I stumbled out past the scores of silent, waiting faces, not catching anyone's eye.

Seasonal Migration

Every summer, before the Second World War, my parents and I, my little brother, Toto, short for Theodore, and Mrs. Fraser, the English governess, would leave hot, humid Alexandria for the pure clean air of Switzerland. The car came along, too. It was an English Humber, a temperamental thing that sometimes refused to start, and overheated continuously, sending us scurrying with picnic bottles and mugs in search of the nearest stream to cool its fuming radiator.

Before leaving, however, came all the preparations. The initialed pigskin suitcases with cloth covers, along with the heavy cabin trunks, were brought down from the box room and aired on the terrace before packing. Toto and I had our own small suitcases to carry, containing precious possessions we could not bear to leave behind. Miniature cars for Toto, along with a pretty doll, one that he could undress. Colored pencils, a Kodak camera, and an autograph book for me, in case I ran into Edward, Prince of Wales, who would one day be king.

After the packing came the goodbyes, to Hannah, the gambling cook, who was always in debt; to Gamal and Soliman, the *suffragis* who waited at table; to Abdu, the kitchen boy, who was not a boy at all but in his fifties; to Sayed, the gardener, and to elderly Nagibeh, the Lebanese housekeeper, who had been with the family longer than I had.

"What shall I bring you back?" I would ask her in Arabic.

"Snow!" she always replied, laughing and crying at the same time. She hated to see us go. More often than not she said that all she wanted was to see us back in good health.

As we walked out the front door to be driven to the harbor by Ibrahim, the chauffeur with gold teeth, all the relatives and friends we had in the world came to see us off. They poured out of cars like marines making a landing, carrying large boxes tied with pink and blue ribbons, of chocolates and *loukoums*, dried figs, and crystallized dates.

"*Bon voyage, ma petite chérie!*" they cried, snuffing the air out of my lungs with overwhelming embraces and emblazoning my cheeks with red lip marks.

Many more of them were at the docks, not only to see us off, but to inspect our cabins on the SS *Ausonia*, the Lloyd Triestino ship that sailed between Alexandria and Genoa. They had more farewell gifts, *baklawa* and *pistaches*, *fruits confits*, *marrons glacés*, and sheets of dried apricot paste. From soft pillowy Aunt Julia, we always received homemade rose-petal jam because she thought we would miss it in Switzerland.

"Why don't you spend the summer in Lebanon?" they asked, "at Sofar and Beit Meri, like us? We could all be together!"

Pale little Toto looked at me out of big brown eyes and made a grunting noise with his teeth and tongue. I giggled. We leaned over the railing looking down at the noisy disorderly crowd who were pushing, shouting, waving handkerchiefs, and yelling to passengers on deck.

"There are our trunks!" Toto pointed to a stream of barefoot porters, the hems of their tattered *galabiyas* gripped between their teeth. Bent in two, they heaved and groaned as they came up the gangplank, heavy trunks on their backs. It had taken Gamal and Soliman together to bring an empty one down from the trunk room.

The SS *Ausonia*'s fog horn let out a deep agonizing howl that made me shiver in the July heat. "*Bon voyage!*" There were final smothering embraces.

Toto laughed and pointed to my cheeks. "This orange one here is from Aunt Julia, and this purple one is from Aunt Adèle, and the big pink one. . . . "

The SS *Ausonia* left the quay and slowly moved away until Aunt Julia's plump kind face became a blur that melted into the horizon. A fresh sea breeze cooled our faces as the ship gathered speed. Stewards appeared with consommé and cheese sandwiches, and Father asked for deck chairs to be placed in a good spot out of the wind.

As soon as we left the shallow coastal waters my head started to spin and I turned green. Clinging to the railings I hurried to the cabin I was sharing with Toto and Mrs. Fraser.

"Fancy being seasick on a mere three-day voyage on the Mediterranean!" Mrs. Fraser scoffed. She stood tall, ramrod straight, elegant in a midnight blue suit, with a long pleated skirt and a green cloak thrown over her shoulders.

I had hardly been in my bunk three minutes when I heard a familiar English voice moaning pitifully in the hallway. Clinging to the walls came our English governess.

"These silly Italian ships . . ." she groaned, quickly disappearing into the bathroom.

Toto put his ear to the door. "I can hear her," he giggled, his eyes sparkling with mischief. "She's going ugh, ugh, ugh!"

A moment later Mrs. Fraser emerged, moaning, "Oh, I'm so ill I could die!" Her elegant clothes awry, she dabbed her cheeks and forehead with a dainty lace handkerchief steeped in eau-de-cologne. She dropped onto her bunk fully clothed, one arm hanging limp over the side of the bed.

"Mama, where are you?" she cried. For some reason she always called my parents Mama and Papa.

It took Mama and the stewardess to undress Mrs. Fraser, who continued to moan that she was very ill. "I need sustenance, Mama. Bring me Brussels sprouts and bananas. It's the only thing I can keep down!"

Every hour the stewardess, who was as fascinated as the rest of us, brought her a big tray of Brussels sprouts and bananas. Mrs. Fraser sat up, swallowed the whole thing like an ostrich, and promptly fell back again moaning that she was going to die.

"*Inglesi?*" the stewardess whispered each time she came in. "English?"

Mother who was spending most of the time in our cabin nodded in the affirmative and tipped her.

"What is the wretched woman saying?" Mrs. Fraser groaned.

Father was a good sailor. Mother was not, but hid it well. Toto always insisted it was his dolly, not him, that was sick. He threw bits of cold turkey at me in my bunk, and I threw them back. Cold turkey and mineral water were the SS *Ausonia*'s diet for seasickness.

"Ridiculous!" Mrs. Fraser let us know in between sprouts.

As soon as we sailed into the calm waters of Genoa harbor, Mrs. Fraser and I were resuscitated, but each in our own way. With trembling hands I managed to dress, after a fashion. My mouth tasted sour.

Mrs. Fraser, on the other hand, not only got back her bravado, she even looked like a queen, in a burgundy outfit and a sky blue cloak. She wore something resembling a tiara on her head. She was so regal that when we disembarked the Cook's man who was to forward our heavy trunks to Lausanne mistook her for mother.

"Mama, Papa," she announced on her first voyage with us, "I speak fluent Italian. Leave all customs formalities to me." My parents who only spoke a smattering of Italian were delighted. With pride we watched our Mrs. Fraser stride toward the customs officer in uniform with a feather in his cap.

We soon realized that in spite of the high speed gibberish no progress was being made. The customs officer was not marking our beautiful pigskin suitcases with white chalk. We listened to our so-called linguist in action.

"Now look here, *prego* . . . *yo, yo, yo*, no that's Portuguese. Nonsense! Here are the *baggaglios*. Don't look at me like that, especially with that *plume de ma tante* in the ridiculous hat." She dabbed at her nose with her dainty lace handkerchief. "I've sailed the world not once but twice, and I know all about customs. Oh, how infuriating! Yes, this suitcase is mine, and this one is Papa's, and this one is *la madré*'s, the mother of the two *bambinos*." The customs man stared and shook his head.

Mrs. Fraser turned to us exasperated. "Papa, Mama, the wretched man doesn't speak a word of Italian." She swung her cloak, nearly knocking me off my unsteady little legs.

"*Va bene, va bene!*" the customs man quickly marked our luggage and disappeared as fast as he could.

With churning stomach and jaundiced eyes I watched the Humber roll off the ship, dreading what lay ahead. I looked up at Father. His eyes gleamed with happy anticipation. He couldn't wait to get his hands on the steering wheel. Mother took my clammy hand. Toto made grunting sounds with his mouth and pretended to throw up.

"Little boys should be seen and not heard," Mrs. Fraser scolded.

~

It was time to leave for Lausanne. Suitcases were strapped onto the luggage rack. Reluctantly I climbed aboard the Humber, clutching my little suitcase and trying to think of the handsome Prince of Wales who would one day be king.

Father turned the key in the ignition, but the Humber was in no mood to obey the first time. Or the second and third. Eventually it did. With every mile I slid further and further down my seat until I was semicomatose. My decline was even swifter than on board because the devilish Humber had an overpowering smell of leather, guaranteed to send me reeling. At every turn, every bump, I became queasier and queasier, clammier and clammier.

Father had not noticed. "*Je fais du cent à l'heure!*" he cried ecstatic, as he crouched over the wheel in an exciting world of his own.

"Stop, Papa!" Mrs. Fraser shouted, "my lace hankie has flown out the window!"

Father jammed on the brakes. The contents of my stomach shot out, over Father's head to splash onto the dashboard and windshield.

"What you need is a good dose of sprouts to settle your stomach," Mrs. Fraser said.

At last we reached Lausanne. Face ashen, hair clammy with sweat, I tottered unsteadily on my skinny legs into the grand old hall of the Lausanne Palace. Manager, concierge, bellboys, all of them familiar faces, were there to greet their faithful clientele from Alexandria, Egypt. I knew that flowers, fruit, and Swiss chocolate would be waiting in our rooms.

As we went up in the lift with the iron gate, my queasy stomach rumbled basso and alto.

"Do be quiet," Mrs. Fraser hissed. "It's most unladylike."

But Jules, our favorite bellboy who operated the lift, grinned. "Is that Egyptian belly music your stomach is playing?"

～

Other relatives were in Lausanne too. My grandmother (my mother's mother), my aunts, uncles, and cousins were there, and we all had rooms that opened into one another. They had large terraces with flowers and shrubs, and they overlooked the lake. With my cousins, Nadia, Simon, and Harry, Toto and I ran from terrace to terrace, not just to visit, but to peek into other rooms. We met some interesting people that way.

"Where have you been, you naughty girl?" Thoroughly annoyed, Mrs. Fraser looked down at me from her lofty height. "Don't you know it's bath time?"

"Sorry, I was with Toscanini. He played the piano for Toto and me."

"Little girls shouldn't lie between their teeth."

"He signed my autograph book. But he didn't know where the Prince of Wales was."

"Let me see that." Mrs. Fraser snatched it out of my hand. Her eyes popped out of her head. She gave a little laugh. "Fancy that—Arturo Toscanini."

"I told him you ate Brussels sprouts and bananas, but that you were sick anyway."

"He said it served you right." Toto's eyes sparkled.

"Hold your tongue, naughty boy."

"Like this?" Toto pulled his tongue out and wrapped his fingers around it.

～

From Lausanne we went up to the mountains. High up in the Alps it was quiet and peaceful. There were only a few cows, but—alas—half of Alexandria was there.

"*Chérie!*" the Alexandrians cried in amazement, even though we had all been on the same boat together. "What brings you here?"

Sometimes we went to Villars, sometimes to St. Moritz, sometimes I didn't know or care where because I was dizzy. If there was something I hated more than ships it was cars.

But Father was happy. Higher and higher he drove, from peak to peak, round terrifying hairpin bends that my system could not take.

"How much longer?" I gasped on our way to St. Moritz, my lips dry, my eyes closed, so as not to see the Jungfrau that seemed to be tilting every which way, as the car hung on the edge of a precipice, revealing valleys below. I saw cows and chalets all upside down. I heard bells. I was ready to expire.

Mrs. Fraser poked me in the ribs. "Don't sit like Quasimodo. Do try to think of edelweis, dear."

It was in St. Moritz that Mrs. Fraser suddenly produced an autograph book of her own, tied with a blue ribbon, that she claimed to have had "since the year dot."

"Who is this?" I asked, pointing to an illegible spidery signature. "Is it someone very important?"

"That's our vicar in Norwich, dear. He has arthritis."

Mrs. Fraser, however, was now on the lookout for a celebrity to match my Toscanini.

It was in the hotel one evening, on our way to the dining room, that, like many of the other guests, we were drawn to the slot machine. Not any old slot machine, but one where for a franc, if you were lucky, or many many francs if you were determined, a crane reached down into a mass of colored bonbons, and came up with expensive Swiss watches, French perfumes, and silver cigarette cases and lighters.

A small crowd had gathered around a man in dinner jacket who was putting one franc after another into the machine.

Mrs. Fraser dug her fingernails into my bony shoulder. "Oooh, that's Howard Carter who discovered King Tutankhamen's tomb." Toto and I threaded our way to the front to get a good view. Holding a fistful of one franc pieces, Howard Carter was chanting, "Abracadabra, abracadabra, hashamaasha, wooloo, wooloo, woooolooo! Bring me that cigarette case!" But the magic words failed to work. The crane missed its object and came up with only a couple of bonbons.

"Oh!" Everyone was disappointed. Undeterred, Howard Carter put in another franc and came up with a few more magic words that were followed by something that sounded very much like "damn." He shook the slot machine, unhinging it from the wall. The crane swung about and finally landed on the cigarette case that it promptly picked up and dropped into the waiting drawer. Cheers greeted his success.

"Here, you take it," Howard Carter said to one of the guests. "Now let's try for that lighter there."

"Jolly good sport, isn't he, Mama?" Mrs. Fraser said as we went in to dinner. "I shall ask him to join us for coffee. I know he'll be delighted to meet us and sign my autograph book." She gave a little laugh.

"And mine?"

"If you behave."

"He may be with friends, and not be able. . . ." Mother began.

"Nonsense! He'll be only too happy."

Whatever magic persuasion of her own Mrs. Fraser used it worked. After dinner she brought him to the lounge to have coffee with my parents as though she had known him all her life. "Mama and Papa are simply dying to meet you," she said brightly to my parents who appeared a little stunned.

"Don't you think, Mr. Carter, that little Toto resembles King Tutankhamen with those big brown eyes, and that pale delicate face?"

"Ah!" Mr. Carter peered at Toto. My little brother sat quietly, neat as a pin in his gray suit and tie. The big brown eyes were all innocence, the light brown hair was slicked down with water. I knew that Toto longed to swing his legs and hit the table with the coffee cups, and make the grunting sounds that infuriated Mrs. Fraser, but at the moment he looked like an angel.

"At your age, Toto, Tutankhamen was already a Pharoah," Mrs. Fraser said, her tone reproachful. "He does look like a Pharoah, doesn't he, Mama and Papa?" My parents looked at one another, and then everyone laughed, even Toto.

Thus it was that we heard how after months of fruitless excavations, Howard Carter made his dramatic discovery. With his friend, the Earl of Carnarvon beside him, he peered through a hole into the antechamber of the tomb and, by the light of a flickering candle saw, as though through a mist, statues, alabaster, and gold everywhere. "Wonderful things," Carter said.

Toto's little mouth fell open as he sat mesmerized. I could picture him as a boy Pharoah making weird noises with his tongue against his teeth, crying out "hashamatasha, wooloo, wooloo, wooolooo!"

No history before or since ever seemed so alive, though it was strange to hear the story of King Tutankhamen told by Howard Carter himself, high in the mountains of Switzerland.

~

By the first week of October the seasonal migration was over and it was time to return to Alexandria. I was glad to be going home. Switzerland was all right for a holiday, once you had got there, of course, but there was no place like Alexandria in the whole world.

Once again Toto and I leaned over the ship's railing and watched the city come into focus. The pilot's launch flitted across the water, the green Egyptian flag with its crescent and three stars flying in the wind. The pilot climbed aboard up a rope ladder, followed by a handful of officials and policemen in white uniforms and red fezzes.

There by the lighthouse was the familiar harbor scene again. The yacht club and its jetty, around which clustered gleaming white cutters, motor boats, and dinghies. Nearby, the King's yacht, the *Mahroussa*, sparkled in the sun. British destroyers were sending out signals and shrill whistles, and on the deck of one of them sailors still in summer uniforms were putting up flags and bunting.

"They're having a party tonight," said a wistful Mrs. Fraser, who now stood beside us.

Father took our passports and hurried into the dining room which had been cleared of tables and chairs and assigned for disembarking formalities. Everyone shouted and shoved, in an attempt to reach the green baize table where immigration officers were stamping passports with an air of great importance.

Slowly the ship docked and the gangway was lowered. The noise from the dining room now became deafening. I could hear it all the way out on deck. It was always like that.

On the quay, their fenders dented, hub caps missing, windows broken, taxis stuffed to overflowing honked and honked as they inched their way through the noisy undisciplined crowd. A Rolls Royce with a uniformed chauffeur waited patiently for its owners to disembark.

"Can you see them?" I asked Toto, as I watched a *chaouiche*, a policeman, come to blows with a rug salesman. "Son of a dog!" the perspiring *chaouiche* shouted. "*Yalla, imshee*, go!"

"There's Aunt Julia." Toto pointed to a kind beaming face in the middle of a crowd of black-veiled women with babies on their shoulders.

Yes, she was there, and so were all the other relatives and friends who had seen us off.

They had seen us too. "Toto, Jacqueline!" They waved and blew kisses. Toto and I looked at one another and ducked.

It was hot now that the ship had docked. Flies came to greet us, and the Swiss Alpine air was nowhere about as we came down the gangplank, Father, Mother, Toto, and I, and Mrs. Fraser, like a duchess, in yet another stunning outfit that she claimed she had made herself out of "bits and pieces."

"Isn't it a beautiful October day?" she said.

"Why do English people always talk about the weather?" I asked.

"Don't be impertinent and do smile at your relatives!"

I heard Toto make grunting noises as aunts, uncles, and cousins engulfed us in over-affectionate embraces.

"*Chérie*, how you have grown!" they cried, pinching my cheeks. I had not grown an iota, and would have been a perfect mate for Tom Thumb. I cringed as the kiss I knew would follow was firmly planted on my perspiring forehead.

Of course they brought *loukoums* and dates and figs, and huge apples from Lebanon, and the sickly rose petal jam that I couldn't stand the sight of. Of course they followed us home, so that a line of cars stretched the length of a block.

Into the blue drawing room we went, the blue room for the homecomings, with the distant and not so distant aunts and uncles, and the cousins, once, twice, and thrice removed.

"Do you remember me?" asked one elderly aunt, beckoning me to go and sit beside her.

I nodded. How could I not? She had a bladder with a faulty valve and it dripped under the blue velvet couch.

"Doesn't the poor dear remind you of my great aunt, Mrs. Walton, Mama?" Mrs. Fraser said.

Mother smiled tolerantly. That none of us had ever set eyes on Mrs. Walton was an example of Mrs. Fraser's reasoning at its best.

Gamal, the *suffragi*, came in with a tray of little cups of Turkish coffee and glasses of mulberry syrup. Soliman followed with petits fours and crystallized dates, and the talking went on and on. Everyone spoke at the same time, tongue, hands, expressive eyes all going at once.

Toto and I fled to the pantry where Nagibeh, with tears of joy, thanked the Blessed Virgin over and over again for our safe return, smothering us with kisses, as though we had returned from a dangerous safari. She had sent us brightly colored postcards of angels that Hassan, the gardener, had written for her, because she could neither read nor write.

Finally, the relatives and friends departed and the house was quiet. I had a bath and supper, and slipped between the cool white sheets in my room with the nursery rhyme pictures around the walls. I lay awake a long time listening to the dogs baying at the moon. I heard the whistle of a train approaching Sidi-Gabar Station a few miles away. I knew that if the whistle sounded close tomorrow it would bring the searing, dusty *khamseen* wind blowing in from the desert. After the serene sound of Swiss cow bells, the nocturnal sounds of Alexandria that first night home always made my skin crawl.

A piercing meow rent the air and I sat up in terror. Cats! I had seen them one evening, their eyes green and luminous, jumping over the garden wall to cause havoc in our garden. Even Al, the German shepherd, dared not fight these wild marauders, and so they raided our hen house and rabbit hutch, and pounced on our beautiful white doves. I shivered and lay down again.

"Mrs. Fraser. . . ." I called out, "do you like cats?"

"Do think of edelweis," she replied.

I slid further down the bed and pulled the sheet over my head.

Proxy

MOHAMMED ABOU and I had never seen each other—not even in photographs—but he grabbed both my shoulders and kissed me hard on the mouth when we met. I was not his son, but his son, Kadir, was safe in my house in Minneapolis, so he kissed me as if I were the lost boy himself.

We could hardly speak after that first kiss. I looked away in embarrassment and he kissed me again.

I've seen pictures of a lost child reunited with his family. There was a bewildered joy in those faces, an emotion as overwhelming as death. We aren't accustomed to that fierce joy beyond happiness and laughter. Perhaps the human psyche wasn't constructed to sustain the shock of reunion, just as we're not meant to be forever separated from our children. Kadir was twelve years old the last time his father had seen him. He was twenty-three when I met his father in Ethiopia.

The father's face pulsed with emotion. Kadir shows nothing in his face. He covers his mouth when he laughs and turns away when he is sad. He had given me a cousin's phone number in Addis Ababa, but he didn't tell me anything about the rest of the family. I knew two of his cousins' names, Anisa and Ekram, but not the names of his parents or brothers or sisters; neither one of us thought I would see them.

I'd arrived in Ethiopia on a Saturday, stayed with friends, and we'd called the cousin, Anisa, on Monday morning and arranged to meet her at my friend, Innes's, office at the University. Innes and I were waiting on the steps when an old car with three people in it pulled up. The driver was a plump, mature woman swathed in the traditional scarves and skirts—Anisa. A man in a khaki sports coat and white skull cap sat next to her, and a younger woman in jeans and a denim jacket was in the back seat. The car stopped; they got out.

I stepped forward and introduced myself.

"I am Ekram," the young woman in jeans said in English, "and this is Mohammed Abou."

I put my hand out, but he grabbed me by the shoulders and kissed me. I realized immediately that he was Kadir's father—the name was right and he had his son's angular build. My instinct was to embrace him, but he was in charge and all his emotion was in those kisses.

We stood there laughing and crying. Nobody knew what to say. Finally Innes herded us into her office and sent out for coffee.

"Mohammed Abou has been looking for you," Ekram said. We were sitting on metal folding chairs around Innes's desk. "He went to every hotel and to the airport."

"I am so sorry," I said. "Tell him that I'm sorry. I had no idea he knew I was coming."

When Ekram conveyed my apology, Mohammed leapt up and kissed me again. Every vein in his sharp face was visible. The room could not contain his emotion. At first I thought he was simply glad that Kadir had found a good home with us, but it was more than that. I was living proof that Kadir was alive and well. Mohammed didn't kiss me because I had been Kadir's guardian for the past five years; he kissed me as if I were Kadir himself, his son in the flesh.

When the coffee came, we clutched the cups gratefully, glad to have somewhere to put our hands, but too nervous to drink. I was so rattled that several minutes passed before I remembered to take out the pictures I'd brought of Kadir. Mohammed stared at the snapshots of the son he hadn't seen in eleven years and then at me, back and forth. Anisa and Ekram giggled over Kadir's long hair.

I don't know what I expected from this meeting. Until that morning I hadn't known it would happen. Harar, where Kadir's family lives, is over five hundred kilometers from Addis Ababa. I didn't expect to go to Harar; I didn't expect his father to come to Addis. I was in Ethiopia to gather material for a novel and had some notion that Kadir's cousins would have me over for dinner, to meet the branch of the family that lived in Addis Ababa and that I might see them two or three more times before I left Ethiopia. It hadn't occurred to me that I would move in with the extended family for the duration of my time in Ethiopia, that I wouldn't be free to do *anything* else. It hadn't occurred to them that any other arrangement was possible. They invited me to lunch that afternoon. I told Innes I'd see her later, got in Anisa's car, and disappeared for two weeks. They kidnapped me.

〜

Eleven years earlier, in 1978, Kadir, with his two older brothers, attended a demonstration of students in Harar. The students were congregated on the main square when the soldiers appeared. Kadir is hazy on the sequence of events or even why they were there—he just went with his brothers. His oldest brother was killed outright, the next, Nasser, thrown in jail, and Kadir ran and hid. Three days later Nasser was released from jail. He found Kadir, but they were afraid to go home.

It took them thirty-three days to cross the desert to Djibouti, hiding during the day, walking at night with others fleeing the cruel dictatorship of Mengistu Haile Mariam. The period in which Kadir fled came to be known as the Red Terror. Every family lost somebody; every family wore black for years.

Kadir and his brother lived hand to mouth for six months in Djibouti, on the Red Sea, where the hottest temperatures on earth are recorded, until the United Nations declared them official refugees and took them to Egypt. Kadir spent four years in Alexandria, went to school there, and was the first Ethiopian to come to Minnesota under the Unaccompanied Minors program established at the close of the Vietnam War. His brother is in Atlanta. They never saw their family again. When I think of Kadir's story, I imagine my other three children, Anna, John, and Alex, going downtown for some rally and never coming home again.

〜

I spent five days at his cousin, Anisa's, house. On the second day I realized that Mohammed had come to Addis Ababa for the sole purpose of taking me home to Harar to meet the rest of the family. I didn't think it was possible. All internal travel by nonresidents had to be approved by the Ethiopian Tourist Organization and I had already been refused permission to go to Dilla where I'd taught as a Peace Corps Volunteer. We went to the E.T.O. anyway and learned that since Harar is one of the historical cities in Ethiopia, I could go on the approved government tour and stay at the government hotel for one day only. That wasn't what Mohammed had in mind.

"Is there no other way?"

"Only if you are visiting a relative," the clerk said.

I looked at Mohammed Abou. "I am visiting a relative," I said. "Give me the form."

When I got to the blank asking for my relationship to the person I was visiting, I wrote, "my son's father," and gave Mohammed's house and *kebele* number. The clerk read over my application without comment, asked for fifteen dollars in American currency and told me to return in three days.

It was four days before I got back to the E.T.O. office because nobody in Anisa's household had a sense of urgency and Harari etiquette wouldn't allow them to let me leave the compound alone, much less go across town to pick up my travel documents. I pointed out that I was forty-five years old, that I had lived in Ethiopia for two years previously, that I spoke Amharic, that I knew my way around Addis and, in fact, had walked all over the city, alone, for two days before I called them, but if I opened the compound gate, they ran after me: "What do you want? Where are you going?"

I quickly learned that if I told them where I was going, they would go for me or, in the case of the travel papers, reassure me by saying, "Don't worry, we will get them."

One morning I tried to go to the post office to mail some letters. "Okay, Sammy will go for you." Sammy was Anisa's teenage son.

"Okay, but I also want to buy some aerograms."

"He will buy for you."

"Thank you," I said, "Here is the money." But Anisa wouldn't let me pay for my own aerograms. I put the money on a table, Anisa threw it back; I left it there and walked away; she grabbed my purse and put the money in it. This happened every time I needed something; I couldn't bear to have them pay for my film, my aspirin, my postcards, and they couldn't bear the sight of my money.

I particularly wanted to take the bus to Harar, especially since I'd been refused permission to travel anywhere else. I was eager to travel overland, to soak up as much of the Ethiopian countryside as possible before I had to leave. I tried to explain this to Mohammed Abou, but he closed his face to me. No, the bus was too rough for me.

I knew flying was expensive. "How much is it?" He wouldn't tell me. Finally, I relinquished all desire for souvenirs or toiletries, and stifled my need to pay my own way—I was in Ethiopia for three weeks and probably didn't spend fifty dollars.

~

At home, Kadir is the first person to clear the table after dinner; he *notices* when the garbage bag is full and takes it out without being asked. He remembers everybody's birthday; he is solicitous of his new relatives, particularly his grandparents. It was clear from his first week as a member of our family that he had been raised by people with definite expectations of correct behavior.

I told him once that he was a perfect son and he didn't deny it, but his manner was self-effacing. Our only conflicts are when I ask him to do something that clearly violates his sense of propriety.

"Kadir, look at me when you're speaking," I say. "I can't tell what you want."

He turns his face towards mine, but the eyes won't follow. He covers the side of his face with his long hand. "I can't, Mom."

I know that he really can't look straight at me when making a request, that it is against his cultural norm for child to parent, but it is frustrating that it takes so long to figure out what he wants—especially when I want to give him whatever it is. Kadir is one of those people who is so generous and unself-centered that your natural instinct is to give him more than he asks for—because he seldom asks.

∽

The more I tried to tell Mohammed Abou exactly what I needed or wanted to do, the easier it was for him to refuse me. "I really want to ride the bus to Harar," I said, looking him straight in the eye.

Impossible.

∽

Mohammed and I finally left Addis on Friday. We kissed Anisa good-bye at the entrance to the airport, showed our tickets to a soldier at the door and were passed along a phalanx of taciturn, armed men who funneled us into the main departure terminal.

We were without translators for the first time. My Amharic had reappeared rapidly during my immersion into the family, but I was slow to realize that Mohammed didn't speak Amharic much better than I did even though it was the national language. He was fluent in Oromo and Arabic in addition to his mother tongue, Aderage, but not Amharic. It was also our first extended period alone together and we each fell into one of the predictable strategies for communicating with a person with whom you don't share a common tongue. I began speaking loudly, slowly, and distinctly, as if my increased volume would overcome my inability to speak Aderage. Mohammed, on the other hand, pressed his lips together and gestured at me silently and imperiously as if I were incapable of interpreting any sound at all.

The din and confusion in the terminal were overwhelming. Dozens of people pressed toward uniformed airline agents behind a long counter. The numbers one through eight were posted at regular intervals high above the counter, but there was no sign in any language to indicate which agent we should approach. Neither of us knew how to proceed, so I collared a man in an official-looking uniform and asked him which counter was for the flight to Dire Dawa. Number seven.

"Sabat!" I shouted at Mohammed Abou, pointing at the number seven swinging over a counter some distance away. "Sabat!" There were maybe thirty-five people huddled around the agent at number seven. "Let's get in line there," I yelled slowly, for some reason imagining that an orderly queue would work.

He pressed his lips together, grabbed my arm and pulled me to the front of the crowd at number seven. I pulled back, embarrassed at breaking in line, but he slapped our tickets on the counter and the agent took them in spite of the thirty people ahead of us, tagged our bags, stamped our tickets, gave us the appropriate coupons, gave the bags back to us, and sent us to the gate. None of the people Mohammed had dragged me past protested; neither did the agent.

Our tickets were scrutinized by another armed soldier—this happened seven times in all—then we queued up to go through the metal detector, with ten people ahead of us. Mohammed again tried to push to the front. Because I was still under the illusion that I knew more about airport etiquette than he did, I tried to take control of the situation. "No," I explained loudly, "there is no hurry. Let's just get in line like everybody else." I even allowed a portly man to take his time to pass through ahead of me. Mohammed gestured at me furiously over the fat man's head, but I went through on my own. When we got to the gate, Mohammed motioned to me to sit down. I did. He paced in front of the cloudy window for a bit, then sat on the edge of the seat across from me with his elbows on his knees and his hands clasped before him, staring out the window where the plane would appear.

"Well, we made it," I said. "It's fine."

The sound of my voice startled him. With a clenched smile he acknowledged my ability to speak and lit a cigarette. He was ready to be in Harar.

~

I'd traveled to every province in Ethiopia when I was a Peace Corps Volunteer and had been to Dire Dawa where our plane would land that day, but I'd not gone the extra hundred kilometers to Harar on the eastern ridge of the Great Rift Valley. I was excited to be going at last. Harar is a famous, walled city that has been a center of trade and Islamic learning in the Horn of Africa since the seventh or eighth century. Great Harari caravans carried fruits, vegetables, coffee, saffron, *khat*, and slaves to the provinces of Ethiopia and to the Red Sea coast. The city is still known for the ninety-nine mosques within its walls and its ornate basketwork and fine silversmithing.

When explorer Richard Burton approached Harar in 1854, he was warned that he would be killed if it were discovered that he was an infidel, but he entered one of the five gates without incident and described the city as poor, infested with smallpox and characterized by "lax moral habits." Shortly after Burton's departure, the Emir of Harar decreed that all women should clothe their legs in the tight-fitting velvet pants that Harari women, including Kadir's sisters, still wear under their voluminous slips and skirts.

The French poet Arthur Rimbaud entered Harar twenty years later, unaware that Burton had preceded him. Rimbaud fancied himself a "Northern barbarian" and was confident that *he* would be the first white person the Hararis had seen, but when the gates swung open at dawn, Rimbaud was greeted by a blue-eyed Capuchin priest whose first words were, *"Vous parlez français?"*

Burton and Rimbaud arrived on foot with camels. Mohammed Abou and I arrived from Dire Dawa in a low-slung Peugeot station wagon cum taxi that deposited us at the bus park outside the walls. Mohammed grabbed my bag and we entered Harar on foot through the western gate. His posture changed as we entered the city. He walked with his toes pointed out, each foot flying forward before it touched the ground, claiming every inch of earth, nodding to bystanders who called his name. He was not entirely oblivious of me stumbling behind, but clearly was ready to be home.

I stumbled on the rough road because I was staring at everybody staring at me. *"Ferenji!"* somebody called. It pleased me to be called *ferenji*, foreigner, after so many years. I waved, but Mohammed shouted something at the boy who called to me and sped up. Just before we made the sharp turn down the narrow path that led to his compound, an old man stepped in front of me. "Cuba!" he said.

It took me a minute to understand what he said, then I remembered that the Cubans and the Russians had occupied Ethiopia ever since the United States left after Emperor Haile Selassie was deposed. "No," I said. "American."

"Ah! *Vive* American!" he said and grabbed for my hand. In the days that followed, people grew misty-eyed when they learned I was an American and asked if I knew Mr. Bob who taught them in the Peace Corps or Mrs. Susan. The conceit of Rimbaud was seductive. It was easy for me to imagine that I was special there, the first American who had been to Harar in fifteen years. The Hararis greeted me with the nostalgia of a people who had suffered under the hands of the foreigners who succeeded us. By the time I got back to Addis Ababa a week later, I had begun to believe in American benevolence until I spoke with a man who was inspecting the box I was sending home.

"Oh, you are American? Yes, well, this office was the office of the American Mapping Mission." He shrugged. "Now it belongs to the Russians. It is the same thing. We do our work on your desks."

$\sim$

Mohammed shouted something and I ran to catch up. We hurried through the central square, down a rock road, past the mosque where Mohammed worships, and up a sharp right into a narrow, rock path between two eight-foot walls. Without warning he stepped through an arched gate and we were in a compound filled with people who were grinning at me. Mohammed appeared to make a hasty introduction, then issued a string of orders. He'd delivered me safely and now was impatient with the drama of the moment.

I was trying to discern which woman was Kadir's mother and I approached the wrong person. That woman covered her face with her hand to hide her laughter—just as Kadir does—but shook her head furiously. They all laughed and pushed Mama forward. She was a short, shy woman with long hair braided in buns around her ears and covered with a scarf. She kissed me on the cheek, one, two, three times. We stepped back to look at each other. She was smiling broadly and I was wiping tears from my eyes. She'd been waiting for me, Kadir's stand-in, for a long time. She didn't try to speak and I was incoherent. "I am so happy to be here," I repeated several times. It was all I could think of to say.

Hamza, a cousin, spoke English and began telling me who everybody was, but I couldn't absorb it all. I met Kadir's sisters: Asiah, Khadije, who had a new baby, Besmata, Zeinabou, Mariam, Sa'ada. They kissed me shyly. Kadir's two younger brothers, Abdusalem and Abdukadir, were even stiffer. I learned their names later; at the time, I didn't know who I was kissing and crying over.

We were standing in the courtyard. Three other houses opened on the same courtyard and people were crowded at all the doors to gawk. There were chickens in the yard and several cats. A raggedy girl, who I later realized was a servant, was filling a pot with water at a spigot in the center of the courtyard. Suddenly, Mohammed Abou said something and everybody was quiet. Mama hurried a couple of the girls to the kitchen on the opposite side of the compound, the boys faded back to the wall, Hamza grabbed my bag and he and Mohammed escorted me into the house.

The house was a traditional Harari house. One wall of the central room was completely open to the courtyard; there were five levels to that room, not as stair steps, but in L's and U's that differed in elevation by ten or twelve inches. Traditionally only men sat on the highest level, women the next, boys on the right, girls on the left, and the lowest, common area was in the middle. Each level was layered with carpets and the walls were adorned with baskets, quotations from the Koran, and various niches that were originally sized to hold specific oils and holy books.

Up a narrow staircase was the room where I slept in a big double bed—Kadir's parents' room, I assumed; there was a second room at the same level that the girls shared. This room contained a double bed and walls covered with forty brightly painted trays and plates that were startlingly wonderful to look at. Below the girls' room, with a door that opened onto the courtyard, was the boys' room. Kadir's sister Shukuria and her new baby slept in an alcove off the ground floor. Normally she lived in Addis with her husband and nine-year-old son, but she was spending several months in Harar with her mother during her confinement. All the girls and women worked continuously while I was there, except for Shukuria. Her sole responsibility was to take care of her new son.

The furnishings of the common area consisted of embroidered pillows and a television set that they turned on each evening, thinking I wanted it. The programs were in English and none of them ever glanced at it.

They had been cooking for days before my arrival. They seated me on the floor on the upper level of the main room and brought on the food: a large plate of plain pasta; chicken stew with hard boiled eggs; a plate of tomatoes; a plate of *injera*; boiled meat and potatoes; potato chips; another plate of cold tomatoes, carrots, potatoes, and beets; boiled greens; fried chicken; fried hamburger; cabbage and potatoes; bananas; a huge platter of white rice with raisins. Mama set the rice in front of me and all the raisins flew off.

I was handed a warm Coca Cola and told to eat. Everybody was watching me. I took a piece of bread and they all grinned.

∼

At our round table at home I sit next to Kadir and each night I see him carefully remove the potato peelings or the tomato skin or the apple peeling and hold these inedible parts in his left hand below the table. He is so thin that I am always after him to eat, eat, eat. "There are a lot of nutrients in the skins of things," I tell him.

"Yes, Mom," he says, but he continues to conceal the peelings beneath the table. He has trouble with other food. I cook only brown rice because the whole grain is more nutritious and has a fuller flavor, but after six weeks in our house, Kadir pointed to the rice on our table. "This has no taste. You should try white rice."

∼

I ate as much as I could, but my stomach was churning with the strange tastes. I kept seeing those flies lift off the rice.

"*Bie, bie*. Eat, eat," Mohammed Abou urged every time I paused. He filled my bowl full of food I couldn't possibly get down and waved his finger at me whenever I faltered. "Eat! Eat!"

Every meal progressed like that, with Mohammed shouting, "Eat, eat," and me eating as much as I could to please him. Between meals they paraded me around to neighbors and relatives who fed me again. By the evening of the second day, I had a migraine. Kadir's mother brought me fried ground meat swimming in grease and a bowl of canned pineapple for supper. It appeared that I was the only person who was going to eat. "No, I can't," I said. "You eat, please."

They were desperate for me to eat. Mohammed, Mama, the three sisters who live at home all entreated me to eat. "Please," Amira said, so I tasted the meat and swallowed a chunk of pineapple. The pineapple tasted like aluminum. "Excuse me," I said and rushed past them, across the courtyard and into the latrine where I was repeatedly sick to my stomach. They could all hear me.

When I came back, the food was out of sight. "I am sorry," I said. Maria insisted on washing my feet; Sa'ada stood with me as I brushed my teeth in the courtyard, then the three girls took me up to bed and left me alone. I pulled the sheet up over my head and cried, ashamed to be sick and unable to eat what they gave me and thinking of Kadir with the potato skins in his left hand under the table.

~

After we ate that first day, we lounged on the carpets for the coffee ceremony. Asiah roasted the green beans over a charcoal fire, then ground them with a mortar and pestle as we watched, then made the coffee in a clay pot over the charcoal fire. The men smoked cigarettes or chewed *khat*. Incense burned in the corner of the room as we waited for the coffee. My lungs were filled with the smoke and incense in the unventilated space—I wondered how they could breathe—but nobody commented on the density of the air.

"This is how we relax," Asiah's husband, Abebekar, said when coffee was served. "All the family taking coffee together, talking, praying. Do you do this in America?"

I sipped the rich black coffee and admitted that we didn't.

When the coffee was finished, I got out the pictures of Kadir to show his mother. Mohammed hadn't let me show them when I first arrived. He'd wagged his finger at me when I pulled the small albums out of my bag as they were bringing the food, and spoke his first word to me since we'd left Anisa in Addis. "No."

Kadir's sisters were impressed with the pictures, particularly with Kadir's long hair. "He is so old," Amira said.

I nodded. "Americans say he looks like Michael Jackson."

His mother looked at each picture for a long time before turning to the next. When I told her the photo books were hers to keep, she grinned and nodded. She had prominent, white teeth that made her smile memorable. When I think of her now, I see that radiant smile and her short body bent to some task. The only times I saw her not working was when she was praying or looking at the pictures.

I expected to be left with the women in Harar as I was in Addis, but Mohammed controlled my schedule there. In Addis, he'd been subdued. At home in Harar, he was imperious and impatient, the center of everything. I was never alone with Mama or the girls. Mama and I never really spoke—she was too shy and too busy. If I tried to help her, Mohammed dragged me away. If one of the girls sidled up to talk or sit with me, he ordered them to some task. I was his responsibility.

When things got too awkward, I wrote in my notebook. Mohammed was relieved to have me occupied and smoked and talked to the men who came by.

Every time I looked up, somebody was staring at me. Khalid, Mohammed's grandson, sat very close to me, whispering and staring the whole time, reporting my every movement to the others.

They prayed without embarrassment in front of everyone, including me, while the others kept on talking. Asiah wrapped her feet in a scarf, (her head and hands were already covered), and stood as she began praying. I was clearly in the way, but I didn't know where to move to. I was sitting where they put me, on the floor with three pillows behind my back—the only person with pillows. Asiah finished and Mohammed began his prayers with little Khalid. They prayed, kneeled, touched their head to the rug, stood up and continued praying. Nobody seemed to mind that I was there writing. In fact, a couple of days later, when the girls were praying, they ask me to take their picture. "No, I can't," I said. "It isn't right."

"Yes, please. Show them how we pray in America."

～

There are ninety-nine mosques within the walls of tiny Harar. There are two in Minneapolis. The one at the University of Minnesota meets at 1:30 on Fridays—Kadir was in school on Fridays—so on a Saturday I drove him to the Islamic Center of Minnesota. We passed several large churches as we looked for the address. "That must be it," Kadir said, indicating a particularly impressive church.

"No, I don't think so," I said. A few minutes later we found the Islamic Center in a small frame house.

"This is the wrong place," Kadir said.

"It's the right address," I said. "I'll wait for you while you check it out."

An hour later he came out, subdued. "How was it?" I asked.

He shrugged. "It was good."

"Were there other Ethiopians?"

"No, they were Pakistanis and Indians."

He never went back.

～

Everybody in Harar asked if Kadir was praying. "It is hard," I said but my inability to explain why it is hard for him to pray went beyond the language limitations. Kadir doesn't observe Ramadan or all the dietary restrictions either, not because he doesn't care, but because the world he's landed in is so alien to those things.

In Harar the voices of the muezzins in the mosques fill the air five times a day. The early morning streets are crowded with men in white robes returning from the mosque. Asiah and Abebekar go to Arabic lessons from six until seven thirty every morning. Kadir's mother prays as his father carries on a lively conversation, even interrupting her from time to time. She answers his questions and goes back to her prayers.

We've taken Kadir to our Unitarian Universalist Church, to the youth group with our other children. He goes and he has friends there, but he doesn't pray. We don't hear the call of the muezzin in Minneapolis. None of us pray.

～

I was in Harar because Kadir couldn't be: it was still too dangerous for him to go. While I was there, it occurred to me that if Kadir became an American citizen, he could travel to Ethiopia as I had, on an American passport. I had met a refugee in Addis Ababa who had done just that. Kadir was desperate to go home. His parents are in their sixties and he's afraid that they'll die before he sees them again. I told Mohammed that Kadir wanted to come home.

"No," Mohammed said, "he must finish school first." (Kadir was in his second year of college then.)

"But it would mean so much to him. He wants to see you and his mother and sisters and brothers. Then he can finish."

"Yes, he will finish. Then he will come," Mohammed said.

We had this conversation without a translator and I struggled for the words to explain the hole in Kadir's heart, to explain how much he needed to see that everybody was all right before he could get on with his life. Kadir had received his first pictures from his family the second spring he was with us. It was the only time I'd seen him break down. He held the picture of Sa'ada, his youngest sister, and sobbed into his arm. When I asked if somebody had died, he lifted his head and showed me the picture.

"No," he said. "It is my sister. She was a baby when I left. Now look." She was ten in the picture, twelve when I met her. I saw the same hole in Mohammed Abou's heart, but he closed it. "No," he said, wagging his finger, "he must finish school first."

~

The telephone rang and Mohammed shouted for Amira to get it. Neither he nor Mama ever answered the phone.

"Hello," Amira said. She listened, then looked at me, smiling broadly. "It is for you."

It was Kadir. "Mom, is that you? Are you really there?"

"Yes, yes, Kadir. I'm really here, in your house. Do you want to speak to your father?"

"No," he said. He wanted to talk to me first. "How are they? Is everybody all right?"

"They are wonderful," I said. "Really. Everybody is fine. They look wonderful."

"My mother?"

"Your mother is amazing. She is so strong. She works all the time."

"Everybody is fine?"

I could hear the relief in his voice. He didn't trust the family to tell him the truth. "They don't want to worry me," he told me before I left. "If something is wrong, they never tell me." But he believed me.

"You didn't tell me your house was so beautiful," I said.

"You like Harar?"

"I love it."

"How are you talking to them?"

I imagined him trying to imagine me sitting on the carpets, leaning against the green wall under the framed exhortations from the Koran. "Some English, some Amharic."

"My father is speaking English?"

"No, your sisters." I paused. "Your father *controls* everything though."

Kadir laughed.

I looked at Mohammed watching me speak English to his son. "Your father is here, waiting to talk to you," I said to Kadir and handed the phone over and stepped back. My job was done.

⁓

When I left Harar, Mohammed asked me to choose among the exquisite baskets that adorned the house. I protested; he insisted. I chose one. "For Kadir," I said.

"Take another," he said.

"One for Nasser in Georgia," I said.

"And another."

"No," I said, "it is too many."

He insisted. I protested. How could I carry all those baskets home, much less to Kenya where I was going next? I refused adamantly. He insisted. I refused.

I left Harar with twenty-seven baskets, two kilos of *berbere*, a kilo of honey, and a pair of gold earrings in the shape of the Lion of Judah. I had been greeted as the prodigal son, with passionate kisses; I left as the obedient son, showered with gifts from the father who loved him.

The Feast of Abraham

THE BOAT RIDE from Algeciras had not been exceptionally turbulent, but the woman, Jean, could feel her heavy lunch not quite moored in her stomach, and the memory of the waves' gentle rocking still upset her equilibrium. She lifted her suitcase and followed Hassan through the baggage inspection line, fumbling through her purse for her passport as they approached the *douane*. Hassan helped her heave her bag up onto the long metal table in front of two uniformed customs agents, idly puffing cigarettes, their heads lost in a cloud of black-tobacco smoke. The smell made her feel slightly sick, and she tried to swallow. She had never been inside a coal mine, and yet this was the odor she was sure it would have.

She extended her passport across the table to the two men, holding it open to the page that had been stamped on the boat.

"*Amerikaanya*," one of them said to the other.

"*Zid, zid*," the other said. "Move along." He picked up her bag by its thin leather straps and tossed it toward the end of the table, where it landed on its side with the thud of an overstuffed carcass. Jean slid the bag to the floor and stood to one side to wait for Hassan.

The two agents had taken his passport and were inspecting it. Then one of them began going through his suitcase. He picked up Hassan's electric razor and stared at it, then put it to his face. The other made buzzing noises, and they both laughed. They took out the sociology text which was the subject of a paper he presented at the conference in Madrid the week before. After leafing through the pages and finding nothing of interest, they lay the book to the side with his razor. The rest was just clothes and a few toiletries, but they went through every item, one by one. Then one of the men held up a pair of boxer shorts with a hole in the seat. His partner made a lewd comment, something about having it both ways, then pointed at Jean and laughed. Then they piled his effects back into the bag, pushed it to the end of the table, and handed him back his passport.

The one who had been laughing yelled something to Hassan as he tried hurriedly to rearrange his clothes. Jean noticed the razor in the man's hand. He tossed it in their direction, and it landed with a metallic clank on the tile floor. One of them apologized; they both laughed.

"What was that all about?" Jean said.

"They're thieves, all of them, the *douaniers*. They were waiting for me to give them money, to make them stop. The razor might have been good enough, but they prefer bigger items, or cameras."

"Shouldn't you report them?"

"Everybody knows what goes on. Besides, they're just civil servants. You can't feed a family on what they make. So they have to take what they can get through intimidation. People see the uniform and get scared."

It was early evening, but the air retained the heat of the afternoon sun, and the streets were full of vendors hawking maps, postcards, and every sort of local artifact: hand-painted pottery, silver teapots, long wooden kif pipes, djellabas, rugs. The water seller strolled lazily back and forth, the brass cups strung to his shirt clanking together as he made his tour of the port.

"Need a taxi?" a man said to Hassan in perfect English.

"No, sanks," he said, absent–mindedly. He looked at Jean and laughed. "I'm gone five years, and they start speaking to me in English."

"And that's how you reply."

"Things change so quickly."

"I know." She was starting to feel queasy again and sat down on her suitcase to rest.

"You okay?" Hassan asked.

"Just a little nauseous. The boat didn't help."

"I'll get something for it. Then we'll go check the train schedule." He hailed a young man who was casing the port. Jean heard them whisper for a minute and made out the word "*chocolat.*" Hassan held out a hundred-franc note. The man said something under his breath and spit on the ground, then walked away.

"No luck?" Jean asked.

"Told me to go back where I came from. Said no one sells small quantities anymore."

They walked down the long dusty street that led from the port to the Tangier train station. Two boys passed them, leading a sheep. One had the animal tethered at the neck with a piece of rope, while the other goaded it from behind, slapping its haunches with a small stick.

When they got to the station they found it was locked. Through the grimy glass doors they could see the empty terminal. The station clock read seven. A middle–aged man was seated outside on the ground, counting the brown beads on a string attached to one of his belt loops. "It's clow-sed," he said in broken English.

"I guess we'll have to wait until morning," Hassan said, squinting through the fingerprints on the glass at the timetable above the closed ticket counter. "It looks like there's a train for Rabat at six-thirty."

"There seem to be a couple of hotels up that way," Jean said, pointing toward a dimly lit side street.

The first two hotels that they checked were full, but there was one more a little way up the road. When they reached it, they entered a long narrow hallway lit by two weak bulbs hanging from old fixtures, one on either wall. The registration desk at the end of the entranceway was empty. A man in a white crocheted skull cap and white linen gown lay on a cot beside the desk, reading a book. When he saw them enter he looked up over the book, then cast his eyes downward and resumed reading, stroking a long gray beard.

"Have you a room?" Hassan asked.

The man set the book down on the cot and swung his legs around to the floor. He slowly slid his feet into a pair of brown leather slippers, then stood up and walked behind the desk. Jean looked at the book on the cot and recognized the lettering from Hassan's own copy of the Koran.

"You have a marriage certificate?" the man asked.

"What?" Hassan said.

"A marriage certificate," the man repeated, not changing the steady tone of his voice, looking over Hassan's shoulder at Jean.

"No," Hassan said, as if he didn't understand. "We've just arrived this evening. We need a room. We're going to Rabat, but the train station is closed."

"Of course it is," the man said. "I still need to see a marriage certificate."

Hassan began taking out his papers. His Moroccan passport, his French *carte de séjour*, the letter from the university in Rabat, inviting him to teach for a year. "Listen, we're engaged. We're going to be married in the spring. We have an *acte de concubinage* in France. It's legal. She's my common-law wife."

"Not here," the man said. "Here, the laws are different. You forget the laws of your country."

"She's not feeling well. Please, understand. It's just for one night," he said, rifling through matchbooks and napkins and instant train station photos they'd taken along the way for some evidence of commitment he'd left out.

"I can give you two rooms. The last two that I have."

"How much?"

"Seven hundred dirhams," the man said.

"Seven hundred?" Hassan looked helplessly through his billfold. "That's robbery. What is this, the Ritz?"

"This is a good hotel. I run it, and I say that's the price for two rooms."

Jean couldn't follow their argument word for word, but understood enough to feel somehow responsible, as if her place in the scheme of things were an object being haggled over. She kept her eyes fixed on her shoes; the tips of the soles were coming away from the uppers and flapped like two tongues when she walked. She hoped Hassan would know of a place to fix them, before the fall rain set in.

"You have the nerve to dress like a holy man?" Hassan said. He picked up the bags, and Jean followed him toward the door. "Fuck you, your mother, and your god."

"As you wish," the man said, watching them go out the door.

"What now?" Jean asked, sitting down on the cement steps outside the hotel.

"You need to eat something. We'll go to a cafe and sit down. We'll figure something out."

Jean watched a young boy on the other side of the street approach a group of British tourists that had been with them on the boat. He was talking to them and making gestures as if to lead them somewhere. A man gave him a coin, and the tourists walked away. The boy flipped the coin in the air and then put it in his pocket. When he saw Jean watching, he walked across the street toward her.

"*Vouz voulez boire quelque chose?* You drink some tea?" He looked at Hassan. "*Schdup 'ntay?*"

Hassan nodded, and the boy picked up Jean's bag and led them down the street to a small cafe. He stood in the doorway, lopsided from the weight of the suitcase, and waved for them to come in. He set down the bag next to a small table by the window. Hassan gave him two francs.

"*Ingliziiya?*" he said, nodding at Jean.

"*La, Amerikaanya,*" Hassan said.

"Lots English now," he said to Jean. "*Amerikaanya, mneezien.* Americans is good." He turned to Hassan. "*Schdup 'ntay?*"

"*La, juuj cafés crèmes.*"

"I bring you coffee, lady. I work for Si Mohammed. I bring customers."

Jean watched him at the counter. His nappy hair was white under the light, and his face was prematurely lined with long diagonal creases extending down from his cheekbones. She would have thought he was an elderly midget except for the elfin glint in his eyes, still full of unanswered questions.

"He's odd, isn't he?" she said. "Like a little old man."

"It's the hash. I had a friend like him when I was growing up. Too much of it turns the hair completely gray. It ages them."

"How old do you think he is?"

"Thirteen, maybe younger."

"How could his mother let that happen?"

"A lot of things happen we can't control." He touched her hand across the table and squeezed it. She bent her head and pulled her hand away.

The boy came back to the table carrying a tray with two coffees and two *pains au chocolat.*

"You tired," he said to Jean. "You eat and feel better."

"You speak English very well," she said.

"I speak *ingliizi, arabi, italiani, fransoui, allemani.* All the important words. You need hotel? You need cafe? What's you name? I take you. English the best. American sailors teach me."

"Do you know a hotel where we could stay?" Jean asked. She had started to lose hope until they met the boy. She took a small bite of her *pain au chocolat* and chewed it slowly, then sipped from her glass of coffee. It had a thick syrupy taste; several sugars had already been added, and the steamed milk rose up in a white foam around the edge of the glass.

"Hilton," the boy said. "Big rooms. I take some English there this morning. *Flooz kteer,*" he said, rubbing his thumb against the tips of his other fingers. "Lots money."

"We don't have much money," Jean said. She thought about a long hot bath, a firm bed, but knew it was out of the question. When Hassan accepted this teaching post, they resigned themselves to doing without, to not having everything that they wanted. His father had died the previous spring and that left only Hassan to look after his mother and sisters—four women whom Jean had never met and who had already changed her life forever.

"No rooms at Hilton now," the boy said. "It's *Aïd* now. Lots tourists come for *Aïd.*"

"It's the feast," Hassan said. "I forgot. That's why the train station was closed. I should have known when I saw the sheep."

"What feast?" Jean said.

"The Feast of Abraham. It's the biggest holiday of the year. Every family slaughters a sheep. You remember the story, don't you? God telling Abraham to kill the sheep instead of his son."

"Yes, I remember. It was Isaac, wasn't it?"

"Yes," Hassan said.

"What a lousy sense of timing we have."

Hassan reached for her hand and held it, then began stroking her arm. "It'll be all right," he said. "In a week you'll be fine."

"If I had known in France, we could have taken care of it."

"But you didn't know. We weren't sure until Spain. You can't keep thinking that way."

"You stay here," the boy said. "Cafe open all night, for people who have no *flooz*, no money, like you. In the morning you go on train."

The air was getting cooler now, and Jean pulled a sweater from her bag and wrapped it around her shoulders. She took another bite of her croissant, hoping it would stay down.

Hassan whispered something to the boy in Arabic. The boy smiled. "No problems," he said, taking a small box out of his pocket and placing it on the table. "You have tobacco, I have *chocolat*. Okay?"

Hassan put a pack of Marlboros on the table.

"Just like American sailors. Always Marlboro. I like Marlboro."

The boy opened the box and took out a small bar of hash and some rolling papers. He spread out two papers and licked the edges, then pressed them together lengthwise. Then he peeled the paper off a cigarette and emptied the tobacco onto the two papers. Hassan gave the boy his lighter, and he began heating one end of the bar of hash until it was soft. He looked up at Jean for a moment. "I cook," he said, then gently cut into the softened end with his thumbnail, rolling the small pieces of hash between his thumb and index finger and sprinkling them in with the tobacco.

"What you name?" he asked, looking up at her.

"Jean," she said.

"Djinni," he repeated and laughed. "I have cat named Djinni, nice cat. I don't believe in djinn."

"Moroccans believe djinn have supernatural power over people," Hassan said.

"It's Jean," she said again.

The boy began rolling the paper together, until it was tight, then put the joint in his mouth and pulled it out between his upper lip and his tongue. "*Filtre ou sans filtre?*" he asked, laughing. He ripped off a piece of cardboard from the cover of the rolling papers, rolled it into a tube and inserted it into the thin end of the joint. "I make filter for Djinni. The devil smoke with filter, too."

The boy lit the joint and then passed it to her. She took a deep drag and held it in for a three count, then exhaled. She did this two more times. Her nausea had started to go away with the coffee and croissant, but this was the best remedy.

"I know all about woman. Sailors tell me. American sailors the best," the boy said.

"What do they teach you?" she asked.

"Fuck, they teach me lots. They teach me 'You place or mine?'"

"They taught you that?"

"They teach me a lot about woman, not nice woman like you. They teach everything, shee-it," he said, proud at that last one, holding onto the vowel so that it came out with a southern twang.

Jean watched the boy as he spoke. He had switched to Arabic and was talking to Hassan, trying to explain something. She felt like everything that was complicated was made simple here. And the simplest things they could complicate. Like the way Hassan, a doctor of sociology, kept saying "*aventrement*" to her, as if it was her stomach they were going to remove. It wasn't as if he didn't know the real word, it just got stuck and came out wrong sometimes. Or perhaps there were some things they had no words for, the very thought was so foreign. At home—

at least, in France—I would just go and have it done, she thought. Pay a hundred bucks to some clinic, and it would be over. Simple.

"That man over there, see how his face is burned, that from a woman," the boy said to her in English. "She said she fix him a tajine first, to eat before bed. Then she heat up the oil and throw whole tajine in his face. You can't trust a sida."

"A what?" Hassan asked.

"A sida. The woman that come into the cafe looking for man. That how you get sick. Everyone call them sida now, like the sickness. Not a nice lady like you wife."

The cafe owner called to the boy from the counter. Two new customers had come in. "I think he's a djinni," Jean said when the boy had gone. "What were you two talking about?"

"He told me he's twelve years old," Hassan said. "He's been working here since he came to the city two years ago. He's got ten brothers and sisters and had to leave the countryside because there was no food and his parents couldn't feed so many kids. You see this stuff all the time here."

Jean began to shake. The nausea was gone, but she couldn't stop shaking.

"It's all right," he said. "Si Mohammed feeds him and lets him sleep in the back room at night. He gets a tip when he brings in new customers. He's not unhappy. You can see that."

"I'm sorry," Jean said, unraveling the paper from a sugar cube on her saucer.

"What we're doing is right," Hassan said. "You know it."

"I know."

"When we get to Rabat it'll be over like that. Abdeslam gave me the name of a good doctor. He tried to tell me about a nurse who does the same thing, but I got a good doctor for you, a very good doctor. And I'll be right there with you."

The boy came back to the table, lugging a large calico cat by the scruff of its neck. He sat down at the table with the cat on his lap, took the sugar cube that Jean had unwrapped and held it in his palm under the cat's nose. The cat's pink tongue licked the edges of the cube. The boy placed the cat in Jean's lap. "You nice lady," he said. "Djinni keep you warm tonight. She sleep with me every night."

Jean cradled the cat in her arms and kissed the soft orange fur on its head.

"I tell Djinni, she my *xaruuf*. I kill her like Ibrahim." He dragged his index finger across his neck, made a slitting sound, and laughed.

Jean held the cat tightly to her and stared at the boy. The cat began kneading her chest with its paws.

"Joke," he said. "No problems. Djinni know it joke." He scratched the cat under its chin. Djinni closed her eyes and purred softly.

"I'm going out to buy a newspaper," Hassan said. "Looks like we'll be here for the night. You'll be all right?"

Jean nodded. She watched him through the window as he walked toward a small kiosk across the street.

"You husband good man. He come here to teach, he come back. Others leave, never come back," the boy said.

"He is a good man," Jean said, "I know."

"What he teach?" the boy asked.

"Sociology."

"Soo—" the boy tried, then cocked his head to one side and looked at her.

"Sociology. He studies people. How they act together."

"Like me," the boy said, smiling. "I study everyone. Maybe someday I teach."

"I'm sure you would be a good teacher," Jean said.

"You okay, lady? You husband say you sick. I get more coffee?"

"No, thanks. You should go to bed."

"I wait for you husband, then go." He sat with his elbows on the table, his chin resting in his hands, watching Jean bounce the cat in her arms. "Djinni like you," he said.

She stroked the soft black and orange fur on Djinni's head and smiled at the boy. She felt safe, more settled; her earlier uneasiness was gone. She propped the cat up on her shoulder, its paws clutching her sweater, and patted it gently on the back.

Hassan came back with two Moroccan newspapers, one in French and one in Arabic, and the *Herald Tribune* for Jean. The boy stood up and said good night. "The good djinn sleep together," he said, rubbing his tired eyes. He kissed the cat on the head and went to his mat in the back of the cafe to lie down.

Jean looked at the newspaper for a while. There was an article about the celebration of *Aïd* on an inside page, along with a photo of a young boy smiling, standing next to a large sheep, his father in the background looking proudly at them both.

She felt her eyelids growing heavy and closed the newspaper. Djinni was asleep, curled up on her lap. Hassan pulled his chair closer and put one arm around her shoulders so that she could rest her head on his chest. She didn't awake until she heard the first cry of the muezzin, calling the people to prayer. Then others chimed in from the peaks of far-off minarets like a resounding, hypnotic echo of the first.

"Prayer better than sleep," said the boy, mimicking the call of the muezzin as he unloaded two coffees from his tray onto the table. "Si Mohammed say coffee better than prayer." He laughed and placed two large pieces of bread on the table, along with some butter and jam.

Jean rubbed her eyes and took a sip of her coffee. Through the window she could see the orange haze rising out of the water and over the port. The air was warmer, and the vendors were already scrambling for position on the street, opening their cases and cartons, taking out their wares.

Djinni stood up slowly on her lap and stretched, digging her claws into Jean's legs. Jean picked up the cat and handed it back to the boy, who held it in front of his face, offering it a sugar cube from between his teeth. The cat licked at the sugar, and the boy smiled. He sucked the white cube into his mouth and kissed the cat on the back of the head.

Hassan sipped his coffee and spread some butter and jam onto a piece of bread. He handed it to Jean and then fixed one for himself. She took the piece of bread and tore it in half, handing the other piece to the boy.

"You eat," he said, handing the bread back to her.

"You eat, too. We'll all eat together." She pushed the bread in front of him and stroked the back of his head. The hair looked wiry but was as soft as fleece. He bent his head toward her, and she brushed his cheek with her thumb.

"This our *Aïd*," the boy said.

"Yes, it is," Jean whispered, biting into the soft, fresh bread.

Hassan watched them both and smiled.

"You come back to Si Mohammed's?" the boy asked.

"Yes, we'll come back to see you," Jean said.

"And Djinni?" he said, holding the cat over his head and smiling.

"And Djinni."

"And you will speak *arabi*. You husband, good man. He teach you *arabi*. Like sailors teach me English." He smiled and took her hand. "When you come back, you not be sick."

"No, I will be better by then."

"You wait," the boy said, standing up from the table. "I have something. You wait." He ran to the back of the cafe and returned a short time later, carrying a white sheepskin rug.

"For you," he said. "It from *Aïd* long time ago. My mother give it to me."

"I can't take it," Jean said. "Thank you. I just can't..."

"Yes, cold no good for nice lady. No nice lady come in cafe before. I want you have it. Si Mohammed give me one later," he said, pushing the skin into her hand.

"Okay," she said, "but just for now. I'll bring it with me when we come back."

"Good," he said, with a firm nod, as if closing a difficult deal. "We go train now. I take you."

Jean clutched the soft wool of the rug and held it against her face. The boy picked up her suitcase and took her hand, tugging her along toward the station. Hassan followed closely behind, watching their joined hands swinging between them, wishing he'd brought a camera.

Tanzania on Tuesday

WHEN I LIVED in East Africa, the day began with a discreet knock on the door, then a lovely cup of tea was arranged on the bed table by an unobtrusive servant. The soothing brew was sipped in bed so you could gradually untangle your mind from the muddled dream world before you seized the vicissitudes of the day. It's ever so civilized—you savor the sweet, spiced tea before you get up out of bed and cautiously shake out your shoes. It is important to inspect both of them carefully in case scorpions have crawled inside during the night. Scorpions are nasty when they are rashly aroused from a warm snooze by cold toes.

Today, there is no cautious servant to knock politely on my door and softly awaken me with tea. Now I must stagger from my warm bed to the kitchen and prepare my own cup of Earl Grey. However, after all these years, I still take the tea back to bed. It is a lovely transition from the inner world of dreams to the outer world of solid surfaces and the grouchy scorpions at work who feel I have stuck my foot into their business.

The treasures we bring back from far away places are usually not purchased in souvenir shops. Like my morning tea in bed, the real gifts of a journey are not for sale. They come to us unexpectedly and frequently have nothing to do with what we planned. When I traveled in Africa, I learned that the vacation, like the day, begins at the beginning, not when you get where you plan to go. Often we do not ever recognize an unusual event until it is over. It was years before I finally realized that I had met the world-famous archeologists, Richard Leakey and his mother Mary, while I was hitchhiking. I was on a vacation from my teaching post in Somalia in early 1970 and was so interested in getting to my destination that I paid little attention to those who helped me on my way.

Several friends from Somalia and I decided to go to the Ngorongoro Crater in Tanzania, a place famous for its teeming African wildlife. Lions, zebra, rhino, elephant, gazelle, ostrich, and many other species of animals graze and hunt in the one hundred and two square mile floor of the crater. The deserts of Somalia do not support this variety of wildlife and I was eager to finally see African animals while in Africa.

Unfortunately, travel in East Africa was expensive for someone on a Peace Corps salary. Despite limited financial resources, I had an unlimited desire to travel and had learned to rely on the resources afforded by youth and wit. My girlhood friend, Diane, and I arranged to meet four other friends on a Tuesday morning in Arusha, Tanzania, at the foot of Mount Kilimanjaro. We did not have enough money to take a packaged tour and so the six of us planned to pool our money, rent a car, and drive to the lodge at the crater's entrance. We looked at a guide book to East Africa and arbitrarily selected the cheapest hotel in town for our meeting place. The lodge at the crater was expensive so we decided to spend as little of our precious money as possible getting there. Besides, after living in Somalia, anything listed in a book seemed luxurious.

Diane and I spent the first night of our journey in Nairobi. In the bar I heard that the Kenyan government had recently instituted a policy of "Africanization." In order to increase the number of African-owned businesses, severe restrictions had been placed on Indian-owned businesses. Many had decided to leave, but the shilling was a soft currency and worthless outside of Kenya. Indian merchants were eager to acquire hard currencies such as pounds or dollars and the black market was thriving.

With my American passport, I could change as many Kenyan shillings into dollars as I wanted to. According to several people I talked with, certain Indian shop owners would exchange large American bills for double the official exchange rate for shillings. If one had the nerve, felt sympathetic with the Indians, and was willing to risk an African jail cell, small amounts of money could be parlayed into enough funds for a trip to Ngoronoro Crater, car rentals, new underwear (mine kept disappearing in Somalia), and expensive hotels.

Monday morning I gathered together all of the American dollars I had and set off in search of an address scribbled on a scrap of paper. The streets of Nairobi were busy and colorful in the mellow morning air. I walked across town, with my head held a little too high, and my chin jutting out, as I tried to disguise the fact that I was up to no good. I stopped and poked nervously around in several stores to make sure that no one was following me. I scrutinized the swirling blend of Asian, African, and pasty-white faces as I walked along. The Africans were gay and talkative with expansive mouths framing white teeth. The Asians were purposeful, and had thin lips stretched in a line over narrow chins. The Europeans looked worried and dour with mouths that pursed into vertical wrinkles.

I found the little shop and waited until it was empty to approach the tall Indian at the back counter. "Change money?" I asked, a little too loudly. His jet-black eyes glinted, betraying instant interest. Hand gestures are different in every culture, but facial expressions are universal; the eyes divulge what we seek to conceal.

He motioned meaningfully to a young man slouching in the back who stared at me while he closed the door and lowered the tattered shade. He positioned his narrow body in the shadows and watched the street. I felt the muscles at the back of my neck pull my shoulders up. Suddenly the danger involved in this illegal transaction became real, not idle barroom conversation. My neck ached and I began to think that maybe this was not worth the danger. However, once the journey began, it often takes more boldness to turn back than to continue.

"How much you want to change?" my confederate in crime asked in the hurried Indian-English accent.

"What is your rate?" I replied, stubbornly following the procedure that had been described to me. I had been told that it was important to bargain in the black market.

"I will give you twelve shillings for small bills, thirteen for large ones," the Indian replied. His white turban did not move when he spoke; only his thin bottom lip went up and down. The official rate was seven shillings to a dollar. The black-market rate was almost twice that. Large bills had a higher rate because they were easier to smuggle than smaller ones.

I wanted out of there so badly that I did not care to prolong the transaction. I was ready to drop my money on the counter and run outside to the safety of the honest daylight. "Okay," I said too quickly, keeping my eyes away from his searching gaze. The shop owner surmised I was not an undercover agent because my hands trembled as I yanked the dollars out of my purse. He held each bill up to the light and smoothed them out on the counter as if they were fine silk, then disappeared into a back room. It occurred to me that I could be the one who had been tricked. The Indian could be an informant calling the authorities now that he had evidence of my illegal actions. He would probably take some of the cash and turn the rest over to the police. I began to sweat, the air in that little shop was so close and so still. I noticed the nearly empty shelves for the first time and wondered what kind of business this was.

The merchant pulled the tasseled curtain back and returned with a handful of Kenyan shillings. He proceeded to count them very carefully and slowly onto the counter with long delicate fingers. He was demonstrating the accuracy of the amount, but I didn't care how many shillings he counted, I wanted to be out of there as fast as possible. When he finally finished his tortured accounting I scooped up the pile of bills, threw them into my purse, and rushed out the door.

My heart pounded as I walked away. My shoulders ached and I quickly gave up any attempt to appear nonchalant. I couldn't wait for the traffic to clear and burst across the street, almost getting run over by a zebra-striped minibus of tourists going on safari. Finally I ran into the safety of my hotel, unlocked the door to my room, and locked it again behind me. I leaned up against the door, panting for breath, and realized that I had run halfway across Nairobi like a stampeding wildebeest, mane flying, tail in the wind. I waited, straining to hear pursuers come running up the stairs to haul me off to prison where I would languish for years before my case ever came to trial, living with cockroaches and filth in a dark cell with nothing to eat and a rag for a bed.

No one came. The hallway was silent. I went over to the bed and sat down, still waiting. Silence. I began to relax and slowly feelings of euphoria at having actually succeeded stole across my mind. My hands, unbidden, reached into my purse and pulled out an enormous wad of money. It was thick and heavy and, elated, I thought that there is nothing as wonderful as free money. I counted it on the bed, stacked it up and held it, then counted it again. I decided that this game was, after all, rather fun. I had almost doubled my money. It seemed so easy in retrospect, so simple once I had done it.

It was eleven o'clock. Diane and I were taking a bus from Nairobi to Arusha at 1:30 from the marketplace outside of town. I was seized by the sudden and irresistible urge to change money again. I could take the Kenyan shillings to the bank and, with my American passport, change them for American money which I could exchange again on the black market. Unable to resist, I went resolutely back to the bank and boldly asked the clerk to change my ill-gotten shillings into dollars. "Going home," I said to the bank teller, and I was going home, eventually. Then, with the crisp new bills in my purse, I hurried back to the Indian shop.

It was closed. The door was tightly shut and the shade was drawn. I couldn't believe it. The black market, like the rest of the country, closed for lunch. I paced in front of the store trying desperately not to look obvious in case the police did not close for lunch. Maybe they waited in front of shops like this for stupid tourists who dared to change money on the black market. Maybe the shopkeeper and his son had already been arrested and dragged off to the dank jail cell. I knocked lightly, then rapidly, on the door. No answer. I rapped sharply, then insistently, feeling stupid and hating myself for the greed that trapped me in this terrible position.

The shade was pulled aside and, after a quick glance, the door opened. I slid into the dark interior and smelled saffron rice and spices from the lunch being served in the back room. I could hear several children playing. My ebony-eyed merchant came out, wiping the remnants of the rice off his beard. He looked startled but quickly summed up the situation.

No words were exchanged this time but the routine was the same. The guard at the door, the lingering touch on the dollars, and the visit to the back room. Long before he finished counting an enormous pile of shillings onto the table waves of fear began to ripple across the waters of my mind once again. The bank was also closed for lunch and would not open again until two o'clock. I would not be able to change all these single shilling notes for anything easier to carry on the trip to the crater before the bus left at one-thirty. If I was going to catch the bus with Diane I would have to take this money with me. The stacks of notes were too big for my purse. My confederate in crime rummaged around the vacant shelves behind the counter and found an old paper bag. I crumpled up the bills and stuffed them into the dusty bag. Well, I thought, I will just look as though I've been shopping, and I hurried out the door.

Walking through the streets of Nairobi in the bright light of high noon with a shopping bag full of illegal shillings is not an experience I want to repeat. Everybody stared at me, hundreds of people followed me down the streets. Fat women surrounded me at corners and bumped into my bag to make sure it was the one full of money. I was tempted to run screaming to the American embassy and beg for protection when I heard my name being called. I knew I was trapped and my eyes brimmed with tears over my greedy foolishness.

"Jeanne?" Diane said, suddenly next to me. "I've been looking all over for you. The bus leaves for Arusha at twelve-thirty!"

Suddenly catching a bus, any bus to anywhere, was all I ever wanted to do in the world. "Let's run to the hotel and get our stuff," I said, hoping I could fit the shillings into my already overstuffed suitcase.

Diane and I had enormous suitcases full of practically everything we owned and little that was of any use in Kenya. High heels, sweaters, hair rollers, and lipstick were quickly packed and we both lugged our ponderous bags down the hallway. I told my horrified friend what I had been up to that morning. Diane was too nice to offer her real opinion of my escapades. She was a clear-headed sort of person, straightforward and open. She had long dark hair, matching dark eyes, and a high innocent forehead. Everyone loved her for her sweetness and thoughtfulness. I was jealous that everyone liked her so much and hoped her better nature would rub off on me, but it never did. She offered no comment other than, "I can't believe you actually did that!" leaving me to wish for the third time that day that I hadn't actually done that. I waved frantically for a taxi to take us to the bus station and away from the scene of the crime.

I insisted in putting my suitcase with us in the back seat of the cab over the protests of the driver. "Oh, really, it's not heavy at all," I lied, wrenching my arm and smashing Diane as I 'lightly' swung it into the back seat. "My treat," I said, eager to divest myself of the ill-gotten gains as soon as possible and because I had noticed that several notes were sticking out of the sides of my suitcase. I struggled to pull the exposed shillings out of the closed bag because I was afraid that if I opened it the money would explode all over the cab.

The taxi driver dropped us into the middle of an open field swirling with buses, dust, bleating goats, unhappy chickens, and large unwieldy bundles carried by sway-backed women who chatted cheerfully. Diane and I dragged our suitcases to the area indicated by the driver, but none of the buses there was going to Arusha. Motioned on by one driver after another, I stopped to think what to do. A young boy approached and shyly said, "Hello," with a wide grin. Obviously proud of his English, he wanted to practice it on the whites.

I was quite happy to meet someone who spoke English and asked where the buses to Arusha were. "Away this morning," he replied.

"Are there any buses going there this afternoon or evening?" I asked with sinking heart.

"No, memsahib," came the cheerful reply. "That bus gone for the week. Nothing more until Thursday."

I couldn't believe it and asked again. "No," he said, "maybe somebody go there later but nothing go today." He could not understand my growing anxiety. Africans do not have such a thing as a two-week vacation. They work when things need to be done and stop when the job is finished.

"How about a minibus?" I stubbornly continued.

"None go there."

"A cab?"

"Nobody."

"A train?"

"Not to Arusha."

I turned to Diane who was sitting on her suitcase. "Well, I guess we won't be able to meet the guys in time to go to . . ." she started, but I was thinking of the money stuffed in my suitcase.

"Come on, Diane," I said. "We're going to hitchhike." One of Diane's problems was congeniality. A less kind person would have quickly disabused me of my impulsive notion. Diane, however, only frowned and obediently followed me up the hill to the road leading south toward the Serengeti. I stubbornly stuck out my thumb in what I hoped was the hand-signal for a ride. Diane watched from the side of the road and murmured something about this not being such a good idea.

Plenty of people hitchhike in Africa, I told myself. I simply didn't admit that plenty of people did not include two white women with big suitcases outside the native market in Nairobi.

A car pulled up and a short, well-dressed Kenyan motioned that we should get in. I resolutely put Diane in the back with the two suitcases and climbed into the front. This man was clearly amused by his passengers. He offered to take us outside of town to A104, the road south to Arusha. Any car heading south on A104 would go across the Masai Olobolodi Plain to Arusha.

Luck or fate was with us and almost immediately after he dropped us off at the end of the paved road from Nairobi, a second car stopped. This ancient vehicle was stuffed with a family from New Delhi. Father and wife sat in the front with two small children and a baby. Mother-in-law, Aunt Fatima, and three giant adolescents peered out of the back seat. I protested that they would be crowded but not fast enough to prevent our suitcases from being placed into the trunk next to a picnic basket. Diane and I were welcomed into the back seat next to toothless Aunt Fatima and the giant smiling mother-in-law. She moved over enough so I could sit down and then encompassed me with her body when she leaned back again. The family was excited about their picnic and only the car springs groaned about the extra passengers. Soon we left Nairobi and any hope of turning back. I could tell that Diane was upset but she was either too polite to say anything or she couldn't breathe.

An hour down the road, at a little African tea shop, we emerged from the back seat when the light-hearted, stout-bottomed family turned off the main road and went into the park. I felt as though I too had come into the world out of that woman's body when I got out of the back seat. They drove off with many waves of good-bye and good luck.

Although I was glad I could breathe again, the tea shop was a dismal affair. It was only a lean-to with two chairs surrounded by broken-down trucks and discarded car parts, proudly displayed next to the road.

I asked Diane to watch my suitcase, winking in case she forgot the contents, and went to see if they had any bottled soda. Diane tried to appear nonchalant while she sat on the suitcases but she couldn't quite pull it off. She was immediately surrounded by curious loiterers and I could see her talking with another middle-aged Indian while I waited for the dusty sodas.

"He will take us after he finishes some business here," she said proudly when I handed her the warm coke.

Regrettably, I was so relieved I didn't bother to question Diane about our benefactor any further. We sipped the tepid soda and watched the inhabitants of the tea shop as they watched us. Shortly a gray car pulled up and our new Indian friend emerged. This time I jumped in the back with the two suitcases. Diane had to sit in the front and make small talk while I got to marvel at the glorious African scenery and watch for animals in the distance.

The road to Arusha is mainly level, and even though it is not paved it wanders placidly over the rolling open country of Kenya. Everything seemed to lope along, the car, enormous birds floating on the hot air updrafts overhead, and distant giraffe startled into motion by the sound of the car. Soon I was lulled into an even contentment. Unfortunately, as is so often the case in Africa, my serenity was abruptly called into question when the car came to a halt in the middle of nowhere.

Much to my utter amazement, the driver opened the door and motioned for us to get out. I thought it must be some kind of a misunderstanding and insisted that this was not Arusha. "No," he said, flashing a smile. "I really must get back. I can't take you any farther."

There was simply nothing to be done but to climb out of the sheltering arms of the little car and stand there next to the road. Cars make very loud and rough sounds when they are turning around in gravel. He waved cheerfully out of the window as he sped off and we both watched the car disappear over the horizon in total disbelief.

"I thought he was going to Arusha."

"So did I," replied Diane. Africa is a mysterious place and here we were confounded by yet another mystery. Why anyone would drive for two hours out into the plains and then drop two women off in the middle of nowhere was not explainable by any logic I knew. If he had robbed us I would have understood, but this was inexplicable.

The sun was still high in the sky, but night comes quickly near the equator. The light fades rapidly in a free fall and the darkness sweeps away everything in its path. Diane and I were sharing similar fears. Despite the heavy suitcases, we had no food or water with us and we had not passed a single car on the entire trip. Obviously this was not a very well-traveled road. I did have matches and money to burn, but the thought of spending the night was frightening. Diane, placid as usual, had opened her suitcase and was brushing the dust out of her hair. I paced the tracks in the road, looking for the spoor of cars in order to ascertain how many passed this way.

Then right out of the blue, Diane made a negative comment. "I don't think hitchhiking was such a good idea," she said. I sat down next to her and put my head down between my knees.

"Well, I wish you had said something before," I replied, suddenly angry that she hadn't balked back in Nairobi.

"Before I had a chance to really consider it we got that first ride," Diane apologized. This irritated me since I knew everything was really my fault. I thought again about how hard it is to stop something once you got started.

When I looked up to heaven for forgiveness I spotted the wisp of a dust cloud off in the distance. "Hey, Diane," I shouted, "there's another car coming! Surely they'll pick us up." After the family of picnickers, I was confident that no one would complain they didn't have enough room for two stranded tourists. I got up and dragged my suitcase to the edge of the road and calmly watched the horizon. The dust cloud grew larger and larger and the rumble of the car on the gravel grew louder and louder. It appeared it might even be a truck convoy from the size of the dust which soon covered most of the blue line of the horizon.

Slowly it dawned on me that the approaching car was not following the road which curved away in the opposite direction. I stood on my battered Samsonite to get a better look but couldn't see anything but dust streaming across the plain like a brush fire. Perhaps it was the pounding noise, maybe the size of the disturbance, but something convinced me that this was not a vehicle. Slowly and with great difficulty my mind finally gave up the idea of another car. I realized that this was actually a herd of wildebeest stampeding across the open plain of the Serengeti and heading directly toward us. There was no place to hide and no place to run. My feet felt like stones. My heart beat wildly as if it wanted to fly away. Hot urine ran down my legs and into my shoes.

Diane saw it at the same time. We both watched the hooves of death in horror. The distance between us and the wildebeest was disappearing quickly. Diane crouched into a little ball behind her suitcase, an effect I found so futile that I countered by standing up on my suitcase and waving my purse. Final thoughts like "If this is death I shall meet it bravely," did not enter my mind. There were no sudden revelations, no bolts of truth. The meaning of life was not made clear to me while I stood facing the moment of death. I felt ridiculous standing on top of my suitcase but the truth is I couldn't think of anything better to do. I knew it was futile and stupid but I had to do something. I had to confront the raging dust and snorting demise approaching me in slow motion.

The animals were spread out over the plain in a V-shape with the lead animal running straight for us. They were spaced farther apart than they looked from a distance. I could see the bloodshot eyes of the leader as he plunged along, head down, beard waving, hooves spitting up clods of dirt as they hit the ground, tongue hanging out. I saw him see me, Diane's suitcase, and then I saw him jerk his head to the left. The body and slashing hooves followed the head and went around us. So did the animals behind him. He ran by us and one by one the rest of the herd followed suit. Some to the left, some to the right, but none of the panting creatures even came close. Soon we were surrounded by dark animals and dust. Diane and I stood there and watched in amazement. The herd had been moving quickly but they were not being chased. They were not even stampeding. They had moved around the obstacle in their path and Diane and I were alive in the middle of the pulsing drama of Africa.

They pulled away exactly as they had come. The thunderous roar of hooves became pounding then rumbling. The thick fog of dust settled on the ground, the suitcase, on Diane and me. Diane's face was streaked with tears. They rolled down the side of her cheek in a furrow and dripped off her chin to stain her shirt with brown spots. I was crying too and shaking with relief. Suddenly it mattered that I had wet my pants. We laughed at each other and hooted at the blue sky, wild with primitive relief and joy.

"I guess animals aren't as stupid as they look," I said.

"Only some animals," Diane replied, giving me a reproachful look.

"You could do a commercial for Samsonite!" I joked.

"I loved the bullfight scene," she remarked dryly. "You waving at four thousand tons of wildebeest." Diane made the remark from inside the bowels of her suitcase. She emerged with a little bandana to wipe off our faces and bobby pins to hold her hair in place. Clouds of dust billowed out into the still air when she attacked her long brown hair. I was afraid that if I retrieved clean pants we would have a cloud of money springing out of my overstuffed suitcase. However, I was confident that if the Nairobi police had been following us, they probably thought I was dead, trampled to death and no longer in need of incarceration, so I changed my wet pants.

Intent on repairing tangled coiffures and my dignity, we did not notice the car until it was almost next to us. Startled we stood there dumbly and watched a well-equipped Land Rover come to a stop. Out jumped a young man, white, and obviously British.

"I say, I do say! What a surprise! I mean, can we offer you a lift?" he said.

"Yes," we both replied at the same time.

"What's this now, did you girls see that tremendous herd of wildebeest? Quite a sight, no?"

"Actually we did have quite a view of the wildebeest," I began, but he just rambled on.

"Used to be hundreds of thousands, but now the herds are diminishing rapidly. But, we can talk in the car, right?"

"Right," I said. Diane closed her suitcase and tied her hair back neatly. I rolled my wet pants into a little ball and stuffed them into my purse.

"I'll put the tots in the boot, then," he said. I hesitated wondering what he meant. I was torn between my desperate desire for a lift and fear about what tot he wanted to put in his boot.

Gallantly he picked up both suitcases and struggled with them to the trunk of the car. He placed both tots in the boot and, giggling, we got into the back seat. Our new friend was driving with an older woman. She greeted us cheerily, with another very British accent. Richard introduced himself and his mother, Mary Leakey, and we drove off again. At the time neither Diane nor I had heard the name.

"We are meeting friends in Arusha," I explained. I described the Indian driver who dropped us off to see if they could offer an explanation.

"Strange chaps these Indian blokes," Richard replied. "He might have been nervous about crossing the border which is quite near here. They are having a bit of a time because of the Africanization laws. I don't know what will happen in January when they come into full effect. There won't be a food store left in Nairobi."

"It is a terrible puzzle," agreed Mary. She was in her fifties, with a serious look about her as if she spent a lot of time thinking about puzzles. Richard was ruggedly handsome. He drove as if he loved the road and the open plains of Africa. He talked as if he owned the place.

"Where are you headed?" I ventured, just checking before I allowed myself to think that we would actually make it to Arusha.

"We are going up to Olduvai Gorge. It's outside of Arusha so we will drop you there on our way back to our camp." Richard seemed delighted to be going back to the camp.

"Olduvai Gorge?" I asked, since I had never heard of it.

"Yes, we are working with some rather old chaps up there," Richard replied and his mother laughed.

"How old?" asked Diane.

"Very old," said Richard playfully, watching her face in the rearview mirror.

"I don't really know," continued Mary. "We are not sure yet, but a couple hundred thousand years."

"It's an anthropological dig," explained Richard. "Quite an interesting area."

I looked over at Diane to see if she would continue the conversation but she seemed as uninterested in digging around to look for bones as I was.

When we reached the outskirts of Arusha, Mary asked if we had booked a hotel for the night. She frowned when I told her the name of ours, the Star.

"There is quite a nice little hotel I could suggest," she offered, echoed by Richard.

"We are meeting friends at the Star early tomorrow morning so we need to stay there," I replied firmly. I suspected that proper British folk did not stay in hotels frequented by the natives and I bristled at the snobbish attitude. Diane and I, like most Peace Corps volunteers, prided ourselves in going native.

"Actually," continued Richard, "the good priest at the Catholic Church quite near to the Star would take you in for free. He does that quite a bit, I understand." He looked meaningfully at his mother then into the back seat.

"Good idea," she replied, too enthusiastically.

"No, I think we will be fine at the Star. It's only for one night," I replied.

"Quite sure, then, are you?" he tried again and Mary turned around to search my face for signs of weakening.

"Yes, we are all set."

Reluctantly, Richard stopped in front of the Star Hotel and helped us with the suitcases. They drove off waving cheerily, after Richard pointed out the Catholic Church with instructions to talk to Father Benjamin if we changed our minds.

The Star, as we anticipated, was in the African section of town. It was haphazardly built and had run down quite a bit after that. The sign above the door was so faded it could hardly be read, and the rough wooden door had lost its handle and was filthy. Diane went defiantly inside but I glanced up the street to see how far away the Catholic Church actually was. On this point, Diane was more stalwart than I. If it was an African hotel, and therefore not suitable for whites, she would definitely stay.

There was no hotel lobby, only a bar with a long front counter and small tables scattered capriciously throughout the shabby room. The interior was dim and smoky. A customer or two lounged at the tables and there were two or three men behind the bar, all African. If there had been any talk before we entered, it ended. No one moved. Interest was betrayed by the rapt attention in every single pair of eyes. Diane and I stood there, befuddled since we did not see a hotel desk where we could check in. As soon as he understood that we were confused, the bartender took control of the situation.

"Yes?" he asked in English, leaning with both elbows on the counter and propping his head up on two fists.

Relieved that language would not be a problem, I responded that we were looking for a room.

"This is the Star," he replied quizzically.

"Yes, we need a room for tonight."

"For you?" He rolled his eyes but did not move.

"Yes, we would like a room for two."

"There are some other hotels," he said carefully, reminding us of the unspoken, but unbreakable, separation of the whites from the Africans. He was as uncomfortable as Richard and Mary had been with our intention to stay in a native hotel.

"We want to stay at the Hotel Star," answered Diane firmly.

"The rooms are not ready."

I thought this strange since it was already quite late, but Africa has its own time, its own ways. I tried to signal to Diane that perhaps we ought to take a hint and go elsewhere, but she ignored me.

"We will have dinner, then," Diane replied. She was not going to be deterred. "Can a room be ready later?"

The bartender had backed off from his captious pose and was wiping the bar with a gray rag as he thought. He reluctantly gave in. Perhaps obedience to white people had been too deeply ingrained, perhaps he was curious, or perhaps he, like everybody else, liked Diane. At least that is what I accused her of later. He shouted at a surly-looking man at the back of the room. The response must have been negative because the shouting began again. "This man is taking you to a restaurant where you can have dinner," the bartender explained.

"We can eat here," Diane said.

"No, not here," came a very firm reply.

Our surly friend had roused himself and the bartender shouted for someone else to take our suitcases. I was surprised at the way he treated his customers but things in Africa didn't make sense so frequently that I had given up trying to understand. I watched reluctantly as our suitcases were carried away and felt in my purse for my passport. Numb with fatigue and hunger, we didn't think a suitcase full of money seemed important enough to drag around. I followed Diane out of the door into the quickly falling darkness.

The restaurant, as expected, was in a much better part of town. Our driver refused our invitation to join us for dinner. He would not enter a restaurant that contained white faces at the tables and black ones bringing food. We assured him we would get a cab back to the hotel, but he waited outside the door, as if he had been assigned to guard us. During dinner, Diane and I tried to puzzle out the bartender's obvious discomfort with our staying in the Hotel Star in the first place and then his insistence that we needed a guard to drive us to dinner.

Our guard seemed in better spirits on the drive back to the hotel. The Star was jumping when we returned. The bar was filled and the tables were mostly occupied as well. Loud music drifted out into the street. However, the noise and laughter stopped immediately when Diane and I entered. The bartender seemed to sigh but he hurriedly sent someone round with a key to escort us to the back of the bar. We were rushed up a back staircase through a curtain made of strings of beads. The bar noise resumed as soon as we had passed through the hanging beads. Diane and I were exhausted and grateful for the sight of our suitcases, two metal beds, and a bare bulb in the little room. I tipped the boy and he shuffled off down the empty hallway. We could hear the noise from the bar below us, but I was so tired I didn't think it would bother me in the least.

It *did* bother me. First we heard laughter and drunken people stumbling in the halls. Doors slammed, more laughter, then bed springs squeaking. Soon other people staggered down the hall, slamming into the walls and often into our door. I made sure it was locked and we put both the suitcases against it, just in case. Then there were loud, angry voices, and footsteps running down the hall. Someone threw a glass and it shattered on the wall.

"Jeanne, I think we're in a brothel," Diane said calmly from the edge of my bed. Oh God, I thought, she's right.

The fighting stopped but the respite was brief. A loud man and a woman went into a room across the hall and we heard the dull thud of fists striking bones. She screamed and cried but no one came back upstairs.

We pushed Diane's bed against the door, braced it with suitcases and the dresser, and slept in my bed. Or tried to sleep. I was actually more frightened than I had been of the wildebeest. That had seemed like an act of God. Clean and mighty. These fights and flights seemed wrong and grotesque, ugly and awry.

It was a long night. I finally fell asleep in the early morning. However, my tumbled dreams were disturbed by a knocking on the door. I awoke, frightened, and saw that Diane was terrified as well. Her big brown eyes were rimmed with red. My thoughts stumbled about hoping that the knocking would end. It became more insistent despite the morning light and the silence in the bar below. Finally, I called out across the little room, "Who is it?"

"It's tea, memsahib, your morning tea," came the voice from the other side. Diane and I clasped each other and laughed. I told the boy to leave the tea outside the door, and when his footsteps disappeared down the hall, we pulled the iron bed and our suitcases away from the door. The tea tray was neatly covered with a white napkin and the tea was hot and sweet. Diane and I sipped it slowly and listened to the soft murmur of people on the street outside. It was a mellow transition from the vicissitudes of the night to the serendipity of the day.

Cape Town,
South Africa, 1994

In HARARE, Zimbabwe, on New Year's Eve we are waiting for midnight and glancing at the television with our Shona friends, Lovemore and Christine. There before us is a gruesome reminder that in South Africa politics is everyday life. A popular nightclub, The Heidelberg Tavern, in a suburb of Cape Town, was attacked by armed men who shot and killed five young people and wounded eight. Three young women were shot at point blank range as they huddled in the corner begging for mercy. Christine watches the report and softly says, "shame." Lovemore and David go outside to look for fireworks. Christine and I talk about what it's like to be a mother. We don't talk about the shooting, but I was apprehensive and tell myself it's okay to go to South Africa now. The political situation has changed, and it's not politically incorrect to go. But I was less anxious about going to Maputo, Mozambique in the middle of the war in 1987 than I am about going to South Africa in the midst of the peace process.

It's a long way from Harare to Cape Town in more ways than one. We have to change planes in Johannesburg, and I wonder if we'll fly over Soweto. Before we land I look for the sprawling townships, the high density suburbs, but all I see are miles and miles of big houses on large plots of land with swimming pools gleeming from the yards. Off in the distance skyscrapers tower into the cloudy sky from the downtown. Quickly, we pass over one area with dirt roads and tiny boxes close together that must be an "African" area, but is too small to be Soweto.

The wheels touch down smoothly, and we walk toward immigration with our required visas. In the recent past entering South Africa involved long waits and potential hassles with the authorities. That's changed. The immigration clerks sit behind sophisticated computers and take down the information in one's passport, but it's fast, efficient and no problem. This is the new South Africa. In less than an hour we retrieve our luggage, pass through customs and are on our way to Cape Town in a comfortable, European-made Airbus where South African wines are complimentary.

Cape Town is said to be one of the world's most beautiful cities. I can attest to that fact. The sweeping deserts and rugged mountains of the Karoo lead to this jewel of a city on the southwest tip of the African continent where the Atlantic and the Indian oceans meet. We land at sunset in fifty-mile-an-hour winds. A British expatriate, Robin, who recently moved back to Cape Town after three years in the U.S. rented a car for us and booked us into a posh hotel on the newly renovated Waterfront. We speed along the freeway, the craggy peaks of Table Mountain forming a dark silhouette against the rose-colored sky, the lights of the city flickering at its base like a moon-shaped bowl of diamonds. The warm winds, the black mountains, the city lights promise excitement even for a jaded traveler like me. I feel as giddy as a kid going to Disneyland and keep reminding myself that this is South Africa.

The Victoria and Albert Hotel is four star, luxurious and expensive. Staying on the waterfront is like staying in the middle of Ghiradelli Square in San Francisco. South Africans say Johannesburg is their New York and Capetown their San Francisco. At first glance I can't disagree, except that there are more black people in San Francisco. I keep looking for black Africans, but there aren't any. The man who carries our bags is a milk chocolate color, what they call a "cape colored," people of Malaysian descent who were brought to South Africa in the sixteenth century as slaves and have intermingled with Africans, whites and peoples of the Indian subcontinent.

We stash our suitcases and go out to our friend's favorite bar for a beer. The bar is one of many on the waterfront, bustling with white people talking, smoking and drinking. We take a table outside on the patio. We could be in any generic tourist resort: Cabo San Lucas, Puerto Vallarta, the French Riviera, San Diego, the Cornish Coast. I ask Robin what he thinks is going to happen after the elections in April. He smiles and says, "We don't talk about it." I didn't come all the way to South Africa not to talk about it, but it is our first night and the winds are blowing our words away anyway. Later in the hotel room, David says all the women looked "slutty," an unusual thing for David to say. I don't know what he means; I think the fashion of short tight skirts, tight jeans and low-cut necklines is more or less the same in any summer tourist resort.

I go to sleep disoriented. This is not the Africa I know. The next day we set off toward Seapoint, the place where Robin said the Jews live. I can't tell if Jews live there or not, but it is obvious that wealthy people live there. Modern luxury apartment buildings constructed of stucco, glass and steel overlook the narrow road that twists and turns along the Atlantic beaches. Late model cars—BMWs, Mercedes, fancy sports models—are parked in every available space. In the area of Seapoint a promenade goes along between the road and the sandy beaches, but as we drive farther on and climb into the mountains the scenery is more like Big Sur, sheer granite cliffs on the left, ocean beaches a long way down on the right. Luxury apartment buildings are replaced by private villas built into the cliffs overlooking the ocean. Everyone is white and nicely tanned. The road signs are in English and Afrikaans. I try hard not to feel instant prejudice against this language which I associate with the cruelty of apartheid, but on a gut level I do.

The scenery gets even more spectacular as we come to a road called Chapman's Peak Drive where layers and layers of sedimentary rock shoot up from the road on a diagonal. The beaches, a thousand meters down the other side of the road, are deserted. The day is hot. David and I are thirsty. Soon we come to what looks like a beach town on the ocean side of the road. Cars are parked along the steep, narrow roads that access one beautiful house after another. We turn in and follow the road down, but there is no cafe, grocery store or gas station. At the bottom are armed security guards who direct us back to the main road. We joke with each other that if we were this rich we wouldn't ever have to go to the store; someone else would do it for us. We joke, but knowing what we know about Cape Town, about South Africa, driving around the place feels surreal.

Why are we here? We decide to be just tourists and do what tourists do in Cape Town—go bird watching and to the beach. For two hours we walk through tropical foliage and around ponds at a bird sanctuary and view most of the African birds we're familar with and then some: louries, rollers, owls, wydahs, widows, penguins, even the Australian Cassoway, a huge bird that has been known to claw humans to pieces in the bush, the stuff of nightmares. By the time we get to the beach and stick a toe in, the wind has come up and the water of the Atlantic is freezing, worse than the Northern Pacific where we live. The locals say the Indian Ocean beaches are warm so we drive across the cape. By the time we get to Simon's Town, the home of the South African Naval Base and Museum, we're tired and decide to skip the beach and have tea instead. The traffic is terrible. Even though we are going north to Constantia for dinner with Robin and Patricia we choose a circuitous loop to the south toward Cape Point to see the scenery. The only difference between California scenery and the landscape here are the baboons sitting on the hoods and tops of cars along the road. This is the place to go if you want to commune with the baboons. The price? A mere piece of bread. We drive up and over the top of low mountains, craggy brown piles of rock, scrub bushes and gray boulders separated by dry grasses. Unfortunately, we end up in Fish Hook where the beach traffic is bumper to bumper.

We talk. I tell David that the shopkeeper whom I'd bought a dress from asked me how I liked it here, adding quickly that Cape Town is the best part of South Africa. What's not to like? I risked adding, it's odd there are no Africans here. She nodded. "Yes, they're all up North, in Jo'burg and the Transvaal." David had a similar exchange with the Indian merchant next door. These people see themselves as a different part of South Africa, the non-black African part. So how will they like the African National Congress being in power? In April everyone will vote in free elections and the polls indicate that the ANC is a sure winner, but the way they're structuring the government, each person votes for a party, not a person, then the party picks its representatives for regional and national positions. In other words, the party rules, which means the politicians have less accountability to their constituents and more loyalty to their party. But will the powerful armed forces and police go quietly over to the side of the same people who've been the bitter enemies of the white National Party? Will the impoverished colored population—we know it's there even though we can't see it—of the Cape Province like the ANC anymore than the National Party? We ask these questions of each other and speculate this way and that as we inch toward the richest suburb of Cape Town.

After a swim in the pool we have dinner on the terrace of Robin and Patricia's rambling rancher that looks out over the city to False Bay, a choice piece of property with hillsides of vineyards surrounding their acre. I'm not an expert, but the South African wines taste as good to me as the best wines of Napa and Sonoma. They are incredibly cheap and an innocuous topic for dinner conversation. When Patricia and I are alone in the kitchen I ask her about the killings in the Heidelberg Tavern. A friend of hers had been there earlier in the evening, and his son and girlfriend were there when the armed gunmen arrived. They fled out the back door. Patricia seems to take this in stride, not seeing it as political, but as bizarre and random as the gunman going berserk on the Long Island commuter train. Still her main concern for her children is security. Cape Town is beautiful and inexpensive by Western standards, but the trade-off is potential violence, not just random crime, but political and racial violence. When Chris Hani was murdered, she says, they were preparing for a major race war. Around their house they have walls with an electric gate and three dogs. She doesn't hire housecleaners or a gardener because then they'd have access to the house and grounds. She has a fortress mentality. On the other hand, Patricia is selling real estate; the economy is picking up now that sanctions are gone. Headlines in the daily newspaper say: Boom Times Ahead. Gold shares are setting record highs. The time is right to invest in South Africa. Maybe. The complexities and contradictions are glaring.

We leave Cape Town the next morning for Saldana, a town to the north on the west coast of the Cape Province. I want to experience the country and get closer to the Karoo, the dry, arid landscape of several excellent novels. We pass the marine industrial section of Cape Town and continue straight into brown, barren rolling hills. Another hot day, a relentless sun, nothing to see. An hour later we pass the South African Nuclear Power station on the Atlantic coast, definitely a "first world" place, and shortly come to a sign for Yzerfontein. In the book we'd borrowed (we couldn't find any travel books for South Africa before we left the U.S.) Yzerfontein is called "a sleepy fishing village." We turn left and drive toward the ocean. There are no ramshackled fishing cottages or anything shabby, only more modern development, large fortress-type houses lined up lot by lot.

The white sandy beach is vast and sparsely populated. We walk toward an outcropping of rocks, passing several white families. Over the rocks to my surprise are colored families, some even look close to black. They look as surprised to see us as we are to see them. After our walk we drive through the town, hoping to see more signs of diversity, but we come instead to a real estate shed advertising "Sunny Acres." The realtor, a retired service station owner, was very pleasant. He says he gets along well with the "Affs." "They're not like us," he smiles, "but they're wonderful people once you get to know them." Things are looking up, he says, the Americans are coming back; a few days before he sold a lot to an executive from Kodak. What did the lots cost? For sixty thousand U.S. dollars you can buy a lot and for a hundred thousand dollars build a five-thousand-square-foot house on it. Sure beats California. He is unaware of the recession in the U.S. and seems to think we don't have social problems, not like them anyway. "You don't have politics," he says. Who lives here? I ask. "Retirees and Cape Town commuters." It's the country life for them.

On to Saldana where we check into the Oranjevlei, a farm turned into a quaint guest house with grandmothery rooms, a delapidated tennis court and postage stamp sized swimming pool. Summer is the brown season in the western Cape, and the farm sits exposed on the top of a brown hill with more treeless hills rolling several miles to Saldana Bay, where fishing and canning are real economic operations. The man who shows us around is a white Zimbabwean from Bulawayo who fought in the war they lost to the blacks in 1980. We don't want to talk about that so we sit in the pub with a local farmer and talk about AIDS, farming, and our impressions of South Africa. The typical Cape Afrikaner seems to be a liberal, carefree type of guy, not very well informed about the rest of the world, but happy to share his opinions. The farmer tells us that the people in the Cape don't like what they call the "Jo'burg Afrikaners." Coincidentally, after he leaves, a middle-aged couple from Jo'burg come in to have a drink, and we talk to them too. The woman is wearing a four-and-a-half carat diamond the size of a nickel. She and her husband agree, "Our blacks are a lot more aggressive than the Cape coloreds, and there aren't any blacks to speak of down here." I detect a tone of resentment in her voice, as if the people in the Cape had a better deal with "their coloreds."

In the middle of the night I wake up to the door of our room shaking, as if someone is trying to get in. When I open the door to investigate I see a thick, cold, windy fog, what is called a *guti* in the eastern highlands of Zimbabwe. As I listen to the wind howl in the dark I finally feel like I'm in South Africa, the desolate Karoo frontier of novels. By breakfast, the sun is hot with not a cloud in the sky. In search of a hat and a laundry we go into town. In the stores I'm immediately greeted in Afrikaans which is disturbing though understandable since I'm white Anglo-Saxon looking. On the way back we pick up three different groups of colored people hitchhiking, hoping to hear a bit of the other side of the story, but sadly, the colored people speak only Afrikaans and no English at all. I think of the schoolchildren who protested and died because they didn't want Afrikaans to be the official language of instruction. They are trapped in the language of their exploiters, a language unique to South Africa.

In the evening we drive forty-five minutes to go on a riverboat tour billed as "bird-watching with snacks." We see two birds, eat snook pâté and converse with Germans, two Australians, a South African photographer and the boat owner, Nick, a fourth generation sheep farmer who is turning to boat tours to make a living. Farming this water-poor land, he explains, can't compete with Australia and New Zealand to produce lamb, beef or wheat. We are the first Americans he's had on his boat, for him a sign of the changing times. Back at the farm we have delicious lamb for the second night in a row.

The following day we head inland through wide valleys of bright yellow fields toward the black mountains of the wine country and stop in the small town of Tulbagh at another farm guest house, less rustic than Oranjevlei. The elegant main house dates from 1792 and is decorated with English and French antiques. The front garden is filled with red, pink and white roses. Our host, Buck, a friendly Boer, is the great-great grandson of the original farmer. Over a bottle of wine he talks a blue streak about himself, his work, his travels, his hobbies, the latest one being this guest house. When he hears that David is a doctor he says the other guests he expects are a doctor, Professor Steyn, and his wife. This is the man David was told is his counterpart in infectious disease in Cape Town. It really is a very small world, especially when narrowed down to white, upper-middle class professionals in South Africa.

Without really planning to we end up spending the weekend with LeFrans and Kate Steyn, I think upsetting poor Buck who didn't get to entertain us or them with his Vortrekker stories. LeFrans comes from a solid line of Afrikaners. His father was once ambassador to England. Kate is half-Afrikaner and half-British which is significant in this country. He apologizes to David for not seeing him in Cape Town, but he wanted to go on holiday after the tourists from the Transvaal had gone home, the local prejudice again. Both LeFrans and Kate are well educated, well informed and liberal, pretty much like us and, of course, we get along. Our first conversation was about the historical similarities and differences between the U.S. and South Africa. LeFrans says the most important difference is that Europeans initially came to South Africa for reasons of commerce alone—to exploit natural resources and return to Europe. Whites initially went to the U.S. with no intention of going back. I wonder out loud what the U.S. would be like if the settlers had met with an organized population of Native Americans who continued to reproduce, hold their cultural ground and win some wars. Imagine a highly industrialized, modern European civilization on the East Coast of the U.S. coexisting with a majority population of Native Americans west of the Mississippi. Would we be negotiating democracy and majority rule? Sadly, that wasn't our history. We killed off the Native Americans and soon outnumbered them.

Buck rouses us early on Saturday morning to go champagne–tasting with the Steyns and another couple, Mr. and Mrs. Hook. We ride with the Steyns and chat about how they liked living in Denver for a year and other preliminaries of getting to know each other. When we reach the champagne vineyard, we follow Buck. He seems upset and mumbles, "what are these people doing here?" I look around just noticing there are people sitting on the steps, strolling around the grounds, children and their parents, older people, well dressed and smiling, obviously having a good time. We're quickly wisked off to the champagne cellars, Buck and Mrs. Hook seeming tense and annoyed. After a brief tour we adjourn to the tasting room for a glass of champagne. The people are still there, a young man strumming a guitar, others sitting at tables tasting as we are. "What a disgrace," Mrs. Hook was livid. "What are they doing here?" I look at Kate, questioning; she leans toward me and whispers, "The colored don't usually come here. She's not used to it."

After champagne we and the Steyns go for a sumptuous lunch at a beautiful garden restaurant. I sample a tasty local specialty called Bobotie, a minced lamb pie with Indian condiments. We order more wine and talk about politics. Kate says she's going to vote for the African National Congress, but LeFrans says he's not sure. He'd like to be able to split his vote, nationally and regionally, the issue that David keeps talking about. One-party rule hasn't had great results in Africa. The big problem is what he calls "the lost generation," the schoolchildren who came of age protesting in the mid-seventies and grew up without education, living essentially in a state of seige. They are angry, uneducated, unskilled, living in poverty and many of them are armed. One can buy an AK47 for one hundred rand, thirty U.S. dollars. What opportunities can the ANC give them? Are they able to kill with ease, having already been dehumanized? The sort of terrorist violence at the Heidelberg Tavern is no rational political strategy, but the product of desperation, of being left out in the past and in the future. Their goal was to terrorize and be remembered. If Mandela comes to power he will be the one sending the Casspirs into the townships to keep order, and no one knows how "the lost generation" will react to that.

LeFrans is the first person I ask who has any idea about the demographics of the Cape Province. He thinks there are about two hundred thousand whites, two hundred thousand black Africans, and three million coloreds. Population statistics from 1989 estimate the total population of South Africa to be 36.5 million: 75% African, 13.7% white, 2.6% Indian, 8.7% colored. The majority of the Cape Province (the coloreds) will go from being ruled by the white minority to the black Africans, a regional minority. Kate speculates that many coloreds will vote for the National Party, the known rather than the unknown. They are the workers of the Cape: the maids, the servers, the truck drivers, gas station attendants, shop clerks. Having jobs makes them a group with something to lose. Redressing economic and social disparities in a society with such an enormous gap between the rich and poor and such diverse cultural traditions will not be an easy task. Nelson Mandela is a hero, but he's not a magician or miracle worker. Under apartheid the racial classification scheme is extremely complex; the colored group was initially divided into seven sub-groups, but suffice it to say that it's *how* the classification scheme ordered and controlled everyday reality that makes it so important. Apartheid is finished, but the world it created still exists and isn't going to go away overnight. We finish our lunch on this perplexing note.

Sunday we exchange addresses and hopes to meet again in Cape Town. David and I are returning to spend our last five days in the city. Buck plots a route for us through Franschoek, a French settlement in the wine country near Stellenbosch. This town, he says, has wonderful food and wine. I've had so much wonderful food and wine already I can barely zip up my jeans. The route is quite scenic, the lush greenery and flowers a big contrast to the open brown hills, and the restaurant, Le Rouge Ballon, is wonderful, as advertised. Late in the day we arrive at the Underberg Guest House in the Cape Bowl section of the city. The Underberg is a lovely old Victorian, and the owner who greets us sounds typically British. He tells me later that he's an Afrikaner, his father having sat in the first Parliament on the opposition side with Helen Suzman in 1961. In the small lounge there is a photograph to prove it.

Early Monday morning David goes off with Robin to give a lecture on AIDS at the hospital. I decide to spend the day in the museum and botanical garden complex near the Underberg. The National Art Gallery isn't open so I go to the South African Museum of National History and educate myself on the history of the only surviving indigenous peoples of the Cape. When the Europeans first arrived they met the Khoi-Khoi, a group they called the Hottentots. Farther into the bush were the San—called the Bushmen by the Khoi-Khoi because they had no name for themselves. As I look at the life-size models of these people I recognize the features of many of the colored people I see on the streets. The Khoi-Khoi had heart-shaped faces and were a light brown color. The Bushmen were small and yellow brown. The black Africans are in the north, and the Europeans didn't run into them until they began trekking north. Two rooms house the exhibit on the indigenous peoples and the rest of the musuem is devoted to whales, fossils and the animal life. The most interesting part of the people exhibit, aside from the clay models that were created from the last surviving "pure" Khoi-Khoi and Bushmen, is a series of recent newspaper articles lambasting the museum for putting the indigenous peoples in the same place as the animals while the history of the whites is in the South African Cultural Museum. The curators have posted disclaimers apologizing for any misunderstanding and saying they don't mean to imply that the indigenous people are closer to the natural world than anybody else. One could get that impression.

David and I meet back at the guesthouse and ask our host for restaurant recommendations. He gives us several. The Cafe Paradisio, he says, has a "buzz" to it, meaning it's lively and trendy, a good place to see the locals eating out. In the course of the evening I discover there's a "feminist" writer staying at the Underberg, and I resolve to meet her. So far even though I've met several well educated folks I've met no one who'd read as much South African literature as I have. She might be someone who has, and I am curious to know what feminism is in South Africa. I spot her at breakfast the next morning and waste no time striking up a conversation.

Andrea is the associate editor for what she calls the only feminist magazine in South Africa, *Femina*. She hands me a copy with a pretty picture of the actress, Meg Ryan, on the cover. She is as eager to talk to me as I am to her. She lives in Jo'burg, but is working in Cape Town for a month to fill in for another editor who's having a baby. She asks me to read her article on abortion in the magazine. I agree, knowing abortion is a hot topic in Africa where it's strictly illegal but is done anyway. Briefly, we discuss politics: the headlines this morning are about a thirty-two-year-old colored photographer who was shot while on assignment with ANC politicians in a township. Andrea knew the man whose newspaper photo showed a nice-looking young guy with a camera around his neck. She speculates that the armed wing of the Pan African Congress, a formerly banned political party to the left of the ANC, may or may not be responsible for the Heidelberg Tavern attack. Possibly, it was the mysterious "third force," a group composed of ex-military, police, right-wing fanatics, and who knows who else. We make a date to have dinner together. She says she wants to interview David about his AIDS research.

If *Femina* is the only feminist magazine in South Africa the feminists are really in trouble. The article on abortion is informative, but the rest of the magazine is movie stars, diets, fashion and an interesting spread on "nice men," complete with photographs, biographies and eligibility status. At dinner when Andrea asks me what I thought of it I try to say this as politely as I can. She agrees that the feminist movement here is in bad shape: small, mostly white and facing an uphill battle with the diverse ethnic traditions. Our dinner conversation is strange. Andrea doesn't ask David any questions about AIDS. She asks him about Prozac, the anti-depressant that thirty million Americans take. Tonight she seems different from the woman I met this morning—meeker, more deferential. I mention the film, *Taxi to Soweto*, a hilarious, well–done movie about a white madam in Jo'burg who is hijacked to Soweto. The director, a young man with a brilliant career ahead of him, recently committed suicide, she says. I find this hard to believe, then she tells us of two painters who committed suicide and a poet too. Why? They were all believers in a new South Africa. The dream of the revolution, flag-waving in the streets and victory parties, isn't working out quite right. The thrill of success seems to have been dulled into everyday dreariness by the toil of negotiation and compromise. The revolution isn't a revolution. The idealists, romantics and committed white activists don't have The Cause to fight for anymore, or an enemy so easy to recognize. It's depressing to go back to humdrum what-am-I-going-to-do-with-myself-today existence. Andrea glances up at David with disappointment, realizing he doesn't know anything about Prozac, then says she is depressed herself. By the end of the evening I am worried about this young woman who's had bad luck with men and knows too many people who've committed suicide.

We leave the Underberg Guest House the next morning to spend our last few days with our friends in Constantia. The next day we wake up to rain and fog. "Unusual for summer," Patricia says. After ten days of hotels and guest houses we are back in the chaos of a family with two children and three dogs. David wants to get back to work so he and Robin leave early for the hospital. Rebecca and Jonathon are carted off to riding school, and Patricia has an appointment to show a house. I'm left to wait for the electrician. Caesar, the doberman, is an intimidating dog, and workmen won't come in unless they are assured that he won't attack.

In fact, the other dog, Teddy, a mongrel collie, is more likely to attack. As soon as I settle down to write the phone rings. Melissa Steyn, LeFrans's sister, invites me to lunch, volunteering to pick me up. I accept. Then I spend the rest of the morning trying to figure out how to get the electronic gate open. "Sometimes it works and sometimes it doesn't," Patricia tells me later. I don't like being trapped, even inside a luxury house.

LeFrans and Kate were right about Melissa. They said I should meet her because we have a lot in common, and we do. Her home is near the University of Cape Town in a nice, but not posh, area of small houses. Like myself she married and had a daughter as a teenager. I went to college and worked after my daughter was born, and she lived for fifteen years as the wife of a farmer in the Karoo without electricity or running water. When her marriage failed she got an Honors in English which means one year post-graduate study, and now teaches at the college level. I also went to graduate school after my marriage failed and taught college. I am pleasantly surprised to discover I haven't overlooked any major South African writers in my study of their fiction and poetry. I tell her about my meeting with the editor of *Femina*. "That's not a feminist magazine at all," she laughs, then tells me about a feminist journal that's published quarterly. The black women, as I've seen in Zimbabwe, don't have time for women's liberation, she says. They're too busy working and taking care of children, their own and their employers. Activist white women are more often working on issues of race and economics; they haven't yet had the luxury of focusing on their own oppression. In the context of this society where colored women do the domestic labor for them they aren't as burdened by dual responsibilities of home and work. They're less likely to see a need for women's liberation. I shift the conversation to politics, asking my usual questions. Melissa echoes the observations I heard from LeFrans and Kate. The Cape Province may become the most conservative in South Africa. She thinks many colored will vote for the National Party, but has no doubt that Mandela will win the election. Like everyone else she doesn't know what's going to happen. She looks down and shakes her head from side to side, a gesture of apprehension, then she looks up and smiles, "I hope it's going to be better. We'll have peace."

There's so much we don't do in Cape Town. We never swim in the Indian Ocean. We don't ride the cable car up Table Mountain. We don't drive the famous Garden Route that runs east and north toward Durban. Our last days we relax in Constantia, take walks through the vineyards, swim in the pool, read, write and eat at another superb restaurant, the Rosenhof. Patricia has a natural talent for stand-up comedy, and she entertains us with funny stories of her encounters in real estate. I might have gone out more if it weren't for the fun I had listening to her stories and jokes. The current events were providing plenty of material for comic relief—the trail of Lorena Bobbit who cut off her husband's penis, and the hung juries of the Menendez brothers. If your children blow you away when they grow up you know something was wrong with your parenting. My attempts to get either Robin or Patricia to talk seriously about South Africa are futile, and that's okay. My head is filled with ideas, questions and information. I'm ready to go back to my Africa—Zimbabwe. I like the slow pace of the developing as compared to the developed world.

On our last day David and I take Patricia out to the prissy Constantia Cape Farm Stall for lunch. We settle ourselves in with several tables of well-coifed and dressed middle-aged ladies and order steak and kidney pie, quiche lorraine and salad niçoise. The food is good. Patricia says this place is famous for their Sunday breakfasts; local folks come to eat in their pajamas and slippers. I laugh, thinking this is another joke, but she keeps a very straight face and says, "It's the God's honest truth." This part of Cape Town is a homey, safe place indeed, and the idea of going out to Sunday breakfast in pajamas and slippers has a certain appeal.

As we leave Robin says be careful on the N1, the freeway that takes us to the airport. When the government decided a few years ago to bulldoze the Cape Flats, the less desirable suburb of Cape Town, thousands of homes were destroyed and thousands of people were displaced. But people came back and rebuilt their modest houses so the government built a huge sand dune along the N1 to block the view of the area. Angry young boys sometimes come running across the top to throw rocks at passing motorists, a problem the commuters have to endure. We drive by the dunes without incident. On the plane, David asks me if I'd like to live in Cape Town, and I think about it. No, I decide. It's a great place to visit, but I may as well live in California.

THE AMERICAS

Cuba's Special Period: Dial 911 and Wait Forever

SHORTLY BEYOND the gate of Jose Marti International Airport, a huge fading sign proclaims "It is time to greet the revolution." Perhaps, but it appears the best the revolution will muster is a weary response. Everything I see is decrepit, falling down, falling apart, rusting, languishing. What is stunning is the worn, patched (and more often unpatched) look—all the buildings in degrees of disrepair. Everything once painted is now so faded and peeling that colors have lapsed beyond recognition. Dwellings and storefronts seem hollowed out, the glass broken or just plain gone. I'd think them abandoned except that laundry is strung from most windows. The sparse vehicular traffic is composed of Fiats, Russian Ladas, and American cars from the forties and fifties. Twice we pass ancient red buses jammed beyond belief. People are literally hanging onto the outsides, tenuous toeholds at the bottom, their hands clinging to door and window frames. Most of the traffic, though, is bicycles, many with an extra rider perched behind the seat or on the handlebars. As we enter the city of Havana, the remains of a billboard tell us that, "With the revolution and socialism, we have all that we want." Another mile, another sign: "This is our victory."

We are a group of writers, a photojournalist, and an illustrator. Most of us have no previous connection to one another. The string that has drawn us together for this ten-day trip is a common interest in Cuba, the restriction of visas (by our government, not Cuba's) to ones issued for professional education and journalistic purposes only, and the practice of the Cuban government of giving entry to various agencies and professional groups. There is an obvious down-side to a Cuban-arranged itinerary, but we are determined to see the party line and then beyond it to lives of the Cuban people. A freelance writer always prowling for unusual material, I've paid my money and come at least partly because I've recently received a substantial grant providing for time and travel. The luxury of the decision is so great that it begins to haunt me even as I get my first glimpses of the city.

Although we were booked into the Havana Libre (the Hilton until it was nationalized after the revolution), our Bureau of Tourism guide, Nelia, tells us we have been moved. The tropical "storm of the century" that severely damaged the eastern United States in March, 1993, was even more devastating to Cuba; now, two weeks later, four major downtown hotels are still closed due to extensive flood damage. Not to worry, she says, the Hotel Capri is also "a first-class hotel."

We enter the lobby and stand around for nearly thirty minutes, nervously shifting our weight from foot to foot as Nelia, a diminutive thirty-two-year-old woman, talks to front desk personnel. None of us, high-school Spanish notwithstanding, can understand a word of the rapid-fire exchanges, but Nelia looks increasingly pained. She suggests we sit down, and gestures toward nondescript brown sofas some distance from the desk. Foam rubber is spilling from split seams onto the bare floor. Next to the sofa into which I finally sink is a Formica table crusted with dirt from the last time a dying fern on it was watered. Around me, on the walls, are the remnants of elegance: ornate gold trim, shaped into leaves surrounding recessed arches, within which have been set pieces of sculpture.

It is another fifteen minutes before Nelia comes. "We are so ashamed," she says. "There is so much crowds because the other hotels are closed that there are not rooms for you yet." We will have to go out to lunch and proceed, she tells us, on a tour of the city, before checking in at the hotel. None of us is happy about this, but we collect a few possessions, cameras, and the like, which we are loathe to leave with our luggage. Kate Dahlgren reluctantly lets go of a heavy bag of soap and patent medicines which a woman back home begged her to deliver to the mother she has seen only once in the twenty-eight years since her father fled the revolution, with her in his arms. The mother had remained in Cuba because she feared that she and her second husband, an Afro-Cuban, would be subjected to discrimination as an interracial couple in the U.S. This is only the first of many stories and fragments of stories we will hear of the sadness of families divided by ninety miles that might as well be nine thousand.

Before leaving the hotel, we ask to use a rest room. The elevator to the basement has a uniformed woman to push the self-serve buttons for us. Full employment. In the bathroom, there are no seats on the toilets, no soap, no paper towels, no toilet paper in the stalls, though here, as at the airport, an attendant hands me two thin sheets of toilet paper as I enter.

It is a ten-minute drive along the Malecon—a broad boulevard separated from the sea by a thick, concrete wall—to Old Havana, the section of the city constructed as early as the sixteenth century. We are taken to a mansion built around a courtyard. It was once owned by a wealthy family but was seized and nationalized after the revolution and now serves as a restaurant, though we do not yet know that this place, like any Cuban attraction at which food or consumer goods are available, is limited to foreign tourists who must pay with American dollars. We are served a five-course meal, much more than any of us can finish. This begins my experience with the vast discrepancy between what is available to Cubans, whose ration cards often entitle them to buy what isn't available at the distribution center, and the relative luxury of what is reserved for tourists, as part of Castro's desperate plan to attract tourism dollars to replace the economic subsidies of the former Soviet Union. Relative luxury is the operative term here; by United States standards, the "tourist" conditions are abominable. It is nothing less than painful to realize that we are receiving the best Cuba has. The revolution's achievements in education and health care are still remarkable, but are not what captures attention any more. In the Cuba of 1993, everyone is underprivileged, everyone is struggling, everyone is deprived. To be sure, it is not Somalia. While I am in Cuba, I do not see homelessness; I do not see people dying of starvation. What I do see is a country in steady decline, an educated, resourceful people lacking more and more of the essentials with which to be resourceful, unable to purchase many basic foodstuffs and raw material or finished products. When something breaks, there are no parts to fix it and there is no place that sells a replacement. Blackouts to save energy are common and unpredictable. The cumulative impact of the American embargo has been difficult; the end of Soviet subsidies has been devastating. Where are they finding hope? Who do they blame?

After the meal, Nelia leads us on a walking tour of Old Havana, during which she frequently asks if we'd like to stop for a drink at one of Hemingway's haunts, or points out a place where we can shop for souvenirs. Each of those places has a blue and white sign in Spanish and English: *Tiendas Intur compras faciles.* . . . Tourists easy shopping. I will come to realize that part of Nelia's job is to get us to spend dollars anywhere she can, and that what is in these shops, uniform from one to the next, are the same trinkets, rum, and cigars. It takes a little longer to grasp that Cubans are not allowed in them and pesos are not accepted. Why not? Because the goods available there—which often do include such items as canned meat and milk, shampoo and razor blades, in addition to souvenir trinkets—are reserved for tourists, on the theory that tourists must not experience any deprivation or they will not come here for their vacations. The miniscule supply of these precious items that Cuba is able to import is channeled by the state directly into the tourism industry. Cuban individuals are not allowed to have dollars. The law, consistent with socialist theory and practice, is that any dollars procured must go to the state which will use them for the benefit of all citizens by buying, on the dollar-driven world market, goods to be rationed among all citizens. (Of course, the relationship of the law to the reality of the flourishing black market is limited; later in the week, when Nelia has come to trust us, she will tell us that virtually all consumer goods are illegally available, but only for dollars.) The state's second task, after the difficult one of gathering dollars, is to find countries outside of the eastern European bloc, now in their own state of collapse, willing to defy the American embargo, especially in the light of the October 1992 Cuban Democracy Act—which extended and tightened the blockade by forbidding foreign subsidiaries of American companies from exporting to Cuba to unload any freight in the U.S. for six months.

During this walking tour of narrow, cobbled streets, Nelia points out historical and architectural features. Most of us, though, are much more fascinated by the children, who continually approach us with outstretched hands, chirping "chiclets" or "chocolate" in heavily-accented English. We easily identify prostitutes, lounging in doorways that open onto the street. Everywhere, laundry is draped from balcony to balcony. A teenaged boy approaches Ed Thornburg, the illustrator in our company, and, as Ed turns to respond to the begging he anticipates, the boy suddenly leaps up and snatches Ed's white baseball cap from his head, tearing off down a narrow street. As though in a movie, we stand dumbfounded, watching him for a long time, a long-legged figure growing smaller. Nelia is obviously embarrassed, as she has been by the prostitutes and begging children, some dressed in tattered red and white uniforms of elementary school "Young Pioneers." She apologizes on behalf of Cuba; this is obviously not the picture the Bureau of Tourism has in mind.

Finally, we do stop, in a tourist shopping "mall," housed in an ancient mansion-like building, built around a courtyard much like that of the restaurant. We order rum mojitas, three American dollars each. I find the bathroom unusable: seatless, unflushed and unflushable toilets, no water, no soap, no paper towels. Even recognizing that I'm probably doing permanent kidney damage, I skip it, though I've been waiting since lunch.

After another length of time, a source of consternation to Nelia, who recognizes the fatigue and impatience we're no longer attempting to hide, our bus reappears, and we proceed on the city tour, past points of pride: the stadium of the Pan Am games, which looks like an athletic complex that could belong to a small, strapped U.S. college, the capitol building, *La Plaza de la Revolucion*, the hospital, the University of Havana. These landmarks are thin slices of bread sandwiching ruins; the consistent aura of poverty and disrepair throughout the city is what affects us.

Returning to the hotel, we get rooms at last. Kate and I have twin beds in a room the size and structure of an average American hotel, but there the resemblance abruptly ceases. Filthy, worn carpeting, torn in many places, is coming loose from the floor. Mismatched, ugly orange lamps sit crookedly on ancient pine and formica tables. Plaster, crumbling from the stained walls, lies on and in the carpet shreds. One window is simply missing. There are no screens. The drapes are moldy, plasticized fabric, long past salvageable. The bathroom appears to have been cleaned, and there are four small, neatly-folded threadbare towels, but no hot water. No washcloths. A half-roll of toilet paper. One handle on the tub has been rigged, one is simply missing. Large sections of the walls are missing plaster; what is there is mold-stained. We meet our first cockroach, a bold one out for a late afternoon stroll. Welcome to Cuba.

That evening, Kate and I walk several blocks to the Malecon, then to the National Hotel, where we have a drink and share a sandwich. In a kind of reverse culture shock, we walk on the marble floor of the wide, elegant lobby. The *diplotienda*, or tourist store, in this hotel is stocked with all manner of things the Cubans cannot buy. The only expensive clothes I've seen are all here, on women waiting to enter the chandeliered restaurant. Other guests are still wandering in from the columned portico overlooking the sea, where they had been sitting to gaze at the waves over their cocktails. This place, crammed with apparently wealthy South American tourists, is the one, brief glimpse of opulence I will see in this beleaguered city. As we leave, Kate points out the ununiformed guards at the ornately landscaped entrance drive; we realize that we were allowed in because we are not Cuban. Over and over, we will encounter this tourist apartheid; already I am feeling apologetic, strangely embarrassed, strangely ashamed.

Disconcerting, also, is the continuing sense of vulnerability. We were warned that we'll probably be watched, that the safest assumption is that our rooms will be bugged. Also, we've been told that petty theft from hotel rooms is common. My passport, tickets, letter of assignment, and cash bulge in a flesh-colored body wallet under my clothing. All this seems at once necessary and stupidly self-important in a country where people spend much of their lives in lines hoping for an inadequate ration of a basic necessity, and the owner of a scrawny rooster scratching in a pan in a tiny overgrown yard a half-block from the hotel could end up in jail for "private farming."

When we return to our room, a party of roaches scurry from the light. Water trickles from the faucet, and I leave it running for a half hour to see if it ever becomes hot. At nine o'clock—the schedule discovered quite by accident—hot water comes on, and Kate and I rush to shower, not knowing for how long, or when we'd have it again.

~

In the morning, we have breakfast in the basement of the hotel in the none-too-clean dining room, where the tablecloth has obviously been used at least several times this morning, if not for the past several days. The buffet includes eggs scrambled with some sort of grain, as well as both hard and soft boiled eggs, and a fried, fatty, processed ham. There are trays of cut fruit—papaya, pineapple, oranges—and a sugared/honeyed bread. A cold potato and cucumber salad, and a cabbage slaw are also out, though little touched. Most of the tourists here—although they are not nearly as well dressed and lack the aura of wealth evident at the National Hotel—are Spanish-speaking. In spite of a great effort to attract Canadians and Western Europeans, the most successful campaigns have been in Latin America. After this first hotel meal, we meet in the lobby to begin the real business of the trip: meetings and interviews to acquaint us with the impact of what Castro has deemed the "Special Period," since the disintegration of the Soviet Union and Russia's subsequent withdrawal from its "unbreakable friendship" with Cuba.

Our schedule, which includes morning and afternoon meetings each day we are here, has been arranged by the Cuban Institute of Friendship with the Peoples (ICAP), which means that we will hear exactly what the state wants us to hear. When reality differs from the party line, as is almost always the case, we will have to discern it for ourselves. Although we knew we'd not be allowed contact with dissidents, we have yet to realize what lengths our hosts will go to to prevent us from casual conversations with ordinary Cubans; we are supposed to gather our material only from sanctioned sources. This morning we are met by Nelia, whom we are delighted to see; she was going to ask to be replaced, she told us yesterday, believing her English too rusty to meet our needs—extra-intimidating, she says, because we are writers. She has been assigned very few English-speaking groups because there aren't that many that come. Although her English is halting and she lacks the vocabulary to translate nuances, we have all been taken with her natural mixture of shyness and warmth. This morning, she is joined by Olga, an ICAP representative. We are told that she will be with us this week to help Nelia translate. None of us quite buy this, however, because her English is certainly no better than Nelia's. Nelia, we notice, seems very careful about how she answers our questions in Olga's presence and, once we find out that Olga is a member of the Communist Party and Nelia is not, we become certain that as Nelia is there to watch us, Olga is there to watch Nelia.

At any rate, both women kiss and embrace Kate and me in greeting, and Olga stumbles through an explanation of ICAP and how she had planned our week's program. We head to the bus just outside the hotel, where Roberto, our driver, waits. I've become intrigued with Nelia and Olga, and begin a process of asking them about themselves, noting a decrease in Nelia's candor. Yesterday, when I asked harmless personal questions and gave empathetic responses, she revealed that she was still single at thirty-two, but engaged to a plumber, and had majored in English at the University of Havana. Now, she lives with her mother, father, sister, and brother-in-law in the outlying province of Havana. She acknowledged that it is very difficult for her to get to work, because often the bus simply doesn't come, or bypasses the stop because people are already hanging off the side; there is simply no space for even one more body. She says there is no room in their tiny apartment for her fiancé, who lives with his family in the city, nor is there room for her with them. I ask why they don't marry and get a place of their own. The answer: they cannot get an apartment in Havana, and the impossibility of transportation makes it absurd for her fiancé to move away from Havana city, in which he, like Nelia, works; two of them would then face the problem. Kate says that in Amsterdam, from 1985 to 1986, there was that kind of housing shortage and there were waiting lists for apartments. Nelia replied, "At least there was a list. Here there is none."

~

After repeated attempts over a period of several days, Kate makes contact with Mousi, the Cuban woman whose daughter has sent supplies of soap products, chocolate, medicine, and one hundred dollars, which she's asked Kate to use to buy food at a *diplotienda* for her mother. Mousi had said she would take a bus into the city and meet us in the hotel lobby, and that she'd be happy to allow me to interview her. After an hour and a half, she has not appeared. We walk to the Malecon again, frequently approached by young men asking to exchange pesos for dollars, or calling *chica, chica* with a lewd grin. An Afro-Cuban persistently follows us, asking in English for five dollars for shoes, he says.

Back at the Capri, there is still no sign of Mousi. We give up and go to the dinner buffet. The food is plentiful. Fish, chicken, and meat platters are stacked on the hot table. Other tables are heavy with potato and cabbage salads, a mélange of hot vegetables, and trays of cut fruit. Several kinds of heavily-sugared pastries are set out for dessert. I am ravenous and guilty. Cubans might have a ration for one-half chicken a month. Beef is unobtainable. Milk ration cards are given only to people with elementary school-age children, but on the Capri's beverage table, unlimited milk is ours for the pouring.

Journalist Jon Hughes, who has been here before, tells us that Mousi would probably not have been allowed in the lobby, even to visit a hotel guest, or might have been stopped by the police to be questioned as to why she was in the area of town where the tourist hotels are concentrated. Sean Hughes, a photojournalist and Jon's son, has been told by a Cuban with whom he tried to begin a conversation that people can be arrested for talking to tourists. Kate and I feel naive, confused. Has an attempt to do a favor endangered Mousi? Jeff Hillard, too, is carrying money to pass to a relative of his aunt. He, however, has not yet been able to make contact. The phone in our room works only intermittently; his, he has found, does not work at all.

At eight-forty-five, the hot water is turned on. Exhausted, I stand a long time in the shower. I intended to go to sleep early, but, though I am in bed by nine-thirty, sleep is impossible. Kate and I are assailed—from across the street—by a huge gathering in a pavillion. We can see uniformed guards on the street. A hugely-amplified speech goes on for several hours. Due to the missing window, there is no way to muffle the speech or the pounding music which follows. A single song is played over and over and over.

~

Esther Perez, the vice-president of the Cultural Center for Latin American Arts and Literature known as *Casa de los Americas*, refuses to paint the Special Period only in black. This is particularly impressive as they had forgotten we were coming, so engrossed is the whole staff in work to save literary and artistic treasures that were flooded in the recent storm, without any equipment or money with which to do it. While mourning all that was damaged or ruined, they are scrubbing and drying books and folk craft, trying to resurrect anything they can. A brilliant sun washes the courtyard where lines are strung to hold the damaged artifacts aloft. Paintings are off walls—the water rose that high—and are being sorted as to which might be restorable, which are not. It was from this hopeless task that Esther is called to receive us. In bluejeans and sleeveless shirt, this articulate, consummate professional shows us around the devastated gallery and library areas. There are simply not the resources with which to tackle the damage, yet of the Special Period she says, "We are in the midst of a crisis, but we know the system works. . . . There is also the question of solidarity. Hitchhiking and bicycling were not Cuban traditions. Now, though, state vehicles must stop at designated places to pick up anyone in need of a ride, or they will be fined. It's amazing what you can do without and not give up, learn not to even miss. You must remember that we have lived through this before. Most people believe that we are going to overcome this. Our problem is this: how do you reinsert a country into the world market economy while preserving social-ism? This is what we must address. We are making all gestures possible to the United States. . . ." Her voice trails off on the last sentence. "To no avail," is the implicit end. "The Special Period is a challenge to the imagination," we are told.

I find that the positive spins of solidarity and challenging the imagination are not applied by other people, especially non-party members, when we have an excursion to Santa Maria beach.

Nelia—who asked Olga if she could invite her fiancé, and was told no—accom-panies us, as does Olga, with Olga's two-year-old son. The forty-five minute Sun-day morning bus ride takes us through East Havana's suburban and semi-rural poverty. Hovels appear stacked into the hills, strung together by the ubiquitous laundry lines. Along the route, we pass an occasional pathetic-looking horse or burro, tethered on the shoulder of the road. Near the beach is a huge, Russian-built, barracks-like "city within a city," a concrete apartment complex that seems to go on forever. Our rail-thin sixty-three-year-old driver mentions that this is where he lives; he bicycles the distance to Havana daily. I resolve to begin smug-gling breakfast food to him tomorrow morning.

Roberto delivers us to a large tourist hotel, open for business, although a sig-nificant part of the construction was abandoned in progress. A rusting crane looms over a cement shell. A hole has been dug for a pool, which lies open, unfin-ished and weathered. Beyond a fringe of cabañas stretches the spectacular: palm trees on fine sugar sand, and turquoise water extending to a line where it turns cobalt blue.

I take a long walk on the beach by myself. Some distance from the hotel, I am approached by a young Afro-Cuban man, who points to my watch by way of ask-ing the time. As I hold up my wrist, he speaks in broken English, asking if I am from "America." He becomes very animated at my response, saying that his name is Miguel and that his father has been in Miami for thirteen years, since the Mariel boat lift. He writes the thirteen in the sand, unsure as to his pronunciation. He and his mother, who is blind, stayed behind. "Why didn't you and your mother go with your father?" I ask. "It was not possible."

We stand and talk a few feet from the water for perhaps twenty minutes. An archeology student at the University of Havana, he says "very much I want to go to America, but it is not possible. When I finish my studies, I must do national service." Then Miguel gets to the point. "Do you like Cuba?" he asks, refining his question to "do you like socialism?" after I respond to the first question with a slightly evasive "I like the people very much." I take a deep breath and try to reduce a complex collection of notions to one-syllable words.

"I think socialism has brought good education and health care to the people but I feel bad because I see they are suffering, too. It seems they do not have enough food and cannot buy what they need." He responds with a question: "Why does the United States blockade Cuba? No one understands for what you do this."

Even if I could speak Spanish or Miguel could better understand English, my answer would sound halting and inarticulate. The truth is I have no idea. I know we've done it for over thirty years and that it was supposed to bring the communist revolution to its knees, apparently considered undesirable even if Batista was corrupt, fascist, cruelly destructive. I know that Cuban exiles in Florida are vociferous and politically powerful in a politically significant state. When I came here, what I *didn't* know was that the embargo includes food, medical supplies, educational materials, clothing, every essential of daily life for adults and children. I tell Miguel the truth, a poor answer: I don't know.

What music do the American "jung" people listen to, he wants to know. "Madonna? Whitney Houston? Michael Jackson?" He says, "Cuban young have no discos, no fun. I have Walkman, but no batteries for six months. Cubans cannot get batteries, only tourists can get batteries." This begins a persistent theme of the one and a half hours I spend with him: the frustration of the Cuban people that so many commodities are reserved for tourists. Miguel is no exception to the rule that Cubans are almost universally dealing, or trying to deal, on the black market. Without quite putting me in the uncomfortable position of being asked directly, he wonders aloud if I might have extra batteries with me. He describes his Walkman as one he'd traded old roller skates for, and pantomimed how the back cover long ago "few off and was lost."

In fact, I do have spare batteries with me and suggest that if he wishes to walk me back to the part of the beach clearly reserved for tourists—I've walked about a mile into another beach area crowded with Afro-Cubans—that I will give them to him. He readily agrees, but begins, as we walk, to say that he could have "big trouble" for talking to a tourist, that if he's seen by the police, they'll wait until I'm gone and then stop him and say "for what are you talking to that stranger?" Miguel goes on to defend himself ambiguously against this projected attack. "I like it, my country. Why? I can't don't like it. Police think maybe we talk bad about Cuba, but I don't talk bad about Fidel." He indicates that when I go onto the tourist beach area, he'd stay several hundred yards away.

When I return with the batteries, I also bring some pens, gum, and five dollars, wrapping the booty in the T-shirt he hands me. Miguel talks on. "Is much better I have dollars than just batteries, can buy many batteries with dollars," one of his frequent references to the black market.

"Could you get in trouble for this?" I ask.

"Oh, yes," he replies. "Cubans caught with dollars can go to prison. We can only have what is rationed to pay for with pesos. Everything good is for tourists."

I ask Miguel if his mother ever talks about the revolution, and what does she think of it. Taking the question to be about socialism, he nods and replies, "She say whole country is bullshit; with blockade, can't buy, no eat, no nothing."

About the Soviet Union, he says, "Ah, now is good, I think, is capitalist. Capitalism is good: you work so much, people work, they buy what they need."

Cuban television, Miguel goes on, daily proclaims how bad the United States is, "but I no believe. You have drugs, yes? Whores, yes, but not so many. Here has so much prostitution. The young girl, she want dollars for bluejeans, for fix hair. Thirteen, seventeen, fifteen, she go to tourist, say 'you like girls? I fuck with you for dollars . . . hey Dad, I fuck with you.' You can't help it . . . you need shoes, you can not get them other way. Is not possible."

What else is not possible? "I am here on beach; I get hungry. Over there is restaurant. I can no eat there, only serve. Only you can eat there. For me, for Cuban, is not possible. I take bus to beach. Maybe bus come, maybe no. I can no have car; only government work drive car. If I have car, is no good. Gasoline is only for government. Police ask where I get gas, I go prison. For Cuban, to drive is not possible." Very little is possible, it seems.

Later, at the beach hotel, I interview a Bureau of Tourism guide, Eddie, also a graduate in English from the University of Havana, who is there with a Canadian group. He's a long-time friend of Nelia's who speaks with surprising candor about the Special Period and how it is presented to Cubans by the state. "We are always supposed to compare before the revolution to after the revolution," he says. "Always the rationale for not criticizing the government is that things are so much better than Batista days . . . . Before 1989, things were far better than now, in that there were things to buy without a rationing card; the black market was not much. With the collapse of the Soviet Union, everything . . . ." Eddie's voice trails off as he dramatizes a drowning person rising, gasping for breath, and going under.

Eddie and Nelia explain their status with regard to the Communist Party in answer to my question. Children under fourteen are all sent to school as "Young Pioneers." At the age of fifteen, some are selected to join the "Young Communist League." Eddie says these are the children "who have obtained good grades and behavior. They must be the best—honest, noble, kind." Eddie was a member, but Nelia was not. I ask if everyone wishes to be chosen. "No," he explains. "They must be first in everything and of them is expected more sacrifice, more work." At age thirty-one, those who have been Young Communists may, by invitation, join the Communist Party. Eddie was not given the chance because, "sometimes I liked fighting. You have to be the best." I ask Eddie, "if you could, would you join the Communist Party now?" Eddie and Nelia exchange a look and a half-laugh before he looks back around the table to me. He draws a breath and says, "Yes." I comment, "I get the feeling you couldn't tell me if the answer were no." He laughs again, looks me dead in the eye, and says, "I couldn't tell you."

∼

After our return from the beach, the group sits around the hotel bar in an elaborate debate about whether there is any danger to Mousi in her contact with Kate. The revised plan—developed after a second phone contact is finally made, and Kate learns that Mousi waited two hours for a bus that never came—is that Kate will take a cab to Mousi's flat to make the delivery. (Only tourists are, of course, allowed to use a cab.) Dallas Wiebe insists that everyone is being watched and the notion that Kate can take a cab to Mousi's flat, deliver the packages, and videotape an interview without endangering Mousi's ability to ever travel to the United States to see her daughter is nothing short of criminally naive. Reporter Lew

Moores disagrees, saying that things have loosened up somewhat. He believes that the economic collapse is so great that more trivial matters like watching us have fallen by the wayside. In fact, he says that what he's seen come over the wire services in the last year about Cuba has included some criticism of the regime attributed to specific sources and there have not been reprisals as long as there's been no direct attack on Fidel. Dallas—poet, fiction writer, literary critic, editor—says that this confusion is nearly an example of magical realism, the literary movement best exemplified in the work of contemporary Latin American writers such as Gabriel Garcia Marquez, which holds that there are no blueprints to follow. In this realm, reality is presented alongside alternate realities, and we are left bewildered as to what we are to think, and what anything means. That pretty well sums up where we are.

～

One night, I spill some sweet bread crumbs on my bed, and frantic not to encourage the roach population by feeding it, I rush to the bathroom for a towel in which to collect them. When I came back, Kate is smoothing the cover. "I was going to put those crumbs in the toilet," I say to her. She replies, "Oh, there weren't so many; I just brushed them on the floor over there," offhandedly indicating an area of the ragged carpet on the side of my bed. "You did WHAT?" I hiss, through gritted teeth. Now, each time I kill one, I tell her it was carrying a little sign saying, "Socialism thanks you, Kate." She is amused. I am not.

～

Late afternoon. We have gathered in Jon's room, where Jeff is trying to place a phone call to the distant relative for whom he's carried in money; he repeatedly either can't get a dial tone, or gets a busy signal halfway through the sequence of numbers. We wonder what would happen in an emergency. Once, I became so tired of waiting for the elevator—and felt so in need of exercise as an antidote to the sedentary hours of meetings at which, no matter what the hour, we are served rum—that I tried to take the seven flights of stairs. I made it up two before I encountered a locked door. This was, of course, the only emergency escape, and it seemed an apt metaphor for this country—spirited, brave, and crumbling all at once. Jeff never is able to get his call through. Here, one could dial 911 and wait forever; we have only until Friday.

～

Another day: at the lunch counter in a hotel, the waiter approaches Kate and me and, in a low voice, says "por favor. Could you take my money and buy me a bottle of dark rum? It is not for me, it is for the doctor who is treating my child. At one point, he stops talking and, indicating a much older man by a barely perceptible inclination of his head, says, "That man is my boss. Please to have the rum in a bag and let no one see." He slides a a five-dollar bill under my plate. Apparently, Cubans cannot even purchase Havana Club rum in Havana.

～

I am alone in the bus with Nelia and Roberto, both non-Party members, trying to find what they feel about the state of their country. Nelia, who is wearing a hot pink Gucci T-shirt, and a denim above-the-knee skirt, both clearly black market items, is telling me what happened to her last night. The memory is still smarting like a slap. She'd gone back to the restaurant in Old Havana, the one she'd taken us to the first day, with her fiancé, with an "invitation" she'd been given—stating a specific date and time—at which she and another Cuban could return to this tourists-only restaurant. She'd have to pay full price; the privilege was that she'd be allowed to go there at all. These "invitations" are given to Bureau of Tourism guides in a gesture of gratitude from the restaurant for bringing a group there. When she and her fiancé arrived, she was refused admittance; someone had forgotten to copy her name down when the invitation was issued. She was humiliated and furious.

This incident is the catalyst to Nelia's speaking more frankly. She says she trusts me and that she regrets that sometimes through the week at the meetings, "things have been said that are not quite true." She has wished, she tells me, to stand up and disagree, but would lose her job for doing so. Guides have been fired for less. Also, she is unsure of Olga, has not worked with her before, and does not know if she can be trusted. Therefore, she has kept her own counsel about such things as whether or not there are reprisals for writers critical of the government, or whether the Cubans she knows were supportive of the execution of General Oachoa, a decorated hero of the revolution convicted of drug trafficking, and probable scapegoat for the state. We've been told in her presence that Cubans universally agreed with the execution. She did not, she says. She then asks Roberto in Spanish if he was, and he says no. Roberto has grown increasingly expressive since I began my smuggling career. The first morning I offered him a small, napkin-wrapped pastry "for later." He rubbed his stomach saying, "I eat now. I very hungry."

～

The University of Havana Department of Foreign Languages has asked me to come speak to some classes, and one morning I try to call to confirm that I am coming, using a phone at the Editorial Jose Marti, where I am interviewing an award-winning writer who also works as a translator there. The connection is repeatedly broken: I place the call four times. I need a cab to get across Havana; there are no phone books in Cuba; therefore I cannot get a phone number and must walk to a tourist hotel where they are based in clusters. An editor walks with me and we converse in broken French. (Her French is better than her English, and my French is slightly better than sign language.) She asked about the possibility of "less tension" between our countries and said that she thinks Cuba has done what it can to make overtures. Her tone was a strange combination of hope and despair and, after arranging a cab for me, she embraces and kisses me warmly, as have all the women with whom I've met.

At the University, I meet with the English teacher who handles the courses in American literature. She wants to know what has happened since 1950; she has no idea of literary movements or major authors since then. She wonders if it might be possible to get her a complete copy of *The Great Gatsby*, *The Sun Also Rises*, and *A Farewell to Arms*; she has only excerpts in Spanish. She begs for one copy of an anthology of contemporary American fiction and poetry, with some introductory material on the various authors. I ask her what good one copy would be, other than to put in the library, as they have no photocopying equipment, nor paper. American copyright laws notwithstanding, she explains that when she obtains anything, she begins typing it onto stencils, the whole book if she can get it. The stencils remain stacked in drawers until they come by some paper and start running off some copies. The assistant chairperson asks for videotapes of American movies; until last month they had only a broken Beta cassette player, a first generation model obtained before the Special Period. They have just acquired a used VHS machine, but have no way to copy their Beta tapes.

Asked to speak to an English class, I enter another stifling, filthy room with one small blackboard on dark-painted, peeling walls. The furniture is vintage 1945 American high school, wooden and in disrepair. Indeed, the five-story building, some distance from the beautiful, small University area where administrative and official functions are held and which would do any small American collegiate institution proud, is a story in itself. The entryway to the Department of Foreign Languages is piled with uncollected garbage, much like New York City during a garbage strike. The building almost looks bombed out, missing windows, and the interior, dark, narrow halls crowded with bodies. A few posters of Fidel and Che, and one large student painting of revolutionary icons are the only adornment I see. What makes it seem familiar and comfortable are a few touches: the students carry small notebooks, something like the blue books in which American students write final exams. Test scores, hand-penciled by the faculty on flimsy beige paper, are posted on a few doors, and the din of student chatter fills the hall.

Another faculty member asks me to visit her class on American government. Language majors study not only the language—grammar, speaking, reading, writing—but the history, culture, literature, government of the countries in which the language they have chosen predominates. The fourth-year students in the class I am with are knowledgeable, articulate, eager for clarification about exactly what "indeterminate sentence," "burden of proof," and "plea bargaining" involve. Because the reference books used by the faculty member (who reads the book and presents the material in lectures since the students have no text) are generally from the twenties through the forties, the students are under the impression, for example, that women and minorities do not serve on juries. I have no sense that there is any propaganda intent in any of the misinformation, only that the embargo has been amazingly effective in preventing the Cubans from receiving current and accurate educational material for which they are anxious; the corrections I made were received with gratitude by the teacher.

When it comes time for me to leave, the students follow me down five flights of stairs to await the cab which I'd asked to return. It never appears. A Palestinian student with a car, and more importantly, the dollars with which to buy gas on the black market, is sought to drive me to my next appointment. I try to give him what I would have spent in cab fare. For the first time, someone in Havana refuses to accept a gift of American dollars. I've left the American Literature teacher with a full yellow legal-pad—the only one I've brought from a stack of two dozen in my study at home—which she received as though the sheets were gold leaf.

∼

During our last dinner in Cuba, Jon and I notice that Nelia is sitting by herself at the lunch counter—separated by a half-wall from the main dining area, and, apparently, the only place where Cubans employed in the tourist industry are allowed to eat. When several of us cross to join her, she tells us that her fiancé has just left to bicycle across the city to his home. She is spending the night at the hotel because she must accompany us to the airport tomorrow morning at seven; given the unpredictability of transportation, the Bureau of Tourism can only insure that she can be on time by accommodating her at the same hotel. This is the only circumstance—essentially business—in which a Cuban may stay here.

We chime in, asking why her fiancé didn't stay with her. Embarrassed, she fumbles with the explanation: he is not allowed because he is Cuban. Jon and I get very caught up in this, taking it as somewhat of a challenge. We urge her to call him to come back; we'll get him in the hotel. She is obviously excited by the prospect. They've never had a whole night of privacy, never been alone for more than a few hours at one of their homes, but she declines. The *policia* will not let him approach. What to do with his bicycle. He will not quite yet have arrived at his home; to turn around and bicycle back will take another hour and a half.

Jon and I, brashly confident, tell her to call him, that we'll work out a plan. A half-hour later, I pick Nelia up at her room. Jon and I have chipped in for me to take Nelia, presumably on business for which I need her help as translator, by tourist cab to Tony's house, to pick him up. Twenty-five minutes later, the driver shows me the meter, which reads $7.75. "You pay me two times that, *si*?" Si. On round trip cab rides, the drivers turn off their meters for the return to their post, and pocket the untraceable extra dollars, without charging the tourist more than what she or he knows would be the correct fare. Tony, still amazed, is waiting at his front door. He, Nelia, and the cabbie chatter animatedly in Spanish, presumably about the insane American woman.

As we make our way back to the Capri, an eerie indirect light emanates from a few dim windows behind archways, bathing parts of buildings as though in moonlight, leaving others in unfathomable shadow. But moonlight could not reach there; these are alley-width streets with high, old, balconied tenement flats. Everywhere there are people on the streets. Dark women, in pale dresses or skintight shorts, entwine with men whose hands cup the women's rears in open doorways. Couples, arms draped around one another, walk down the center of the narrow street; practically no cars come here. Children play impromptu baseball, though it is close to ten o'clock already. The driver slows to a creep at one point to call "*Ola!*" to a woman who runs to the window of the cab to place a wet kiss on his lips. The scene repeats block after block: backlit couples, children, this vaguely ancient world variously luminous and shadowed.

We pass through this neighborhood to the Vedada section of central Havana, where the Hotel Capri deteriorates daily. Outside, we review our game plan. Nelia shows her room key to the doorman, as she must gain admittance, and proceeds to her room. Tony and I stand outside, in full view of the *policia* watching the hotel, and talk for a few minutes—a charade made immeasurably more difficult by the fact that neither of us speaks the other's language—before I put my arm through his and draw close in an unmistakable indication that we are a couple. We pass thus, unquestioned by the doorman, into the lobby. I am conspicuously holding my room key and a tip for the elevator operator who is simultaneously not supposed to allow his fellow Cubans into the hotel and to please the tourists. He opts to please the tourist and his pocket at once, takes us to the seventh floor, and the deed is done. I take Tony to Nelia's room, and go on to my own, thoroughly happy with this circumvention of apartheid. Back home, I will worry that we were all naive, that Nelia may have lost her job or worse, that the *policia* wouldn't have stopped me anyway. It was Nelia they would stop, well after I was gone and would never know.

～

Our last morning in Cuba, I again smuggle my eggs out of the dining room to Roberto. Will anyone bring him eggs tomorrow? We ride to the airport, passing hundreds and hundreds of bicycles, as well as a few motorbikes with overfull sidecars and rickety carts harnessed to bony animals. Roberto slips in a cassette that Ed gave him, and the Beach Boys blare out, "good, good, good . . . good vibrations." Nelia takes the microphone to say goodbye, and that she and Roberto are very sad we are leaving. She has tears in her eyes. She puts a hand on her heart and says she loves us.

We arrive in Miami after an unexplained four-hour delay in Cuba during which we were kept in the large, hot waiting area where the duty-free shops try to coax out a last few American dollars, and cigarette and cigar smoke hang visibly, thickening the tropical air. Exhausted, brimming and drained at once, we are catapulted back to the future. A four-hour layover stretches to six due to air traffic problems. Bad weather over Atlanta, another big storm on the east coast. We've known nothing about it, having not heard a newscast nor had access to a newspaper other than the Party's weekly, *Gramma*. While we wait, the world rushes to fill the void, and La Habana fades a little into the dust of its crumbling and its hunger, ninety miles and lifetimes away.

Four Viuda Stories

How the *Viuda* Who Keeps to Herself Found Herself in Some Perplexion

THE PHONE RANG, and thinking it might be another strange message to deal with—using a second language, the simplest request for coffee and toast can take several bouts of word-search and *Sí* or God, yes, *Gracias* like you'd sat in at Yalta for the conference that settled the world—thinking that this call would almost certainly present her with a problem, the *viuda del norte* (the widow from the north) dropped her towel—it was early morning and she had just bathed—and spoke into the phone: "Hello?"

There was much static on the line, and then a man began speaking hurried Spanish and the *viuda* feared it was another caller from the tour company, like the call yesterday from which she had barely gathered that today had been cancelled. Yes. Today had been cancelled. The City had closed certain streets because of the smog. Your money will be repaid. That had taken ten minutes, at least.

This man, unlike the other from yesterday, made no attempt at English. He spoke very rapidly, long and long, not one word of which the *viuda* could understand. She kept saying to him, "*No comprendo*," until at last he asked rather clearly, "*Quieres amor?*"

"Oh, no," said the *viuda*, grabbing up her towel and hanging up the telephone with ugly haste. "Oh, no, *gracias*."

That was an obscene phone call, she concluded with wonder. And to think, all she could say was no, thank you. She did not want love and she lied.

The *Viuda* Reveals Herself a Traveler and Speaks in Tongues

She speaks to her ghost, her lately deceased ex-husband, who being dead now and cannot reply, which seems suddenly and all at once—because it was not acceptable to her before—remarkably sad. As there is no one else in this *restaurante* (*La Hacienda*, this time) who speaks any but the crudest menu English, she figures she might as well.

I was reading something interesting on the plane, she tells the lost husband. About *Exiles*. James Joyce's *Exiles*. A play. One of those works you scoffed at, in life. But *n'importa*. Is that French we hear, at the next table?

You think I falter here in Spanish; you should have been with me, in France. In Nice it was. Excellent fish there—*poisson*. I knew that much, and asked for the sole. *Le sole*. I didn't recognize anything else.

In the book on the plane was a part I underlined. It was an extended thought about that, how we exile ourselves, full of "rancor and nostalgia."

It makes me smile, even now. Am I full of rancor and nostalgia? Or is it the veal. A rack of young veal, with tiny, roast-charred ribs. *Delicioso.* The herbs are basil chiefly, I think. Rosemary is for remembrance, and rue. The proper exile eats veal with rue—and sage.

The wise man who wrote this book, having gone on to discuss *Ulysses*—I underlined it with my traveling red pen—says: "Steven Dedalus suggests we go forth into the world expecting to encounter external phenomena but always meet ourselves." I could have sobbed. I understood.

Here I am, drinking my J & B with *Peñafiel de manantial*—*agua mineral* (she examines the bottle *vidrio reciclable*. *Vidrio* is glass. Aha. *Vidrio reciclable*, as in *viuda*, an older woman, a witch or odd widow, a recycled life.

In Nice, I was surprised when it poured down rain in the afternoon. The wind came up about noon, rattled the stained white umbrellas of the cafe. That was the best place I had, for French. "*Omelette.*" Ate *omelette con jambon et fromage*. No *con. Avec.* Remembered teaching Bubba the dog not to eat *jabón* nor *jambon*—the soap nor the ham. *Sopa de jabón* is soap soup . . . another life. Worlds ago, yet here in time.

It rained hard there, with thunder over the hotel. How odd. That taxi driver overcharged me, too. Do they simply haunt the airports, knowing the confused and befuddled old *viudas* have no comprehension of *pesos? Francs*, there. Five to one. Three thousand to one, incredible *pesos*, here.

In Nice, it was an elderly woman taxi driver, with gnarly tanned hands on the wheel, driving like a pro, with her little black pug dog up front beside her. Oh, I was so glad to finally find a taxi. "*Merci*," I said to her, and to her dog. Oh, "*Merci, perro*—no, *chien.*" And I looked around at the hillside dwellings and buildings of Nice, thinking this is a place not like any place before. "*Merci, beaucoup.*" Giving her a pile too many francs, to see her smile. Not sure, myself what a tip should be. "*Un pourboire?*" It must have been way too much, for her smile.

And in the park near the hotel, another old woman was walking her dog, a big black shaggy affair. I talked to her. I held up my fingers, to show somehow I have two dogs at home.

Her dog had come up to my hand, all panting and eager. "*Allo, allo*," oh, *perro*. No. *Chien*. Oh. "*Il aime beaucoup un petit caresse*," she said to me. I could have wept: I understood.

And then it rained. Much rain. How odd.

The sole there was excellent, delicate and white. The chef himself, a young man in black trousers and a black and white striped shirt, came out with his personal razor to debone the sole for me, after it had been cooked and laid out on the plate—a work of art in frail white fish flesh—with almonds, and that broad-leaf bitter parsley—slick, slick with the razor and he lifted away the bones, all in one piece, and laid the flesh back on the plate. It was memorable to see.

Broad-leaf parsley, rosemary no doubt, a bit of thyme. It's no wonder our *viuda*—in common company—has so little to say, she being so thoroughly confused, most of the time. "*Merci*," she said to the stout black-clad waiter who had brought her more of the *Hacienda*'s delicious crispy bread.

He looked at her, startled.

"Oh," she said. "*Gracias*, I mean."

I do as well as I can with *gracias*, and *merci*, she told the ghost of her ex-husband. But one can't go through the whole world, on *gracias* and *merci*. And the shade of her other self said, with his usual touch of cynicism, "Why not?" Why not, indeed.

SHE OBSERVES SEVERAL *CONTRA TEMPS* REGARDING THE *PIÑATA* AT THE PLAZA SANTA CECILIA

First of all, the Plaza Santa Cecilia is a nightclub, off Garibaldi Square where the mariachis hold forth, and our *viuda* was in some perplexion going into a nightclub named for a saint, but that is not unusual in Mexico, she was assured by others of her group who seemed unconcerned at the anomaly. Our *viuda*, who was not really a witch and not even really a widow, but a little of both, settled down to enjoy the show with *cerveza*, a foreign brew, because she distrusted the water even in the form of those innocent-seeming ice cubes.

Santa Cecilia, she remembered—having in her youth belonged once to a Society of St. Cecilia, a choir—was the patron saint of music, so she was not surprised when there was a great deal of whanging and twanging from mariachis of the better sort, and when one woman vocalist who, despite heavy fleshy bare arms and a somewhat ratty hairdo, had a good, if loud, passionate voice, and sang with gusto out at the audience about the wonders of love.

There was also a most sensual Oriental girl who swung by her hair out over the audience, taking off a series of ever smaller robes—starting with glittering black gold, and moving to scarlet, there were seven outer garments that she discarded—until she was swinging her bare bottom and pale legs right and left over the cheering crowd, looking untouchable and inscrutable as a hanging, swinging china doll.

There were also folk dancers who seemed determined to add a new lewd meaning to the square dancing they did, popping their bellies up out of their hips with wild abandon, so that the *viuda*, who was in a thoughtful mood, worried a little about all of those silver buttons which seemed destined to come loose. It was a sexual, sensual show and then in the middle of it, the mariachis switched to a Christmas carol, and a procession came across the stage, carrying a creche with the Christ child and Mary, and they went around the stage to great applause, as much as the naked Oriental girl had received.

"Isn't that sweet!" cried someone at the same table with the *viuda*, leaping up to take pictures.

The *viuda* had to be quick, to grab the beer bottle so it would not topple over, so she did not have to say anything about how sweet or not sweet she thought this pseudo-village procession was, which was probably just as well.

The guide who had brought the group to the Plaza of Saint Cecilia was a stocky, swarthy man in brown. In features he was very much like Fernando Lamas, and his thick white hair was worn brushed back, enhancing that look, but his whole aspect was one of someone who had been stepped on. That is, if a tall younger man looking like Fernando Lamas had been compressed by a great weight on his head, causing stoop-shoulders and a pronounced hooking of the nose, he would have looked much like this guide. The guide, who was drinking tequila in small shots, smiled vaguely at the *viuda*. "Is Christmas," he said, and then perking up a little, he added, "Soon they will have the breaking of the *piñata*."

"Oh," she said.

"How wonderful!" cried the lady from Miami who had thought the creche scene was sweet. And someone else, probably the lady's husband, said "What a treat!"

The *viuda* had scarcely said a word all night, so she thought she would say something now. But everyone else at the table was speaking up on the subject of *piñata*, so she kept still.

"The *piñata* is a symbol of evil," said the loud-mouthed young boy from the University, as if this would be great news. "*Es muy símbolico.*" This young lad was the child of displaced Cubans, and liked to show off his language skills. He had annoyed, in this way, both the Spanish and English speakers in the group most of the night. "That's why the person who hits at the *piñata* has to be blindfolded."

The *viuda* continued to hold her peace, which was not unusual. But she was thinking, I did not come across these mountains to be lectured by a young idiot about symbols. This is my vacation from symbols. She did order another *cerveza, por favor.*

The Guide leaned back in his chair, sipping at an empty tequila shotglass. "You are right," he assured the sweaty young boy. "The child or the person who hits at the *piñata* is blindfolded so the evil don't get in his eyes."

"Are you sure?" asked the *viuda*, feeling more and more cross. "*¿Seguro?*" She was perverse. "Maybe to give the Devil a chance?" It was a funny thought at that, *el diablo* needing a chance for anything, and she began to smile.

The young boy leaned across the table, urgent. "If the blindfolded person breaks the *piñata*," he announced, loudly, as if she were insane and loudness might help bring her to her wits. "The evil is broken, and all these candies and gifts fall out."

The *viuda* accepted the fresh beer, with thanks.

The nightclub provided a large, round *piñata*, hung above the stage in the same place and probably on the same scaffolding as the swaying Oriental girl. Customers crowded up onto the stage, for a turn at it, including some of the group with our *viuda*. She, of course, stayed quite still.

As it happened, most of the people who went up to flail at the hanging prize—symbol of whatever—were quite drunk, so there was much noise and rowdiness, and the mariachis played faster and faster, to encourage the flailers and the shouters and the screamers.

Muchos borrachos y muchas borrachas, thought our *viuda*, somewhat to her surprise thinking it first in Spanish. Very drunk men and women. But her mind kept toying with the other idea: If you don't see the evil, but you manage to destroy it, you get a present. What kind of devilish logic is that?

And the ghosts of three of her ex-lovers, including her ex-husband, all ex-Catholics, spoke up out of the darkness around her. "Oh, *viuda*," they said, in chorus. "Didn't you ever listen to us?"

Now the dancers around the *piñata* were screaming and yelling and jumping up and down to encourage the blindfolded player, a woman from the *viuda*'s own party, a divorcée from Columbia, with reddish curling hair and thick thighs encased in bright orange leotards, cinched with a wide silver belt.

"Orange," said the *viuda*, to dispel the ghosts of her lovers. "*Naranja.*" And, "Legs. *Piernes?*" Someone yanked on the *piñata*'s rope, to make it harder to hit. *Piernes naranjas* leaped and whacked away with the stick, but she wasn't any place close. The *piñata* hopped merrily above her.

This went on for some time. Then someone else took the place of the orange-legged woman. The *piñata* remained unbroken. Our *viuda* sipped her beer, and pondered. Why should it be rewarded, to be blind to evil? "It's symbolic," giggled the three ghosts of ex-lovers. "And you being human, and female, are foolish enough to miss the huge joke."

"It's a joke?" She doubted it. She also wondered why she had always been attracted to cynical men.

"Ignorance is bliss," sighed her ex-husband, the bitterest of the lot.

At about that time, the management decided that the competition for the prizes had gone on long enough, and let the *piñata* drop into hitting range. But because of the drunkenness of the blindfolded man with the flail, it was some time before the ball was accidentally shattered, and shining bits of presents flew out.

"Blind faith," murmured the *viuda*. "That's got to be part of it." Her ghosts had no response. But the orange-legged woman had scrambled for, and won, a pack of cigarettes from the *piñata*. She came back to the table, grinning. All was well.

Our Viuda Makes an Excursion into Taxco and Never Once Mentioned the Silver There

It was a day of expectation and strangeness. The *viuda* sat at the foot of a potted palm in the hotel lobby, waiting for the driver, and at once was weeping, as a foolishness came over her with the music which was piped into the air—with plenty of violins and an accordion to cause the tears—"*La Vie en Rose*," a song from her shadowed past. The driver came in and did not look at her nor did she look at him, so in this way many moments were lost. When at last they found each other, he scowled: it seemed she had been under the wrong tree. It was a day for patience and learning, also, the *viuda* could tell.

The driver's vehicle, an aged, dusty blue car waiting in the garage was not as expected. As Reuban explained—for this was Reuban—due to yesterday's tours being cancelled, many tourists had gone away on their own, and there were not enough left to afford the taking of a bus. There were left only—and he was obviously unhappy about it—the two sets of *novios*, honeymooners, and herself.

They were speaking Spanish together, the *novios*, as she inserted herself into the back seat with one pair of them, so she smiled and said "*Buenos días*," thinking that would be a safe thing to say. They all smiled: Reuban, the driver, did not. And so they drove away, the *novios* twittering away in their language, and the *viuda* thinking strange thoughts in hers.

The cancelling of the day before's tours had been a frustration. On her own, the *viuda* had looked for a *museo* where the works of a woman called Frida Kahlo were supposed to be hung. But the *museo*, when found, was closed. *Cerrado*. An iron-sounding word. Tomorrow she would see the works of the Kahlo woman's husband—Diego Rivera—but that was not what she had hoped.

Around her, the *novios* and the driver Reuban made much conversation, in Spanish, but being in a sad, petulant mood the *viuda* purposely did not hear. And outside, of course, inevitably miles and miles of Mexico City were flashing by. What she was thinking, rather sourly, was that she was annoyed with the Spanish language. It is sexist. Here there were two *novias*—the young brides—but you must speak of them in the masculine, *novios*, because the men were included there. The *viuda* had been born too long ago to care much about the current rage for feminism, but it was irksome to her anyhow, that the masculine ruled over gender, gramatically speaking; and that it is easy to see the works of Diego Rivera but as for the works of his wife, which are reputed to be stronger and more colorful and clearly more interesting, well. She sensed an insolence in Spanish males, reflected in their use of words.

Now suddenly she realized that Reuban, slicking back his dark hair as he drove, was speaking English. Must be to her. She must listen. "*Miel*," he said in his slithery way. "Tha's what you say, honey?" Rolling his eyes around at the young people he wanted to know did she speak any Spanish.

"*Poco.*" Inevitable word.

She looked away, hoping that "*poco*" would be enough. She would not like to struggle on, putting sentences together, and further, it was not wise to distract him from watching the road, where there was much traffic, a wrangling and tangling of cars and trucks and hawkers pushing and pulling their carts.

Reuban said this was a holiday, so there was very little traffic. You should see it when it's busy. As another guide had said that in the middle of frantic, dashing London traffic, she assumed it was a routine they all do. The *viuda* was not amused.

The old blue car had to stop for a traffic light then. Horns were honked. A policeman whistled. It was a funny tweety whistle and the novio in front giggled and said "*pájaro muerto.*"

"A dead bird?" asked the *viuda*, astonishing everyone, including herself.

But then the *novia*, the young bride beside her, turned to ask, in absolutely American English where was she from? And as it turned out, both couples were Americans—the pair in back were from Puerto Rico, and the pair in front were from Miami, recently graduated from Dade County Community College. . . . They only spoke Spanish with Reuban for the exercise, you know.

On that trip, which turned out to be a lovely trip, the *viuda* learned many things, including how fast an old blue car could be forced to go, once out of traffic. They went up and down mountainous roads, through fields of sugar cane, and later, where wheat was being harvested, the *viuda* tried to express what she suddenly could not remember—the English word for "sheaf." There were donkeys and goats along the roadside, but as the others now all spoke English, the *viuda* was sorry not to learn what they were properly called.

Cuernavaca, she knew, meant horn of a cow, and was pleased to see that lovely city. Reuban, warming to his small group, told everyone they were visiting the favorite vacation spot of the Shah of Iran, where the Shah had come, and been made welcome because of course he had all that money.

Leaving the blue car a while, the *novios* went together to shop and to find *gelados*, an icy confection, but Reuban and the *viuda*, mindful of the seriousness of touring, went into an old Catholic church—surely one of the oldest in the New World. Here there was a half-restored mural, depicting the death of a saint quite unknown to the *viuda*. This saint, whose name the *viuda* never learned, was a martyr who went from Mexico to Japan as a missionary, but there he was crucified. He was pictured in agony on the cross, with fire about his head. As Reuban told it, this man, dying, had predicted that the place in Japan where he was being slaughtered would end in a rain of fire, and as that place was called Nagasaki, he had gained much posthumous fame. The mural had only recently been uncovered, said Reuban, when they took out a really ugly altar, and went to clean the wall.

Besides being famous for its extremely old church, and its flowers—and there were gorgeous flowers everywhere—Cuernavaca is famous for honey—which gave Reuban more opportunities to roll his eyes, and lick his lips as the two couples returned carrying many packages, and their cones of ice. "*Miel*" and "*La luna de miel,*" he seemed to love the sound of his own voice, slavering over the words. "Taxco," sighed Reuban, "is *famosa* as a place for the *luna de miel.*"

As they drove on through the mountains, now taking an excruciatingly narrow road, where the slimmest burro standing by the roadside was an obstacle, Reuban told them much about the city they would see, and where the *novios* would be staying on, leaving the *viuda* once again on her own. He waxed poetic over the riches of Taxco, the old mines, the jewelers who now made more with their craft than the mines could pay out, the Cathedral, one of the oldest naturally in the New World—famous for the tons of gold in its walls—the Cathedral of Saint Priscilla, *San Prisca*, built by a grateful mine owner, on top of a fabulous lode, the painting—no crummy mural but a true work of art, the only one in the world that showed, in one corner, the Virgin Mary very pregnant. . . . Here he giggled and looked around.

As if in anticipation of the old hotel high above the blocks and blocks—like children's building blocks, the houses perched on Taxco's mountains—the *novios* on the drive up to that place fell strangely silent. They seemed not to hear a word of all those tour-guide encomiums. Only the *viuda*—who knew she must find her own way home—was listening. The *novios* and *novias* spoke only to each other, hands fluttering softly, like *pocos pájaros*, little birds, speaking the language of love, silent but most effective: as any tourist through this life should know.

Goin' Out to Come Back

As I TEARFULLY waved good-bye to the airplane winging away from the Caribbean island of Grenada, Mitchell, my taxi driver, mopped his glistening black forehead and said kindly, "Write your hosbon that I'll take his place while he gone."

The thought of my "hosbon's" reaction suddenly made me laugh. I climbed into the front seat and peered through the army of white plastic saints glued to the dashboard, all eyes on the precipitous mountain road ahead.

Like a coral link in a sapphire necklace, Grenada lies twelve degrees north of the equator and averages eighty-three degrees Fahrenheit in the trade winds. This secret haven in the Caribbean measures twelve by twenty-one miles of tropical alps, is edged by eighty-five miles of irridescent-watered beaches, and now harbors over a hundred thousand friendly inhabitants of Afro-English descent.

My 'hosbon' had completed his government research into Caribbean agricultural cooperatives and flown back to Washington, D.C. to make his report. I, on the other hand, had become interested in the island and its people and hated to leave—particularly in February. Secretly, I had begun to fantasize a new life as a Grenadan farm woman: life in a tropical Eden where nutmegs roll to the ground and exotic fruits hang from the trees and five acres can support a family.

So I stayed behind, alone. Maybe forever. Who could know?

Mitchell zigzagged the old taxi around potholes, waving and shouting at pedestrians. "All right!"—obviously a greeting, not a judgment of road conditions.

He stopped beside a straw-hatted woman who eyed me curiously and leaned in the window to chat. Mitchell explained, "Her hosbon leff on de plane." "Oh," her smile a yellow snaggle. "She cry?" "Yas." "Tha's good," she approved.

For twenty-two miles we shared the fern-lined, cloud-topped mountain road with careening buses named "Trial de Luxe," "Baby Cyclone," and "Born to Lose," but Mitchell cautiously followed a small and slow van labeled "I Am Nothing" down to the harbor and St. Georges.

The capital town is a cluster of candylike houses whose rooftops are tiled with red clay cookies originally shipped as ballast from England in the 1700s. The colorful Carenage rings a blue deepwater harbor where rusty freighters load bananas, cocoa, nutmegs, and copra, and white cruise ships unload tourists. Yachts, dinghies, steamers, and schooners bob gently in the swells. Flags snap with a festive air.

Gaily painted trucks dubbed "Never Despair," "Live and Let Live," and "Study Your Head" jostled in the busy traffic. As if an answer to all life's problems, a black hearse pulled ahead of us, advertising in large letters, "Why live in misery and unhappiness when you can die in comfort and joy?"

Grenada's history, like its mountainous terrain, has had its ups and downs. After being discovered by Christopher Columbus shortly after America, for the next hundred years nobody else came to investigate. In 1609, a ship of British colonists landed but were soon frightened away by fierce Carib Indians. Mapped into both the British and French land grants, Grenada was bought in 1650 from the French "Company of the Islands of America" and the purchaser, M. du Paquet, tipped the Caribs some knives and hatchets, two bottles of brandy, and a large quantity of glass beads. A year later, their friendliness having vanished with the brandy, the Caribs resumed hostilities. Outnumbered and rather than surrender to defeat, the Indians leaped off a cliff into the sea, a site now called, "Le Morne des Sauteurs."

Grenada passed under the French crown in 1674. Within a hundred years, the population grew to 1,263 whites 175 free people of color, and 11,991 slaves working sugar and indigo plantations. After the Seven Years War between Great Britain and France, Grenada was ceded to the British. The French still hankered after the island and, during the American Revolution, recaptured it. In 1783, it was returned permanently to the British by the Treaty of Versailles.

On February 7, 1974, Grenada achieved independence from Britain and, although still a member of the British Commonwealth, now operates as a democracy. The fete-loving people celebrate ten official holidays, most followed more soberly by a "Recovery Day."

Possibly the most important date in Grenada's history was 1873, when nutmeg was introduced from the East Indies. Grenada is, after Indonesia, the world's main supplier of nutmeg and mace (the nutmeg's secondary spice). The sale of this spice averages nearly half of the total value of Grenadan exports and is a primary source of income to approximately six thousand farmers.

~

Mitchell and the plastic saints left me off at an old wooden building, the harbor offices of The Grenada Cooperative Nutmeg Association, where a bent bucket with a hole in the bottom hung from the corrugated tin roof and served as a rainspout. I climbed the moldy green stairway and opened the glass door into the office. Ceiling fans swirled tropical heat into the staccato clickings of busy typewriters. A farmer dozed on a wooden bench in the corner.

From my husband's research, I learned that this cooperative had been established in 1947 as a producer's marketing group. Similar to the Banana Co-op and the Cocoa Co-op, membership is open to all growers. Most of the six thousand nutmeg growers were women.

The executive secretary stuck his head out of his office and grinned, "You still here? W'ap n'in?" (a West Indian greeting meaning "What's happening?")

I explained my idea as research: Was there a farm woman I could visit as a paying guest for a few weeks?

"Possible, possible . . ." he mused, rubbing his chin. "One of the Nutmeg Board members is a woman. Mrs. Alexander has about eight acres, I think, outside Grenville . . . I'll telephone her. Wait here."

He returned, smiling. "She say next week will be fine."

Elated, I thanked him and ran down the stairs to the dock. A dinghy named "Be Courageous" bobbed in the water. The oarsman sang as he rowed me across the harbor to my cottage.

During that week, it began to rain. From my chameleon- and gecko-studded porch in L'Anse aux Epines (pronounced lan-su-peen), I watched sky-waterfalls come looming across the hills like veils of lavender gravel. Suddenly, the rain hit. It rattled like small stones. Clackety-whish-boom! Wind tugging at the roof, wrenching at the palms, tearing at the garden. Just as suddenly, it stopped. Silence. Whistling frogs piped up. At first, hesitantly. Then slowly they swelled into a shrill jinglebell chorus. Big frogs in the ditch made hollow knocking sounds, others clacked and thumped. And on the beach, the sea sighed with an exasperated slam. Bang. Sigh, sigh, sigh. . . . Bang! It was glorious.

Grenville, population 2,000, isn't a place a tourist would go except to catch a plane at nearby Pearl Airport. On the opposite coast from St. Georges, Grenville is a jungle of buildings with blowing curtains and rusting roofs where everyone knows everyone else and where children were hopscotching in the streets the evening I arrived.

To my surprise, instead of living in a farmhouse, my farmwoman hostess and her family of five owned a boutique and a bar and lived upstairs. Mrs. Alexander's husband tended his bar under a sign, "No Loitering." In an adjoining room, she ran a tiny store displaying straw hats, seashell jewelry, and clothing.

It was said, "In Grenada, it be a scratch for a livin'." A neighbor ran four businesses from a delapidated shed: a barber's chair, a photography booth, an upholstery section, and a carpentry shop.

Mrs. Alexander, whom every called "Missus Sepp" (her husband's name was Septimus), greeted me, her brown face brimming with friendliness. Attractively trim in a purple-flowered shirt, matching turban, and slacks, she instructed her children to stop staring and take my straw hat and satchel upstairs while she proffered a chair and table. Approving that I preferred a "sweet drink" to alcohol, she briefly disappeared behind the bar into the kitchen, re-emerging with a cool refreshment from a bottle of "gingah," which she'd concocted by "biling fresh gingah from the garden with sugah an' watah."

The women in the community had been alerted to my arrival. They began to drop in for a chat, their soft, high-pitched voices as musical as nursery singsongs. "Oh Grey," they sighed. "Thing are so es-pen-sive on the island and the chil'ren are all leavin' for Canada and the States—where do you think they should go?"

Fortunately, I'd resisted ordering Grenada's famous Rum Punch, for there was a sense of Orderly Righteousness among the feminine community. Missus Sepp represented Organized Virtue. She was president of everything she wasn't chairman of. She organized good citizenship programs for children and arranged benefits for the poor, the sick, and the aged. A devout churchgoer, she murmured, "Please God," after every proposal. "Tomorrow we go to the Banana Boxin' Plant. Please God." This lent a disconcerting sense of mortality to any plan. As a government supporter, she saw altruism everywhere.

"The government acquires farmlan' from the rich to give to the poor," she explained. "It raised women's wages from twenty cents a day to four dollars and the men's from twenty-eight cents to five dollars." (One dollar Eastern Caribbean equals fifty cents, U.S.) "But most men and women both work. Prices are so high—we eat from the lan'. Please God, that's only how we manage."

I followed Missus Sepp through her red-carpeted living room decorated with red plastic flowers and through a doorway hung with inch-wide red plastic ribbons up the stairs to her own bedroom. It was to be mine. Gold satin draped every window. A double bed with a gold chenille bedspread, gold pillows, and a golden mosquito net knotted at the ceiling gave me the feeling of being the heroine of *The Princess and the Pea* fairy tale, particularly when Missus Sepp untied the gold netting and it cascaded around the bed.

I fell asleep with a sense of feminine luxury, surrounded by plaster saints, frilly dolls, and elaborate perfume bottles. Outside my golden canopy, mosquitoes whined to the tune of whistling frogs and chimes tinkling in the wind.

Next morning in the kitchen, dressed in a fresh slack suit, Missus Sepp grated a black ball of homemade chocolate 'from the garden' into hot water, milk, and sugar for 'cocoa tea.' Over a breakfast of fried ham and 'coocoo' (corn mush), I asked about women's rights in that country.

She wiped her hands on her apron and sat down. Her West Indian dialect was a lilting song. "I own my own lan'. You know, when a woman marr-ees, a mon wil take what he can an' then leave her. An' what has she? When West Indian men marr-ee, they settle the woman into the home an' aftah she have the children, he get a woman outside, an' is away from the home, a *lot*! He go with men in the rum shops an' to par-tees. The woman stay home. So she owns her own lan' as securi-tee. Aftah all, she is responsible for the children an' the communi-tee. And Please Jesus, when a woman gets sick she has to know that she doesn't have to drag herself to work!"

Three of Missus Sepp's eighteen brothers and sisters were outside children and according to Grenadan custom, her father provided for them. She clicked her teeth disapprovingly as she told of a genial St. Georges bachelor, father of forty-seven children, who'd invited his friends born in the same month as the baby to a christening fete to pledge their monthly support.

Birth control? Missus Sepp shook her head. "A mon must not interfere with the will of God. There is plen-tee of lan' an' everybody has food to eat." She looked at her watch and began to clear the table. "First, Please God, we'll go to the Nutmeg Plant. Many of the women who own lan' work there."

The sun was already hot at nine in the morning. Donning sunhats, we walked down the dirt street past delapidated board houses obscuring the sea. The sweat trickled down my back as we reached the three-story warehouse.

We entered the concrete building and passed a large table stacked with workers' handbags. Our eyes smarted from the spicy pungence and gradually adjusted to the golden light of nutmeg dust. A gentle roar, like a sea rolling a beach of pebbles, came from women seated on crates and stools, their skirts spread wide to hold wooden trays of brown nutmegs, as they deftly rolled and sorted them for shape and size. Almost playfully, they tossed the nuts into jute sacks marked 60, 80, 100. The tiniest nuts were 110s—110 to a pound.

A giant cracking machine upstairs added to the din. It tumbled four hundred pounds of nutmegs an hour when a shipment is on. Nutmegs are warehoused in shell—only cracked and sorted when an order arrives. The "cracks" rattle down wooden chutes to waiting baskets handled by barefoot women. Humming and singing, they dunk the gurgling baskets into large concrete sinks of water to stir up "floaters." Defectives float and are reserved for extracting nutmeg oil.

Good nutmegs are then hoisted upstairs and dried in a stifling dormitory of four-layered wooden bunks with wire bottoms. On a hot day, continually rotated by long wooden rakes, nutmegs dry in seven or eight hours. We climbed more stairs to the top floor. There were huge storage crates of mace. It crinkled in my fingers like starched, yellow lace. I peered out the window. Below, a rooster and two hens picked over mountains of nutmeg shells. Missus Sepp remarked, "Shells make a good garden cover. When I go to the nutmeg distillery, I always bring back a bucket of ground dust. It make a fine fragrant fertilizer."

I dawdled and smiled at the women, hoping someone would speak with me. Dorothy Felix, herself the color of nutmeg dust, grinned, displaying bad teeth. "I been sortin' here since 1950. Let's say I make a hundred dollah a month." She sighed. "Oh, we hoff to know how to spen' for food an' then we save some for school."

Dorothy had three sons. Primary school was free but secondary school cost thirty dollars EC per term.

The flat of her palms expertly rolled and separated the nuts as she chatted. "I own my own home but I haven' got a spot. I'm payin' twelve dollah. But the mistuh tell me when I come to pay this month that I have to pay some more. I don' know the mox-i-mom. It's a board house so it is a removable."

I was puzzled. Removable? Spot?

They laughed merrily. The American lady didn't know about moving a house to a new spot? Dorothy owned a Jenny House, a prefabricated wooden shack. So named after the disastrous hurricane Jenny of 1955, when the government of Surinam donated hundreds of houses to Grenada. A "spot" is a spot of land, sometimes overlooking spectacular sea vistas but more often a mere few yards of dirt where tiny shacks huddle with just enough room for a clothesline, a few chickens, and a dog. Retailing at seven hundred dollars EC, Jenny Houses can be moved on the back of a truck and set atop concrete stilts.

Dorothy confided, "I never marr-eed. Well, I will not say I did not want to get! Sometimes you don' get the oppor-tun-i-tee. An' then if you do, maybe you not like it. The children's father didn' wish. He help me very seldom. So—we hoffing it very hard down here. We hof to try. We don' givin' up!" She smiled and shrugged with a gesture which would soon become familiar as Missus Sepp guided me around the Grenville countryside, introducing numerous farmwomen.

Without an automobile, "push come to shove an' you travel how you can." Missus Sepp and I climbed aboard the new schoolbus, one of four donated by Canada, for the Banana Boxing Plant at Birchgrove. The bus squeezed through the tiny jungle roads like an elephant through a tube. The schoolchildren in navy and white uniforms behaved quietly and disembarked decorously.

Finally, after all the children had been deposited, the bus lumbered down a narrow road through the rain forest to the boxing plant. We stepped down on the moist, leaf-covered soil and Missus Sepp thanked the driver and waved good-bye to him.

At the tin warehouse, trucks pulled up to the tin shed loaded with bananas packed in dried fronds, and people with banana-laden drogues on their heads unloaded their wares. Every banana farmer was a member of the co-op. Here, bananas were inspected, washed, sprayed, and trucked off to the freighters in St. Georges Harbor. At the end of the day, leftovers were sold to grocery stores or given to gleaners.

I'd wondered how my hostess would manage our transportation away from the boxing plant after the schoolbus disappeared, but somehow Missus Sepp had materialized with an old dented Austin with a driver. We sputtered down the mountain in a backseat cloud of exhaust fumes. An East Indian woman in high rubber boots, green tam, and khaki pants walked down the road ahead of us, her cutlass swinging at her side. We billowed to a stop.

Sarah Joseph jabbed her sword indignantly toward her banana fields. "They don' be content to rob the lans'! They stan' on the road and ask for a free ride, too!" Her bananas had been stolen. "No one want to work these days an' they take the free bananas off the stations and then complain about the government!"

Sarah taught arts and crafts two nights a week in the government evening school and occasionally worked as a domestic. Without a husband, her ten children help farm her eight acres of bananas, yams, and twelve nutmeg trees.

She swung her cutlass, motioning me to follow. We slipped and slid down the steep slopes, Janet—one of Sarah's kids—chopping banana fronds and leaving them for mulch along the way. At a clearing, she handed me a nutmeg. Inside the split peach-like fruit nestled a shiny black nut wrapped in scarlet lace. She picked off the red sheath. "That be the mace. When it dry, it be yellow. Don' put it in your purse," she said and stopped me. "It decay. Keep it in the air." Sarah said, "Now I dig tania for you." The tip of her knife turned up the soft, dark cinnamon soil. "It be a cousin to dasheen. It be nice." She pulled up a long tuber and handed it to me. "Cook it. If you eat it raw, it scratch."

From the road above, Missus Sepp shouted. Janet flashed me a quick smile and yelled, "Hold strain! We're comin'! We're comin'!" and ran up the hill, her gray hair flying. More slowly, weighted by the heat and humidity, I followed to rejoin Missus Sepp in the car.

The rattling cloud-chamber putt-putted around chartreuse mountainsides and pastel houses fenced by flowers. We pulled up to a garage where a large woman was loading bananas onto a truck.

"This is Mrs. Forrester, of the very best fam-i-lee," Missus Sepp introduced her. The countrywoman blushed, smoothing out her shapeless dress. "Oh, I am so spotty, I been pickin' bananas."

She complained about the packing plant. "These be the rejects—but nothing is wrong!" She angrily tore into a banana. The flesh was white and unbruised. "Nothin' wrong but they don' accept it! A little mark comes on at the hot an' wet season—we lose a lot! It is very hard. Very low price an' we have to go to so much processes!" A chicken pecked around her feet and she nudged it away with her dusty shoe. "When it's planted, we pay a man's day pay and the land use is expensive. An' we got to treat it like a baby, you know? You see that boy there? He the last boy to stay with me. One girl in Canada. And my first boy, he gone to the States. But this one got so fed up he don' want to stay. He can't stand it again. I don't know how I can do all this myself. My husband be dead. I close my grocery store an' go to the fields."

I looked at her corpulent form. "How often do you go to the fields?"

Indignantly, as if I'd asked her if she neglected a sick child, she said, "Every day! But, oh, well—I can't control the field. That be a man's. I have to tell a man how to crop the banana trees, what leaf to cut, dig the drains an' things like that. An' we've got nutmegs. Oh, so much work an' so little to come out of it! It's from

God's word, you know. We shall not live by bread alone." The two women nodded meaningfully.

More chickens gathered around our feet and were clucking up a clatter. Mrs. Forrester shooed them away, still talking. "Ah well, a banana a day keep the doctor away. But we cannot save any money. Everything is so expensive an' al produce so low."

The two women argued about the government's regulation of prices. Mrs. Forrester turned to me. "Oh, I'd like to be a lady like you, goin' around askin' questions. . . ."

Missus Sepp indignantly defended me as an American agricultural expert on a research mission. Mrs. Forrester's mouth fell open. Then quickly, on pretext of showing me her land, she grabbed my hand and pulled me down the hill into the banana fronds out of Missus Sepp's earshot. "Please God. Oh save us! Tell the United States! Things are very bad in Grenada!"

Her story tumbled out: Government corruption. Bribery. Police brutality. Strikes. Docks shut down. A disaster economy. Money donated by Canada for road repair never reaches the roads.

She glanced nervously over her shoulder. "Mrs. Alexander be a government supporter. She make me vex. She won' tell you how people are sellin' off their lan' before the government take it. My cousin owned a big cocoa plantation. The best of his lan' was taken—with a government I.O.U.—they parceled it out in half-acre plots to people from town. The creatures cut down new cocoa plants to build their huts an' tied their animals to cocoa trees—which died. Once the crops an' exports fail, this country will eat its own children!"

Later, when I asked Missus Sepp about island politics, she praised the government as a savior to the poor. Besides, she added, many world-funded agencies such as the Caribbean Development Bank in Barbados and CARICOM (Caribbean Common Market) are working to solve economic problems common to most tropical islands. Please God.

One bright, sunny morning, my thoughts were more on the people, not their problems, as Missus Sepp and I walked up the street to meet her cousin. Her pretty relative wore her black puff of hair like an exploded bomb. She smiled. "My name is Felici-tee. It mean hoppiness." Surrounded by dogs and children, she was hanging sheets on a clothesline beside her unpainted house adjacent to her husband's watch repair shop.

"She's tough!" Missus Sepp said admiringly as we all piled into Felicity's battered car. Besides owning farmland, Felicity was a seamstress and taxi driver. She floored the accelerator. I wondered at the scar on her chin.

"I been drivin' a cab eleven y'ars," she laughed. "I go up an' do cutlass at my garden every day. I have two acres. My chil'ren help. You have chil'ren?"

"Two," I answered, "but mine are blonde," pointing to my own dark brown hair.

Felicity's smile vanished and her eyes brimmed. "Oh, that's bad," she said quietly. After a minute she said, "Your hosban be blind, too?"

When I explained, she laughed so hard the car slowed to a near stop and the children rolled on top of each other in convulsions of mirth.

The woman wiped her eyes and pointed. "This is my lan'. As time roll on, things get mor expensive. I bought here for one thousand five hundred dollars. One acre. Another piece I bought for three thousand. But that is more cultivated an' near the road an' you can put a house on the spot."

We tromped through the tangled underbrush. The children scattered and began to whack at the cocoa pods which hung like orange and red balloons from the trees.

Felicity proudly recited her crops: "We grow orr-inges, tangereens, guavas, pears, cassava, pigeon peas, golden hopples (apples), nutmegs, cocoa, bananas, bluggo—it be a kind of banana you cook—tanias, dasheen, potatoes, coconuts— here, eat the jelly, it make you strong as a lion!—cashew nuts, mango, star hopple, sugar hopple, sapodillo—it be a sweet fruit (bile the leaves for tea, it help you relax)—yams, sweet potatoes, an' avocado."

We piled back into the car, wedged between sacks of vegetables, fruit, and children, our mouths filled with sweet, sticky juice which dripped from our chins.

During the nights under my golden canopy, like the sleepless princess atop the pea, I pondered the quality of life. Perfection is explained by its flaws, please God. Easier surely, would be farming flowers. Like Mrs. Nurse whose tiny stilted house was surrounded by exotic flowers on a small acreage. To my questions, she'd answered, "The antherium keep coming the whole year. Yes, we make enough off the flowers to live. You have to be contented and not live above that."

Red antheriums pointed phallic fingers as we walked through the damp, palm-shadowed garden. She pointed to a palm stump. "Antherium be a kind of parasite an' she take water from the log. When she be a baby you have to pet her an' pet her. See this one, she feel the wood is there so she reach for it. She smell it."

"How many plants do you have?" I asked.

She looked around vaguely. Then she said, "Oh, 'bout ten thousand."

Finally, the day came to visit Missus Sepp's "garden." Jute sacks, buckets, cutlasses, children, and a picnic lunch were loaded into Septimus's old car. On the way, he stopped by the beach to order "sea eggs" from a diver. (Later, Missus Sepp would remove the meat of the white sea urchin, season it, cook it, and stuff it back in the shell.) Straw weavers waved to us from their huts where they sat with laps full of bleached grass blades. The car strained uphill until the slice of sea rounded into a shimmering bowl of blue. At the end of a dirt road, we stopped.

"When we come to the garden, we always say hello to the people," Missus Sepp said as we got out of the car and the children ran ahead. With the sun beading sweat down my back, we walked along a ridge where unpainted shacks perched above a dazzling view of jungle and sparkling sea. I pictured myself living there.

One of the Jenny Houses was vacant. I wandered inside. A cool breeze swept through the wooden shutters into the darkened room and four sleeping bats swung gently from the ceiling. Through the cracked floorboards, the green of the earth shone beneath. There was a rusty metal-grilled table for cooking callalou soup over hot coals, and out the window, a coldwater spigot for washing. The simplest of toilets lay in a corner: a calabash bowl.

Outside we walked toward a woman picking over her drying cocoa pods, ants crawling between her sticky fingers. She looked up and laughed. "My! You got fat!" Missus Sepp said. "How's it goin'" to which the answer was a shrugged grin. "I try. . . ."

Under the shade of a cinnamon tree, another woman peeled the bark, laying it to toast and curl in the sun. She gave me a bunch of fragrant sticks to take home.

Farther down the road, an old woman rose from her stained mattress to greet us and chat, her feet wrapped in red wool kneesocks and her head in a pink scarf. She shuffled into her kitchen and emerged with a gift "for the nice 'meri-can lady who don' think she too good for us": a perfect brown egg. I thanked her through the tears and sweat which mingled to run down my cheeks.

Missus Sepp's eight jungle-fruited acres dropped downhill to a stream and climbed up the other side. Cocoa trees ballooned with red and yellow fruit like a tropical birthday party and underfoot lay the scarlet sheathed nutmegs. A perfect place for a picnic.

Afterwards, we piled up a pyramid of cocoa. The children split the fruit with cutlasses and scooped out the slippery white pods into their buckets. After several hours of picking, we stuffed the car with a harvest of cocoa beans, nutmegs, oranges, sapodilla, dasheen, pumpkin, bluggo, and bananas. Nothing would be wasted.

Back at Missus Sepp's, we dried and roasted the white cocoa pods till brown, then ground them into a chocolate paste and shaped them into fist-sized balls. We steamed the breadfruit with pork and coconut milk to make "oil down," a national dish. The cooked bluggo resembled a nutty potato and the green elephant-eared dasheen went into callalou soup. A feast fit for royalty—even for a spoiled princess.

～

When Mitchell drove me to the airport, his array of white-faced saints still stared from the dashboard. He looked at me from the corner of his eye. "You cryin'?"

I was sad to leave such warmth and richness, humor and grace. I felt pale in contrast to the rich skin tones and rollicking spirits.

I nodded. "But don't worry. I only go out to come back!" (Grenadan for "I'll be back.")

He grinned. "Tha's good!"

～

Postscript: This piece was written in 1974, long before the U.S. invasion of Grenada during the 1980s.

Sal Si Puedes

A ROCKET EXPLODES outside my living room window and for one supercharged moment everything around me stops. I grip the table, hyper-aware of the heat, the heavy stillness in the air, the smell of garlic and sulfur drifting through the open window. Sweat rises like blisters on my neck and back and between my breasts. My bare thighs stick to the vinyl chair. When the second detonation comes, I recognize the shrill whistle of a lone firecracker and release my grip, relax my shoulders slightly. Then curiosity takes over and I move to the window, peer out at the night skyline over Panama City. A Roman candle shoots up from the center of the banking district. Its long white tail falls over Paitilla Bay. I'm mesmerized for a moment. Then there's another series of blasts and this time the whole sky erupts with fireworks. They're harmless, really, I reassure myself, but a part of me is fighting the urge to duck below the window and huddle against the wall.

In the street five floors below me, someone lights a bunch of cherry bombs. The noise ricochets off the cement buildings and more firecrackers explode at the other end of the block. Then they're everywhere—on the ground, in the sky, all over the city in a beautiful and frightening display. I move away from the window, and instinctively on hands and knees, crawl to the phone. If this were New Year's Eve or the start of Carnival, I wouldn't be worried, but it's an ordinary Wednesday evening in a country that has been on the edge of something tumultuous for months. My fingers are trembling as I dial Nilda's number. "God, it's just fireworks," I say out loud. Nilda answers on the third ring. The noise outside is so loud that I have to shout. I try to keep the panic out of my voice as I ask what's going on.

"He just made a speech on Channel 2. Didn't you see it?"

"Who? Noriega?"

"Not on the phone," she hisses. She's warned me before not to say his name out loud like he's something sacred, a god, omnipresent in our phone wires, our cars, our living rooms. I'm not usually paranoid and have managed so far not to take her seriously. She waits for a lull in the noise. "He accused your government of wanting to go back on the Canal Treaty. What you're hearing is a celebration. Panamá standing up to your President."

I don't say anything and she asks if I'm all right. I am, of course, but I hate being alone, which I don't tell her. "It wouldn't be safe to come over now," she says. "The *Fuerzas* . . ." She doesn't finish.

I tell her I'll see her in the morning, put the receiver back, but don't get up from the floor. It's March of 1988 and I've been in Panama for six months. Most of the time I experience the political distress as a nuisance. The demonstrations keep me from getting to work, the strikes make shopping impossible, and the supplies on grocery store shelves continue to dwindle. I have a thousand dollars sitting in an account in Citibank that I can't withdraw because the banks have been closed for over a month. The U.S. Army now cashes my checks, so I'm not without money. But Nilda doesn't understand why the U.S. won't intervene. I'm called on to defend a government I don't believe in. When I mentioned peace talks, she laughed and mumbled, "Democrat" under her breath. She reminded me that Reagan sent the marines to Grenada. Why shouldn't he do the same for the Panamanians?

I lean my head against the wall. The fireworks have stopped, but not the noise. The Opposition Party is giving its rebuttal by way of banging on pots and pans. I hear my neighbors at their window with a kettle and a metal spoon, shouting something I don't understand.

It's still hot, even though it's after nine at night. I'm in my underwear and a T-shirt and the marble floor feels cool on my bare legs. I miss Ann, my lover in Minneapolis, and think about calling her, but we just talked this morning and I don't want to appear needy when things may finally work out for us.

∼

In the morning I pick up Nilda at her apartment for work. It's seven-ten and already so damn hot that perspiration collects on the inside of my dark glasses where they rub against my eyebrows. I crank up the air conditioner in the Nissan ZX. Nilda adjusts the vent so the flow is blowing directly on her face. Neither of us mentions last night, not the fireworks, nor my call. Traffic is practically non-existent and there's an eerie, artificial calm in a city that is usually jammed up like an L.A. freeway. I tune the radio to the Armed Services station where they're playing classical music. Then they report the weather—eighty degrees, clear sky; I wonder if it's a tape they punch in every morning at this time. They never mention what's going on in the city except to announce areas of tension in town. They don't use the word "demonstration," but talk about "congestion" or "expected traffic delays."

We pass the American Embassy on Balboa Avenue. It's recently been whitewashed to cover the red paint splatters that resembled blood stains. We cruise through the spider web of streets in El Chorrillo, nicknamed *Sal Si Puedes—Get Out if You Can*, and just as I think we'll make it through in record time, I catch the flash of red lights in my rearview mirror. *Shit.* I slap my hand on the steering wheel and pull over to the curb. A burly Panamanian Defense Forces cop in tight, navy blue pants with a yellow stripe down the leg strides over to my car. "Speak English," Nilda warns. "Pretend you don't understand."

"That shouldn't be hard." She turns away and looks out the window.

"*Licencia*," the cop says. He pushes back his hat that sits like a saddle on his large head, and mops his brow with a dirty handkerchief. I hand him the ticket I received earlier this week when I was stopped by another cop and had my license taken. The ticket is a temporary substitute until I show up at the police station next week with my fine of fifty dollars in cash. What it doesn't state is that my violation was really for driving an expensive car, which I'm sure I am also guilty of this morning. The cop reads the ticket, turns it over, then gives it back to me. His disappointment is evident. He can't give me another citation, because there is no license to confiscate and no assurance that I'll pay again. The system is not computerized like in the States. They can't cross-reference, check for outstanding warrants or issue more than one ticket.

"Maybe I'll just hold on to this," I wave it at Nilda, "not even pay the damn fine." She eyes me warily, a look that tells me that the *Fuerzas*, like the United States Internal Revenue Service, are not to be messed with. Having my Nissan ZX shipped down here was not one of my wiser decisions.

I'll admit I was ignorant when I first arrived in Panama. That was in October, during the height of the rainy season. Some days it poured so long and hard that I'd wake up in the morning to find two feet of water running like a river through the street outside my front door. Just as I thought I'd lose my mind, the last drops of rain were rung out of the clouds and the sky cleared to a gorgeous blue—a color I've dreamed about back in Minnesota on dark, cold, January days.

We pass by the burned-out hull of an overturned car and piles of charred garbage cans and tires—the residue of the strike. I have to veer around the debris. There's no sign of the men and women in light blue T-shirts with brooms and dustpans who clean the streets. The government has been paying them in rice and beans since the banks closed a month ago. They joined with the dock workers and the electrical employees, and took their frustration out in a city-wide strike.

Nilda stares out the window. I don't know what she's thinking. I try to keep my opinions to myself. I've always been against the war machine, but with the banks closed and the embargo tightening like a noose around the necks of the people, the pressure is building. Noriega appears dug in with no sign of budging. Lately I've started to think that Nilda may be right, that Reagan should just send in the goddamn marines and take him out.

When I pull into Corozal Army base, the sentry holds up his hand for me to stop. "Now, what the hell is this?" I gripe, and point to my vehicle pass, displayed on the dashboard as required. He motions for me to roll down the window. "I wish we worked for the air force," I say to Nilda and slap off the AC fan. "They're much more civil." She's not smiling. We've never been stopped at this gate before. The soldier is dressed in camouflage with his pant legs folded on the crease and neatly tucked into his polished black boots. His helmet is so low on his forehead it covers his eyes. "Can I see your ID, ma'am?" He's half my age and looks hotter than I feel with sweat trickling down the side of his face. I fish my wallet out of my purse, flip it open so the yellow contractor's ID card is visible.

"What is this about?" I ask without disguising my impatience.

He scrutinizes my card, then peers through the window, beyond me, to Nilda. "I need hers, too."

"Oh, come on."

"Just routine, ma'am."

Nilda keeps her eyes straight ahead and passes me her green Civil Service card. I hand it over. "Don't you guys remember faces? She's only worked here for the last three years." But he's new, I can tell by the way he studies her card before he gives it back. Meanwhile, cars are pulling in behind us. I glance back to see today's PML—personal movement limitation—hanging on a post at the exit. It's still at *Bravo* which stands for *No unnecessary travel*, the normal state of things recently. During the strike it was bumped up to *Charlie—Stay home and batten down the hatches*. That's when I made my decision to leave Panama.

The soldier gives me one last look before waving me on. "We've had to tighten up since the strike, ma'am," he explains. I roll up the window, flip the AC back on high even though we're only going up the street. "Do I look threatening?" I ask Nilda.

"I don't think he's worried about you. You don't look Panamanian." I lean forward, and pull the back of my blouse away from my skin. Leather upholstery is not the smartest thing in the tropics. The air inside the car starts to cool, but I can't stop a complaint from rolling out. "God, it's hot."

"This is Panamá," Nilda says and smiles for the first time this morning. I love the way she pronounces it, with the emphasis on the final *a*. In all my life, of all the things I've known and learned, the correct pronunciation for the name of this country was not one of them. It's amazing, the things you can get by without knowing. I did look at a map when I was offered this job to see how closely Panama was situated to Nicaragua. I needed reassurance that at least one country would separate me from a war zone.

"The dry season is almost over," Nilda says, "then we'll be back to the humidity. " She looks at me. "Of course, that means you'll be picking up your battle with mildew."

I grunt. We're almost to the Data Processing Center where we both work. I hardly want to get into a discussion about my future in Panama, mildew or no mildew, when we have less than a block to go and are already late.

In November, when we were just starting to be friends and the political situation was heating up, she commented that I probably would leave soon. I assured her I'd be here for a year, minimum. That was the term of my contract, which I didn't know was negotiable until this week. It's more Noriega's fault than mine and yet, the fact that I'm able to leave makes me feel guilty.

Nilda is the administrative assistant to Major Wilcox who heads up Data Processing. She acts like his personal sentry, regulating who gets past her desk to see him and who is re-routed or sent away as a bother. When I first met her, I viewed her as more of an obstacle than a possible friend. Then one morning I blew a fuse in my apartment and couldn't communicate to the building attendant what I needed. By the time I arrived at her desk to ask for help, I'd had a cold shower, a shouting match in English, Spanish and sign language with the attendant, no coffee and a near mishap on the drive to work.

Her laughter disarmed me. "You're going to tell me that you can install this entire computer system but you can't change a fuse?" Her English was impeccable, like a native speaker's. She's a small woman and was dwarfed by the big desk. I fought an urge to look under and see if her feet touched the floor.

"Just tell me how to say 'fuse' in Spanish and I'll call the apartment owner."

"And then he'll tell you how to change it and you won't understand a word he's saying."

"I'll manage." My pride was at stake even though she was right. I'd had four years of high school Spanish, but you'd never know it.

"I've heard you practicing with Captain Sanchez," she smirked.

I actually blushed. Sanchez is waging a one-man campaign to awaken the Spanish language sleeping in my brain. He's my counterpart in the Army. It's the oddest system. They match each civilian with a military person of similar training. It's as if we civies, left to our own devices, might muck something up or not do things exactly according to Standard Operating Procedure. Only God knows what havoc that would cause. Sanchez's training was on weaponry, computerized tank scanners and radar systems. Once a month he's out of the office for three to five days to "play soldier," as he calls it, on the Atlantic coast, where they make him paint his face green, crawl through the jungle on his belly and shoot at fake targets. If I look past his uniform, he's a nice guy.

"Give me the number," Nilda said. "Tell me exactly what's wrong and I'll make the call." While she was on the phone, I helped myself to the Major's coffee since he was nowhere in sight.

"The Señor will send someone over this afternoon," Nilda said when she hung up. "He thinks it's the hot water heater because it happened to the last guy who lived there. You must have a nice place if it comes with hot water."

I nodded. "It's a condo, in Obarrio." I could see on her face that she knew I lived in an expensive area. She straightened the papers on her desk. "Thanks," I offered. It was an awkward moment, and I didn't understand it until that afternoon when I saw her walking toward the gate where the taxis lined up. I pulled over and offered her a ride. She hesitated, glanced down the street. I took off my dark glasses. "I'll take you right to your door just like they will. And charge you a lot less." That made her laugh. I knew it was the ZX, and the hot water heater, and the apartment in Obarrio, a middle-class neighborhood where people with large well-kept homes also owned apartments like mine and rented them out. She insisted on getting out at my place and walking the five blocks to her own apartment even though I tried to convince her that I owed her for making the call. We stood for a few minutes outside the building; the rain, for once, had stopped. Then I said, "Sometimes I feel like such a pig. Here I am in your country and I can't even speak the language." I wanted to offer her something to lighten my guilt, so I added, "Your English is so perfect. I bet people mistake you for an American sometimes."

She squinted up at me and pressed her lips together into a single slit, then opened her mouth, closed it again. "I am an American," she said. "I just live in a different hemisphere than you. What you mean to say is do people ever think I'm a *North* American."

"Of course." I stared down at my pumps. The humidity was ruining them. I'd noticed a light green fuzz growing on a pair the other day. From a block away on Via Brasil I heard a long blast on a horn, screeching tires, the distinct sound of metal colliding with metal. I was sure I'd just wrecked my chances for a friendship, but when I looked up at Nilda, she had her head tipped back and was eyeing the height of my building.

"What floor do you live on?" she asked.

"The fifth."

"Is it a good view?"

I nodded. "Would you like to come up? Have a beer?"

In the elevator she said, "I've never been in one of these buildings. I've always wondered what they look like inside."

$\sim$

"Look at that." I point to the marine guard in front of the American Express Bank. He's wearing fatigues and clutching a machine gun in his hands. I turn into the parking lot slowly, nose the ZX up to the front of the building, and then ease it around the tight driveway to the back. It's a damn nice car, looks sleek as hell, charcoal gray with shiny black painted bumpers and has headlights that pop up from the hood when I turn them on. I only wish it had tinted windows, but they aren't something I thought about when I bought the car in the dead of winter in Minnesota. Sometimes when I'm driving, I like to pretend I'm in an old spy movie, like the reruns they show on the Armed Services channel. Or I make something up—*Nancy Drew Goes Global*, or Kinsey Millhone in *N is for Noriega*. Around the back of the building is another marine stationed at the top of the stairs in front of the data processing door. "It's getting scarier around here," I say, strengthening my case for leaving.

"At least we can cash our checks," Nilda says. I'm sure she knows people holding worthless paychecks, waiting for the banks to reopen. Her boyfriend Edgar lost his job, and the university where he was studying engineering was closed by the government after too many student demonstrations.

"I know I should be grateful, but I'm not used to this. We don't see soldiers patrolling the street corners in the States."

I back the car into the one remaining shady slot next to the building, a parallel spot, where it won't get nicked or banged by some thoughtless fool throwing open their car door. Nilda's out as soon as I turn off the engine. It's after seven-thirty, official army starting time.

"See you at ten?" I shout before she reaches the top of the stairs. It's her usual break time, and accompanying her to the snack bar next door has become a ritual. Why should it be any different today just because we were carded at the gate, just because my office is stuffed with packing boxes that I brought by in the dark two nights ago, just because I haven't settled on the exact words to use when I tell Nilda that I'm leaving Panama? She waves and darts inside.

I'm a systems analyst hired by the army to install an upgraded computer system. On Monday, after only six months into a three-year project, Major Wilcox told me that if I wanted, the general in Washington overseeing the program was willing to terminate my contract. He said now that the system was installed, they could use their own people to keep it running. He gave me a choice, then sat behind his desk with his hands folded over a neat pile of papers and waited for me to decide. I was shocked and I think he saw it. He picked up the papers and reshuffled them. My relief must have come through because he started filling something out on one of the forms. He looked up once and asked what date I wanted my household goods packed.

"Captain Sanchez knows the system," I said. "I'm sure he can run it without me." Wilcox nodded and went back to writing. I couldn't help wonder if he was as relieved as I was. I had the feeling that he saw me as a liability, a woman driving alone from town to the base with the personal movement limitation at Charlie.

I knew he would give those forms to Nilda to type, so before I left his office, I asked him to hold off on them until I had a chance to tell her myself that I was leaving. He looked at me a little funny, as if he didn't see the point, but agreed. It's Thursday today, and I'm pressing my luck by waiting any longer to tell her. As a friend, I owe her to hear it from me directly.

I straighten my skirt and tuck in my damp blouse, then reach into the back seat for my blazer with my official name badge affixed to the lapel. The heat and mildew are not the worst parts of living in this country. The worst part for me is that being afraid has come to feel normal. When I reach the top of the stairs, I'm tempted to say something smart to the pink-cheeked marine, like, "Ever thought of getting a real job?" but nothing fazes these guys. They look beyond you, as if you don't exist.

Inside, I remove my sunglasses and nod good morning to Sheree, the receptionist. Her father sent her to Panama from Jamaica to find a good job with the Americans. She sends half her pay home to her family. I'm tempted to ask her if she has gotten used to being afraid, but I don't know her well enough.

I unlock my office with a single key that slips into the slot above the door knob. My co-workers in Minneapolis would have a fit if they saw this flimsy lock or the simple wire mesh screen over the window. The main frame there is housed in a section of the building which is secured with an electronic alarm system and can only be accessed by punching a code number into the key pad on the wall outside the door. There's such a thing as overkill, but even with the marines' finest stationed outside, I still look forward to returning to the key pad.

My office here is drab. The linoleum floor is worn and scratched and the walls are dirty gray, stained from mildew and humidity. It smells like an old gym locker and I can only guess what the climate is doing to the computer hardware. I kick an empty box out of my way and close the door behind me. It seems like weeks rather than months since I unpacked the piles of books and manuals, the files, disks and computer parts that clutter the room.

On the wall, in front of my gun-metal gray, army issue desk, is a snapshot of Ann and me when we went cross county skiing in northern Minnesota. We're bundled from toe to chin and look happy. It was taken before I discovered she was having an affair. I pretended for a long time that I didn't know, even though the clues were all there, the way her voice changed and her face colored when she talked on the phone or mentioned the other woman's name. I didn't worry about it at first, because she was a business acquaintance, someone Ann stayed with when she was in Chicago. Then I found a letter, lying on our desk, under the latest issue of *Rolling Stone*, which I picked up to read. I have to admit that if I hadn't read that letter, I never would have left Minneapolis without her. I didn't say anything about going until I was offered the job. We were eating dinner, not exactly together, but coincidentally at the same time, each of us with our own carry-out item, picked up on the way home from work. She was unwrapping her deli sandwich when I told her. Secretly I hoped she'd beg me not to go, but she just stared at me with an open mouth.

"I know about your affair." I said it as if I was saying, I know it's going to rain tomorrow. "I read her letter."

"You read my mail? You actually read my mail?"

"It was lying open."

When I left, we didn't actually split up our stuff. I didn't want to bring anything valuable, other than my car, which was the only thing I really cared about at that moment. I took the old couch and chair from the basement, the dishes we'd been saving for when we bought a cabin, my dresser, the guest bed, and the card table and two folding chairs. I didn't want to have to worry about selling off my stuff if things didn't work out and I wanted to ditch my contract. No matter what happened, I'd foot the bill to have the car shipped back.

Yesterday morning I called Ann to tell her I was coming home. I waited for her reaction, wondering if it would be better to stay with one of our friends. The first month I was in Panama, I resisted the urge to call her. Instead I tried to calm myself by swimming laps in the hotel pool where I stayed until I found an apartment. When I couldn't sleep, I paced around the patio area, soothed by the yellow garden lights, the sweet smell of tropical shrubbery, the glow of the white underwater lights in the pool. I believed that by walking round and round in a circular pattern, I would eventually work the loneliness out of my body.

Once I moved into my apartment and was grounded by the familiarity of my own things—the musty furniture from our basement, my favorite books and a few pictures that had hung on the wall in our house, I could finally talk with her. We were cordial at first, then friendly, and more recently silly and joking, moving closer to our old selves. In our conversations, neither of us has mentioned the reason I left, and to this day, I have not said the other woman's name out loud.

Yesterday morning, to Ann's silence, I suggested that I stay somewhere else. "No," she said quickly. "Come home. We'll work this out."

"What about. . . ?"

"It's over. Please, I want you to come home."

～

I ease the tape off the back of the photo, smooth out the curled edges and slip it between the pages of a computer manual, then toss the book in a box. The task of packing overwhelms me, and I slump down in my swivel chair, twirl around one revolution. Then with my toes on the linoleum floor, I push off and spin the chair around until the room becomes a blur. Wherever I stop, I tell myself, that's the area I'll attack.

I haven't worked up the courage to explain my relationship with Ann to Nilda. The army would probably have me fired if they knew I was gay, but that's not the excuse I've used. I've been more afraid of losing her friendship, afraid that if she knew, she wouldn't like me anymore. It sounds juvenile, I know, but when you're far from home, things that haven't mattered for years, suddenly pop up in the forefront again. My friends in Minneapolis would be disappointed to see that I've slipped back. The more radical ones would disapprove, but I wouldn't say that I've been completely deceptive. It's not like I've gone on dates, even though Nilda did try to fix me up with one of Edgar's cousins. And then there's Glenda Werness who works in the American Express bank downstairs and has an unmarried son she wanted to set me up with in the worst way. I met them at the Balboa Union Church in the Canal Zone the first month I was here and desperate for community. We went out for breakfast, and I found myself considering whether or not he was my type. I was amazed that I'd been almost willing, just so I could fit in.

At ten I go down the hall, poke my head in Nilda's office. She motions for me to come in and close the door. I pull a chair up to her desk and hope she hasn't already heard that I'm leaving. She leans forward and speaks in a low tone as if she's sharing a secret. "I just heard from Sheree next door that the soldiers are stopping cars and searching them." Her dark eyes are wide and as she speaks her eyebrows lift and disappear under her straight black bangs.

"My soldiers or yours?" I tease and lean back in the chair.

"The *Fuerzas*," she hisses. It's not a joke. This is the first time I've really seen her scared. "We were lucky this morning," she says. "When you go home today, take off all your jewelry, put it somewhere safe, like the toe of your shoes. And take your cash out of your purse."

"You're coming with me," I state. She nods. "Where'd Sheree hear this? On

the radio? Has it been substantiated? Has the army made a statement?"
Nilda waves her hand to calm me down. "It's just rumors. Besides, when have you relied on the army for information?"
I get up. "Let's go get a cup of coffee."
On the way to the snack bar, she tells me that she has a friend who works in the allergy clinic at Gorgas Army Hospital in the Zone. "She says they've turned it into a M.A.S.H. unit. I think your President might finally use his troops to help us."
I hold the door open for her. She passes through with her head high, her chin jutting out, like this last piece of information is a sign of victory. Reagan has finally seen it her way and is coming to his senses.
The contrast of air from outside to inside hits me with a force and I'm chilled. Nilda orders two coffees and I procure us a couple of powdered sugar donuts. Thanks to the U.S. military and their daily cargo runs, we're exempt from the embargo here on base, and everything that's available in America is available right here. Almost everything.
"I don't think you should get your hopes up," I say once we're in the booth. "If Reagan does decide to invade, it may not happen the way you imagine. They can't just drop a bomb on Noriega and miss everyone around him."
"You know what I like about you, Jean?"
"Tell me," I say, dunking my donut. It's a little stale, freshness being sacrificed for the familiar. I should have stuck with the local fare, had the *empañadas*. Now *there's* something I'll miss.
"You remind me of my friends I had in college, in the States. Optimistic Democrats. They loved to talk. Talk, talk, talk, always wanting to find a peaceful, non-violent solution to things. The cleanest way to the end, where no one would get hurt, especially not the *norteamericanos*. The truth is, I've never known the Democrats to get anything accomplished."
I dump coffee whitener in my cup, swirl it with a spoon. I don't even like this stuff, but I can't look at her right now. It's not the first time we've had this conversation. She thinks Reagan is brilliant and says that most Panamanians hope Bush wins the election this fall.
"Since the canal was built, we've relied on the U.S. Why should it be different now?"
I tilt my cup, debate drinking the last swallow. Donut crumbs floating like lumps of flour in gravy help me decide against it. I wipe my sweating palms on my skirt under the table. "I have something to tell you, Nilda." Now I look at her. "I'm going home. The army is canceling my contract because of the political situation." I want to explain it all, about the army's liability and my not being a regular employee and having base privileges, but I know it won't take away her blank stare.
She turns away, first toward the counter where the Cuna Indian man is cleaning the grill and getting ready for the lunch crowd, then beyond me, to the window that's behind my back. I imagine the view she sees, the cyclone fence with rolled barbed wire on top, marking the boundary of the base, and beyond that the jungle. Thick, green, and wild. It would grow right over the street and up to the buildings if it weren't held back.
"I'll miss you," I say.
"I've known all along that you wouldn't stay."
"Well, eventually—"

"No, I knew you wouldn't last a year."

"This isn't easy for me."

"Of course not," she forces a smile.

"I'm not sleeping well. I'm scared all the time. And I keep thinking about Mel Gibson in that movie, *The Year of Living Dangerously*. I'm afraid something will happen and I won't be as lucky as Mel was to make it out of the country at the last minute."

"I didn't see the movie." Her voice is flat. I don't know what to say. I don't think I'm handling this well. "You can understand my being scared? You must get scared sometimes?"

"Yes, but it's not like I can run away. This is my home."

I tap my foot nervously under the table. "I wouldn't have made it this long without you. You've been a good friend."

"Sometimes I hate working for your army," Nilda says bitterly. "People are always leaving. The only reason I do it is because it pays better than anything I can get in town. And there's the PX." She looks down at her cup. I wonder if she's going to cry. It wouldn't be polite of me to watch.

"I have to get back to my office. Will you come over tonight, have a beer, watch me pack?"

She doesn't look up, but raises her hand. I wait until she slides out of the booth, then follow her outside. The sun is so bright I have to squint. We walk back to data processing in silence. I don't even feel like making a comment about the heat.

～

The day before I leave, I relinquish my car to the shipping company. I take one last walk around it, touch the hood. The guy checking it in, smiles. "Don't worry," he says in a Jamaican accent. "We'll take good care of it."

That night I take Nilda out to dinner. When I propose the invitation, I think it's a good idea, a farewell gift, but once we're seated at a table, and I see the tentative way she picks up the linen napkin, I know it's all wrong. The place is too expensive, which alone wouldn't bother me. But Nilda opens the large menu, then closes it and looks around like this is her first trip to Disney World. I'm sure this will be the only time she'll ever eat here. We'll spend on one meal what she and her cousin could eat off for a week. I wanted this to be really nice, our last time together, but now I'm embarrassed. I wish we'd gone to our usual place, Napoli's, and had bad pizza and Panamanian beer.

"Edgar's going home, too," Nilda says. She picks at her salad with her fork. "He hasn't found a job and can't pay his rent. His father owns a coffee farm in Chirriqui. He says there's nothing to keep him here."

"He said that?"

She shrugs. "He's under a lot of pressure. I'm sure he didn't mean it about me."

"Why don't you come to the States. I could help you find a job. I have plenty of friends with good connections."

She laughs. "I wouldn't go to the States."

"Why not? It wouldn't have to be forever, just until things blow over down here."

She looks a little shocked and sets her fork down hard. A piece of lettuce flies off the end of it and lands between our two plates. "Until things blow over?" I see the flash of color come to her cheeks as she draws her mouth into a tight line.

"Nilda." This is our last night together, I want it to be memorable.

"You *norteamericanos* think it's so easy. When things get bad you think we should all go and live in your country where it's so much better."

"Hey, I'm only talking about for a while. It's getting worse here. Every day the line outside the passport office gets longer. Fifty people or more a day are waiting to get their *pas y salvo* exit papers. Do they all know something you don't?"

"They have reasons to go and I have reasons to stay."

"Like what?"

"My family, Edgar, my cousin and her husband. They wouldn't be able to eat every night if I didn't have privileges at the PX. They rely on me and I won't desert them."

"I'm just thinking about you. If Reagan sends in the troops like you hope he does, people will be killed. It won't be safe once the shelling starts."

I take a sip from my glass of wine. It's too sweet and I don't care for the dressing on my salad, but I eat it, knowing people are doing without tonight. I'm used to fighting to get my own way and usually I'm able to convince people that I know what's best. And I do feel I'm right about this, but Nilda's anger is unexpected and throws me off balance.

"I went to college in the States. I know what it's like to live in another country, to be that lonely and far from your family. I don't ever want to do it again. You change after awhile. You lose some of who you were before you left. The longer you stay away, the harder it is to fit in when you return. If you stay too long you realize you don't fit in either place. I'm still Panamanian. This is where I belong."

I feel my shoulders relax for the first time in days. This isn't my country, I don't know what I'd do if it was. But I understand wanting to be around the people you love when things are unsafe.

After dinner, I take Nilda to her apartment. We don't hug, but when she says good-bye, she touches her fingers to the back of my hand resting on the seat between us, and tells me that she'll have a reason to check her post office box. Now that I'm leaving, I can admit I'm a little in love with her, not that I ever would have done anything about it, but admitting it makes driving away all the harder.

I back the rental car out of the lot and glance behind me in the mirror. She's standing on the steps in front of the building, looking out at the empty street where I'm about to head. On the corner there's a small band of Panamanian soldiers, wearing the same uniforms as their North American counterparts, with the same helmets down over their foreheads. The only difference between them and the U.S. soldiers is the insignia on their sleeves and the short rubber hoses hanging off their belts.

Throwing Bombs

CHARI MELÉNDEZ and I went out driving every night. It was my third visit to Puerto Rico since teaching there ten years before and Chari—who'd spent the ten years going to college and going crazy and being shipped up to Massachusetts to live with her brother and having another breakdown there, plus getting married and pregnant and battered—Chari still didn't know how to drive.

I rented the car partly to give her driving lessons, and partly because having a car in Puerto Rico gives you so much freedom and power. *That* I remembered very clearly.

Sunday night Chari and I were driving around and we found her oldest half-brother parked outside the pharmacy—not the one on the plaza, the one down Calle Porrata-Doria, the one owned by the Arabs. It was Mother's Day and Tato Meléndez was sitting outside in his silver station wagon while his wife, inside, picked out something to buy herself for Mother's Day. Something from him.

It was eight at night and the pharmacy was mobbed.

It wasn't very romantic—not nearly romantic enough for me, unmarried still at thirty-eight, or for Chari, divorced at twenty-six—but Tato, forty-eight, sat waiting patiently for Millie in the evening heat.

"*¡Bendición!*" Chari called—Your blessing!—and Tato, as her elder, blessed her. Then he smiled at me. "*Díos me las cuida las dos,*" he said. May God take care of both of them for me.

Tato smiled again, and Chari and I could see that he was sober and we knew that was the real Mother's Day gift: Tato staying sober all day.

That was what Millie had asked for, of course; the most she could hope for. The pharmacy was named "*Farmacia Rincón*"—The Corner Drugstore—and I'd been in it earlier, asking after the owner's youngest son, the one who'd been my student. Arvid married, his pharmacist brother told me. "Arvid went to college in the States, and he's a photographer, and he'll be so sorry he missed you—he and his wife were just here to visit last month."

Ten years ago Arvid Bey had been the San Sebastián High School photographer and school joke. When the ceiling plaster fell in my room, I was glad—it gave me an excuse to rearrange the desks into a circle—but the other faculty were horrified. "Did it hit any students?" they asked. "Arvid Bey," I told them, and they laughed. Even the principal laughed.

Mostly, though, I remember Arvid from the day a senior class field trip took all but five of my students. We spent the period singing American pop songs, and Arvid explained to us that Billy Joel's "Just the Way You Are" was *not* about keeping women stupid—as I insisted—but in fact written for *him*, Arvid, to sing to his dog. To prove his point, Arvid had us sing it again—"*Don't go changing . . .*"— while he, at the end of each line, made appreciative dog noises.

Now Arvid is married and lives in the States. No children, his brother said. "Not yet."

Tato Meléndez is married too, of course; all twelve of the Meléndez children have married, even Chari. Tato and his wife Millie have eight kids, nine counting the illegitimate daughter Millie had first and was so grateful to Tato for accepting as his own.

Tato is married but yesterday it was me in the driver's seat of the silver station wagon. Me driving and Tato drunk. A drunk Tato who knew, vaguely, that he could memorialize his alcoholic father, not just by drinking, but also by womanizing.

"*Me estás tirando bombas,*" Tato said. You're throwing bombs at me, and he meant my smiles. He meant my smiles were exploding like bombs right in the middle of his marriage.

People disapproved. The family said it was a shame how Tato drank. He should find God, they all said, but by then I was sick of the family's knee-jerk fundamentalism. A little bit I loved Tato for drinking in spite of them. What a shame, they said. Such a pity, they said, and I knew they wanted me to such-a-pity back, but instead I left with Tato, saying only: "*Me encanta pasear.*" Driving around enchants me.

How could they expect me to agree with them, anyway, when they all knew I hadn't *found* God either?

"*¡A pasear!*" Tato said. Drive around.

"*¡A pasear!*" I said, smiling back at him.

"*Me estás tirando bombas,*" he said, and I liked it because I'd always liked Tato, and I always knew he liked me back, but Tato didn't usually admit to it. "*Díos me la cuida siempre,*" Tato always said after we'd flirted a little too heavy. May God take care of her for me always. It was a declaration of disinterest, that Tato desired nothing more than God's protection of me on his behalf.

Tato's wife had her own forgiving phrase: "*Elena siempre buena conmigo.*" Elena is always good to me. And she meant that even if I *seemed* like the kind of hussy who flirted with other women's husbands, she knew I would never *actually* encourage Tato, never *actually* threaten her marriage. I had a mantra too— because sometimes the pattern of married or otherwise unavailable men in my life made me feel locked into an endless search for Mister Wrongs. My mantra went: *The attraction is not JUST because he's married.*

And that was the truth because I *did* love Tato. I loved that Tato used to greet me "*¿Cómo estamos?*"—How are we?—back when it was too soon to use the familiar *tu* form but he didn't want to offend me with the formal *Usted*, and I loved that Tato started dropping by his stepmother's house for his morning coffee after his father died and all Doña Luz's kids were either married or in the States, leaving her alone in the house with her grandchild. His visits were such a comfort to Doña Luz and they were so much chivalry from such a poor man.

Just like his chivalry toward me, the one who keeps throwing bombs at him. Loosely, *paseando* means "driving around", but more precisely it means "passing by people's houses and dropping in on them unexpectedly, with no apparent reason. "*Paseando*, Tato and I stopped at the new house of his brother Sixto, the Meléndez sibling the closest to my age. "*Mi casa es tu casa*," he said to me. My house is your house. Sixto also said, "*Más llenita*"—A little bit fuller—and *Six* meant "fatter." He meant the twenty-five pounds I'd gained since my skinny schoolteacher self. But I deliberately misunderstood him. "Fuller?" I asked. "It's that I just ate at Doña Luz's house." I patted my stomach, and at first Sixto tried to correct me, but Tato was laughing and finally Sixto laughed too. *Paseando*, Tato and I stopped at the basketball court to see Millie's cousin, a man as black as Millie was white, darker even than Tato. Millie's cousin made some sense of Tato's kids: the way they alternated between blond and dark.

Tato didn't have any real business anywhere.

"Stop here," he said and I did.

"*Toca*," he said. Touch, and I knew he meant "Sound the horn," but I didn't want to.

"Touch what?" I stalled.

Finally Tato leaned over and leaned on the horn himself. I looked up and saw eyes at the kitchen louvres.

"*¡Ya!*" I said. "Enough."

A woman's eyes peered out, and there were probably lots of people she knew who might drop by—sisters, cousins, people in the church—but she didn't recognize Tato's car, didn't recognize me, and so she turned and yelled for her husband to go out and see who it was.

The husband came out wrinkling his nose at me—that Puerto Rican rabbit-nosed gesture for "What do you want?"—but then he saw Tato. The two of them were buddies in the U.S. Naval Reserve so he went around and leaned in the passenger window, standing there and doing all the talking because Tato was too drunk to hold up his end of the conversation.

"*Bueno, negro*," the man said finally, slapping Tato on the back, "*cojelo suave*." Well, friend, take it easy.

"*Mucho gusto*," he said to me. Nice to meet you.

"*Igualmente*." Likewise.

"*¡A pasear!*" Tato said, and I did, but by this time I felt cruel, that I was making a spectacle of Tato and his drunkenness and would-be infidelity.

But then, from a house in that same housing development, out ran Aldito Luna, one of my students from ten years ago, the one I was so sure was being fucked by his older cousin Hugo.

"Missy, Missy!" Aldito ran waving at me and I stopped the car in the street.

"*¿Aldito?*" I laughed, but it was Aldito all right, a little chunkier, a little less blond, but still Aldito, still bending like a noodle as he brought his head down to the car window to kiss my cheek in that Puerto Rican greeting gesture.

Partly I was sure that Aldito was being sexually abused back then because I'd been told it was so prevalent: that all over the island the mandatory virginity of Catholic girls turned teen-age boys to butt-fucking. And partly because there was a giggle that Aldito and his friend Frankie had, a sophomore's giggle of submission that they giggled before the mighty senior Hugo. That giggle struck me as sexual; it struck me that Aldito and Frankie were the boys whose sweet bottoms were saving Hugo's girlfriend for marriage.

I liked Hugo Luna too. He was a huge dark-skinned boy with an odd over-powering body odor, and I knew he hated English and got his test answers from one of the sophomore girls, but he was very sweet with me. It was only his put-down of homosexuals that got to me, because it was so blame-the-victim—*I fucked you because you're gay and wanted me too*—and because there was *so* much homophobia in Puerto Rico. I was tortured, imagining sweet Aldito—who *was* a little swish the way he fawned all over me, but I liked that too—I was tor-tured imagining that Aldito would end up locked into homosexuality. It's terrible to feel out of control of your own sexuality.

Finally one day, after yet another homophobic put-down, I told Hugo that in *my* country, the one on *top* was considered just as much a homosexual as the one on *bottom*.

This was pretty crude language from the Missy and there was no response from Hugo, but Aldito looked at me fish-eyed, that corner-of-his-eye look telling me something. "You guessed right," it said? Or "Thank you?"

Something, and I never thought I'd done enough, but that eye, that side-long look of Aldito's, had stayed with me ten years.

And now here were Tato and I *paseando* and out into the street came Aldito. He told me he was an engineer—though everybody in Puerto Rico was an engi-neer and I thought it must all be euphemism like "janatorial engineer" and "mar-keting engineer"—but Aldito had gone to the University of Puerto Rico at Mayagüez, he said, and now he was an engineer and married and had a baby. He wanted me to come back and see his baby.

"Yes, hello," he said to Tato when I introduced them. "You're the uncle of the Vidal who makes the wedding videos?" he asked.

Tato looked very drunk but managed a very formal: "*Corecto.*"

"Look, Missy," Aldito said, switching to English to make sure I understood, "The sign, it says Familia Luna Figueroa"—Figueroa is his wife's name and that's his brother-in-law helping work on the roof—"but look the sign, Missy, and return to here, because Missy, *mi casa es tu casa*. My house is your house."

Aldito and I kissed cheeks again. I was so happy I was almost crying.

"*¡Adíos!*" I called, and Tato and I went back to driving around. We only quit when he told me to drive home—"*¡Rapido!*"—but I wasn't fast enough and the poor drunk ended up peeing in his pants.

Peed all over himself, the family said, and they clucked and *Díos mio*'ed. "Dear God, what a pity," they said. If only Tato would join the church and put his prob-lem in the hands of the Lord, they said.

"*¿Verdad?*" they asked me. Isn't that so?

But let Tato pee on himself, I thought. The point was seeing Aldito and his not-so-badly-scarred-he-can't-have-a-wife-and-a-baby life. And the point was Tato, sweet Tato who'd worked for $3.49 an hour at the Chevron petroleum plant until it shut down but nevertheless managed to support his family, and afterwards man-aged to become a schoolteacher, and so what if he got drunk? The point was Tato being sweet to me and admitting the chemistry that's always been there, admit-ting that even now—with me "full" as anything—even now my smiles still threw bombs at his heart.

Me encanta pasear, I told his family. Driving around enchants me. And now it was Sunday night, Mother's Day, and I was *paseando* with his sister Chari. The two of us were happily discussing Tato and Millie, Aldito and Arvid, and what *we* fantasized for our own lives—what careers would suit two hardworking intelligent women? Was it worthwhile dating a man who'd been married twice before? Could they ever change?

We knew nothing was perfect, but that night, for the two of us, anything seemed possible.

ASIA

Apples

I**T ALL STARTED** with a bushel of apples. Yasin Pekdemir appeared at the door of our apartment and asked if I would like to buy them. The money would supplement his scholarship at Robert College as would the small fee he received from his duties as a "surveillant" or resident assistant in the prep school dorm. Who could say no? Yasin had been one of our favorite students at the Turkish prep school where my husband and I taught, just a few miles north of Istanbul, on the European side of the Bosphorus. Eager to help, I bought several bushels of apples, as many as I could find room for in our apartment. Yasin told me how his father, uncle, and other villagers pooled their resources each fall and rented a truck to transport all their apple harvest from their Anatolian village to Istanbul, to sell in the market. For years, Yasin's father gave him all the money from the sale of the apples, the family's only cash crop, to help with his college expenses.

All that fall and into the winter, I planned menus around those apples. At first, we ate lots of crisp, small apples. They were remarkable, with a wine-like flavor. As the apples aged, I turned them into apple pie, apple cobbler, apple brown betty, apple crisp, apple sauce, apple jelly. I cooked red cabbage and apples, chicken and apples, and a few other forgotten gastronomical variations on the apple theme. The cupboard where I stored them had a wonderful, fruity aroma and scented the whole kitchen.

One day in midwinter, Yasin mentioned that his father and uncle were back in town for a few days. I asked him to invite them to dinner, and I would fix them apple pies from their own fruit. Messages went back and forth, they accepted the invitation, and we agreed on a date. When the appointed time came, they arrived promptly at the door. They resembled most village Turks, wearing shabby suits so ancient that you could not tell the original color, handknit sweater vests, slouch caps, and scuffed, muddy shoes. Their clothes would have been in style in Western Europe and the United States in the 1930s. At Ataturk's behest, these outfits had replaced the fez and Eastern dress of the Ottoman Empire. The father and uncle had cheeks red from the cold, and bristling moustaches. They smelled of tobacco and that sweet essence of apples. We shook their gnarled, calloused hands, and they removed their shoes and came into the living room.

We exchanged greetings and polite compliments in Turkish. The great thing about Turkish is the language has an expression for any imaginable social situation. We had rehearsed the Turkish social expressions appropriate for this particular occasion: "Welcome to our house, your son and nephew is a fine student and an upstanding citizen, and we are very fond of him, you honor us with your presence and we shall honor you with a meal and apple pies made from fruit from your orchard, and may it help sustain your son and nephew in his honorable efforts to obtain a higher education and bring honor on you, your family, your village, and all of Turkey." Following that effort, which evoked from the men a similar set of polite, social responses, my husband and I had to resort to English. Yasin translated.

I returned to the kitchen to complete preparations for the meal, which included some Turkish favorites, roast leg of lamb with lots of cloves of garlic tucked into slashes; *iç pilav*, rice cooked with bits of tomato, onion, lamb liver, currants, and pine nuts, dusted with cinnamon and sprinkled with the drippings and crisp bits of meat from the roasting pan; salad with *beyaz peynir*, the white goat cheese Turks prefer, cured black olives, chunks of tomatoes, and slivers of onions; stuffed eggplant, called *imam bayıldı*, or "the imam fainted," due to the cost of the olive oil used in the dish; lots of *ekmek*, the substantial yellow, slightly sour crusty bread; and, of course, the *pièce de résistance*, apple pies.

I summoned our guests into the dining room, where they tucked their napkins into their collars and began to eat with a gusto that would have warmed the heart of any cook. Round and round the table the platters went, as conversation gave way to the concentration appropriate for serious eating. In no time at all, the lamb roast was stripped to the bone. The eggplant and the mountain of *pilav* disappeared, and the salad followed. Chunks of bread mopped up the good, yellow olive oil and the juice from the lamb.

I returned to the kitchen to prepare the coffee in the Turkish fashion, with a long-handled copper device in which the powdered coffee and water are brought to a boil three times and the foam allowed to subside twice, before the coffee is poured into tiny cups. Then I brought out the apple pies, still warm from sitting in the oven, two traditional double-crusted ones and a Dutch apple pie with a crumb crust. Their eyes lit up with pride, as I explained, in halting Turkish, that these were made from their own apples. In less time than it takes to say "May you enjoy your food," the pies were devoured, as I hurried back and forth from the kitchen with fresh cups of coffee.

Yasin's father and uncle pushed their chairs back from the table, with huge sighs of satisfaction. They thanked us for the meal and expressed a desire to return our hospitality. They invited us to visit them in their village, whenever we could come, and promised to show us the apple orchards that had produced these succulent apples that had been made so cleverly into that great American dessert, the apple pie. Then they rose, shook our hands, slipped worn, baggy socks into scuffed shoes, and bowed their way out the door, with an *Allahasmarladik* (Allah's blessing), the traditional farewell. We gave the prescribed response (laughingly, laughingly)!

I thought about the apple orchard each time I used apples during the following months. The image became more elaborate and detailed as the winter dragged on and the pile of apples diminished. Yasin, my husband, and I began to plan a trip to Yasin's village, Dundarlı. When spring vacation arrived in April, we set off in our Volkswagen to drive from Istanbul to the village.

As we drove along the main east-west road that bisects much of Anatolia, and then on more primitive roads, the image of the apple orchard, with trees beginning to blossom white and fragrant in the mountain spring air, filled my mind. Finally, we arrived in Dundarlı. The village consisted of about sixty low, stone dwellings resembling blocks that had slid down the mountainside. There were no street lights, no paved roads, no signs of the twentieth century. The bare winter branches of cottonwood trees provided scarce protection from the wind for the houses on the rounded mountainside. When I questioned Yasin about the lack of trees on the mountainside, he explained that the forests had disappeared long ago, as the villagers burned them as fuel against the long, bitter winters.

We drove up the winding path to Yasin's house, and as we pulled into the yard, the family emerged from the flat-roofed, two-story house. His father, whom I recognized, his mother, with a head scarf tied under her chin, younger brothers Sabri and Sabit, and his sister Fatma were all torn between shyness and curiosity about the foreigners and their eagerness to see their son and older brother. We were greeted with much ceremony and warmth. Before we had even settled down on the floor cushions, Yasin's mother sent a neighbor down the street to have the village tailor make me a pair of *shalvahs*. She explained that I could not sit on the floor properly, wearing a dress. Within a half hour, the neighbor returned with a huge, roomy pair of dark blue flannel trousers. The elasticized waist and wide legs made it possible to pull the *shalvahs* over the bulk of my skirt.

We ate a special meal that evening. In honor of our arrival, they had slaughtered a chicken, a rare occurrence in this poverty-stricken village. We ate yogurt, salad made from greens collected on the mountainside, bulgur, and unleavened flat bread. Afterwards, we drank small glasses of tea, more common in villages than coffee, and made plans for the following day. The village schoolmaster would escort us to the neighboring village to inspect the grade school. And of course we would have to visit the apple orchards, on the way back from the school.

We all spent the night on pallets in the one room on the upper floor. In the room below us, the heat produced by the goats and sheep rose and warmed the floor boards on which we were sleeping. Everyone slept in their layers of clothes, and I was grateful for the *shalvahs*, which also helped me stay warm. That night, I dreamed of the apple orchard, but without the blossoms, my dream modified by the unrelenting cold in the mountains.

We all arose early the next morning. After a cup of tea and some bread and a visit to the outhouse, which was conveniently located in the farm yard behind the dung heap, we were ready for our trip. Yasin's uncle and the schoolmaster met us at the bottom of the hill, with a small donkey in tow. They explained that we would have to ford a cold, wide, stony mountain stream, and the donkey was to carry me across. The school was about a mile's walk, and the orchards, it turned out, were downstream, about halfway between the school and Dundarlı. Yasin's father and uncle, two of many brothers, had inherited separate plots of the orchard from their father, and we would see both of them.

The trip across the river to the village with the grade school went quickly. We were received like visiting dignitaries and asked to inspect the school. The schoolmaster proudly pointed out a small library that Yasin had established by collecting his classmates' textbooks at the end of each high school and college term and bringing them back to this little village school. At age twenty, he was already a local hero, the only young person from these two villages to get a high school education, and soon, if Allah willed it, a college education.

My mind pondered the significance of all this, and the contribution made by the apples, as we started the trip toward the family orchards. Back across the stream we went, me on the donkey and the men gingerly hopping from rock to rock to avoid soaking their shoes in the icy water. Another half-hour's walk took us to a small stand of gnarled, bare fruit trees, set into the rocky, desolate landscape. As we approached, Yasin announced, "Here we are! My father's orchard!" We stopped and stood there, our mouths gaping. We were speechless. This was it? Six old apple trees huddled for warmth against the mountainside?

I put out my hands and placed them on the rough bark of the nearest tree. I waited, somehow expecting to feel a vibration or to sense the sap running inside the trunk—something that would account for the power of these trees to catapult Yasin out of his village and into a life that his father and uncle could only glimpse. My fingers felt nothing but the rough reality of the knotted, tough old trunk, firmly rooted in the rocky soil, with its branches reaching toward the sky.

Afraid that our silence would offend Yasin and his uncle, I glanced at them. Their faces were creased with smiles of satisfaction at our reaction. Interpreting our silence as awe, they stood there, solid and strong as the apple trees.

There Are Seventy Peoples in the World

"**W**ATCH OUT for Israeli men. My wife says they're terrible womanizers." That's Bob, my seat mate on the plane to Tel Aviv. His daughter Beryl, seated behind us, reading my tour pamphlets, informs us, indignantly, that she's just found out the Wall is segregated. "We'll have to find another place for my Bat Mitzvah."

"A thirteen-year-old feminist," Bob says proudly. "And Zionist. She's here to find out what Israel means to her."

I'm thinking that's why I'm here. That's what I told Rebecca and David when I left them in care of their father, my ex. "That's why I don't want to go with you," David said. "I don't want to find out."

"I'm afraid she'll want to stay," Bob says *sotto voce*. "My wife says, 'Don't worry. American kids are too spoiled to live in Israel.'"

His wife is coming tomorrow. They never fly together. Her family was killed in the Madjanek massacre. The Nazis made the Jews strip naked and dig ditches. Then they shot them and threw them in, piling up live ones on the corpses.

～

When I was here thirty years ago with my parents, rusting tanks lined the road from Tel Aviv to Jerusalem, black metal skeletons, corroded relics. Moshe, our Israeli driver, told us, "They'll be here forever, to remind us." Moshe had fought with the Palmach, saw his brother's head stuck on a pole. "The Arabs," he said. *Gott veht shtrofn.*

"God will punish," says my mother, translating.

Moshe died in the Six Day War and is buried near his brother. It's 1985, the tanks gone, and in their stead, there's a shiny steel column. The road is merely beautiful. "It might be California," I tell Menachem, my cab driver.

"Is nice, California? I like to get there," he says. "Jobs here how-you-say 'lousy.' In Russia, I am engineer. Here I drive cab like stupid Yemenite."

Proster yid, my mother would have said. "Vulgar, low-class Jew."

～

"What state do you belong to?" asks the small, straight-backed Asian boy seated across from me in the Hotel Mizpah lobby.

I have just finished a breakfast of burned toast and squishy hard-boiled eggs, and now I'm drinking bitter coffee, studying my Israel guidebooks, waiting to meet my tour group.

115

"I belong to New York," I answer, wondering what that means.

"I belong to Wisconsin. I'm here with my father. He's a Catholic priest. He adopted me from Vietnam five years ago. Now I'm American. So we're related."

"We're related."

"Shake." He extends his hand. "Are you going to Bethlehem to see where Jesus was born?"

I nod yes, though we're going to Bethlehem to see the mayor.

"My father says Jesus is from Vietnam, too."

⁓

The tour group assembles in the hotel lobby with fifteen minutes to get acquainted before today's bus trip. Two psychiatrists and their teenage children, a sociologist, several journalists. I am the only painter. I forget everyone's name immediately, except for Roger Blum, chairman of New Roots Foundation, which sponsored this trip. He excuses himself for the small speech he is about to make, "really a speechlet," he promises. We laugh politely.

"This is not the usual tour to see how our desert has bloomed, but to get a perspective on the human diversity, to visit with Israeli Arabs and Jews, see the real Israel."

I think of Adela in *Passage to India*, wanting to see "the real India," and feel anxious.

As we board the bus, Roger's wife, Angela, tall, blonde, in khaki jumpsuit and white cowboy boots, tells us she converted when she married Roger. Her nail polish matches her lipstick. I wonder about her toenails. The driver hands out paper fans and orange drinks, warns us we're in for a hot day in the desert.

⁓

Our first stop is Yarka, a hilly sandswept town which has the only steel fabricating plant in Israel. Mahmoud, the manager, in jacket and tie despite ninety-degree heat, leads us to the conference room. I'm woozy after three stifling hours in an unair-conditioned bus. When will we eat? Would it be rude to ask for the bathroom? The teenagers poke each other and jiggle in their Grateful Dead T-shirts. Their mother whispers to sit down, take off their mirrored sunglasses. They shrug and remove them.

After Mahmoud hustles up bottles of Israeli orangeade, we settle down. Standing behind Sulemein, the Druse who owns this factory, Yaakov, the Polish engineer, addresses us. "We built this for an idea, one Pole and six Druse brothers. Money, too, but more an idea." He folds his suntanned arms on his chest and waits for a signal to continue. Like Yaakov, Sulemein, wears a short-sleeved white shirt, but resemblance ends there. With his large, muscled arms, stiff bearing, and patronizing air, he embodies his namesake the Emperor who built Sulemein's wall around the old Jerusalem. We should be sitting at his feet.

"This factory *is* Yarka," Mahmoud says. "Every family in the village has someone working here."

Later, Mahmoud introduces the workers, describes how they fabricate steel. I sketch the men in goggles carrying blowtorches and think of the mills in Pittsburgh, where I grew up, where the steelworkers were called Hunkies and Polacks and lost their jobs when the open hearths shut down. The building is oppressively hot and I have jet lag. The woman I think is a travel writer closes her eyes and naps standing.

I ask myself where are the women? "Where are the women?" I ask Mahmoud, as we leave the plant and a hot blast of air hits me in the face. How do Jews from Russia and Poland, accustomed to below zero winters, learn to live in this heat? Perhaps they keep a small, cool pocket somewhere inside.

"We are going," Mahmoud says, escorting us up a dusty road to a shoe factory that looks like an old airplane hangar. I sketch a field of embroidery skirted women stitching shoes on ancient sewing machines, surrounded by mounds of sandals and sneakers. We're toured around them. They're impassive. How would I like to be on view like this?

"They are liberated, these women." Mahmoud knows we will want to hear this. "It may not look like much, but they no longer must live with their fathers, they no longer must work in the fields. They can leave the house, make a salary. They can choose whom they marry."

"What if they don't want to marry?" I ask.

"Why should they not want to marry?"

"But what if they don't?"

"I cannot understand. This has never happened," Mahmoud says.

∼

Mahmoud's house, where we are invited to lunch with his family, might be a suburban American ranchstyle, though there are no other houses around it. Where is the rest of Yarka?

Inside, women in Bedouin dresses, black with red and blue embroidered yokes and sleeves, heads covered, are setting a large dining room table. They greet us shyly, extending their hands to indicate that we should sit; then they withdraw to the kitchen. We take our places at the table among the male members of Mahmoud's family.

"We are waiting," Mahmoud announces.

The women serve small cups of coffee. We drink and chat about the heat. Some of the men talk steel. We wait—no one asks why—for five, ten, fifteen minutes. More coffee. I wish I had brought gum, Trail Mix, anything to put in my mouth. Finally a group of handsome, dark-skinned men in plain black robes and black headresses file in, sit down along the wall. It takes me a moment to realize they are not Greek Orthodox priests, but Druse elders, a frame to our picture. I'd like to set up an easel and paint them. What if I open my sketch book on my lap and draw under the table? No, not these guys. I'm sure pictures or photos are a breach of sacred etiquette. I'm sure that like Chassidim, they would hide their faces.

Mahmoud bows to them, thanking them for their long journey. I see them leaving a movie-like oasis set with palm trees, dismounting from camels.

I concentrate on their faces so I can get them down on paper later, while Mahmoud begins a brief history. "We are Druse. You in America may not know of us. We are Mohammedans and separatists who left Egypt a thousand years ago and spread throughout Syria and the Middle East. Like you, we consider ourselves descended from Abraham and Sarah. We are mountain people, good fighters. We are the only Arabs allowed to join the Israeli army."

I decide to find a bathroom, lock myself in and make sketches. But first I have to pass through a surprisingly modern kitchen where women are preparing our meal. Dishes of food are everywhere, on counters, tables, the floor, where the older women sit, rolling dough balls and chopping meat. All are in Arab dress except for one pretty young woman in stockings, high heels, a bright blue sweater and short skirt. I introduce myself. She tells me her name is Darva. I ask why she's dressed differently from the others.

Darva motions me into a room lined with low sofas and embroidered cushions and shuts the door. "Do you think my skirt is too short?"

I assure her it's not.

She tells me she left Yarka four years ago to go to the University at Beersheba. "I found a man who would take me with him to college and married him. He is very handsome besides, and I love him, but mostly I love him because he is modern and understands how I want to be. My mother is not sure whether to be ashamed or proud. Most of all, she thinks my skirts are too short." Darva says this in one burst, as though she may not have another chance to express herself to a modern American.

I would like to stay and talk, but it's rude to be absent any longer. Darva asks, "Will you write to me about America?" We exchange addresses, and I return to the dining room where Mahmoud is at fever pitch.

"They like us for scouts," he is saying, "but not for citizens. We are told to be a minority here as you have been throughout history. We are not equals. "Dr. and Dr. Morton, the psychiatrists, look glum at this news. The journalists are taking notes. I pull out my pad and finally I'm able to draw.

"We are not accepted here and we suffer for it. We don't want guns, we want a connection to this country. We give our lives to it. We deserve a place." He wipes his face and loosens his tie.

We all clap.

Mahmoud thanks us several times and begs us to eat. There are little footballs of spicy ground meat; lamb in sweet tomato sauce; several kinds of rice and other grains I can't identify; cold salads and warm bread; delicious sweet desserts and more coffee. The Druse women serve us, except for Darva. Before we leave, she introduces me to her husband who looks like a cowboy in jeans and denim shirt. On the bus back to Jerusalem, tired and full of food, I drift off, thinking of Druse men, wondering where Mahmoud expects us to take his message.

∼

After several days, I lose track of time. Seminars, lectures, dinners with board members, meetings, one at our hotel with a group of West Bank settlers. Their leader Hannah Benjamin is as well known in Israel as Meier Kahane's protégée, a candidate for the Knesset, and an astonishingly beautiful woman in *sheitel* and makeup. "You Americans must come to Judaea and Samaria, and see the land God gave us."

"God gives real estate?" Dr. Morton, the psychiatrist asks.

"You must be ignorant of the Bible," she answers.

We are not going to the West Bank, whoever gave it. Arab boys have been throwing rocks at cars. Last week an American tourist was stabbed in Nablus and a Palestinian man died in an Israeli jail, beaten to death, according to the Arabs.

"You Americans must come and join us," Hannah continues. "God said, 'Be fruitful and multiply.' Arab women bear more children than Jewish women. Six, eight children. Soon we will be outnumbered."

Janessa, the sociologist, asks Hannah if she thinks modern Jewish women want such large families.

"Modern!" Hannah spits it out. "What has that got you but TV and drugs?" When she stops talking, she looks like wax.

∼

At the Battered Woman's Shelter in Jerusalem, the director, a bitter young Sabra, shows us an Egyptian woman with a scarred face and blacked eyes. "This is how men of the Middle East treat their women."

"Surely all Middle Eastern men don't beat their wives," Vera, Janessa's partner, says.

For an answer, the director points to a slight, scared Yemenite girl of sixteen, raped on her wedding night by her husband. "Her mother held her down while he raped her. Look at her face, her legs, she still has bruises."

"But *all* Yemenites don't rape their wives, do they?" Janessa echoes Vera.

The director asks if this is our first trip to Israel. She tells us the new immigrants, meaning the Sephardic Jews, were brought up in a different culture.

Janessa asks if there are gay groups in Israel. She'd like to visit one.

"The rabbis don't go for that," the director says. "We have enough trouble protecting straight women."

On the way out, her assistant gives Janessa a list of lesbian groups in Tel Aviv and Haifa.

∼

At the Ghetto Fighter's Museum, we circle a neat scale model of Treblinka, a glass case marked Personal Belongings: a squashed tin cup, the bald, cracked head of a toy. It's too neat, too clean, too disembodied. I want the world to see ashes on the toy; the day's rations, a filthy crust in the cup. Not this antiseptic miniature with background photos of stacked human bones. How do you exhibit lives going up in smoke? I've heard somewhere they have stacks of real hair the Nazis cut and saved.

Get a grip, I tell myself, and leave the tour for the Vilna Room, where I search the portraits for my mother's face, though I know she left Vilna for America when she was three. Otherwise it would be my cracked head, my father's bones in the stack, my mother's hair. . . . When I return and take a place at the group table, the poet Haim Guri is describing a movie we will see of European Jews who survived the camps and had no homes to return to. Guri reads in Hebrew and is translated:

> You must know where you come from
> and where you are going
> and how you will be judged on the Judgment Day.

"Speaking of judgment," says Dr. Morton, as platters of bread and cold cuts are passed around the table, "I must raise a question here." He describes our visit to Yarka, repeating the gist of Mahmoud's speech. "After what we've suffered, I can't understand how Jews can ghettoize the Druse. Why can't they vote in national elections? Isn't Israel a democracy? Why can't a Druse be in the Knesset? Don't they fight for Israel? Don't they give their lives?"

A hush like electricity. Knives and forks stop in midair. A man sitting across from me winks. Am I seeing right? Should I wink back? He shrugs his shoulders and smiles. Then the cloudburst. Everyone is talking or shouting, in English,

Hebrew, Yiddish. "You're nothing but tourists," someone hollers, "traitors. You call yourselves Jews?"

A heavyset blond man to my right stands and delivers a long, ardent speech in Hebrew. Someone translates. "General Netanyahu says many Israeli soldiers suffer emotional problems from serving in the army, and often refuse to fight. It's the paratroopers who started Peace Now." Another voice: "Did you hear that, Americans, paratroopers." Netanyahu is pounding the table, yelling, translated, that Israeli planes, at their own risk, have refused to drop bombs on civilians.

I assume they are talking about Lebanon, but it's impossible to ask a question and be heard. I take out my camera and start snapping pictures, like a TV reporter about to witness a massacre, knowing I'm part of the story, hoping I won't be strafed and left for dead.

Someone shouts, "To avenge ourselves, how many of them do we have to kill?"

"Who is them?" Mrs. Dr. Morton shouts back. "What are we avenging?"

"We are avenging the holocaust, our dead," an Israeli woman answers. "Who are you Americans to come here and complain about the Druse, to tell us what to do?"

"We're family," I say, surprised to hear my voice above the melee. "Family always has the right to criticize each other."

"What kind of family?" she says. "You want to criticize, come here and live. Then you can talk. Don't send us money and advice."

"Right," someone else shouts. "Don't come plant trees and go back to your air-conditioned movies." Roger clinks with his spoon on a glass. "I think we should finish lunch," he suggests. But how can anyone eat.

As we leave for the screening, a stranger across the table walks over, takes my hand and leads me out of the room asking, "Who are you?"

How should I know?

We kiss in a small room down the hall. I cling to my straw hat, my camera, my map.

~

In Italy, it's Stendahl's Syndrome. In Israel, it's Ishmael's. All tourists are exiles, circling Diaspora, reflected in a mirror that scrambles identity, a foreign alphabet, words written backwards. The text is Elan's question: Who am I? The screech of shifting gears, the Aramaic pitch of street vendors' amplified, all the noise like stones in my ears, muffling answers. A fish on land, tuned to love songs of the deep, I pick up sounds on other frequencies.

I leave the tour that evening, and we roam the city. He's my personal guide, he tells me, a Virgil to the real Israel. I tell him this is more than mixing metaphors. As we walk down a Jerusalem street, the pavement disappears in front of us. We're enveloped in fog.

"There is never, ever fog in Jerusalem," Elan says, his arms around me. "Maybe once a decade." He kisses my forehead. "Maybe it's right we can't see through it." He kisses my ears.

I assume this means he is married. I hold on tight, close my eyes as he kisses my mouth, ruffling me with pleasure.

"I can offer you this," he says, "something sweet in your mouth. Memories."

"What a line." I laugh. So I'm right. He is married and can't make commitments. "Jews have always been good with words."

"I'm an actor. Words kept us alive for thousands of years."

"As actors?"

"As Jews."

I'll take his sweet words, fill my mouth with them, my shoes with sand. When I go home, I'll spill them out.

∼

Some days I leave the tour and we go driving, north to Safed and Tiberias on winding mountain roads bordered with Arab villages, houses colored like the hills. We pass thick clusters of sabra cactus, the reddish prickly pear for which native Israelis are named. After dips and bends, the road opens out to the Sea of Galilee, a blue lake with grassy slopes and white stone settlements, a pastoral valley of such tranquility I can't believe it's Israel. We drive south through the Hebron hills to Beersheba, an ancient trading post edging the Negev Desert. In the Bedouin Market, I decline an Arabian saddle, a copper and brass coffee set, a photograph of me on top of a camel.

Elan is second-generation Sabra, his mother born here, his Polish father a pioneer before Israel was a state. Elan grew up on the kibbutz where he lives with his wife and two daughters. An actor and director at the Habimah Theater, a soldier in every war since he was old enough to be one. "The best kind of Israeli lover, a soldier-artist-farmer, a real Jew," he says with mock heroism, a guide to the "real" Israel.

One evening, instead of wine, he brings me a book about Israeli artists and one of Israeli poetry, telling me again as I unwrap the poetry that words are something he can give. He has inscribed the fly leaf, *All journeys have secret destinations of which the traveler is unaware. Martin Buber.*

When I complain that the words he gives me aren't his, he says, "An actor knows it's better to take another's words. In two weeks you will forget me. But never Buber."

I learn it's a country of words, each stone, each word heavy with meaning. We drive down the road from the Mount of Olives, where Elan says Jews who come to die in the Holy Land want to be buried. I say the road is beautiful. Elan says the Arabs took the gravestones from the cemetery to build the road. In Israel, every act, every object is a metaphor. Every day is a question, "What does it mean?"

∼

At King David's Tomb, looking out over the hills, the red-headed rabbi asks our group, "What is the holiest of holies?" He answers with this excerpt from an old folk tale:

Among the holy lands in the world is the Holy Land of Israel. In the land of Israel, the holiest city is Jerusalem. In Jerusalem the holiest place was the Temple, and in the Temple the holiest spot was the holy of holies.

There are seventy peoples in the world. Among these holy peoples is the people of Israel. The holiest of the people of Israel is the tribe of Levi. In the tribe of Levi the holiest are the priests. Among the priests, the holiest was the high priest.

There are three hundred fifty-four days in the year. Among these the holidays are holy. Higher than these is the holiness of the Sabbath. Among Sabbaths the holiest is the Day of Atonement, the Sabbath of Sabbaths.

There are seventy languages in the world. Among the holy languages is the holy language of Hebrew. Holier than all else in this language is the holy Torah, and the holiest part is the Ten Commandments. In the Ten Commandments, the holiest of all words is the Name of God.

On the Day of Atonement, the high priest enters the holy of holies and there utters the Name of God. And because this hour was beyond measure holy and awesome, it was the time of utmost peril not only for the high priest but for the whole of Israel. For if, in this hour, there had, God forbid, entered the mind of the high priest a false or sinful thought, the entire world would have been destroyed.

Every spot where a man raises his eyes to heaven is a holy of holies. Every man, having been created by God in His own image and likeness, is a high priest. Every day of a man's life is a Day of Atonement, and every word that a man speaks with sincerity is the Name of the Lord.

"And every day of a woman's life?" I ask minutes later. "Every word a woman speaks with sincerity, isn't that, too, the Name of the Lord?"

"Right on," says Angela. "Aren't Jews supposed to be progressive?"

"My wife is always reminding me of that," the Rabbi says. "I guess anything as old as Judaism is can stand a little touch-up."

"Want to hear a neo-feminist neo-Jericho joke?" I ask Angela, as we start down the winding narrow steps. "Joshua comes home and his wife asks him where he's been all night. 'Out fighting,' he says. 'Out screwing,' she answers. 'You said you'd be home before dawn.' 'I wasn't screwing,' he insists. 'It was just a long night. And anyway, it isn't dawn yet. The sun isn't coming up.' 'That's a good one,' she says. 'Next thing I know, you'll take the credit.'"

"I love it," Angela laughs.

The rabbi, who's leading the way, stops. "That's sacrilegious."

"You must be kidding," Angela says.

"God should have the last word."

I say, "There shouldn't be a last word."

Angela wants to know if she can unconvert.

At ground floor, we're overwhelmed by the smell of urine from public toilets.

⁓

Beryl, the girl on the plane, was right, the Wall is segregated. On one side, bearded men in black hats, grieving a Temple destroyed two thousand years ago. On the other, women they're afraid to look at.

"Why are they so scared of women?" I ask Elan.

"Pleasure frightens them. What is pleasure compared to God?"

⁓

"It's a little like trying to find the Rabbit Hole," Angela confides. Looking for the Dome of the Rock, we wind and turn through the Old City's cramped alleys. Bright colored dresses, bead strings in shop doorways, rugs rolled out on narrow pavement, carts pyramided with pastry, jumbled sounds and smells. Several false starts down wrong alleys until we reach the wooden wall, and walk, like Alices, through a small door, Israeli soldiers on one side, Palestinian on the other. After noisy claustrophobic streets, a blue sky so vast I feel disoriented. In the middle of this horizonless heaven, the great Mosque of Omar, magnificently tiled in cobalt blue. Soldiers take our bags, packages, shoes. Inside, another vast space: fantastical, ornate, with green, blue, white and yellow tiles; striped gray and streaked purple marble; far away, at the top, stained glass windows. The stone floor is filled with worn rugs—my mother would have called them *shmattas*—and in odd corners, people kneeling, rocking. In the center of the mosque, a chest high wall of plastic surrounds an enormous rock where Mohammad's horse took off for heaven, its footprints still on the rock.

There's no one around to tell me it's sacrilegious to pray here. I kneel on a rug, rock back and forth like the men at the Wailing Wall, wondering which Holiest of All Words to pray for. Closing my eyes, I see the white horse lifting off like a jet, forelegs folding in ascent, the prophet on its back, his bright yellow robes like a sail.

~

Shepherds leading their flocks on the road from Jerusalem. Jericho is hot and smells of oranges. Elan and I buy two at a fruit stand and eat them immediately. I want the pungent smell, the sticky juice on my fingers forever.

At an outdoor cafe, lined by date palms and roses, Elan tells me the soil, fed by underground streams for thousands of years, has made Jericho an Eden. "If it were mine to give, I'd give you the Groves of Jericho, which Antony gave Cleopatra," he says. Instead, he gives me milk for my ersatz coffee.

Up the dusty hill, I hear a guide quoting Mark Twain to a group of bible students, among them, my Vietnamese friend from the hotel, holding his father's hand. He smiles at me and I wave. I would like to ask him if he's been to Bethlehem yet, what he thinks of a white Jesus. I'd like to ask him if he misses Vietnam, if he remembers his mother.

Elan and I walk around the empty site. "Nothing here but dirt," I whisper, as we approach a large, roped-off hole in the ground. There are hills in the distance, a vast blue sky. I lean over and look down a dark emptiness.

"It's Old Jericho. Tel-es Sultan. What were you expecting?"

"History," I say. "Something you can touch. Words. Anything."

Elan reads from a plaque: "'Ten thousand years old, the oldest city of continuous human habitation.' What that means," he says, "is the dustbin of history."

Elan and me, sweeping out our dust for ten thousand years. I sweep, he holds the dust pan. "Just a hole," I say, straightening up, and there's a man in a dirty robe, standing right where Elan is standing, talking to us, finger pointed at the sun. "It won't stand still," he says. "Make it run."

~

In Bethlehem, we are ushered into the mayor's presence. An Arab, the mayor is known for his even-handedness with Arab and Jewish Israelis. Most Arabs consider him a traitor; many Jews, an enemy. The man in the middle, the unpopular peacemaker, often the target. Someone is always planting bombs outside his residence. He has survived repeated attempts on his life. I wonder what his wife thinks about this, if she is proud of him or wants to leave town with the children, if she says, "Remember Jesus? Someone will nail you up, too. I want a normal life."

Hellos and small pleasantries are passed around the table with the usual small cups of coffee. The mayor gets a special cup. Maybe he has a taster.

Sitting at the head of the table, he's so short his feet dangle from his chair. I admire him for this. It shows he is willing to be seen as human.

A lot of talk about Arab-Israeli cooperation, how this group will work with that, how that group, etcetera. I am more interested in the mayor's feet, which seem the most important thing at this meeting.

〜

On my last day in Jerusalem, in the Old City Market near Sulemein's Wall, I buy my children Macabbean coins. I want them to know about the freedom fighters. I also want them to be pacifists.

I buy them each a Roman tearbottle, buried for hundreds of years, the surface spotted and glistening. I'll tell them not to hoard their tears, not to take them to their graves, which might be dug up to make roads for armies.

For myself, to remember this trip when I am back in my American life, I consider embroidered Arab dresses, earrings with green stones from the Dead Sea, a Bedouin egg basket made of velvet and straw. I decide on an ornate Bedouin wedding veil with silver coins, amber beads, and large cut out ovals for the eyes. When the shop owner holds it up, it looks like the shape of a woman's body. I hold it over my face and imagine my bridegroom facing me.

〜

Our last evening in Israel, we go to a Palestinian film, *Wedding in Gaza*. Israeli soldiers, one of them a woman, must attend the wedding because it's after curfew. The groom's brother plans to kill them, but his girlfriend talks him out of it. The female soldier drinks too much wine, and goes to sleep in her hostess' house. Waking, up, she takes off her army uniform and puts on an Arab dress. I think of my Bedouin veil.

The bride, robed and in a long white veil, waits for the groom. He comes for her on a white horse and lifts her veil with a sword, takes her back to his house to consummate the marriage. Scared and angry at his father, with whom he argued before the wedding, he can't get it up. His bride saves his honor, penetrating herself with her finger and smearing the sheet with blood.

Meanwhile the bridal horse, which has run off to a mined field, is coaxed back by the soldiers and the groom's brother before he can blow them all up.

"I think it's right it's a white horse," I tell Elan, as we walk back to the hotel. "Maybe it's Mohammad's, come back for one last time to carry us all off."

"Maybe," he says. "And maybe the Messiah will come for me tomorrow in a rusty truck."

"Maybe there are many real Israels, besides the muscles on your arms, besides the Jewish farmer, the Jewish actor, the Jewish soldier."

He looks at me in the Jerusalem moonlight to see if I am mocking him.

I take his hand to assure him that I'm not. "I think the real Israel may be the mayor's feet, the Druse's steel, the smell at David's Tomb."

He thinks I'm pushing it.

"I wonder if Beryl has been Bat Mitzvahed yet, if my Russian cab driver will emigrate to California and learn to love blacks, if next year all Israeli paratroopers will refuse to fight."

"And if a Druse, maybe Sulemein, will be elected President."

"And the Messiah, created by God in Its own image, decides to come."

"And brings peace, not a sword," Elan says.

"And when she does, turns out to be a woman."

"That would be sacrilegious," he says.

"I wonder," I continue, "if she will speak seventy languages and every word she speaks with sincerity will be the name of the Lord."

"You are an American," he says.

And a Jew, I think. But I let him have the last word.

RACHEL HALL

The Intelligent Woman Traveler

*Should you droop or feel ill en voyage, it will probably
be due to one of two basic reasons: Either your body is
reacting to the new physical situation inherent in the
act of travel itself, or you are suffering from the same
illness you might have had at home.*

FRANCES KOLTUN
*Complete Book for the
Intelligent Woman Traveler*

THE ISRAELI SOLDIER next to me groaned in his sleep, shifted his weight, so his
gun nuzzled my thigh. I had grown accustomed to seeing men with guns since
arriving in Israel—the airport security guards bent over my open luggage, their
Uzzis grazing my T-shirts and nightgowns; the suntanned soldier at the beach,
wearing only a black Speedo and a gun strap, which he shifted periodically to avoid
getting tan lines; and this young man,who told me earlier he was on his way home
to be married. Would he wear the gun during the marriage ceremony, I wondered—
a kind of warning to us all: One is never safe.

I scooted closer to the window and looked out at the greenish-black pines on
the mountains and the curving highway that led us to Jerusalem. My brother David
slept too, leaning into a Bedouin woman whose almond eyes were darkly lined in
kohl. I had learned to stay alert, to keep my foot hooked through the straps of my
duffel bag, to keep my money and passport in a pouch under my shirt. I would
not be caught off guard again. Across the aisle an Orthodox woman sat surrounded by her three little girls all wearing long-sleeved dresses and baggy tights
despite the ninety-five degree heat. The oldest girl kept looking at David's Walkman. He looked out of place on this bus with his ice-blue eyes, his tiny pug of a
nose. In the window, my dark eyes looked sunken and my hair was frizzed and
coming out of its braid. I look like my mother's side of the family, Jews from
Ukraine, known for their devotion to the Torah. Though it was pointless, I pulled
my hair off my neck and attempted to smooth the frizz with my palm.

From the back of the bus I heard shouting in Hebrew. David jerked awake as
the bus pulled over onto the shoulder of the road. A tall man in a black hat and
a dark wool suit led four boys in identical suits to the front of the bus. The boys,
all under ten, had shaved heads except for the long, limp tendrils which hung down

in front of their ears. Outside they lined up, their black-jacketed backs to the bus, and they pissed in unison.

"Is that some sort of ritual?" David asked, rubbing his eyes.

"Shhh," I hissed. I smelled someone's garlic sweat coming from the next row and I thought: Cleanliness being next to Godliness is clearly a Puritan innovation. I planned to remember that to include in a postcard to my husband, Giles. It was just the sort of witty dispatch I was aiming for.

"The old guy looks like Abe Lincoln," David whispered, as the man solemnly led his boys back down the aisle. David took off his earphones, and I could hear the tinny sounds of the Grateful Dead: "A friend of the devil is a friend of mine."

"Got any water left?"

I handed David the last of my mineral water, which he gulped before readjusting his earphones and shutting his eyes.

"Thanks," he said.

In high school my brother talked about writing *Cliff Notes* for *Hair* and Pink Floyd's movie *The Wall*. That summer he had planned to follow the Grateful Dead around and write sociopolitical and economic commentary on their concerts. "Free enterprise at its best," he said of the parking lots at the concerts. "You can get whatever you want: brats and sauerkraut, LSD, peyote buttons, holographs of Jimmy Hendrix." He claimed to love this scene: the music, the wild, dancing people who followed the Dead everywhere. What kind of name was that, anyway? I was amazed at how easily my brother could hop on the bandwagon. If he'd been around in the second century, he would have been one of the Jews convinced by the pagans to worship their graven images and carved idols.

David's summer plans had changed when my father's Aunt Ruth died and left us money "so that we should see the Promised Land." Clearly, Aunt Ruth hadn't trusted our father to properly instill in us our Jewish heritage. Since leaving my mother, my father had been married three times, to women increasingly younger and paler, with names like Molly or Becki, which he modified into Malka or Rebecca. On a shelf in his living room he kept a brass Menorah, an antique seder plate, and two sepia-colored photographs of his grandparents—their mouths thin, grim lines, their eyes wide and bewildered. "The Jewish shelf," David and I called it privately as we left, overfed on Becki's dinner rolls, creamed corn, and au gratin potatoes.

I had intended to wait and take this trip when Giles could get away, too. I planned to work through the summer at the *Tribune*, where I was responsible for "Action Line," a weekly column that addressed reader queries. I was called upon to expose fraudulent mail order companies, to locate eating disorder clinics, to uncover the origin of the word "skivvies" (it began as navy slang for underwear). And of course there were questions of etiquette: If a couple divorces within the first year of their marriage they are, indeed, expected to return wedding gifts, despite the humiliation and hassle. Sometimes it was just a matter of flipping through a couple of dictionaries, but other times I had to yell at people, threaten them with the law. "You, in charge of 'Action Line,' *action*?" David said, "the irony, when you won't even tell Giles to scram."

"The job doesn't have very much to do with action," I told him. "Mostly, I gather information."

A couple of weeks ago, I'd returned home from work early and found Giles sitting on our futon looking deep into the eyes of one of his students—a volleyball player who had missed a lot of classes and needed extra help. When she saw me, she removed his hand from her thigh with an agility that must serve her well on the court. Myself, I walked into the kitchen and began making the bernaise sauce I had planned to dollop on the T-bones I bought for dinner. I understood then why the German Jews stayed in Dusseldorf or Berlin, kept dusting their dark walnut furniture, polishing the silver that had been in their families for years. I kept beating the egg yolks and trickling in the melted butter. Later, I listened silently while Giles told me about his infatuation with his student, Bertie, short for Roberta. "I think it's just a passing thing, Miriam," he'd said.

The next day I made reservations—a funny word: I have some reservations, I am reserved—to join David in Israel, the Promised Land.

Two weeks later Giles still hadn't called and asked me to return, though I had many times imagined the call, Giles's pleading and my judicious Old Testament response. I practiced the way I would sternly exact promises of devotion. In Tel Aviv, David and I stayed with distant relatives, two elderly aunts who kept calling me by my mother's name. "Esther," they'd said, "you've turned into a lovely woman, lovely." "Thank you, I'd said, willing to accept even misguided compliments. I kissed their powdery cheeks before we left.

The bus lurched forward as I opened the packed lunches they sent with us— thick, dark bread, cheese sweating from the heat, and ripe plums. A good healthy lunch like the ones my mother had made for me as a child. Giles had told me about his childhood meals, food I would've envied. Mayonnaise sandwiches on Wonder Bread, butterscotch Snak-Pak Pudding, Ho-Hos in glittery foil wrappers, and thermoses full of Cherry Hi-C or slightly flat Dr. Pepper. But I was trying not to think about Giles. Even his name—a good Anglo-Saxon Protestant name— seemed to me somehow intrusive. Giles's relatives came to America in the 1700s, but now his family lived in Moral, Nebraska. "I sure pulled one over on them," he used to say after we drank too much or spent a Sunday in bed, or committed some other supposedly immoral act. I'd never felt so tiny and dark and Semitic as the first time we visited Giles's family in Nebraska. His sisters and brothers all towered above me, smiling teethy grins. That night Giles sneaked into the guest room where I was sleeping beneath a needlepoint of Christian quotations and for the first time he couldn't make love to me. He stayed soft, though we tried, even moving to the pale blue carpeted floor where we didn't have to worry about the noise.

The bus pulled into the station. I put the uneaten lunch back in my pack. As David and I gathered our belongings from the overhead racks, the children wove in between us rushing for the door.

"I'd rather wait than push," I told David, and he was too groggy to argue. We watched everyone file out. As we approached the front, the bus driver held out a cigarette and fumbled in his pockets. David pulled a lighter from his pocket and lit it for him.

"There you go, man," he said, smiling.

"Thank you," the bus driver said in English.

"Hey," David asked, "do you know any place we could stay in the New City, cheap?"

"Yes," the bus driver said, "I will take you. It is on my way, anyhow."

People were always charmed by these men—David, Giles, my father. If you were with them, you might reap the benefits too: a free round of drinks in a restaurant, extra pillows from a flight attendant, the biggest piece of pie.

The bus driver drove us to a pension near the center of town. He told us it was run by an elderly Austrian woman. He slowed the bus in front of a bleached stone building. We thanked him and began to descend.

"Hey, look," David said, pointing to a sign written in Hebrew, Arabic and English above the bus door.

HAVEN'T YOU FORGOTTEN SOMETHING?

"Sounds like Mom," he said.

I hoisted my pack to the ground. Unlike David, I always did what our mother wanted me to—kept my curfew in high school, didn't take acid in college, used caution in all my actions. Even my journalism degree had been her idea. About my marrying Giles, she'd said nothing. David always threw caution to the sweeping gusts of Kansas wind, the wind that was probably right then whipping through the lawn in front of Giles's office. I was determined not to argue with David and ruin the trip because it would prove Giles right; it would prove that I had changed, grown less fun, and too picky, nervous and easy to not love. I believed that if David and I could get along, it would be some kind of proof that Giles and I could, too.

We had no problem getting a room from the girl at the desk. She pointed to the bathrooms and the lobby where we were free to watch TV. A thin, gray-haired woman peered out a doorway. "The owner," the girl said, waving.

David and I dropped our packs in the airy room which had two cots and big, glassless windows that opened onto the street. The ledges were covered with vines and soft, purple buds, the kind that survived the heat by disappearing in the day and blooming in the cool of the night. We decided to take a walk and get something to eat.

All the buildings in the area were made from the same pinkish-white stone. A law, the aunts told us, so that the New City would match the Old. We found a café where we ordered falafels and beer and took a table outdoors. The street was busy with other tourists lugging backpacks and young merchants in loose, gauzy clothes holding trays of dangling earrings. They approached our table and shook their trays near David. "Only three shekels. Buy some for your lovely lady."

I felt myself blushing, though people had confused us as lovers before on this trip. The earrings, tiny threads of silver and brass, sparkled on the blue velvet.

"No thanks," David said.

A waitress came and took our drink order. David wanted a good vodka tonic, but they had only Israeli vodka, so he settled for a Macabbee beer.

I was tired from the traveling and my beer made me woozy.

"What is it, Miriam?" David asked.

I realized that I'd sighed loudly. "I miss Giles," I said.

"Why?" David demanded. "Why are you staying with him? Are you happy?"

His string of questions confused me. I tried to light a cigarette with a flourish to distract David, but he was firm.

"Why are you doing this to yourself?"

"I'm married, David. It's not just like one of your flings, you know."

"Yeah, I know, but does Giles know?"

"It'll work out," I said.

"You saw how far that got Mom," David said.

"This is different," I said, grinding out the cigarette, but I remembered our mother's silence and the parade of women who sauntered through our family room to our father's study.

"Well, what are you going to do?" He tilted back on his chair. On the table our beer sloshed.

"I'm thinking, I told him.

"That's your whole problem, Miriam. You think too much. You've got analysis paralysis."

We both lifted our beers and drank at the same time as if we were toasting. The beer fizzled in my throat.

"I just need to figure out why he's done this," I said. "Then I'll know what to do."

"Excuse me, you are American?" the woman from the next table asked.

Her English was clipped and sing-songy. She was an Aryan dream of blond curls, tanned skin, eyes as blue as the Mediterranean. She sat with two other women and a man. They were from Denmark, she told us, on their holiday.

"We're from Kansas," David said.

"Near Chicago?" the tallest woman asked, pushing a veil of blond bangs from her forehead.

David explained that it was in the middle of the country. Our mother used to say the middle of nowhere after our father dragged her there from New York.

They'd seen *The Wizard of Oz* and we laughed, our origins settled. The man, Henrik, introduced himself and the others: Janna, Eva, and Alexandria. "Join us," he said.

"I'm David, and this is my sister, Miriam."

The waitress came to our table as we scooted our chairs over, and David started to order more beer for everyone.

"Wait, do you have pitchers?" he asked.

The waitress didn't understand.

"You know," he said miming the pouring motion, "a big, communal container from which we could all imbibe."

The waitress smiled and shook her head.

"Clearly one of America's greatest inventions," David said. "It's things like pitchers of beer that make you proud to be American."

Janna smiled at David and pointed to his tie-dyed T-shirt with a Rolling Stones emblem spanning the front. "I saw them in Copenhagen," she said. "People went crazy, shoving and pushing. Some people from my town were crushed." She said all this with the same lilting speech, so it sounded like a happy tale, a nursery rhyme.

Henrik and Alexandria sat close together and Henrik held her hand, stroking her knuckles with his thumb. I looked away quickly and picked at the brown and gold label on my beer bottle.

"Do you want to?" David asked, nudging my shoulder.

"What?" I asked. Janna had scooted close to David and her bare feet were propped on his chair. So this is how it starts, I thought, wondering if Bertie's toes were this tanned, the toenails this glossy with pale pink polish.

"Come with us to the Old City," she said. "We'll go to the Arab market and grab some dinner there. We were there last night and met some great people."

"Let's do it," David said.

"Haven't they warned Americans not to go there?" I asked.

"No, it's perfectly safe," Janna said. "We were there and look at us. We're fine."

"But you aren't American," I said.

"Come on," David said, "let's go."

Janna led us down King David Street and then through some winding alleys. If I'd separated from the others, I'd never be able to find my way back; the alleys had the same overflowing garbage cans, the same gray cobblestones. Even the skinny, meowing cats look alike.

"We're almost there," Janna said, stopping. "But first . . ." She pulled a hand-rolled cigarette from her shirt pocket. She lit it and inhaled. "Here, try some," she said handing the joint to David. "We got this in Spain before we came here. I smuggled it in my bra." She laughed.

David looked at her chest and took a long drag, before passing it to me. I welcomed the thick smell, the feeling which reminded me of summers from my adolescence, summers when David and I were allied against our parents. We'd sit in our downstairs family room and smoke when we calculated our mother would be doing laundry. We practiced offering her the pipe without flinching. "Wanna get loaded, Ma?" we planned to say. "It'd be good for her," David insisted, filling a water pipe made from an Aunt Jemima syrup bottle.

Janna and David giggled as she slipped her hand into his shirt pocket and pulled out a regular cigarette. This alley seemed suddenly too dark, too narrow. I could see Henrik and the others up ahead. Eva stopped and took a picture of some weeds pushing through the stones. My heart beat fast against my rib cage like, I imagined, some melodrama villain throwing himself against prison bars. I wanted to tell David this, but he and Janna were too far ahead of me.

When we arrived at the Jaffa Gate, I only saw Arab men in gauzy head dresses. I remembered the warnings, the newsclips of terrorist casualties. I wanted to turn back, but I couldn't think of a way to suggest it without seeming uptight. The women were covered in black, navy, or maroon from head to toe. Only their dark eyes showed as they regarded our bare arms and legs.

"Shouldn't we cover our arms or something?" I said, but no one listened. My feet, in new sandals, throbbed.

"Come on," Janna said, leading us to a narrow street lined with shops. Pale cotton clothes hung above us, their price tags fluttering in the lazy breeze. The shops overflowed with brass pots, painted pottery and jewelry made from tarnished coins. The air smelled like garlic and grease and manure. I saw that David had bought a falafel loaded with tomatoes and tahini and was sharing it with Janna. I hadn't been eating much on this trip. My travel wardrobe of shorts and jeans hung on me, baggy and loose. Maybe it was from smoking, but I was suddenly famished. A little sauce trickled from the pita onto the cobblestones as David and Janna passed it back and forth.

"Can I have a bite?" I asked.

"All gone," David said, popping the rest into Janna's mouth. "You can get one back there." He pointed to a gray cart.

I started tallying all my generosities to David—the last of the sunscreen, the harder mattress in the pension in Haifa, the window-seat. And hadn't I paid for our one nice dinner in Tel Aviv? I stopped. No big deal, I told myself. I started to go back to the cart when I noticed two black-bearded men staring at us from a cafe, their arms crossed. The younger man spit and it landed right in front of me on the dusty ground. I jumped back.

"Never mind," Janna said taking my arm. "It's okay."

I tried to believe her as we walked past stands of fresh fruit, live chickens squawking. The sun was going down and my sandals were cutting grooves into my feet. All the other tourists had already gone back to the relative safety of the New City. We were conspicuous here—the five beautiful blonds trailed by me. The others, including David, looked Scandinavian, exempt from ethnic rivalries, as neutral as Switzerland. I felt marked JEW by my darkness, the angle of my nose, and my kinky hair.

"Let's go look at the mosque," David said.

"Don't you think we should head back before it gets dark?" I said, adjusting my sandals. There was a coin-sized blister ready to burst on the back of my foot.

"We're almost there," Eva said.

"But we aren't dressed right," Henrik said rubbing her bare shoulders. "Women aren't allowed to show any skin."

I felt a rush of love for Henrik, for Muslim traditions, for Allah himself.

We wandered back the way we had come, passing through the shops. David looked through T-shirts and Coke logos written in Hebrew, bracelets hanging on rods like skinny, wooden arms. The shopkeepers used long metal poles to close up their shop gates. It sounded like a hundred garage doors closing behind us. As we passed some children playing jacks with small pebbles, my blister burst and I felt the fluid under my heel. The raw skin on my foot tingled as dirt from the street blew into the cut. Up ahead Janna held up pairs of earrings. "We'll take them," David said, handing the shopkeeper paper shekels. In the cases, all the earrings looked the same, but on Janna, I saw they were beautiful. I should've bought a pair, an exotic souvenir. They would flutter in the Kansas wind as I came down the airplane stairs and walked into Giles's arms.

Janna walked back to our pension with us, but the others said good night after we made plans to meet up with them the next day. Next to me, David had his arm around Janna and was rubbing her back in slow circles.

"Oh, yes," she crooned. "Right there."

I slowed to look in the shop windows and to let them walk ahead. Tomorrow, I planned to let the others go off. I would buy souvenirs, earrings or something.

When we got back to the pension, the owner, a birdy little woman, was sitting very still at the front desk.

"Can you help me," she said in heavily accented English. "I've lost my key somewhere." She stared straight ahead. "I can't see a thing."

"Let me look," David said, moving behind the desk.

I longed for cool water on my face and on my feet. I was exhausted from traveling, from the dope, the walking.

"I have inoperable cataracts," the woman said. "I can't see a thing."

David said the key wasn't there, and she moved to let him search the other drawers.

"I don't know where she put it. I have a girl who works here in the day, helping me since my husband died," she said.

Janna and I sat on the tile, which felt cool on my legs and feet. The woman's eyes were pale and milky, and they gazed slightly above us.

"Last year he died. Eighty-six years old. We met in this country, I was a volunteer nurse and the first woman he met when he came off the boat. I gave him a shot. Tetanus. Right here," she said, holding her shoulder.

"Were you born here?" I asked.

"Oh no, I came here from Vienna when I was nineteen. In Vienna, my father had a bakery. I was famous there for my apple strudel. You know what it is, apple strudel? I'll make it for you."

"You don't have to do that," I said.

"People came from miles around to eat my apple strudel. If there was a celebration anywhere in Vienna, you could be sure my apple strudel would be there—the crispy sweet crust, rich and tart at the same time. That's the secret."

"It sounds great," David said, still looking through the desk drawers. I could see, even from where I sat, that they were a complete mess. Some of the papers were yellowed with age.

"In Vienna, I left eight brothers and sisters and my parents. They wouldn't come with me to Israel. Eight brothers and sisters all killed by Hitler." She began to cry.

I stood next to her, holding her hand. I felt the bones beneath her skin. At one time, she must have been quite beautiful, I knew from the way she moved with me to the couch, allowing me to fuss over her.

"I'm so proud of this country." She made a sweeping gesture with her arms like a tour guide.

"It is very beautiful here," Janna said. She joined us by the couch.

"Yes," she said, "and they will never know this beauty." She began her story all over again. Vienna, the strudel, the brothers and sisters killed, murdered in the bakery by Hitler, she repeated like a litany.

I held her hand and listened. Her sleeveless cotton dress revealed that she wasn't marked a victim by the blue numbers I'd seen tattooed on others' arms. What did I know about loss this size? I could think only of my father leaving for the final time, the toaster-oven in his arms, his new girlfriend waiting in his new car, my mother folding his shirts into squares, stacking them into cardboard boxes. The luggage, she'd said, was a wedding gift from her side of the family. If it came to that with me and Giles, I had long ago decided he could have everything. I knew the way the small losses—the fern stand for the cedar chest, the albums for the books—would only compound and draw out the bigger loss.

"I had my husband," the woman said, "and he is gone. Died at eighty-six. He was so proud of Israel."

"Here it is," David said producing the key from under a stack of papers.

"Thank you, God bless you," the woman said. "You must stay in Israel." She dropped my hand and clutched David.

"Grad school," he said. "I'm going to school in America."

"Listen to me," she said. "Once before my husband died, we went to America to visit his relatives. They lived in a flat in New York. There were cockroaches this big." She made a fist with her bony hand. "One fell into the soup I made, and I swore I would never go back. But we needed to when his great-aunt grew ill. I wanted to bring the cousins something to show them how beautiful Israel is. So I take them tomatoes grown on the kibbutz, beautiful, juicy tomatoes. At customs, they tell me no, I can't bring any vegetables into America, but I explain to the man that I must show my relatives in America. He looks around, and nods, putting the tomatoes back in my bag. He is a Jew too and he understands. He lets me take the tomatoes to New York. You can't get tomatoes like that in America, let me tell you."

"That's wonderful," Janna said. "You have done so much."

"I must rest now. Tomorrow I make apple strudel," she said.

"Shalom," Janna said.

"Good night," I said. I listened to her heels click on the tile until she reached her door.

"It's so sad," I said. "She's so alone."

"I think she's amazing," David said. "She must be at least eighty and she's running this place. What a survivor."

"Or a walking statistic," I said.

"I loved that story about her tomatoes," Janna said.

"Yes, but she's lost so much—her brothers and sisters and now her husband," I said. If we'd lived in Nazi Germany, David would've assessed the situation correctly and escaped, while I would've stayed on, disbelieving. I shivered.

"You only see the bad side, don't you?" David said.

My beautiful brother, what did he know about suffering? Women fell at his feet. Colleges and universities begged him to attend. He could walk on water. "It is bad," I said. "It's horrible and you can't deny it just because it doesn't feel good, David."

"Hey," he said standing, "I know it's tragic just as much as you do, but she has reasons to be happy too. She said so herself. You *like* to feel bad, Miriam." He pulled Janna up by the hand. "And it's a real drag," he said, leading Janna upstairs to our room. She looked back at me and shrugged.

I stayed in the lobby watching TV. The Israeli programs were subtitled in Arabic, the Arab shows in Hebrew, suggesting benevolence, compromise, brotherhood. I tried not to think of David and Janna moving together in our room.

In Kansas, Giles would be getting ready for work. I decided to call him. The phone rang and rang. Finally, I placed the receiver back in its cradle and curled up on the couch. I woke in the early morning to the gray static of the television.

In our room David and Janna lay crowded together on the cot. As I shut the door, Janna stirred and pulled the sheets over her legs. Tapes and clothes were scattered all over the floor. The empty bottle of wine had been used as an ashtray, and the room smelled like smoke.

By the window, the purple flowers were open, their petals heavy with dew. I gathered my towel and robe and headed for the shower.

When I returned to the room, Janna and David were up.

"We're going to get coffee if you want to come," Janna said.

"Come with us," David said. He was bent over, tying his boot. "Janna knows a good place close by."

We ordered coffee and the nutty pastries Janna recommended. I thought of the Austrian woman's hands kneading dough, sprinkling chopped nuts to make pastries like these. The flaky crust caught in my throat.

"Today let's go to the Knesset," David said. "They'll be meeting this afternoon." He wiped his hands on the cloth napkin.

"I need to buy some gifts," I said. "I promised I'd bring souvenirs back for some people I work with and I should write postcards."

"Correct me if I'm wrong," David said, shaking his head, "but I thought this was a vacation."

"I want to buy gifts, David," I said. "What's wrong with that?"

David poured more cream in his coffee and took a generous gulp.

"We can meet you back at the restaurant where we met last night," Janna said. "At eight o'clock?"

"Here's the room key," David said. "I'll keep the outdoor key since the doors don't lock until after ten anyway."

I spent the day shopping. I found bracelets made of braided silver and brass, candleholders painted with vines and a pair of full cotton pants for Giles. The pants hung low between the legs, in case, the storekeeper told me, Mohammed is born to a man. I imagined Giles explaining this to his family, his arm draped over my shoulders.

Even in the evening, the heat was intense and I felt it baking my skin brown like Janna's. Back at the pension, I looked for the Austrian woman, but her door was closed and I didn't want to disturb her. I showered again and put on a loose dress. I wanted to call Giles, to tell him about my day and about his gift and how he might at any minute surprise me, give birth to a miracle. Wouldn't our life change then, I would say. The connection had a kind of echo, so the rings trilled twice, but I listened for a long time anyway. Taking my postcards, I headed to the cafe at eight o'clock.

It was already crowded when I got there, but I didn't see David or Janna. I took a seat at the bar to wait. There wasn't room for me to write my postcards because I was crammed in between a couple quarreling in Hebrew and a heavy man from New Jersey. He was telling the bartender about sending his daughters to Hebrew school.

"And the youngest, Judy, she tells me she wants to marry this Buddhist guy. Well, it turns out, his parents are Catholic, and he's just, I don't know, playing the field. Buddhist my ass, I tell Judy."

I ordered a beer. In my head I composed a postcard to Giles. I described the flora, the fauna, the ethnic food, the architecture. I understood informative reporting, but I didn't yet know the words for what I really wanted to say. "What would you do if you were me?" I had asked Giles before I explained I was going to Israel. "I'd kick me out," he'd said, knowing that I wouldn't.

I finished my beer and still Janna and David weren't there. At nine, I ordered another. The couple next to me had stopped fighting and were whispering and giggling. The woman rubbed the man's muscular thighs. She wore red stiletto heels and a short flouncy dress. Her top was cut low revealing a blue, lace bra. In the mirrors behind the bar, I looked young and naive in my sundress, hopeful beyond reason.

At nine-thirty, I checked out front for David. The tables were covered with pita, salads, lamb gyros and I realized I hadn't eaten since breakfast. Where was David? I remembered my mother's nervousness sitting at our kitchen table, her hand on a cup of tea, waiting for David to return from one party or another, the clock ticking, one a.m., two a.m. I imagined a car accident—these flimsy European cars buckling into each other, Janna and David mangled by the side of the road.

I decided to walk back to the pension to see if they were waiting for me there. The streets were dark, lit only occasionally, but there were lots of couples walking, pushing strollers, holding hands. The women gracefully maneuvered their high heels over the cobblestones. During the day, people on the streets seemed sluggish and grumpy from the heat, but at night, in the cooled air, they were festive. In front of me some teenage boys were throwing a stick to a bony black puppy, its paws too large for the rest of its body. It darted and pounced, wagging its skinny tail.

"*Bo hana,*" they shouted and hurled the stick down the street. The stick flew into the middle of the street and the dog bounded after it, just as a taxi sped around the corner. The boys shouted *"Bo hana, kelev, bo hana!"* The dog's legs went taut and he froze in the car's oncoming lights, like the possums on the Kansas back roads, their eyes blinded into beady, red discs. The taxi screeched to a halt and only nudged the puppy. The driver jumped out and started ranting in Hebrew, while the dog ran off limping. "Funny animals," Giles used to say about the possums, slowing the car, switching off the lights for a second, "they just wait there for you to hit them." But, I understood that frozen feeling, the weight of disbelief.

I kept walking, scanning the boulevard for David and Janna. The street to the pension was unlit. I walked quickly to show I had a destination. I heard noises from the alley, people talking on their balconies. At the pension, I realized that David had the outdoor key. I shook the door and waited, but no one came. The lights were out in the lobby. I was alone and hungry. My brother was probably screwing Janna in some olive grove. I didn't want to return to the restaurant, but I was beginning to feel chilled in my sun dress.

I walked to our window on the second floor and yelled for David. No answer. I heard a phone ring in an apartment somewhere and I thought of the phone ringing at my house, Giles asleep in his student's arms. Where was he? I sat hugging my knees on the pension steps. Next to me the purple flowers were in full bloom. Their vines crawled down the front of the building. Even they knew when to open and close, to protect themselves from dryness and from heat. I'd thought that if I was quiet and agreeable things would be OK, but I had forgotten, in this country fortressed with tanks and missiles, entire armies, how to protect myself.

I looked away and saw David and Janna weaving down the street. David was carrying a wine bottle and he stopped and took a swig.

"To those who believe bad wine is better than no wine," he said, handing the bottle to Janna.

She laughed and drank.

"Miriam, what are you doing here?" David asked when he saw me. "Didn't Henrik and Alex tell you we went hiking in the mountains instead? You're supposed to be with them."

Janna stopped and lit a cigarette, but David kept walking towards me, his blond hair shining in the coppery light. He was grinning like all the charming, unreliable men in my life. Suddenly, I was furious at him for abandoning me. I swiped at David with my hand and knocked the wine bottle from his hands. It hit the cobblestones and shattered, sending a spray of wine onto his shirt.

Goddamnit, Miriam, what are you doing?"

"You bastard," I yelled smacking his chest. "How dare you do this to me?" He tried to hold me back, but I kicked him harder and harder, his knees, his shins, his balls. With each movement, I felt lighter, stronger. I slapped David hard on his upturned nose and it began to bleed.

David grabbed my arms and pulled me down. We rolled together on the grass. I struggled under him, scratching his back and kicking.

"Whoa, Miriam, knock it off."

"Ssshh," Janna said.

I felt David's blood on my face and tasted it like soil in my mouth. His eyes had teared up and I saw that we did look alike, the way his cheeks jutted out, tapered to a pointy chin. I relaxed my grip.

"We had plans," I said, "and you changed them without telling me." David rolled over me and pulled a bandana from his pocket for his nose. He was sweating.

"Jesus Christ, Miriam," he said. His voice was muffled by the bandana. "I'm sorry."

I could smell the wine and David's sweat and the peppery scent of the purple flowers. "You won't do it again," I said, standing and brushing the grit from my palms.

Bashfulness Is Required in the Kingdom

For Mary Merlin, esteemed colleague

"SAUDI ARABIA has a desert in the sad heart of it," writes one of my English composition students. After a bit more scrutiny I realize she may mean southeast; her writing is close to illegible. Teaching English to young Arab ladies in Riyadh is pleasant and undemanding, and on the whole I am enjoying my time here as a young married woman, off on an adventure in a foreign land and even earning a respectable salary. My students, all Muslim, are mainly Saudi or Palestinian, though there are sprinklings of Syrians, Bahrainis, Yemenis and Egyptians. They're university students of eighteen to twenty-two years old, and they're eager and attentive; they fight for the teacher's attention: "Missus, Missus, Missus," they call out as they lean forward, arms flailing toward me. They are generous in their affection; it's not unusual for them to take my arm as they accompany me down the college corridor. But they quickly determine the religious status of all their teachers: "You are Christian?" they ask with disgust and incredulity. I can't explain that I'm nothing really, for atheism and agnosticism are blasphemous stances here. However, the non-Muslim and thus infidel status of me and most of my fellow Western teachers is generally ignored; the students accept us graciously, kindly, with open arms.

The mores in this land are intricate and inscrutable. I come to the country with a simple Panama hat: excellent sun protection, I think, and quietly elegant, to boot. But when I wear it I find locals doing double takes and generally staring at me in a perturbed way. A fellow teacher named Mary, a stalwart widow from Minnesota whose children are grown, informs me that that type of hat is slightly taboo—the broad brim is seen as flirtatious.

"But I'm covering my head," I say. "I thought that's what they liked."

"Nope," Mary tells me. "Hats are not the thing here."

I learn that it's perfectly acceptable for non-Muslim women to appear in public bareheaded, but their hair must not be loose and flowing. Mary takes me to the *souq*, the ancient labyrinth of shops in the center of the city, so I can buy the ankle-length skirts and dresses that are *de rigueur* here.

We think of our students as girls though perhaps half of them are married and have children. Child care is not a problem for almost everyone lives within an extended family. There is a pervasive girlishness at the college, and the typical student dress throws a Western woman off a bit. Below their floor-length skirts they wear candy-colored high heels. The skirts are usually cut very narrow, so the girls mince around, knees close together. The university dictates that all students enter and exit the college completely veiled in black. The trip between Mercedes or Nissan Laurel and the college entry gate is made as Hugh Hefner fantasy material: slim, veiled virgins in spiked heels, knees somewhat bound.

Once inside the college, the girls roll their black silk capes into tiny bundles and stow them away in their purses or book bags. The college consists of four two-story oblong buildings, and there are small garden areas here and there. Between classes the girls sit strewn among the oleander and fuchsia, laughing, chattering, eating ices or tabbouleh salad. They are in the loveliness of full bloom, but one notices a surprising number of crossed eyes and unchecked acne problems. Clothing is generally polyester and mismatched, though certain students have startlingly lovely collections of silk blouses. The university suggests the girls wear green skirts, so one sees every shade of green. Among the students there is an evident weakness for T-shirts covered with Mickey Mouse or P.L.O. symbols and slogans. T-shirts with English expressions are also popular, but the language barrier creates oddities: one student occasionally wears a shirt that announces "Piss Artist." Another girl sports "I'm like wine. I improve with age." We Western teachers goggle at that one, for alcohol is verboten in this land. And a third girl sometimes walks around with I-like-to-screw in pictogram across her chest: an eye, the word like, the number two, and then a drawing of the metal bit.

Most of the girls wear gold chains and bracelets. It is the soft, dully gleaming twenty-one karat gold that is prevalent here. No silver is seen; it's inexpensive and looked down upon. No traditional heavy Bedouin crude beads or tarnished metal adornments are worn; that's the style of their grandmothers and the girls love what they consider modern, up-to-date. And yet traditional henna use is quite common. The reddish rust tone is in their hair, on their fingernails, and even on the palms of their hands and the bottoms of their feet. "Beautiful. It's beautiful, Missus," they say when I ask them why they do it. They explain to me that a bride might henna her legs from toe to knee so that her groom finds her especially enticing. "Very beautiful, Missus."

These delicate and amiable women are the sheltered nucleus of this exotic Islamic world, and so the women's college is a very cloistered affair. No males except repairmen may set foot inside, and only well after college hours. There are a number of male teachers but their presence is strictly via video.

The Saudi girls seem happy with their lot; I try to scratch through to any interior discontent, but I only seem to find more layers of a very simple-seeming happiness. They are cheerful, smiling, giggly, pliable. But then perhaps they have no reason not to be; they are the pampered children of a people who were used to eeking out a minimal survival until oil brought them every imaginable material comfort. The girls live amidst parents and grandparents who tell them tales of an arid and dusty past; it seems they realize how charmed their lives are.

The Palestinian girls possess a more western complexity; they haven't known insulated, trauma-free lives. They carry passports that label them refugees, and I've heard a Saudi girl remind them of it. "I'm not one of these refugees," she said haughtily, throwing her head back toward some of the other students, when I asked her where she was born. Palestinians in Saudi Arabia are second-class citizens who can't own houses or control businesses.

Arab students are accustomed to learning by rote, the way they learned the

Koran. Some sit through months and months of daily English classes and still say "me" for "you." "What is your name?" my workmate Mary asked a particularly obtuse girl every morning for nine months, and every morning that girl turned to a classmate for a translation of the question. "You develop a lot of patience here," Mary says, and she's right. The prevailing atmosphere is gentle and relaxed nurturing; after all, we students and teachers are together in the complex five days of the week. There are no Saudi instructors who teach English, but it is clear that Saudi teachers on campus have authority over us infidel Westerners. We give them a wide berth and they mostly ignore us, but in a pleasant enough way: there's a tacit agreement that we don't share a language of any sort.

The students too are not overly curious about western teachers' lives nor about Britain or America. Their knowledge of the U.S. seems limited to Disneyland and Michael Jackson. They are puzzled when they come across the term "hot dog" in a grammar exercise: "You eat dog in America?" one Saudi student quietly asks me, her face pale with disgust. I learn at some point Mohammed didn't care for dogs; the Koran instructs the faithful to wash their hand seven times after touching a dog. "Oh, no, it's not really dog," I tell them, and then I hesitate for I can't go too far in explicating hot dogs for aren't they usually made of pork? And of course pork is not a topic for polite conversation here.

⌒

As an exercise I instruct the students to ask each other what countries they'd like to visit.

"Bahrain," says a little Bahraini named Huda.

"America," says a Palestinian named Awatif.

"Qatar," says Jamila, a Saudi. "Men from Qatar very handsome, beautiful."

"Are they?" I ask, impressed with her ability to make fine distinctions, for to me all Gulf Arabs are equally lovely—the most breathtaking people in the world with their piercing dark eyes and their flashing white teeth.

"No. Bahrainis are the most handsome," says tiny Huda.

Flurries of discussion in Arabic.

"Kuwaitis are handsome, aren't they?" I say, trying to steer the conversation back into English.

They register my remark, but they continue to twitter in their own language. Amid the hubbub Jamila says to me, "Missus, I can only marry from my family. I can only marry a man from my family." She belongs to one of the four tribes that ruled this part of Arabia previous to the reign of the Al Saud, the current ruling family.

"Why?" I ask.

"Because we only marry our family. Our family old, old. Powerful before . . ." She hesitates, glances about. "Powerful before Abdulaziz." She pronounces the name of the first Saudi king with slight disgust. "Our family from before that. Our family thousands, thousands years old."

"I see. So your family wants to stay together to stay strong."

"Yes. But I don't want to marry from my family. But I must. I can't choose. Before wedding I see pictures only. If I don't like pictures, I say no to man."

Huda, the Bahraini, has been listening, and now she jumps in. "She can't have love first. She can't marry the man she love."

"So you can't choose at all?" I ask Jamila.

Jamila shakes her head, and Huda draws a finger in a quick line across her throat. "If she fall in love . . ." she says, laughing.

∽

I teach three different groups. The group with Huda, Awatif, and Jamila includes twelve students—six Saudi, five Palestinian, and one Bahraini. This is the usual mix.

Western teachers receive only one instruction when they sign their contract: not to speak to students about sex, religion, or politics. Everyone understands that controversial classroom discussions will be the basis for dismissal, for non-renewal of contract, perhaps even for quick escort to the airport with immediate exit/no re-entry visa stamped firmly into one's passport. However, all three topics come up frequently, of course. One day my students ask me what my name means. "Christine, Christine, Christine," I hear them whispering to each other.

"It's a Christian name," I say, feeling a bit tentative. "But it's just a name. Jewish people probably don't give it to their children. But Christian people probably aren't thinking of religion too much when they give it to their child."

There's a pause, and the girls look at me skeptically. But all of a sudden they come to life.

"When you learn Arabic, you be excellent, Missus," says Awatif.

"You have a son, you give him Muslim name," says Jamila. "You name him Hussam."

"Hussam? What does that mean?"

"Hussam mean knife. Knife for war."

"Knife! But that's so cruel, so hard," I say.

"Yes, Missus, power, strong. Good name," they say. A number of the girls are named Hend, and later I learn this means scabbard.

"I bring you Koran, Missus," says Manal, a Palestinian. Then the girls quickly confer among themselves in Arabic.

"What are you saying? Say it in English," I ask. It's my mantra with them. They look at me, reluctant to speak. "Missus," Jamila finally says, "you must wash before reading the Koran. You must wash all body."

"And the eight days, Missus, the eight days that fall down on a woman," says Huda, "you must not read Koran then."

"I see, I see. But why? Who told you this?"

"That's what it says," they all say. "That's what we're told."

"Missus, sometimes when I read Koran, I cry. It's so beautiful," says Manal. All nod in agreement. "Beautiful, beautiful, Missus," they murmur. It is a widely held Arab belief that Arabic is the most beautiful sounding language in the world, and I too come to believe this, especially as I listen to the daily calls to prayer that are broadcast aloud throughout the city. The sound is lush and melancholy and resonant. I feel charmed to live in this special aura, for the people's devotion is touching, deep, genuine. Even the most flighty-seeming girls are devout in word and in practice. Every college toilet stall is material evidence; all are equipped with spray hoses so that the faithful may wash private parts and feet before prayer. And every day the restroom floors are flooded. We Western teachers, unaccustomed to our long skirts, curse to each other as we slosh through the wet restrooms.

∼

The students lean over the banister on an upper landing and watch for the approach of the teachers. When the teachers are sighted, the students giggle and rush off toward the classrooms, hand in hand. To me they seem innocents without enough objects for their affections but I realize it's partly that I'm more used to Western taciturnity. One of the Palestinian girls comes up to me one day and asks if she can talk to me for a few minutes. She is obviously upset and on the verge of tears.

"What's wrong, Awatif?"

She blushes and shakes her head and looks away. I put an arm around her.

"Oh, what is it? You can tell me."

"I love you, Missus," she finally blurts out. She covers her mouth with her hands. "I love you all my heart."

"Oh," I say. It is the first declaration of love I've ever had from a nineteen-year-old girl. "You live at the hostel, don't you, Awatif?" The hostel is a student dormitory and is considered a pathetic place to reside; the great majority of the students live at home or with local families.

"Yes."

"And do you have sisters at home?" I find I'm automatically scrambling to change the subject, to twist the matter into some recognizable formula.

"Yes. In Al Jouf."

"Oh. So you must miss your sisters. You must want to have a sister here. Well, you and I can be friends," I say.

"I love you, Missus," repeats Awatif. "I love you like my sister."

"That's nice, Awatif. It's nice to love people," I say, sounding as lame as I feel. "We should get to class now."

She gives me puppy-dog eyes for a few weeks. I usually don't have to deal with problems any more difficult than this one. We teachers are lucky here. These students are as eager to please as small children, but they're quieter and less restless. Teaching in the West is more of a challenge because the students there test the teacher constantly; they don't accept your authority until you've proven yourself. Here there's very little battle of wits with the students. That's why Manal, one of my Palestinian students, irritated me so very much at first. She stuck out; she was the nearest thing here to a class mischief-maker. She'd stroll in to the class late and hiss "sssssalaam alaykum" to everyone, and she'd draw out that initial "s" needlessly, annoyingly. Then she'd joke in Arabic throughout the class and distract the other students. I could feel my antipathy toward her growing until I realized that she was the only one who had a healthy disregard for teacherly authority. Generally the girls are the meekest of lambs: one day I sat atop my desk cleaning out a folder as the girls worked on compositions. I took a pile of old memos and ripped them in half. All the girls' heads jerked up at me; I read fear in all their eyes. They thought I was ripping up unsatisfactory student work, or some such thing. "It's nothing," I said sheepishly. "It's just trash, old things." Manal wasn't there that time, but if she had been she would have laughed at the other girls. It's a blessing that she's here; perhaps she'll teach the other girls something about assertiveness, about individuality.

∼

I bought myself a traditional Bedouin dancing dress but I found I couldn't get my head through the opening. It was tunic length; I thought it might look great with black pants, if I could only get my head through. Finally I took it to the college and asked the girls. They immediately started to laugh. "For little girl, Missus!" "Oh, of course," I said. Tunic length. Stupid me.

Anyway, a week or so later, Huda, the tiny Bahraini, brought me an adult-length dancing dress. It's a traditional Gulf Arab garment; this one is red chiffon-ish stuff, heavily trimmed in gold sequins and brocade. It's lovely and the perfect thing for costume parties back home.

Huda weighs thirty-five kilos and her feet dangle a few inches off the floor as she sits at her desk. If she and I stand together in conversation, I have to fight the urge to squat down like you might for a six-year-old. Her figure is a perfectly formed woman's figure; it's just minuscule in scale. She's been banished to Saudi Arabia by her strict parents who feared the more westernized social milieu of Bahrain. "I play too much with boys there," Huda tells me. "My parents very angry." She's clearly homesick for Bahrain. Every time I ask her to use a verb or invent a sentence, she brings up Bahrain: "I would like to go to Bahrain." "Bahrain is a beautiful country." One day she tries the patience of Jamila, the Saudi. "If you marry Saudi boy, you stay in Saudi Arabia," Jamila tells her, an edge of malice in her voice. "You never go back."

"I not marry Saudi. Never," Huda laughs. "I marry Bahraini, Kuwaiti. Not Saudi."

I nod and smile and move back to a grammar issue, but I'm storing this little exchange in my memory as a bit of evidence that there is general recognition among these students that this country is a cage for women, gilded though it might be.

Huda tells me she loves to write and keeps a diary. "I write songs in it," she says. I'm very impressed and ask to see some of them. She brings her diary in and lets me examine it, but I'm disappointed to see that it contains only lyrics of Western pop hits: oooooh, love to love you, baby—and other stuff of that ilk. But then I realize she is practicing writing English and on top of that I am touched by her romantic streak.

The students are fine makeup artists; all highlight their dark good looks with eye makeup and lipstick, and many use elaborate foundation lotions despite their youth. They look like China dolls, and it's all for each other. If they don't have time to apply their morning makeup, they tend to sit in the back of the room and huddle behind a book or to make some excuse to run off to one of the restrooms.

~

One of the students brings a friend into the class. They sit together in the back of the room. "Where do you come from?" I ask the visitor.

"From Yemen."

"Oooooooooooh," cry out many of the girls in disgust, as if they've come upon a squashed lizard. They turn and look at the Yemeni. She blushes and shrugs. I stand in front of the class, shocked and at a loss.

"Oh, no," I say to them. "You can't . . . you can't say things like that. It's not right."

"Yes, Missus, Yemen very bad," says Jamila. "Very poor and dirty."

I see that the visitor is struggling to maintain a brave face, and I change the subject. Later I feel guilty about not lecturing the girls on prejudice, but then I realize it would be swimming through mud.

~

Mary and I discuss how much we miss the exuberance and energy of American students. The girls here are attentive but tentative, birdlike, and easily scared. They very rarely ask questions about anything; analysis and curiosity are not parts of the educational fabric in this part of the world. I never yell at the students or display the slightest annoyance—I've taken the cue from them, for they always seem completely pleased and delighted with me.

One day the girls invite various teachers to a college activities evening. Mary and I decide to go together. It turns out to be a sort of amateur-hour variety show. Two sisters roller-skate, a group of eight does very simple acrobatics, another group in pink leotards performs a very childish and inexpert ballet. All legs are covered in baggy warm-up pants; "Bashfulness is Required in the Kingdom" proclaims a bulletin at the entry to the gym. The bulletin goes on to specify that lady swimmers must cover their legs. These rules are enforced even though all sports activities are strictly sexually segregated: women may not even bare their bodies among one another. Mary and I whisper to each other and plan to remove the notice to keep as a souvenir, but there are too many young Arab women wandering about and we as teachers certainly can't be caught stealing. "Be sure to jot down the main points when we sit down," Mary says to me in an undertone.

The audience at the show is all female, of course. Some spectators are dressed in trousers, but most wear elaborate full-length party dresses, frothy concoctions of lace and gold lamé and fluorescent polyester. Girls walk around distributing chocolates, hard candy, and bottles of water. The show makes my blood run cold after a while; here are twenty-year-old girls performing at a level of six-year-olds at a dance recital. There's a booth of judges, all princesses of the Al Saud. In front of them are stacked piles of gold medallions, elaborate china tea sets, and other prizes. Mary and I gaze at their splendid clothes and royal visages. Every performer wins a prize, and all prizes are first prize. It's all very pleasant, but I feel stifled, hemmed in by what I perceive as excessive treacle. I am comforted that Mary sits at my elbow and we can exchange glances. There is one piece that has a zestful panache—a wedding dance in which a Jordanian student takes the part of the man. She dances with verve and imagination, and the audience howls at her imitation of a male. The other acts pale in comparison.

Throughout the show our students run up to us in their fancy dresses; they show us their prizes. We nod and smile and give compliments, but I feel hypocritical, unethical, and I notice Mary shifting around in her seat. I'm thinking I have to help these young women realize how thwarted, how aborted their lives are. I can't pass my horror off as simple cultural chauvinism. Mary and I go home bored and depressed and slightly nauseated—the evening lasted seven hours and only that candy and water were available.

~

One day I walk into the classroom and all the girls are in heated discussion. It's something quite unusual.

"What are you saying?" I ask.

"Oh, Missus," says Jamila. "Jews very handsome. Jews most handsome men in world. Do you think?"

"Jews?" I repeat, not thinking I'd heard correctly.

"Yes, Missus."

"Yes, some of them are very handsome," I say, opting for neutrality. "Just like people everywhere, some are very handsome, some not."

The Palestinian girls murmur indistinctly. "No, no," says Manal. She shakes her head at Jamila.

"I wish I marry Jew," bursts out Jamila.

"No, no, Jews terrible," says Manal. She flings her hand forward, dismissing the subject.

"There are handsome people everywhere," I say lamely, trying to steer the conversation into safer territory. "What about Italians?"

"Oh, Italians!" say the girls. "Yes, Italians!"

I can't decide whether the discussion of Jews was meant to tease the Palestinians or was conceived from the exotic and untouchable picture these girls seem to have of Jews.

~

One of the students comes up to me and says she saw me in the gold *souq*—the multiple small shops of the gold market. Everyone living in the Gulf always has a moderate gold fever. Westerners frequent the gold *souq* as one of the few legal leisure activities here; in addition, they convince themselves the gold is a good investment akin to stocks, bonds. And the locals too are regular purchasers of gold; brides traditionally are given much gold jewelry, and it is considered their bank account.

"I followed you around," this student is telling me. "I watched you shop in the gold *souq*. Me and my mother," she says, giggling.

"Why didn't you come up and say hello to me?" I ask, slightly horrified at being spied upon.

"Our faces covered. You not see us." She giggles again. "We follow you around, we watch you."

I nod and quickly start speaking of something else for I feel bemused and a tad violated. But perhaps it's fine that I served as entertainment for the girl and her mother.

~

I ask the girls to make some comparisons between Riyadh and Jeddah.

"Jeddah very nice," says Manal. "In Jeddah women don't . . ." She makes the sharp gesture downward across her face that the students use as shorthand for the word veil.

"Oh, I see. They don't veil." I write the word on the board for the umpteenth time. "They don't cover their faces."

"Yes, very nice, Jeddah," says Manal.

A pregnant Saudi student turns to her. "Good Muslim women do . . ." She finishes the sentence with the same downward hand sweep. "In Jeddah, yes."

"I see. Good Muslim women veil even in Jeddah," I say.

The pregnant girl nods vigorously. Manal, seated behind her, shakes her head and shrugs.

～

"S'cuse me, Missus," Jamila says in class in the middle of a lesson. "Was this book written by a man?" I pause, wondering what she has in mind. "Because you see it says 'women talk, men listen'," she explains, smiling and pointing to one of the exercises. The students laugh. I'm pleased; it's a novelty for a student to make a joke in English.

～

Faten, a married Saudi student, always wears a large, crudely worked but valuable gold necklace. "See what her husband give her?" says Jamila, touching Faten's necklace. Another student says something in Arabic and everyone laughs.

"Tell me in English," I say.

"She say we all too old to marry, Missus," says Jamila.

"We very old. We too old to marry. Get marry here at fifteen. We nineteen, too old," says Manal.

"My mother marry when she twelve years, Missus," calls out Jamila.

"Here twenty old woman. Twenty-three very very very old. Twenty-three only marry old man—forty, fifty."

"My aunt and uncle tell my father 'get husband for her, get husband—she too old.' I nineteen," says Jamila.

"What do your parents say?" I ask.

"They say no, I too young to marry. I only girl in family, I young one in family, they want to keep me at home. They love me too much, they say," says Jamila.

"I see, I see," I say. Now that the opportunity has arisen, I think over other marriage-related questions I'd like answered.

"Do many men have more than one wife?" I ask.

Responses burst out.

"If I marry and husband take a second wife, I kill him," says Jamila immediately. She is smiling but definite.

"If he take a second wife, I leave him," says Manal.

A Saudi girl rubs her thumb across her fingers and laughs and shakes her head. I can guess that she's saying it's not that easy.

"What are you saying, Kadija?" I ask her.

She chatters in Arabic to the other girls. They laugh. "She says, Missus, that if husband give her twenty-five thousand riyals before marriage, if she leave him she must give it back."

"If he take another wife, I kill him and her. I kill them both," says Jamila.

"Does it happen very often?" I ask her.

"Yes, Missus, my brother, my biggest brother have two wives. He marry one and she have one baby, but her mother not good. Wife's mother not good. So he leave first wife and marry a second wife. She have five children with him. Then he go back to the first wife and want to keep second wife, too," says Jamila.

"So how does the second wife feel?" I ask.

"She angry, she cry, she very sad. But now she say yes, now she used to it."

～

Occasionally there is a chink of light. "Missus, I move to Milwaukee," Manal tells me one day out of the blue. She still comes to class late; she still hisses "sssss-salaam."

"You're moving to Milwaukee?" I ask. She might as well have said the moon. "Milwaukee, Wisconsin? Milwaukee in America?"

"Yes, Missus. Milwaukee America. I study English there. My sister there now studying engineering."

"How wonderful!" I say. I'm thrilled for her. It seems crystal clear to me that a young Palestinian girl would be much better off in the midwest of America than here, here in the sad-hearted desert. "It's very cold in winter there!" I say to her. "You'll need very warm clothes!"

Manal brings in her sister, who's in Riyadh on semester break from the University of Wisconsin in Milwaukee. "Milwaukee is very nice city," she tells me. "People in Milwaukee very nice, very friendly. People in Milwaukee like the P.L.O. I love Milwaukee. Chicago very bad, very dirty, but Milwaukee nice."

"Oh yes, Milwaukee's a wonderful place," I tell her. The words echo in my mind for a split second and I realize I'm just blustering. I know Riyadh better than I know Milwaukee. But still, Manal's imminent escape from the Kingdom makes me very happy for her. The two sisters invite me to their home for a farewell party. I notice their passports lying on a tabletop, and I ask if I may take a look. Manal flips hers open to the page with the entry visa for the United States. I look at it and then look at it again. It's a three-month tourist visa. It specifies non-student, non-worker status. Manal's sister notices the expression on my face when I look up. "No problem," she says. "We change it there. No problem."

I hope she's right. I don't worry about it too much; the important thing for Manal is to get out of the Gulf and marry a nice Milwaukee college boy. A month later I hear that she's very homesick and cold in Milwaukee. I don't worry a single speck. She'll survive, I feel.

∽

The mid-semester exam reduces the students to tears. A crowd of seventy takes it in one room. One starts to cry and then another and suddenly it seems that dozens of them are weeping. We Western teachers stand with hands on hips, looking at one another, wondering what to do.

∽

Awatif, the Palestinian who told me she loved me, worries me more than the other students. She's a sweet but bumbling eighteen-year-old who follows Western teachers around like a puppy, pleased with the slightest show of attention. She possesses a lopsided smile and a propensity to grab and hug when no other students are around. She's short and femininely rounded, and she wears her hair loosely on top of her head in a Victorian bun. Sometimes she looks slightly dirty, so I've asked her about her home life. She no longer lives in the hostel; her brother has moved to town and she lives with him. She does all the cooking and cleaning. They fight a lot about the television and the stereo, she says, and who gets to use what when.

During class I've sometimes noticed her smiling at me in a pleased-cat sort of way; she's clearly paying no attention to the lesson at hand.

"You happy, Missus?" she asks me one day after class.

"Yes, Awatif. I'm happy. Are you happy?"

"You happy, Missus, I happy," says Awatif.

Awatif's native intelligence has not been cultivated carefully; many western teachers smile grimly when her name comes up. Whatever the case, she never scores high enough to pass any of the English proficiency tests although she returns semester after semester. The only time I've seen her unhappy was at the end of a final exam session. She performed miserably and she knew it, so she refused to give up her exam paper. She seemed to think that if she stewed over it long enough, she would come up with some correct answers. We Western teachers were anxious to escape from the exam room, so three of us ganged up on Awatif and took the paper. I'm ashamed I didn't do more to comfort her at that moment; I still remember her captured-doe look as she held on to the exam booklet while we three infidel bullies tried to take it from her.

But the truth is, Awatif doesn't work very hard. I don't think she knows how to, and I haven't had much success in helping her improve. Everything she hands in is done in a hasty, slap-dash way. At first I'd administer bromides like you're improving! or keep working! written in block letters across her papers. But Awatif got in the habit of coming up to me and demanding a more judgmental response. "Good, Missus?" she'd ask, holding up a miserable piece of work. "Well, not really, Awatif," I'd say. So I began writing harsher comments: poor work! your handwriting is terrible! correct all these verbs! i can't read this! But even this wasn't clear enough for Awatif.

"Good, Missus?" she asked me one day, holding up a paper upon which I'd written all wrong! do this again!

"No, Awatif. This is not good. Do you see what I wrote?"

"Not good, Missus?" Awatif asked, and I noticed a twinkle in her eye; she was flirting with me.

"No, Awatif," I said, smiling at her. "It's not good. Please write more carefully, work more slowly."

She never has, of course. Everything is always done devoid of capitals, verb endings, punctuation. One day I sit correcting papers and find that Awatif has handed in a particularly atrocious piece of work on a filthy sheet of paper torn from a notebook. I am short-tempered this day, so I block in BAD! across the top in huge red letters. The next day I return the papers. When I happen to look over at Awatif, I see her huddled over her desk, crying. She has crumpled the paper and thrown it under her seat. She mopes and weeps quietly through the rest of the class. I feel a little annoyed with both of us; she is acting like a baby, and I'd been mistaken in giving such a negative response.

The next day Awatif comes up to me after class and hands me a tape cassette. She's given me tapes before—third-rate pop groups such as Boney M and Bananarama—the same stuff all the girls listen to. This time, however, the tape is a peace offering.

"For you, Missus. Michael Jackson."

"Oh! Michael Jackson. Thank you, Awatif."

"You angry by me, Missus?"

"No. Why?"

"Because yesterday I throw paper under chair. I sorry, Missus."

"Oh, that's all right, Awatif."

"Tape very beautiful," says a beaming Awatif. "Michael Jackson very beautiful. He American, like you."

The tape is a copy she's made herself, and it reeks of perfume. And she's inked carefully on it: To Mrs. Cress, my fraind and sester—remember me. She's even made a delicate, tiny drawing of an arrow-pierced heart.

⁓

One day in class I notice that something is wrong with Awatif's nose; there is a perfectly round, nearly dime-sized burn on it, just slightly off dead center. I can't imagine how she'd gotten it; I glance at her frequently trying to figure out possible origins. It looks like a burn from a car's cigarette lighter. The more I look at it, the surer I am that that's what it is. Oh god, I think, what chasms of mystery.

"What happened to your nose?" I ask Awatif after class.

She looks slightly upset. "My brother. He mad at me because I forget to wake him up."

I feel suddenly frozen. I have to force myself to speak. "Tell him not to do that again," I say slowly and clearly.

"He good man, he make mistake," says Awatif. She gives a little wave of her hand. "He not bad."

That day when I get home I send a friend in the States twenty dollars to send me a Michael Jackson T-shirt; it will be a gift for Awatif.

⁓

Awatif strikes us as innocent and mildly retarded, but she's got a devilish streak. Lately she's begun querying us about sex.

"What meaning orgy, Missus?" she asks in the middle of class, pronouncing the word with a hard g.

"Pardon me?"

"Orgy, Missus. What meaning orgy? O - R - G - Y."

"Oh." I pause. "Well, it's a party, it's a kind of party." I keep my face bland. "Where you have too much of something. For example, if two people eat a lot of chocolate, an entire cake. That's an orgy of chocolate."

"Party, Missus?" asks Awatif, scrutinizing my face closely.

"Yes, like a party." I immediately realize this definition might be a mistake; parties are among the few highlights of these girls' lives, and they write about them often in compositions. Now they might refer to them as orgies.

The next day Awatif comes up with another request, but this time I am on guard.

"Missus, what meaning planzation?" she asks, again in the middle of the lesson. The other girls perk up their ears; they see the little smile on Awatif's lips.

"Planzation?"

"Yes. Planzation."

"Hmm. Planzation. Do you mean plantation?" I sort through possible sexual aspects of the word.

"Planzation," she repeats.

"There's no such word as planzation, Awatif. You must mean plantation. It's a large farm."

"Large farm, Missus?" repeats Awatif, giving me a skeptical look.

"Yes, a large farm." The other students lose interest and their faces relax back into incuriosity. I realize Awatif must mean implantation. She's perhaps gotten hold of some sort of sex and reproduction manual.

Sure enough, the next day Awatif has another query, but this time she asks a different teacher, a Scottish woman named Jane.

"Hingman, what or who's a hingman?" asks Jane as she strides into the teachers' office and heads for a dictionary.

"Who wants to know?" I ask.

"Awatif from your class."

"Hingman?" asks Mary. "How is she spelling it?"

"Hingman," I say. "Oh. Hymen. She must mean hymen. She's into sex lately."

We teachers enjoy a brief laugh about this, but I feel a passing stab of regret that I can't rescue Awatif, that I can't do more to improve her lot.

⌒

Not much later than this Awatif gives me another tape. "To my fraind Mr crass" this one says across the label. I'd devolved slightly from Mrs. Cress. "I remember you every day" is scrawled across the tape. "You my dear and my fraind (forever). Love, love, Awatif." I listen to the tape at home; it is Arabic music but too garbled and badly recorded to enjoy. But I keep the tape because of Awatif's written messages.

⌒

"You have brothers?" Awatif asks me one day. "Brothers in America?"

"Yes, I do. Three brothers."

"You have pictures, Missus?"

"No. I didn't bring any, Awatif. Oh wait a minute, I've got a picture of my husband here in my purse. Would you like to see that?"

Awatif gives me a blank look. "No pictures of brothers?" she persists.

I shake my head. She's looking into my eyes. We gaze at each other and say nothing, paying a kind of fleeting respect to this escape fantasy of hers.

⌒

The failing students who retain little English come back semester after semester even though Mary and Jane and I and all the western teachers try our best to dissuade them. But our powers are limited; flunking out rarely occurs in Saudi universities no matter how richly the student deserves it. Awatif is a classic example, a student who stays in the beginning English courses term after term. And yet we don't especially mind; it makes for a bridge between semesters.

⌒

And so back to the college for a new semester after vacation escape to westernized lands where I can wear jeans and drink wine in sun-splashed cafes. Awatif, the sweet, the crafty, the nebulous, grabs me and kisses me twice on each cheek.

"Welcome, Missus. Welcome."

"Hello, Awatif. What are you going to study this time?"

"Of course English, Missus. I like it too much. I want to read Shakespeare."

"OK, Awatif. That's fine," I say. The vacation has put me back in the grip of Western efficiency, of perceived practicality, so I become didactic: "But I want you to know that you'll never succeed. You'll never be able to take courses beyond the beginner's level." This is sad, but true. Awatif's English is not good enough to meet even the very low standard of the English literature department.

"It is hopeless, Awatif. You won't be able to go on to advanced English. It is hopeless." I feel like I am doing Awatif a service by ladling out this bitter medicine. "Hopeless, Missus?" Awatif says. She has been watching me carefully and is on the verge of tears.

"I'm sorry, Awatif. Yes, it's hopeless."

~

The next day Awatif comes up to me, beaming happily. "Not hopeless, Missus," she scolds me. "You say hopeless. Not hopeless. Nothing hopeless."

I feel reproved and I conjecture that she's spoken to someone who's bolstered her confidence, someone Muslim. Or maybe she's prayed about it. Good Muslims would never call anything hopeless; all is in Allah's hands. So Awatif, Muslim that she is, continues studying English, confidence unabated.

~

As the academic year draws to a close, the students finish the English workbooks. As I leaf through the last lessons I notice Awatif's scrawl to me on the final page of her book: "Don't forget me my dear and my fraind for ever for to ever. Awatif."

She still never bothers to concentrate during class. She seems to feel she'll absorb lots of English by osmosis; she isn't wrong, of course. "You give me the hope, Missus," she says to me. "You give me the hope." I decide to quit giving her advice; it's a breach of good Islam for me to be so arrogant as to feel I can predict the exam results. I warn her to study hard, however. She just laughs. "But Awatif," I say, and I break off, frustrated.

"But Missus," says Awatif, starting to giggle.

"But Awatif," I say, looking into her smiling, child-like face.

"But Missus," says Awatif. "But Missus." We are both giggling now.

"I'll see you tomorrow, Awatif," I say.

"Good-bye, Missus," she says. "Good afternoon."

~

At first it didn't bother me that Western men, especially the sexually-deprived single men, salivated over the veiled Arab virgins. I was blinded by the novelty of the land. But after a while I become more and more angry at the confines, the enslavement, the subjugation of these young women. Seeing them draped in black makes me turn away in horror and disgust and sympathy. I hate seeing them mincing along in their ridiculous high heels. It reminds me of Chinese ladies of a past era, Chinese ladies with tightly bound feet.

~

I don't really teach anymore. The semester has drawn to a close, the exams are soon to be given. Everyone has cabin fever although the campus is still lovely and there are new plantings of flowers. It's impossible to teach. I just sit in front of the class and giggle and all the girls giggle, too. Sometimes for variety we have hysterics. The girls lose patience toward the very end and begin racing up and down the corridors, slamming doors, turning off lights, crowding into restrooms to redo makeup. Teachers too feel the freedom of summer beckoning, and we let the students enjoy their energy, the energy of that cusp between childhood and adulthood.

It's time to leave Saudi Arabia for the summer, and maybe forever.

Tiny Huda invites me to visit her in Bahrain and to stay with her family for as long as I wish.

Awatif asks for my New York address.

Jamila gives me a gold ring with a sapphire.

I fly out of the Kingdom on Air France, and I find I can breathe deeply.

Iran: Private Perceptions

TEHRAN, MEHRABAD AIRPORT, OCTOBER 1964

IRAN AIR FLIGHT 505 approached in the middle of a very dark night. Passengers scrambled for their carry-on baggage—Yves St. Laurent tote bags stuffed to overflowing, sacks of fresh fruit spilling, orange peels rolling down the aisle.

The sudden surprise flurry of activity when everyone should have been strapped in their seats caught me unaware and for a moment dissipated my intense excitement.

Children shrieked, women clutched at long black veils, stewards ran up and down admonishing passengers to please be seated until the plane had landed, all in vain. A man in a turban and a long robe whom I could only presume to be a *mullah* was saying something I presumed to be his prayers.

My sleepy two-year-old awoke to the confusion and light and, rubbing his eyes, crawled to the window seat and looked out with me peering over his head. It seemed a spread of black velvet cushioned a million tiny flecks of gold, winking and beckoning; light from the sprawling city reflecting against the Elborz mountain range, a shadowy shape looming to the north.

Pressing close to the window, the full panoramic view still escaping my breadth of vision, it was clear to me that at least one of my preconceived notions about Iran had to be discarded—it was not all desert.

A crisp winter wind scooted across the runway, our first breath of Tehran, as we made our way the short distance to the gates of Mehrabad. About midway across I heard it. My name being called by a chorus of voices.

The entire family had come to greet us near midnight and stood shivering on the balcony of the airport, waving and calling to me. This, apparently, was the nature of things in Iran; it seemed that all passengers had their own delegation to greet them; every arrival was a celebration.

Preferential treatment to foreigners was in evidence at every turn. Customs officials with limited English or French smilingly processed papers; baggage carriers rushed forward with carts to help load luggage; pretty girls obligingly waved the foreign passenger on through the checkpoint with hardly a bag opened, while Iranian passengers were halted and searched as though being examined for contraband. Taxis lined up outside, trunks open, ready to lurch into the night.

The family all came forward, surrounding us, taking turns holding my son Eric and hugging him (though he was by my first marriage, he was always accepted and cherished), then me, kisses from everyone. I felt at home.

Hooshang, my Iranian husband-to-be, had not told me much about Islam, only that it was no longer practiced by "more educated Iranians" and that the *mullahs* had lost most of their power and prestige in recent times.

"They are hardly more than beggars in most cases," he once said disdainfully. Now, across his shoulder, I saw the one from the plane watching and imagined it was with a disapproving look.

"Come on," Hooshang told me as he hoisted Eric onto his shoulders. "Dinner's waiting! And remember what I told you back in the States: Don't smile at strangers! This isn't Texas."

Diary Notes, Tehran, January 1965

The oldest of the family servants is also the most notorious in the neighborhood. She comes from the Kurdish tribe that inhabits the northwestern region of Iran and is famous for its independence and a certain ferocity.

A tale that circulates through the family regarding Tayeh's past seems to attest to that. They say she once had a husband and two children; before she left her tribe, her husband had greatly wounded her pride and in some way incurred her wrath to such an extent she deemed it necessary to punish him to avenge herself.

So she took their children to a deserted hut, locked them in it, and went away, leaving them to starve to death. It was then that she came to Tehran, soon afterwards coming to work for Mama John (dear Mama). That was over thirty years ago. In spite of the way she pampers me, because I have the good fortune to be engaged to her favorite, I can hardly bear the sight of the old woman.

Henna-red hair peeping from under a filthy, faded scarf; run-down shoes and a man's grubby old suit coat with sticky handkerchiefs hanging out of the pockets, the same pockets that hold the pistachio nuts and almonds she insists on offering me constantly; gnarled hands so toughened by hard work, weather, and age that they can carry a pot of boiling water from the stove without twitching a muscle.

Half her face lies dead; she was paralyzed years ago. The mouth is weak on that side, the eyelid collapsed, the cheek sagging. Yet her great kindness makes me feel guilty for rejecting her. (Eventually, she wins me over.)

Several days following my arrival she approached me in the kitchen (they find it a little shocking that I want to cook on occasion) and clutching the soft pouches that hang from her chest to waist she began jabbering excitedly. From her gestures I gathered she was relating to me the fact she had nursed my husband when he was a baby, to which I responded in English, "That's disgusting!"

Cackling and chortling to herself, she tottered away up the stairs, thinking, no doubt, I had just commended her for her service.

Tayeh's room is a chill, musty basement storehouse. The odor assailing one's nostrils on entering is a peculiar mixture arising from the various jams, pickles, and spices she hoards there, mingled with the smell of age and mildew.

It took months to be able to step into her lair without covering my face with something or holding my breath. A tiny bulb hanging from the ceiling by a singular cord about a foot long illuminates the room. Four thick black strings are strung, two by two, from one corner to the opposite, whereon she hangs wet clothing on cold or rainy days.

The general grime and clutter of the room made me squeamish in the beginning to taste her jams and preserves. But they are wonderful and I can't resist them. Fig, a tart, strangely-shaped cherry, plum, and the tastiest of all: that made with rose petals.

Heaped on the fresh *barbari* bread she brings daily from a nearby bakery, they make breakfast worth rising for, served with hot tea and goats-milk cheese.

There are no supermarkets, or only one facsimile, so Tayeh or Gharib go running off to neighborhood shops for everything from two eggs to a bunch of parsley every time a meal is prepared. And everything is prepared fresh; canned goods are on the shelves now but very few and they're generally shunned as unhealthy.

I made Southern fried chicken for Hooshang's father, Agha Jahn (dear Sir, the usual endearment for fathers), once I wearied of Iranian fare and he absolutely loves it. He thinks it's the best thing he's ever eaten.

Tomorrow we go to the ancient site of Rey, which lies south, between Tehran and the holy city of Qom.

REFLECTIONS ON REY, JANUARY 1965

We piled into Ron's Landrover early in the morning to make a day of it—a drive to the ancient town of Rey, by 1965 more of a southern suburb of Tehran on the road to Qom.

Sussan, Fereydoun, Vida, and I, with Ron driving. Ron is a Peace Corpsman and the only American I ever knew who could discuss any topic in Farsi and translate even legal documents from Farsi to English or vice versa.

It was suggested that since we were going so far south and near Qom, we females might want to wear headscarves, but, as on many occasions, we threw caution to the wind. It was a cool, dry day and my liberated sisters-in-law scoffed at the idea of even minimal covering.

Our purpose in traveling to Rey was to view the carpet washing. Only Westerners vacuum their oriental rugs; the proper care is beating, broom-sweeping, and washing, and as seldom as possible, to preserve their condition and colors. My rug merchant had already cautioned me not to wash a carpet more than every ten years unless something threatened to stain it.

One of my first big shocks in Tehran was driving down the street over elegant Persian carpets.

I practically leapt out of the car the first time it happened, telling my husband that we had just run over someone's carpet and shouldn't we stop and pull it onto the curb.

"They would be very angry if you did," he responded, or something to that effect. The reason, he explained, was that some people were convinced that since the best way to knock the dust out of rugs was beating them, driving a car over them would be even better.

"But," I asked in bewilderment, "won't it just settle back down on them?"

He assured me we would leave ours to more traditional care. The last time I left Tehran, a few weeks before Khomeini returned in 1979, they were still driving over rugs.

In Rey, the task of carpet cleaning had become a cottage industry, where individuals and carpet dealers alike took their precious cargo. The oriental works of art lay all over the ground, all over the mountainside and stacked in heaps at the edge of flowing spring waters.

Everything was done by hand from start to finish, just as in their creation. Iranians value their rugs even more than the rest of the world, which pays handsomely for its admiration, and they pay far higher prices than might be expected at the source.

A carpet is everything to some: an investment, a bed, a seat, a place to eat, sleep, pray or make love, a decoration, something to roll up in and keep a blizzard at bay. Carpets come first among acquisitions—they are transportable. Land comes second.

We watched as rugs were first hung up on strong lines and beaten until dust flew no more; then they were soaked briefly before shampooing, men generally doing the beating and women the scrubbing. Rinsed and draped around massive stones and the side of the mountain to have excess water stroked (never squeezed) out, they were left to partially dry. A final stage, once they were no longer heavy with water, was to hang them back on lines to dry completely.

Walking to one end of the bustling workplace, Sussan showed me thousands-years-old bas reliefs, predating Islam, etched into the mountain, of brave Persian kings and noblemen, lions, and mythical beasts.

I asked if something shouldn't be done to protect such relics but she said there were so many all across the land they had yet to even be unearthed. She said the government was just beginning to piece together its ancient history and explained how the present Shah was instilling a sense of pride in the people for their pre-Islamic heritage.

Tehran, Autumn 1965

The old matriarch of our family had been dead seven days. It was time to go to the mosque to properly mourn her passing. Muslim ritual directs the faithful to gather on the seventh day after death to mourn their loss.

Unfortunately, the mosque was not available on the seventh day so the ceremony was postponed until the following *chahar-shambe* (Wednesday), making it actually the tenth day, but no one minded the slight discrepancy, least of all the deceased.

Bi-Bi, as she was affectionately called, was some one hundred years of age, insisting vehemently that she was one hundred and fifty if a day, with hennaed hair the color of a bright autumn maple leaf. And it was autumn when she passed on—hopefully to the Seventh Heaven.

She was no taller than an eight-year-old child, her body bent forward by time and osteoporosis, but with spirit undampened by the vast and sometimes wearisome panorama that had passed before her faded eyes.

She had seen shahs come and go, and seen the end of a long-lived dynasty. She was not, however, concerned with kings or kingdoms so long as they did not disturb her afternoon tea or deprive her of her favorite smoke.

Her daughter, Habibeh, was with her the last night she slept at home. At some dark hour of the morning when most of the world was at rest storing up energy to face the coming day, Bi-Bi-Jahn (dear Bi-Bi) was perhaps thinking of storing a little energy to face the 1001 prophets. She rose quietly and toddled off to the kitchen to brew a bit of chicken broth.

Habibeh did not realize her mother had been up, until morning, when she awoke and saw the near-empty soup bowl by her bed. Bi-Bi had joined the prophets.

Her grandsons would tease Bi-Bi at every opportunity, for she was far more fun than women their own age. At one hundred, she no longer had to hide behind the rigid Muslim rules of behavior for proper Muslim ladies. She could, and did, say what she thought. Just the day before, Fereydoun had been to visit her. Tweaking her craggy chin that jutted forward, he leaned over and whispered, "Bi-Bi! Guess what? I found the perfect man for you today."

Brushing him aside like a pesky fly she retorted, "Listen, stupid, I know I have beautiful hair and I don't need you to find me a man! I can find one anytime I want!" This was followed by a high-pitched cackle and a sharp poke to the ribs for Fereydoun. Bi-Bi had outlived her only husband and his three younger wives.

There was some confusion before the ceremony concerning proper attire for me, but it was decided that a *chador* would not be necessary as I was still, despite my Muslim marriage, considered a foreigner at the very least and an infidel at worst, so I chose instead to wear a black lace mantilla a friend had brought me years before from Mexico. Secretly I was a bit disappointed not to have an excuse to don one of the beautiful floor-length lace *chadors* worn for such occasions.

Although the late Reza Shah the Great had banned the wearing of *chadors* in Iran some thirty-five years before, it was still customary in 1965 to shroud one-self for mourning.

Most of the women wore no cosmetics; aside from the inappropriateness, they were going with the expectation of weeping and it would only become streaked. The row of black figures sat phantom-like against the wall to our left as we entered: daughter, daughter-in-law, two granddaughters, and the wife of a grandson. The other empty chair they told me to take as wife of the other grandson. This service was reserved for women; the men, whose service would be held later, sat about the courtyard in convivial attitudes.

There was only a handful of mourners as it was early yet, but there were to appear some fifty or more female visitors before the conclusion; mostly near the conclusion so they would not, I later calculated, be obliged to sit so long. Much to my discomfort, members of the family sat facing the host of mourners; draping my mantilla over my nose I could glance about the room and observe, if not fully understand, all that took place.

As the women sat chattering quietly to one another, a servant brought several small tables with ashtrays, matches, and clusters of the spindly Iranian cigarettes, Homa. Everyone took advantage of the offering and soon gray billows of smoke wafted toward the ornate domed ceiling. The servant returned with delicate cups of Turkish coffee. Some refused, preferring the *estacons* of tea they knew to be coming next.

The *Qur'ani* (reader of the *Qu'ran*) entered, sat to the far left facing the congregation, kicked off his shoes, and picked up the *Qu'ran*. Solemnly leafing to a certain text, he placed one edge of the open book against the right side of his nose. The acoustical effect was splendid.

His clear, rich voice rang out across the room, through the mosque, and into the court beyond in the opening prayer for the deceased.

Everyone respectfully extinguished their cigarettes, set aside tea or coffee, and dutifully tucked themselves away under folds of *chadors*. The *Qu'rani*'s plaintive yodel rose and fell, reaching deep into the hearts of his audience with painfully sad words as though intended to wring forth tears. Words of "beloved mother," the good mother, kind mother, the one who cared for us throughout our childhood days and made those days safe and happy—storehouses of sweet memories.

Soon lamentations rent the air, the black apparitions sat trembling beneath the weight of the dirge. Then almost as suddenly as they had begun, they ceased. The *Qu'rani* also, apparently to take a break and rest his voice. *Chadors* were quickly pushed away from pale faces, everyone reached for a cigarette, and again tea was passed around.

A soft babble arose among the visitors and continued even after the *Qu'rani* resumed his elegy, nose twitching. But eventually his pitch rose higher, became more insistent, again prodding, pricking, racking the mourners with remembrances, his own face contorted with professional fervor.

This, then, was to be the climax of his performance, as he rocked back and forth rhythmically, stockinged toes gripping the rung of his chair as though in fear of drifting heavenward himself, putting heart and soul into the carefully memorized verses.

By this time even I was crying. I would attend other ceremonies over the years in Iran and come to understand more fully the power of public mourning and the inner relief brought by expressing grief, so unlike the Western tradition of restraining oneself and stifling emotion.

But just at that moment I could not help but imagine Bi-Bi perched invisibly on the railing, swinging a tiny foot as she was so prone to do, and puffing a Homa herself, enjoying tremendously the whole display.

The *Qu'rani* expertly brought the mourners back to normalcy, and (it had been an arduous two hours) ended his exhaustive song. The service continued for another half hour or so while the *mullah* delivered his oration.

As soon as the women were outside their floor-length veils were deftly bundled into their handbags, lipsticks and powder puffs whipped out, and away we went, back into the world of the living.

AHWAZ, PERSIAN GULF, MARCH 14, 1967

Here we are in Ahwaz, one of Iran's oil boom towns in the southern region, near the Persian Gulf. It's fascinating; it must be just like California's gold-rush days. Only here, newcomers are putting gold into the land: oil rigs.

Hooshang came to the capital for me and we took the train, which was an experience itself. The flat, desolate, and sandy land around Ahwaz is at first glance deceiving, especially if you arrive as we did by train, on an early spring morning. It looks just like any other sleepy-slow little Iranian town with familiar sounds of donkey carts, the soft shuffling of workers along the roadside, and a rhythmical muezzin's voice sounding from a street loudspeaker, calling the worshipers to prayer.

But the area's industrial activities have turned the Gulf village into a city surely destined for worldwide recognition. The town itself and the hotels are becoming populated with expatriates from all over the world: English, American, German, Dutch. The register at the strikingly modern new Hotel Ahwaz is lined with names from a dozen nationalities.

The minute we come in from the streets of town to the hotel at dinner time, the change of pace is startling. There's a sense of urgency in the air. Most of the hotel's occupants are not tourists. They're here on the various projects now in operation here and in Abadan, where the big refinery is: foreign consultants and technicians, Iranian supervisors, interpreters, directors, and trainees.

It's clear these are people with no time to waste, and they often carry on their work into their dinner conversation, over after-dinner drinks, and during hands of poker in the hotel's cozy little lounge. They're up again next morning at dawn and back out on the job, compacting the sandy soil of Khuzistan, surveying new sites or directing bulldozers.

Some evenings we visit with Hooshang's aunt and uncle who live here with their eight daughters. Poor man, he wanted desperately, as most Iranians seem to, to have a son, but finally gave up in despair.

Their home is typical of others in this hot climate (the pavement melted last summer and bogged down tires at 145 degrees), with the mandatory flat rooftops where they can set out cots and mosquito netting to sleep at night and a large inner courtyard with a fountain to help cool the air.

They love water and flowers, I guess because they're so scarce. That must be why they draw them into miniatures, weave them into carpets, and carve them over copper, brass, silver, and gold.

Last night the air was heavy with dust; a caravan of nomads had arrived on the outskirts of town, on their traditional spring migration to higher, cooler climes before the onslaught of the Gulf summer.

Their women wear tribal dress and spurn the customary veil of the city women. Gold earrings, nose rings, tattoos, and bracelets are their adornment and their brilliant-colored clothing is in high contrast to their sooty darkness.

As we drove past on our way back to Hotel Ahwaz, one lone woman stood with a child clinging to her back, just at the edge of the camp.

We drove close, but slowly, so as not to disturb the camels. So close that we passed within a few feet of her; we stared at one another across worlds and centuries. Her fierce black eyes locked onto mine with a steady, and, I thought, slightly defiant gaze. Flies were clustering over the baby's lips. For the first time since I've been here, I felt like an intruder.

We'll be here a week before starting the long drive back. I'm looking forward to a stopover in an Arab village en route, where Hooshang knows the sheikh.

Tehran, May 1975

It took one solid month after my return to Tehran in early 1975 to locate a livable and affordable home in what had become one of the world's three most expensive cities. My first sojourn in Iran had lasted but four years; I planned for this to be a permanent return.

In my interview the month before, I had neglected to inquire as to how much rents had increased in the six years I had been away. That they had doubled or in some cases trebled laid waste to my budget, and the salary that had sounded so generous at the time would, in fact, be barely sufficient.

My children and I were returning at the crest of the Shah's "White Revolution," so called because it was bloodless. It was an economic revolution, as technological progress surged across the country bringing with it thousands of foreigners feeding at the seemingly bottomless trough of Iranian petro dollars.

Arriving in the dead of night at the Hotel Imperial on Takhte Jamshid, a few blocks from the ill-fated American embassy, we stepped over Japanese businessmen sleeping on the lobby floor in their once neatly pressed pinstriped suits. Only through *parti-bazi*—the system of name-dropping and knowing the right people—as an employee of one of the Shah's major projects, was I able to hold the hotel to its previous confirmation and secure a room.

Setting out daily in search of a suitable home, pouring over newspapers first, I made every available personal contact through family members and old friends. The search continued throughout May and June, when temperatures and tempers are steadily climbing and by the time I answered an ad at Shiraz Avenue #46, I was near collapse.

Another woman, an Iranian, arrived shortly after I had signed the lease and burst into tears when informed it had been rented. She had spent three months looking. Iranian landlords practiced a sort of reverse discrimination, refusing to rent to their own when there was the tempting prospect of a foreigner coming along to pay two or three times as much, then leave at the end of a short contract, allowing them once again to hike the rent.

At fifty-thousand rials (about seven hundred and fifty dollars U.S.) a month plus bills, it seemed a bargain for four bedrooms with a large garden and small servant quarters. The reason the rent was comparatively low was due to its down-town location. Most Americans preferred clustering together above the Tehran American Club in the hilly northern suburbs, and practically all foreigners took houses somewhere in the foothills—Shemiran or Tajrish—to get above the city's pollution.

The ad had been in the paper one day; it took me five minutes to know that I wanted it, but when he mentioned that the domestics living on the premises could either stay or go as I wished, my decision was made.

While it was true there had been many modern improvements to homes and general living conditions since I first lived in Tehran, I had no doubt as to the value of a good housekeeper and cook, particularly as I was now a single parent with two children and a career to manage.

She had been hovering about, appearing suddenly from terrace-side when hearing our voices and had little to say. She watched me ever so closely and seemed extremely pleased when I spoke Farsi with her and told her I had two children. That I had been married to an Iranian and could communicate with her diminished my foreignness and her evident anxiety. Her name was Soghrah.

She had a wonderfully amiable look to her florid, full face, so beloved of photographers framing cheerful peasants in the countryside. It was that certain, kind, sparkling-eyed look of trust and innocence which she had not lost despite her many years in the harsh, cynical capital. It was a face not often to be seen.

～

My new landlord had offered Soghrah to me as he had his property, but she seemed eager to participate in the decision, so I had asked if she would like to stay on and work for me.

Well, yes, she would, she said, but she would have to discuss it with her husband and son and then we could see whether I liked her work and still wanted her.

Years later, after the revolution had begun and the children were off to England and the two of us would sit about consoling one another in the darkness of curfew hours, she would tell me how, in fact, it had been she who had to see whether she would accept me or not.

"If I hadn't liked you," she said, taking my hand in hers, "I wouldn't have stayed a minute! We don't need the money, you know, and it wouldn't have mattered how much you paid me. If I didn't like you, I wouldn't work for you."

They lived in a tiny one-room brick hut in the garden: Soghrah, the old man—*Hadji Agha* he was called, for he had made the *hadj*, or pilgrimage, and their children. He was the youngest son of six children, Ramazud. Adjoining the living area was a storeroom and adjoining that, jammed against the back garden wall, was their toilet. They went to the public *hamum* (bathhouse) weekly for bathing.

Now I realize it was nothing short of a miracle that kept Soghrah in our household, as we managed to offend frequently so many of her traditional and religious beliefs. One such violation occurred when my favorite summer pastime became known: sunbathing in a bikini.

In retrospect, we foreigners, as well as many of the Western-educated Iranians, were incredibly insensitive to ages-old customs and mores. All this was, however, encouraged by the Shah and his court and their behavior.

Soghrah's solution to my indecency each weekend was one befitting a diplomat. Either the entire family would leave the premises during the hours I chose to expose myself, attending to their weekly house calls on friends and relatives, or out came the sheets.

Lying smothered in cocoa butter and coconut oil, I heard the outer doorbell ringing, followed by a frantic scrambling through the garden and then I saw Soghrah whipping out a bedsheet, arms stretched as far as they would go to either side of me, as she swooped and flapped around me in a protective arch like one of Persia's mythical half-human, winged creatures of yore. The old man shuffled out quickly and escorted his eldest son, Hossein, inside the hut.

"Soghrah, what are you doing?" I asked, to which she intoned: "I am shielding you from the insult of their eyes, *Khanum* (madam). You must understand, Iranian men are lascivious!"

It did not occur to me then to think that to the truly devout I was the insult. I cannot say that we (foreigners as well as middle-to-upper class Iranians) were oblivious to the feelings and beliefs, the traditions of the masses; we simply disregarded them. A breach of etiquette for which the entire world would pay.

TEHRAN, 1977

We clustered from one house to another, in a continuous round robin of feasting and drinking and vaporous intrigues of the heart, my new community, the community of expatriates.

Entertainment, even in the capital, was scarce by Western standards: an occasional fairly new movie from Europe or the States, but most were a decade old. Back in the sixties I had seen *Dr. Zhivago* the first time in Farsi; more were given subtitles by the seventies or were available in their original language. Nearby ski slopes were a wonderful weekend escape for the sports-minded, or just for lolling on a sun deck and visiting. Seeing and being seen.

Scattered nightclubs with dance bands and good food, a few more with international vaudeville-style shows of sword-swallowers and dancing girls brought some relief.

The expatriate grows weary; he imports what morsels and articles he can and shares; creates his own ambience. Tonight Claude's; tomorrow, Patrick's; Thursdays, Rheingold's; and Friday the Arab ambassador's residence for a poolside party celebrating . . . who knows? There was always something to celebrate in Tehran. The group would swell and thin as they came and went over the years. Some stayed briefly; others, like Carlucci, would never leave.

All suffer periodic bouts of homesickness. Homesickness for a lifestyle no longer accessible, whether they come from Paris, France or Paris, Texas: a certain way of having a table set; a particular delicacy or common food one had grown inordinately fond of without knowing it; manicured lawns with white picket fences or *maitre d's* who can call one by name and lead one to a favorite corner.

Feelings toward the choice of exile are as the shifting sands. For fleeting moments love of adventure and the often royal treatment the Third World provides them with prevail over a thinly-disguised disgust, and the condescension of the *conquistador*.

"Nothing works." It is the refrain of the expatriate. The telephones were splendid for making a call to London or New York but we couldn't call across town without at least five attempts. Central air and heat was on the blink, elevators stood without moving or became lodged between floors, electricity went off all over town in patches, daily. Refrigerators clogged and stoves threatened to explode. Traffic was indescribable.

Women did not drive, not out of any religious taboos (as is the case in many places in the Muslim world), but out of fear for their lives. Brawls in the midst of afternoon rush hours over someone cutting in front of another were common enough to cause any big stir.

One of my cab drivers ran a man on a bicycle down once only to become so enraged at him he withdrew a knife from the glove compartment and threatened to finish him off on the spot for being so stupid as to ride in his path. I like to think that my entreaties were what saved the poor peddler's life.

TEHRAN, FALL 1978

Incongruous headlines vie for readers' attention: "Isfahan under martial law after bloody riots;" "People and Places: The return of Shahyar Abdo to Tehran . . . has caused quite a stir amongst the young female population we understand. He is, of course, one of Iran's most eligible bachelors. . . ." That was August; it's November, and today's papers tell us what we've already heard by word of mouth: "Mobs run wild. Bloody riots erupt after troops open fire at Tehran University."

My new job at Farahabad Racecourse at least takes me out of the center of town where most of the rioting occurs. Overlooking the racecourse from the private club set aside for members only, we toasted the opening in June. By August, we closed. Reopening sporadically, and when the authorities advise us we may do so without being bombed or otherwise targeted, we hardly know from week to week if the races witll be held.

The forty-five-million dollar racetrack with stables housing thoroughbreds shipped in from Australia, New Zealand, and England, got off to a roaring start, with some eight to ten thousand attending opening day. We had expected no more than thirty-five hundred, with all the unrest and rising Islamic fervor so in evidence.

As public relations and advertising director for the Tehran Racing Company, with the responsibility to get out the crowd, I felt the turnout was gratifying. Downstairs in the public enclosure, women in long veils queued alongside those dressed in high-heeled, short-skirted fashion and their husbands and friends, to place their bets.

Upstairs in the club, imported scotch and soda fizzed while still larger bets were placed, imported models modeled imported *haute couture*, and small syndicates formed to buy the imported twenty-five-thousand dollar racehorses. Many were bought by individuals.

As weeks pass and demonstrations become increasingly violent, authorities caution us to keep a lower profile, so I've cut back on the advertising. We're leaving it up to the columnists and sportswriters to keep us in the news.

Members gather early on Fridays (the Muslim Sunday) for lavish luncheons catered from the Intercontinental Hotel downtown, known for its excellent cuisine.

September 7th would become known as "Black Friday."

We knew that demonstrations were planned that day but stubbornly pressed forward. The city was unusually quiet and streets relatively empty as club manager Nina Akhavan and I rode to the track.

The day's lunch offering was spectacular, with every sort of edible spread out before us. No more than a half-dozen members showed up by one o'clock. We picked at the buffet and strolled about the vacant clubroom trying to be gay and rushed to the balcony when someone called to us, "You can hear the gunfire now! Something's going on." We stood sipping our drinks and listened, watching the by-now familiar spirals of smoke dotting the horizon.

Our French chef from the hotel was still nowhere to be seen, though a few more members came straggling in chattering with rumors of something dreadful. When the chef finally arrived, white-faced, he described the massacre of Jaleh Circle. His chauffeur had driven headlong into the midst of it, arriving at the circle just as soldiers descended and opened fire on demonstrators. (We later learned of the predawn radio broadcast announcing a ban on demonstrations that day; virtually no one heard it at the hour it ran.)

Estimates of casualties, as always, varied radically. A CBS cameraman who was at the scene told me he was certain no less than five hundred had died that day; the government figure was first twenty-nine, and the final figure was ninety-six.

A bomb blasted an American company's van, killing the American advisors in it; I took the children out of Tehran American School and put them in boarding school in England. I'm making plans for my own departure in order to leave before the next significant mourning period that falls in December. Riots almost always break out at those times; then more are killed, setting off another cycle of mourning.

"You're an alarmist," my Iranian friends tell me. "Everything will be over in six months and you'll just turn around and come back. We've been through all this before."

Banks and liquor stores burn all over town, and cinemas. Banks because they represent the Western usurer (usury, or interest, is forbidden in Islam); liquor stores because Islam forbids drinking alcohol; cinemas because they show the decadent foreign films, corrupting Islamic youth.

We've begun to hold very limited races on weekends. The crowds have thinned. Guards are posted.

Tehran, November 1978, The Last Party

"Saltanatabad to Farmanieh . . . left to police station on left-hand side, one more block to Italian School on right side just past turn—right on Mehrmandust three *koochehs* on left turn into 3rd *Dorigar* (at curve) white wall, three door garage, second house on left #6, third button from bottom."

These directions were found years later, scribbled in the back of my battered old address book; names and notations a time machine that took me back to that night, our last big party before the expatriates began the exodus.

Directions in Tehran were always interesting. It took a page to get them all down for one's first visit anywhere. Narrow, meandering *koochehs* (alleys, usually unpaved) and avenues ten kilometers long that changed names at four different junctions, unmarked dead ends, and a numbering system to boggle the mind of any unsuspecting tourist who thought that numbers run in sequence, gave one a sense of embarking on a treasure hunt.

Actually, the numbers were in sequence. It's just that the sequence had been changed so many times; somehow, the old numbers were not always erased.

Guests never arrived before nine in Tehran, but since curfew had been set at eight-thirty p.m., everyone rushed to this, Mustafa's going-away party, knowing they were going to spend the night at their host's. Once the troops and gendarmerie were out, no one ventured about before dawn.

(Memories of a heavy iron gate as it slammed shut each night on the stroke of eight-thirty; stores and shops shut down, their metal roll-up doors clanging down; streets deserted, and nightly blackouts swooping across whole sections of town. The silence broken only by occasional crackling of gunfire; someone shouting an order; a curfew-breaker's feet on the pavement as he ran for cover.)

The last guest came scurrying into the foyer ten minutes to curfew. The international crowd of expatriates was more subdued than in the past.

"Remember last year's New Year's party at Djamshid's?" Everyone agreed it had been wonderful. That was the New Year's Eve President Carter came to express to the world his full and undying support of the Shah.

We had all cringed at the gesture. It was not long after that we began to know. Reality was hard in coming, but many sensed the die was cast by spring after destructive rioting in the northern city of Tabriz. Women began to discuss the possible wisdom of wearing headscarves to work.

The party was a sparkling polyglot of Frenchmen, Arabs, British, Egyptians, Germans, Iranians; such gatherings knew no barriers to nationality; shared pleasures created a sense of family.

Mustafa and his new bride were headed for Egypt; Hossein and Nazali would be off to Canada; Herbert was returning to Hamburg; Michel to Paris; and James, well, he thought he might like to cover Alexandria next—anything but going back to England, thank you.

Everyone looked lovely, had outdone themselves. They knew it was not just Mustafa's farewell they were saying.

Set high in Farmanieh, the posh home—perched on a ridge—overlooked the city. Everyone always said Tehran was beautiful—at night. And looking down on it that clear, cold, winter's night, it seemed to have outdone itself, too.

There were no blackouts; its light, spreading over twenty-five kilometers in all directions, twinkled and winked at guests as they danced past the broad expanse of glass terrace-side.

By sunrise, Michel was making blintzes, David was sizzling the bacon, and half the guests were dozing. As all awake sat around the dining table with thick, black coffee and fortified themselves for departure and another uncertain day, sounds of life returned slowly to the streets and *koochehs* below.

"*Shalvar . . . shalvarrrr . . . shalvariii. . . .*" The vendor's melodious voice carried over the high walls and into our special little world. As did the *muezzin*'s from the minaret.

November 1978, Farewell

Iranian frugality wasted nothing. Soghrah was no exception, stunned the first time I chastised her for chopping up the spinach stems and tossing them in with the leaves, and told her to discard them. (She set them aside and added them to their own stew mixture that evening.)

Once the season for tomatoes drew to a close and the soft, overripe fruit filled stalls, it was bought by the basketfuls and her daughters would all come over to visit and spend the day mashing it into wonderful thick paste, the like of which I have yet to discover in a can.

A wife's worth was often judged by onlookers by the number of gold bangles she wore, and nearly forty years of wedlock had endeared Soghrah to *Hadji Agha* to the tune of some ten or more wide gold bracelets she never removed, not even for scrubbing floors.

After a time with me I bought her some gold hoop earrings, to signify her worth to me—which was truly greater than I could afford to demonstrate—but her ears became infected immediately from whatever primitive method she used for piercing and the hoops were replaced with ugly coarse string.

She tucked the hoops away somewhere and promised some day she would wear them for a grand occasion. I often wonder now if she has ever enjoyed that occasion.

Within the confines of our high walls she wore typical provincial garb: long-sleeved shirts or sweaters usually of bright hue, long cotton skirts generally festooned with floral print, over thick, dark stockings, cheap plastic slippers, and a head-covering of indescribable wrappings. Outside, she never stepped two feet without her *chador*.

My attachment to Soghrah grew quickly and took firm hold. In fact, I can't contemplate her rosy-cheeked face, standing in the garden with the family, smiling for one last picture, without feeling a rush of warmth and some sadness.

She was cheerful most of the time, and always willing to learn new things. We traded many secrets of our respective culinary arts, but the one thing she could never conquer was ironing. Clothing so bothersome as to require pressing back into shape shouldn't be worn.

When only a few days remained before my departure, the two of us drove down to the big main bazaar in the far south end of Tehran to shop for some last minute items I wanted to ship or take with me.

Often the scene of bloody riots and demonstrations, the bazaar had been quiet recently, but nevertheless, I decided to wear a headscarf as a precaution.

Though my contract would not be up for another two years, I was breaking it; the handwriting on the wall was too clear.

The bazaar trip was nostalgic because I always enjoyed my visits there, and thought how little changed it was from the first time I had seen it some fifteen years before, and how this would probably be the last.

Row on row of gold glitters along the gold bazaar; Western jewelry shops seem meager by comparison. Artisans painstakingly work in intricate designs, weaving fantasies in arabesque on brass and copperware. Peddlers push their carts through the narrow passageways, dimly lit beneath aged, domed ceilings; donkeys bray and somewhere a radio plays a yodeling Persian love song, almost always of broken hearts.

Goods are separated into certain passageways or sections, and as you go round a corner you may be faced with brilliant swatches of fabric in the fabric bazaar or just as suddenly find yourself surrounded by auto parts and tools.

On my last trip there we went for spices I could not find in the States or would find very dear. It's the easiest of areas to locate, as one's nose leads the way. Bay leaves and teas, cinnamon and allspice, cloves, za'faran, mint, sumac; a thousand and one scents to draw one nearer.

Sensing my nervousness and tension one night long before, Soghrah had brought in from her cupboard a dried flower for a tea she promised would bring relief for jangled nerves. It was a dark, royal purple leaf she mixed with rock sugar and dried limes. When I returned to the States I found it had become popular in health-food restaurants: hibiscus. But not knowing then when I might come across it again, I sacked a bagful to carry home with me.

Dried limes, hard and black, were another must, as they are difficult to come by away from Iran's hot, arid climate where they're quickly dried, and are used in so many favorite Iranian dishes. We wrapped up our shopping tour in the gift section and headed home just as the merchants began rolling down their tin doors for the night.

The early evening sunset was a jeweler's inspiration—the sun a heavy gold coin hanging against a lapis lazuli sky—as we moved out into the streets to the parked car, the same streets that would in a few days be teeming with angry, hate-filled slogans and the visage of the exiled ayatollah.

As the time drew near for me to leave, Soghrah and I inclined to avoid one another, lest we become tearful throughout the day. She had been the helpmate I needed, a mother figure and friend, and we would not see each other again.

She ordered her son the taxi driver to come and fetch me in the early morning hours for the drive to the airport; it was a cold, but dry, November dawning just before Ashura, Shi'a Islams's darkest mourning period.

Kalighat

To Mercy, Pity, Peace and Love,
All pray in their distress:
And to these virtues of delight
Return their thankfulness.

For Mercy has a human heart
Pity, a human face:
And Love, the human form divine,
And Peace, the human dress.

WILLIAM BLAKE
Songs of Innocence

K ALIGHAT, the Home for the Dying Destitute, was the toughest assignment in the convent, reputedly reserved for the mature. I had kept asking Sister Ruby for it until I got it; I was greedy for challenge. The place glowed in the light of literature. It had been written about, repeatedly. I had read the poetic accounts of Malcolm Muggeridge, Desmond Doig, and Edward Le Joly; I *had* to work there.

In 1952, Mother Teresa conceived the notion that the *dharmasala*, the dormitory for pilgrims to Calcutta's famous Kali temple, would make an ideal Home for the Dying Destitute. The municipality of Calcutta refused to turn over a portion of a famous Hindu pilgrimage site (after which Calcutta is named) to an obscure group of Christian nuns. Undaunted, Mother Teresa and her sisters accompanied by Father Henry, their chaplain, and lay Catholics marched through Calcutta's streets from six to nine p.m. They chanted the rosary and novenas, praying to be permitted to take in dying homeless people from the streets and nurse them in the dormitory of the Kali temple. The publicity worked in their favor. (Mother has a supernatural explanation, of course.) A wing of Kalighat, the temple of Kali, a devouring, destructive goddess, was handed over to Mother Teresa. She rechristened it *Nirmal Hriday* (The Immaculate Heart) in honor of Mary, conceived without sin. In the temple, Kali-worship continues, goats sacrificed daily amid chanting and singing.

In Hindu iconography, Kali, the Black One, is a hideous, black-faced hag, smeared with blood, her teeth bared and mocking tongue protruding. She is naked except for her ornaments—a garland of skulls and a girdle of severed heads. Her four hands brandish a sword, a shield, a severed head, and a strangling noose; her symbol is the ill-omened left-hand swastika. Until the nineteenth century, the "Thugs," a religious organization that murdered and robbed in the service of Kali, made ritual sacrifices of their victims at this temple. A male child was sacrificed every Friday evening.

The head priest of Kalighat had opposed the occupation of his temple by these Christian nuns. Groups of angry Hindu youngsters threatened Mother Teresa's Missionaries of Charity. They burst in and broke furniture, to the terror of the patients. The head priest—supposed to be a celibate *Brahmachari*—had a son he did not acknowledge, the story goes. That son, dying of tuberculosis at twenty-four, sat begging outside the Kali Temple, coughing blood, a dread shadow, scrupulously avoided. Looking out from the temple window, the priest saw the sisters lift his son onto a makeshift stretcher and carry him into their section of the temple. "How can they touch him, or stand to be near him?" he said. "These Missionaries of Charity must be genuinely good, not Christian fanatics." He stopped opposing them. The sisters retained their wing of Kalighat which is now Mother Teresa's best-known home, almost as famous as the Kali Temple.

~

We entered the quietness of Kalighat after a long jeep trip through Calcutta's streets raucous with the high-decibel blare of radios with film songs barreling from megaphones, the shouting and incessant horns. We recited the rosary above the din around the jeep as the rule decreed we should, no matter how unpropitious our surroundings. Our voices growing hoarse and our throats parched, we trolled through the fifteen "mysteries" of the life of Christ: *Joyful*—The Annunciation, The Visitation, The Nativity, The Presentation of Jesus at the Temple; *Sorrowful*— The Agony in the Garden, The Scourging at the Pillar, The Crowning with Thorns, The Carrying of the Cross, the Crucifixion; and *Glorious*—The Resurrection, the Ascension, The Descent of the Holy Spirit, The Assumption, the Coronation of Mary as Queen of Heaven.

This chanting was meant to be a barricade against distraction and doubt. Just as well perhaps. While we hurtled through the angry honking of buses and cars, the cackle of the red rubber horns on the three-wheeled autos called "bone-shakers" and snaked amid stray dogs I sometimes saw hit (willfully? out of unfathomable malice?) it was not easy to clasp simple verities: There is a God, that God loves me, as he loves every human on this crazy street. It was easier to believe that God had hurled the world into motion and then absconded, a notion I had heard denounced from the pulpit as atheistical absurdity.

Hail Mary, full of grace; the Lord is with you. Blessed are you among women, and blessed is the fruit of your womb, Jesus, we chanted as our jeep swerved through street children, trams, lorries, scooters, and dangerously lurching buses with youths leeching onto windows, railings, and roof. I usually kept my eyes closed. To open them meant to contemplate the possibility, no, the probability, that our driver would collide with rickshaws dragged by scrawny men who looked tubercular and crammed with housewives and their purchases; hit a sacred cow, crush a child, and so cause an ugly communal riot for us to sort out. I remembered the time my father had to bail out a Jesuit professor, his colleague, who was nearly lynched for hitting a poor Hindu boy with his posh car.

~

Entering Kalighat is akin to entering a city church—or, for that matter, our chapel at Mother House in the center of Calcutta. You are stunned into stillness, into a guilty awareness of your racing pulse and distracted mind. The silence shrouds you until you are aware that it is not silence, not really: there is the rustle of supplicants, rosary beads rattle, bowed heads breathe. So, in Kalighat, after your jangled spirit laps up apparent silence, you hear soft sounds—low moaning, a tubercular cough, patients tossing in pain and restlessness.

Still, Kalighat felt like holy ground. I often sensed the presence of God in the dimness and hush of that place. *Bhogobaan ekane acche,* Mother Teresa whispers in Bengali as she goes from bed to bed: *God is here.* Her creased face looked sad and sweet. This is *Bhogobaan ki badi,* God's house, the sisters tell new arrivals, believing that Kalighat is sanctified in its very stones by the thousands who have died peaceful deaths there. Perhaps the light created this aura. The light spilled from high windows through a filigreed lattice, spilled into the dim room with a stippled radiance that made working there epiphanic, an annunciation.

In this place Malcolm Muggeridge, curmudgeonly Catholic convert, experienced what he calls "the first authentic photographic miracle" as he filmed a BBC documentary on Mother Teresa in 1969. The cameraman insisted that filming was impossible inside Kalighat—dimly lit by small windows high in the walls—but reluctantly tried it. In the processed film, the part taken inside was bathed in "a soft, exceptionally lovely light," whereas the rest, taken in the outside courtyard as an insurance, was dim and confused. Muggeridge writes: "I am absolutely convinced that this technically unaccountable light is Newman's 'Kindly Light.' The love in Kalighat is luminous like the halos artists have seen and made visible around the heads of saints. It is not at all surprising that this exquisite luminosity should register on a photographic film."

Perhaps Kalighat had that sense of being holy ground because it was an ancient Hindu pilgrimage site. I wondered whether the devotion of generations of Hindus, no less than Catholics, had hallowed the ground. Surely, I reasoned, all kinds of God-hunger are acceptable to Christ who chose as his symbols bread and wine, who offered his flesh to eat, his blood to drink. Perhaps what happens in a pilgrimage spot is not that God descends to earth in a shower of radiance and the earth ever after exudes his fragrance. Perhaps it is we who make spots of earth sacred when we bring our weary spirits, our thwarted hopes, the whole human freight of grief, and pray—our eyes grown wide and trusting; our being, a concentrated yearning. Perhaps that yearning—which is a glimpse of better things— makes that spot sacred and lingers in the earth and air and water so that future pilgrims say, "God is here."

~

On our way to work, we frequently picked people off the pavements where they lay dying and transported them to Kalighat to die, in Mother Teresa's phrase, "within sight of a kind face." "Stop," we cried to the driver, who then helped us carry them into the jeep. (Occasionally we picked up a drunk who cursed us on his return to consciousness.) Most people we picked up were as emaciated as famine victims; they lay on the pavements, a feeble hand outstretched for alms. And yet there was no famine in Calcutta; our prime minister protested that nobody, simply nobody, dies of starvation in India.

These people had probably worked all their lives. But in a land where wages are so exploitative and low that families can go hungry after ten hours of work, how can an illiterate worker save? The poor have no insurance; there is no social security. "Naked they came into the world, naked they depart." Many end their lives destitute on Calcutta's streets. They waste away as they grow too old, weak, or sick to scavenge for themselves or even root for food in the open garbage dumps.

For these people who are kicked aside, cursed and ignored, Kalighat is an inexplicable miracle, a last-minute respite, a stepping into grace. In her speeches, Mother loves to quote the dying man she brought to Kalighat from the streets of Calcutta— "All my life I have lived like a dog, but now I die like an angel"—which was, perhaps, just what he said, or, perhaps, a composite of many experiences.

～

Kalighat consists of two L-shaped wards, accommodating about sixty men and women, rows of low cots, snuggled even into every cranny. The Missionary Brothers of Charity, the male branch of the order founded by Brother Andrew, an energetic and down-to-earth Australian ex-Jesuit, help out in the male ward; they sponge patients, change soiled clothes, hack off elongated and hardened toenails. I saw them as I entered the male ward to dispense medication—sweet, serious, humble and hardworking men. Perhaps I perceived them in cliches since I never actually talked to them. A postulant hobnobbing with men would not have been approved of. We mainly worked in the female ward, an oblong room bathed in dim light from the ornate windows filigreed in an esoteric Hindu pattern whose symbolism I did not understand.

Iris, a tubercular Anglo-Indian patient, was Kalighat's presiding Fury. She hobbled all over the ward on her walking stick which she thrashed around when enraged. Her puckered brown face was a maze of hate-lines, and as she limped, she cursed: "Those bloody Muddses, I hate those swine, they . . ." "What's the matter, Iris?" people asked, mocking her—for every one, of course, knew her story by heart and was fed up of it. And as if it were new every morning, she'd repeat her tale of the Muddses, her distant relatives, these people she had helped who, in her old age, assaulted her, evicted her from her house, and pushed her down the stairs so that she broke her leg.

"Those bloody Muddses," she muttered, her rosary of hate. She was fond of me and would stroke me, telling me that I was nice, her smile surprisingly sweet. Every one had to be very good to me when Iris was around, or she would brandish her stick at them, reprimanding, "No, this is a *nice* sister." Poor Iris, balladeer of old grievances, anger always at boiling point for old wrongs. Her grudges had driven her crazy, cruel Erinyes devastating her long past the initial injury. I often talked to her, asking about her childhood in pre-Independence India, to try to divert her mind from the injustices in which it was stuck to happier memories. I realized how wise Mother Teresa was when she admonished, "Forgive. Never allow yourself to become bitter. Bitterness is like cancer; it feeds on itself. It grows and grows."

～

I tried to feed a round-faced old lady, too weak to feed herself. She could barely swallow her rice. She kept pushing away my hand with the next spoonful. I relaxed; I could see that I would be sitting on the edge of her bed for a long time. So while I tried to feed her, we talked. Her son had deposited her on the streets from where the sisters had eventually picked her up. "I haven't seen my four sons for years," she cried, her meal still uneaten.

I gave up on the rice and fed her the mango. She loved that. She fixed her eyes on the diminishing fruit, then asked for more. There was no more. So I folded the skin in two and drew it between her lips, again and again, until she had sucked the last drops of juice. Suddenly her eyes lit up with love. They streamed. She caught me, pulled me to her, and rocked me in an embrace, crying, "Ma. Ma. Ma," her mind reverting to memories of childhood, her face grown baby sweet.

I hugged her back, not even trying to remember if she was tubercular, forgetting my mask and *Mycobacterium tuberculosis* spread by the respiratory route. During that insomniac night, I thought of her. The next evening, I sneaked out a mango from the convent kitchen and concealed it in my saree. I went straight to her bed. It was covered with a white sheet. She had died in the night.

〜

Death was a constant in Kalighat, that Home in the temple of the goddess of death. Only the ostensibly dying were admitted. About half recovered with rest, medication, and nourishing food. For the rest, this was the end. When we entered the ward, stark white sheets, the color of mourning in India, covered the beds of those who had died the previous night. In the face of death, its inevitability, how trivial much of life seemed. "Teach us to number our days," the Psalmist cried, "that we may apply our hearts unto wisdom." I realized why the novice-mistresses preached detachment to us. *Guard your heart*, I admonished myself, chary of emotional involvement with one who might soon be a corpse in the morgue or burnt to ashes on the shore of the River Ganges.

In a place like Kalighat, perspective is everything. My parents, on their monthly visits, grumbled that it was a grim place, daunting and unpleasant—and so it is until its strange charm, its eerie radiance, works on you. I loved Kalighat for its tiny miracles. An old, almost bald woman with a wicked, shriveled face occupied a bed in a corner. Everyone avoided her: she was nasty. When she could sit up, she'd curse all within earshot. She spat gobs of yellow phlegm all over the floor, perversely ignoring her spittoon. Once, as I tried to feed her, she lost her temper and slapped me, sending my glasses flying across the ward.

Dealing with her was not a pleasure. So other patients had often eaten their dinners and fallen asleep while she hadn't been brought her tray of gruel and boiled vegetables. One evening, chiding myself for my fastidiousness, I braced myself and took her tray to her. As I approached, she smiled, and her face briefly became numinous. It glowed. No one had ever seen her smile. I hugged the memory to myself as a shaft of grace, a cryptic divine sign—though perhaps it was a trick of the light. But I remembered Gerard Manley Hopkins, my favorite poet:

> . . . *Christ plays in ten thousand places,*
> *Lovely in limbs, and lovely in eyes not his*
> *To the Father through the features of men's faces.*

〜

Most patients in Kalighat, too old or weak to walk, crept around the ward or to the bathroom while squatting on their haunches, slowly moving one tired leg after the other. Since their diseases were highly infectious—cholera, typhoid, and, especially, tuberculosis—we had to be vigilant. Sister Luke, the stern-faced nurse from Mauritius who ran Kalighat, ordered us to use masks all the time that we were in the ward. These we sewed ourselves, a double strip of thick cotton cloth, covering the nose and mouth. I often disobeyed orders and dispensed with my mask, partly because it was stifling with my nose and mouth covered, and partly because my smile helped in this difficult work with difficult people. (Months later at home, when I grew too weak to get out of bed, and coughed blood, dread symptom, and X-rays revealed a shadow on the lungs, indication of TB, I looked back on those days of idiotic, uncalled-for faith with bemusement. I then had a sense of inviolability, common to children and puppies, a half-conscious sense that Providence would protect the simplehearted—and the foolish.)

The actual work dispelled vestigial illusions of the glamour of being a "Flit on, cheering angel" Florence Nightingale of light and mercy. It was "hands-on," occasionally repellent. I often forced myself through the chores by sheer willpower. I reminded myself that I had decided to imitate Christ, and to be a saint in the tradition of Francis, Damien, Schweitzer, and Dooley as I fought nausea and changed sheets fouled by the "rice water" stools of cholera patients, the blood and mucus filled feces of those with dysentery.

Why do you do it? foreign volunteers asked. No one assigned me this chore. (On the contrary, as one of the better-educated sisters, I was given the more "prestigious" jobs which required some expertise: to give the patients their daily medication and injections, to set up and administer an intravenous drip when a patient was admitted delirious with typhoid, or with the cold, withered skin, sunken eyes, and icy hands of the cholera victim.) No, I chose. I was struck by the paradigm of Christ, "who, though he was rich, yet he became poor." Born amid a stable's dung, as literally as we cleaned feces; homeless during his ministry; dying naked on the cross. *Come follow me*. "One must go as low down as possible to find God," I reasoned with eighteen-year-old intensity. And what did I equate "God" with? Joy. Certainty. Peace.

"Oh the mind, mind has mountains." The romance of the spiritual life, its Pilgrim's Progress through internal hills and valleys, shed a gleam on everyday chores—washing clothes or windows, or scrubbing the stainless steel plates left pyramided on the courtyard floor after the patients' evening meal. We hoydenishly hoisted up our sarees (a rare glimpse of legs) and squatted on our haunches to scrub the endless pile of plates with our scourer, a piece of coconut husk, and home-mixed detergent, ashes and shavings of soap. Western volunteers helped, professing amazement at our primitive methods of washing clothes and dishes. "Mother has been offered dishwashers and washing machines many times and has refused," I'd explain, smugly and self-righteously—repressing my annoyance at her rigidity on the days when I was exhausted.

⁓

I dealt with the new admission who was brought in on a stretcher—a teenager with a prematurely haggard face, her hair an uncombed, matted mass that I could see we'd have to cut off. How to unravel it? When I undressed her for a sponge bath, I saw that her thighs were bloodstained. Her vulva was a raw, feces-encrusted sore. I involuntarily moved back, overcome by the stench. A group of men had slashed her crotch with blades, she said.

"Why did they do that?" I asked, quite ignorant of perversion. I gathered from her faltering reply in Bengali that she had been forced into prostitution, and that there were all sorts. . . .

"How old are you?"

"Eighteen."

She was my age. I stood, staring at the pus, feces, blood, and raw flesh, wondering what to do first, when Sister Luke appeared. She pushed me aside, grimness on her long, serious face. "Go away, child, go away," she growled, as she bent her sinuous body down to the patient. Sister Luke later explained that the girl had venereal disease, something I'd never encountered before.

Sister Luke was good-hearted, but her volatile temper and gruff, no-nonsense manner scared patients, postulants, and volunteers alike. My parents, visiting, were shocked and upset to hear her scream at the patients. Indeed, her behavior was far from the ideal for workers in the Home for the Destitute that Mother Teresa recommends in the Constitution: *Death, sacred to all men, is the final stage of complete development on this earth. Having lived well, we wish for ourselves and for all men to die beautifully. We train ourselves to be extremely kind and gentle in touch of hand, tone of voice, and in our smile so as to make the mercy of God very real and to induce the dying person to turn to God with filial confidence.*

Since she perceived me as responsible, Sister Luke, a trained nurse, entrusted me with deciphering the doctor's scribbled prescriptions, and doling out the evening medication. She put me in charge of giving injections and intravenous drips when I came on duty. In the absence of professionals, we picked up the elements of nursing from one other. I am sometimes appalled, remembering our amateurishness, but then recall that we looked after people we carried in from the streets, whom no one else cared about, and that we did alleviate their pain.

One evening, I balanced a tray of medicine—Chloramphenicol, Ampicillin, Streptomycin, para-aminosalicyclic acid, isoniazid—sorted out in little cups, in one hand as I left the office to begin my rounds. I tripped. Hundreds of pink, white, and parti-colored pills raced over the floor. Sister Luke had locked the medicine cupboard. Terrified to ask her for a fresh dose for the hundred patients, I began to pick the pills off the floor, intending to use them anyway. The colored or unusually shaped pills were easy to separate. I slowed down at the homogenized mass of white pills, a desperate Psyche, hope and guesswork intermingling as I sorted, when Nemesis descended.

"What *are* you doing?" Sister Luke stood over me, her hands on her hips.

I told her.

"You blessed child. You stupid child," she shrieked, throwing the tray into the trash, cups and all, tossing me the keys to get a fresh dose.

Sister Luke had probably sworn freely before she became a nun. Perhaps her favorite swear word had been the Anglo-Indian "bloody." Anyway, she had ingeniously transmuted worldly expletives into heavenly ones. "Get the blessed bedpan to that blessed patient," she'd scream. Sister Luke was admired, almost hero-worshiped, by all who worked in Kalighat, for she was dedicated and unpretentious, so "blessed" became a common expletive for all "Lukies."

For the first few weeks, I scrupulously followed the doctor's charts as I gave the patients their medication. But as the medicine and dosages grew familiar, I began to trust my memory. Teachers and friends had often commented on my "photographic memory," and I was proud of it. I made a point of smiling at Krishna, an emaciated pale-faced teenager with close-cropped hair, as I gave her

her medicine. ("Smile five times a day at people you do not feel like smiling at. Do it for world peace," Mother Teresa said. I'd cheat though, selecting targets whom I liked, at least a little.)

Too frail to sit up, Krishna lay on propped-up pillows, a faint smile on her face, her eyes huge and haunted. She looked classically tubercular, like Severn's portrait of the dying Keats.

One evening, Krishna shivered feverishly, face flushed, eyes streaming. Her forehead burned. Pulling out the thermometer, I read: a hundred and six, the highest I'd recorded.

I went to Sister Luke. "Sister, the girl with TB has a very high temperature."

"Which girl?"

"Krishna."

"Oh Krishna!" She laughed. "You know, Krishna was severely malnourished when she was brought to us. She looked as gaunt as a TB patient. We thought she was going to die. But she is recovering nicely. I think we will be able to discharge her soon, or send her to Prem Dan. You say she is sick?"

Malnutrition! I flushed. Krishna was not sick. She had starved. And I had given her the dosage of Isoniazid for a severely tubercular patient. I had been cautioned never to dispense these pills carelessly.

"Krishna is feverish," I mumbled, and slunk away, stunned, too cowardly to tell her what I'd done. *If I have to confess, I will, but please, oh God, oh God, heal her.*

A Calcutta volunteer doctor was at work. I feigned jocularity. "So Doctor, what happens if you take drugs for TB when you don't have TB?"

"You want to kill yourself, Sister? You could pop off. That's potent stuff."

I had guessed that already; why did I ask? Miserable, remorseful about my hubris, I dashed to Krishna's bedside with paracetamol for her fever and laid my hands on the surprised girl's head. "Now Krishna, listen. You are not feeling well, right? I'm going to pray for you. Right now." I prayed desperately, imploring for her life.

No result. I had other duties, but every few minutes, I stole to Krishna's bedside, praying for her, for a miracle. Gradually Krishna's fever subsided, her temperature returned to normal, though she was very weak.

I felt close to Krishna after all this. The severely malnourished girl had grown too weak to walk. And since she lay all day on her jute-strung cot, her legs atrophied. As she grew stronger, I helped her to walk again, walking beside her, her arms around my shoulders, or walking in front of her, holding her hands, until she regained balance and confidence and strength.

Krishna walked, shakily but unaided, before I left Mother Teresa's congregation. I saw her discharged, another Lazarus restored, another woman returned to Calcutta's Darwinian struggle for survival, but with an ounce of hope. One drop removed from the ocean of misery—but the ocean would be greater were it there.

A Playwright in India

APRIL 30TH

I ARRIVE in Bombay at two in the morning. I ask a little Punjabi girl on the plane if I'll see an elephant right away. She shrugs, saying "acha" with a slight tilt of her head.

A car meets me at the airport and takes me down roads of swaying palms and Casuarina trees. Heat is over the city like a moist cloth. A calf, skinny and spotted with his own dung, strays into our path and the car swerves as a matter of course. At the hotel, my room overlooks the sea. But this is the Arabian Sea, one so steeped in mythical lore that it seems unreal. All waters—rivers, streams, the sea—are sacred in India, being symbolically one, the Holy River Ganges. When dying, an Indian must have at least a drop of Ganges. I try to imagine Iowans desperate for a drop of Iowa water on their deathbed.

My hotel is Indian. A small, brass bowl filled with rose petals rests on the dressing table next to a basket of mangoes. Candles are discreetly placed in table drawers for when the lights will sooner or later go out.

Hindus give the world an elephant to support it, but they make the elephant stand upon a tortoise. And indeed, everything goes slowly: Wait for the elevator, wait for dinner, wait at the pharmacy, wait for phone connections.

MAY 1ST

I go to the NCP (National Center for Performing Arts) to see the set and meet the cast. There is a security check to get into the theatre. My play is being performed in the Tatta Theatre, an experimental space, a black box with three hundred seats. It could easily be an off-Broadway house. I meet my actors. Harsh Nayyar, of course, was in the New York production. But the others are new faces: Shernaz Patel is a new Indira Gandhi, Yasmin Palsetia a new Kamala. Everyone is energetic and excited. We send out for "Bombay Hamburgers"—except these burgers come in little square boxes with curious Sanskrit lettering on the lid. And they're no cousins of the McDonald sandwich; some are stuffed with vegetarian filling, some have meat—grainy and coarse.

MAY 2ND

We will have four performances of my play here at the Tatta Theatre before moving it to Delhi. Today is the Bombay opening, and I stand nervously in the lobby and watch the people come in: A woman in a gold-brocaded sari, an elderly man in a khaki shirt and blood-red *dhoti*, young girls with anklets jingling and flowers in their hair, a grandmother carrying a muslin purse and wearing gold embroidered shoes, a pious man, the mark of Vishnu freshly and neatly painted on his forehead. There are no Westerners in the audience. Three bells are rung at five-minute intervals. After the third bell, the lights go down. I hover by the back row. How will the Indian audiences react?

Suddenly, Indira is heard, her real voice on a recording opens the play. A spot singles out Nehru's desk in Naini Prison. I am suddenly in awe at my own arrogance in writing about an Indian dynasty.

The theatre is very quiet. I can't tell how the audience is liking it. Someone coughs, and I fear the worst (a cough of contempt?) Then Nehru's mother says Indira should have been a boy. The audience laughs. Now I feel they're with me. Still, I can't relax. Finally, lights down. Quiet. Generally, there is no curtain call in India. But because I am an American playwright, my actors come out to take the Namaste (hands folded with bowed heads). There is applause. Later a woman stops me in the lobby to say she wants to come back and see the play with her daughter, a comment I am to hear often.

May 4th

The play is going well. A full house. I have a press meeting after the matinee. In Bombay, theatre is an event. Every magazine and newspaper is present.

I go shopping in the late afternoon. I pass men fixing betel leaf cones, women dusting the steps of a sweets shop with dirty rags. Street photographers display their smiling victims on a sandwich board. An old astrologer with his cards carefully placed before him on a blanket tugs at my skirt. A Muhammedan barber smiles at me, his razor and scissors on a small crate, his profession clearly written in red Hindustani letters. Everywhere are leather handbags, jeweled elephants, colorful silks, Tibetan brassware, bracelets of agate. Vendors hawk their wares with slow natural movements, stepping calmly over stagnant drains, rotten grain, fresh cow dung and urine. Sometimes I can walk for hours and nobody bothers me; other times, I am persistently followed until I have a dragon's tail of beggars following me. I am warned not to give money or I will be mobbed and suffocated. To escape, I hail a rickshaw; the old driver sweats in the sun as he pedals to keep me and the rickshaw from bouncing out of control. His skin is like dried banana peels.

May 8th

Early morning and we're off to Delhi for ten performances. Early mornings are precious in India, a freshness before the heat. Now it's calm, a kind of caesura, a time of respite. The muezzins give their call from the minaret. Indian gardeners flail the grass with long, flexible bamboos to remove the dew so it won't scorch the grass when the sun is high.

It's an hour and forty minute trip on Air India; I'm made aware that it is an Indian airline because we are served tea, jalebies, cream cakes (Indians love sweets), and a dish of variali (green seeds) for digestion.

We land at the Indira Gandhi International Airport, and the airport's name foretells a good luck omen to me. Traces of cardamon seeds litter the terminal. Outside the entrance, old men lie huddled beneath scraps of rags, sleeping on their *charpoy,* the portable string bed that is so cool in the summer months.

A car is waiting and the actors, director, producer, and myself are driven to the hotel by a man in a turban and a beard; he could be the magi in a Christmas play.

Delhi is the Washington, D.C. of India and the center of the city is imposing and grand, linear and masculine, with all the aura of the grand thirties. There are open, green parkways and red brick, Victorian houses that serve as offices. I recognize every method of transportation from the beginning of civilization to the twentieth century: cars, tongas, yekkas, jeeps, cycles, bamboo cars, donkeys, scooters, rickshaws. Suddenly, I see a billboard five stories high advertising my play, my name under the title a story high. I shout, and the driver stops. I persuade him to drive around the billboard five times.

We arrive at the Maurya Sheraton to find that our stage is a banquet hall. The hotel personnel scurry around frantically to build platforms and line up chairs and hang lights. By the end of the day, the room resembles a theatre. There are over a thousand seats. I am used to having my plays produced off-Broadway with a capacity of two hundred to three hundred seats and I worry that ten performances will not fill up the room. I worry that the acoustics are bad.

May 10th

Since the Sheraton is one of our producers, we are given coupons by them to purchase our food. Our rooms are spacious. And free laundry service—my blouses and skirts will come back washed and ironed and folded like works of art (they will never have it so good again).

The Sheraton has two dogs as their mascots. I meet Bernie and Bertie, St. Bernards, as their trainer, Man Bahadur, walks them through the lobby. It is love at first sight. I romp with the dogs on lounge chairs and sofas. I laugh to learn that the dogs have an air-conditioned room in the hotel. But many people do not find this fact amusing, not here in India where people live in cardboard boxes and mud huts in the one-hundred-twenty-degree heat—places where they say even rats and bugs won't go because there is nothing to eat.

I take the scooter-rickshaw into Old Delhi, pass the Old Fort on which site stood the city of Indraprastha, home of the heroes of the Mahabharata.

Old Delhi makes me use all my senses at the same time. There are smells of powdery jute, raw cotton, fumes of rubber baking in the sun, joss sticks, muglai curries, musty damp pepper, Bengali sweets. Buildings lean toward me, plaster blackening, peeling, sun-scorched and monsooned. I enter a tea shop and the rust on the iron handrailing comes off like pollen in my hands. The wooden shop door opens with a single clear whine on its hinges, serving as a doorbell. I order tea and drink from a battered brass tumbler. Bananas bright as sunflowers hang by their ends over the window like chickens in a butcher shop. Suddenly hungry, I order pancakes; they're served steaming hot with sesame oil, ginger, green chilies, red peppers, shredded onions and coriander leaf. The man who serves me points to a banyan tree near the door and says: "A blessing rests on the shop where falls the shadow of a tree."

I take the scooter-taxi back to the hotel. Hot air rushes in my face. Every time we stop for a traffic light, beggars reach in and pinch me, moaning for rupees. The sound they make is like a chant, an elemental urge, and I soon learn to recognize this whine as a desperate litany.

I watch rehearsal. The actors walk through their blocking. Half of the action cannot be seen from the back of the room. We build up the levels. The lights are focused. Props are set.

MAY 12TH

As a means of good luck, I go out in the early morning and buy a picture of Saraswati, the Hindu goddess of writers and books. There is a heavy scent of incense in the air. I watch a man, bare from the waist up, wash himself by throwing cups full of muddy water over his shoulders. A woman peers at me from the ancient fold of a purdah veil. Suddenly I feel the tenderness of India, an almost convalescent sensitivity.

When I return, the hotel has elaborately prepared opening night. Pictures of Nehru are in the lobby, placed artfully in museum style. A *charkha* (spinning wheel) and handcuffs from Naini Prison are showcased in a small circle of light. The ushers are in Khadi and Nehru hats, and a sumptuous dinner along with Ka Khana (prison gruel) will be served after the performance, dished out by waiters in jail uniforms. Black plaster prison bars line the lobby walls.

Cabinet members begin to arrive. Limousines rarely seen in India pull up to the hotel entrance. Soon over a thousand people have filled the hall until there is not a seat. Women in smooth braids and silken saris are forced to stand by the wall, joined by other latecomers.

The lights go down and a spot appears on Nehru's desk; the crackling recorded voice of Indira is heard and the play is off.

I clutch the arm of my chair nervously. This is a political town. What political baggage will the audience bring with them?

Harsh (Nehru) gives his line to young Indira: "I wish to be known for my inconsistencies." And a man in back of me says, rather loudly, "And so he is." Indira is cautioned by her father "not to do anything in secret." And a woman across the aisle groans audibly in apparent irony. I am told repeatedly after performances that most Indians still hold a warm memory for Nehru, but many harbor contempt for some of the despotic measures used by Indira.

Finally the play ends. There is a spurt of applause. I am called up on the stage for flowers, along with the cast, director, and producer.

MAY 14TH

The reviews are out and I am praised for dramatizing the unusual father-daughter relationship of Indira and Nehru, something the Indians themselves had never considered.

Relieved about the reviews, I let an assistant of my director, Samir, take me to his grandmother's house for a typical Brahmin meal. We climb up the stairs of an old apartment building with swaying pillars and railings of timber posts rotting with age and monsoon. By each door, there is a mailbox decorated with flowers—a prayer for the mail to be delivered. As we enter, Samir's grandmother is drying her hands on the end of her sari. Behind her are two enormous colored pictures of Ganesha, the elephant God, the figures hidden by the faded strings of jasmine along the frames. Two cucumbers hang from the ceiling, wrapped in banana-fibre. On a brass tray I'm served chopped-flower petal rice and Saru (a well-seasoned sauce) and sweet mango slices, dhall, onion, tomatoes, curry leaves, gingelley oil. I eat with my God-given hands, Indian style, pinching the rice and playfully adding Saru to it, the way we use biscuits to sop up gravy. I drink gray tea that tastes of iron and wood smoke and nibble on anise seeds coated with sugar. Samir's grandmother tells me an old story of a Sikh who, coming back to India after a long journey, sits on the dock and weeps when he suddenly encounters Indian poverty again. It is a very typical Indian tale, one that shows the country's depths of sensitivity yet also reveals the way the Indian mind regards poverty both passively and poignantly.

When I leave, Samir's grandmother gives me a stem of red bananas as a gift and I walk outside into the Indian darkness, a mysterious purdah no longer forbidding.

MAY 18TH

The play has had a standing-room-only reception. And now it is time to go back to Bombay for three more performances at the Nehru Auditorium. The mascots, Bert and Bernie, arc brought to the hotel entrance as the troupe and I depart. I turn my head to take one last look at my favorite Indian dogs, and I see them "salaam" me, full on their knees, as the car pulls away and heads to the airport.

In Bombay, I check in at the West End Hotel. I'm told this is where Peter Brook stays. It is a small hotel, with one ceiling fan and one wall gecko. The rate is four hundred fifty rupees (thirty-five dollars a day), and it is rather on the level of the Empire Hotel in New York City, except that this hotel has a sign on the wall that states: "Visitors' servants are not allowed to sleep anywhere in the hotel or hotel premises." I am happy to be back in Bombay. It is a beautiful city, the sea breeze never failing to cool in the evening.

MAY 20TH

The temperature reaches a high of over a hundred degrees. Statues of gods in Bombay are curtained with straw matting every afternoon to protect them from the sun. And I have to put Scotch tape over the addresses on my postcards because the heat makes the ink from my ball-point pen smear and run.

I see a little girl swimming in the sea with her father, a dried pumpkin tied to her back to keep her afloat. Boats nod at their moorings. There is always the smell of sun-baked dust, the honey smell of fuzz-buzz flowers, of thorn trees in the sun and coconut oil.

If in Iowa City we worry about winter ice and snow, the counterpart in India is the monsoon. Advertisements everywhere read: "With MRF tyres, you're ready to take on the Monsoon Challenge. Play safe before it rains."

Along Chowpatty Beach, unlike any beach in America, there are horses, camels and monkeys romping in the sand—chipmunks, too, with stripes on their back, stripes that got there, so Indian stories tell, when the god Siva stroked them with his sacred fingers. A man with a cobra lets his charge spring at me, and I draw back more in amazement than fright at the snake's sweet beckoning head.

In the evening, I go to the Nehru Auditorium for rehearsal. It is an imposing theatre, cold and elegant, and the actors work diligently to bring across an intimacy and warmth in preparation for tomorrow's opening.

MAY 21ST

It is early morning, the ennui of hot Bombay. I wake up more lazy, more fatigued than when I went to bed. I walk to a teashack, a corrugated iron shed with jute cloth awnings. Before I am served tea and sweet mangoes, the waiter, flapping sure-footed in Indian rubber chappals, shines the brass tabletop with a tamarind rind. When I tip him later, he smiles, his teeth red-tinted with betel juice. He ties his two rupee tip to the end of his *dhoti* in a small bundle. Behind me are tiers of sweets dripping with syrup from shelf to ceiling and colored drinks and bottled pepper-mints. At a nearby table, merchants wearing khaki coats with big pockets like shopping bags, jabber in Tamil. Outside the door, a young girl sits on her haunch-es, bathing a child with a pan of water, her faded blue sari rolled up to her thighs. A man next to her grooms himself loudly, blowing his nose, coughing, splashing his face with a bowl of brackish water. A student nurse in a blue and white sari hurries to the Bombay Hospital a block away. A child with rickets sits on the blan-ket of papers and rags and sucks poinsettias, drinking the sap from the stems for milk. Figures with bare, emaciated legs carry brass lota-pots in their hands, going to the sea for ritual bathing and to say their prayers. Beggars walk in the streets of pipal trees, red stone minarets of mosques, golden domes of temples, and shrines of the Goddess Kali with her bulging tongue and garland of skulls. Every-where I see stagnant drains, fresh cow dung, urine, dust, flies, bulls, calves, albi-no cockroaches; added to this are smells of human and animal breath, sticky sweat, musk, garlic, incense, sour milk, ghee, sandalwood, fresh and decaying fruit. Thomas Jefferson once said: "If the good God saw fit to create so many varieties of trees, creatures, everything, who are we to say that there should be one way?" Of course, the philosophy that prevails here is that there is a unity behind all this diversity of India's five hundred million and all its sixteen major languages—not to mention dialects. I have seen India's poverty in the movies, but the flickering images I am observing now are not contained on a reel—these are the images with-out the frame, overwhelming and wrenching. And why, I ask myself, is there always some callousness in the simple act of watching?

I walk down the streets, always so full of contrasts: A copy shop next to a man loading sticks on a donkey, a contact lens center next to a stand for scooter rick-shaws. One open-air restaurant, trying to ape Americans, calls itself a *Coffee Home*, and next to it is the *Monalisha*, a beauty parlor. A schoolbus goes by, a cart full of children pulled by a pony braided with coral-tree flowers. Everywhere are movie posters heralding lust as if it were hope: *Bade Ghar Ki Beti, Parayaa Ghar, Caribon Daata*, (and *Roger Rabbit*).

I arrive at the Nehru Auditorium at seven p.m., one hour before performance time. Over one-thousand long-stem roses have been ordered and wait on a table by the ushers. This was Nehru's favorite flower, and now each member of the audi-ence is handed a rose as he/she enters the auditorium. Again, I am startled by the number of people. All one thousand seats are full. Long-stem roses loom up pre-cariously from the seats, sometimes unexpectedly poking out over shoulders and armrests. Women in disco saris sparkle in silver- and gold-metallic thread. A bell rings for complimentary drinks. There is a rush to the bar. Thirty minutes later, the play begins. Some people have trouble hearing in the back, and I squirm with anxiety. But when the play ends, there's a healthy applause.

May 23rd

After breakfast, I stop at the PEN Center at Theosophy Hall, which is only a few blocks from my hotel. I meet the president, Nissim Ezekiel, a respected Indian poet. Nissim and I have tea, and he tells me about his first visit to New York City, how he was so lonely at first, and how after he saw his first cockroach, he felt at home. In the afternoon, I go to a Hindi children's play, *Bem Bim Boom,* at the Center for Performing Arts. Although I can't understand the language, the situations are universal: The bully, the nerd, bickering brothers and sisters. The actors are wonderful—both adults and youngsters. The music consists of sitar and taba (hand drum). It is as much fun to watch the audience. It could be a children's matinee anywhere in the U.S., except that these little children wear white Nehru hats instead of Mets' caps.

I go walking at Churchgate. There are hundreds of people waiting to cross the street, a rope strung across the sidewalk to keep them in check, as our traffic lights keep us in check. Suddenly, a street-guard drops the rope and we sweep across the street like cattle. Though a primitive traffic light, it is still effective.

The buses in Bombay are as tricky as New York's 104 and M-10. I take the 314 bus and get off at the Government Colony Terminus, then get in line to hop back on the same bus and continue my trip.

I see the last performance of my play at the Nehru Auditorium. The house is once more full and the audience claps warmly at the end. In two days, we will begin taping the play for Indian television.

May 24th

I wake up with a very sore throat. Luckily, the Bombay Hospital is across the street from my hotel. I sit in the infirmary next to a mother and daughter. The daughter's arms and legs are bandaged. The mother tells me her daughter is the victim of "wife burning." In Bombay alone, she tells me, there are as many as three hundred and fifty cases a year. And what causes it? The husband's family is disappointed at the amount of money the bride brings and they literally burn her—often to death. Even though dowries have been outlawed in India for the past eighteen years, it still does not prevent this calamity. Many daughters-in-law work like laborers in their husband's house. In some Indian states, bills have been introduced to change the law so that if a bride is abused within five years of her marriage, it will be regarded as an act to induce dowry. "Aren't there any organizations to help?" I ask. "Yes," the mother says, "there are some; one group is even taking on just wife burning alone. But women need to be independent for anything to help." Then her daughter's name is called. They both walk into a white, open-air corridor as jasmine in wild undergrowth suddenly scents the air. I never see them again.

I return to the hotel with a bottle of sticky throat syrup and some pills. My bed has been changed but there is no toilet paper, no soap, and no clean towels. Every task requires a different person, so that I have to wait as each member of the hotel crew makes an entrance and exit. Everyone has their station in life. Stations, classes, that's what the Gita says. Most of our problems we cause ourselves because we don't know our limits. "And do thy duty even if it be humble, rather than another's even if it be great." This is the Gita, fifteen hundred years before Shakespeare.

May 25th

I go to a studio in the early morning. We are shooting the play. The sound is not working properly, and we only get six minutes of film after ten hours.

In the evening, I see *Last Tango In Heaven*, Bombay's big Broadway musical. There are three or four glaring audio commercials before curtain time, but nobody seems to mind. The play is slick and glitzy with its main theme being an Indian government minister who goes to heaven where he causes chaos and destruction even there. The government minister is described in the program as: "One of the common species that thrives internationally despite efforts to make them extinct."

All week I have practiced looking in a mirror and saying "kulfi" with great sophistication. "Kullll . . . . . feeeee." Kulfi is an Indian ice cream of burnt milk and saffron which my Indian friends order for me. I have a passion for it. So after the theatre, I go to a restaurant and say to the waiter with great confidence: "Kulfi." He brings me a cup of coffee.

May 28th

We have finally finished the TV tape, so I accept an invitation from my director, Vijaya, to visit Film City. I'm driven to an outdoor park one hour from Bombay. We turn down a narrow road and into a lush, hillside area. Banyan trees line the path. The car comes to a stop in front of an oil drum, and a man wearing a plaid shirt over a *dhoti* runs out to remove the barrier and we travel to the interior. So this is where all those Indian films are made! I step out of the car and on my left is a street of shops where twenty young people are dancing in a TV commercial. On my right, under a row of jack-fruit trees, is a scene from a Marathi drama on its twentieth take. I hear the actor mumble a few English words to his co-star: "I can't afford to eat, and you want a car." Then he reverts back into Marathi. Farther down the trail, an entire Indian village has been created on a hillside, along with a mosque, for the TV series *Discovery of India*. I can't believe that the mosque is only white clapboard. I move closer to touch it, then walk inside the hollow shell. I look out the window and down on the sea and suddenly feel a cool breeze. Walking back to the main area, I see a man swinging by a rope on a tree in what appears to be a movie about Tarzan. And everywhere there are stray dogs sleeping in the shade and directors on moving cranes holding black umbrellas over their heads to protect themselves from the intense heat. I sit down in the shade to watch a take of a boy riding a motorcycle wildly through an archway. He doesn't come in at the right time, so the director makes him repeat the action. I suddenly feel a tap on my shoulder; a man in wide, cotton pajamas is passing around squares of coconut to the crew and I am offered some. I hungrily chew the fresh white chunks which are sprinkled with sugar. The coconut, I learn, is always broken as an offering to the gods—for luck.

After a lunch of rice, lentil, curd rice and mango pickles, I am put on a train to go back to Bombay. It is Sunday and first class is not safe as it will be empty. I am put on a second class lady's car smelling of sandal-oil perfumes. Women and children sit squeezed together. A little girl pushes between standing passengers whining for money. An old woman scoots along on the trunk of her wasted body—no arms or legs. She wears a good-luck Ganesha medal and shoves a cup in front of her for coins. A passenger next to me says that beggars maim themselves to make more money. And if India is one of the poorest countries in the world, then to merely comment on the poverty is meaningless. It is a tourist's cliché to wince. It is no mark of my sensitivity to feel outrage. I look closer, and the beggar child has a smile on her face. The woman with no limbs is so insulated in her journey that she is as private as if she were covered by a veil. It is my stares that desecrate them, my sense of indignation that creates their indignity.

Women and children lie on the streets as I get off the train. Mother and child curl in a peaceful ball of sleep amid a background of wall-to-wall mud houses; they rest unaware of me and every passerby. I have never known the serenity on their faces.

Back at the hotel, I hear newly arrived tourists speak of poverty in India. They typically announce their wrath. I can only agree. But somehow, I am aggravated by their standard remarks on what is so very evident. It is not flattering to find my compassion so blatantly imitated.

May 30th

My last day. Several people call and invite me to lunch or dinner. But I want to walk through the streets alone and say good-bye to Bombay.

I have a cup of coffee at the corner sweet shop, then walk along Marine Drive until I arrive at the sea. I watch the boats and people along the water's edge. I buy a mango from a fruitseller and eat it for lunch, sitting beside a mangy dog who has billowed his head into his paws, shrinking into himself as if he were afraid to take up too much space.

Before I go to the airport, as one last gesture, I let a child of eight approach me with a string of jasmine. I buy one strand and give him ten rupees—too much money for a wrist of flowers. I hold out my arm and he ties the blossoms into a bracelet. His eyes are large, his face serious. I smile at him and hold up my flowered hand, "Bye, bye," I say, flattering myself into thinking that perhaps he knows that I'm leaving. Then I turn and happily walk away. But suddenly he starts to hiss at my back for more money, the flower-boy turning into a greedy beggar. I've been continuously warned not to overpay, and now I've ruined my last encounter. He dogs me for a block, mumbling an old man's incantations for "more . . . more." But then, as if the gods have miraculously granted me a farewell gift, he stops and is silent. I hear a voice suddenly young, and I turn to find him smiling at me. "Bye, bye," he calls, grinning boyishly, for all the world like a kid from Iowa, "bye, bye."

JUDY RAY

Shiva Was the First Dancer

EK, DO, *teen, char; ek, do, teen, char.* In this resonant room Wesley and I first learned the Hindi numbers, to four over and over countless times, and never beyond sixteen, basic beat of the musical sequence. *Ek, do, teen, char*—flat feet mark the rhythm on the stone slab floor. Double time. Double double time, till they barely lift yet slap down sharply.

Wesley had initiated the inquiries about drama or dance programs, in addition to the German class she's attending at the University. Clear-eyed and freckle-faced at nineteen, wearing her pink sundress, she had described her drama activities and aspirations as we visited college departments. Then, following hazy directions to an off-campus place, Wes and I eventually found our way down the narrow side street that runs between a bleak, concrete block of apartments and quiet homes secluded behind walls. We couldn't at that time read the Hindi sign outside this particular house set back from the alley, but assumed it indicated the Dance Centre. I began this program with Wesley to take the place of belly dance classes, of aerobic exercise. Now for an hour each afternoon I found myself in another world, a centering world, the Jaipur Kathak Kendra being its outer shell.

At three in the afternoon the gray-haired guru, a little portly but with back erect, glides down the alley, his feet in their pointed shoes turned out at forty-five degrees. He wears an off-white *kurta*, the long loose shirt of cotton or silk, over a snow-white *dhoti*. In winter he adds a brown waistcoat and carries a Kashmiri shawl for the evening chill. As he steps into the Kathak Kendra he removes his shoes and prays, with a happy smile, to the gods, Krishna and Lakshmi, whose pictures hang above the door. Then the cheery, cheeky maid comes forward in her long Rajasthani dress of primrose yellow to offer him a drink from the clay water jar.

No shoes are worn inside the dance rooms; sandals line up at the door. The musicians on their corner rug tune up to the harmonium's pitch with tap-tap of hammer on wedges around the *tabla*, and whining of strings from the *surangi*, which looks like a rectangular fiddle played upside down. It has a hide cover, and four gut strings are stretched over a lower layer of metal strings.

Wesley and I tie the heavy *ghungrus* around our ankles—a hundred little bells on each string that wraps half a dozen times around. Then the *namaste*, brief sequence of homage to Krishna, to the guru, to dance, to music, to Apollo, to grace, to tradition, to ritual—all flood through my alien mind as the arms circle wide, fingertips brush the floor, palms press together before the face, then fleetingly touch each instrument. All is ritual. The precision of this classical Kathak dance is ritual. Yet Krishna is not my god. Shiva the Destroyer is not my god. And certainly Ganesha, whose picture hangs before us above the guru's cushion, is not my god. To a nonbeliever, this god might appear ludicrous—Ganesha the elephant headed, in this pastel rendering with his voluminous yellow pants billowing around his porky figure seated on a pink lotus. But he is a favorite household god of good fortune. In sandalwood he even sits in our own living room, and I have begun to appreciate his benign presence.

Long ago these classical styles, including Kathak, were "temple dances." The interpretive mimes still portray devotional moods and scenes from the religious epic, *Ramayana.* The bold emblem of Kathak Kendra, and of all the classical dancing, is the ageless Nataraja, four-armed Shiva holding fire, an hourglass drum, a cobra around the wrist, and poised on one leg with that classic twist of the balanced body. Now, however, new forms are being choreographed as pure dance— "Kathak Without Krishna" reads the headline of a newspaper review—and in this primary stage that is all we need to know.

Ta tei tei tat, ta tei tei tat. The gap-toothed guru speaks the rhythms, sitting complacently on his cushion, watching our hands try to draw in the air the designs he sees, and that we strive to see. For our first few lessons we had joined a class with another teacher, a class of several small girls stamping rhythms in unison. They perhaps ranged from ten to fourteen years old, all slim, even skinny, with slender feet and long hands that I envied. It seemed they could quite naturally bend their hands back from the wrists, open elegant fingers out like lotus blossoms. Wes and I are blessed with wide feet, wide hands, and have to work harder on looseness of movement. We felt like giants, aliens, among the small girls. One day the guru came in to observe the group class, and seemed to be asking for the director, Mr. Patni, about us, although I couldn't understand the conversation. Next day we were told we'd have our future classes in another room, just the two of us, under the direction of the guru, Pandit Gauri Shankar from Bombay.

To teach us new parts of the dance routine or rhythm—a few steps or gestures at a time—the guru gets up from his cushion to demonstrate: long feet slap the concrete, hands swoop with the fluid control of a hovering, diving bird. Sometimes I stay on after our session to watch the two boys, about fifteen and seventeen years old, who follow. I can see now how their advanced routines are built on the basic patterns we're beginning to learn, but they are so fast, so precise, the hands sliding, the spins sliding. It inspires me with the desire to get whittled down from a rigid self-conscious self to become singing feet, drawing arms, totally in harmony with the *tabla's* talk.

⌒

I notice an interesting passage from Sri Ragini's *Nritanjali*, which I find in the library:

> Dancing and music in India were considered excellent regulators of the emotions. The venerable Brahmins who defined and practiced the fine arts in the past believed that ill-regulated emotion ruined life and destroyed happiness.

It sets me wondering how many of my emotions are "ill-regulated." Perhaps the desire for control is why the dancing seems so urgent, so obsessive, even in this elementary stage.

One day in December, after I've been watching the boys practice, Guruji says, "Very hard work. Kathak is a five-year course." I express regret that we will have only a few more months, and he replies, "You must stay. Kathak is five years at least. You must stay on." There's that phrase, "staying on." Not, in my mind, staying on past an outmoded colonial era because the place has become home. But staying on to be taken in new directions, to absorb new rhythms day by day, to learn all discipline through this one discipline. Then I wake myself from these fantasies of changing the choreography of my life, and decide to enjoy the dance for these given moments. Wesley and I cycle down to the Kathak Kendra every weekday afternoon—unless there's a religious or national holiday, which we sometimes discover only when we find the place closed up for the day.

Sometimes Guruji gives us the rhythm notations to write down, the spoken rhythms. These are strange dictation sessions as we struggle to understand the thickly accented English spoken through missing teeth. And a new rhythm seems a breakthrough—after weeks of 1 2 3 4, 1 2 3 4, we go to 1 2 3, 1 2 3, 1 2!

In class our guru sometimes calls out, "see your hands," when we stare straight ahead instead of letting our eyes follow our hand movements to give them emphasis. "Where the eye is, there the mind is, where the mind is, there *bhava* (expression) is; where *bhava* is, there *rasa* (aesthetic experience) is." That maxim speaks to the developing process and message of the dance.

Another passage from *Nritanjali* reads:

In Hindu music no liberties are taken with the rhythm. . . . Modes of melody are so thoroughly mastered that the instrumentalists are in a sense creators of an infinite variety of melodic and rhythmic patterns within the prescribed forms. . . . Hinduism defines *sound* as the primary symbol of creative energy or of the activity of Nature, the drum being its emblem.

The *tabla* player for our dance sessions is usually the guru's elder son. When I ask his name, he smiles and says, "Ravi Shankar. Yes, like the sitar player. I think he visits your country many times." This Ravi is very tall, and seems especially so when he puts aside the drums at the end of a session and uncoils from his cross-legged position. I am amazed at the variety of expressions he bears: in fact there seem to be great changes in his appearance from day to day. Sometimes he appears darker complexioned; sometimes round faced; sometimes hollow, sunken faced; sometimes very young; sometimes somber as a shade; sometimes smiling with the red-stained slightly buck teeth protruding.

It is in March that Guruji, looking sad and tired, tells me one day that Ravi is leaving, returning to Bombay. "Already he stayed longer because I needed him," he says. "But he wasn't happy here."

Musicians' families often become musicians, inherit the disciplines. This guru's two sons, tall and lean as poplar trees, both have the rhythms in their blood. Ravi speaks the insistent language of the *tabla*. The younger, whom we have watched dancing, is also learning that instrument, though one day, playing a new rhythm on the bigger drum, he says, "Do you know disco? Is this disco?" There's the tiny tongue of modern style flickering into that very traditional world.

The rooms of the Kathak Kendra always echo with sound—a patter, a jingle, a hum, a drum. One afternoon, though, all is centered on slow, winding strains coming from a back room. Wes and I stand at the door, then slip in to join the half-dozen musicians, the guru, and the Centre's director, who have tucked themselves on a rug behind a new *tabla* player. He is short and stocky, with a glinting gold tooth. Across the room his daughter, maybe seventeen, two braids framing her serious face, leans over the great wooden bowl of a regal *sitar*, the neck of which rears high to seven carved knobs. Her small capable hands pluck strings below, press hooped frets of silver above, as the music winds its subtle way around the rapt listeners. The always sad-looking, woebegone *sarangi* player seems unusually at peace as he closes his eyes. The guru nods. The director sits stoutly, seemingly impassive, until I notice the gleam of appreciation in his eyes. Gradually the *tabla* joins the intricate circles. The small man smiles as he drums, then almost tosses away with laughter as he acknowledges with excitement, enjoyment, their duet and the crescendo of the *sitar's* singing strings. His daughter smiles back, playing the sliding delicate notes of this difficult instrument with masterful assurance.

～

Then one January night Wesley and I find ourselves on the performing side of foot-lights in a theatre, the Rabindra Rang Manch of Jaipar, participants in a dance program with other Kathak students. In view of the guru's remarks about years of study and our very amateur status, it seems absurd that we are to step out on that stage to stamp and twirl the elementary routines. But the guru wants it that way, perhaps to show the process as well as the polished performance, perhaps to show off his two foreign (and therefore exotic) pupils.

At rehearsal, our usually placid Guruji becomes a whirlwind of energy, super-vising every detail of the show. As excitement rises, he stammers and stutters his directions in guttural outbursts. He checks the arrangement of musicians and instruments in their downstage corner; the exact position of the cut-out Nataraja image upstage so that it might appear to dance, too, in the spotlights; the staging of each dancer's routine; the brief announcement I am to make in English to explain our presence; the trays of lighted candles to be carried for the votive finale; the maneuvering across the stage of a "boat" silhouette with long-necked bird as prow; the choice of cloth-of-gold a boy will wear to match most closely a bright painting of the god.

Wesley and I are to wear the full, long Rajasthani skirts, so heavy with silver embroidery that at rehearsal their swinging weight sends us off balance on the turns. Matching veils, usually covering the head and blowing light in wind, are draped across the chest. I am assigned magenta; Wes is all in yellow, making blonder her blonde hair. No blouses in the Kendra wardrobe fit us so we're sent off on our bicycles with Mr. Patni, the Kendra director, deep into the heart of the city. From busy Johari Bazaar we turn down an alley, zigzag into the maze. For one careless moment I glance aside, and run into the backside of a man who has just stepped back from washing at a pump and has bent over to adjust his san-dals. He jumps, startled. I apologize. Bystanders laugh, so he laughs too. Goosed by a foreign woman's bicycle!

Then in a tiny room, like a packing case, a tailor takes our measurements, and swatches of cloth to be matched. Our arms stretch from side to side of this place of business: there is barely room to turn around, to string out a tape measure, to run a sewing machine. Yet the task gets done: on performance night the new tight blouses are ready, bougainvillaea and sunflower colors perfectly matched.

The dressing room shimmers like a palette of primary colors spangled with gold, streaked with the oiled black of long braids and tassels, glittered with bangles, earrings, nose rings. Visiting musicians— singers, *veena* player, drummers—join the regular group in a close, gossiping circle and share the blue smoke of weedy cigarettes. Both the brothers play *tabla* today, the younger one left-handed, in mirror image.

For our brief sequence the sad-eyed *sarangi* player, muffled as always with a woolen scarf, wails his strings mournfully to accompany the harmonium's repetitive song, while from the *tabla* flows the rhythm's current as strong fingers play over taut tuneful skins with a relentless tumbling patter. *Taram tei, taram tei*, the *tabla* commands a jump. Then we must spin, three times, three-times-three turns, but with precision, not abandon. I miss the pink lotus of Ganesha from the wall of our dance room as I try to find something to sight on in the dark theatre.

The star dancer, in a Kathak outfit of tunic and tight pants, blooms in white and silver—a swan, a snowbird, a snowdrop. After all other acts of homage, displays, and storytelling, she turns the whole stage into a battlefield. She leaps from side to side in increasing frenzy as in mime she pulls the bow again and again, dramatizing the fight between Rama, divine hero, and Ravana, the ten-headed demon.

~

Leaving behind heroes and demons after the show, David and I stop to visit a carnival at the edge of the walled city. I'm suitably garbed for the freaky place, still wearing the very heavy theatre makeup, eyes black-ringed, and a tear-drop red *bindi* painted on my forehead with little white petals around it. Past the ferris wheel there's a tall ladder and diving board over a small pond for a suicidal dive; a magic show; puppet show; booths to have our instant picture taken against exotic backgrounds; a booth urging use of Western-style toilets, showing posters of dirty streets and samples of toilet bowls; stalls of bangles by the thousand, pendants, woven picture rugs in garish colors. But the most bizarre fact about this carnival is its emptiness. Where are the crowds? All day long, all the roads and alleys and corners teem with people—selling, buying, sweeping, sleeping, dreaming, spitting, talking—yet here in a carnival where we expect crowds we wander almost alone under the flickering red and green lights.

Despite the excitement of the Kathak show, it's the daily routine of practice, of learning, that we'll miss when we have to leave this place. On the day of our last class I set our little Panasonic tape recorder at the front of the room. The musicians take this session seriously, tune up carefully, listen critically to the playback. Guruji wants me to dance through the routines and to have the *ghungrus* (ankle bells) recorded, too. He tells me to wear double strings on each leg, which means about four hundred little bells! I can barely lift my feet for the fast sequences, but we get through it, and this twenty-minute stretch of cassette tape is perhaps my most prized acquisition of the year. I feel the intensity and centered wholeness of the art. I take that out of the shadowed rooms, persistently counting in my head, to shape the ambient chaos.

JOAN K. PETERS

Foreign Exchange

THEY WEREN'T actually porters, just construction workers hired on the spot, willing to abandon eighty-cent-a-day work for the windfall of $2.10 plus tips.

There were three of them: scrawny, sinewy men whose muscles cabled their calves and thighs. They wore scraps of tattered fabric patched together to make a shirt, a vest, the seams undone and pieces hanging in frayed flaps. One had only a *dhoti* so threadbare his buttocks stuck out. But another wore a multicolored beanie, its octants alternating bright red, yellow and green, though no one else in Nepal wore beanies of any kind.

Barefoot, they climbed the twelve-thousand feet of our trek, jumped stones to cross the shoals, and raced over fields of scree that forced me, in my rubber-soled Reeboks, to tiptoe. Carrying eighty pounds each in baskets on their backs, they bolted up the crumbling mountain stairways bent at an angle to balance the loads that were secured by a strap around their foreheads.

Only Dhan Bahadur, the eldest by many years, called attention to himself. For one thing, he wore the beanie. For another, he was an animated man with mischievous eyes and high color in the sharp Mongolian curve of his cheeks. The beanie gave him an almost dapper air. More so, when he donned the sky-blue T-shirt I discarded after a muddy plunge into a shallow river.

He was quick to smile when I caught his attention, and to laugh, roguishly, as I teetered across the slippery stones. At my first dumbstruck view of the great Himalayan peaks, he tittered: the kid falling for the old magic show. "Beautiful," I said in his language. "*Raamro,*" he repeated pointing out a terraced grainfield that cascaded into the valley like some lime-green wedding train.

At rest stops he sometimes crouched by my side to watch me apply a coat of sunscreen to my face or write in my journal. The journal slayed him. He would point at my scrawl and guffaw to the two Sherpa guides, though never at my expense exactly. In fact, I thought he liked me.

The other two porters never lifted their eyes from the ground nor spoke. They nodded when given directions, and squatted separately at rest stops to smoke in silence. At meals, each built his own fire at the outskirts of our eating area, cooked identical meals, ate, then disappeared into the nearest village for shelter since they had no tarpaulins or blankets. Those nights I needed long underwear in my sleeping bag.

Mingma, the chief guide, told me they didn't have big enough pots to cook together. I didn't pursue it, but obviously they could have eaten together the way the cook and kitchen boy did. Maybe it was their caste, I thought. Maybe they wanted no company at all, except for Dhan Bahadur, who occasionally wanted mine.

With the uncanny ease of a bilingual child, Dhan Bahadur moved in and out of the two groups: sociable with me and the guides, silent and solitary with the other porters who had begun, even by the second day, to seem like a distinct species: half man, half mountain goat. Everyone, including the villagers, treated them that way and eventually I did as well.

I never even learned their names.

But Dhan Bahadur was different from all six members of the crew: as easy as they were rigid, as indifferent to class as they were attentive, as spontaneous as they were predictable. Why, I didn't know. I only managed to learn he was sixty years old and had "many" children. Questions were a social blunder.

Our interactions fell so quickly into the category of the incomprehensible I adopted an uncharacteristic passivity. Across an ever-widening chasm of foreignness, this much was clear: only Dhan Bahadur was gregarious, and only he was friendly to me.

~

I hadn't craved company. My fantasies were of being alone. After years of work in a claustrophobic profession, I sought what people do in remote and pristine places—a cleansing, a sharpening of my sense of the essential human spirit, an experience of the remarkable in nature. But except on the most popular, litter-strewn paths, a woman alone couldn't go into the Himalayas with nothing but a backpack. Porters and guides were a necessity. So I'd arranged for the retinue, picturing them, from God knows which Hollywood movie, as silent shadows who appeared at intervals with a bowl of rice or a finger pointed to the correct fork in the path. Then there they were: seven very particular men. Until I saw them, I didn't really understand that I wouldn't be alone.

Yet I wasn't disappointed. In the dusty outpost of our embarkation the electricity of greetings excited me. I switched fantasies to how we would become friends, a sort of temporary tribe, laughing and talking together. I imagined all this despite the fact that I was the only female among them, the only foreigner, their employer, and incomparably richer than even Mingma.

Mingma might have been a friend. He spoke English. His status was equal to mine. But Mingma was a sullen man of twenty-five who did his job and nothing more. I doubt my femaleness was Mingma's problem since he'd lived for a year in the States and, anyway, Dhan Bahadur, who'd never been out of the district, was warm. Kancha Lama, Mingma's young assistant, liked to scare me out of my wits on the high cliffs and the river crossings, but it was less for my delight than for the amusement of Dorcha, the cook, with whom he began to hold hands. Dorcha and his kitchen boy, Ek Raj Rai, were exceptionally nice but they spoke no English and were too busy cooking to bother with me.

You might imagine that for someone who wanted seclusion and nature, the group's impenetrability could have been a relief. In fact, it didn't bother me at all when I *was* alone. But most of time I was part of the convoy of seven men. We hiked the trails in a line, we rested together, and protocol dictated that I take my meals with the gloomy Mingma. Though I appealed to them for privacy, they seldom let me out of sight. They occasionally let me lead, which made me feel less like a prisoner being marched to the authorities and more like an explorer. Explorer was my final fantasy. Over each new rise was the possibility of revelation. I could reach a numinously beautiful summit and pretend that I was Keats's Cortez, "Silent, upon a peak in Darien." Most of the time, though, they were there.

Such was the difficulty: to be at once constantly with people and unable either to dismiss them or connect with them. Nor did this apply only to the crew. No matter what pasture, gorgeous grainfield or beautiful bluff we camped on, we were never far from a village. Within minutes, I was surrounded by twenty to forty Nepalese standing at my tent flap to survey my equipment, or at the edge of my tarp to watch me eat. I eagerly distributed portions of my meal and displayed my things, but since Mingma wouldn't translate, our communication was limited to such questions I had mastered such as, What is your name? Can you (to children) sing a song?

Mostly, to the mutual frustration of both the villagers and me, we just stared. Once I even stood on my head to amuse three little girls. It was twilight and they were my only guests. Combed and dressed in brown capes pinned under their chins, they looked so biblical, so solemnly expectant, I wanted to give them more than a candy bar or a song. But the gesture was too bizarre to charm them. They didn't giggle or respond in kind. They seemed puzzled when I held out my hands to play a circle game. Finally, unable to bear the blankness between us, I retreated to my tent.

~

That blankness made me appreciate Dhan Bahadur all the more, although our relations were strained as well. On the very first night, when Dhan Bahadur had come to inspect the contents of my tent, I offered him a Marlboro. Instead of taking the one I had teased from the pack, he put his palms together. I tapped several into his open hands. From then on, he appeared nightly at my tent, cupped his hands, and smiled.

I didn't resent it. In the first place, he seemed as curious about me as my foreign goods. In the second, I'd brought the Marlboros to give away. It was natural that he ask, I felt. Anyone who is that poor can't be expected to luxuriate in a cross-cultural friendship, wordless no less, without an interest in property. I certainly had my share with friends wealthier than I. And Dhan Bahadur was charming about it. If the evening were clear, he'd stay and have a smoke, the two of us looking out at the declining sun.

The first time he sat beside me under a shady tree, he took my umbrella whose duck-billed handle stuck out of the zipper of my pack. Sitting with it nose to nose, he quacked and chuckled, looking over his shoulders at me to see if I was amused, which I was. Then he quacked at everyone in the group, pretending the umbrella was biting his arm, then his nose, then the nose of the cook. I sighed. I know, old man, you want the umbrella. But I liked my umbrella, which had been a gift. Its handle was hand carved. So be it, I decided. It was dishonest to give what one didn't give freely. He had a right to ask.

He had his generosity too. At the first rhododendron forest, four days into our trek, I picked a bloom for my hair. Every day after that Dhan Bahadur brought me a fresh flower. Once, without any embarrassment or lechery, he tied a stem into my buttonhole, fumbling at my breasts. With Dhan Bahadur, my property was a substitute for words. At rest stops, we looked through my binoculars together, examining the mountains or two men ploughing a grain terrace a thousand feet away. I showed him how my camera worked, moving the telescopic lens so he could see the different depths of field. He posed for me proudly in elegant, stylized postures: profiled, straight-on with his fists tightened at his waist. I tried posing for him, too, though the camera bounced down a foot and up again whenever he pressed the button. Only one of his pictures came out: me from the knees down, my Reeboks blurred next to an even blurrier chicken.

Whatever Dhan Bahadur asked for beyond a rote response and trekking etiquette, it was always worth it. For the pleasure of sitting together outside my tent, of feeling that affinity between me and another, that mysterious accord, however slight. But it was difficult to maintain.

In the second rain during that first week of climbing when we'd gotten to know one another somewhat, he pointed to the poncho I was struggling into. He clearly meant that my umbrella would suffice and he could use the poncho. I gave it up without hesitation, glad for the opportunity to be helpful. But in every rain after that the poncho was automatically his and, as I learned, carrying an umbrella on a slippery trail can be a hazard. Still, he had the supplies to protect and I liked his presumption. It meant he had spirit. It meant we had a bond. But then I got drenched and then I skidded into the mud flat bordering a watering hole, umbrella and all.

Near the end of the first week, when we came to a village store that sold liquor I bought a bottle of vodka for the porters. Dhan Bahadur was at my side throughout the transaction. He seemed to know without being told that this expensive gift (three day's salary for a porter and a noticeable portion of my surplus cash) was for everyone. Yet at the next shop in the next town where vodka was available, he just pointed, rather insistently, I thought, and carted off the bottle without a nod.

Gradually my posessions were becoming the focus and the issue between us. Whenever he sat down by my side now I found myself wondering what he was after.

I'd begun to feel hustled on all sides. The children never stopped asking for pens, my supply of which was depleted. The adults needed more than leftovers and tea biscuits, more than I could possibly give. I was overwhelmed by my property, by the disgrace of having in a place where no one had been put, by the inescapability of class. My trek had turned into a traveling zoo featuring me. My binoculars and sunscreen, my well-fed American face defined and limited me more than I'd understood. It seemed this mutual gaping, this accentuation of shame and need, was all that could come of standing at the chasm's edge and I was tired, then, of foreignness. Of crowds surrounding my picnic tarp, the peering into any little air opening of my tent, the relentless and silent scrutiny. I just wanted to be left alone and, not a moment too soon, I was.

~

Deeper and higher in the interior, Anapurna and the neighboring peaks rose above us like a phalanx of paleolithic sphinxes. In circles at their feet, the endless webs of grain terraces seemed to hold some kind of agricultural tremolo for an astonishingly long time. I began to notice people less. I'd grown stronger, too, more goatlike myself.

Lambchop, as I now called Kancha Lama, carved a walking stick for me. I would have parted with my camera before giving up that stick. For leverage and balance it was better than a third leg, and it didn't ache. The crew didn't have to watch me so closely. I could lose myself among them, enjoy the more abstract sense of group: being a part of the line, snaking up and down the mountains like a single organism. Their banter and songs charmed me, Lambchop's friendship with Dorcha, even his idiotic pranks. And we were a group in certain ways: all of us tired at the day's end, thudding to the ground, panting, when we came to a shade tree. Neither the chasm of foreignness, nor even their need bothered me as much. I was so absorbed by the mountains that mere people, including myself, almost seemed beside the point. If this wasn't revelation, it was enchantment, beyond my fantasies.

After nine days, we came to Sirandanda, our highest camp, where we would stay four nights. I had my tent pitched on the other side of the summit from the crew's. We were well away from the nearest village, whose white Buddhist flags waved in the distance. In fact, our camp was its burial ground, a kind of Stonehenge of monuments positioned where one could see down on three sides of the mountain at once. In one direction were ranges of mountains vanishing into an infinite horizon, in another the terraces, and in a third a six-thousand-foot drop to the river where we'd camped two nights before.

Every morning I went off alone with nothing but a daypack. I stopped when I pleased, ate a Tiger's Milk Bar under a tree where I could watch a herd of oxen graze. Afternoons when I returned to camp, I read under the shade of a rhododendron tree. Once a golden eagle with a six-foot wing span whooshed by my nose. Aside from that I was alone.

Without the crew or my vast duffel bag of possessions, villagers treated me more casually, less like a department store encountered for the first time. Away from the jagged dynamics of the group I found what I'd come for: the place ravished me. Under the weight of its ancient gaze I felt like the world's child. It seemed to me, too, that the less I looked to people, the better our relations were. Everyone, including the crew, began to respond differently. On the third morning in Sirandanda, Mingma brought Dorcha to my tent to see if I had some medicine for the rash on his neck. I tried the cortisone cream, which cured it overnight. While I was at it, I gave Mingma some Sudafed for his cold.

The next morning, Dhan Bahadur sat himself down at my tent door and pulled up the blue T-shirt to show me his back. Along his spine were black mushroom-sized lumps. Whatever they were, and surely they were from carrying packs and cement blocks some fifty years, they were beyond my counter-girl expertise. Nonetheless, when he grimaced to explain that they hurt him, I rubbed some cortisone cream on each. More, he gestured, his whole back hurt. I brought out my Nivea and massaged some into his back and shoulders. When I was done, he still looked unsatisfied, even indignant that I wasn't doing more. So I poured some Nivea into his open hand and told him to rub it all over, which he did, even through his hair.

As I walked the path alone not an hour later, villagers waited. One man had a badly cut finger which I attended to with wet wipes and bandages. Another man brought me to his wife who complained of general malaise. Since she had no fever, diarrhea, or vomiting, I gave her mint tea.

I liked this ministering. I liked being a healer, feeling that I had something more meaningful to give than biscuits or pens. I thought I'd found both the mountains and a relationship with the people who lived in them; I even felt some mysterious correspondence between the two. My contentment was so great, I considered that it might point to a new direction for my life. That night and the next, as I lay stargazing on the *stupa*, I played with the idea of applying to some world health organization.

Then, on the morning we were to leave Sirandanda, Dhan Bahadur showed up to complain about itchy eyes. "I can't put cortisone in your eyes," I explained, shaking my head as I moved an index finger from the tube to his eyes. Judging from the tightness of his lips he was vexed. Perhaps he believed I was hoarding my goods.

At the morning rest stop on the second day of our descent, Dhan Bahadur sat by my side and, smiling weakly, lifted the bottoms of his feet to me. They were thickly calloused, an inch at least, and creviced into sections like animal paws. One crevice, which he pried open to show me, was bloody. I was horrified both at his condition and my inexcusably stupid assumption that the porters' feet, or their backs for that matter, simply toughened over the years. I felt helpless again. My extra sneakers wouldn't fit him. Bandages were no use on the bottom of his foot.

The whole time I examined Dhan Bahadur's feet, he talked softly, trustingly, explaining, I suppose, how much they hurt and how long they had been like that. Slowly I slid my fingers along his bony shin, my heart sinking. My supplies were so much red candy in a plastic play-nurse kit. Even more slowly I raised my hands so I faced him, palms held out. I saw in his eyes that now he understood both I and my supplies were limited.

Later that day when we stopped in someone's farmyard to make our lunch, I asked Mingma about the children, who seemed dangerously unhealthy. He said they were very poor. The clinic costs money. I was sure I saw a dirty look on his face. Mingma had never liked my medical act. Although the Sudafed had made him feel better, he refused a second pill and sniffled miserably for the rest of the trip.

The bravest of the children, apparently deaf, waved her hands at me while she opened and shut her mouth rhythmically, the way a fish does. Her brother, whom she had left by a tree, had a withered leg. All of the children were dotted with sores. When I sat against the tree drawing pictures with the little boy, the mother emerged from the house, pushed her way past the knot of children, and set a baby girl in my lap. Her face was covered with scabs. Though I rocked her she didn't coo or follow my eyes. With a pantomime of rubbing salve on the baby's face and putting a pill on her tongue, the mother begged me for medicine. I made Mingma translate that I had nothing strong enough, but when I told him to say I would give her money for medicine, he refused. "She'll expect it from everyone," he said. They would pay her for firewood, that was enough. That, I knew, wouldn't buy an aspirin.

In the afternoon, another man stopped me to look at his wife. She was lying on a mat, ashen and pained. I could have given her something, aspirins or antibiotic, but I hadn't a clue what was wrong. I didn't want to play shaman then, or benevolent Westerner in an impoverished land. I didn't want any hype, not theirs or mine. And yet it seemed as inescapable as my duffel bag of things. I was sorry, I said. I had nothing to help her. The whole entourage—guides, cooks, and porters—stood and watched.

A day's walk from Sirandanda had changed everything back. Once the group reunited, all the former tensions re-emerged. People crowded out nature's sublimity. Dhan Bahadur never asked for doctoring again. He'd become so annoyed with me, or so disillusioned, our former affection was gone. Halfway into our descent, we had to singly cross an insanely shaky suspension bridge. It listed so far to the right people hung onto its rusty cables to keep from falling into the torrent below. I had to force myself to take the first step and once I did, my eyes pinned on the survivors at the other end, I lurched like an accident victim learning to walk. Even so, as I reached the center, Dhan Bahadur smacked into me and tried to push past with his enormous basket although the bridge was only wide enough for one.

"No," I screamed, clutching the cables that felt no sturdier than coat hangers. Tears sprang to my eyes as I looked down, as his huge basket shoved me farther toward the edge. At that point, I just screamed as loud as I could. But Dhan Bahadur only stopped when Mingma shouted at him from the shore. He stopped and waited, though not without annoyance. I was still trembling as the last of our group landed on the other shore, yet no one inquired or apologized. Dhan Bahadur never perceived or acknowledged my terror. Either way, some essential compassion seemed lacking. More so when he came as usual for his cigarettes that night and took time out for another quack.

~

By then I was disappointed, too, not only in Dhan Bahadur, but in the whole trip. I had not anticipated how anticlimactic the descent would be. Climbing had been difficult, but it was the unraveling of an adventure, which, by the fifteenth day, was being tied up again. It was, in every way, a coming down, and not only for me. There were no more songs, there was no chatter on the paths.

As we neared the town on the highway where a car would pick me up, the villagers seemed tougher and more mercenary. It was "give me money" from the children instead of "give me a pen." No one smiled, no one offered the ritual "*Namaste.*" Strangers still crowded around my tent and tarp but in a slightly menacing way. It was poorer, meaner land, more densely populated and dirtier than the higher areas. Their windows weren't trimmed with red and blue molding. Their daughter's hair wasn't braided with red rope. When I coiffed one little girl with a barrette as I'd often done before, she peered in my mirror, then held her hand out for a coin.

The crew was naturally impatient to get back, get paid, and go home. Mingma didn't seem to care where we stopped any more, either to lunch or to camp. I felt the trip was over, that it was a packaged tour, stupid and rote. That I was being marched out the door.

With only two days to go, I doubted I could recapture the rapture I'd felt, but I wished all the more for some contact with the loveliness of the place. Mingma, however, became devious. He wouldn't stop at the scheduled camps. Our last two improvised ones were ugly and uncomfortable. When I asked him about it, he never answered.

On our penultimate day we hiked hours longer than usual with a half-hearted assurance at lunch that we were heading to the scheduled camp near Bisile Danda. My itinerary listed it beside a stream in a little wilderness outside of town. It was sunset, however, and we were not near any wilderness.

"Camp," Mingma said, pointing to the congested village directly below us on the path as we came around a hill. My tent had been pitched next to the animal watering hole in the town square. The stench, the mosquitoes, and the crowds watering their buffalo were alarming. With houses on three sides of the square and a drop down the mountain on the fourth, there was no privacy at all, and no rest. At least twenty-five people had already formed a circle around me.

"Where are we?" I asked. In unison Mingma and Lambchop said, "Bisile Danda." I wandered a half mile or so down the path where a schoolboy who spoke English told me he had never heard of Bisile Danda, which meant that it was at least a three-hour walk from where we were. This town was Malti Ghira. There were no streams nearby, nor any woods. He himself had never tasted fish.

At dinner I asked Mingma straight out why we'd come to Malti Ghira. Bisile Danda was full up with trekkers, he said. But we hadn't met another trekker from the day we left. Whether they understood I'd caught them in a lie, I don't know. If they were contrite, they weren't showing it. Why they did it I didn't understand. The car wouldn't come earlier to pick me up and we were ahead of schedule now.

~

The heat and the misery of our last day's hike was unrelieved. If the crew was out of sorts before, now they were explicitly sour. Like convicts, we walked stone faced. Lambchop and Dorcha were not holding hands. Dhan Bahadur wasn't quacking any more. The plains were dull after the heady mountains. Haze blocked the view. The air was thick, the grainfields yellowed, patchy and ill-kempt. Their shadeless heat was agonizing. Iowa in August, after the High Sierras. A dark laugh at the idyll above.

It took only three hours to reach our final camp, one so ghastly it made our last days' breathless pace seem lunatic. With a full day left, we would be part of a transient slum where some two hundred squatters lived in a narrow communal field. Horses, oxen, and cows grazed among their makeshift tents, covering with dung every inch of ground between the river and the sharp rise to town.

In town, trucks were everywhere: thundering in both directions, parked in rows on either side of the highway and next to the squalid sleeping mats scattered outside four tumble-down buildings. Over their doorways, professionally painted signs read, "Hotel." There were a half-dozen liquor stores but no clinic or school. Ragged children roamed aimlessly up and down the mud lane. One restaurant cook chopped chicken on a cement floor outside the toilet I had come in to use. Frantic now to salvage this finale, I headed back down to the camp with a peace offering of a bottle of rum.

Not a minute after I arrived lightning cracked across the sky and it began to pour. In the tawniest light of the loveliest afternoon, a rapprochement would have been difficult; in the rain, I was at a loss. I watched the cooks and porters scurry to gather up their pots until I noticed Dhan Bahadur watching me. With a puzzled smile that was supposed to explain I had wanted a party, I hoisted the rum bottle by its neck. Moving faster even than usual, he grabbed it, indicating with gestures aimed toward town that he was on his way. "Wait," I yelled, scrambling through the cow pies to where Lambchop was digging a drainage ditch around my tent. He caught up with Dhan Bahadur and explained something or other. The next thing I knew, the group huddled under the kitchen tarp to drink together as they thought I'd requested. I stood outside in the rain. There was literally no room for me, nor, I think, could they imagine that I would sit in the kitchen or share a drink with them.

As dumbfounded as we all clearly were, we all knew the fiasco meant wet supplies for the porters and no drainage ditch for me. But there was no repairing the situation, nor could I move. I got soaked watching the wordless crew dutifully drink their rum, then slunk off across the dung field to my tent.

In the morning the porters, who generally didn't arrive until breakfast, were already assembled when I woke. Of course, I knew why. My guidebook explained that on the last day everyone got tipped 15 percent of their salaries (twenty-five dollars for the guide, five dollars per porter, etc.) and spare clothing should be given as gifts. But the ceremony itself intimidated and distressed me. Not only did I fear another social fiasco, I also felt the sharks were circling.

It was an overcast day. The earth was sodden from the night's rain and the riverside reeked. A kind of nausea overtook me at the thought of such a bleak, commercial conclusion to the trip. On a desperate impulse, I popped out of my tent and asked if I might take a group picture. They assented and quickly formed a row. Each man stood about half a foot from his neighbors, as if in no relationship whatsoever. With steely seriousness, they stared at the camera. Not even Dhan Bahadur, who was familiar with posing, responded to me. Still, through the whole deadly scene, I couldn't stop coaxing them to smile. I snapped some unpromising photos and returned to my tent to get on with the morning's real event.

It's not as if I hadn't given this any thought. My last three nights had been devoted to planning. Castoffs, I had decided, would go to the "lower" staff. The cook and the guides clearly clothed themselves adequately without my help. I thought I might insult them by offering not only my old, but now filthy things. Lampchop, who wore a *Save the Earth* T-shirt certainly wouldn't want my plain one. Dorcha's new jeans fit him so well they couldn't have been hand-me-downs.

For the others, I selected carefully. My unworn safari shorts would go to the porter in the decrepit *dhoti*. Then I would hold out a pile of my two striped bath towels and two white T-shirts for each person—in descending order of rank—to select what he liked. My plastic rain poncho, now unfortunately torn, would nonetheless go as an extra to Dhan Bahadur who had worn it throughout the trip.

Even with a plan I was dizzy with the inadequacy of my offerings, the subtlety of the procedure, and the seven dour faces awaiting me. At the same time I still hoped the gratuities would express some feeling for each of them. I even imagined that, unlike the photo, the gifts might revive whatever connection I had had with Dhan Bahadur and, to whatever extent, with the group before the descent. The worse I felt, the more ardently I wanted this.

I began with tips then went to my tent and brought out my paltry pile. The sight of the prize safari shorts on top reassured me. I walked straight up to the porter with the *dhoti* and smiling, handed him the shorts. He grinned. Encouraged, I brought the pile to Dorcha, who chose a T-shirt and smiled, then to the nameless porter, who chose a striped towel. Poised now on a near lightheartedness at the thought the gifts made them happy, my guard was down. Just as I turned to the porters to distribute the remaining towel, Mingma exchanged his worn face towel for my plush striped one, explaining that porters only use their towels to cushion the basket straps. I couldn't think how to refuse him. Rattled by the watching eyes, the judgments, and the inevitable disappointments, I mistakenly turned to the porter in the *dhoti*, who instantly snatched Mingma's grotty face towel—

and tucked it into his waistband next to my safari shorts. This left nothing for Dhan Bahadur.

Praying this awful ritual would end well, I handed my poncho to Dhan Bahadur who, knowing it wasn't intended as a main selection, threw it on the ground in a temper. He pointed to the grotty towel, which was by rights his, and shouted at the porter and at me. I pleaded with the porter, but he wouldn't give the towel up. Even Mingma couldn't make him. Dhan Bahadur, meanwhile, was banging his fist on the ground and hollering like a six-year-old. I rifled through my pockets for an extra dollar, which he accepted, but never stopped ranting. The torn poncho lay rumpled in the mud.

In this state, I left him. Obviously, reparations weren't the issue; I'd already wounded him. On a rock by the river's edge, I waited for the entourage to eat breakfast. It had started to drizzle and darken. While they packed, I watched the brown water swirl over the rocks and float debris onto the shore: an empty fruit cocktail can, a flip-flop whose unhinged tong stuck up like a wishbone. In one spot the rising water dislodged a dry cow pie and carried it downstream.

At my back I felt Dhan Bahadur's hurt. I'd even begun to wonder if I hadn't meant to wound him. From the corner of my eye I saw him sitting next to his pack, sulking while the others bustled. He was the only one I cared about. By the time they were ready to leave I was frantic to let him know how much his warmth had meant. But even if I had thought of something to say, Mingma wouldn't translate and I didn't trust Lambchop. Right before Mingma called us, I pulled my umbrella out of my daypack, rushed to his side, and held it out to him. He looked at me forlornly.

"Quack, quack," I said, humiliating myself, for I am not a quacker.

He looked away.

I touched the duck's nose to his arm and by the second nudge, he accepted the gift.

He grinned, but so listlessly I withdrew, assuming that I'd ruined our friendship or that none had existed, that the chasm of foreignness was simply too wide and his poverty too urgent.

~

Having deposited me with my knapsack and duffel bag at the highway, the guides went off in search of the car. The porters and cooks dispersed. Groups of trekkers paraded up and down the road, a constant turnover of people entering and leaving the mountains. Children surrounded me, demanding money. No warmth seemed possible.

In the Himalyan perfection of Sirandanda I hadn't cared, but that was an interlude—a taste of nirvana, a vacation. For a second I had seen, as the mystic said, how the landscape looks when I am not there, but that's only ever the briefest glimpse. I *was* there, and the villagers too, and the crew of seven men. Yet we were to be left without one good feeling for one another, without any connection at all, though we'd been together for three weeks. I'd reacted so strongly to them, but maybe they had seen the likes of me come and go too many times. Maybe *they* were tired: of foreignness, of memsahibs, of cameras and sunscreen. I didn't believe I was entitled to more, but I hadn't the colonialist's heart to shut them out, nor the Marxist's idealism.

The guides heaved my things into the trunk of the car. I didn't look at them. It was just the relief of departure I wanted. We said perfunctory good-bye's. No one pretended to care. I wasn't smiling, nor were they. As Mingma opened the door for me, Lambchop stepped away and lit a cigarette.

Just as I leaned down to climb into the car, Dhan Bahadur appeared. Reaching into the back, he took my stick from the floor and gave me his own bamboo one instead. For a second I was almost indignant. My stick was longer and heavier, more suited to my height. I actually thought Dhan Bahadur might be appropriating it the way he had my poncho, hustling to the end. But instantly I realized that had to be ridiculous. Sticks were abundant. It must have been a gift.

A warm flush spread over my cheeks and shoulders. I *salaamed* to thank him and he *salaamed* back. We did this several times, but stiffly, the tension unabated. We did this until the driver called me into the car, then we nodded our heads at one another, unmistakably uncertain and, like everyone everywhere, trying, despite it.

Clutching his stick, I leaned back against the seat and was driven off into the black fog of diesel fumes.

CATHERINE WATSON

Tibet:
The Search for Shangri-La

MY MOTHER HAD DIED, and in the emptiness that followed, all I wanted was to be far away from home.

Travel has curative powers for me, and I turned to it as to a healing drug. I craved a place so distant and so difficult that it would take full concentration to survive the present moment, with nothing left for the future or the past.

I chose Tibet. I wanted escape and epiphany; I got dust and distraction. In the end, they were almost the same, and I was grateful.

~

We began the overland trip from Katmandu, Nepal, just after dawn on the morning of the Lord Buddha's 2,531st birthday. It seemed auspicious.

All sorrow comes from craving, the Buddha had taught: Extinguish craving, and you extinguish sorrow. That is a good banner to travel under. Travelers who expect nothing are never disappointed.

Unfortunately, we expected a great deal. We couldn't help it. For centuries every foreigner who has set out for Tibet has gone with expectations. Or because of them.

Tibet is Shangri-La. The lost paradise of the Himalayas. The Land of Snows. The Roof of the World. The Forbidden Land.

In many ways, it is still forbidden, the way blocked for most travelers by high costs, by the whims of the Chinese bureaucracy, and, in our case, by a landslide that had cut the road between Katmandu and Lhasa.

Barriers, we assured ourselves, only make some things better. But that was before we had to climb the landslide.

~

Our budget tour headed east, then north, by bus through the fertile, crowded Katmandu Valley, into the foothills of the Himalayas, along the Sun Kosi River, which forms part of Nepal's border with Tibet, and finally across it, over the Chinese-built Friendship Bridge.

Once in Tibet, we went steeply uphill—on foot at first, on moist, landslide-ravaged mountainsides from about five thousand to seventy-five hundred feet, and then by small vans that carried us up another ten thousand feet, over the passes of the Himalayas, and finally onto the great Tibetan plateau and into Lhasa, the country's ancient capital.

Prevailing winds follow much the same route, pushing clouds up and over the mountains. As they rise, the clouds lose their moisture on the Nepali side, leaving Tibet in the rain shadow, with skies as clear as blue glass and land as sere as sand.

The rain shadow makes the Himalayas different, too, one side from the other. Glimpsed from Nepal, their great snowy peaks had shimmered like white curtains in the sky, a congregation of angels.

When we met them again in Tibet, they had changed. Sturdier, plainer, more of the earth, they looked like the broad, brown backs of work horses tossing distant white manes.

⁓

Although we had seen many small landslides in Nepal, we were not prepared for our first sight of Tibet. The landscape looked as if it had been unraveled, like a badly knitted sweater.

We hired a gang of rag-clad, barefoot porters to carry our backpacks and suitcases from the Friendship Bridge to the village of Zhangmu, where we would spend the night.

As if the mountain slopes were city sidewalks, the porters trotted straight uphill, following a trail so narrow that only one person could negotiate it at a time, and so steep that I thought it was a mistake.

Some of the landslides that had disrupted our road were natural, but the largest was man-made, the result of Chinese blasting for a new roadbed. Not that the cause made much difference in the climbing. Though we were only a mile in the air, we weren't used to the altitude, and many in our group of seventeen found the two-hour climb exhausting.

I stopped every few minutes to rest, gasping for breath, blaming the altitude for a sudden, puzzling confusion, and wondering why thrice-weekly aerobic workouts hadn't left me in better shape. Then a wave of fever and nausea hit me, legacies of my last meal in Nepal, and I realized that my distress was caused by germs, not altitude.

We climbed again the next morning, up the muddy scar of a landslide that had obliterated not only our road but a third of Zhangmu, before we reached the vans that would carry us on to Lhasa.

What I saw in those first days of climbing and riding was filtered by illness and shrouded by whirling dust; it seemed not quite real.

Months later, I remember the journey to Lhasa as a dimly lit, exotic movie— a dizzy blur of thirst and fatigue; of eerily treeless mountains; of roads so rough they made our teeth chatter; of passes so high we got headaches riding over them; and of dry, dirty villages with strange names like Tingri and Xegar Dzong.

But even sick, I realized that Tibet had given me what I needed: a present tense so consumingly difficult that I could not think of anything but *now*.

⁓

The brightest spot in those first few days was the town of Shigatse and the golden-roofed monastery of Tashilhunpo that appeared to float about it against Tibet's cobalt sky.

Still shaky and out of breath (Shigatse is at 12,800 feet), I stepped through the great monastery gate into the courtyard of what could have been a medieval city—

or the setting for *Lost Horizon* if James Hilton had chosen to locate his Himalayan paradise in a desert.

Buildings rose around the courtyard like a heap of blocks, painted white or salmon-pink and adorned with fluttering awnings and the golden figures of deer— revered because deer were the first creatures to whom the Buddha preached.

Needing a map, I pulled out a guidebook and was instantly mobbed by Tibetans: first an old couple, then a clot of children, then a family.

They were pilgrims, come from other parts of Tibet to pray at the Tashilhunpo shrines—all wearing black clothes made of thick wool, all beaming and smiling and holding out their hands, all murmuring the same unintelligible syllables over and over.

Dalampich, dalampich, dalampich. . . .

I could not have felt more alien on the plains of Mars. Then a man reached forward and touched my guidebook, and I understood. They were speaking the one English phrase all Tibetans seem to know:

Dalai Lama picture.

In other countries, the poor beg for money. No one we met in Tibet ever did. The only things they wanted from us were photographs of their exiled religious leader, and they knew that tourists' guidebooks often contained them.

Forewarned by other travelers, I had packed prints of a recent picture of the Dalai Lama and now passed out a few. The reaction was startling.

The Tibetans looked transfigured. They grinned, bowed, clasped my hands, held the pictures to their chests, tapped them on their heads.

One old lady wept.

So did I, at the thought that something so small could be so important, and that belief could persist so long and so intensely.

Soon it will be thirty years since the Dalai Lama and his family fled the troops of the People's Republic of China.

By any standard but Tibet's, he should now be nothing more than a mildly interesting, half-forgotten institution, like the late Duke of Windsor, or the former royalty of Montenegro.

But where those gentlemen were mere earthly rulers, the Dalai Lama has the force of heaven on his side.

Tibet's devout Buddhists believe that he is a manifestation of the Chenrezi, the Buddha of Compassion, who chose to reincarnate to help human beings. This Dalai Lama is the fourteenth in a series of such reincarnations. That makes him as much a god as he is a king.

He was a boy of sixteen when the Chinese troops seized Tibet in 1950 and, despite admonitions from around the world, kept it.

Tibet was bigger then, covering all of the Tibetan plateau, an area roughly the size of Europe.

The borders have been redrawn, so the Tibet Autonomous Region (TAR) of today—in theory, a self-governing subdivision of the People's Republic of China— comprises only about one-third of the old country. Historic Tibet's eastern districts, Amdo and Kham, where a Tibetan guerrilla movement exists, have been absorbed by neighboring Chinese provinces.

The population of the plateau has changed too, and the Tibetans are no longer in the majority.

According to the Office of Tibet, in New York, approximately seven and a half million Chinese and six million Tibetans live on the plateau now, either in the TAR or in China.

The Office further estimates that 1.2 million Tibetans died "as a direct result of the Chinese occupation"—either during the fighting or later, from executions, suicide, illness, and famine.

The cultural price was also high. More than sixty-two hundred monasteries were operating in Tibet before 1950. Today there are perhaps fifteen, though others are being restored under the more benevolent aegis of the current Chinese government.

$\sim$

At first, the Tibetan government tried to coexist peacefully with the Chinese invaders. But tensions worsened as more and more of Tibet's traditions were undermined, and more Chinese settlers moved into the country.

The situation exploded in the spring of 1959, when Tibetans attempted to throw the Chinese out and failed.

On a March night, the Dalai Lama and his family dressed themselves in peasants' clothing, slipped out of the Norbulinka, or Summer Palace, and escaped on horseback over the mountains to India. He was twenty-three.

Now he is middle-aged, the religious shepherd of a scattered flock, a Tibetan diaspora of one hundred thousand exiles.

There are colonies of Tibetan refugees all over the globe—in Nepal, in Switzerland, even in Indiana—and the once-cloistered Dalai Lama has had to become a world traveler to visit them from his headquarters at Dharamsala in northern India.

Back home, a generation of Tibetans has come into being and grown to adulthood in his absence. His palaces—the one-thousand room Potala and the smaller Norbulinka—have become museums.

And even he has suggested that the end of the reincarnation may be approaching, that when the people of Tibet no longer need a Dalai Lama, he will cease to reappear.

But there are no signs that the Tibetans at home have stopped needing him. They believe, in fact, that this Dalai Lama is going to come back to Tibet.

His picture is on every altar, in every active temple.

In the palaces, the beds he slept in are littered with offerings from pilgrims—coins, crumpled bills, handfuls of barley, and skeins of the gauzy white ceremonial scarves called *kata*.

Pilgrims bow when they pass the Potala, because it was his home, and in the Norbulinka they touch their heads and hands to the wall that bears his portrait.

One afternoon, as a friend and I lingered in the Potala at closing time, an aging monk hurried up to us, glanced around to see if any Chinese guards were watching, and struck a defiant pose, head up, shoulders back.

"Take my picture!" he commanded. "The Chinese will kill me if they find out, but take it! Send it to the Dalai Lama in India. Tell him that his monk says, 'Come back!'"

We sent the picture.

$\sim$

You can tell the losers in a culture clash. They're the ones running around in native dress, the ones selling trinkets to tourists, the ones who are bilingual. Winners never need to learn the other language.

That makes Tibet feel a lot like an Indian reservation in the American Southwest.

It was worse in Lhasa, a city of sixty thousand, where the natives are out-numbered by the newcomers three to one. That means Lhasa is not a Tibetan city anymore—it is an outpost of modern China.

"Lhasa is a disappointment," I wrote in my journal on our second night there.

Not that we weren't grateful for our spotless rooms at the Lhasa Holiday Inn, or for its abundant hot water and clean towels. It even had piped-in oxygen, bub-bling in bottles by the headboards—more than a courtesy, considering we were at 11,800 feet.

But as we sprawled on the comfortable beds, drinking Coke and watching *Death on the Nile* on the hotel's closed-circuit TV, we felt we were anywhere but Lhasa. And we could have been.

It was, I wrote, "a shell of a city, like Christmas morning after the gifts are opened and nothing is left but the wrappings. The Jokhang Cathedral (Tibet's holi-est shrine) looks as if it were restored by Walt Disney.

"There are better Tibetan souvenirs in Nepal than there are here. Better, healthier Tibetans, too.

"Cities of dreams ought to be left there. Without Shangri-La, what will I dream about?"

~

But Lhasa grew on me. Partly it was my own improving health and increasing acclimatization: Each day meant we could walk farther and climb more stairs before the altitude took our breath away. And the more we walked, the better we knew the city.

The other reason I liked Lhasa was the Tibetans.

In Tibet, a tug on a camera strap meant curiosity, not threatened theft. I'd look around and discover a child, an old person, once even a monk, solemnly exam-ining the peculiar block of metal and glass that swung from my shoulder.

It was a little like trolling: I never knew what I'd find on the end of the line.

They would smile up at me, blameless as cherubs, and then return to the cam-era, poking fingers and noses into the lens. I found I could make instant friends by directing their eyes to the viewfinder.

Innocent or not, though, it was disconcerting.

So was their habit of close inspection. Old people were especially fond of it.

Prayer wheels spinning, the great mantra of Buddhism moving on their lips—*Om mani padme him: O, though jewel in the heart of the lotus*—they would stroll to within a few inches of my face and then stand there, smiling benignly and eye-ing me head to toe, even when I didn't have Dalai Lama pictures to offer them.

At first, I thought they were addled. "Think of this as a nation of outpatients," agreed one of my equally disconcerted companions.

Frankly, I thought of them as chronological relics, mementos of another age, until one evening at the Jokhang Cathedral, when the tables turned.

The Jokhang is the pilgrims' ultimate goal, the religious center of Tibet, so important that the modern Western world offers no parallel. If Tibet were Europe, the Jokhang would be Chartres, Westminster Abbey, and the Vatican, rolled into one.

Pilgrims stream around it, close to four thousand an hour, in a river of black robes and rakish hats, men with red tassels in their hair, women with turquoise nuggets strunk on their braids, some people wearing charm boxes, some with daggers at their belts, some carrying statuettes of the Buddha as tenderly as if they were living infants.

Standing beside that fantastical parade, in my blue jeans, denim shirt, and pink sneakers, I suddenly felt idiotic and laughed out loud. I was the real curiosity, the one that didn't fit.

It was as if I'd been invited to the world's most elaborate costume party and had underdressed. The Tibetans who saw me laughing laughed too.

～

Though most obvious at the Jokhang, it is true everywhere: Prayers are in the wind in Tibet, fluttering into heaven with each gust on a prayer flag, each spin of a prayer wheel.

"Wheel" is a misnomer. The little machines look more like tin cans tacked loosely to the end of a stick. Twirl the stick to spin the can, and the written prayers it contains are wafted up to God.

People carry prayer wheels with them, so they can continue praying while doing other things, but prayer flags pray by themselves, whenever the wind blows.

Prayer flags festoon the high passes, mark bridges, bless the corners of houses and fields, protect painstakingly-made irrigation ditches, even adorn the living backs of yaks, Tibet's totem animal.

Scraps of thin cotton printed with Buddhist scripture, prayer flags are vivid when new—red, blue, yellow, green, or snowy white—but they weather badly. The dyes fade, the blowing dust stains them, and the wind worries them rapidly into rags.

A line of old prayer flags, fallen beside a pass, looks like laundry hung by elves—poor elves, at that.

So there always is a market for new prayer flags in Tibet. In Lhasa, you can buy them by the meter in the festive clutter of Barkhor Bazaar, the market street that encircles the Jokhang Cathedral.

The market is there because the pilgrims are there, and they are there because the Barkhor is one of three sacred ways that the devout must follow in Lhasa. It is by far the busiest, given that pilgrims must circle the cathedral, clockwise, at least three times; most do many more circumambulations than that.

Leaning on walking sticks, swinging prayer wheels, keeping count of their progress on Buddhist rosaries, the pilgrims form an unending parade, while prayer flags whip and rustle on the long poles in front of the temple and sacred juniper smoke rises like incense from its hearths.

Whole families walk together, the elderly leaning on younger arms, toddlers on foot until they get too tired, babies in their mothers' arms. Young men go by in little gangs, kidding each other, clowning around. Nearby in the crowd, as inevitable in Tibet as in Tallahassee or Timbuktu, cliques of young girls are walking, whispering to each other and managing to stay within eyeshot of the boys.

Some people prostrate themselves before they enter the Jokhang. Some prostrate themselves as they circle the temple. And a gaunt handful, their eyes wild by the time they arrive, make their entire pilgrimage this way.

Starting upright, hands raised prayerfully over their heads, they bow, kneel, lie down, stretch out, arise—over and over again, like devout inchworms, all in the name of God.

~

I liked to go to the Barkhor in the late afternoons, to watch the pilgrims and sometimes to join them for a turn or two around the temple.

Their pace, I found, is not fast but relentless. Stop for any reason, and you are left behind. Linger too long, and the pilgrims you started out with will come round again, catch up with you, and keep on going. They don't look back.

But they do shop. Lhasa's merchants recognized the market potential centuries ago, and the pilgrims' way is crowded with their booths.

On one circuit, I discovered a man making refills for prayer wheels—rolling thick pads of paper scriptures into tight cylinders like stubby fireplace logs.

He kept shop on the open street just beyond the guy with the performing monkeys, and just before the man selling hand-carved home altars.

Before them were the vendors of bread, yak cheese, charm boxes, hair ornaments, gold teeth, red felt boots, sheepskin cloaks, black wool dresses, Tibetan rugs, jewelry studded with turquoise and coral, the lady with bolts of prayer flags, and the group of novice monks, swathed in maroon robes, chanting for donations in the middle of the street.

~

Inside, Tibetan temples are as black as caves, lit only by the flames of butter lamps and their flickering reflections in the golden skins of the Buddhas.

The lamps are fueled with *ghee*, clarified butter made from the milk of yaks. The burning butter gives the temples a familiar smell, like the lobbies of old movie theaters.

Butter lamps look like goblets made of brass, full to the brim with melted *ghee* and continually refueled by pilgrims who spoon the stuff out of jars they bring from home. Before it melts, it looks like whipped honey.

Sometimes the pilgrims are too generous, and the lamps overflow. There are splashes of butter on the temple floors, butter on the railings, butter on the wall hangings, and buttery smudges on the faces and limbs of the protective deities.

Except for the peaceful Buddha, the exotic figures in the chapels are difficult for Westerners to comprehend. Like the Dalai Lama himself, most represent incarnations of spirit—energy made flesh.

But with their demonic snarls, bug eyes, and multiple arms, they look anything but serene. A few are considered so frightening that they wear cloth veils over their faces, to protect worshipers from shock.

Then you realize that these horrors are the good guys, showing off their powers against evil. Like He-Man, they're who you want on your side if times get rough.

Tibetan worshipers press together near the altars, concentrating on the figures they most revere, and there the buttery air is warm and full of human smells—old clothes, unwashed heads, the milky breath of babies.

That gives a cozy intimacy to the temples, despite their high ceilings and dark, drafty rooms. Ultimately, they seem not much different from medieval cathedrals in Europe: the same devotion, the same little flames glowing in front of holy figures, the same smells of oil and incense.

The gods are different, the demons more garish. But is Christian hell any less horrible than Tibetan? Is its heaven any sweeter?

Surely not. The blessings, too, are kin.

That was clear as early as the first temple at Tashilhunpo, when I glanced up at its huge Buddha and was jolted, as if physically hit, by the serenity of the Buddha's face.

It was like that every time, at Gyantse, at Drepung, at Sera, monastery after monastery, until I came to treasure—to long for—that sudden relief, that inoculation of stillness.

∿

Leaving Lhasa, we looped briefly north, through natural pastures where herds of yaks, looking like long-horned cattle under shag rugs, grazed at the foot of snow peaks.

Then we cut south into a region of blowing sand, crossed the young Brahmaputra River by ferry, and rejoined the main road, retracing our path through the dry valleys to Shigatse and the Nepali border beyond.

It was just as dusty as before.

When we got down past Zhangmu, the Chinese were blasting on the new road, so we waited with a clutch of porters for the shattered rocks to stop flying. We moved only when they did, and then straight downhill.

Up or down, those mountainsides were hard going. Even at the end of the trip, acclimated and in good health, my knees shook when the descent was over.

We walked back across the Friendship Bridge, went through Nepali customs in one of the roadside shacks that constitute the border hamlet of Kodari, and were picked up promptly for the long ride back to Katmandu.

We were on the other side of the rain shadow now—the wet side—and it showed. In the rich, slanting light of that afternoon, Nepal—poor, dirty, overcrowded Nepal—looked like a garden.

New rice gleamed neon-green in the paddies, and ripe wheat fluttered like gold leaf in the fields and lay in yellow drifts on the road.

Yes, the road: At harvest time, inventive Nepali farmers spread sheaves of wheat on the pavement and let passing traffic do the threshing. When you drive over the stalks, the liberated wheat kernels sound like fine gravel, leaping at the undercarriage.

∿

One image stood out from that golden afternoon—something so commonplace in Nepal that I would not have noticed it before our arid days in Tibet.

As we whisked through a village, we saw people bathing at a public tap, women in saris sluicing water over their brown toddlers. One little girl, naked and wet, suddenly darted away down the street, jumped over a sleeping dog, and then froze for a second in a shaft of sunlight.

Glistening there, she could have been a symbol for the miracle of water.

We had seen nothing like it in the Tibetan countryside. Back there, water was too precious to be wasted on anything so purposeless as a bath.

Back there, the dust devils were still whirling, even over irrigated fields, and the yaks were trudging, and the people, still wearing the black woolens they'd worn all winter, would still be looking up whenever a bus went by, to smile and wave at tourists they would never see again.

I thought of the dust blowing in clouds through the wretched villages. Of the costume party at Barkhor Bazaar. Of prayer wheels and butter lamps and monstrous demons. And finally of old people with their constant chants and innocent, smiling faces.

Shangri-La exists, I know now, but only where it always did: No nearer and no farther than the Tibetan soul.

The Encroaching Forest: Southeast Asian Memories

PLANTS & HOUSES (NORTHERN THAILAND)

A FEW MONTHS after I come to live in the house, I begin to realize that nothing in the compound exists without effort or purpose. The lush, tangled gardens surrounding us serve as constant reminder that until only recently the neighborhood belonged to the encroaching forest. The house, a perfect cube with glass walls and a frame and floors of solid, polished teak, is just big enough for Khun Ma and Khun Pa, my host parents, their daughter Nuan-wan and me. Gleaming and new, the house sits unobtrusively in the space it has claimed for itself. With all the glass louvers open, it is as if it has no walls at all and we are living in the midst of tropical wilderness.

It takes a while before I notice things: that the family never buys medicine, and the lemony bushes hedging the house repel mosquitoes. I attribute it to sheer luck that trees droop heavily with red finger bananas, fat pomegranates, and softening, sugary guavas whenever I'm hungry, that twigs grabbed randomly to chew are always flavorful, that a rambutan, with its rubbery red and green antennae resembling sea life, slipped inside somebody's sheets never fails to elicit a terrified shriek. I never question the fact that every morning I awake to the fragrance of mango, orange, and fig trees ripening in the sun outside my glass walls.

Once she sees my interest, Khun Ma spends hours trying to teach me about the surroundings she has created. I trail her through the gardens, a basket looped over my arm, as she pinches annatto seeds and sniffs galangal root. "I planned *every* plant you see in this compound," she says, handing me a stalk of lemongrass to test. Its clean, hot bite sears my mouth, and she nods briskly. "As a developing nation we need to know our environment in order to liberate ourselves."

At the dinner table she is continually fishing one leaf or another out of the soup. She holds it aloft and announces: "This prevents sore throat!" or "This one is clearing your sinuses!" Attentive, I nod at what to me looks hopelessly like yet another plant, indistinguishable from all the others.

～

The house has three different cooking or eating areas, all of which translate into English as *kitchen*. The first, a sleek room with Western appliances, is where we take our meals. Here, thanks to the maid, Phi (Older Sister) Niew, a steady supply of hot drinks and chilled fruits appears to replenish itself magically all day long. The second kitchen, located behind the house in a small cement building containing

Phi Niew's quarters and the laundry, keeps bulk foods and the baking oven—quite rare in the tropics. The last, my favorite, is simply an open clearing in the garden where a slab of cement has been poured on the ground. The wok and gas burner stand on one side, the chopping board and mortar and pestle on the other. This is the real kitchen.

There are two sounds I associate with the kitchen: the metallic staccato rhythm of Phi Niew's heavy Chinese knife against the worn chopping board, a solid cross section of tamarind tree, and the steady, hollow *thwap* of the wooden pestle against the side of the mortar as she pounds chili peppers, seeds spraying into the air and tears streaming down her face. I sit for hours on the warm cement at her feet, half asleep from the soothing sounds of her pounding. Giant flies hover just out of reach, driven wild by the stench of warm meat. I close my eyes and pretend that the noises are that of trees being cleared in the nearby jungle.

One evening early in my stay, a sudden wave of heat sweeps through the house as we are eating dinner, followed by an unprecedented chill. Immediately the kitchen is flooded with the overpowering perfume of night-blooming jasmine. There is a deafening crack, as if all the glass panels in the house have shattered simultaneously, and it begins to rain.

"First rain!" someone cries, and the entire family leaps up from the table, shouting directions to each other in *pasat nua*, the local dialect, which I don't speak. They seem excited but not upset, so I try to stay out of the way. Each person grabs a basket and rushes outside. No one thinks to direct me, and I am too surprised and too new to the household to demand an explanation.

Once everyone leaves, I run to the louvers and peer out. I can hear them laughing and calling to each other in the rain, but the wind blows their words away, and I am blind outside the glass perimeter of light. I chart their progress from inside the house, following the sounds from room to room. They move along the outside corners of the house, keeping low to the ground. I wonder what they could possibly be doing.

After twenty minutes family members begin to straggle in, flushed and triumphant. Nuan-wan extends a basket for my inspection: it is crawling with plump black beetles.

"Good thing we remembered!" Khun Ma rejoices. "The first rain last season we forgot all about them!" She turns to me, laughing, and promises, "I'll roast them for your breakfast tomorrow!" I grin weakly.

The next morning I find a basket of small bugs awaiting me. I wonder how to begin. The almost weightless creatures are still intact, their tiny legs permanently curled in the air above them. I stir them with one finger, and the dry bodies make a faint rustling sound.

Phi Niew comes in and shows me how to peel off the head casing and dip the body in chili sauce. The crisp insect pops on my tongue, the rich, oily taste of nuts or fried meat flooding my mouth. Relieved, I smile. Khun Ma walks in and beams to see me. "And *twice* the protein of meat!" she crows.

⌒

Another morning I accompany Khun Ma to a Buddhist temple. We see two nuns at the front entrance holding meager posies in the folds of their white robes. Their faces shine as brightly as their shaven heads, and I linger to smile at them.

Khun Ma smiles sadly. "See how they sell flowers to support themselves?" she whispers when we are out of earshot. "They can't even take the vow not to touch money!" On the car ride back, she will explain how using money relegates nuns to a lower spiritual plane, even though they are forced to support themselves. While monks receive food, clothing and shelter from the church and devout lay people, nuns are nobody's concern.

Inside we prostrate ourselves before the altar three times and light three sticks of incense. Like Christianity, Thai Buddhism is based on a trinity: the Buddha, his teachings (the *dhamma*), and the community of monks. The importance of the number three runs strong throughout Thai society, even secular life. Everything must be done, said, allocated in threes.

We leave the temple, and I look back, trying to imagine what makes these hungry nuns smile so. A beautiful nun with a glowing face hurries after us and hands me a golden blossom. "For you," she says, before returning to her post.

I am stunned at the gift. The flower looks fake, its petals so thin they could be made of paper. While Khun Ma and I are talking, I put it down and a full, heady perfume fills the sunny car. The fragrance reminds me of summers as a child, when I would ease my way through a cloud of bees to reach the orange trumpets on the honeysuckle vine and suck the nectar.

When we reach home, I find that the flower has burned up, leaving nothing but a scattering of pale, scented ashes across the dashboard like incense.

～

The best time of day is early evening. This is when I like to emerge into the quiet cool and ride my moped around the neighborhood. I pedal down narrow roads overhung with giant wild banana and coconut palms, leaving a cloud of red dirt behind me. Dwarfed, I feel on the verge of discovery.

I pass young housemaids with smooth, shy faces who look up from their laundry to smile at the first black woman they have ever seen, children sprawled asleep on porches, mouths open, still wearing their school uniforms. A new cluster of houses surprises me, almost hidden in the underbrush: modern glass-and-stucco bungalows, all pastel whimsy and odd geometry. Traditional wooden stilt houses, simple except for handmade lace curtains behind scrolled window grilles.

One evening, just as the sun is fading, I turn a corner and come upon a middle-aged woman in a clearing. Dressed in a bra and *sarong*, she rakes weeds into a roaring bonfire. She works furiously and does not look up. As the sky turns to night, the thick black smoke of the fire billows up around her and she disappears before my eyes.

I start for home feeling a bit unsettled. I hurry back, thinking about the first time I took out my contact lenses. The entire family stopped what they were doing and watched me, speechless. Eventually we worked out a system where each morning I wash and rinse my contacts, then place them on the counter near the back door. Phi Niew boils the case for ten minutes while making breakfast in the garden kitchen and then brings it to me in a little cut-glass bowl, still steaming. She walks slowly, her eyes trained on the sterilized treasure clutched in her hand.

As I approach the compound gate, I notice for the first time the tall cement walls surrounding the house, tops glittering with barbed wire and crushed glass.

～

Besides the glass house, there are two other houses in the compound. The old house standing cool and dim in the back, everything about it worn smooth with years, is quiet with sleeping children and women. Khun Ma's mother lives there with her teenage daughter-in-law, her grandchild and the maid Nong. Hidden in the garden between the two homes is the family shrine, a miniature house shaped like a temple with a traditional three-tiered roof. Every morning Phi Niew and Nong pass between the houses, delivering the food they have prepared. With each trip they pause at the shrine to leave offerings for the ancestors—balls of sweet rice, waxy jasmine blossoms, tiny cups of green tea.

One morning Phi Niew looks distracted at breakfast. I notice her worrying a cold sore at the corner of her mouth and watching Nong carefully. As I help clear the table, she tells me that years ago Khun Ma took in a foster child, a teenage boy who had been orphaned when two car accidents within one year claimed first his mother and siblings, and then his father and his mistress. When he himself was twenty years old, a truck hit the motorcycle he was driving, and he was killed. Because it was a violent death, Khun Ma engaged a spirit medium to hold a special ceremony that would recall the soul from its exile on the side of the road and grant it peace.

According to Phi Niew, the medium went into a trance, selected the boy's favorite clothes from a large pile in front of her, and put them on. Speaking in a young man's voice, she demanded foods that had been the boy's favorites. After eating and answering a number of questions to establish the authenticity of the spirit, the medium said the boy wanted to confess to murdering his father's mistress. The second car crash had not been accidental. Everyone was stunned. The medium then bowed before Khun Ma and begged forgiveness for destroying her motorcycle and leaving this world. At the end of the session, the boy's spirit moved to a tree above the shrine between the houses and refused to be born again.

A year or so later, Nong, who passed the tree regularly on her way to and from the two houses, was struck ill. She had a high fever, and large blisters covered her face and her body. Khun Ma took her to doctor after doctor, but no one could cure her or explain the illness. Finally they went to another spirit medium who said that the spirit of the orphan boy was lonely. He had seen Nong and was trying to kill her, so that her spirit would join him in the tree. Khun Ma and the medium made offerings at the shrine beneath the tree, and Nong recovered that night.

Phi Niew ends the story with a shy smile. "It is nothing," she assures me, touching her own sore. "Perhaps a reminder."

Nong says nothing. Grabbing a load of dishes, she disappears into the vegetation between the two homes. It is difficult to see her, though the walls of the house are glass, but I can smell the plants she brushes against, leaving a fading trail of lemongrass and ripening persimmon behind her.

Later, as I wheel my moped out from behind the house, I think about the boy whose spirit has climbed a tree and refuses to come down, about how even death could not destroy his ravenous loneliness. I wonder how offerings of orange sections and sticks of incense are supposed to help him. So far, no food, no scent, has helped fill that hungry space in me. Only movement.

I leave the compound and ride toward town. This time along the road I recognize meaning in things I previously could not even see. Nearly every few miles there is a cluster of white flags and strings and chalk lines. The highway is crowded with them. They are not, as I had always assumed, traffic markings, but sites where spirit mediums have lain the souls of countless transit victims to rest.

Now I understand why the third home is crucial to the compound. It serves to remind us that death drives along the side of the road with us, eating the same food we do. The thin white string and chalk lines not only bind the spirit's essence to earth, but show how slender is the boundary between the two worlds. I see why Khun Ma works so hard to make ancestral offerings and engage spirit mediums: It is, after all, a full-time job helping those who have suffered violence, those who are lonely, those of us in trees who refuse to be born again. Sometimes the work is not so much saving those who have left their souls at the side of the road, as it is keeping the survivors alive.

LOVE TOURISTS (SOUTHERN THAILAND)

It is a neon night in the sex resort, the balmy air weightless against our tanned faces. Thatched-roof bars strung with bright paper lanterns and girlie calendars line both sides of the town's only road. This is not what we expected.

Things have changed since we were here last. Then it was a cheap student vacation. Scott and I slept on the beach and bought fresh crab and coconuts from the native islanders. No one paid attention to us, two friends from school. This row of bamboo bars, looking like something from the set of a South Pacific movie, did not exist. Now the entire city dedicates itself continually to sex. Packs of men on "love tours" swagger the Strip, undressing all brown women with their eyes. Arab men, American men, Australian men, German men, Japanese men. We learn to walk with Scott's white hand proprietarily on my brown arm.

Local teenagers crowd the free discos. Flamboyant, heavily made-up mixtures of fashion and race, they do the latest dances from London and New York, next to tourists who could be their unknown fathers. Their younger siblings haunt the streets and bars, draped in chains of jasmine, selling packs of Lucky Strikes. The police maintain paradise by rounding up beggars, revolutionaries, the deformed, anyone who ruins the ambiance.

As foreigners fluent in the native tongue, we attract attention. Countless vendors approach just to hear us speak. Pawing through a basket of goods, I come across a find. "Look, Scott," I cry, holding up a flat yellow box. "No way!" he shouts, smiling. "I can't believe it! Chiclets!" We buy the gum and keep moving.

Grinning pimps swarm everywhere, pressing business cards against us that advertise the skills of their sisters and daughters. Scott pushes away their advances, shaking his head *no*, holding up his hands to ward them off. There is a flurry, two men shouting, a brief scuffle, then somebody flees and a fan of cards falls to the street. The squares of paper lay face up in the mud, boasting *Live live American-style show! See pussy eating banana! See pussy to blow out candle!*

We ignore the offending cards like roadkill, stepping over them to enter the safety of a quiet, open-air bar. We sit on rattan stools and order drinks and giant saffron prawns. The drinks—local rotgut whiskey distilled from rice—are dressed up with pastel paper umbrellas. As I take a sip of the harsh fermented rice, I feel a softness at my knees and look down to find a young boy beaming up at me. The child grips my leg, one tiny hand steadying himself, the other clutching a wire loop strung with plastic bags of pink shrimp crackers. His huge eyes meet mine easily. His unself-conscious touch in this place of pimps almost makes me cry.

Scott and I both bend forward on our stools to reach him. The boy stands bravely between us, beautiful and so very, very small. He wears a scruffy yellow sweater over a powder blue safari suit. I reach out and cup the point of his chin loosely in my hand, half afraid of leaving a stain on his translucent skin. He flushes and ducks his head. Scott asks his name at the same time I ask his age.

"Thum," he replies, too young to be surprised that we speak *pasat thai*. "I am five." He is the size of a three-year-old American child. He braces himself sturdily against our barrage of questions and answers each with great seriousness. Yes, he has already eaten. No, he doesn't go to school yet. Six, he has six brothers and sisters. At the mention of his siblings, his face blooms into smile. We ask him what time he goes home, but he is either unable to understand or unwilling to answer. Already it is after ten o'clock.

I ask the price of the shrimp crackers and Scott grimaces comically. "Oh no!" he says. "I *hate* those things!" Thum hoists the wire loop up to show that someone has carefully drawn the number *three* in red marker on each bag. Three *baht*. Ten cents. I hold up one finger. One bag. He gnaws his lower lip as his tiny fingers wrestle to pull a bag off the wire loop. After an effort, he hands me the crackers in exchange for three coins. I reach for the box of Chiclets and Scott begins to laugh. He shakes his head. "God, you're a pushover!" he says.

I hold the gum out to Thum, who immediately sets down his wares and pads his palms together, tiny fingers splayed. He bows to me, bringing his hands up to his forehead in a *wai*, a sign of respect and thanks. He is a child, so instead of returning the gesture as I would with an adult, I hold out my palm. As he brings his hands down into mine, I feel the faintest brush of his fingers across my skin. Only then does he accept the box. In perhaps just another year he will learn to put away such gifts to sell to the next tourist, but tonight he is still a child. Painstakingly he shakes out one piece of gum and puts it in his mouth. Again his face flowers into a smile. He labors to find his shirt pocket under his sweater, managing after several tries to slip in the box. "I can't believe you're giving him all our Chiclets," Scott moans in mock distress. "*All* our Chiclets!"

At that exact instant someone takes Thum by his left arm. We look up to protest. A teenage girl stands in the street behind him. She starts to pull Thum away, her resolute expression silencing us. A split second later a policeman takes his right arm. The policeman's grasp is gentle but determined. The girl looks at the policeman. She does not let go of the boy. The policeman returns her look. He gives his head a single, firm shake, and then Thum is gone, our hands around the space where he used to be, our silent mouths still open.

A few moments later a dark *Nissan* police truck creeps by, clearly on a sweep. Half a dozen child vendors lounge calmly in the open pickup bed. The studied boredom on their faces resembles that of their sisters, the painted bar girls who throng the street, looking on with only vague interest.

The policeman tosses his shaking body into the back of the truck, and Thum crouches where he lands. His face crumples and he begins to scream, his three-year-old's body shuddering with the force of his cries. I hardly recognize him, the intensity of his unhappiness almost unreconcilable with the soft child of five minutes before. The girl flutters, distressed, near the back of the truck, her hand still warm from holding him. She says nothing. None of the other children move. Thum is by far the smallest and the youngest among them. The truck moves on. Minutes after it has disappeared, Thum's shrieks still hang on the warm night air.

Long after life in the street has resumed, long after we have finished two plates of prawns in silence and several drinks each, we still do not look at each other. Though we don't know it, we are already checking out, already getting ready to leave. A few days later, in the final incident that prompts our departure, one of the posh international hotels burns to the ground, and the remains of at least five native women are found chained to beds. But tonight we dream of children. "No," Scott finally says, shaking his head curtly and once again holding up his hands. *No.* He may be saying *no* to what happened, *no* to what will happen, *no* to this place of pimps. Perhaps he is saying *no* to action, or to responsibility. But this time innocence is not as easy as walking away from the obscenity of business cards. We are here, and even if we never speak of this again, we have already by our presence said *yes.*

Coffee Break (Java)

I come upon the Jakarta Pizza Hut feeling a bit extravagant and giddy. I have spent days trudging around fetid, steaming Jakarta, my least favorite Asian city, black tears of pollution streaming down my sticky cheeks, getting the bureaucratic run around. I am tired of being in transit, tired of worrying about potential thieves and fakes, tired of trying to squeeze myself into native life. At last my traveler's checks have been replaced, and in two hours I have a flight out of this labyrinth of rubbish heaps and open sewers.

I stand outside the Jakarta Pizza Hut, bastion of Western culture, feeling at once compelled and repelled. It looks like any Pizza Hut anywhere in the U.S., and I haven't eaten for thirty hours. Still I hesitate. I pride myself on being a true traveler, able to withstand hardship, scornful of Western luxury. As I ponder, it begins to rain—big black drops that sizzle ominously as they hit the street.

The Jakarta Pizza Hut is nearly empty, and I am ushered to a table with all the pomp and ceremony due a dignitary attending a state funeral. A second waiter presents a menu with great flourish. Two others, apparently joined at the shoulders, take my order. Already drunk at the mere thought of my first cheese in a year—and soon to discover that I have picked up lactose intolerance along with other native customs—I develop a craving for wine. A fifth waiter passes by, and I call out in *bahasa indonesia.* Caught off guard, he nearly topples over in his eagerness to stop. He leaps to my table, responding immediately in English. Then, apparently taken aback as much as I, he stands speechless, blinking at me.

The fifth waiter at the Jakarta Pizza Hut is distressingly perfect. Indonesians tend to be lovely, but his classic beauty is universal, completely lacking ethnic stamp. He is tall and well built, with luxuriant, blue-black hair and sculpted features. His dark eyes gleam with what I choose to interpret as sincerity; his dazzling smile relaxes into a generous mouth. Dressed conservatively like a Connecticut college boy, he is well yet not overly groomed—unlike the pretty island boys in clicking-heeled shoes who prey on and are preyed upon by foreigners. Though such smooth beauty does little for me, I am suitably impressed. I tell him that I want to order a glass of wine and ask him please to send my waiter.

"Yes," he answers promptly. "A glass of wine. Certainly!" He leaves, glancing back over his shoulder. Almost immediately he reappears and places an entire carafe of wine on the table. I am surprised, but a year on the road has taught me not to question any perks along the way. As I thank him, I notice my gestures becoming expansive and more gluttonous.

After a year, the simple act of having wine with a meal is thrilling. The cheap juice enters my system like a fun childhood friend who doesn't really care what's best for me. One time I glance up just as the fifth waiter happens to be passing by. He feels the movement and falters in his path, watching me out of the corner of his eye. Confused, I look away.

A bit later I raise my head to find him facing me, standing perfectly motionless with his arms folded behind his back like every uniformed native in every tropical travel poster. At my gaze he promptly glides forward, "Yes?"

"Oh no, nothing!" I protest, wondering if I had indeed summoned him.

He asks in faltering English what I am reading, and it pleases me that his first question is not where am I from and why am I alone. His name tag reads Sudirman.

"About Bali," I answer, touching the book. "It's where I'm going next."

He steps to my right and picks up the book, his movements respectful yet confident. I wonder if he comes from money. As it turns out, he is a student at the National Institute for Hotels & Tourism, and this job is his field experience rather than his livelihood. Though I attend the occasional gala expatriate event, most of my friends are hungry priests, artists, activists. Sudirman is not the kind of Indonesian I usually meet.

He offers politely to take me sightseeing. I thank him then tell him that I'm leaving for Bali tonight. "Tonight?" his eyes widen. "Then please, when you return, to come here—or to my home. May I?" he asks, opening my book and writing his address inside the cover. I am explaining that I do not plan to return, that I hate Jakarta, when the twin waiters appear and stand behind him, clearly impressed by his self-assurance. We are all impressed. I laugh to see them peeking over his shoulder, and they blush, nodding to me.

Sudirman looks up, smiling, and touches one of them and then the other lightly on the cheek. "My friends," he says tenderly, and something in my chest shifts. He turns back to me, still incredulous at my news, "You don't come *back* from Bali?" He considers this, smiles, then suggests gently, "I think you had better cancel?" He widens his eyes and nods encouragement, "Yes, *please* to cancel your flight to Bali."

Bali. The place everyone in Indonesia seems to be dreaming about, travelers and natives alike. I am only passing through Jakarta on my way from one such dream place to another, my loose itinerary based on adding excursions to newly-discovered locales. What keeps me moving is the belief that the best in travel is the unexpected that appears and disappears along the way. What can't be planned or held. I don't need Sudirman. I don't need any of his possibilities. I've never stopped moving for anything or anyone before.

I consider the fifth waiter's proposition anyway, twirling my empty wineglass. I wonder what would happen if I stopped. *I wonder.* With all this wine and cheese in my stomach, I feel almost as warm and relaxed as if Bali were inside me. *Should I cancel?* Sudirman nods, smiles, waits; and I realize that I spoke out loud.

I have been avoiding local pickups, though in Central Java I almost regretted this decision. It had been the month of Ramadhan, and the entire city sat up every night, gathering at tiny candlelit stalls to watch flickering shadow puppet plays and wait for the four a.m. meal. On every dark street corner Muslims grouped together, murmuring and laughing quietly. Crouched among the *wayang* musicians, sleeping children and their dogs in my lap, I could have fallen easily in love and stayed on, settling into the rhythm of the sleepless city.

I think about rushing back to the guest house tonight before my flight to say good-bye to my Jakarta family: Edina from Berlin and Bud from Portland whom I keep running into throughout Southeast Asia. They've been feeding me ever since some neighborhood kids stole my traveler's checks. Mary, the beautiful Malaysian anthropologist who brings us treats from Embassy fêtes. Rudy, the Sumatran owner who's been letting me stay for free. Later he will take me to the airport, kiss me on both cheeks and the forehead, and say, "You shouldn't trust anyone, even me. You're always welcome. Send a telegram if you run into trouble." I think about arriving to yet another unknown city at night with my bag that never completely unpacks.

I hadn't noticed Sudirman leave, yet suddenly he appears with garlic bread and another carafe of wine. "You have decided?" he asks, putting them down. "You cancel?" We laugh, appraising each other, and he nods slowly until I am nodding too. "Tomorrow and tomorrow," he says with a smile. "Keep canceling."

"Okay." I tell him. If I didn't stay for something in Central Java, I can stay for something, here, now. "I cancel."

He pours the wine. "It is okay, I visit after working tonight?" His question is a formality.

A young well-dressed couple enters the restaurant, and after excusing himself, Sudirman runs over to shake hands with the man. Another waiter takes the opportunity to refill my glass and ask where I am from, why I am alone. I pay the bill, which consists only of the order taken by the Siamese twins. As I expected, there is no garlic bread, no two carafes of wine.

Sudirman returns and walks me out. "I finish at twelve o'clock," he says quietly, and his words reach me like a caress. I feel them like they were the back of his hand against my cheek. "Don't fall asleep."

Startled by this sudden intimacy, I step back. "But I'm exhausted!" I warn. He smiles, says nothing. "Well," I say. "You better really show up, then!"

"I will. Don't sleep."

~

At eleven-thirty we are all lounging at the guest house kitchen table, debating the best cities in Asia to receive mail *poste restante,* when Sudirman strides in, immaculate in pressed royal blue corduroys, polished loafers, and a long-sleeved, blue and white, tuxedo-style shirt. Gleaming in the light of the dingy kitchen, he is even more than I remember. I realize that I hadn't really expected him to come.

"Uh, hi," I say, at a loss.

He places two large pizzas on the table, bows to the circle of stunned foreigners, and sits down next to me. I feel as if a gentleman caller has wandered into my mother's parlor. After a moment he holds out his hand and asks, "Will you walk?" As we stand up, the group of travelers rips into the pizza boxes with a cry.

Edina turns to me, stuffing cheese into her mouth and shaking her head. "There you go again, Faith!" she mumbles between bites. "Just this morning you were broke, hungry, and hating this Jakarta. Now we are all indulging in expensive imported food! How *do* you do it?"

Later, when Sudirman and I return from our walk, I find the kitchen dark, the pizza boxes empty. All that's left on the table is a matchbox with *Pizza Hut: Jakarta • Singapore • Bangkok* emblazoned across the cover and a picture of a prickly *durian* on the underside. Though the flesh of the *durian* fruit is reportedly rich and intoxicating, the stench is so overpowering that no Westerner I know has ever tasted it. There are countless stories of travelers fainting in *durian* fields or abandoning cars they thought were about to explode because of ripe *durian* in the trunks. It is the quintessential Asian fruit. Days later, when I awake, rested, the wine and lactose purged from my system, and move on, this will be my only souvenir.

The Splendor of Fruit (Burma)

It is dusk in Rangoon. I sit smoking in my room at the famed Strand Hotel. I am alone and feel as though I am the hotel's sole occupant. Since my arrival I've seen no evidence of any other guests. Because of delays in Bangkok I missed the friends I was supposed to meet. I am pleased at the way things have turned out, pleased to have been left behind. Solitude seems fitting in Rangoon. Closed to the West since the 1940s, Burma is a country that has been left behind.

After the harsh, modern reality of Jakarta and Bangkok, Rangoon feels like an abandoned movie set. I can picture the dramas that took place: mysterious foreigners with strange appetites lounging downstairs in the smoky lobby; opium smugglers vanishing into the murky lighting of Rangoon's black market; colonial wives escaping the capital to summer in the cool hills of Maymo. Dressed in tennis whites, they sit fanning themselves on the verandah. Below, native servants crouch in the garden, transplanting imported strawberries by hand.

The post-war flight of the British must have been similar to the departure of a film crew: the fantasy cut short; the elaborate, impractical structures beginning to crumble into disuse. Today rotting colonial mansions house small cities of the homeless. Families squat in the echoing halls of deserted ministries. Outside, the sons of military officials rumble through the streets in the country's few cars— antique fin-tailed Cadillacs, their radios smuggled over the border from Thailand.

Listless, I do nothing. At seven p.m. the city is no cooler than it was at noon. A book of stories by Somerset Maugham lies abandoned on the dresser next to a half-empty bottle of beer. The warm, root smell of malt clings to the open mouth. *Mandalay Beer* is notorious among travelers on the Asia circuit. Perhaps its foul taste is due to a missing ingredient that can't be imported from the West. Perhaps it is simply a matter of local preference. Either way, the result is a dark, yeasty concoction, served warm in a country without ice. It is still fermenting as it touches the tongue.

The hand-drawn label on the bottle depicts a famous pagoda not in Mandalay at all but in Pagan, miles to the north. Pagan, where my friends are. Burma's ancient capital. *Village of 100 temples.* Favorite among the four cities to which each closely-guarded phalanx of tourists is rushed. I think I understand the marketing strategy: Mandalay is the country's most famous city, Pagan's temples its most-recognizable image.

The Strand Hotel used to be the center of colonial society, and being here is like stepping into someone's faded memory. I close my eyes to fix the scene: the bed covered with soft chenille nubs; the fragile, yellowing lampshade that coughs like an old drum at my touch. Draped over the rattan whatnot, my freshly-washed underwear drips slightly like someone perspiring. The carpet is indistinct; years ago it may have been red or violet but can no longer remember.

I open my eyes, and Maugham stares out. As reflected in the dresser mirror, the room makes an old photograph, stained and curling at the edges. Something about the reflection is wrong: me, a black woman holding a cigarette. When did I take up smoking? It is difficult to isolate my own memory. Originally I must have been dreaming of menthol and thought that cigarettes would keep me cool.

Burmese cigarettes are made of cloves. Their warm, cloying scent hangs over the entire country. There is no escaping the fragrance.

Suddenly it is an hour later—eight o'clock. The ceiling fan whines, languidly revolving its arms. Even on high speed it is virtually useless. It swirls cloves and malt into the thick atmosphere, unbreathed in years. Sporadically the air shifts like a musty animal, placing a damp, scented hand on my shoulder, the back of my neck. In search of anything cool, I leave my suite. The hallway is as wide as the street outside. My bare feet slap against the cool marble, and I am tempted to lie down on the unswept floor. I pass through anterooms and parlors and sitting rooms crowded with dark furniture: Settees and writing desks. Dusty ebony and teak. There is no sign, no sound of anyone else. At the end of the dimly-lit corridor, the communal bathroom gleams white.

I enter and sit on the edge of the claw-footed bathtub. The room is easily five degrees cooler. Everything in the long, narrow space is white: Glittering white tile walls and floor. Oversized white ceramic fixtures. Stubbly white towels. The only spot of color is the pale orange toilet tissue that feels like its made of corrugated cardboard. Envisaging a long, cool bath, I twist the bathtub knob, and a ribbon of rust sputters out. I remember that there is also a soap shortage. I climb into the tub and mop up the rusty water with toilet paper. The tissue is the exact same color as the water. Once the tub is dry, I take off my shirt and lie on my stomach. Pressing my face and chest against the cool, hard porcelain, I dream. Of ice cream. Cold beer. Lemonade.

It is nine-thirty when I awake, blue light streaming across my body. The light comes from the open window above. If I stand up and climb onto the edge of the bathtub, I can just squeeze my head through the narrow opening. The window faces a shanty town behind the hotel, leaning on the verge of collapse: Wormy planks patched together with scraps of cloth and cardboard; the eerie glow of battery-run blue lights after curfew. Noise and light spill out of every crack of the structure: Michael Jackson on black-market cassette. Voices raised in laughter and anger. The cries of children and dogs. In contrast, the dark street is utterly barren, as hushed as the hotel corridor. I am protected and trapped.

～

In my best Gloria Swanson imitation, I sweep down the grand staircase to the hotel lobby. Two white-gloved attendants in frayed uniforms spring up, leaving their conversations behind. They usher me through a stately set of glass doors off to the left. I enter another series of empty formal rooms, pale blue walls stretching to twenty-foot ceilings. I wander, already having forgotten why I came, until something feels out of place: An English-language newspaper strewn on the floor; an abandoned slab of papaya growing soft on a plate. Someone has recently been here—only a hotel guest would be allowed to do this. I hurry ahead.

The dining room, an elegant, Old World affair with ornately-carved ceilings, is nonetheless empty. Everything stands ready: Tables swathed in snowy linen, set with china, crystal and silver; wicker screens curving inward to isolate private conversations. A young waiter, his face dramatically scarred by pockmarks, rushes towards me from his post. His manicured nails are the color of raspberry sherbet.

Leading me to a chair, he suggests that, "Madame is wanting a nice bottle of *Mandalay* beer?"

"No," I respond, staring hungrily at his hands. "I want fruit. Lots of fruit. Any fruit. All the fruit you have." Anything to relieve this thirst.

In what seems like seconds, he returns with a large silver tray and begins to pile dishes and dishes of fruit atop the table until every inch of cloth is covered. He works quickly, silently. I gape at the staggering still life. At the splendor of fruit. The musky perfume of mango and pineapple. The whimsy of rambutan with its red and green tentacles. Plum-colored mangosteen, so quick to stain. Huge juiceless pomelos, tinted rust. With a flourish the waiter places before me a cut-glass bowl set inside a larger dish of chipped ice. "Chilled strawberries," he declares proudly at my startled look. "Just brought down from Maymo hills!"

I begin to understand the colonial aesthetic: the addiction to privilege; the seduction of creating a role and starring in one's own fantasy. This, then, must be progress: for the right price, now anyone—even a black woman—can play.

Shadow Puppets

HARRY AGUNG put me on the bus for Parangtritis, telling me there was a *wayang kulit* going on at the seaside, a shadow-puppet show to celebrate the annual wedding between the Sultan and the sea. When he saw me off, he cautioned me not to wear green near the water. "The goddess gets jealous," he called as I boarded.

The bus arrived after dark. Parangtritis is a small, one-street town, renowned during tourist season for the availability of psychedelic mushrooms. But in February, all the hotels and shops were boarded up. For the first time since my arrival in Indonesia, no one attempted to sell me taxi rides, hotel rooms, food, or souvenirs. The few children playing in the empty street ignored me. A man in a conical bamboo hat tugged along a pair of white oxen. One turned and bawled at a calf galloping anxiously after her.

I went into a small restaurant to ask where I might find a room for the night, but no one was inside. A handsome Indonesian woman called to me from a building next door, which turned out to be a *losmen*, a cheap hotel, attached to the restaurant. She showed me into a room smelling of cat piss and lizards. Her son brought gas lamps, lit them, and placed them around the room and just outside the door. She unfolded heavy straw mattresses onto two wooden beds, and added a sheet and pillow to each. She gave me a tiny padlock and key for the door, and showed me how to close and latch the wooden shutters at the windows should I leave the room.

They went out. I sat down, intensely relieved by the polite quiet with which I had been greeted. For the first time in weeks I was alone. I had finally escaped Ellen and Herbie and all the other expats telling me I was doing everything wrong, showing off their superior knowledge of Indonesia and the Indonesian "mind."

I hid my possessions under the bed and went next door to get something to eat. Traditional *wayang kulits* usually start late and go on all night. I planned to catch up on letter writing while waiting.

A couple sat at a table inside. The woman was thin and tanned, with waist-length brown hair, dressed in tight white jeans and a loose backless T-shirt. She had a New Zealand accent. She seemed completely unaware of the inappropriateness of her near nudity. I envy such women, next to whom I always feel a little drab in my attempts to offend no one.

She was talking to an extraordinarily colorful Indonesian man. He too had waist-length hair, cut into a short mane around his face. He wore an orange and green tie-dyed cotton jersey vest, which bagged from his shoulders, exposing his nipples. A dark purple sarong was tucked up between his legs into short ballooning pants slit at the sides to his hips. Brightly embroidered slippers protected his feet. Heavy rings were on every finger. I was most struck by his unexpectedly round face. Most Indonesians are painfully skinny by American standards. He was by contrast almost decadently plump.

I sat at a table on the porch beneath a fizzing storm lantern, ordered fried rice and eggs, and wrote while half listening to their conversation. The man drew clothing designs for the woman, who was interested in importing samples to Australia. They haggled prices.

The proprietress of the restaurant and hotel brought me a guest book to sign. A tourist couple passed on the street. A yellow cecak lizard ran down a pole onto my table and sat gulping insects attracted to the light.

A tall young foreigner materialized out of the darkness onto the porch and joined the couple. His arms looked squeezed dry, the arms of a habitual drug user or someone who had been sick for a long time. His short, messy hair stuck out from a green headband. He was barefoot, in a tight, knee-length, ragged blue sarong, and a sleeveless red T-shirt with gray and white ribs painted on it. One arm was completely tattooed. Amulets and talismans dangled from his ears, neck, wrists, and ankles.

He sat down next to the Indonesian man without looking at him, then spoke to the woman in an aggrieved whine about some look he claimed the Indonesian man had given him that afternoon. The woman made light of it. He yelled back at her angrily, "You don't know! You don't understand. I!! . . . have a magical mind!"

The Indonesian got up and walked to the edge of the porch. He stood staring into the dark, ignoring the argument behind him.

The woman said, "Well, Sean, I have an entirely scientific mind."

"I know." He fumbled, "It's just . . . I need . . . I must. . . ." The Indonesian went back to his seat. Sean still did not look at him. The woman tried to get Sean to leave with them, but he refused. He sat frowning as they left, then went into the back of the *losmen.*

I continued to eat and write. I felt embarrassed by Sean's outburst. While he seemed angry with the Indonesian man, he disregarded him completely, as if the Indonesian had been invisible.

Half an hour later, the Indonesian man returned alone. He sat down across from me at my table. I stopped writing. The gas light sputtered and lowered, then flared up again brightly, passing shadows like the flames of fireworks over his face.

I braced for the usual twenty questions: "Where are you from? Are you alone? Are you married? How long are you here? How old are you?"

But without preliminary, he asked, "Why do foreigners put themselves here?" as he raised one hand to eye level, "and us here?" the other hand at chest level.

His hands in the light seemed cast in silver. I could feel him staring at me, but couldn't see his eyes past the glare.

"I don't know," I said, thinking back to everything I had seen since arriving on Java. "Perhaps they're afraid of losing themselves in a strange country. If they didn't put themselves above you they would be forced to look around, see things differently. That's frightening."

"You?"

"Yes. I'm frightened. So many things are different here. I don't know who or what to believe."

"But you don't put yourself up here. You're open."

I suspected he was flattering me, but answered truthfully. "Well, I came here to be changed. If anything, I feel lower than you. You are all my teachers. I can't talk, eat. I don't know how to dress properly or be polite. I'm a child here. How can I act as though I know everything?"

"Then why are foreigners so impolite? Why do they talk as if we don't exist?" He asked this without anger in his voice, seeming genuinely puzzled. He seemed to be trying to comprehend why Sean, whom he had thought a friend, now would not talk to or look at him.

I had no answer, so I ordered tea for us. He told me his name was Andra, then asked, "Do you mind talking with me about these things?"

"No. I think about the same things a lot."

"You are honest with me."

I asked him to sit next to me so I could see his face. He shifted seats, then ordered fried rice. "I'm starving," he said.

I was surprised again. I had never heard an Indonesian state hunger. They usually ask me if I've eaten yet, and will not eat unless I join them.

Friends of his entered the restaurant and sat in a dark corner of the porch, playing guitar, drinking tea, and laughing. They all wore bright clothes and a lot of jewelry. They were all obviously stoned. After quick greetings and curious glances, they ignored us. They were what Ellen used to call disparagingly, "Land Crocodiles," the young Indonesian men who survive by scamming tourists.

Andra's liking of food made him seem less dangerous, different from his friends. I trusted the softness of his face, hands, and stomach.

Sean reappeared, staggering up the steps. He ignored me as he came up to confront Andra. "How many beds in your room?" he demanded.

"One."

I saw the lie in Andra's body while he maintained a polite face. Sean said angrily, "I have nowhere to sleep." He stood over us—dingy, gaunt, spoiled—waiting for Andra to solve the problem.

"Do you have money?" Andra asked mildly.

"Yeah." Sean sounded affronted, as though he should not have to pay for himself. "Oh, never mind. Don't worry about me." He flapped his hands and turned back to the darkness, his back rigid and steps fumbling.

Andra ate in silence. The proprietress and her son began folding up chairs and clearing condiments from the tables.

"Why are you here alone?" he asked me.

"I'm going to the *wayang kulit*. It's supposed to happen tonight somewhere."

"Ah. Yeah. . . . I come with you, okay?"

I hesitated, unsure of the place or him. "Oh. Okay. It starts pretty late. . . ." I didn't want to be rude. He had been pleasant, unthreatening. I decided to overlook the redness of his eyes, the lack of constraint in his speech.

I wanted to ask him how it felt to dress colorfully and act so freely in a country where I have been repeatedly told blending in and discretion are prized over individuality. I am used to being stared at or approached because I'm white and tall and alien. But how strange it would be to make a life out of befriending the aliens while being rejected by almost everyone else.

It was after ten when we left for the shadow-puppet ceremony. There was no electricity in town, on the streets or in the houses. Soon there were no houses.

Andra walked close to me, but not touching. The proprietress sent her son after us with a flashlight, but he didn't turn it on. None of us spoke.

I had a sudden moment of paranoia. What if they jumped me? Was I a fool to be walking in the dark with these two unknown people? But my worries came not from the ones walking beside me, but from Ellen's warnings, her disdain for men dressed like Andra.

After about half a mile, I began to hear the far off clack of wood on wood, then the staccato falsetto of a man's voice speaking an ancient dialect: the puppet master. We turned left onto a dirt road curving back to the beach. Ahead the whole village stood around a flourescent-lit hut. A generator ran nearby. Shadows of gods and goddesses danced on a screen at the end of the bamboo and leaf walls. The Sultan and his family, dressed exquisitely, sat inside on folding metal chairs. Villagers stood outside peering between the leaves at the far-off shadows. I was conscious of their quick looks at me and Andra as I went near the entrance to watch the puppets over their heads. The boy who had accompanied us squeezed in amongst them. Andra stood off to one side, bored. He shifted from foot to foot, then moved behind me, sighing occasionally. I suggested he return to town without me.

"Never mind. I wait. It is Indonesian." I went on watching the shadow puppets. They faded on and off the screen, dancing, fighting, singing at each other, all accompanied by the high, inconstant beat of wood on wood.

Andra got something in his eye. I took him to a light, but found nothing. Then it began to rain. First just a few drops, then it poured down. Andra pulled me into a food stall and ordered tea. We sat together companionably. Thin old men lounged on benches in the corner, staring at us. We gazed out at the rain, which all but hid the lights of the *wayang* just a few yards away. Andra reached past me for the ash tray. Long, dark scars ran in parallel strips across the width of his inner arm. One was raised the length of his arm, like the gash on a loaf of bread.

"Knife fight?" I asked, pointing.

He gave me a little smile. With his right hand he mimed cutting himself with a razor, sprinkling granules into the wound, then holding the skin closed to keep them in.

I looked away, inadequate to the revelation of his addiction.

He told me.

He came from a well-to-do family in West Java, the youngest of four children. By the time he was twelve, all his siblings had left home. His father and mother were unhappy together. "One night, I knew in a dream how to help them." He showed me how he'd broken his bedroom window and climbed out. I couldn't imagine him, a frail twelve-year-old, flinging himself out naked into the night. Had it really occurred, or was it part of the dream he was telling me?

He left home, he said, to unite his parents in grief over losing him. He told me this unself-consciously, as though it were perfectly logical. He traveled a long distance alone, first to his sister's house, then to his brother's. They didn't want him and thought he should go back. He ended up with a cousin.

I couldn't follow the next part of the story. His English became less fluent as he moved back and forth in time with an almost embarrassing intensity, as though reliving the past for my benefit. He didn't have the careless, relaxed attitude with which Indonesians usually describe hardship. Like his comment, "I'm starving!," it showed an uncommon strength of feeling for himself.

I wanted to touch him and say, "You must forgive them," but was afraid he would take it as criticism, and said nothing.

He told me he had been a junkie for four years. I missed what led up to it, but it had been when he was a teenager. To reassure me, he said, "Now I dislike drugs. I don't take them." I believed him.

"Look at my eyes," he said.

"What?" I didn't know what he expected me to see.

"They are always red now. Friends ask, 'What you been smoking, Andra?' but I smoke nothing."

Then he told me, again without transition, about waking up in a hospital, blind. With his eyes open he could see only yellow darkness. He had overdosed, or had some bad heroin, and for three months was close to death. Sometimes he heard his sister praying in one corner. Once he felt her lay her hand on his chest to be sure of his breath. When he did not die, she wept to have him back.

Still he continued withdrawal. He described itching unbearably, screaming with fear of remaining blind, his body uncontrollable with pain.

One day he came to consciousness in an insane asylum, just as they were wheeling him to electro-shock therapy. He struggled and broke away, screaming, "I'm not crazy!" The doctor who had ordered the treatments had not read his records, had no idea of the history of his abused body. Andra grabbed a bottle, broke it, and held the doctors and attendants away. They called his brother, who told them he really wasn't crazy, just a drug addict coming out of withdrawal.

Again I was startled by the violence of his story. It seemed impossible. The scars I could understand. They were part of the ritual of need. But looking at his soft face, hearing his gentle voice, I could not envision him, thin, shaking, anguished, terrified. I couldn't imagine that much passion in him.

The rain had, if anything, increased. The townspeople, not allowed into the Sultan's shelter, held banana leaves over their heads or crowded into the doorways of the little *warungs*. We waited for the rain to stop.

His friends took turns reading my palm and making prophecies in Indonesian. I was restless. I joined the people in the doorway and stood staring out towards the opening of the *wayang*, which seemed very distant. The clacking singsong of the puppet master continued unceasingly.

Andra came and stood beside me. I was cold, but he was shivering. I took my sarong from around my neck and draped it around him. He shifted it up around both our shoulders. We stood close, but not touching.

Well after midnight, the rain slackened. We decided to brave the wet and run back to the hotel. The mud was ankle deep. We removed our shoes and ran barefoot, squelching, laughing, leaving the watchful villagers and his boring friends behind.

Once on the paved street, we redraped the sarong into a damp umbrella across our heads, continuing barefoot. It was so completely dark that I could not even see the silhouettes of trees against the sky or the edge of the road. I felt disconcerted, dizzy, and wildly silly.

A car blinded and then passed us. It stopped and began to back up. As it pulled closer, Andra said, "Wait." Pulling off the sarong, he turned to face the car. It quickly sped away.

"They thought I was a woman because of my long hair and big body. They were coming back for another look." He ran ahead of me, laughing, then minced with a swaying walk, the sarong pulled around him like a skirt. I had to admit it was hard to tell from behind, and laughed with him.

It seemed a much longer walk back, but finally I saw the haze of gas lanterns in town.

He asked if I'd had any experiences with drugs or drug addicts. I told him I'd had a boyfriend who had been a cocaine addict and had stolen money from me. He touched me on the shoulder, halting me. He looked at me seriously. "Yes. Addicts are bad. They will always steal from you, even if they say they love you. You must be careful."

I wondered for a moment if he were warning me against himself.

At the *losmen*, we stood on the porch for a few moments. "Goodnight," I said awkwardly.

"Wait. I have something to ask you."

I sighed and stepped back, thinking, "Here it comes. He couldn't leave it alone."

"You are my friend, right?"

"Yes."

"Even though I just met you I know that, or I would not ask this."

I waited.

"Please let me stay in your room tonight."

I shook my head, annoyed.

"There are already four in my room and only two beds. It is very crowded, and you also have two beds. . . ." He smiled, unabashed.

I thought, "If I cannot trust, what else is there?"

I pulled myself up tall and said, "All right. But I don't want anything else. You understand? If you touch me, I'll kill you." I was amazed by my own ferocity as I said this, by my own conviction not only that I would try, but that I was physically capable of killing him.

I could not explain to him that it was not my body I was protecting, not my sexual honor, but the honor of my trust, my intuition. I couldn't bear to lose it, to have him betray our sudden and unlikely friendship. I could hear Ellen saying, "Look out for those creeps, those land crocodiles. Don't dare bring one home." I defied her propriety. I defied every foreigner who had told me I didn't know what to do, that I didn't have any idea what was really going on in the "Indonesian" mind.

He thanked me and disappeared in back of the *losmen*, to take a bath by lamplight.

I was not wholly oblivious to self-preservation. I went into my room and tried to move the beds apart. I was dismayed when even an inch gap between them blocked the edge of the door and made it impossible to open. I pushed them back together, then put my backpack well under the bed and hid my money and passport under the mattress.

He returned carrying his wet clothes and a gas lamp. He was divested of ornament, dressed only in red bikini underpants. I nearly laughed from surprise, but caught myself.

Despite the tight, round belly protuding over his red underwear, he was beautiful. The lamplight cast low, red shadows across his soft brown skin. His face was in darkness, surrounded by his long black hair.

I wanted to stare at him, but didn't want it mistaken for an invitation.

Flustered, I grabbed my towel and the other lamp, then went to bathe in the outhouses. I returned in a long T-shirt and underpants, and hung up my clothes on a peg. Andra was already in bed, lying against the wall. I quietly closed the door and blew out the lamps.

The sky had cleared. The full moon was rising and lay a space of light between us. With a quick rustle, Andra rolled toward me. He lay directly alongside, but only the hairs on my leg and arm tickled with his closeness. He whispered, "Tell me a story."

I told him about my childhood, my friends, then a long joke which he laughed at politely but didn't really get. Then he told me a story about some animals. I thought it was a Javanese fable and listened with all the rapt attention of the amateur anthropologist, until I realized he was telling me a dirty joke.

He took my hand. We lay in silence.

I was very sleepy, but too aware of him, too guarded to relax. At the same time, I felt a deep sensual pleasure lying beside his warmth, having intentionally chosen to trust him. I thought, "If he tries to make love to me, how will I respond?"

Then I thought, "I should tell him to tell his friends we didn't." I imagined my embarrassment in the morning. I was about to speak to him about it, then realized I couldn't. It would be the same as saying, "I don't really trust you." As a matter of face, he would probably brag about me to his friends. If he promised to tell them the truth, that we hadn't made love, then I would be forcing him either to lie to me or lose face with his friends. I sighed and let it go. I knew if I was to trust, it must be completely.

At that moment he rolled up on one elbow and pressed against me. I lay relaxed, not allowing him to sense my wariness.

He said, in the small voice of a child desperately needing to be cared for, "I don't want you to think I'm a bad man. I don't want *you* to think I'm a bad man." Then he leaned over and kissed my forehead. "Thank you." He rolled back across the light dividing the narrow beds. Soon I heard his breathing change and deepen as he fell asleep.

I lay wide awake. Cecaks were calling in the roof of the *losmen.* I heard bats winging by outside, lizards running overhead. The moonlight softened. The room grew darker. The ceiling seemed much higher, diffuse and pale.

I had. . . .

How can I explain it?

I had an extraordinary feeling of exultation. Of perfection. I felt, there is no other word for it, redeemed. Nearly in tears, I lay awake, aware of his breathing, the moon, my own hot skin on the hard bed.

At dawn, he quietly got up and left, perhaps to protect me from the shame of others seeing him exit my room. I pretended I was asleep. After he was gone I finally did fall asleep. When I awoke again two hours later, the flawless ecstacy of the night was still with me. I was unconcerned about facing his friends, Ellen, anyone.

He had freed me to trust.

The Memory of Unusual Things

"**A** WOMAN, nearing forty, gets married. She is ready to have children, but after some trying finds she is unable to conceive. She consults a doctor. Was it this difficult with your first child? the gynecologist asks. I've never had a child, the woman says. Yes you have, the doctor tells her. And then the woman remembers. She was raped repeatedly by her father. She bore a child by him and gave that child up for adoption and then forgot. This a true story," a woman in a swimming pool said to me. "I know someone who knew that woman," she said. It was raining. Drops of rain were falling on my face as the temperature of my body dropped. The woman, whom I had just met, told me this story as we breaststroked the perimeter of a small blue pool in central Java. She was a middle-aged woman herself, who had recently left her family for the love of another woman. She was resting in the pool after a month-long trek in the Nepal Himalaya with her youngest daughter and had continued her trip alone in order to grieve, or in order to stop grieving, I cannot now remember which, because when alone her face possessed the transparency of one in the process of remembering. My lover and I came upon her during these pensive moments over the course of a week at our hotel, notebook open where she sat eating hot soup, recovering from a malaise of the stomach. The pool was being retiled that week, and after breakfast the screech of power tools drove us from the hotel into the hot streets of Yogyakarta. We went to the famous bird market where fire ants whose eggs are sold as bird feed bit our ankles as we walked. Parakeets and mynas, a large number of cocks and pigeons. Small caged bats sold as decoration for the house.

At night I gave myself to the abandoned pool. And there was the woman floating beneath the stars. We introduced ourselves that first night and when I told her I traveled with my lover, also a woman, she began to mete out stories to me like lengths of rope. "I cried inconsolably with my daughter in Nepal," she said. "I can no longer bear the company of men."

One night when I came down to swim a small creature had taken the woman's place in the pool, perhaps a large moth, beating its wings frantically and rhythmically back and forth. I didn't have my glasses on but my lover, leaning over the balcony, correctly identified the thing as a bat, unable to shake the weight of the water from its wings and rise. She found a net by the side of the pool and scooped the animal up. We peered close to its face and it beat its wings as if to escape until we let it be. My lover, herself a lover of unusual things, rose in the dark to check on the bat, but sometime in the night it had dried and flown away. This pleased my lover and soon she was able to sleep. The woman from the pool took a night train through Java to the coast, then a boat to Bali where we would see her again at a beach in Sanur, and again at a pool in Ubud where we each paid five hundred rupiah to swim.

Arbor (Kyong-Ju, South Korea)

Because all had been destroyed by war, everywhere the countryside bore the mark of intention: pink azalea, yellow forsythia, cabbages and greenhouses congregated like brethren in the fields. We rode a bus down the coast, stopping in rest areas where hundreds of people spilled forth from small cars to eat ice cream, drink coffee, to photograph each other in the car exhaust, and smile, which signified holiday to them. Arbor Day. Cherry trees blooming in the long lane that wound down to the village which had become our destination by virtue of a guidebook we had purchased in another, hotter country, one not so gracious to our pink and tender skins. Here the sky produced a fine mist which clung to the pink blossoms lightly so as not to knock them from the trees, coating them a translucent silver as if they were, every one of them, encased in a fine webbing of light. Quiet, though many people traveled the streets of the town, women selling tangerines on the corner where the bus, after many hours, let us out.

~

We took a room in the English-speaking hostel, slipping our shoes off and letting our feet marvel at the heat coming up from the floor. *Ondol*, the native word, but this was a modern building so the heat we felt was electric, not the smouldering charcoal of the past. This was a modern city, everything having been destroyed by war, though the *kimchee* pots that lined the tiled roofs and small walled gardens gave the place a feel of self-sufficiency that spoke to us of older times, my lover and I, happy to be in a climate more like the one to which we had grown not exactly native I would say but familiar nonetheless, like mockingbirds looking easily for food in the snow.

In the morning we strolled the market for food, pointing to the piles of noodles when we wanted to eat: fish soup, meat soup, the wilted, peppery leaves; dried fishes, pickles and radish, heads of pigs on the table declaring the richness of the broth. Women smiled their approval when we began to eat, no matter whose table we decided in the end to grace, words passing among them all like a multitude of eggs in the briney air. Garlic, spoons, a cup of tea and thank-yous bowed slightly from the waist.

In the afternoon we visited the vast green burial mounds the town had long been famous for, among the lines of schoolchildren carrying umbrellas, red, and elderly people walking also in a gray mist which made us feel both reverent and excited. The grass in the park was clipped and sure as a horse, teams of labor women dressed in gray scrubbing dead bark from the trees. They stood on stepladders to reach the higher limbs, and when they lifted their hands from their individual buckets the yellow of the gloves they wore shocked me, like flowers blooming on the leafless trees. Ginseng tea so sweet I couldn't drink it and chose instead the local coffee into which we stirred spoonfuls of dry, whole milk, turning it the color of the uniforms.

It was later that we entered the baths.

Unsure what to do and ill-prepared, we purchased soap from the attendant as we paid, removed our clothing gingerly in the dressing room, and entered, fully naked, the place for washing, awkward and timid as girls. Inside—such treasures!—sinuous fog and modesty tempered only by intent, each woman squatting in front of spigots with her own basket of useful things: loofahs, washcloths, bottles of fragrant shampoo. Children splashed near the drains in the floor and old women gossiped, but softly, as they washed, gesturing to the hired woman to come and scrub their backs. Muscular and bored, she wandered among us in black underpants and a nylon bra, also black, a spider wielding rough cloths in her hands. Should we, or should we not have, admired the bathing women? My lover, the studious one, watched the way they scrubbed themselves a few square inches at a time, and set to work at once on herself. I rose to enter the square stone tubs, unfurling at last to my full body's height, a giant among the native women methodically washing, achieving their weekly godliness in a climate of extremes: the hottest water, the coldest water, the steam I tried to linger in but could not stand.

What family did not come to the temple next day? Families lined the paths and covered the hills with their resting, portable braziers sending smoke into the air like offerings for the gods. Women entered restrooms in Western suits and came out again in traditional gowns, colorful sashes tied beneath the breasts, satin skirts ballooning in front to the ground. Lilac, saffron, shocking pink, women like flowers, like birds! A thousand cameras photographed the national pose which seemed, to me, apologetic: tilted heads, folded hands, men pulling boughs of blossoms to their faces. Cherry blossoms hushed the ground, even the vendors were peaceful selling their treats as we passed: ice cream, sugared corn, dried squid softened over a flame to wave like flags in the hand. We entered the grounds temple. We peered inside the shrine where the Buddha was kept in his most magnificent repose. People left coins and lit candles on the altars, women in their modern heels kneeling. Wafts of monks walked quietly home, somewhere a bell, the faithful falling easily into silence. Ponds full of koi seemed especially well kept. I sat on a bench while my lover roamed, and can see her even now in my mind's eye examining the tiles of the temple roof, how simply and elegantly they fit together, how she came in that moment to admire without envying them, which was the gift of that place.

We packed our bags. We bought oranges and cookies for the long trip home. When we left Kyong-Ju the guest house owner gave us each a pair of flowered socks, white with fawn-colored heels and toes. "You will come back," he said. On the bus a conversation that came to center around the subject of plot, how a lack thereof leaves one restless and yet how little a story requires in order to succeed, like the river we were crossing was successful though it was low that time of year, edged by people hoeing between turnips in their rows.

Rita's House

"**N**UKARIN KA MINTA?" the old lady Persing asks. She sucks a thin, homemade cigarette, the burning end in her mouth. She removes the soggy stick, and asks again, through craggy, black teeth, louder, "Nukarin ka minta?" I lift higher my market basket overflowing with turnips, onions, rice, instant coffee, a secret hidden roll of Joy toilet paper, a bouquet of midget bananas in my hand, so she can see where I've been.

But I don't answer. I point to home with my lips, point toward the river, excusing myself. She raises her eyebrows, smiles, leans against the doorway of her tiny bamboo house. Dark shadows behind her leap. A pig squeals shrill in the dirt, and I jump back, startled. The old woman hoarsely laughs phlegm; blows me on my way with her withered hand.

When I reach my house, first I reach Persing's daughter, Rita Garcia—the landlady, the witch, the one who cooks the gruel with bloody-bloody soup in my front yard every day, the one who wants me out of her house so she can move back in. As I approach her food stand, we smile fake, size each other up and down. Her wet black eyes pilfer through my load of stupid American shopping, though I do have rice. I want her to know that, yes, I do eat rice. I adjust my bags.

"You buy so very much food," she says. She stirs a big pot of brown bloody-bloody, and I watch as chopped intestines float fast like dizzy rigatoni. I shiver in the heat. "You are hungry?" Earnestly I shake my head, pat my stomach.

"Mengan na ku," I tell her I've eaten, tell her I'm full. "Where is Ryan?" I look around for her miniature washed-out boy, her life, her wispy little sickly only child, the one she brags of and beats on. In the early mornings, I have peered through window slats and seen her whipping him senseless back by the water pump.

"Ryyyy-aaaaaaan!" her voice rips apart the silent afternoon, and then, embarrassed, she giggles. "That my little baby he is a so sick. And my mother and sister, they give to me no moneys for the food to my baby." She tries again, she tries—sad stories about her horrible life, her estranged husband, her poor child—so that I will give her money. And I want to. But I pay rent for the house; I pay more than enough for what I get. Her husband left behind a half-completed, crumbling cement box—an empty gray cavern with wide open windows, rats, snakes. The rains spray in and puddle yellow on the floor like urine. If you touch the wall, it crumbles. I pay her out of my small teacher stipend. I pay her more than most people in the barrio make in two months. And yet.

231

I sigh sympathetically, hoist my purchases up, and head for the house. But Ryan pops from behind the corner, his skimpy tank top dirty and full of holes, his nostrils caked hard with green snot. He sticks a finger in his mouth, kicks in the dirt, and then makes a mad dash for his mother across the dirt yard.

"*Si, Ryan, 'gunda Americana.*" She swings Ryan onto her hip, and sways with him, pointing at me. "*Magunda,* say 'beautiful,' Ryan, say, 'bea-ut-i-ful Americana.'" Ryan digs his face into her chest, as if to actually climb back inside her body.

I feel ashamed, silly, big, ugly, and unlock the padlock on the plywood door to let myself in. As usual, pigeon crap chalky white all over the cement floor, all over pots and pans, all over the hard wooden couch. Freshly-hatched mosquitoes buzz out of my damp towel, their stripes vivid and heavy on their bottoms. Pink lizards dash under the table, out the window, up the walls. To at last be home, I breathe relief.

I sweep up bird droppings, set water to boil on the kerosene stove, dump rice in a special tin to keep out rats — and then the rain. It comes on suddenly, like a bout of hysterical sobbing, and refreshes the end of each day. Bamboo leaves click and ticker in the wet. The tin roof pounds.

I go to shut the plywood door, but see Rita still outside, not yet gone back to her mother's house down the road. She sits on a wooden bench with Ryan's head on her lap, smoothing his hair. A patchwork of pastel rice sacks hangs over bamboo poles and protects them from the rain. Rita sings sadly, and sways back and forth watching the rain, watching nobody go by. She hears me as I try to sneak shut the door, and turns. Her eyes snap at me black, then she smiles sadly, and I simply cannot shut the door, shut her out.

"You are cooking the rice?" she asks, pulling Ryan closer to her. She kisses his wispy nothing hair. The green river flows behind her, rising, and could swallow her up. Rain taps at her homemade tarp. Ryan whimpers, squirms, and rubs his eyes.

"*Wa,*" I say, forgetting my own English. "I am cooking rice." I am suspended in the doorway—in or out, in or out, my mother used to say—and I want to be in, but I feel guilty. Me, in the big empty house. Rita, out in the yard, out in the rain. Me in her house, but her going back down the muddy path to her mother's, to what's old, to cramped walls of bamboo, to aunts, sisters-in-law, a dozen skinny children with scabs on their legs, flies in their eyes.

But she chose this, I think. She agreed to rent me her house for two years while I taught at the Refugee Camp in the next town, Mariveles. She said she needed the money. I said I needed a house of my own, peace and quiet. She said she would live with her mother. She said no problem. And it was fine, for awhile. She kept to the other side of the barrio, and I had silence under the bamboo trees. In the mornings, I trudged off to catch a dusty Phillipine Rabbit bus that wound its way up the coastal mountains, where my class of Vietnamese students filled the classroom, waiting for English. I'd come home again, kick off my shoes, pore through a *Newsweek* if I could get my hands on one, drink lukewarm water to beat the heat.

On days off, which were many, I scrubbed my laundry back by the pump, and laid the underwear to dry over huge banana leaves; nobody saw. I walked to town for coffee and bananas, stopped to talk to the old women selling live chickens and rice, the ones who wanted me to marry their sons. But always the relief of coming home; home to my own big house, to the quiet, my peace.

Then one morning I woke up to the sound of my own pump handle squeaking back and forth. Jumping out of bed, I peered out, and saw Rita back behind my house, rinsing little Ryan's little ragged T-shirts amd hanging them on the rusty line. She filled up all the rusty lines and the banana leaves with their clothes, and began to do this regularly. Then it was the food stand in front of my house. Her house. It started out with a small wooden table where she laid bags of fried corn, Skyflakes crackers, hard green guavas, garlic peanuts locked in tiny brown sacks, stalks of fresh sugarcane, and Stork menthol candies. This soon drew a crowd, and hordes of children emerged, leaned their elbows on the table, deciding, then hung around to play all afternoon. Then their mothers came, and smoked, gawked at me, looked in my windows, laughed at my height, said I was fat. Then the grandmothers. I felt encroached upon; the store was growing. Rita banged around in my yard at the crack of dawn, and stayed until dark. When she started cooking bloody-bloody and ox tongue for the rice farmers passing by, I knew I was in trouble. No more quiet. No more alone.

I smile back at Rita with effort, and click the door shut. Inside, the water boils madly and streams down over the pan to extinguish the weak flame. Too hot and irritated to cook a real supper, I wonder why I boiled water in the first place. At the kitchen table (which is crawling with ants), I unpeel a midget banana and eat one, two, even three, and jump as a pink lizard falls down splat! from the tin roof onto the table where I'm sitting. It remains in place as if paralyzed, panting in shock, its black, bugged eyes alert, then disappears. I throw the banana peels out the back door by the pump and notice that it has stopped raining. Night falls. Across the river horses snort their hay, dogs bark, the old man, Salvador, plays his beat-up guitar. There is a knock on the front door, and I slip back into the house, breathing heavily.

Again the knock. Two sharp taps of a knuckle. "Helen?" It is Rita's voice. "Helen?"

"Just a minute," I answer, even though my name isn't Helen, but Ellen. I turn the bent nail up so the door flies open, and there stands Rita with a newspaper over her head like the roof of a house, even though it has stopped raining. Ryan stands shyly behind her leg.

"Oi! Ryan! Say hello to Tita Helen," Rita says, but she cannot pry Ryan off of her leg. He clamps his arms and legs around her thigh and will not budge.

"Hello, Ryan," I say. I do not know if I should invite them in. Surely she would invite me in, feed me her last Skyflake cracker even if it meant she would go without. "Can I help you?" I ask stupidly, but Rita sidesteps me and enters her house. My house. She flips off her thongs at the door and seats herself on the warped wooden couch.

"I have so many problems to my husband," she sighs. Ryan grabs a purple pen off the table and scribbles on his leg.

"What is the problem?"

"My husband went to Saudi and gets a new girlfriend. He gives me no moneys for my baby."

"How is Ryan now?"

"He is so sick my baby."

"Why? What's the matter with him?"

"He not eating, and when he is eating, he is—" She raises her hands and flings them from her mouth, to indicate throwing up.

"I'm sorry to hear that."

"And my mother I think she is not wanting me to her house. My sister fight me. And I get no moneys for the food of my baby."

I look at her quizzically. I don't know what to say.

"My mother is wishing me out the house. I fight my sister."

I nod, confused. Should I offer her some rice? Should I say that I'm sorry, but . . . but what?

"You know," Rita says, sitting up, clasping her knee, "I know how Americans like. In Clark Base, I cook the food for the American boys they like very much hamburger prench pry. I bake." She laughs. Her face is soft, almost jowly with dewiness. Her eyes are rimmed in harsh black liner, and she seems made-up, despite her dirty, stained T-shirt and pants. She looks around the room and catches me— bird's nests in the rafters, spiderwebs, dustballs, and birdpoop on the floor. Again, I feel ashamed; big, messy American.

"I just haven't cleaned the house yet," I say. Ryan spins the pedals on my bike, spinning them with reckless little-kid pushes so that he's almost knocking the whole bike over.

"Ryan! Ryan! *Malucut!*" She runs to her son and swats him hard on the arm. Squatting by the big blue bicycle, Ryan throws back his head and wails. Hot tears roll out of his pinched-shut eyes. Rita laughs as any mother nervously laughs at her crying child getting a haircut, getting photographs taken, wanting treats in the grocery. "Ryan is very naughty."

"Hmm," I say, not knowing what to say. Ryan's piercing wail is unsettling, and I shift in my chair. As his crying subsides, Rita smoothes her hair and stands up.

"My baby and I will stay with you tonight." She looks sternly at me. "My mother has a too much problem in her house. It is too much not happy there." She surveys the room and walks over to a glass cabinet she has left in the corner full of her clothes, her husband's old clothes, Ryan's clothes. Through the glass I can see a balled-up black sweater glittering with silver threads, shiny double-knit seventies shirts with big collars, a puffy down winter coat bulged into a corner.

I stand up. "But Rita, we had an agreement. You know how I like to be alone." I scramble for nice words as she scrounges through her glass cabinet. She pulls out a big purple and green folded mat. She shakes it out to full size; the smell of mold and must wafts up and makes me sneeze. The straw mat does not lay flat, but remains lumpy with folds it has known so many years.

"Me and my baby will sleep on this." She gets on her knees and smoothes out the purple and green woven mat. I look at Ryan, then look at her, angry. Everything is ruined; I have nothing to say about this?

I place one bare foot on the purple mat. "Look, Rita, I paid you rent for this whole month. I don't mean to be rude, because I know this is your house and everything, but I'm sorry. I just can't do this." I feel awful. My heart pounds wildly and sweat rivers down my temples and neck. I feel large and oxlike; big pushy American. Can she understand? Am I out of line?

Rita sits back on her knees on the straw mat. Ryan runs to her, lies bellydown on the hard mat; he knows it as bed. Rita's marble eyes meet mine, and nothing is said. She runs her fingers through her permed black hair, and sighs. We have come to a hard place. I don't want to give in. I want this house, and I want to be alone in this house, now.

"We never sign papers," Rita says. She has a trick in her eye, a glimmer of sneak. She reaches for my palm-spine broom and sweeps the dirty floor. Dead cockroaches, garlic skins, bamboo leaves, dental floss accumulate in a pile.

"What do you mean, we never signed papers?" I step in front of her so she cannot sweep me away.

She sweeps around me. She doesn't answer. Ryan has fallen asleep on the green and purple mat, one arm over his eyes to keep out the glare of the bare lightbulb overhead, the other arm spread straight out. Bright blue veins run like magic marker from his armpit to his wrist.

"We never sign papers mean we never sign papers." Rita sweeps the dirt heap up into a *Manila Bulletin* and throws the whole mess out the back door by the pump. "It means we have no agreement, and is my house." I watch her as she eases the back door's slam with her rear end. "If I say Helen she moves out the house, she move out." Rita dips a rag into my pan of once-boiled water, wrings it out, and wipes the sticky kitchen table clean. As if uncomfortable with what she's just said, Rita laughs and says, "I'm, what you say, make a joke with you." She averts her eyes.

"I can clean up. You don't have to do that." I stand up to try to stop her cleaning. I lean one arm stiffly on the table. "Rita, can we talk about this tomorrow? *Masakit ku.* I'm just not feeling very well." And suddenly I'm not. My head aches, my stomach feels caved-in and jagged, probably from not eating all day.

Rita sits me down on a wobbly wooden chair and rubs her oily hand over mine. "Me and my baby Ryan, we just stay with you one night." She tilts her head and smiles. "*Sige? Walang problema?*" She pats my hand to convince me it's okay.

I sigh, roll my head back to ease the kinks, and stare at the tin-roof ceiling. Dozens of pink lizards cling to the metal, darting after flies and mosquitoes; one bare lightbulb swings dangerously off a coiled black cord. What can I say? It's *her* house. But I look around to see what a home I've made: old coffee jars lined up against the window full of sugar, munggo beans, rice, tea, coffee, a world map hung precariously over the delicate cement with tiny turned-in nails, a stack of musty rat-chewed paperbacks, wildflowers woven into a wreath, seashells hung with fishing line in front of the door, an intricate, pink snakeskin pressed between two pieces of glass. To think that when I came there was nothing on the walls, nothing in the house but a wobbly wooden table where she and Ryan ate big plates of rice and little else, in the dark.

"Rita, what's happening at your mother's? I thought you said it was a good arrangement for everyone." I sit on the wooden couch and swat mosquitoes on my legs, my arms, my face. Rita cannot stop cleaning. Now she is on her knees sopping up the urine puddles from the afternoon rain; puddles I never bother with because they dry by morning. But she dabs them up with old rags she has left behind—tiny old Ryan clothes that have split apart with wear.

"My sister is a jealous of my baby cause she can have no baby to her." She rises, goes to the back door, wrings out the rags, and comes back in. "I have the baby, my sister have no baby, and my mother say I am not working to my family." Rita's face twinges, as if something has truly hurt her, and her voice wavers. "Because I am lonely to my husband."

It is then that our eyes lock, and she turns away. She puts a hand to her heart, to her face, her back to me.

Suddenly there is a light tapping at the door, and at first I think it is only the wind; never visitors at night. Another light tapping, and I walk to the door slowly. "Who's there?" No answer, and so I lift the bent nail and let the door swing open.

"*Oi! Lewan si Rita?*" It is Rita's mother, Persing, the old lady I speak with in tangled Kapampangan or not at all. Her milky cataracted eyes search for her daughter, then spotting Rita in the house, she scolds. "*Sus Mari Josef! Nukarin ka minta? Makiramdam ya!*" Her gray head pokes in, the rest of her stays outside. It's late! she scolds. Where've you been?

"*Lungub ka,*" I say, inviting her in. She's my favorite—a spicy, flamboyant old woman, a smoker, a drinker; she holds me around the waist when we talk, rubs my back. But she won't come in. She shakes her head and tosses the butt of a shriveled, wet cigarette out into the yard. She carries on in Kapampangan fiercely, shaking her finger, pointing to Rita, pointing to Ryan, scolding, stomping her foot. She waves Rita outside to talk, and again, Persing rattles in lisping Kapampangan: You are welcome in our house! Come home now, come! It is shameful! Leave this one to her alone!

And then she is gone.

Rita comes back inside, looking sorry, sorry, sorry, ashamed, and I am sorry, sorry, ashamed. I shut the plywood door. I want the old woman to stay, to clear up this mess, but again, it is only Rita and I in the house, and Ryan asleep.

ANITA FENG

Digging to China
with a Spoon

TRAVELING FROM HOME to a far away other, there is a third locale, one that serves as kingpin to catapult me into the unknown. It is a moment without a map leading up to it—a transitory realm, or changing room, where I am stripped of all the dulled perceptions accrued over the years like parasites. From there I will walk through the streets of China with my eyes as wide open as my baby's, acutely aware. For Tasha, it is her natural state of wonder. For my husband it is a natural state of euphoria on returning home after eleven years' absence. But as for me, I will be changed. I will grow silent and passive, watching the inner workings of another world.

That moment intervenes as China comes to meet us at the gate area in the Los Angeles airport. Milling around in a thick aura of cigarettes, impatient to return, China is as enthusiastic as a child dressed in gray business suits, wash-and-wear dress pants, jogging suits or China Air uniforms. China applauds as one at the arrival of its airplane. Photos are taken, gifts exchanged and compared. Just as we find an empty seat to put all the baby gear down, China rushes toward us with open arms, not to speak with my husband or me, but to pluck our baby out of my lap. Out of my heart a small cry calls out, but we are strangers! Strangers! China lifts up our baby, high above her head and carries her off to the other airline attendants. Isn't she wonderful, China says. Tasha's mouth forms a small "O". Her eyes, perfect instruments of wonder, interview each passing face with unblinking awe. With only eight months to her credit, she already understands this is not the American way. Immediately, for the sake of that lovely, small mouth—sweets, crackers, rice cakes, bits of fruit find their way into it. China laughs as Tasha refuses, laughs as she accepts, or throws it on the floor, or grabs hold and will not let it go. There is no dark shadow of lawsuits and abuse and simple disengaged reserve. How old is she, China asks? *Ba ge yue*, eight months old, my husband says.

Throughout our one-month stay we will never be alone. Wherever we go, if we stop for a moment, or walk along slowly enough, a crowd will form. A woman will ask if a picture can be taken, not of the Great Wall behind her, but of Tasha next to her. I will grow accustomed to the next question, after the admiring clucks and baby talk. In spite of my toneless, near-fatal Chinese, whenever someone sees our baby and then asks in that appreciative blur, I will know what to say. At least in this one case, I will relish my understanding and reply, fluently, *Ba ge yue*. As for what follows from that point on, the world of ideas and their expression disperses into ten thousand directions and China divides into the billions of faces that she truly, inevitably has. From here on, I have a lot to learn.

~

We walk past the length of the apartment building where the faded red slogan from the sixties reads, "Down with anyone who is against Chairman Mao!" Barbed wire near the doorways guards the greenery of a few tenants. In what used to be the courtyard where my husband Nick played as a boy, two rows of buildings serve as minimal shelter for the latest influx of people swelling the population of Beijing. A bare light socket, a bulletin of notices and directives, bicycles wedged into the corners of the entryway and along the wall, are all covered with dust. The corridor is gray and the dust is gray. The walls, floors and ceilings are molded in uniform concrete.

A neighbor peers around the edge of a door to get a look at Feng Zhe's son who's come back with a foreign wife and baby after so many years. She calls out to him, "Is that really Xiao Ge?" His parents have lived here over forty years: through the Great Leap Forward, the Cultural Revolution and Four Modernizations. They have raised three children here, lived through their own youth, middle age and the beginnings of retirement. The things I see first, on entering their apartment, are the unpainted concrete walls and floors, a solitary fluorescent bulb hanging from twisted wire that comes out of a hole in the ceiling, and three colorless curtains pinned across the windows.

In the midst of this bleak space used as living room, dining room, office, and spare bedroom combined, a stereo and tape-deck system with huge speakers flaunts one side of the room. Shiny and new, a refrigerator sits in the hall, a washing machine in the kitchen. The appliances make it difficult to open doors. One must pass sideways to get by them. They have the place of honor, but nothing relieves the monotony of the walls.

I had known what to expect, and had intended to keep my mind open. Nevertheless, the objects of these rooms, understandable as accruements of the modern world, are combined or missing in such ways that I can't make any sense out of them at all. I am thinking that I am thinking like a materialist. I am baffled and overcome with exhaustion. Under the glass that covers the desk are two pictures: one of Paul Newman, the other of Meryl Streep. Nearby are several sets of Mao's complete works. A sense of dizziness comes over me filtering these first hours of reunion and introductions as if the words spoken have passed across a great distance. Through the melodic and rapid-fire Chinese, I catch an occasional word such as: time, hungry, Tasha, or Xiao Ge—the name that belongs to Nick in China.

As my surroundings settle into focus after a few days, new layers emerge: a cabinet with glass doors, its key at rest in its lock, comfortably worn chopsticks standing in a glass jar, the teapot of boiled water always warm on the dining room table, Mother-in-law's daily departure at predawn to practice walking Qi Gung in the city park, a bamboo mat spread over the surface of a bed to ventilate the heat, Father-in-law's precious books of Tang Dynasty poems, a family chronology with stories and histories stuffed in the back of a drawer, a beautiful mirror etched with a pair of lovebirds sitting on a bough (a marriage present for Nick's parents) propped up in the corner of a back room.

Gradually I manage to uncover more aspects of Nick's home as he bravely tries to translate it for me. Back and forth he runs between being Nick to his wife, and

Xiao Ge to his parents. There are so many details, one protectively tucked away inside another. There are reasons and subtleties and whole other vocabularies that cause the rooms to be silent, contradictory and vague. I learn the reason why there is never any light bulb in a building's entryway. At the time of the Cultural Revolution, the Red Guards liked to destroy public facilities. Shooting light bulbs with a slingshot was fun. Soon enough no one bothered to replace them. After the Cultural Revolution it was for another reason. Because of careless bureaucracy or poor management, there was no separate meter for that light bulb; instead it was connected to the meter of the apartment closest to the entryway. Naturally, the people living there didn't want to be the ones to pay for it, and the fixture has been empty ever since.

I learn that Nick's parents have never painted the walls or floors because they don't own them, because the expense and sheer logistics of buying paint make the idea seem ludicrous. Money is difficult to come by. With the long understanding of how government policies can change overnight; how, in the face of desperate need, money that has been saved penny by penny may need to be used to line someone's pocket, to buy a ticket, or pay for emergency medical care. I have also learned that belongings mattering the most are put "safely" away. At one time, poems from the Tang Dynasty were considered artifacts of the old, corrupt society. Owning such a volume could be dangerous—one never knows. Certainly a bound volume of family letters and histories smacks of bourgeois thinking. In a variable political climate, owning a refrigerator and washing machine can be safer than owning a book of poems.

Nick and I dig around in the overstuffed drawers of the cabinet looking for traces of family history. I feel the silence keenly, as if we are engaged in a secretive act. There was so much that I wanted to learn about his parents. I had imagined asking about their youth engaged in underground support for the communist revolution. I had imagined I would be able to ask, within the privacy of their home, about Tiananmen Square, what they heard or saw. But Nick explained, when nothing was forthcoming, that if there are more than two people in a room (which I would always require, one extra being needed for translation), no matter how loved and accepted I am, it is unlikely that I will ever have that kind of conversation, at least on this first trip. On several occasions I cannot bear the silence surrounding our amiable conversation over a table covered with food, and I plead illness or exhaustion to go back to our room, close the door, and wring the silence between my hands until I feel its shape, and bury it in my pillow.

⁓

Although the Beijing city bus shakes us up all the way down Chang An Avenue, the passengers are transfixed as one audience on my Jewish nose and the magic trick of our half-Chinese baby, an enigma. Someone takes courage to ask my husband the obvious, who am I to you? Someone else asks, "Can you really talk to her in the foreign devil's language?" Another leans over, scolds our child and kindly pulls the thumb out of her mouth.

Nick says, "In America, this is considered impolite."

"Is she Russian?" A woman wants to know, open to my being from Mars.

Nick, who has been away from China for twelve years, says with a note of friendly expertise, "Once you are out in the world no one can tell where you come from, who you are. Even if a Chinese leaves China, people don't know the difference."

We pass the enormous likeness of Mao in the square, the mole on his chin the size of an average man. Bicycles vie with taxis, pedestrians en masse. It was foolish to think I could see the bullet holes sunk into lampposts as we barreled past. The glare of sun barely infiltrates the dust, and one can't help blinking laconically over the view. Out of the corner of my eye, I catch sight of a banner over a storefront: Accumulate Celestial Dollars Restaurant. Our child has been lulled to sleep; the world leveled by its revolutions. She clings to her small and perfect thumb, half in, half out; and at the next jolt of changing gears, gravity itself will let it fall.

∽

Long before the Warring States, the Three Kingdoms, Five Dynasties, and the Gang of Four; long before the written word, China was a matrilineal society. There was no hierarchy or evidence of war among the people. Kinship and clan ties were very strong. The people lived clustered in a circle of dwellings surrounded by a moat. Beyond the moat was the burial ground where ancestors were laid to rest, with food and utensils to sustain them in the afterlife.

The population of such a community was probably less than what you would find in a single work unit's housing compound in Beijing. My in-laws' apartment complex houses several thousand people densely packed in similarly sparse rooms. Although not circular anymore, the buildings form a square around the courtyard. Children wearing the Young Pioneer's tell-tale scarf, play in a mound of gray dirt. They quickly become the same shade as the earth and the concrete behind them. Old men and women come out to do Tai Chi or Walking Qi Gung with their arms waving out from their sides. Others meet to talk or sit at the curbside. Well before dawn, all the garbage and refuse has been hauled away. Babies in bamboo carriages blink into the early sun. No babies are crying, and none are being scolded. They will come out again in the early evening when the oppressive heat lifts slightly, when a man will walk through, chanting, "Knives sharpened, knives sharpened," with the sound of his steel blades to accompany him.

An old woman with stooped shoulders stands off to the side, near the entrance to the street. Her expression is terse and her eyes busily dart around corners, lips pursed in intense concentration. She has a unique armband, and when I ask Nick about it, he explains that this is the neighborhood committee chairperson—usually an elderly woman assigned the task of listening for trouble, tasty gossip, or the seeds of political insurrection.

There is a moat just outside the housing complex. A few people line the banks to fish, or swim, or wash, but most are bicycling over the bridge in a huge wave of black heads above spinning wheels. They carry everything: bags of onions, coal, watermelons, mattresses, box springs and briefcases. The moat is so long and extends so far through the city that it is difficult to tell which side was intended for the living and which for the dead. I catch sight of a man bicycling past on a three-wheeler that holds his wife and his mother, who in turn, holds an umbrella over his child sitting on her lap. And the man is smiling. And within that semicircle of his smile lies the persistant shelter of generations, the realm of family that overreaches history, nearly invisible yet strong enough to carry them through a perpetual crowd. And I consider that something of the ancient ways remains.

∽

The old White Cloud Temple is within walking distance from my in-laws' apartment. At the entrance to its alley there is a massive construction site, the whole thing cordoned off with warning tape and boards. Construction vehicles grind over reddish dirt, shifting stone, excavating a muddy abyss into a modern foundation. No one knows what it will be. The dust raised by the project covers the whole area for blocks. The alley is so narrow that a small truck speeding through forces us to flatten against a wall. Watermelon rinds are everywhere over the street and doorsteps, as well as cabbage leaves and refuse kicked around enough to have lost all aspect of original form. When bicycles come through on the six-inch-wide sidewalk, the children, mothers and old men who live there shift into doorways at the last possible moment.

We see an ornately carved archway to the left. Underneath it, a plywood ticket booth cancels out the initial effect of grandeur and antiquity. We pay for two kinds of tickets, one for the Chinese that is one-tenth the price of the other, for foreign devils. The temple is very old, having been graced by emperors, pillaged by Red Guards, and recently renovated during the current relaxed attitude toward religion. We see elaborately painted gods, religious and mythical dramas painted on the lintels of various doorways. There is a stone garden and enormous statue and a bronze incense burner. The monks are dressed in robes with white leggings, their hair tied up severely at the top of their heads, the elder ones with beards reminiscent of old masters from another era. A young monk, while drawing water from a well, scrutinizes the three of us thoroughly. I am uneasy, as if I had intruded on a living artifact or gained admittance to a human zoo.

My husband is undeterred by any sense of intrusion in the air and his intense curiosity leads us from one pavilion to another. In one of them, alongside a platform of religious figures, there is a stand with a beautiful brass gong and mallet, and a bell and small wooden drum. What are they for, we wonder. Nick tries them out, one after another to see if they might delight our baby. What pure, resonant and piercing sounds they make! Immediately monks come running up. One of the older ones, red in the face, is shouting and shaking his fist. He urges us out, muttering a litany of temple protocol, ending with the sin of holding hands.

As we find our way back, I wonder about the original nature of Tao: the free and easy wandering of Chuang Tzu, the Taoist strategy of simplicity and spontaneity according to the laws of Nature and "chi," vital energy. In between pavilions, we pass long straight rows of dormitories. In one to the left of us, we hear someone playing the Chinese zither behind closed doors. It could be the music of rain, for its refined, cascading notes that transcend the world's categories of "this" and "that." Nick wants to stop and ask if we might listen for a while. I suggest that we not, but at least walk slowly toward the exit, listening as we go.

∼

"*Tongzhi! Tongzhi!*"

Tongzhi is Chinese for "Comrade." The first part of the word, Tong, means "same"; the second part, zhi, means "ideology." Since the Communist takeover in China in 1949, all people have addressed each other as *Tongzhi*: men, women, cadres, street sweepers. In the early days, before the famine of the Great Leap Forward or the repressive acts of the Hundred Flowers Movement and the Cultural Revolution, before the whole nation served as spies for each other, people generally believed in the principles behind the word, and tried hard to dispel the old feudal system and outdated practices of ancestor worship and superstitions.

"*Tongzhi!* We need a taxi to take us to Baiyun Lu."

The state-owned taxi's driver cracks down his window an inch, unwilling to exchange any of the cool air conditioning for the scalding heat outside. "No. We can't take you there. The road is blocked. Construction everywhere."

We are standing on a busy street corner, with two suitcases, a stroller, backpack, and baby. Nick asks the taxi driver if he can drive around the construction site. We'll pay extra.

"Too much trouble, too much time. Go talk to the Pedicab drivers." As the window rolls up, the draft catches on a portrait of Mao dangling from the taxi's rearview mirror. The tassels spin. Mao smiles on both sides of the card, but in a different pose on each.

Nick was surprised when he first saw these pictures of Mao prominently displayed in buses and taxis. After all, Mao had been in disfavor since the disaster of the Cultural Revolution. Mao's supreme authority seemed a far cry from the call for Democratization in Tiananmen Square in '89. What is going on here? And what is Mao doing in the midst of this steady surge of private enterprise?

We found out that a few years ago, around the time of the massacre in Tiananmen Square, there occurred another event in the south that stirred up great numbers of people all across China. Two cars were driving down a road. The first had a picture of Mao displayed on the windshield; the other did not. The first car crossed the bridge safely, but as the second crossed over, soon after the first, the bridge collapsed and the driver was killed. Now, as a result, the cult of Mao has been revived. Several such incidents have been reported, and all types of people believe that Mao's spirit has the power to protect them.

We walk over to the Pedicab drivers who are eyeing our combined weight with concern. But these are private-enterprise drivers, an entirely different matter from state-run taxis. Nick, worried now about Tasha and me, approaches a strong, broad-shouldered man and begins, "*Tongzhi* . . ."

"Hello," he says, a gold-capped tooth showing out of the corner of his smile. "No problem! I'll take you for forty yuan. Get in, get in!"

Nick can't believe his ears, this being more than a taxi would charge, more than a week's pay for a high-ranking government-paid worker. But we have little choice. The Pedicab driver throws the suitcases and everything else in front of the seat and Nick and I climb on top, Tasha on my lap. The driver takes one mighty heave on the bicycle pedals, his portrait of Mao quivers on the handlebars and we're off. Fearlessly he launches into oncoming traffic. His T-shirt with the word "LOVE" printed in large English letters across the back is soaked through in a minute. When his momentum is fairly established, he flourishes a wet rag and wipes the sweat off his forehead with a dramatic flair. He turns over his shoulder to glance at us and says to Nick, "Mister, you must've been away from China a long time. People don't say Tongzhi like that now-a-days. It's gotten to be a little old-fashioned around here." He barely slows at a red light, crossing in front of an oncoming truck, ringing his small bell at the truck's blaring horn. No way is he going to lose momentum now. Somehow he weaves through the interchange without getting hit. He looks back again to see my tense face, Tasha contentedly asleep on my lap. Obviously Tasha must trust in the powers of Mao as much as he does. "How old is your baby?" he asks.

"Eight months old."

"Eight months old!" The driver slaps his thigh. "When's her birthday?"

"November 1," and Nick can't help adding as if it would matter to anyone but him, "twelve o'clock noon."

"Amazing! I have a son born on the very same day, at ten in the morning. What a coincidence. Say, does she have any teeth yet? No? Well, neither does my son. Has she started spitting out her food? That means a tooth is coming any day now, you'll see."

Nick and the driver continue to compare the merits and accomplishments of their offspring. On the topic of their most precious babies, it is clearly a matter of "same ideology" all the way. At his parents' doorway, Nick counts out forty *yuan*. The driver gives Tasha a kiss, tickles her under her arm and then drives off, not without another flourish of muscle, and his rag across his face.

∼

In 1966, in the great rallies of Young Pioneers that filled Tiananmen Square, Mao spoke of "cultural revolution," calling upon the young people to lead. Thousands lost their footing in the crazed rush toward him. Thousands of shoes fell from thousands of feet. Those who tried to retrieve their shoes were crushed, some to death. Those who remained upright swooned into the multiple arms and shoulders of a whirlpool, carried backwards and away from the Gate of Heavenly Peace.

In 1992, a small stylish woman takes a designer umbrella as gauntlet and pries a curve of air between the people to make space for herself on the city bus. A head taller than her, a young man bristling with sunglasses, fake Rolex and rings, advances. His briefcase, with severe weight at its four corners edges her out of the way. The sheer corruption of shopping bags shoves aside our raw nerves. My own mind has been crowded out and lost. Where is my husband's hand? Move, move! The heat and sweat, a slippery hold on nothing as a man shouts, Make way for our foreign guest! Another shouts back, breathless, Why the hell should I? Who cares about foreign devils when I can't move my ass? I am tall and strong, I say to myself, but I've lost my footing. Lost the power to direct myself. Even unable to fall, I have the eerie impression that I have just entered prison by some terrible mistake, the bars pressing against the valves of my heart, the doors sliding shut. Nick tells me later, we should have known.

∼

When bicycling across town, I always take note of the babies, how grandly they ride in the midst of rushing traffic. How precious they are, those babies. They sit like little emperors and empresses in their bamboo seats, the future of China ferried through the Beijing city streets on the fronts or backs of bicycles, bells clanging, cleaving their way through the dust. But how difficult it is sometimes to have one of those babies, and then keep one. Just one.

My sister-in-law put her name on the work unit's list of hopeful young wives waiting their turn to become mothers. At the time, Guo Ying didn't live with her husband because they were assigned jobs in different cities, but she applied for a transfer and as luck would have it, at last the confluence of lists and quotas and back-door influence had the right result. In her third term of pregnancy she took leave of her husband and job for Beijing. There she could depend on her parents and good medical care that only Beijing could offer.

When a woman gives birth, it is the event of her life over which she has the least control. It will come according to its nature. And_it will come according to the world in which it is born, which has its own agendas to keep. Two days after a troubled delivery, a diligent night nurse happened to notice the baby wasn't breathing well. The doctor on call was busy preparing Bai Cai (Chinese cabbage) for winter storage, reluctant to leave her task at home for the hospital again. It was so impossible to accomplish the basic tasks of daily life! Was it really that serious, she wanted to know. It was an emergency. The baby near death. But the baby had to be transferred to the specialist hospital. No, they were not equipped to deal with this case here. And the parents must pay up front for this new hospital, two thousand *yuan*. It's the middle of the night! My mother- and father-in-law who are very old ran back and forth, to relatives, influential friends. They summoned the hospital ambulance that sat at rest in front of the hospital's door. The driver asked, "Are you a senior party official? If not, I can't help you. Now how can I take a bribe? What if a senior official should have an emergency? Then where would I be? I can't take you. So you are a cadre, a party member, so what! Call a taxi if it's that bad." But where is a taxi at this hour? And who can imagine how long that will take?

The baby was transferred in time, and made a slow recovery. The mother was ill. A wet nurse was hired. All of them lived on top of each other in the cramped Beijing apartment. All had colds and bouts of depression. It was decided the sickly baby should go to the countryside where the air was good, and stay with the father's family in southern China. Guo Ying had to return to work. It would have to be a relationship of covert care and love incognito. After almost a year had gone by, just before we came to China, Guo Ying and her husband had finally been granted vacation time to visit their son. When I talked to Guo Ying on the phone, she apologized for not being able to see us in Beijing since they had used up all their time. She was sorry that she would not meet her little niece. Perhaps next time. "Tasha must be a lovely baby," she said, "When we visited our son, he had grown so much. Now he is healthy and strong. But he didn't know me, and screamed whenever I came near. Perhaps next time will be better."

~

What is vast as the universe and cloistered as goldfish in a fishbowl?

All around us bamboo rises delicately as grass, with its refined sense of green sprinkled throughout the forest. We have taken time off from city life to come to the scenic countryside surrounding Hangzhou. Slopes invite our gradual ascent up a hillside west of the Pagoda of Six Harmonies, through the Nine Creeks and Eighteen Gullies. Ancient stepping stones lay scattered and untended because an emperor once walked this way. In deference to the blessings bestowed by his footprints, the stones have been left as they were and never altered. The streams run their harmony over roots and pebbles, between heaven and earth. Two solitary travelers, we cross over, thinking of the legendary goddess who crossed from the east bank of the Milky Way to the west to meet her cowherd, earthly lover. Magpies, it is said, grew bald because they were made to form a bridge for them with their heads. Our shoes slip over the wet stones and become soaked through. We are exhilarated in the expanse of nature. We have crossed over east and west and the linear concept of time to find ourselves in a land of wonder.

The ingenuity of nature takes us up a steeper and steeper path until our middle-aged sensibility starts to breathe hard. A man with a cart is going up. Would we like a ride? Yes, we would. We settle in next to a peasant woman. Her husband's family has tended the tea plants growing here as long as anyone can remember, harvesting the famous Dragon Well tea. We should visit them and try some of their tea, she says. As we near the summit, multitudinous hillsides reveal themselves, each planted in rows of deep green tea trees pruned to the size of bushes. The woman explains the qualities and pricing of tea, between tea picked in the spring and tea picked in midsummer. She even hops off the cart to pick a leaf of tea and show us what they look like at the proper stage of harvesting. What good fortune to run into her. Her smile is broad and generous. Here is the real China, we think.

At a leveling-off place, the path widens suddenly to a road. The road is lined with peasants at long tables, on the curb, or on the tailgates of trucks. They have hand-held scales, bags of tea, and they are all shouting, "Tea! Come buy famous Dragon Well tea!" Greenery has given way to a countryside metropolis in the blink of an eye. Where are the magpies? Like a jolt through time and space, loudspeakers explode from above with the strains of music sent down in heavenly directives. Notes that sound like fistfuls of gravel sing in perfect English, Do, a Deer, a female Deer; Re, a drop of golden. . . ." No one seems alarmed at this transition, not even Nick who explains to me, these are the loudspeakers that I grew up with. He laughs. I love this song, he says, You know, the one from *The Sound of Music*? Yes, I reply. Yes, what was the name of that movie star? And my eyes. My eyes turn out of focus, and wide, like those of a fish.

～

After three weeks in China, the strain of my "foreign" appearance has begun to wear me down. There appears to be no way off this stage I'm on. Even in public restrooms, there are no doors to separate stalls. The Chinese women stare at me in such a way, they must be eager to find out once and for all if foreign devils are fully human. I have almost forgotten how to walk naturally, talk naturally, or throw my head back and laugh. Three weeks of polite restraint, of trying to decipher meaning out of safe topics of conversation such as food and health have brought me to an almost complete standstill.

Therefore I surprise myself at the airport in Hangzhou, by leaping into the arms of a group of Israeli tourists. I recognize them instantly by their emphatic volleys of Hebrew, hands in a blur of punctuation spiced with emotion. How handsome and lovely these people are! Less than a minute after introducing myself, we launch into heated debates on the political turmoil in Russia, interracial marriage, the recent changeover of power in Israel, and how I should come as soon as possible and live in Israel, the husband included (grudgingly), there's always room, always plenty of room! What wonderful, feisty people. Even the arrogance of the children accompanying them is charming. Charming. To be verbose and dramatic, to spill out one's beliefs like clear water rapids—how refreshing it is!

Nick, meanwhile, has been approached by a young Chinese clerk from a refreshment stand nearby. She is wringing her hands as she asks, "Excuse me please. I see that you speak English. Would you come to the counter, if you don't mind, and help me."

There, a small elderly Israeli woman is clutching her handbag. Her eyes drill holes into the salesgirl as she shouts at Nick, "That girl has stolen my money! I gave her five *yuan* for a soda and she never gave me the two *yuan* change. And she accuses me of forgetfulness. I remember clearly she never gave me my change. She's lying. Just because I'm an old woman she can't fool me. Tell her that in Chinese."

Nick translates a brief version of what was said. The salesgirl tries to maintain composure and the correct form of response to a foreigner. She smiles and nods minutely in the old woman's direction. Her enviable position of working at the airport could be jeopardized, and her future as well, if complaints are made to her authorities. She begs Nick to intercede and explain that she did give this woman her change, two *yuan* exactly.

The Israeli woman does not wait for translation, but demands, "Give me my change!"

"I gave it to you!" the salesgirl nearly shouts, now in tears.

Nick says, "Okay, why don't you just take a look in your handbag and see if it's there or not?"

"I will not! I don't need to."

The salesgirl says, "Please, I remember it was folded together, one bill showing above the other, open on the right side as you put it in."

Nick says "Take a look. It won't hurt and then we'll know for sure."

The old woman mutters about how you can't trust anyone these days, what a headache it is, just a poor old woman preyed upon by scavengers everywhere, okay, okay I'll look. She finds the two *yuan* just as the sales girl described. She snaps shut the purse clasp, mutters something else, scowls at Nick and the salesgirl, and walks off.

Later on, Nick and I exchange accounts of our encounters with Israelis, and shake our heads, and laugh. I feel, more than anything, the easy affinity that my husband and I share, the peace of our small family settling over us as the definitive gesture of the day. As our plane lands in Beijing at twilight, I am, at least for a moment, released from the oppressive pull of categories: Jew, Gentile, Asian, Israeli. In the face of our daughter (curly black-haired and angelic), they have canceled each other out.

∽

When we first arrived in China, at the Shanghai Airport terminal, there was a brand-new neon sign in English that said, "Elevator Disabled" with an arrow underneath pointing to an elevator. What did this mean? What was it supposed to mean? I stood there, holding up our family, all our baggage dropped to the floor so that I might consider this: does it mean that here is an honest country with the good grace to use a modern, electronically lit-up sign to warn passengers of a permanently disabled elevator?

Halfway down the stairs and laughing, I realized that the essential "for" had been left out. How like the Chinese language, to leave out referent, tense, syntax— all of which can, possibly, be deciphered by the context at hand. How like the Chinese, to withhold certain amounts of information. How like the Americans to be baffled and summarily stopped cold by a missing three-letter preposition.

Weeks later, on an extremely hot day, Xiao Ming (Nick's brother) takes us to see his new apartment in a modern high rise in another part of Beijing. By a successful strategy of influence, he managed to get a hold of it, a rare prize in the overflowing city. After it was built, they waited a year for the plumbing to be installed. Yes, now all is ready, he explains as we change buses. However, they will not be able to move in just yet. The public elementary schools are not as good in this new district, so they will have to wait four years until their son is ready for middle school. They will hold on to the apartment, visit it, furnish it with refrigerator, TV, stereo, and wait. And, he tells us as we enter the usual unlit foyer, it has two modern elevators.

Yes, indeed. One has a sign on it scribbled by hand saying, "Temporarily out-of-order." But the other one works, he tells us cheerfully. A sullen young woman opens the door and several people get on with us. I have all the sympathy in the world for her, working in this stifling box all day. With pride, Xiao Ming points out the digital controls. The door jolts closed, partially, after a few tries. Never mind. Leave it open. I feel the heat like an unbreathable substance. With another jolt we rise. With yet another, we stop after one and a half floors. The light goes out. All the mechanisms have gone dead silent. The attendant lights a match, finds a flashlight, pushes buttons systematically, one after another. She seems emotionally detached, as if to say, this has nothing to do with me. She does not look, or say anything to us. She climbs out to the shaft overhead. Nothing to be done. Xiao Ming looks quickly at Tasha and me. What is going on here? The attendant, back inside again, bangs on the door and shouts for someone to force open the door from the outside. We wait. Tasha is crying and extremely hot. But after a time, the attendant, with the help of some others, forces open the door enough for us to get out, squeezing ourselves sideways to fit. Nick climbs out and I pass Tasha up to him. As we climb the remaining eleven concrete flights, I ask how often this happens. All the time, all the time.

Now I understand! That sign in Shanghai was written as a kindness, to foreigners who might not be prepared for the perpetual breakdowns that the Chinese already understand all too well. It was clear and succinct, a grammatically correct fact.

～

In modern China, as in the old days, the year of your birth decides your fate. What does it matter if a person has exceptional talent, the perfect hands, the perfect ear and heart for the violin? The reading of the tortoise shell, the throw of the I Ching, the latest Party Directive will choose the course of your fate. In what year were you born? Perhaps if you were born in 1953 instead of 1955 all would have come out differently. Perhaps you would not play the violin, and the melodies would be like wind that drives across the vast open plains of Manchuria. According to the words of the Tang Dynasty poet Tu Mu, "Stream flows unfeeling / grass spreads unconcerned." According to the actions of government, human life is cheap.

As a child, Nick had many friends. He was gregarious, good at sports and always at the top of his class for academic achievement. Among Nick's friends, one was a bully who had taken him under his wing, offering protection in exchange for help with schoolwork. Another friend, Xing Wen, lived upstairs. He was a violinist of exceptional talent, two years younger than Nick.

During the Cultural Revolution, when Party policy changed radically and frequently, the three boys met their fate. In 1969, Nick's class was the last to be sent to the countryside for hard labor, in his case, Manchuria. The bully, because he had been held back a year, didn't have to go. A labor shortage had been created by sending a good part of the city's population to the countryside. Therefore desirable factory jobs were available and the bully was assigned an excellent job in the city. The following year, when Xing Wen came of age, there were too many factory workers and only service jobs available, so he was assigned the job of butcher. Needless to say, none of them had any choice in the matter.

One day, after Nick had returned from Manchuria, he heard his friend upstairs playing so beautifully, it seemed as if it came from the domain of heaven, rather than the hellish third-floor heat that it really was. He went upstairs and peaked in the door to find Xing Wen playing in an empty room in his underwear, the sweat pouring from every part of his body in constant streams. He was playing Schubert, preparing for his last opportunity to become a professional violinist. Auditions were being held soon for the very best to enter the most prestigious school of music in China. If he got in, his life might be changed back to its intended course, music.

Nick accompanied him to the auditions. The first round was extremely difficult. Out of hundreds of applicants only a few would be chosen. Those few had to come again for the second round of auditions, bringing written permission from their work units that would allow them to transfer to the music school if they passed. Nick waited for hours while the flying fingers, the bold and facile melodies came from everyone who got up to play. Still, Xing Wen passed, and he was asked to come for the second round. But his work unit refused to grant permission. They needed their butchers. They were unwilling to be moved, bribed, or cajoled. The violinist stayed a butcher.

Now, twenty years later, we go upstairs to see if he's still living there. The man opening the door to us is bald and middle-aged. It takes Xing Wen a minute to recognize Nick but when he does, his tired-looking face is transformed by a mixture of confusion and joy. "Come in, come in!" He introduces his wife and son, and his mother, asking her for watermelon to be brought in. Nick asks him to play for us, and Xing Wen apologizes, it has been so long since he played last. His son, a curious and lively two-year-old will not permit him to play, he explains, because the boy wants the violin for himself. He laughs at the irony of this, gives the boy a kiss and pulls out the old instrument. He asks his wife to take the son into the other room. The song is the same Schubert piece that Nick heard him play that hot summer day years ago except that now the fingers are hesitant, the bowing awkward. Still, the tune is lovely enough to cause tears to well up in my eyes. After, he wipes off the strings carefully, puts the violin in its case, and then offers us huge wedges of watermelon. While we eat and spit out seeds, he fills us in on his life.

"I was a butcher for thirteen years. Finally, I obtained a teaching post in a small new college teaching Chinese Literature. This came about after completing a three-year college course by TV, and negotiating a payoff to my old working unit so they would allow me to change jobs. At first they asked the college to pay an incredible two thousand *yuan*. Eventually, after a full year had gone by, they settled for eight hundred. Other work units were more willing to let people change jobs, but I was not so lucky. You see, it was not really a matter of money, but of bitterness."

He offers us more and more watermelon. I am amazed to find that we are able to demolish the whole thing. But the night is hot. And perhaps we eat as if eating would fill the hungry gap of so many intervening, silent years. He warms to us as we talk. He tells what he saw of the Tiananmen massacre. He shows photos he had taken, of bodies lining the hospital floors where he was admitted for a minor bullet wound in the leg.

When Nick tells him about how he has recently taken up drawing, something he has always dreamed of but never had the opportunity to develop until recently, Xing Wen smiles. Like an eager child, he jumps to his feet and says, "I know what you mean. Would you like to see what I am doing now?" From his desk he takes down a glass case with a tiny figure inside and sets it down carefully in a clearing of watermelon rinds. "What would you guess this is made out of?"

The figure is of a warrior, incredibly detailed and beautiful, with a long pole in one hand, the other held out in a gesture of defense. It is a character taken from an old Chinese novel. His long hair is tied up in back of his head with a blue scarf. The baggy black pants are tied with a red rope, out of which rises a muscular, rippling torso. The toes of his shoes are curled upward in ready expectation. His stance is light and agile, his expression fierce. Looking closer, with my eyes up to the glass, I see a fine network of cracks between the muscles, between the elbow and the wrist, from the shoulder to the center of the spine and along the ankles. The pole is cracked in several places along its length. Only the head is entirely of one piece. And the rope tying the waist is as free and delicate as a brushstroke suspended in midair. I am truly impressed with his skill. I ask him if it is painted clay, air-dried and then painted over.

He is delighted with my mistake and says, "No! It is a very special, ancient recipe of dough. There is no paint. The red lips, the shoes and rope are pieces of dough dyed red. Each colored piece is made separately and carefully, and then very carefully joined into a full figure. I am still working on improving this recipe in order to get rid of these cracks. In fact, some of my most recent pieces have no cracks at all. So far, that is."

We ask to see more. Each one, in spite of the problem with cracking, seems alive and suffused with energy. Indeed, the art is a reflection of the artist. I can see clearly now that the violinist has survived his childhood and the Cultural Revolution, that his spirit proved to be irrepressible, as it was for Nick as well. Nick asks, as we are about to leave, about the other friend, the bully. "Oh him! He's a big man now, in import-export business with gears and motors. He always knew how to make the best of a situation. In the troubled times, when the Red Guards disintegrated in gangs, he was a gangster leader. Now he has a car, and does business with Europe and the U.S."

We were given the little warrior as a parting gift. Somehow it survived the journey without breaking and now it sits on my bookshelf surrounded by books. He faces directly into all those thicknesses of words. His black eyebrows are arched as he considers the nature of that foreign tongue, its mysterious and monotonous script. He is ready to pierce it through with a single stroke of his flour-and-water pole at the first sign of attack.

Island of Serenity

ILENA LEFT her desk at the International Refugee Organization and went downstairs into the milling crowd of Europeans desperate to get out of Shanghai before the Communists came.

For more than a generation Shanghai had been the end of the line for refugees from everywhere: White Russians fleeing from the revolution, Jews and others escaping from Hitler, prisoners finding their way out of Siberia, and all the flotsam from the wars and famines and police courts of the world. Whether they came on foot across central Asia, or by rail or ship from God-knows-where, Shanghai was the stopping place. They had somehow settled in and found ways to survive.

But now, in 1949, the Communists were taking over China, and the future for impoverished foreigners looked bleak. Hundreds crowded into the building seeking help.

Ilena went ahead of a long queue and into an inner office where she spoke urgently to the man behind the desk.

"You're sure you want to do this, Ilena?" he asked.

"I think it is necessary."

"I don't disapprove. I just want to be sure you have thought what it can mean."

"What have I done but think lately? Please give me the papers before I change my mind."

Quickly she filled out the forms and went back to her desk, tears streaming down her face. As she sat struggling for composure her boss came to her.

"What's the matter, Ilena?"

"I have just declared myself stateless so as to be eligible for resettlement. It is a little hard."

"I think you are wise. I've been wondering when you would do it. Of course it is hard, but you can always think of yourself as Hungarian."

"Thank you," she said, "It had to be done, and now it's done."

She went back to figuring the costs of a chartered ship to Israel. This was familiar work. They had already sent two crowded ships. While they had to beg and plead all over the world for two visas to one country or six to another, little Israel, just struggling to get started, had promised to take all Jews who wanted to come.

～

At quitting time Ilena stood in line and squeezed onto a crowded bus that took her to a quiet part of the city where the buildings were in European style. Climbing a narrow stairway, she knocked at the door of her own apartment. Her houseboy, Wang, let her in, and she was met frantically by her two miniature dachshunds, Wurst and Wiener. She sat on the couch and played with them until their frenzy wore off. Then she put on a gaily-embroidered national costume and felt boots and went to the gleaming rosewood piano, a fine instrument she had found in an auction shop. This was the routine that enabled her to forget the world outside. By the time Wang announced dinner she was fully at home and at peace.

This place was her island of serenity, lovingly furnished with genuine treasures, and holding what she had of personal life in a crazy world. The two dogs, the piano, a few pieces of Hungarian art she had found, and the faithful servants, Wang and the cook, Ying—these spelled home.

This was the only home she had known since the night, so long ago, when her father wakened her and said she must put on dark clothes and leave the country. She could go with friends of his, and he would follow later. Everything must be left behind except what she could put in a rucksack.

When she left the house a small, black car came from some distance away and stopped for her.

"This is Laszlo," said her father, "He will take you to other friends who will help you. I'm giving you all the money I can. Keep it out of sight and use it wisely. I will come to join you soon. Good-bye until we meet again."

The little car left the city and headed for the mountains, running slowly without lights much of the time.

Ilena stared at the darkened landscape of her homeland, too shocked and confused to realize the full import of what she was doing. Laszlo did not wish to talk.

Ilena had known that her father was engaged in very secret activities to smuggle people out of the country, but she had never thought that it had anything to do with her. She was fully absorbed in her studies at the university. Her own home, in the house where she and her father were born, was her security. How could she believe that she was on the way to the border in a darkened car with a man she had never met?

In the early morning they pulled up by a peasant house in a lonely area, where a friendly woman took her in and told her not to be seen outside during the day. She had a hearty breakfast, scarcely knowing what she ate, and went to sleep.

The next night a guide appeared with half a dozen other people, and they all set out on foot toward the border. The guide warned them not to speak. Once he hid them in some bushes while he went to scout the way. When he returned he said, "All clear, but follow me closely and don't lag behind."

He set off at a brisk trot, and they followed silently down the mountainside until he stopped under a tree and laughed.

"We're over the border now," he said, "and far enough so they can't see or hear us anymore. You can even smoke if you want to."

The group spent the rest of the night at a house a mile farther on. The guide explained to the hostess, Marta, who Ilena was, and said she could stay there to wait for her father.

Marta told Ilena that her father was an important link in the effort to save people who needed to leave the country. "You should be very proud of him," she said.

Ilena tried to make herself useful as she waited, but she spent a lot of time just resting and letting her mind adjust to the new shape of her world. Maybe when Father came it would all make sense.

Then one day, when a new group of refugees had arrived, Marta came to Ilena. "Your father was a very brave man," she said. "He never counted the risk to himself if he could help others."

Ilena's senses were aroused by the use of the past. She stared at Marta, who went on, "He was killed two days ago as he was arranging transportation for a family. I am sorry. You can stay here until we can make arrangements for you."

Ilena's memories from that moment were confused. She was sent on from hand to hand until she came to a place where she got a job and was supposed to be on her own. But one place after another became unsafe, and she somehow kept going, wherever a way opened. She became adept at sensing danger and seizing opportunities and going on and on and doing whatever her hands found to do.

She was caught in a roundup of Jews for slave labor in Germany. She remembered days and nights in a sealed boxcar, and working long hours making rifle ammunition. Then she was sent on a boat up a river, and walked a long time in a line of prisoners, not knowing where. One day she bolted into the woods, while shots were fired. She lay still, and the guards went on without her. She walked eastward, ever eastward, knowing that the west was dangerous.

She remembered vividly the day when she knew she would survive. On foot in Central Asia, exhausted, hungry and thirsty, she sat on a rock waiting for merciful death. A man was walking over the desert some distance away, too far for her to call. As he came opposite to her he stopped, then turned and came toward her. He addressed her courteously in an unknown tongue, and handed her a loaf of bread and a long drink from his bottle. Then he went on his way.

As Ilena tore off a piece of the bread and chewed it, savoring its goodness, she knew that death was not part of her program. She would survive. When she recovered a little strength she followed the way the man had gone, thinking he knew where people lived.

～

She could barely remember how a truck driver befriended her and brought her to Shanghai, leaving her on a park bench. A White Russian couple who ran a bakery found her there, semi-conscious. Remembering how they had come themselves, thirty years earlier, fleeing the revolution, they took her home and fed her rice gruel and chicken broth until she revived enough to eat regular food. They offered her work in their bakery, which she was thankful to accept but did not want it for long.

Finding that a knowledge of English was necessary for any kind of office work in Shanghai, she found a lesson book in a second-hand shop, and worked to improve the little she had learned in school. Her French, German, Russian, Italian, and Hungarian were of little use until she went to work for the International Refugee Organization, where she was often called upon to interpret for the hodge-podge of people who came seeking help.

～

Now even Shanghai was insecure. Who could know what life would be like under the Communists? She glanced around her beautiful apartment with its treasures, and could not believe that anything could threaten it. This was her home. She could not think of being homeless again. She wouldn't have to. Surely she was invulnerable in the tight little life she had made with her music and her dogs and Wang and Ying. Ying had even learned to make Hungarian food.

Sooner than she could have hoped a resettlement officer called her.

"You can have a visa to Venezuela," she said, "and can leave as soon as you can be ready."

"I'll think about it," said Ilena. "I don't speak Spanish, and I hate to think of learning another language."

"Don't think too long," said the officer, "If you don't take it someone else will, and we can't be sure of finding anything else for you. Time is getting short."

Mulling it over as she worked, Ilena couldn't see herself in Venezuela, She still could not believe that her pleasant way of life was not secure, even if there were a political change in the country. After a couple of hours she went back to the resettlement office.

"I've decided not to go to Venezuela," she said. "Give the visa to somebody else."

"Are you sure? This may be your only chance."

"I have decided."

"I'm afraid you are making a mistake."

The next evening, as she was finishing her dinner, Wang and Ying came into the room together.

"Missy, we want know when you go."

"I'm not going."

"But Missy, we just wait you go, then we go. Must go soon."

Ilena's carefully constructed world came apart. Life in the apartment without Wang and Ying was unthinkable, and she had probably wasted her last chance of escape. She must have time.

"Give me until tomorrow," she said, "I must think."

"Must go soon, Missy. News not good."

The next morning Ilena went again to the resettlement office.

"I must go after all. My servants are leaving and I can't live here without them."

"I'll see what I can do, but there may not be another chance. The world is not very hospitable, you know, and the waiting lists get longer every day."

As Ilena read the papers she seemed to feel a great fist closing on her. The news was very bad. It could not be many more days before the city would be taken. Then who knew what life would be like? Without Wang and Ying she had no safe base. Transportation was jammed.

Each day her mind juggled the puzzle. She obtained the international document for stateless people, but it was of no use without a visa to some country. Even Hong Kong, the only possibility, required permission. She heard that thousands of people were entering Hong Kong illegally, but she had no idea how to do that.

Each evening Wang and Ying begged for her decision. Wang had relatives in Hong Kong, and Ying in Macao. They had arranged for a fishing boat to take them as soon as Ilena's plans were made.

At last the fall of the city was imminent. "Come with us," they pleaded. "We take you Hongkong."

"How can you do that?"

"In fishing boat."

"All right," she said, "I don't see any other way."

They had to wait for the boatman friend to come back from Macao. Ilena collected her last pay and put all the money she could find into silver dollars. Wang bought dingy, second-hand Chinese clothes which would fit Ilena loosely, and an old towel to cover her hair.

"Must wear these," he said. "If see foreigner in boat maybe have pirates."

He gave her a large square of old blue cloth in which to tie up a few of her own clothes and other necessities. Ying procured a large covered basket for the dogs.

The boatman was overdue. The Communist army was expected the next day in a peaceful takeover of the city. Ying cooked an excellent dinner as usual.

"I am sorry," said Ilena, "that you have lost your chance to go because of me."

"Maybe still some chance, Missy. Always some way. You sleep now. Maybe tomorrow find other boat."

Ilena went to bed expecting to lie awake, but she was deeply asleep when Wang shook her.

"Get up, Missy. Boat come. Must go now."

As she put on her disguise and prepared her bundle, she felt clearly that this was happening for the second time.

Once again she set out into the night, knowing only that she was in safe hands.

LISA McKHANN

Lost in Translation

Cynthia knew better than to act annoyed with the man who took her ticket and left her standing in the hot, crowded aisle. It was all part of the routine she'd come to expect. He was changing her berth, trying to pack foreigners together in one compartment. And despite her fluency in Chinese, her regular trips along this route, Cynthia knew she would always be treated as a foreigner on the trains. She squeezed close to the window while other passengers moved along the aisle. Through the glass she watched the throng on the concrete platform contract as more people passed behind her. She stood patiently. The crowd outside thinned, and she could hear the passengers greeting each other and settling onto their berths behind her.

Outside, a lone woman was left squatting on the vacant platform, becalmed. She crouched in the late afternoon shadows of the far wall, a bread woman with her cloth-bound bundle steadied on one knee. She waved a paper fan to one side of her throat and stared blankly at the train. A smudge on the glass brought Cynthia's focus closer in, where she saw her own reflection. The blueness of her eyes was distinct, mirroring her intent gaze. Her thin nose and lips were more difficult to make out. All that could be seen of her black hair were the curves and scallops it created pulled back from her temples and forehead. There were a few light streaks of gray. Her view shifted. The bread woman's rounded form fit within the contours of Cynthia's face. She held it there until the layers blurred, and Cynthia was the woman reflected in her own eyes through the glass.

"*Due bu che*," the man with her ticket interrupted, excusing the delay and leading her to a compartment. He slid open the door for her to enter. Cynthia contained a little smile as she recognized the foreign faces turning to greet her and stepped into the coolness of the air conditioning. Though her eyes acknowledged them, she didn't speak to the couple. Instead, she already settled on the answers to their questions before they'd been fully formed; as if there was no response she could give that might alter the course of their thinking, nothing unexpected likely to come from her mouth. Cynthia knew these rules. She told them that she had lived in Kunming almost two years in a guest house just outside the wall of the university where she worked. That she hadn't been back to the States in that time. That she's vacationed around China and Indonesia. That she had some contact with American families at the guest house, and with other foreigners there, but not much.

She thought of the joke that circulated through the university, one equally enjoyed by both foreign and Chinese professors. An American at dinner receives from his host the first of what should be a long exchange of compliments, polite denials, and counter-compliments. Perhaps he makes it through the first round, complimenting his host in return. But upon being complimented a second time, the American beams, raises his head a little higher, and booms out, "Why, thank you, yes, I'm very proud of that!" Then he proceeds to help himself to more tea. She decided against telling the joke.

"I suppose knowing the language helps," Sally said, "but it must get lonely here. I'd go crazy. Don't you?" Cynthia imagined that Sally would go crazy anywhere. She'd tire of having Doug as her only audience in China. His responses would become too predictable. And she would dislike the stripping away of the beautiful, the unique, the alluring in herself, only to be noticed by the Chinese as different. Cynthia knew how some Americans hated to be alone, and feared the wild responses beyond their boundaries: the Hudson, the Potomac, the Mississippi. Yet she knew, too, how they hated to blend into—and how they would speak and dress and live and buy so as not to be just one of—the crowd. This couple seemed no different, trying to do something unusual for their honeymoon.

To Sally and Doug, though, she simply said, "Yes, sometimes I get lonely, but not very often anymore. I've made some good friends here." Doug wanted to know all about what she taught at the university, her students, her living situation, her daily routine—standard stuff—and in exchange, she asked about them. For her part, the conversation chugged through familiar terrain, leaving her disengaged enough to be aware of the Chinese woman's intent gaze, her mind free to meander back over the ripples of Sally's question of loneliness.

It struck Cynthia as a rude, yet oddly welcome remark. Who but a young American woman could say it? It took a certain impertinence to delve into a stranger's emotional state. Certainly the Chinese woman sitting beside her would never dream of risking such a disturbance. Like Cynthia's Chinese co-workers, the woman might speculate with her old women friends, wondering about this odd, childless, husbandless woman who chose to live her life so far from home. Sally's question reminded Cynthia of the impunity granted to young grandchildren in China, who could circumvent the smooth social rituals as easily as they crawled between the legs of the low, lacquered tables. Sally had that same childish, unrestricted curiosity. Words, phrases, questions spilled out unchecked. Cynthia found it annoying, yet she wondered where the conversation might have gone had she told Sally more.

Sally slipped her foot from Doug's lap and he pushed himself forward on the berth until his feet found the floor. He braced his arms against the underside of the top berth and stretched, twisting his torso and head back toward one corner, then the other where Sally sat. "Well, ladies, I think I'll stretch my legs, go back and explore the *real* train." He let a hand fall firmly onto Sally's leg. "Next time we're going to ride 'hard sleep' for the full China experience, right Sal?" He squeezed her calf. Sally looked across to Cynthia, trying to engage her, it seemed, in a moment of empathy. Cynthia turned her head toward the door, and saw the Chinese woman's smile. Doug excused himself, gave a little nod to the Chinese woman, and slid open the door. A waft of humid warmth slipped in as he left.

Still smiling at Sally and Cynthia, the elderly woman sat forward and stretched a little herself. "*Hao*," she said firmly. Good. Cynthia addressed her formally, asking, "Grandmother, shall we have tea?" She nodded toward the table. "For three women?" The woman nodded, yes. Sally seemed to follow these gestures, and reached to remove the lids from three cups while Cynthia unfolded one paper packet. Cynthia sprinkled green tea leaves into the bottom of each cup, and then Sally pulled the cork from the thermos and filled each with steaming water. With the lids replaced, Cynthia offered with both hands, handle first, the first cup to the old woman. Sally offered Cynthia the second cup with the same motions, and took the last for herself. The old woman held her teacup in open palms resting on her lap.

"You move well together," she said. "You are from the same household?"

Cynthia explained that they were all American, but had just met. She told her that Sally—and here she nodded and said the name again—Sally, and Doug, the man, were just married and were celebrating by traveling in China.

"*Aaah, tai tai*," the woman smiled broadly at Sally, her brown flesh creasing deeply round her eyes.

"I told her you're just married," Cynthia translated for Sally, "a bride, *tai tai.*" Sally smiled and nodded.

"Well, the same country is like the same household, I guess," the woman continued. "You are sisters in the big house. That's why you can just meet and serve tea." When Cynthia translated this, Sally laughed.

"Tell her I would only hope to get along so well with my own sister! And besides, at home I drink coffee."

Cynthia hesitated, worried that this would sound ungracious. She translated anyway.

Rather than the formal smile of politeness she expected, the woman chuckled deeply. "Yes," she said, "even very large families are often not big enough!"

Cynthia laughed in surprise. Sally asked for the translation.

For some time they sat in silence, each occasionally removing the lid from her cup and lifting the rim to her lips. The old woman pulled a tea leaf from her tongue.

"This is great," Sally said. Her head arched gracefully over her cup and she peered up at Cynthia and the old woman through steam. "Peaceful. No crowds."

"*Tai hao la*," the old woman said.

The sentiments of the two women were so similar that it took Cynthia a moment to realize she had not provided the translation. "Wonderful," she said to Sally.

"Uh-huh," Sally said. "It's wild, isn't it? Even when you're both speaking Chinese, I can follow along. Maybe not really, but it seems that way. Her face is so expressive, the sound of the words too."

"It helps when the interaction is simple," Cynthia said. "Then you can anticipate the dialogue." Sitting as they were, turned toward each other in a triangle on the lower berths, she saw that the Chinese woman had been intent upon Sally as she spoke.

"Yeah, I suppose," Sally said. She looked at the woman, and the lines that radiated out from the corners of the woman's eyes deepened in return.

Sally began to ask questions of the old woman, simple things: Where does she live? Does she have children? Grandchildren? Do they live nearby? have they all lived in that same village their whole life? Cynthia translated, though at times it was unnecessary, like when the woman stretched out both arms to show how many grandchildren she had, too many to count, and Sally moaned.

The conversation around her continued. She translated Sally's comments that she has always envied families that live near to one another, that are born and die in the same place, how in America that is very rare. She explained how her own family is widely scattered.

The woman listened attentively as each of these phrases was passed along to her, with mutterings of "*hao*" and nods marking her understanding. "Yes," she began, after Cynthia's final pause. Cynthia shifted her position slightly. "I would not like such distance. Our strength comes from each other. Sometimes my children make me crazy. Sometimes I am crazy. But I get to hold the babies on my lap. I carry my smallest grandson to market day on my back. This way I am needed."

"Yes, you are. That must be wonderful," Sally said.

"Yes, *tai hao la*, wonderful when described from a distant train!" she giggled, and Cynthia rushed to translate.

～

Doug swept into the compartment with another blast of warm air and perched on the edge of Sally's berth. "They sure stuff people in back there!" he said. "They've got them stacked three high, Sal. No air conditioning, and the top bunk is so close to the ceiling there's no room to sit up."

Cynthia explained. Though she had never ridden "hard sleep," she knew from other Americans that the middle bunk was best. "If you get in the lower berth, then the two people above you spend the day sitting on your bed. The top bunk is cramped and hot. The person in the middle has it best."

"So I learned! Some old guys invited me to sit with them at their checker game. They'd pulled a box into the aisle between bunks. All of us—the four of them playing, plus me and a couple of young boys—crowded in."

Cynthia had often wondered how her experience in China would differ were she a man. From what she'd seen, men were given more latitude for movement. They could work their way into the culture more easily, while she still had moments of wondering what her Chinese friends really thought of her, a single woman, alone. She wouldn't feel comfortable lingering in a crowded train car as Doug had, and she knew she wouldn't be invited to take part. It took a lot of time and hard work for a woman like her to establish bonds with the Chinese. She was patient.

"You reek," Sally said, bringing her nose close to Doug's sleeve.

"Yeah, well they kept offering and laughing at me, so I finally took one. They all have stained fingertips from where they hold their cigarettes. Except for one. He stuck the end into the bowl of a long pipe, an opium pipe, I guess—right, Cynthia?" Cynthia nodded. "Anyway, they all offer the others a cigarette each time they want to light up themselves. They had piles of them along the edge of the table."

"Well, just because Chinese men smoke, doesn't mean you have to, you sheep."

"No, I don't have to," Doug said, pausing to look at Sally. "But I wanted to. And I did."

Sally laughed, and this momentarily confused Cynthia. Then Sally reached for the last porcelain cup. "Well, have some tea. It'll clean up your breath at least."

"Thanks, Sal. That sounds good."

Cynthia saw the old woman smile at the young wife serving her husband tea. Cynthia found herself entangled in the simple action, trying to find one context for it. Was it a generous gesture or did it mask something else, subservience, perhaps, or aggression? Or was it just common sense considering Sally sat closest to the thermos?

Sally leaned over the table. Beyond her and through the window, Cynthia recognized the familiar cliffs that came just before Jade Lake, her favorite part of the trip. It would be coming up on the other side of the train. She didn't invite Doug and Sally or the Chinese woman to join her when she stood to leave the compartment. She wanted to be alone. As was so often the case, the work of interpreting languages and cultures had left her drained. It was exhausting to maintain such an acute level of awareness.

"Grandmother, can I get you anything? I'm going out for a few minutes."

"Thank you, no. Everything I need is here," she said.

Jade Lake lay glassy in the evening light. Cynthia watched its surface slip by, mirroring the shapes of clouds above. The lake was always calm when she passed, doubling every willow along its edge. The symmetrical patterns reminded Cynthia of paintings she made as a child, dabbing color on one side of a page, then folding it in half to create its mirror image. Here, two worlds fanned out from the crease of the horizon. Up lake she saw the winged pagoda, its layers of arcing tiled roofs seeming to take flight. Then the white stone bridge spanning a small inlet at the far shore. The arch of the bridge was so gentle that its doubling in the water's mirror transformed it into a chalky band. The five half-circle archways cut beneath became perfect circles with their reflections.

Cynthia stood for some time after the northern edge of the lake had passed behind the window frame. She let the scenery blur before her, not bothering to focus, differentiate, name what she saw. The broad swath of new green from the paddies soothed her eyes. She was relieved to see the colors dimming into darkness.

She reached for the compartment door having decided that she would simply brush her teeth and climb into the upper berth where she could rest or perhaps read. She expected that a polite silence would hang between the Chinese woman and the Americans, and that perhaps Doug and Sally would sit talking softly together. She pushed open the sliding door with downcast eyes and hoped to move directly to her things. But three pairs of feet pointed into the aisle from the berth that she and the Chinese woman had shared. A tentative glance up revealed that her roommates were all crowded onto the berth, Doug and Sally seated on either side of the old woman. In her lap she held a stack of color photos.

"Oh, you're showing her pictures from home? That's great!" she said to them. She could make out the Golden Gate Bridge in the top picture. Doug and Sally stood beside bicycles, her hair blown loose in the wind. The white specks of sails dotted the Bay. To the old woman she said in Chinese, "This is the Golden Gate Bridge in San Francisco, California. San Francisco has a large. . . ."

The woman nodded and smiled, but help up a hand to stop Cynthia from continuing. Instead, she traced with her crooked finger the arch of the bridge, back and forth, back and forth.

"Bridge," Doug said.

Cynthia stood awkwardly. There was no space for her on their berth, so she sat across from them. She watched as the woman nodded at Doug and then at

Sally. The woman left the photos on her lap and held both arms wide, one in front of each of the young Americans. She held her palms face up, steady. Cynthia wasn't sure what she was doing. Her gestures were unfamiliar, so broad and sweeping, so different from the self-contained kowtows, the subtle nods and faint smiles. She was about to say something, to tell Doug and Sally that even she wasn't sure what the woman was saying, what she meant. But then the woman swept her arms upward in a surprisingly energetic arc. Her palms met and she clasped her hands firmly together over her head. Everyone looked up at the gnarled tangle of her locked hands. "*Hao*," she said.

"*Tai hao la*," Sally said, laughing.

The woman lowered her arms and took first Sally's left hand, then Doug's right in her own. She brought them together in front of her. They held tight. Then she covered the knot of Sally's delicate white fingers and Doug's fleshy pads with her own two hands. "Come," she said to Cynthia.

Cynthia slid from the berth to squat before them. She had to stretch to reach her hands in without bumping the woman's knees. She glanced up at the old woman, then added her hands to the mass. The fingers beneath hers tightened and shrank inside the knot. Cynthia squeezed harder, too. The old woman's hands felt much like she'd thought they would. The flesh was smooth. The grip was strong. But there was something unexpected about her touch too, something softer than she'd guessed, yet not soft. And then it was gone, the moment undone in a deep sigh and loosening. *Hao*. It was good.

Cynthia stood, said good night, and climbed into the top berth without brushing her teeth. She lay on her back, her arms folded across her chest. She listened as the others readied themselves for bed. With her eyes closed she could picture their movements around the compartment from the sounds. The old woman's breathing gently rasped with each exhale.

Doug sighed heavily as he let himself down onto the upper berth across from her. "Now, *this* is China," he said to no one and all.

Cynthia wasn't sure what this was and she didn't want to risk pinpointing it with words. She just hoped some trace of it would be there in the morning. The darkness behind her eyelids deepened when the compartment lights were switched off and she imagined the train pushing blindly into night. All the familiar landmarks passed by unnoticed.

After Tiananmen

Tʜᴇʀᴇ's ᴀ ʏᴏᴜɴɢ doctor in this city studying for a specialty in cardiac medicine (in China this is a M.S. degree). He was studying English at the school where I taught from 1985 to 1986, in another province, and the American professor's wife who was his English teacher wrote to suggest that he look me up. Today he comes, tall and rather formal in manner, carrying a big black umbrella and wearing a suit and brocade tie and polished leather shoes with pointed toes. He brings a letter he has received from the professor's wife; she writes that soon she and her husband will celebrate their golden wedding anniversary and she hopes he will be as fortunate in his marriage as they have been in theirs. I remember this couple well, although I have not kept in touch with them. The wife typed her husband's lecture notes every evening, in addition to preparing and teaching her own classes. She had been trained as a nurse, not a teacher, but Chinese universities try to press every available foreigner into service. I would see her following her husband on the campus paths, a pace or two behind and bent forward, hurrying to keep up. In the dining room, when he finished his meal and stood up she, too, would leap to her feet, interrupting her own conversation, and scurry after him. I don't mention these memories to Dr. Hu, but I do ask him if he is married.

"No, but I'm twenty-eight now and it's time for me to find a wife."

We talk of one thing and another. Dr. Hu's English is weak and he's aware of this; he emits a little giggle whenever he gropes for a word that eludes him, or is unsure of one he has used. This habit causes me to feel I should take special pains to save his pride while we talk, and I find myself growing impatient. The rain seems to have stopped, so I suggest that we go for a walk: I need instant coffee and butter.

We set off. A few drops fall, nothing I would call rain. Dr. Hu snaps open his big umbrella and I wave it away: the spokes catch in my hair, and I count only about one block. The coffee is quickly found, but butter is another matter. The one shop that usually stocks it is sold out, and there are so few foreigners in the city since Tiananmen they may not plan to reorder. I decide to try some other shops. As we stride along, Dr. Hu mentions again that he has reached the age for marriage, and he is thinking of settling in this city. He comes from a small town some distance away, but his medical degree will entitle him to choose his place of work. So he asked a friend to introduce him to a local girl. A few days ago the meeting took place.

261

"No good," he says.

"Oh? Why not?"

"Well. It's hard to say. . . ."

"Was she interesting?" (It's simpler, I've learned, to ask only affirmative questions of weak English speakers.)

"I suppose so."

"Then what? Was she pretty?"

"No, not pretty."

"So what happened?"

"We just said some words and go our ways." He giggles.

We walk another block. Dr. Hu points to his brocade tie.

"This cost me ninety *yuan*," he says.

More than a month's salary for a young teacher, I'm thinking.

We try another shop, a shop that stocks imported and Chinese packaged foods, stationery, towels, clothes and laundry soap, but no butter.

"Oh, wait." Dr. Hu is hovering near a display of sweaters. "Which do you like?" He points at two pullovers, one a dark maroon, the other a rich cranberry red.

"But you must choose the one *you* like; it's for you, isn't it?"

"Yes. But I want your opinion."

"Okay, I like the red one."

He asks the clerk to let him try it on and slips off his jacket and his dark blue pullover.

"This one is very old now."

The red sweater fits him well.

He turns around and around, looking doubtful. "Isn't it too loose?"

"No, it looks fine to me; you don't want it too tight."

Though he clearly does: he keeps plucking at his chest and stomach.

A few feet down the counter I see a black T-shirt: just what I need; I found a hole in my favorite one yesterday. I buy it. When I return from paying the cashier to pick it up at the counter, Dr. Hu is still studying his reflection in the mirror, turning to look over his shoulder, turning again to look at the front view with a stern expression.

"Is this good quality wool?"

We both finger it. "Yes, it seems good." I look the sweater over carefully; I've just had to reject two T-shirts because of uneven dye stains.

"Well, I suppose I'll buy it." Dr. Hu takes it off, puts on his blue sweater and coat, goes to pay at the cashier's booth, returns. "I think I'll wear it," he says, with a little smile.

Once again he takes off his jacket and the blue sweater, puts on the new sweater and his jacket. We leave the shop.

I'm down on the sidewalk, heading up the street, when I hear him call from behind me.

"Oh, Margaret! Come back! Come back!"

I race back. "What is it?"

Dr. Hu is standing frozen on the top step of the shop entrance, looking down at his front.

"Too bright! Too bright!" The sweater glows richly in the daylight.

"I think it's handsome."

"Oh, no, no—too bright! Maybe a young woman could wear this. . . . Oh, dear. . . ."

He turns back into the shop; I follow. He speaks to the clerk.

"She says to wait a moment. I'm so sorry to make you delay, to cause you troubles."

"No trouble; I'm in no hurry."

Now he looks at the maroon sweater. "Perhaps I'll try this one. What do you think?"

"Well, you'd better look at it in the daylight."

He walks over to the doorway.

Now I see a sweat suit, a wonderful, bright spring-green suit, with a crazy legend across the chest, something about "Football," and a lot of English words that add up to nonsense. I hold it up to me: it will fit. I buy it.

Dr. Hu is returning from the doorway, slowly. "Too old, I think." He hangs up the sweater, gets a note from the clerk and picks up his refund at the cashier's booth. A few more drops of rain are falling now, but not enough to require the umbrella. But up it snaps.

"I really don't need it," I say; I hate to share umbrellas.

"You use it."

"Oh, I can't do that! It will look very bad! I'm younger than you."

"Yes, I know: you have to take care of me." Resignedly I put my head under the umbrella. The spokes poke at my hair. We walk along; Dr. Hu looks glum. I try to cheer him up. "How do you like your work?"

"So-so."

"Really?"

"Well, I have to work very hard, all day, eight to five. I earn very little money. I thought of going to an economic zone, maybe Shenzhen, but it must be very hot there, and perhaps it's too late to change my idea and go into business."

"So now what happens? Do you get introduced to another girl?"

"What? Oh, yes, I must try again."

I suppose he wanted a new sweater for the next occasion.

"I must get married. I'm almost thirty, and it's not easy for a man to be this old, with no one. . . . In America I could have a lover," he giggles—"but in China we cannot do that."

"So, tell me, what do you want in a wife? What qualities?"

"She must be pretty, and good-tempered, and have good health."

I can't resist. "That shouldn't be hard; I know lots of pretty, kind, healthy girls. I think you'll have a wife in no time." I don't think he even hears me, as often happens when you're struggling to phrase your next thought in a foreign language.

"She must be pretty so I'll fall in love at first glance. That will make me feel it's worth getting to know her more deeply."

I've never thought of love at first sight as having such a practical value.

"You know," he says suddenly, "I envy you."

"Me?"

"Yes. . . . You just step into the shop and purchase something, so . . . surely, with such, such . . . how to say. . . ?"

"Confidence?"

"Yes, that's it! I wish I could do that! No hesitating! So sure of yourself!"

⌒

By the time I've known Dr. Hu a few weeks I'm beginning to think of him as a pest. He is sitting in on one of my classes to improve his English, which is fine, but after class, when I would prefer silence and solitude, he hurries up to the lectern and announces "I will come to your apartment and drink tea." He's very hard to discourage. He uses my telephone to call his hospital's transportation department: if a car is in the vicinity, he can avoid riding a bus home. I've walked past the hospital where he works and lives; it's not so far from this school. But Dr. Hu prefers to be driven.

Today I've weakened again and allowed him to visit me after class. I refuse to go shopping with him anymore. The next time I saw him after the red sweater incident he led me in and out of five overcrowded department stores on a muggy Sunday, where I stood watching while Dr. Hu tried on two-hundred *yuan* wool suits and fussed and turned before mirrors, and ended by buying nothing again. He still has not met the right girl.

"What are the three happiest moments in life?" he asks.

I'm sure he prepares these conversational gambits ahead of time. "I don't know. . . ." Why did I let him come here? I want to sit alone, enjoying the high spirits I usually feel after a class.

Dr. Hu presses on oblivious to my mood. "In China, they are your wedding night, seeing your name on the wall—that you've been accepted at the university; this means a good job, in the Confucian tradition and meeting your best friend when you are far away from your hometown."

Strange there's no mention of the birth of a son.

"What are they for an American?"

"I don't know."

"Finding a good lover," he suggests.

This is a lot on his mind lately. I hate his little giggle.

"China is better for old people, but hard on the young ones. America, I think, is better for young energetic ones but hard for the old. Which system do you think is better?"

I think this is one of his prepared conversations, or an expression of self-pity, or both, and I think the question is silly. I try to joke: "Well, as I'm an old person, I guess I should prefer China."

But I can't keep up this empty exchange. I'm impatient with Dr. Hu's presence, his dumb little textbook dialogues, with myself for tolerating him.

"How long can a government last," I ask, "that is so hard on the young, that keeps disillusioning them, generation after generation, turning them into cynics?"

Dr. Hu loses his grin, and even seems to think for a moment. "Who knows?"

I change the subject. Lately I've noticed many shops remodeling, painting and decorating their storefronts, and whole blocks of sidewalks being repaired. I ask Dr. Hu if these aren't signs of prosperity. I guess I keep looking for signs of hope.

No, he says, quite serious now; the economy is in very bad shape. The government has simply ordered these businesses—most are near the foreigners' hotels—to spruce up by a certain date or suffer consequences. The owners of the privately-owned shops and the managers of the government-owned shops must pay all the costs of paint, labor, plastic facings. Of course, he goes on, some private businesses can make money, but all the government factories are operating under capacity, with many workers sitting at home on partial salaries. "I don't believe any of the figures they've given us in the papers. They say everything is going well, but it isn't."

He looks down at his pointed toes. "I was so hopeful when I entered medical school. I believed that if I worked hard and got good results I would get a good job. But now I know it's only *guan-xi* that counts, just who you know."

"Yes, many students have said that. But isn't this a recent change?" I'm remembering my students of 1985 and 1986, who were so full of hope for their futures and who worked so hard, sitting in the classroom until one or two in the morning.

"In 1985 everything was just the same as it is now. Your students were innocent—and so was I."

"So there has been no true reform?"

"No. I think all that remains for me is to make a life of some sort under the system that exists."

He's grinning, but behind his glasses his eyes look damp. Maybe his empty little dialogues aren't just English practice, after all, but a way of avoiding painful thoughts.

Dr. Hu pulls out another letter from the professor's wife in America. She writes: "My dear young friend, it is so wonderful to hear of your hard work in medical school! China needs dedicated young doctors like you, young men of high ideals. My husband and I are proud to know one of them. . . ." She goes on to say that her husband will be retiring soon and again mentions how happy they have been together. Her insensitive gush bothers me even more than Dr. Hu's cynicism. I hand him back the letter.

"What do you want in your life when you're retired?" I ask him. "I know I don't want to sit on a little stool and watch people pass by!" This is what I always think of when I'm told "China is good for old people." It's what I see here, too.

Dr. Hu perks up a bit. "No, I don't want to do that, either. I would read some books, help my son or daughter raise their children, write something . . . no, *try* to write something. . . ." He looks at the windows, at the damp-streaked apartment buildings on the hillside. "And I'd like to take a trip. To take a trip—that would be best of all!" He keeps looking at the blurry panes. Then he turns back to me. "And I might raise goldfish."

EUROPE

ELIZABETH ANN HAUGEN

Dancing in Stone Footprints

Two DAYS after graduating from college, I went to Greece. Fifteen of us went—eleven students, an archaeologist, a philosopher, the director of the program, and an off-duty pastor. It rained in Athens and we saw pots—in the National Museum we saw rooms upon rooms of pottery: amphorae larger than my dad and drinking vessels the size of my grandma's fine bone-china teacups.

Lydia Shaffer and I walked through the rooms together. Lydia didn't seem particularly interested in the pottery; when I'd pause and gape, she'd move a room or two beyond me. I lost track of time and Lydia as I studied the colors or designs on red-figured, black-figured, and white-slip pottery.

There were vessels just for decoration, just for celebration, just for everyday, for snakes to climb on, for unknown purposes—my mind whirled until eventually the pottery looked the same. Then I caught up with Lydia, in a room filled with teacups. She was standing in front of a case, smiling at the teacups. "Look how delicate these are," she said. "They're tiny. Somebody made these thirty-two hundred years ago. They held these—they drank tea out of these. I can understand them now," she said, turning her to face me. "They drank tea!" She laughed.

In a wild-pine park the next day, I found a snail shell (from the Geometric Period, Lydia said) and Socrates' prison. At least, that's what the nearby taverna hosts and patrons told us. Not the cave with the square room, they said, but the round room behind it.

We couldn't go inside the prison. It was a two-room cave, with metal bars closing the entrance. Stray animal smells wafted from inside. If Socrates ended it in there, then David's depiction with spaciousness and light is generous and optimistic. I mean, it's a dirt cave. I wanted to think the painting implied that Socrates' life created spaciousness and light, but the painting isn't called *The Life of Socrates*.

Pretty dismal way for a hero to go, in the dark. In the dirt.

I always wondered which would be best: to die graciously, with dignity, or to rage a bit and survive by my own determined will. Because if I stood any chance of living, I would be a limp lame fool to let myself die. Sometimes the difference between living and dying is giving a damn. Diseases, bad guys, and cliffs have more trouble killing people who don't give up. If I ever found myself peering over the edge, I would like to think I'd give a damn. I would like to think that I am the one in charge of whether or not I let go.

That is the only way, I think, of legitimately freaking out. Usually freaking out is out of line, out of control, and ultimately harmful. Usually freaking out is self-indulgent and I think it eats your soul—but when it saves, it's worth its weight in snake oil.

Dorothy Monson—probably weighing 106 pounds—shouted at a bear and hit it on the head with a frying pan until it ran away. A logger sawed off his own trapped leg and hauled himself out of the woods on his elbows. Dainty women lift up cars to release beloved crash victims, children pull siblings away from wild animals, old crippled men incapacitate burglars—these people survive via temporary insanity. Adrenaline sustains life and people lose control in order to retain it.

But if I really am positively going to die, I don't want to freak out. I'd end up dead anyway and a bad sport besides. Or if, like Socrates', my life would be better shorter, then I should be ready to die. I have a Norwegian ancestor who wouldn't give his gun to the Nazis. He didn't freak out, as far as I know. He didn't live to be very old, but he never gave his gun to the Nazis.

I suppose it's a matter of identifying your choices.

~

We left Athens for Tolo by bus. The bus held thirty; we were fifteen and I could hang out in my head. Sunshine blared through the windows and saturated the fields. Twisty, demented-looking olive trees and graceful cypresses shouted, "Van Gogh was right!" at me. I know, I know. I mean I believed him; I just had never seen them before except framed or in books. Orange trees, lemon trees, peach trees in bloom jostled past my window but they did not shout. Whether they had nothing to say or presumed my attention I did not know but the cypresses and olive trees shouted at me and I loved them.

At Daphne we stopped to see the Byzantine monastery. Although pieces of the walls were torn out for restoration, golden mosaics and high, small windows gave the impression of lavish holiness. I wandered out of the gold, away from my chattering companions and found one of the cells—a place, I found out later, where monks go to be alone with God. But not knowing that and not having much interest in God anyway, I thought I'd found a clean, dark, lonesome place.

It had the manners of a cave, with only gray and dark gray to see, but with an impossibly high ceiling and walls too close. A single eight-lobed round window allowed in a sharply focused tube of sunlight. The room contained nothing but an altar at the far end, made from the same gray material as the floor. I could not breathe in that room and immediately left.

Then I scolded myself and marched into the opposite cell, across the nave. That one didn't have any more air than the first one. I returned to the first cell and walked inside it. I felt it again—that basement feeling that little kids have when they've turned off the last light and must finish climbing the stairs in the dark.

I could not, would not, for the life of me, walk all the way to the altar. I forced myself to stand in the middle of the room while my heart pounded and my neck tingled. What fear have people given off in this room over the last thousand years for the ghost of it to hit me? I stared at the altar, at the oblique cylinder of sunlight, and at the distant, rounded ceiling. I trembled and wondered whose fear I had but I couldn't breathe and I had to go outside.

I stood under an extravagant old twisted tree with narrow leaves and white flowers, while the outside air warmed me. Maybe I didn't belong in there. Maybe monk fear and Inquisition fear and damnation-to-hell fear, which have probably been steeping in those rooms for centuries, bleed into less saturated bodies. I lit a cigarette and looked at the field with red, yellow, and purple wildflowers behind the monastery. I could smell the flowers through my smoke.

Our bus took us past the Bay of Salamis where Xerxes, King of the Persians, sat on a hill about twenty-three hundred years ago to watch his soldiers trounce the Greek Navy. The Persians outnumbered the Greeks by far, but the Greeks had jammed up the waterway so the Persians had to come through one ship at a time. The unfair odds gave them no advantage—they panicked when they became stuck and they couldn't back out the ships. Herodotus says more Persians died because they jumped overboard and couldn't swim than got killed by Greeks. Whatever it takes, I guess. Xerxes called his own men names and went home for a while.

Our bus driver Yanni took us around hairpins that were never built to accommodate a tour bus. Steep, tree-covered cliffs dropped frequently to one side. I'd never expected Greece to have such lush green foliage; I'd expected mostly rocks. But here was thick, healthy flora—almost rainforest-looking. Much of it dotted with spilled garbage bags and the occasional car. My mind-voice cried out in high-spirited fear, "Yesus, Yanni—slow down!" I stood spread eagled in the aisle like Leonardo's proportion wheel, imagining the long cartwheel I could do.

Little shrines by the side of the road mark the spots where people went over. Grieving families erect them. Most of the shrines contain icons and oil lamps—the flames seem to burn continuously. First I thought what a hassle to keep them burning, but I suppose that's the idea. Some bottles have wine or water in them. Some have refills of oil. The shrines are constructed from rusting metal or gorgeous marble and most of them sit on a hairpin. In some places, the guard rail isn't even replaced; in the ripped-open gap sits a shrine. On one corner, we counted eleven shrines. Dale asked me if that was a bus.

At Tiryns, we saw rocks. It has been such a tremendously wealthy place, it is said, that the giant Cyclopeans were hired to build twenty-foot-thick fortifications. Seven-foot-thick walls remain. In legend, Heracles ran this place. I didn't know much about historical fact—nearby Mycenae had Agamemnon; he's pretty famous. Our archaeologist showed us around surreptitiously—a guide stood near us most of the time. If anyone got to lecturing, we had to break into small groups. Guides at Greek sites have to be licensed by the government and presumably paid by groups who benefit from them. We had our own experts along but in deference to the rules of guiding (and so we didn't get kicked off the sites), we didn't all listen at the same time.

Cindy and I found some beautiful beetles that looked like they had on black and brown printed African dresses. We also saw a brilliant metallic green beetle, and a dusty black scarab with antlers that maybe hasn't changed in design since the walls went up.

I wandered. I stepped on reddish-tan dirt and small rocks. The site area was mostly dirt, but outside the site were fields upon fields of grasses with red and yellow flowers beneath an unbelievably blue sky. The flower smell floated over the dirt and rocks. Sun made them warm. As I walked down two dirt steps I found a small bone-shaped piece of clay —the same reddish-tan color as the dirt. I called to our archaeologist, "Henrik, what kind of bone is this?"

As far as I can tell, Henrik knows everything. Before the trip, I thought he was Moses. Now I think he's God.

Almost every site had pottery shards in the dust. Henrik would inspect them for us, tell us who made them and when, describe where they went on a pot. Then he'd drop them back on the ground—the good stuff was already in museums.

I handed the piece of clay to Henrik and his eyebrows lifted about an inch. He said, "Do you know what you have found." He did not ask that; he said it.

I said, "No."

He asked me and the few other students who had gathered, "What have you all been looking at in museums maybe a little too much?"

We hesitated, feeling ungrateful, "Pottery."

"What were the drinking vessels like in the Bronze Age?" Henrik asked.

Someone said, "Wide, and narrow at the bottom."

"Yes," Henrik said.

"With a stem," another student said.

Henrik looked at me, "You have found the stem." He held the clay up to us so we could tell where the bowl and base would have connected with it. "They stopped making them like this about thirty-three hundred years ago. This particular one is probably thirty-five hundred years old."

He handed it to me. I studied it closely, trying to memorize it. It was about two inches high and shaped like an hourglass or, yeah, the stem of a wineglass. We took turns inspecting it, then it came back to me. As I bent down to set it against the steps where I'd found it, one of the students said, "Aren't you going to keep it?"

I shook my head, saying, "It isn't mine."

Our philosopher, Simone, said, "Bring it to him," gesturing at the site's official guide.

I picked it up again and asked, "He'll care? It's worth keeping?"

She walked with me and acted out "drinking vessel" with her hands, making the top half of an hourglass shape. I handed the stem to the guide; he lifted up his eyebrows and thanked me in English. I said you're welcome in Greek and walked away, grinning.

When Henrik saw some people in our group who had missed all this, he borrowed the stem from the guide to show them. I walked toward them to hear about the stem again, and Henrik handed it to me. He said, "Here—you do this. You found it."

I held out my hand to take the stem and tears flew out of my eyes. I began to sob. This has been sitting around since the Bronze Age and I found it? Henrik said patiently, "Tell us about it."

I said, "This is thirty-five hundred years old," and kept right on crying.

Henrik said, "Hold it right side up."

I laughed and turned it the other way; everybody else laughed and took out their cameras. Simone declared it the Proto-Haugenian Era and when I took the shard back to the guide, he shook my hand firmly and looked me in the eye.

When I pointed out a tall weed covered in climbing snails later, Dale said, "You drank too much last night and you can't look at the sun. That's why you keep finding stuff."

I laughed but the number thirty-five hundred kept running through my head and I felt pensive and raw for the rest of the day.

We stopped at Nafplion on the way back to Tolo. We hadn't planned to stop—people had eagerly been saying "hotel beach" and "swim" to each other. I think the stop at the Castle of Palamidi was Yanni's idea, or some language barrier fluke. It's probably Venetian, the castle. Sits on a cliff that came straight up out of the Aegean some skillion years ago. The sun by now had eaten high noon and gave the sea its flame blue to match the sky. I grabbed my camera, cigarettes, and lighter, shook a small beetle out of my shorts, and hopped off the bus.

Rather than ancient, Palamidi Castle felt legendary. Most of the ceilings are gone; the castle is mostly stairs and windows now. Deep windows because of thick walls are just wide enough to fit an arrow through or maybe a face on a really long neck. They form gorgeous deep lines and angles—each angle of each window conducts a new lesson on perspective. The front rectangle leads through rough beige stone into purple and green flowers and grasses that grow from the stone on the outside of the castle. These volunteer plants lean into the view, asymmetrically framing the rippling blue sea and sky.

Stairs sprout from everywhere and lead to nowhere. From an edge of the castle, I could sit on a low wall and look down the cliff into the sea. From the top of some random stairs, I could look down the castle to the cliff to the sea. At the top of the stairs, though, I found nothing. A small ledge sometimes, or what might have been a hallway once. A path where a second or third floor might have been, but without the floor. I could stand at the top of the stairs or walk the narrow stone pathway, but every time I came back down because there wasn't anywhere else to go.

Occasionally I ran into another member of the seminar. Carrie and I crossed paths and stairs so many times we stopped exclaiming over it, instead smiling at each other and shaking our heads in joy. Sometimes I could see Henrik and his blue, green, and white plaid shirt fifty feet down and two blocks away, standing in another part of the castle. Or it could have been Dave some of the time because he had a shirt like that too.

After learning the castle for about an hour, I found a corner I hadn't yet seen. The side faced the town rather than the sea but still could only be reached by beanstalk. Stairways leading up have little ledges to crouch on, and those deep bow-and-arrow-sized windows. Most of the stairs follow a wall on one side but some have no wall on either side. They lead from an edge to a ledge with a whole lot of space in between. Standing on them made me feel pleasantly disoriented or perhaps non-oriented. Wild courtyards grew tall grass one or two stories below some of the ledges, with no apparent gentle entrance.

I saw nobody in this corner. I felt vulnerable from the heights, small compared to the castle's size and age, and alone. My heart pounded so hard my T-shirt trembled and I began to smile. I grinned, I laughed. I turned my face up to the sun and felt my lungs breathing. I turned my face down to the stairs and felt my muscles: my stomach muscles as I held my body erect. My butt, my quads, my calves as I stepped down each stair. I watched each stair as I stepped on it.

Somebody probably built them level but centuries of feet have put gouges in their planes—skin and dust and skin have slowly and persistently worn into the stone.

I'm vulnerable, I'm small, I'm alone—if I'm only Elizabeth. But see those cliffs, that sea, the sky that stretches from Greece to Minnesota and back. Now see me, made from dirt, water, and oxygen. Through luck—chromosomes and timing and homemade red wine—I became 1) Me; and 2) In Existence. That I have fingerprints is exciting but tied to mortality. That I exist in time in space gives me infinity. I am part of everything. The layers of skin and ounces of brain who dented these stones are part of my world and here's the beauty of it: so am I.

Ahead of me, on what seemed to be the final outside corner of the castle, I saw wide switchback stairs that went down. I didn't know where I fit in time or space, but that didn't seem relevant; I felt less like a puzzle piece than a stew ingredient. I started down the stairs.

I had the castle behind me, cliff and sea to my left, and more and more stairs. Sometimes I'd jump from one stair to the next; sometimes I'd stop entirely and lean over the wall on one side or another. These stairs clearly had not been inside the castle, even when it had an inside. I began to suspect they were the beanstalk. But I also thought they'd twist back up, or branch into another staircase that would take me back to the castle. I still had half an hour before I had to meet the seminar, though; I didn't have to know where I was.

A French-speaking, leathery couple with big white hats and walking sticks came climbing up the stairs toward me. I didn't feel like saying, "Bonjour," "Hello," or "Yassas," so I nodded my head as I caught their eyes. The man looked at me then past me. I turned around to follow his gaze and saw mostly stairs. My head nodded again as I looked back to their faces. Briefly I wished I had the French to ask them where I was going.

I still skipped down stairs as I went. I thought about my friend Aud back home, and something she'd said shortly before we graduated. "I've been thinking about that saying—that you can't understand someone until you've walked a mile in her moccasins. I can't make it a mile. They don't fit. Nobody's moccasins fit me. And mine don't fit anybody else."

The idea haunts me and I have two opinions about it: of course, they don't and of course, they do. Maybe the best thing is to fit inside your own moccasins.

Still, flashes of Lydia-and-the-teacups are the immortal ones. Nikos Kazantzakis says in *Report to Greco* that everything lives while it is remembered—people, canaries, liberty—knowing they exist(ed) keeps them in existence. What a powerful connection. What thrill is it, if not empathy, that makes me dance in stone footprints down the stairs?

My moccasins—my shell, limits, preconceptions—melted; I felt quite barefoot. Emerson's transparent eyeball maybe: transparent barefoot eyeball, with no strings attached. As soon as I reflected on it, of course, I filtered in my thoughts and theories and turned into my own, lone self with stubble for hair and sunburned ears. But my own self still danced on the stairs because my own moccasins fit me and I'm happy in them as well as out.

The stairs continued. I knew the castle had more than one entrance because the tour bus had not driven us up these stairs. All I have to do, I thought, is find the road.

I no longer hopped down the stairs. I half-wished I'd been counting them, out of curiosity. It was too many by now to return up in time to meet the seminar. Once I reached the bottom of the stairs, though, all I'd have to do is walk around the base of the hill until I found a road that went into the castle. It's a cliff on the sea side, but probably more like a hill where we entered. I hadn't exactly been paying attention, but it had to be. Buses don't drive up cliffs.

The bottom of the stairs eased into a fenced, grassy place. A sidewalk-sized path guided me between the steep hill which led up to the castle, and the flowery enclosed backyards of the people of . . . of . . . what town was I in? Nafplion? Or was that just what the Venetians had called it? An enormous white Lab stretched across the path, nursing her puppies. The stray dogs and cats in Athens had behaved sweetly but now I did not know what to expect; I'd have to step over this one. I slowed down my pace, still steadily approaching her. She stared at me. She disentangled her belly from her children and stood.

I tried to tell her telepathically that I'd be very careful when I stepped over her babies, that I'd love to turn around and go back up those stairs, but I really was out of time and it really was a lot of stairs. She let rip a tremendous growl which turned into a flurry of barks and she ran at me.

I froze. Can I reason with a dog, can I outrun her, can I outwrestle her? She's protecting her babies. I'm on a walk. But she stopped running, and she slowly came close enough to smell me. I told myself I was at Customs and waited. She made little snuffling noises then, and sauntered back to her puppies. She picked up each one by the neck and dropped it off on the edge of the path. When she finished, I slowly resumed my own saunter. She stood between me and the pups, even jogging along behind me after I'd passed. "I'm going, I'm going," I said. She licked her lips and returned to her puppies.

The enclosed path became an open sidewalk, but I let nothing come between me and the hill with the castle, so that I could not possibly lose my way. I knew enough Greek to sound out street signs and sometimes they sounded like cognates with words I knew, but none said, "Shortcut to Palamidi Castle." What to do: return to the stairs immediately or look for an alternate route? I vetoed the stairs because there were just too many. Besides, I enjoyed the field trip. I resigned myself to being late, comforted myself that the glass of thick red orange juice I'd drunk hours ago at Mycenae would keep my blood sugar up, and walked: barefoot.

The blank hill drew back, providing room for a large, squat courthouse-looking building. Four tour buses—none of them mine—lolled in a row along the curb. A tiny shrine to a dead person sat next to the sidewalk; it contained a large plastic bottle of commercial water and a framed black and white photograph of a young man with a big mustache and deeply set eyes. He looked bruised from his face's shadows. The wick in oil burned.

Quickly the neighborhood became residential. Pastel-colored three- and four-storied houses placed like walls in a maze replaced orderly and spacious government and business property. Twisted, dead-end sidewalks took me almost inside people's homes. People outside their homes stared at me. I was outside my home too. At the end of something resembling a block, I looked down the perpendicular street toward a more high-traffic area. A long tour bus which looked quite a bit like mine drove through an intersection and disappeared.

My heart tore but my feet didn't move. If I chased it, if I caught it, if it were indeed my bus, then I would be done. If I chased it, if I didn't catch it, or if it weren't my bus, then I would have lost my hill landmark and tired myself out. Would they leave without me?

I ran; not toward the bus but along a street, next to the hill. Any moment now a road might go into the hill. It had been all dead-ends that way so far; my street ran parallel to it and nothing went into it. I ran; I sprinted because I thought I saw my bus and I couldn't bear to walk anymore. I wouldn't have caught it, it wasn't my bus, they wouldn't leave without me but my body had adrenaline and I had to use it.

Soon I stopped. I ran out of space before I ran out of breath; an enormous yellow pile of construction sand blocked the entire street ahead of me, from front door to front door. I couldn't follow the street along the hill any more. I could only go left, away from the hill, which was useless, or I could go back the way I'd come. Back the way I'd come. I would have to. Back across town and up those stairs.

I turned around, sorry to know where I was going. If only I had more time or a sandwich or a map or if I didn't care that everyone had to wait around for me on an air-conditioned bus when they wanted to go swim in the ocean. But I didn't and I didn't and I didn't and I did. I said uncle.

Back through the mazy street, back past the pastel-colored houses. Less exciting, more comfortable this time. People stared at me again—same people, same stare.

Sunlight burned into my retinas. We have bright sun in Minnesota, but spring had been pretty gray. It's yellow and blue and white in the Mediterranean. I tried not to wear sunglasses much because Greeks didn't seem to need them, but they didn't dress as if they felt the sun. An Italian friend explained it to me a month later, "If we start wearing shorts in May, what do we do when it gets hot?"

Gradually the narrow streets opened. Buildings became larger, with yards and grass. With the hill on my left now, the row of tour buses on my right, the black and white dead guy looked at me with as much familiarity as the dog and houses had.

Buildings and streets vanished as the sidewalk herded me onto the path again and I was enclosed between the steep hill and a fence. Beautifully wild, flowered yards stayed on the other side of the fence. Some of the flowers leaked out. I heard a rhythmic clicking sound behind me and turned to see the white dog coming. "When did I pass you?" I asked her. "Where are your puppies?" She showed me her floppy tongue and followed me to the stairs.

Without looking back at the dog, I stepped on the first stair, then the second and the third. I felt resigned but powerful, interested in the difficulty of my task. A few flights up, I passed a young couple who climbed a bit more slowly than I. I walked with them. She had to rest. He walked with me. He waited for her. I couldn't breathe. I had to rest. They caught up. I walked with them. She had to rest. I rested with her. We caught up with him. He had to rest. She walked with me. Finally, we all sat on a stair and panted. I had been counting stairs, but only now announced the current total.

Eventually I went on alone. The sky glowed; the rocks glowed. The stairs, flowers, and sea glowed. I panted; I kept climbing stairs. I gasped; I kept climbing stairs. I finally let my feet stay on one stair. My arms reached out one to each side, and my muscles stretched long. I yawned and yawned; my eyes streamed tears from the yawning and the sun. I'd have laughed if I'd have had the oxygen, but I hoarded it so I could climb stairs.

The stairs switched left, then right, then left again, and always up. My calves, thighs, hips, belly, and heart felt as though they were stretching, loosening, strengthening. My lungs and throat felt fuzzy and swollen. When I could see the castle, I didn't need to rest anymore. I came up the final few stairs, feeling like a mole appearing from underground an hour late, just as Henrik and Arthur walked past. When they saw me they stopped walking. Immediately, Henrik said, "Oh, good. You're all right."

I stared at him and nodded. He looked past me at the stairs. He said, "We wondered if you'd gone down those, but we decided you hadn't. The guide said there are a thousand stairs to the town."

We began walking through the castle, toward the bus. I said, "I only counted 726." I felt dirty, sweaty, and tired.

Henrik tilted his head and lifted his eyebrows, apparently considering this. "Well," he declared, "you're strong."

"I tried to walk around the hill," I said, "so I could come in another entrance."

"Another entrance?" asked Henrik.

"Like walking around the block," I said, "so I wouldn't have to climb back up the stairs."

He laughed. "Oh, you'd have been wishing for stairs. It's probably forty miles around this hill."

"Forty miles?" Oh. This isn't a block; it's shoreline with a fortress on it. Arthur said in a big pastor voice, "I walked a long way, looking for you."

I muttered, "You'd have walked a lot farther if you'd have found me."

Henrik glanced at Arthur and said to me (in his God voice), "Nobody is mad at you. We're glad you're OK." We had reached the parking lot on a cliff now. Henrik looked at his watch. "We're meeting in fifteen minutes, now. Do what you want to do."

I nodded, "OK." Henrik began to board the bus. I called after him, "Um, (ahem) thanks, Henrik."

He turned around, mid-stride. "Yes. You're welcome." Then he smiled and said, "These things happen sometimes."

I said, "Yes." I smiled too, glad of these things. I walked slowly to a low wall bordering the parking lot and straddled it. My right leg hung over the cliff. I looked at my pack of cigarettes and thought no way. No way. Not now. But I had to correct myself. Especially now. My punished lungs asked for more sensation, please, and I pinged open my Zippo and savored the burn. Here's my catharsis, I thought. I let my eyelids drop into a relaxed squint and I let the sea below me go blurry.

Feet on pebbles caught my attention; I looked up to see Carrie and Theresa walking past me on the way to the bus. Carrie called, "Hey, Elizabeth, did you get lost?"

I nodded.

She laughed. "Was it scary?" she asked.

I shook my head no and said, "Yeah. Mostly just a lot of work. But it was great. Not too scary. Mostly just a lot of work."

"You're not a dummy. Glad you made it back."

I nodded again, relieved now and exhausted. Carrie and Theresa got on the bus.

I stepped off the wall and sat on the ground, with my back against the wall. I kept enough consciousness to smoke and listen. More feet on gravel. I opened my eyes a slit. Michelle and Dale came walking, with relaxed smiles on their faces. They had been on the bus, maybe talking to Henrik or Carrie.

I craned my neck up and smiled. Dale asked, "Lost?"

I nodded. I shrugged. I shook my head. "Confused. Not lost. Just confused."

They sat next to me, one on each side, and did not speak. I closed my eyes again. This time I heard the voice before the feet. It was shrill and accusing.

"Elizabeth! I was so worried about you. I knew you hadn't eaten since breakfast and you could have fainted over any one of those ledges. There are so many places to fall from." She drew in a sudden breath as if recovering from hyperventilation. I opened my eyes and looked at her. Cindy had wet eyes and a red nose. Her mouth opened again. "I kept imagining your broken, bloody body at the bottom of any of those ledges." Her mouth kept opening and closing. I stared at it. She began crying. "I knew I'd be the one to find you and I'd have to climb down there and carry your body up (God knows how) and I'd have to go home and I'd have to miss my trip to Italy and I'd have to tell your parents you were dead. Oh, I could imagine what your body would look like. I . . ."

I interrupted her. In monotone I said, "I'm sorry you worried."

Her eyes opened wide and her mouth closed. A huge involuntary breath dove into her lungs, then left. She blinked at me. A few more tears came from her eyes. She looked miserable, all red and blue. "I didn't know where you were," she whispered. She walked to the bus without looking back.

"I knew where I was," I said quietly. I raised my volume a hair so Michelle and Dale could hear me. "I wasn't lost," I said. "I knew where the bus was and I wasn't trying to go anywhere else and then I ran out of time.

"I was just going. Going around in my skin. In the world. Dancing."

They smiled at me and didn't say anything.

I surprised myself by whimpering. I felt elated and tender, as if my skin had opened and let everything in. I squinted against the sun — the same same sun. I glanced at my dirty feet on the old stones. I laughed abruptly and sagged against the wall, where I belonged.

Meltemi

I COULD HAVE been there in a half hour had I chosen to fly. But I wanted to arrive by boat, to let the stress of leavetaking and anxieties of flying wash away gradually in the frothy wake. I wanted to arrive via Homer's wine-dark sea and let the breeze and sun relax muscles still knotted from being forced in one cramped position during the nine-hour flight from New York. I longed to stretch out on a bench in the shade, using my nylon bag of books and writing as a pillow and to rock in gentle swells all the way to Mykonos. The last three weeks preparing for the trip, my mind had become a rollicking polka of lists and endless details, pulled this way and that with sudden intrusions of forgotten tasks, pushing, pushing, then buckling under their pressure and forgetting things, an appointment, a coffee date with a friend. The Athenian taxi driver who drove me to the wharf that morning, silent and angry at some injustice, who tore through traffic, his face grim, one knee furiously bobbing up and down at stoplights—he needed a seven-hour boat ride to an island almost as much as I.

~

It was the summer of 1992, and I was returning to Greece after an absence of eleven years. I wanted to begin the process of marketing my first book, a recently published memoir about the decade I had spent living and painting on the island of Mykonos. At Athens airport, I had walked through customs with a bag of thirty volumes to give away to friends and leave at bookstores as lures for future orders. But mostly I wanted to resume friendships, especially with Greeks I had written about, and paths leading to old, favorite haunts I'd once visited on solitary walks beckoned me. Still, I worried a bit about how it all might have changed.

But was it to be the island that had changed, or I? Since my return to the United States in 1981, many things happened that powerfully affected my life: in the winter of 1982 I lost my younger brother, a fire fighter and my only sibling to a fiery death. After a hiatus of twenty-two years, I went back to school and in 1984 finally took that happy walk to the platform to receive my B.A. degree. In the process, I discovered my love of writing and, after graduation, spent the next several years transposing memories of Greece into something resembling literature. I bought property. I made a number of new friends. I fell in love. In those eleven years, every cell in my body died and was replaced, and now new ones, in their turn, were well on their way to annihilation. I was not the same person who left Greece eleven years before; I felt different inside, more collected, confident, less afraid.

I have been curious and uncertain about how I would react to the inevitable changes a hiatus of eleven years could bring to a place I had once loved for its freshness and simplicity. Old friends who had returned to the island reported that the changes on Mykonos would prove challenging at best. If I could somehow accept this challenge and gather it all into at least a reluctant, if not exuberant embrace, maybe something alive and growing could come out of the experience.

～

From our boat a half mile out from the harbor, Mykonos looked much like always, tranquil and quiet in the midafternoon sun, the hottest time of the day when almost everyone is either at the beach or taking a siesta. The whitewashed town glimmered on heat waves as it swept around and down the ochre hillside like an ancient amphitheater to the circular harbor below.

After a joyful, but hasty reunion—to be continued later at dinner—with American and Canadian friends who met my boat, I arranged to stay at Maria's pensione for three nights while I searched for a house to rent in the country. Maria was a granddaughter of Barba Manolis, my old landlord, and she too had just arrived from Athens, where for a week she'd been attending to her daughter who had suffered a miscarriage. As a gesture of welcome, she and her husband Nikos, a taxi driver, and their friend Soula invited me to go for a swim on the east side of the island, past Panarmos and Aghios to a small spit of a beach near the rock quarry. The persistent yellow cloud of pollution over Athens had worsened Maria's asthma, and she headed for the sea immediately. Nikos, in mask and snorkle, swam out to the small peninsula encrusted with sea urchins.

I too went right into the sea. Cool and clear, its buoyancy totally supported my body. I had forgotten how the high salt content of the Aegean made swimming here so effortless. I dove in and bobbed up like a cork. My Australian crawl and breaststroke had never been so perfect. I turned over and floated like an otter, breathing normally, and realized I could take a ten-minute nap in this position and not drown. I was happy; I was beautiful, swimming in the Aegean once again. My pores absorbed the sun's warmth, my ears the sound of Maria far out, floating with Soula, giving a nonstop report on her harrowing five days in Athens. She paused several times during the account to snuff up water to clear her sinuses. Maria collected this sea water in bottles during the summer, so it would be available when her asthma got worse in the dank, rainy months of winter.

Later we poured ouzos and carved open spiny urchins, dousing them with lemon and sopping them up out of their shells with hunks of crusty bread.

Years before, Maria had a nervous breakdown, and I remember her appearance at a *hirosphyia*, a celebration honoring the pig that was slaughtered and butchered that day. Her eyes held the vacant expression caused by her medication. She had long since reinhabited her stocky body, her beautiful hair thick and piled high on her head and laced now with strands of white. She never removed the freshwater pearls Nikos gave her. The couple traveled in the winter like gypsies, staying in small, out-of-the-way hotels, renting cars and packing lunches of bread, cheese, fruit, and wine. They had traveled everywhere in Europe and the U.S. In the early spring, they returned to the island and resumed their life of hard work, relieved by dashes out to remote beaches, Nikos with mask and snorkel, Maria with a bag of bread and ouzo, taking her cure in the sea.

One morning, Nikos arrived in his taxi with a bundle of fabric: "You will take this cloth and cover the front and back seat of the Saab," he told Maria.

"Don't I already have enough work with the rooms and meals to prepare and the unending laundry? How will she find the time?"

"Nevertheless, you will do it," Nikos says with all the authority of the Greek male. When she left for the kitchen, Nikos confided with a rueful smile, using my Greek name: "In my life, Anna, I have only two problems, my car and my woman."

$\sim$

I had been looking, to no avail, for a small house to rent in the country. One night, in despair of ever finding something suitable during the high season, I arrranged to rent a room on the other side of Maria and Nikos's house. They would remove one of the extra beds, put in a camp stove, a table, dishes, and a reading lamp—all for three thousand drachmas or fifteen dollars a day. It had its own bathroom with shower and looked out on a walled garden. Best of all, I thought (mistakenly, it turns out) the room would be buffered from the wind and road noise by their house.

$\sim$

The most prominent and obvious emblem of the new prosperity was the hundredfold increase in vehicles. Everyone, including tourists, drove a vehicle of some kind. While I saw fewer farmers on donkeys traveling between farm and town, family cars, taxis, three-wheelers, motorcycles, jeeps, buses, cement trucks, trucks transporting dirt and water abounded.

The cacophony created by these vehicles was brain numbing. I began to feel as if I were in rush-hour traffic in the middle of Manhattan: the same tensions, the same fight with the pollution of sound, the same increasingly deadened consciousness. Only here I discovered it never stopped, and I never seemed to arrive home.

This new mobility of Greek and tourist alike had expanded the town out into the country. The road between the main town and the village of Ano Mera sprouted now with new businesses, mostly car-repair shops, gas stations, and cement factories. And a new phenomenon along the road—the migration of clubs from the town and beach communities—now spread out to the once pristine countryside: a Hard Rock Cafe, resplendent with video game room, pool bar, and vintage pink Cadillac sprawled like a poofed and perfumed poodle near the road to Ano Mera, above the Ftelia Valley, where I had once considered living the rest of my days. Despite the buffer that I had hoped Maria's house would provide, the constant drone of taxis through the night, as they transported patrons to and from this establishment, kept me awake until dawn.

The explosion of tourism that occurred with the onset of the 1980s and Greece's inclusion in the Common Market had brought irrevocable changes to the island's culture and lifestyle. Some changes were good, however. Women's work was easier, for example. Maria and Nikos had central heating, a washer and dryer, a full-sized refrigerator, a separate freezer. Her Aunt Dina in town no longer had to run to the bakery oven to roast the flat, round pans of meat and potatoes. Most men stayed at home at night now, relaxing in front of the TV instead of gathering with their cronies in the tavernas to share a bottle of wine, as had been the custom for centuries.

And they all traveled more. In one short decade the island sensibility had been catapulted from one of nineteenth-century agrarian stoicism into a kind of fifties-style nouveau riche giddiness. ("Oh, yes," said the former grocer turned *hotelier*, after planting a moist smooch of welcome on my cheek. "Now the WHOLE town empties every winter. My SON, AnDONY, he is a TRAvel AGENT! We have toured CaliFORnia! Neo YORki! HaWAee! KEEna (China)! This year BORA-BORA!")

This new freedom that comes with wealth demanded the last farthing, however, as evidenced in the unending traffic jams clogging the narrow streets, in the stress and exhaustion etched on faces of those working daily with the demands of tourists, in that dirty yellow cloud hovering over the power plant and, saddest of all to me, in the death of silence.

I had always thought of Mykonos as being a microcosm of the world. For six months of the year the world came to its shores, and the lives of those visitors reflected in miniature all the world's dramas and complexities. Returning after eleven years, it seemed to me that Mykonos had become a microcosm of a world gone awry: at the height of midsummer, it was a small, confined place trying to support far too many people. By summer's end, smiles of welcome became frozen and cracked. Nerves—exposed and ragged from fatigue, and tormented by incessant wind and the sheer boredom of tending shop for twelve or fourteen hours a day—nerves in such divided houses had to become numbed, or they simply died.

It was as if nothing, in fact, could ever again surprise a Mykoniate. The island's freshness, its innocence seemed jaded now and had nearly perished, ground like spent cigarettes by the greed of both merchant and tourist, into the slick marble floors of the latest gold store, the newest discotheque, the most popular first-class restaurant. It was as if their new wealth had not only propelled them once and for all into the twentieth century, but encumbered their spirits with all of its ills as well.

∼

There were many exceptions, of course, besides Maria and Nikos. One afternoon, I decided to go out to Petinaro to visit my former neighbors and see the old house I had lived in for so many years. When Michalis's fourteen-year-old son Andonis saw me standing at the bottom of their stairs and realized who I was, he called his older sister Katerina to come. She erupted in such a warm effusion of greetings and welcome, I startet to cry. They were all grown up, these babies I'd played with and photographed standing all in a row with their cousins, holding lambs only a few hours old. The sight of their mother Frascoula and her warm and long embrace left us both dissolved in tears. She offered me a coffee frappe, and we paged through the photograph album, clucking at how it seemed like yesterday when I had been their neighbor and the children had been so young.

We all proceeded next door to my old house, where my former landlady's son Yiorgos and his wife Katina, who were living there, greeted me with enthusiasm equal to their neighbors'. This house was close to a hundred years old when I lived there and had no electricity or running water. Every day, I hauled buckets of water from a well in an adjoining field and read at night by the light of kerosene lamps. The play of changing light over the irregular texture of its interior walls had been an endless fascination to me while I lived there. To my relief, Yiorgos and Katina had left the beautiful organic walls as they were, instead of making them perfect and sterile with replastering. They had opened up the sitting room and combined it with the former kitchen, making a larger space, which they used as a bedroom. A full bathroom and modern kitchen occupied the space I'd once used as a studio. The kitchen now served as the main living and socializing area with its round table and several chairs dominating the space.

Katina just shrugged and smiled when I asked her how she liked country living. While I think she might have preferred to remain living in town, where her gregarious personality had more of an outlet with all the neighbors so close by, Yiorgas, almost bled contentment. He was back in the house where he grew up, his son and daughter-in-law nearby in a house father and son had built together. He showed off his garden, laid out in neat rows of beans, onions, tomatoes, and garlic; two lemon trees and an olive tree shaded the door to the small barn. None of their lives had really changed that much, except Katina's, perhaps. But for the most part, they all seemed content, unhurried, relaxed, even happy. I left with invitations to return, happy and filled with gratitude for them all.

～

Another morning I took a walk out to Ornos Beach. I chose the high road, a former donkey trail that I used to prefer over the main highway winding beside the sea. Business at the beach had grown from a couple of restaurants into a complete village of hotels, houses with rooms to rent, apartments, and condominiums. Tourists signed on in Stockholm or Stuttgart to come there for their package holidays and found it totally enchanting.

In Constandis's taverna, where I used to come often, the pop star Madonna wailed from one radio by the charcoal grill, while Springsteen rocked from another near the glassed-in refrigerator. Years before I had sat in this same spot with a friend and two sweating bottles of cold beer, silent, watching the sea rise and fall. The radio was on then, too, but quietly, and instead of rock music, the trill of bouzouki shared the soundwaves with the swish of sea on sand. Now it seemed that I rarely heard the bouzouki or the whisper of water on sand. All these gentle things had been swallowed up in the gunning of bus motors, motorcycles, and incessant rock and disco music blaring out from clubs, tavernas, and once-peaceful beach restaurants. I got up and asked the waiter to turn at least one of the radios off.

I attempted to reason it out: maybe they played western music because they thought the foreigners liked it, another concession among so many to the "bottom line." Or, maybe they just preferred this music themselves, the inevitable dilution of a culture. Could the beauty of an individual culture survive only in poverty? Did wealth and the increased mobility and communication that came with it only serve to homogenize a culture, devouring the very things that enriched lives, that reminded us of our uniqueness? What *was* the difference between Tasos Cambanis sitting at home in his undershirt watching a Greek sitcom and Bob Smith in Cleveland with a can of Budweiser and the ten o'clock news?

～

It was two weeks into my stay before I finally ran into my old boyfriend Andreaus. One evening I walked down the road to town, when I noticed a man on a motorcycle coming up the hill at full throttle, hunched down so as to decrease his resistance to the wind. I recognized that posture, that speed, that unarrested intensity. "Andreaus?"

He squealed to a stop and coasted back, laying down his cycle without bothering to set the kickstand. Without a word, he enveloped me in a long, warm hug. Years ago, we had fantasized about this moment. He would be a healthy octogenarian sitting stooped over his cane in a sunny cafe, and I would be an old lady in sensible shoes, stopping briefly on a cruise. We would recognize each other immediately and discover that we had never fallen out of love.

The next night Andreaus took me to dinner at Kunella's, the old fisherman's taverna, remodeled only twice since my first visit there in 1967 and still unfrequented by tourists. We shared a large grouper grilled over charcoal and a tomato and cucumber salad.

He'd gained a layer of fat around his middle and had a barrel chest. His back ached from lifting heavy bags of asbestos and cement. There were white strands among his dark curls. Up until the day before, when he began his annual tribute to the healthy life and quit, he had smoked at least two packs of cigarettes a day and drank without restraint every night. "I have the spirit of a twelve-year-old," he said happily. I play like a child." As if he had learned from Zorba's mistake, he still avoided the "full catastrophe" of a wife and children. "I want to remain free to do all the things I've always done," he said when I asked why.

He had an American girlfriend who taught English in Istanbul during the winter and who spent summers on Mykonos. She was visiting her family in the States as we sat talking. I wonder if she saw what was happening to him, or if she was blind to it, because it was happening to her too. During her summers here, I wondered if she made a home out of the old house in Ftelia, cooking wholesome meals on the three-burner stove, bathing out of a pan of water, draping laundry on the lichen-covered dry stone walls, or if she stayed in a hotel. I realized I was a little jealous.

While I lamented about all the negative changes on the island and in some of its people, it seemed obvious that some change was inevitable and good. But Andreaus has become more of what he'd always been, a Peter Pan, a confirmed bachelor, afraid of any commitment and, regardless of his superficially carefree nature, his heavy drinking spoke of how troubled he might actually have been.

I cared about this man and told him I worried about his smoking and drinking. He worried too, he admitted, because when he had that first drink now, he couldn't stop until the evening ended. His cough came from deep inside his lungs; his earlobes were deeply creased, indicating possible heart problems. Three island men, in their forties as he was, had died in as many years from sudden heart attacks.

As we parted, he whispered "I still love you."

~

The last days of June had been still and very hot. One afternoon at sundown, I noticed that emblem of change over the highest peak on the neighboring island of Tinos: the puff of cloud signalling the beginning of the Meltemi, the fierce north wind of July and August.

Some time during the night it became full blown, careening down onto the island, without hindrance from mountain or counter current, all the way from the Russian Steppe. Shutters rattled, something out on the terrace began to bang against something else and traffic on the road continued all night long as usual, adding to the melee.

I lay awake waiting for some silence so my brain could rest, but none came.

Taxis roared by all night, transporting revelers to the Hard Rock Cafe. Around five o'clock, workers started driving cement and building trucks out to the newest construction sites. There would be no rest, I realized, for soul or body in this place. I picked at my cuticles, a sign of stress that even two days in Athens hadn't inspired. I ached for peace and quiet, my own food cooked in my own time, a view to gaze at. Not isolation, just a sense of solitude, the source of what had been missing, which was that connection with the numinous, the Divine that would make all this madness tolerable.

The Meltemi blessed us because of its cool, northerly origin and it damned us equally to the dust and stress it raised; we were all of us equally mussed, caked in dust and sweat and sea salt—the rich and not-so-rich, the beautiful and the plain. I gave up any aspirations of staying clean and neat. Dust straining the air eventually covered me in a fine layer, collecting in the crevices of my ears, lodging in my nose and stiffening the hair on my head. It dried the inside of my mouth, stinging the delicate membranes of my eyes, causing tears to form that seemed mysteriously near the brink. The Meltemi was a fierce, constant roar in the ears, crowding out thoughts, battering, thumping, buffeting the body in its angry gusts.

I went out in this gale every day to sketch. It was my work. But it had been difficult getting far enough out into the countryside by bus or on foot to find suitable sites. Just eleven years before, the landscape had been a constant inspiration, where farms were few, nestled in the crooks of hills or tucked in valleys surrounded by vineyards and wind-bent stands of chattering bamboo. Now much of the land within a two- or three-mile radius of the town had been developed, and a plethora of new two-story houses squatted in the middle of barren fields as if dropped there by industrial cranes. These were sterile structures, unlike the old houses that were built into hillsides and outcroppings of rocks. These new structures shared no organic relationship with the land and were placed wherever the grown Greek children of the dwindling farming community—or foreigners from Athens or elsewhere—had chosen to build them.

Because I could not endure long walks in the wind and heat any more, I finally gave in and became part of the problem: I rented a motorbike. I could go anywhere I wanted to now. I drove through the hills above Kea and wound through valleys and side roads on the southern route to the village of Ano Mera. I traveled slowly, studying the landscape to make sketches for potential paintings which I would do when I returned to the States.

I also traveled cautiously, aware that the Meltemi could sneak up behind me and sweep me off my feet in one violent blast and, if I happened to be on my motorbike, could, as it had done to many others, sweep me off my wheels and kill or maim me. I began to realize I feared Meltemi, had to regard it with caution, with respect; it was a mirror of something inside me that also called for attention: a sense of fear and at the same time, wonder; dread and at once, curiosity; the deep and discomforting mystery of my own mortality.

～

I encountered the bittersweet wear of time continuously on my frequent trips into town. Around a corner would come Eleni, once a bustling middle-aged housewife, now a gray-haired crone in black. The other day it was Ioannis, a little fatter, more stooped, voice rough as the side of a barn from a lifetime of smoking. And there was Fouskis: I had heard he had become a hopeless alcoholic and was very ill. It took me three and a half weeks to gather the courage to approach him and to say hello. And Costas, whose handsome features had once reminded me so much of my brother, and whose family owned the cafe that I frequented: his young wife Maria, mother of his only child, had become bedridden with multiple sclerosis. With his life falling apart, Costas succumbed to drugs and alcohol. He sat all day in a bar down the waterfront from his family's cafe, his back to the harbor and the tourists passing by, another casualty of the change and one whom I never did gather the courage to approach.

What characteristic allowed some to survive and even thrive on the effects of the increasing foreign invasion, while for others it was anathema? Was it just bad luck, or was it a matter of suffering? The time of suffering came to everyone? To some sooner than others?

Of the beautiful people among the foreigners from years past, there was Kiki, a resident for twenty-odd years and married to a Greek; her aneurysm, the doctors cutting away part of her brain, taking memories lost forever. Or the Swedish couple, Joren and Finn. She a doctor, he, an actor and writer—wealthy, free to travel, they built a villa at a remote beach and came every summer for years. One was tempted to think such golden lives are immortal, but in their late fifties, tragedy struck cruelly: Joren had a totally disabling stroke. The last time she was able to come to the island, they had to carry her from the taxi to her house in a sheet. Finn died a few years later of a heart attack. Beautiful people, beautiful dream house, beautiful dream shattered by the betrayal of the body, that one weak link coiled beneath the carefree veneer of all of our youthful selves.

People have said that I haven't changed a bit. And perhaps it's true that time and good genes so far have been kind. But seeing these people whom I once knew in their prime shocked me and carried its portent of the future: we were, in fact, all getting older; all of us were in a state of slow decay. In only ten years so much could happen to a body, to a face, to a once-fine mind. A time of suffering and tragedy waited to hit each of us, biding its time while we played like innocent children, until the moment arrived when mortality seared its relentless path onto the landscape of our lives. We hung on for dear life, waiting it out. It was in the roar of the Meltemi that I heard its howl. Like suffering, like death, the Meltemi was the great equalizer—wherever it blew, it leveled, it devoured, it transformed.

~

I was confronted around every corner with ghosts. Not only of people, but of images, vague memories, like veils of the new overlying the old. These impressions snuck into consciousness, like dusty shards that slowly took on meaningful form in a handful of dirt from an archæological dig.

I'd be passing a sterile jewelry store with gleaming marble floors and shiny gold pins and rings and necklaces in its window. As usual, the proprietor would be standing near the doorway, watching the endless river of tourists flooding past him, waiting like a bored barracuda for that one who would enter out of curiosity, or need, or greed, and buy. Like all shops in the town, this one had once been someone's home.

I would pass by this same store twenty times in as many days. And then one time suddenly she'd be there, that old woman sitting at a round oak table in the dim interior of her kitchen; she was dressed in black, as she had been for years. She sat with her head in her hands, still, silent, alone, listening to the bells of St.

George slowly tolling the ancient message that someone—a friend, a relative, surely someone she knew in this small community—had just died. And out of this brightly-lit jewelry store with all of us streaming by, her image and the image of the empty street that quiet morning so many years before emerged like a ghost out of the past. The recognition would be but a second or two in duration, if it could be measured at all, but it was complete, and I'd be carried forward by the throng.

I began to realize that I was having trouble identifying who *I* was in the midst of all this. I was Nancy, the foreigner, who returned after having spent most of her life and the most recent eleven fruitful years in an almost totally different culture. I was also "Anna," the American artist who embraced Greek culture as my own and adopted its lifestyle for ten years. How did I fit all this into the context of Mykonos the way it was now? Or, what was harder, how did I fit this new Mykonos into the context of myself, the way I was now? How could I find the will or the space for that "reluctant embrace" I had so hoped to offer?

The pressure to come to some sort of peace with these questions was strong. "I don't know who I *am* here anymore," I admitted to a Canadian friend, who sat with me having coffee on the waterfront one windy morning. I was feeling very shaky, my emotions fragile, ruptured by wind and sleepless nights and the conflicts with noise outside and inside my head. Jan looked at me tenderly. "I'll tell you who you are," she said. "You are one who has returned and is loved."

At that declaration I let loose with weeping. But her comment had set off the hair trigger of something other than just the need to be loved, which we all share. She held me, as what I could only describe as grief poured out of me in silent wracking sobs. I couldn't identify the source, the power of this grief. It was loss of mother, father, brother, loss of the old Mykonos, of innocence, of youth—just a nameless loss of nothing and everything—loss deep, unrelenting, and irrevocable: the old Mykonos, the old Anna were both dead, and neither would ever be the same again.

～

One day I took my motorbike out to Ftelia. The Hard Rock Cafe was quiet at last, its proprietors still asleep after having closed at six a.m. The old donkey trail that I used to follow down to Andreaus's house had been widened into a cement road. I followed it down into the valley past the farms whose owners I once knew. I went directly to his farm, to see once again the house that might have been mine had I chosen to stay. It sat like a white-frosted cake on a slope overlooking the valley. Its corners near the kitchen had been rounded as much by wind and weather as by design, while the opposite end was softened and gentled in its slope to the ground by the round hump of the bread oven. Since Andreaus was at his job, the place was deserted, and I walked freely around the yard baked dry and stubbly by the midsummer sun and swept clean of debris by the wind.

I realized that I missed the presence of his mother, who had made a home out of this rude dwelling and who clutched her bosom in mock dismay, crossing herself every time I arrived. Without her, the farm had lost its soul and been relegated to serving as a place merely to sleep, but without providing any genuine rest. When Eleni moved to town after her stroke, Andreaus sold off all the animals: two donkeys, eight black goats, and a small herd of sheep. No cats sat dozing in the shadows waiting for handouts; no chickens pecked at the hard scrabble.

In the nearby chapel, built by Andreaus's great-grandfather when he first arrived from Turkey in the 1800s, I changed the wick in the oil lamp, added fresh oil and light it. I lit a candle in honor of my deceased parents and brother. I lit another for the father of my former love, Andreaus, for his father whom I never knew, whose name was inscribed in the church wall where his bones lay.

"Watch over your son!" I whispered fiercely.

～

The Meltemi had continued for twenty-one days. I wakened each day, waiting as I came out of the fog of sleep, for some sense of quiet. But always there was the thump of wind against the cabinet door above the bed, wafting open and shut with the wind's vacuum. Then the heavy sense of disappointment: another day of unfulfilled longings to take the motorbike to the north side above Ftelia and visit Aghia Spiridona. I feared traveling alone in that remote region directly into the maw of the wind.

On my last morning on the island, I lay a long time after waking just listening, waiting for the familiar thump, for the cabinet doors to waft open above my head, for its whip through the courtyard where I could hear Maria's cats feasting on the remains of last night's stew. Slowly it dawned on me: I could actually hear the cats eating! A week before I had sat with Maria in her kitchen. "I wish the wind would stop for just one day," I lamented. "I'm so exhausted from it."

Now this last morning I wakened to a new sound: silence, or near silence. Beside the munchings of the cats, there was birdsong and only the slightest rustle of a breeze, the old cossack wind's last remnant, which even at that moment dwindled to nothing. I got dressed and grabbed my bag. Maria called to me as I started the motorbike.

"Anna! You see, we have a fine day! I prayed that the Meltemi would stop for you, for just one day before you left."

That fine day at last I had the chance to go out to the north road above Ftelia. I filled that last day with the fruits of five week's longing. That fine day I made the long-frustrated pilgrimage into silence.

～

I sat on the terrace of Aghia Spiridona, a small chapel high on the hill above Panarmos Bay and the Valley of Ftelia. I chose this church and this scene to paint for the cover of my book about the island. The sea and fields below shimmered in the morning light. It was absolutely still. I would sit there for hours.

～

At seven in the evening, my friend Michelle picked me up to take me to the airport. No longer the small, one-room building of eleven years ago, it was now a fully-appointed international terminal with duty-free shop and a customs and currency exchange to deal with the numerous charter flights that arrived directly from Europe.

I requested a window seat on the left side. All month long, I had seen planes taking off and banking low over the harbor. I wanted to see the town from that height at dusk, my favorite time of the day. I also wanted to see Delos from a height of one thousand feet.

Delos, the small island twenty minutes' boat ride from Mykonos, was known for its vast archæological site covering the entire island. Once a thriving city and a center for trade between Middle Eastern countries and the West, it was best known as the sacred birthplace of Apollo, God of the Sun. Nothing could change on Delos, because no one could live there except rabbits, partridges, lizards, and the men and their families who guarded the ruins.

I had heard that the previous spring Delos had been blessed with a particularly thick carpet of wildflowers: scarlet poppies, violet statice, yellow buttercups, and mustard flowers. But by the time I arrived in late July, all of them had vanished in the arid, cracked earth typical of midsummer. On my first trip to Delos since being back, I picked my way through the ruins of houses, and on the Sacred Way leading to the Temple of Apollo, I searched the Naxian marble lions for signs of eleven years' buffeting by wind and rain; I found none. I climbed the steps to the summit of Mount Cynthus and wound my way along a path to the south rim where I found my favorite spot overlooking the Islets of Prasonisia, whose blinking light, warning off passing boats, I had watched often as it faded to nothingness in the dawning of another day.

In earlier years, I had spent many nights on that mountain, alone, watching the full moon rise over Mykonos, and the sunrise the next day. I went there as much for the enchantment of the moon as to witness Apollo's dazzling splash of light on his island in the early morning hours. He was always evident, not only in his cascade of wildflowers every year—and especially so that year—but in each new day as light was reborn once again, and the dark night, along with its powerful moon and the single, blinking beacon below me were subsumed by his brilliance.

That evening at the airport, after hugs and good-byes from friends who had gathered, I took off in the small plane, my eyes glued to the window, watching the scene below. Lifting higher, we went into a steep turn, banking low to the left over the harbor. The waterfront was teeming with movement and dancing lights as tourists began the first round of drinks in an evening that might not end until six o'clock the next morning. The scene reminded me of the lights of Manhattan, gaudy and yet beautiful, like an old, but well-preserved (and, I realized, beloved) lady of the night, resplendent in diamonds. I thought how appropriate that image was, remembering in its history how the ancient Delians, foreign traders, and pirates used to come to Mykonos for its wild life and abundance of prostitutes.

And I thought how much I still loved this place—*in spite of everything*—that the connection between us was stronger than ever, how in that silence at Aghios Spiridion, I had discovered that the numinous had not abandoned Mykonos; it was just harder to perceive in all the commotion. And if the numinous, the sense of the Divine, could exist there, on that small, troubled island, it could exist anywhere—anywhere a remnant of longing for it remained alive.

As the plane sailed out over the water, gaining altitude, Delos soon spread out below us in the dying light of the day: Mount Cynthus, distorted by altitude into a small bump on the landscape, caught the sun's waning light on its western slope, casting deep shadows, while the rest of the landscape sculpted itself in soft patterns of shadow and light. The few artificial lights powered by generators around the tiny Delos Hotel blinked on. For the rest of the flight to Athens, with my face pressed to the window, I watched the brilliant sky fade from gold, into orange, deep pink, lavender, and, finally, to a dark, fathomless blue, revealing a few stars and the crescent moon, a calm sliver of light in the eastern sky.

The Dome of Creation

I LOST A SON in Bergamo. He was born after six months of a difficult pregnancy and was buried in a small plot surrounded by many other small plots in the town cemetery. From the graves of the children, near the medieval wall, you could see stone houses clinging to the hill, persimmon trees bright with fruit, the serene mystery of the Alps in the blue distance. Bergamo had been our home for a year. By July my husband had completed his course of study. I was several months out of a long hospital stay, emotionally still raw. Soon we would leave for home, losing the place where we had conceived and buried our child.

Now, for healing, for distraction, for some kind of good-bye, we took a train the length of Italy, as if covering the ground with our bodies we would gain some kind of mastery. I wanted to experience this land as passing hills with secure histories of their own, as flashing towns whose existence did not depend on my staying there to know them or love them. We could not know our child. Our love had failed to keep him.

We lived with a huge map of Italy on the wall of our Bergamo apartment—Dan had put it up the day we moved in—and we both had a surprising, passionate feeling about it—the crenelations of mountains, the red veins of roads, the endless meeting of shore and sea.

Sicily is separated from the rest of Italy by a narrow passage—the Strait of Messina, which we crossed on a brilliant day, the water choppy and glinting, the port city low and gray. A ferry carried our train in its belly. We had not believed the ticket woman in Milan who explained this, but then negotiations in Italian always produced surprises.

We stepped off the train in Palermo into an afternoon rigid with heat. After a long and mysterious ride in a battered taxi (two hours in and out of Palermo's dreary sprawl) we made our way to Porticello, where Dan had friends. We understood Porticello to be a fishing village on the coast.

I had expected Sicily to look like the Greece I knew from picture books—harsh but inspiring, a land where temples would spring up as a natural expression of the earth's holiness. Here instead crumbling red hills loomed ominously over the little towns along the bay. Large eroded rock formations jutted awkwardly from the hills shedding rust-colored gravel. A failed mountain. This was the last thing I wanted to find on our journey to the end of Italy.

By early evening we were sitting with Anna and Jimmy Fiumefreddo on kitchen chairs on the sidewalk outside their house. Sitting inside was unthinkable—the two-room cement house trapped the heat, but the street was hardly refreshing. Trucks and motorcycles roared by, kicking up a sticky spray of dust and fumes. Anna had fed us dinner—sardines fried with potatoes and tomatoes—and now she tackled her major worry: how to entertain us properly during our visit to Sicily.

"You must see Monreale, the shrine of Santa Rosalia, and the caves where she hid from the king."

We had been traveling for ten days, stopping along the train's route in Milan, Peruggia, Assisi, Rome, Naples. We were tired. We had imagined a quiet stay in a house by the sea. "But we have no car. It is a terrible thing—we can take you nowhere." Anna and Jimmy, both in their sixties, had been Dan's neighbors some years earlier in Milwaukee, to which they had emigrated as teenagers. Now they had returned to live among their extended family in Porticello. Though they had strenuously urged us to visit, we soon realized they had no extra room, no extra food (the sardines came from their son who worked on a fishing boat), and that our stay meant hardship for them.

"Luckily our neighbor Antonio Zarcone would like to meet you. He is interested in foreigners. He has a car."

Even in the evening heat, Antonio Zarcone seemed propelled. He strode down the sidewalk intensely, a handsome balding man in running shoes. He was a little younger than Anna and Jimmy—fifties—and had a stocky build, but he moved with the intensity of an old cougar—tawny, wary, agile. He did not sit down. After introductions and a brief chat—other neighbors were out too, and everyone was discussing a wedding the next day—Antonio turned to us and said rather abruptly, "What do you wish to see in Palermo?" He spoke no English, but his Italian was elegant and clear, and he had a good ear, which meant conversation was possible. (Dan's Italian was spontaneous and sloppy, mine hesitant and correct. We made a good team.)

Silence. We had no plan, no tourist ideas about Sicily.

"Monreale," I said, the only thing that came to mind. I had read about the famous mosaics in the Byzantine church near Palermo. As soon as I uttered the word, Antonio said, "I will take you there tomorrow. I must be home by midday, so we must leave early. Eight o'clock?"

Why this man was offering to drive two strangers into Palermo on a steamy Sunday morning, I couldn't imagine. But he seemed sincere, insistent even, and we accepted his offer.

～

The next morning Anna insisted on making us an American-style breakfast. We sat in the hot kitchen, arms sticky on the oilcloth-covered table, while she cooked Sicilian sausages in a black frying pan, then added plenty of olive oil to the hissing grease to fry eggs.

Everyone had had bad dreams that night, and we told them at the table—Anna and Jimmy, their son, and Dan. I did not tell mine. I saw a baby whirling into smallness, shrinking until, the size of the smallest sea shell, it slipped between my fingers and was lost. In another dream the child became a thin wafer that was lifted by a breeze and blew off a table. I groped in the grass below, but I could not find it and I knew even if I did, I could not grasp it. My hands were too large.

Anna told us Antonio's story. He and his wife had two children, the oldest a girl who had died five years before. She had been fourteen. Antonio and his wife were stricken with grief. They couldn't bear to stay in their beautiful house—it had chandeliers and suede furniture, a view of the sea, a lemon grove—and they abandoned it. The house remained just as it had been, and they went there to get things occasionally, but they lived in a tiny apartment above a grocery on the noisy street near Anna and Jimmy. The apartment was like a hovel, Anna said, and it was believed they slept on a bed of rags.

They left their clothes on hangers at the house and wore only old things. Antonio quit his job and instead they ran the grocery together. For years they could not bear any outward signs of happiness. The wife was a terrible woman, according to Anna, bitter and shrewish, who caused Antonio endless suffering.

We heard Antonio's knock and gulped down the fiery sausages and sodden eggs. The first thing Antonio said was that he would like to take us to meet his wife. The three of us walked down the street into a tiny shop with canned goods on narrow shelves, a few salamis and cheese perspiring on a counter. Maria Zarcone wore an old-fashioned black dress with a small brooch holding it at the neck. Her hair was pulled back in a bun, in traditional style, showing beautiful gold filigree earrings with tiny pearls, elegant but old. It seemed odd that she wore these precious things to tend the store. She had a gentle face and smiled warmly as she shook our hands.

"*Piacere*," she said. "*Piacere.*" It is my pleasure. She wished us a safe trip.

Antonio had told us the night before that he would give us breakfast. Anna's sausages hadn't settle well, the image of the bubbling olive oil waiting for the eggs was vivid in my mind, but Antonio was so aggressive in his hospitality that we could not refuse a second breakfast. (Nor had we been able to decline Anna's. We were beginning to feel trapped and could not understand if it was the heat or the rigors of travel or the irresistible force of Sicilian hospitality that seemed to be undermining our ability to make decisions.)

We stopped in a bar in Bagheria, a dirty, crowded town along the way to Palermo (a Mafia town, I later read). Antonio said he knew people everywhere, and the man at the counter did greet him by name, though he never smiled. Antonio ordered iced coffee for us and urged us to choose a pastry. Dan pointed to something the size of a tennis ball made of rice and meat, and I picked the plainest thing I could see, a flat cookie with almonds on top. The man steamed up the espresso machine, and poured the coffee over a glass of ice, adding milk. The glass frosted over, and I thought I might be able to drink it just for the cold. Dan and I reacted the same to the first sip: eyes popped open as a jolt of caffeine went straight to the heart. It tasted like a mixture of licorice and tar. The ice shifted in the glass, and my stomach turned. Dan was partway through the rice ball, looking ill. I picked at the cookie until Antonio left to pay, then stuffed it in my purse.

Antonio replaced a very large roll of bills in his jacket, and we set off for Palermo.

He drove very fast.

"I am not like the Sicilians," he said, veering from one curve to the next across the narrow coastline road. "They are timid, set in their ways. I like to do what I want, and why not?"

He swerved around a truck, squeezed past the oncoming cars, and we sped down a corridor of air between the opposing lines of traffic.

"There is always enough space," he said. "Italians are excellent drivers."

Was he suicidal? Maybe grief had left him suspended between life and death, racing down some nonexistent center lane. Whether he crashed or merged didn't seem to matter.

My terror turned to anger. My own grief was a boulder that I carried everywhere. It wasn't so much sadness. To feel pure sorrow came as a relief. Huge, ugly, and uncomfortable, this boulder lodged in my guts, making it hard to breathe. When Dan and I were alone, there was room for tears and tenderness, for whatever the tide of feelings churned up. But being with a stranger could be excruciating.

Introductions stated our names, perhaps where we came from, but never, "and we are grieving for our child." The stranger would look and smile, and not see the most important thing, would offer a hand to shake thinking I could spare one of mine and still hold the invisible burden. The heaviness increased, the pressure built until I had to blurt out our secret or leave. Now I was trapped in a car with someone driven by a pressure of his own, a pressure crazier, more erratic, more aggressive than mine.

I have never liked mosaics. As a ten-year-old I made a mosaic ashtray and though the ceramic tiles seemed colorful and interesting when loose, they lost their vividness when set into a pattern. The gritty, dead-white grout was a nasty substance, and it hardened in an alarming way, trapping the tiles.

The adult impulse to make a mosaic seemed connected to something peculiar. I once saw photographs of a huge tower made by a California hermit of bits of pop-bottle glass stuck into plaster, and another of a shrine made by a Wisconsin recluse of painted bottle caps lodged in cement. They gave me the creeps. These people weren't artists. They were obsessed with a repetitive action like a phonograph arm that stays stuck for twenty years on the same scratch, playing the same break in the music over and over.

I couldn't believe we had come to Monreale to see one of the largest assemblages of mosaics in the world. Suddenly I was tired of being a tourist, sick of eating food I didn't want, angry at sights that had nothing to do with me.

"How many people live in Palermo?" I asked, making a dull attempt at conversation.

Antonio screeched to the side of the road—we had reached Palermo by now—and jumped out of the car. He sprinted through the traffic toward a policeman directing the lines of cars, spoke with him briefly, then ran back to us.

"One million people!" he announced triumphantly.

$\sim$

Monreale, the royal mountain, is an old section of Palermo built on a set of hills. As we wound up the road away from the sea, the pavement turned to cobblestone. The church sat on a piazza where vendors were setting up carts of puppets, postcards, statues, and jewelry. Inside the dark church, nets hung in the enormous domes and apses. A termite problem, the guide said—the tiles of the mosaics were falling off the walls and the nets would catch them.

We walked along a darkened corridor where the guide told the story of William II, twelfth-century king of Sicily and patron of the church, whose son died at seventeen. We stopped at his tomb. A marble boy lay on a marble bed, hands folded on his thin chest. Antonio seemed jolted by this image and abruptly walked away.

When the tour was over I announced with all the conviction I could muster, "I must sit down." The coolness of the sanctuary, the privacy of a pew looked like salvation. The heat was bad enough, but Antonio's intensity was more relentless than the heat. Still reeling from the nausea and fear of the drive, I slumped into a seat.

A huge image filled the central dome: Christ Pantocrator. It was a human face, dark and brooding, the face of a consciousness deeper and older than any image of the gentle European Jesus I had seen. Ruler of the Universe. The eyes held a sort of primal anger, the power of the great seas, of earthquake or volcano, the violence that calls the worlds into being or destroys them.

I felt a little chilled. I thought about the long and bewildering battle I had fought with my body. It was March in Bergamo, the pregnancy in its twentieth week. I was told to stay in bed. For a month I stared at the walls of our apartment. Dan was in class all day, studying at night, and in between he shopped and cooked for me, washed our clothes by hand, read to me. Worried and exhausted, he tried with tangerines and poems and magazines to cheer me.

I felt the baby kick and turn, the gentle thumps of my little companion. But too often sharper pains shot across my abdomen, the walls of the uterus contracting months too soon. By the time I was sent to the hospital, my uterus had become so sensitive that it would react with spasms to the slightest disturbance. I could not leave the bed. I could hardly turn over.

I could not touch my own skin. The doctor said even the pressure of my hand resting on the hill of my abdomen could send the muscles into helpless, violent motion.

This was the universe over which I presided—a universe so fragile the child's own kicking—his signs of life—caused tremors, and each tremor caused a flurry of tremors, and the flurry caused knot-like waves to take over the little sea, preparing for the great landslide that would deliver or destroy him.

~

No one was in sight, so I stood up and walked a bit among the mosaics. I found a glittering expanse of scenes from the Creation, images from Genesis as if they had taken place in this landscape. I felt I had never seen anything so beautiful. Blue and green fish leapt out of waves, palm trees spread their fronds to announce the arrival of plants on earth, and the sea burst forth in a strange and joyous crowd of animals. I stopped and craned my neck. I had walked into the dome of creation.

Who calls the worlds into being? Tears spilled down my cheeks, and I knew it wasn't me and it wasn't Dan who called this child into life. We wanted each other, we wanted a child. But his chance at life and his death were beyond us. We had fought to keep him on our side of day and night.

Maybe our child did not slip through my fingers. Maybe, like the wonderful fish in the mosaic, he too leapt out of the ocean, out of the crest of a wave, and we saw him for a moment, then another wave caught him. Maybe the ache of failure that still convulsed me could be washed away by this same wave.

~

We drove home a different way, passing a horse-drawn cart, along a narrow country road, through the barren hills. The sea sparkled blue to one side, red mountains to the other.

"Antonio, what kind of work do you do?" I asked. I wanted to know more about him. Something in me had snapped and been released after passing through the creation story. Antonio's high-pressure generosity had not let up—in the piazza outside the church he bought me a necklace of white stones and gold beads and insisted we all try the famous Palermo lemon gelato, another exercise in gulping down an unwanted substance—but now, in the car, our journey accomplished, a feeling of relief took over. The possibility of something real blossomed.

"I sell pasta," he said. "To all the small towns. I drive in the company car—not this one." He paused. "But I did not always sell pasta." Another pause. "Five years ago, my daughter died. Everything changed."

"Anna told us you had a daughter," Dan said.

"After she died, I went crazy. I stayed in a hospital for a year. I spoke to no one. It seemed so cruel. It was unbearable that she should die and I should be left, that I could not take her place. I wanted more than anything to follow her."

"How did she die?" asked Dan.

"She contracted leukemia." Antonio said the word with bitterness. "A terrible disease. It is the cells, the cells of the blood become sick. They grow too fast, too big. The doctors can do nothing. It is a terrible suffering—to watch your child slip from your grasp, to be completely helpless. Your heart cannot break in enough places."

He stared hard out the window.

"And now I have no one to talk to. I should go back to my house, they say. They think I am still crazy."

"It is a terrible thing, to have no one to talk to," I said.

"We too have a grief," said Dan, the brave one. "We lost a son in Bergamo. He was born too soon, he was too small to live."

"A son!" Antonio gasped.

Our story came spilling out. Dan spoke.

"The hospital buried him in the town cemetery. We could not find the grave. We had to look through pages and pages of a book until we found his name."

"He is buried in Bergamo? So far from your family?"

"We wandered around the cemetery—it is huge, the only one in Bergamo—and came to a section of small plots, marble lambs and tiny crosses, the infants and children. At the end of one row the grass stopped and the fresh graves began. We found his place. It was marked with a number. A small mound of earth and stones."

"Later we came back with friends and said prayers." Finally I could talk.

Antonio let out a long breath. "These things cannot be borne alone."

~

We rounded the promontory that formed the tip of the bay of Porticello, and the land changed. After miles of raw earth, we entered a cultivated valley, and the sight of living things—brilliant green rows of trees and swirling squares of yellow wheat—took my breath away.

"Where did this come from?" I exclaimed.

"Where there is water, Sicily blooms. Where there is none, she starves. This is my land," he said. "The irrigation system was very expensive."

He pulled off the road onto a dirt path and drove into a grove of fig trees. Dark broad scalloped leaves, pale green fruit suspended like fat globes.

Antonio reached up and pulled a fig from a branch. "*Buono*," he said, biting into it. "*Sono maturi.*"

He picked one for each of us. The flesh was soft and it had a delicious juice.

"When you work in the fields you become thirsty. There is no drinking water here, but with the figs you have what you need. Then you can return to work."

We sat in the shade of the fig trees, the juice running down our arms, the rocky soil hot beneath us.

I thought about Antonio and Maria Zarcone. Grief is like a deportation. After a death you are wrenched from your home, and the inner world that you may not have realized you inhabited becomes a desolate landscape, blasted of comfort or rest. This is where you have to live. You are homeless and you can't escape because it is inside.

Sometimes the only thing that can ease the pressure is to make the outer world congruent with the inner. To sleep on a bed of rags.

Antonio offered us each another fig. We ate them slowly and rested together under green branches, gazing out at the sea. Soon enough we could return to the work.

LINDA LAPPIN

A Quiet Life in the Country

DURING THE LAST hour of my four-hour drive from Rome, I meet no traffic along the lonely road. The late summer night is chilly and calm; a half-eaten moon hangs low over fields of withered sunflowers. Before I turn off the main road onto the gravel track leading up to the village of Poggiarello, my destination, a dark, humped shape bolts from a field, dashes out in front of my car, and then scuttles to safety. I watch it trotting at great speed toward a thicket. This is my first glimpse of a wild boar.

The road up to the deserted village has been badly washed out by the August rainstorms. I park my car outside a large farmhouse where my nearest neighbors, the local dowser and his wife, live. There are eight houses in this village, but only three are inhabited. There to the left, set apart from the other buildings is another old house, facing the forest. This is to be my home for the next twelve months. I have come to house-sit here in Tuscany for an acquaintance who has gone to Australia for a year. But I have really come to see if I can learn to live more simply and more fully, obeying the demands of the present tense.

A dog begins to bark furiously as I go up the steps. The key is waiting for me where the owner told me she would leave it, behind a geranium on a ledge near the door. It is a large, heavy, black iron key, made perhaps fifty or a hundred years ago by a local blacksmith—the sort of key you imagine might have once opened dungeons, worn smooth with much handling. A few weeks ago, when I discussed practical details with the owner before her departure, I marveled at her nonchalance about leaving keys within such easy reach, but she just laughed and said I had been living in the city too long. There was no need to fear intruders in Poggiarello.

As I unlock the door and step inside, I am met by the faint tangy smell of woodsmoke mixed with the pungent odor of dried herbs, the ripe, sweetish smell of straw, and a damp, slightly sour but not unpleasant smell that seems to come from the stone walls themselves. A clock is ticking. Everything is still and seems in perfect order. I stand there for a moment in the dark kitchen, savoring the cozy, familiar, and yet intriguing atmosphere. I have stumbled into someone else's life or into another era, or perhaps into the ogre's kitchen somewhere in a fairy tale and this sensation brings with it an enormous curiosity and sense of anticipation. Then as I grope for the switch and turn on the light, the feeling fades.

I go back downstairs and unload my things from the car, mostly practical objects useful for a life in the country: old clothes; woollen underwear; rubber boots and gardening gloves; kerosene lanterns; the sundry paraphernalia of grown-up girl scouts; a pressure cooker—for all the beans I intended to eat (paying homage to Thoreau); and several kilos of brown rice and other staples. At three a.m. I crawl into bed, leaving a shutter open so that I can contemplate the stars glittering above the dark tower on the hill. I soon fall asleep counting them.

I wake in my new home with a glowing feeling of exhilaration that I have not experienced since my adolescence. From now on until I leave this place, my time will be my own. I will not be straggling behind the calendar any longer. I shall be living in the slow, steady stream of the present which, here in this house of ancient stone, seems inextricably bound up with the distant past.

It's not easy to adjust to the laws of a stranger's house. I spend the first few days getting acquainted: with where things are kept, with the neighbors, the garden, the cat, the neighbors' cats, chickens, and other animals. I explore the most accessible trails through the forest: up to the oak tree, down to the river, up the cypress-lined avenue to the villa where the man who was once landlord of all these houses, fields, and woods lives. My closest neighbors are Guido, a peasant of about sixty, a dowser and healer, and his wife, Giovanna. The other person who lives here year round is a retired banker from Siena. In the tower up on the hill lives a shepherd who keeps his sheep in a field below my kitchen window.

The kitchen is the heart of the house. Here is a picture: high, vaulted ceilings and a red brick floor. An enormous fireplace occupies one entire wall; opposite this are the cooking range and the wood-burning stove. Across from the door stands a huge oak cupboard filled with over twenty drawers. The window faces west, with a view of the mountains. The tip of a magnificent oak tree can just be glimpsed in the distance, above a rise in the terrain. Below the window is an ancient, scarred stone sink. The water in the tap comes from a spring in the forest. In the middle of the room, there is an old, worn but sturdy, oak table where I shall consume my meals alone.

The bathroom, obviously added on as an afterthought, opens off the kitchen and contains all the essentials plus a large family of spider plants. The window is broken. A piece of cardboard substitutes for the missing pane. The toilet doesn't flush. My instructions are to flush it with a bucket of water. This is an ecological measure. Sometimes in the summer, the water supply runs out. Two other small rooms open off the kitchen: one with a window facing northeast, the other southwest with a view of the forest. This is my room. Downstairs is a cantina for storing wine, preserves, and a shed where wood and tools are kept.

On my very first day I explore the garden where the owner suggested I might be able to scrounge up a few vegetables for my dinner. It is quite far from the house, surrounded by a wire fence (to keep out the voracious porcupines) and a hedge of currant bushes. Along the path leading to the garden is a pen of chicken wire where a big black Belgian sheepdog, Giandula, lives. This poor dog is the cast-off pet of someone from Florence who owns a house here but never comes. The local people look after the dog. The garden is in a state of abundant decline, but there are still quite a few tomatoes and plenty of fresh herbs to enjoy: sage, chives, and rosemary; dill, fennel, and coriander gone to seed; basil and tarragon. Below the garden lies a field where dirty sheep are grazing. A trail cuts through the trodden grass, wends its way through a thicket of wild rosebushes and then disappears into the forest. From here overgrown tracks wind back through the trees to a forgotten spot where the remains of the oldest settlement in the Siena area once stood, known locally as Siena Vecchia, dating back to the Iron Age.

On the very edge of the forest is an ancient oak tree, over five hundred years old, if one is to believe the local people's estimate. This giant stands on a sunny ridge preening its leaves in the late summer sunlight. It is of such girth that it would take four stout men to embrace it. Stretching its boughs over the ridge, it leans down toward the meadow below where a muddy pond lies. Beyond the pond, a white ribbon of a gravel road lined with austere cypress trees takes you up to the old villa. Most of those flame-shaped trees are mere blackened skeletons, victims of blight and fire. To the right another dirt road leads down to the Merse River.

It's about three miles down to the river and back. Now at summer's end, a slow stream of cars crawls along the forest track crowded with bathers who have come from Siena for a swim in the murky green waters of the Merse. The name "Merse" testifies to the presence of Celts in this area in the fourth century B.C. This is the name they gave to ponds, marshy areas, and slow-moving rivers. Our word "marsh" no doubt derives from this word. Though I find it hard to believe that this lazy river is as clean as the locals claim, the blazing heat prompts me to investigate. The only thing to worry about, I have been warned, are the vipers, that also go down to the river in the heat of the day.

I follow the track down through the forest. Here and there, beneath the leaves and moss lining the ground, stretches of the track are still paved with stones laid in place during the Middle Ages. This is all that remains of what once in the thirteenth century was a major thoroughfare, connecting the various houses scattered in the woods with the wool workshops and monasteries of the area, leading all the way to the village of Brenna, once the site of an important complex of mills built in the thirteenth century by the monks of a nearby abbey. The village takes its name from the Celtic chieftain Brenn ("brenn" in Celtic means "chief"), who settled here in 390 B.C. with a hoard of blond, robust, and naked warriors after a failed attempt to conquer Rome. Today Brenna is a sleepy little village plagued by mosquitoes, with a few moldering farmhouses, a couple of remodeled vacation homes, and a bar pizzeria.

To avoid the other bathers, I follow the river upstream to where the *steccaia* —a pile work flanked by a huge mound of algae-covered stones—divides the flow into two distinct zones. On one side lie sandy banks and shallow transparent pools strewn with huge white boulders and scattered with the bleached remains of crabs. Each of these boulders is a garden, covered with tall grasses with tiny purple blossoms and plumed sprays of horsetails, all reflected in the limpid waters, the haunt of turquoise dragonflies. There on the other side the river runs deep, murky, and still, its waters opaque, dirty bottle-green in color. Clouds of gnats hover above it. Here the lush growth lines the banks; the tops of tall, lanky poplar trees shiver in the breeze and wild grape vines trail languidly down into the water. Farther upstream a man stands fishing on the bank. He takes no interest in me and I none in him. I wade through the shallow pools, teetering on slippery rocks, hop over the *steccaia*, and plunge in. Opening my eyes I can see nothing underwater and if I remain still for longer than a moment tiny minnows come to nibble at my skin. The river is teeming with insects and tiny fish dimpling the dark surface of the water. I swim a few yards upstream and return, not quite at ease. The river water leaves a silky patina of silt on my skin. As I step back over the *steccaia*, I see a snake glide by along the rocks and disappear.

⌒

At noon, a ray of yellow sunshine falls on the onions piled in a wicker basket on my kitchen table. Spheres of ruddy ochre tinged with pink, a lush magenta under-glow, dry twisted onion tops withered to the palest straw. I look around the room. These old pieces of hardwood furniture—oak , chestnut, and walnut—seem to radiate a presence of their own. Scarred and stained, they have migrated from house to house, century to century, their rough places smoothed by the wear of time and by the endless succession of repetitive human events of which they have been the anonymous participant. What could be more solid than a simple down-to-earth kitchen table? Think of a kitchen table, when you're not there, said Mr. Ramsay to Lily in Virginia Woolf's *To the Lighthouse* in order to illustrate the finer nuances of philosophy. Perhaps Mr. Ramsay could have gone one step further and thought of the kitchen table when it wasn't there: as in a Buddhist mental exer-cise in which you imagine a table full of objects, remove the objects one by one in your mind, then remove the table itself, and then at last yourself.

But I am very much here, alive to the silence of this sunny room. As I sit here I can feel the sensation of my fingers against the warm, smooth wood. There are those who say that natural substances like metal and stone, wood, wool, and silk conserve and concentrate the energy of those who have used them. Talismans are said to make use of this principle. My neighbor, the dowser, claims that he possesses the key to the secret life of things. Through his parapsychological "art" he can unlock impressions accumulated over the years in old objects and make them live again. Though this may sound farfetched, it is true poetically perhaps, that these beautifully-made, old, and rustic pieces of furniture do seem to be liv-ing a life of their own. I am a mere guest or, better, an accessory in their presence.

⌒

There is some debate as to the origin of the house I am inhabiting. The dowser claims that it once housed a community of nuns. The kitchen was probably the refectory, and proof of this was supplied by another neighbor, now dead, who recalled having seen, years ago when he was a child, a stone relief above the fire-place showing people eating at table. This may or may not have been a represen-tation of the Last Supper. If there were monks here in Poggiarello, and documents to this effect do exist, why not nuns, argues the dowser. For hundreds of years, this area was teeming with religious activity. Benedictine and Cistercian monas-teries were numerous and the hills were full of hermits living in caves, like San Gal-gano and San Leonardo al Lago not too far from here whose huts and caves incorporated into the crypts of later churches built to honor them. Ruins of monasteries, convents, and hermitages are frequently to be found in these woods — such as the hermitage of Santa Lucia in the forest behind Rosia. Most of the monasteries in this particular area were under Benedictine rule and were linked to the nearby abbey of Torri. There may indeed have been nuns in Poggiarello.

Nonsense, says the Sienese banker. This house was probably not a convent at all, but rather a workshop of the wool-workers guild. Siena, unlike Florence, had no rivers or streams to provide energy, thus its industries developed outside of Siena in the Val di Merse, an area rich in water resources. The *maestri dell'arte delia lana*, the masters of the art of wool, were based in Stigliano, the larger village below to which Poggiarello belongs. This house probably originally served as a fulling mill, where cloth was cleaned and thickened.

I like to think of the nuns living here, a handful of women living according to Benedictine rule: seven hours a day of manual labor, either in the fields or in the library transcribing books, and then two hours of spiritual study. Here in this house, perhaps, these women lived tending their cabbages and carrots, pursuing a life of inner search—though their intellectual instruction was probably imparted orally, for most of the women living in rural religious communities during the Middle Ages could barely read. Perhaps they sat in this very kitchen, taking their meals together after the day's work.

I awake at three in the morning and hear the faint far away yet distinct sound of chimes, though no church bells ring at this hour today. Ding, ding, ding, and then all is silent. Is it the nuns rising for prayer in the early hours of the morning?

~

Now that autumn is coming, I have been having trouble sleeping. Though I blame the dogs howling at night, I know that is not the reason. One morning, after a particularly sleepless night, Giovanna, the dowser's wife, knocks at the door to ask me to pick up some milk for her in town. She notices how bleary-eyed and pale I look and asks me what's wrong.

"I don't know why," I complain, "but I just can't get to sleep before three or four in the morning."

She looks at me knowingly and says, "Ah, yes, it's the change of season." Then after a pause she adds, "That's the sort of problem my husband could help you with."

Guido, her husband, is the local *mago* or healer. People come to him to ask help for all sorts of problems: where to look for water on their land, how to soothe a bad back, where to find a missing person or object, whether their ailments need medical attention.

Belief in the powers of such people is very widespread in Italy, and not only among ones in the countryside or the uneducated lower classes in the city. To Guido's credit it must be said that many people are convinced that he has helped them in some way. At any rate, he is well known throughout the area and several days a week in the afternoon, he receives a small stream of people who come to consult him, by appointment only.

Guido's career as a dowser began while he was still a young man. After his head was injured in an accident, he suddenly discovered that he had the ability to find underground water with a dowsing rod. He performed this service mostly for his neighbors. Then, when the archaeologists came to excavate the nearby site of Siena Vecchia, they hired Guido to tell them where they should dig. Evidently, he was right on target and as a result his reputation began to spread. Later, his wife convinced him to branch out and to use his talents for healing the sick. He was relatively successful at this, and for the last fifteen years or so has dedicated himself solely to this activity.

There is nothing of the charlatan about Guido. He is a kindly man, tall, broad shouldered, and heavily built, with a ruddy complexion and a face perpetually set in an expression of mild amusement. Though he is in his early sixties, he looks much older and his health has not been very good in the last few years. The only thing unusual about him are his eyes—of a watery, bloodshot blue yet startlingly piercing. This uncanny effect is heightened by the fact that he is walleyed and always seems to be peering sideways at you, straight into your thoughts. Luckily, like many local peasants, he is nonjudgmental.

I decide to accept the offer of a visit to the *mago*. That evening I go over to their house and am invited into the kitchen. His wife greets me and then discreetly withdraws. I sit down at the kitchen table next to Guido. He takes my hand and touches it with a curious silver object, a little statuette of a woman. Suddenly I am overcome by a very odd sensation. I feel as though my mind were being drained, or rather, being cleansed. The dimensions in the room seem to change as does my sense of time, and it occurs to me while this is happening that I am being hypnotized, but I have no idea how this has been brought about. Then the strangeness fades and everything seems normal again, only I feel extraordinarily refreshed. "You'll be all right now," he says. "It was just a bit of nervousness."

Now his wife comes into the room and insists on giving me a paper sack full of dried lime flowers. "Sometimes it doesn't work, so make yourself an infusion of lime flowers before bedtime just in case."

I thank them both and say good night. That night I do sleep well indeed and am not troubled with insomnia again after that. But whether it was Guido's treatment or his wife's herbal tea, I really can't say.

∽

There are many roads through the forest. Once these were heavily trafficked by travelers or woodcutters, monks or farmers. Now, more rarely, hunters come in search of the wild boar or the wild porcini mushrooms. Wherever three roads meet, an iron cross has been driven into the ground. This custom, common practice among country folk, is a vestige of the medieval belief in witches who were said to frequent such places. In times long past, I might have been mistaken for such a person, as it is evening and I am out alone, wandering these trails, in the company of a big woolly dog, black as a shadow—Giandula, who could indeed be my familiar.

Under our feet are slippery slabs of red clay, and here and there an expanse of thick moss finally quenched after a dry summer. A perfect geometry of leaves carpets the path. Looking up at the mountainside through the yellowing leaves of an oak, I spot a strawberry tree: the *corbezzolo*. This small tree with dark, waxy leaves produces a plump little flame-colored berry, the size of a strawberry, lush and inviting to the eye, but inside a tasteless pulp.

In the last few days the rose hips have darkened from russet-orange to deep scarlet, and a few yellow-spotted oak leaves have been tossed to the ground, along with a shower of pine nuts shaken from their cones, scattered in profusion along the sandy trail. I gather a handful for my dinner, soiling my fingers with their fine, black dust. These, crushed with garlic and what's left of the basil, will yield an excellent pesto with a faint yet piquant trace of resin.

Mushrooms have sprung up since last night's tempest. In the fading light, I see a few orange stalks of the delicious *finferle* peeking out from under layers of decomposing chestnut leaves—nearby I notice the glossy black scalloped edges of the *trombette di morte*, death trumpets, which despite their name are one of the area's best mushrooms. I pick some for my dinner. As the twilight deepens, bats flitter out from nowhere and disappear again. There's an eerie feeling in the air, no moon, and the tips of the cypress trees behind me are swaying slightly though

I can feel no wind. From deep in the forest comes the strangled bark of a deer and the dog begins to whine with excitement. I seize hold of his collar, turn around, and head for home. Soon the trees will be alone with themselves and the boars will be on the move. I quicken my pace and am relieved to see a light shining in Guido's house, high on the hill above the pond.

~

I have heard it said that if the house is one of the symbols of the self, then the furniture in the house represents the thoughts and feelings of the self. If this is true, there is no doubt that my host's thoughts and feelings are ruled by the principles of extreme simplicity and order. I have never seen any object that better expresses the organized multiplicity of a human life than the cupboard in my kitchen. It is also a concrete manifestation of that time-honored law of old-fashioned housekeepers, a law which I have never been able to observe: a place for everything and everything in its place. As my host told me, if you need something and can't find it, look in the cupboard and that's where it will probably be. The logic of this intrigues me. If you need something you need only look in the right place for it and you will find it. How often does it happen that things and people are not in the right place. And if only there were a way of knowing where the right place is.

This cupboard occupies an entire wall of the kitchen. Turn the iron key and you will discover over twenty-five drawers and shelves of different sizes, devoted to a vast range of needs, each one labeled appropriately. This allows me an edifying glimpse of my host's vision of a fully-integrated human life, and I lose no time in exploring it. One drawer is for *Medicine*; another for *Patterns, Remnants, and Sewing things*; still another, overflowing with tangled tentacles of stockings and yarn is labeled *Mending*. There are drawers for *Garden things, Tools, Keys, Seeds, Candles, Dish Towels, Drawing and Painting things*; for *Toys and Games, Christmas Ornaments, Empty Jars*; the inevitable *Plastic Bags*, and *Gift-wrapping Paper*; *Letters, Writing things*; alas. even here, *Taxes and Bills*; *Music, Maps, Shoe Polish*, and *Miscellaneous*.

Every drawer has its own peculiar smell: of old rubber and camphor, eucalyptus and rusted iron, onion seeds and beeswax, ether and musty lavender sachets, the stubs of cedar pencils, kerosene, oil of cloves, iodine, hairnets, cloying joss sticks, old crinkled silk, sulphury matches, dusty envelopes perfumed with faded vetiver, lambswool oily with lanolin, candles, chamois skin, citronella, oil cloth, Marseille soap, bergamot, recycled corks still drenched in old wine, lemon oil, quilt batting, dried ink of old newspapers, the worn leather of a battered purse, varnish, menthol, broken crayons, coughdrops, empty cigar boxes, cotton wool, the bitter smell of boar-bristle hairbrushes, paste, bleach, chalk, cocoa butter, peppermints, turpentine, linen tea towels ironed ages ago and wrapped in tissue paper, rock salt. Each smell illumines some dark spot on the aromatic map of my childhood. Surely my grandmother's house smelled just like this. The drawer I find most intriguing is *Miscellaneous*, which is full of curiosities: a broken ceramic plate, postage stamps from exotic places, a hand puppet, a carnival mask of a devil, several porcupine quills, a brass camel, and some old hand-forged iron nails. Even these objects—broken, useless, or frivolous—have found their place in the order of things.

Piled ceremoniously in the fireplace is a bundle of dried fennel stalks, shrivelled roses, laurel branches, resin-encrusted pine cones, and bits of an old crate, all tidily arranged on two trunks of pine. These are the offerings of the summer left here for the first winter fire that must wait until the cold has really come to stay. That day comes in early December. Up until now I have only used the wood-burning stove to warm myself. I throw in a match, the flames leap up, in a second the pyre is consumed.

On this cold evening, my dinner is homemade bread, brown rice, and wild greens, the last of the borage growing wild in the garden and bitter chicory gathered in a field, cooked in olive oil with a little bacon, garlic, and hot pepper. After dinner I draw my chair up to the fire, turn off the light, and watch the flames. This will be my amusement in the evening for many a winter night to come. On the mantelpiece are the finds from my walks in the forest: a jar of feathers and porcupine quills, a fossil shell, a bleached sheepskull. Tonight the cat I am supposed to be caring for, Black Pussy, is keeping me company, honoring me with her rare presence. I have hardly seen her since I moved in. She seems to have been adopted by the cook of a restaurant in the neighboring village. I wrap some apples in foil, put them in the corner of the fireplace, and cover them with ash—that will be my breakfast tomorrow morning. Later tonight, I'll take the priest to bed. That is no sin, however, for the priest is none other than a curious bed-warming contraption consisting of a wooden frame resembling the wings of the Wright brothers' first airplane, and a tin bucket to hold coals and ash. You fill the bucket with live coals, sprinkle some ash over them, and then hang the bucket from the frame and slip it under the covers. This must be done with a certain caution, otherwise you'll scorch the sheets. You leave it in for a half hour or so, then remove it and climb into bed as quickly as you can. There is nothing more luxurious than a bed warmed in this manner, on a winter night, in an inevitably freezing and drafty bedroom such as mine. I have heard different opinions as to why this device is called the priest. One theory is that the name derives from the fact that it only lies very chastely in your bed and warms it and does nothing more. Another theory is that when the covers are pulled over it, it does indeed look as if a very large man with a huge paunch is lying in your bed. Evidently these two qualities are associated in the peasant mentality with the figure of the local priest.

When the flames have died away, I rake the ashes, put reluctant Black Pussy out, and go into the bedroom to look out the window. One brilliant star blazes above the hill in a sky of cobalt. The sharp edges of its radiance presage frost: I touch the black windowpane—the cold is sharp and keen. Next morning I discover that winter indeed has arrived quite suddenly; the sky is swathed in white, and a coat of frost bristles across the farmyard.

Walking early in the morning I see a hoopoe sitting in a frozen field. On my way to the oak tree, I fill my pockets with ripe rose hips and juniper berries. The rose hips are for making a potent infusion against colds, the juniper berries for cooking pork steaks on the coals.

The fire is sizzling and popping for the wood is too wet, too green, too young. I throw a branch of dry, brittle pine found in the shed, probably left over from last year's Christmas tree. In a second the flames blaze up, energy traveling to the tip of every needle. The branch snaps, glows, shrivels, and is gone. Will we too be consumed in this way?

Here before me I have a steaming cup of tea, a plate of glowing lemons, a cauliflower, a blue china bowl whose silky glaze captures the flickering firelight. As I sit here in a strange state of wakefulness and inner quiet, the objects around me seem to acquire a new volume and weight — they seem to inhabit a higher realm of stillness both within me and without me. Now the fire is leaping in the grate. Is it my imagination or is it that these old houses preserve in the resonating stones of their structure, in their wooden beams, and worn brick floors, traces of energy left by those simpler souls who once lived and moved within these walls at their own unhurried pace? At this moment, even the room itself seems alive and aware of me, its temporary passenger.

LISA RUFFOLO

Signora di Lando's Lives of the Saints

THE DAY I MET Signora di Lando, the sky was deep blue, and Florence looked like it was posing for a postcard photo—the ochre and cream buildings along the Arno were sharply outlined against the clear sky, and their reflections in the river made them seem sculpted, like perfect Renaissance exercises in perspective. It was early April, the beginning of tourist season, and I was out, walking briskly toward American Express and trying to forget a nasty letter I'd received that morning from my old boyfriend, Carlo. He hadn't bothered to send it, just taped it to my apartment door, and all day I'd been wondering how he managed to slip in the main entrance, and whether he'd done it before to check my comings and goings. For weeks I'd felt someone had been watching me.

On the Santa Trinita bridge, I passed an older couple in raincoats standing near the railing, puzzling over a street map. The woman was squinting at the traffic—fleets of noisy motorbikes and Fiats—and looked completely lost. I stopped to help them, pointing in the direction of the Uffizi Gallery, then watched as they picked up their cameras and guidebooks, said, "Right, and thanks," then marched off in their new walking shoes. Even after a year, I didn't always feel welcome in Florence, but at least I knew my way around.

I was heading across the river to the American Express office because I wanted to find an Italian tutor. The only Italian I knew came from a six-week course back in Madison, and whatever I picked up from the streets. Which wasn't working. Unlike Parisians, who persist in answering in French no matter what language you use to phrase your question, Florentines always answered in English, even if you spoke to them in Italian. Not speaking fluently made me feel trapped in a passageway, just outside a place I wanted to be in. As much as I loved living in Florence, I didn't really fit in—I was neither tourist nor resident, neither fish nor meat, as the Italians said, one of the few idioms I'd picked up. I hoped that learning the language would make the place I called home accept me as its daughter.

After I crossed the bridge, I followed a narrow road angling away from the river. Stopping a moment at a wall fountain, a silver stream of water pouring from the mouth of a marble angel, I rinsed my hands, then looked up to see a man with narrow-set eyes and a clipped mustache watching me, frozen-faced. "I'm all washed up," I said in my American-accented Italian, getting the expression wrong. I shook water from my fingers. But he only nodded curtly without smiling and headed over the bridge, a cool Florentine response I'd endured before. I patted my hands dry on my jeans, slow, with a feeling I'd done something more than wrong, that I'd offended him somehow.

Continuing down the crooked, shadowy street, I remembered Carlo's letter. Dress yourself in my clothes, he'd written, and you will know how it feels. I thought he was being melodramatic—I'd been dating Carlo when I met Giacomo, though only for a matter of weeks, so I couldn't imagine that he was devastated or heartbroken. Still, the fact that he'd written and delivered the letter disturbed and puzzled me, made me want to stay away from home in case he called or stopped by. Seeing him again would be unbearably awkward—he'd be expertly insulting and cool, his eyes half-closed as he looked down his long nose at me.

Hearing the musical sound of Italian conversation, I paused by a small open doorway to look into a shaded, lush courtyard bright pink with azaleas. Men and women sat at round marble tables and leaned toward one another, making what seemed to be fresh, witty, in-the-know statements—everyone wore amused but blasé expressions. One man in a blue-gray suit sat back in his wrought-iron chair, stubbed out his cigarette, and pulled on a pair of soft leather driving gloves, taking his time, as if dressing himself were a form of leisure, like attending the symphony or playing polo. I thought I might go in for a coffee and read the newspaper I'd folded in my tote bag, but I couldn't see myself in the cafe with my jeans and unstyled hair, everyone looking me over as if they were estimating my place, so I moved down the street, hurrying out of the way of schoolboys on motorbikes.

Then someone riding a motorcycle with a familiar red and black engine cover sped past me, his knee brushing my hip. "Hey," I yelled, my voice loud and low. I recognized the driver's caramel-brown leather jacket, and I stopped and turned away, my stomach crimping as if I'd drunk too much carbonated water too quickly. It was Carlo, and I stared into the window of a shoe store, my heart beating a dull bass in my ears, until I heard the stutter of his engine fade away. What was that all about? Did he only want to get my attention, like a bratty kid? I just wanted to avoid him until he forgot about things, moved on, got over it already.

I scanned the shoes and belts displayed in the shop window on rippling strips of purple and gold silk. When I spotted a pair of leather flats, good walking shoes, with a tiny On Sale sign propped in front of them, I went inside, eager to be off the street, a bell tinkling above the door as I entered.

Two women stood behind a counter with their arms crossed, one wearing a navy jacket and a polka-dotted scarf, the other a sheer white blouse cinched at the waist. They were engaged in conversation, talking rapidly so that I only caught a few words. I looked at other shoes on display, then moved up to the counter, close enough to see the eyeliner the one in the navy jacket wore, how it ended in a curly flourish at the edge of her eye, but neither woman acknowledged me, didn't even shift or glance in my direction.

"Excuse me," I said in Italian, using an apologetic, bright tone, as if I understood they didn't want to be interrupted. "But I'd like to see a pair of shoes in the window."

They both turned to me, their eyelids heavy, as if they'd been napping instead of talking, and looked down to my feet, then up to my head, taking in my running shoes and jeans, my white cotton sweater and short dark hair. No one wore running shoes in Italy unless they were actually running. They stared until I turned away from them and pointed to the window. "The flats," I said. "They're on sale." I knew that last remark sunk me—it was a sign of low birth to admit to shopping sales in Florence.

The woman in the navy blazer tsked and shook her head. "We don't have your size," she said in English. "Too big." She turned to adjust a display of purses, her bangled earrings swinging.

"Well," I said, my face hot. "Could you check?"

"No, no," she said, opening a leather case and selecting a cassette tape, her polished fingernails flashing. "I know we have nothing that big." Then she pushed the tape into a player, and bouncy Italian pop music filled the store, bright as noon.

I left the shop quickly, my face still hot and stinging. These women were not unusual—other Florentine shopkeepers were the same—but I hadn't ever grown accustomed to their rudeness. Where was the famous European courtesy? And why chase away business like that? Didn't they want Americans shopping at their store? Shopping, after all, was what a store was all about. *Veni, vidi, visa,* my sister Cristina always said, watching tourists fill the center of town—we came, we saw, we shopped.

But the clerks' rudeness wasn't about shopping, or even economics. Probably *campanilsimo*—loyalty to what was closest to them—made them treat Italians better. All over the city, I'd seen Florentines bar the gates, pull down their complicated steel shutters, preserve the small social groups they'd been part of for generations to keep foreigners out. I hurried on, hoping that learning Italian would help me become a part of them, that I wouldn't always be outside looking in.

Turning up the busy street that led to the Pitti Palace, I finally saw the familiar blue and white logo of American Express. I pushed open its heavy glass doors, then headed straight for the bulletin board where I scanned the business cards from independent tourist guides and bypassed the language school ads—I wanted a private tutor. Then I saw a thick, textured, cream-colored card, decorated with gold and red scrolls, like a royal document. Signora di Lando instructs English speakers in the Tuscan tongue. The handwriting was old-fashioned, neat and formal with well-rounded, even strokes. There was no phone number, only an address—a number on Via Maggio, the street leading off the Ponte Santa Trinita. Since I was only a few blocks away, I found a pen in my tote bag and copied the address on a strip of newspaper. Then, feeling decisive, on the brink of change, I shouldered my way through the glass doors and headed back to Via Maggio.

The building where Signora di Lando lived was one of the oldest on the street—its double front doors were big enough for a horse to fit through, and rusty circles of iron hung beside them, to hold torches, I supposed. A smaller door was cut into one of the big ones, and I pushed that, then stepped into a cool atrium, the sky a pale blue square above me. I found the Signora's name on a polished brass plate and rang her bell.

A small woman with smooth skin and a squared-off jaw answered the door, tucking her hair under a burgundy scarf. She stared at me placidly, patient as a cat. "Signora di Lando?" I asked, sticking out my hand. " I'm here about the Italian lessons?"

She ducked her head and pulled the door open wider, so I stepped onto the parquet floor of a dim foyer, pushing myself into air scented with furniture oil and eucalyptus. She led me down a hall, a thick Persian runner springy under my shoes, and into a large cluttered salon. As I entered, the light from a window on the opposite wall blinded me so that I could see only the outlines of the things in the room, but as I followed the woman in the burgundy scarf, I saw the form of another, smaller woman sitting on a high-backed wooden chair, a kind of throne, with carved pine cones set on the chair posts and braided gold piping along the cushions. Her slippered feet were propped on a brocaded footrest under which slept a floppy-haired chow.

"Signora di Lando," I said, my eyes still adjusting to the light and shadow, "I saw your ad at American Express. I'd like to take Italian lessons. I'm looking for a tutor. I liked your card." I shifted my feet and bent my knees, as if I were warming up for the ballet. "Oh, here I am speaking English. I assume you speak English." Always, always when I was nervous I went on and on, as if the sheer volume of words could pad and calm me.

Signora di Lando leaned forward on a cane topped with a polished brass ball, her hands cupping and rubbing it as if they were shaping clay. "You will please sit and have some tea," she said, seeming distracted, as if she were addressing the gilded teacup on the glass-topped table next to her. She gestured to a suede side chair, where I sat and could finally see everything clearly.

Signora di Lando reached into a basket on the floor and drew out an orange wrapped in turquoise paper printed with a drawing of a peasant in a red dress. She smoothed out the paper in her lap, as deliberate as a magician, rolled the orange between her palms, then picked up a paring knife from the glass-topped table and began to peel the orange, letting a pulpy spiral fall onto the paper in her lap. I sat quietly, listening to the unsynchronized ticking of three or four mantel clocks in the room, and watched her, intent as an audience.

When she finished peeling the orange, she looked at me, her striking, heavy-lidded eyes magnified by her jeweled glasses. It was hard to tell how old she was—her powdered pink skin was unwrinkled, as if she'd never been in the sun, and covered with a fine blonde down. But her hair was white, a true snowy white, her movements slow, and when she handed me a purplish section of the blood orange, her fingers, thick with rings, were trembling.

"Ah, Valeria," she said, as the woman in the burgundy scarf entered the room bearing a silver tray covered with a teapot, cups, and embroidered napkins. As she walked, the grand piano in the corner played faint chords. Signora di Lando smiled and adjusted a string of pearls at her throat as Valeria set out the cups, then whisked the orange peels onto the empty tray. "We'll have some tea and get acquainted," Signora said, though the look on her face was closed, guarded. "It's so pleasant to meet new people, even in this new way, without them being introduced."

"Oh, sorry," I said, reaching for the tea she offered me, wincing as if I'd pricked my finger. Here was another botched encounter, a social gaffe in a city that defined itself by social decorum. After a year in Italy, I should have had all this down cold. "My name's Beth, Elisabetta," I said.

"Elisabetta. A fine name." She loosened a tasseled shawl from her shoulders, let it drape around her elbows. "Named after the queen of Portugal, no doubt, Santa Elisabetta, who died marching with the Portuguese army."

"Well, I don't know," I said, sipping the tea and tasting a bit of chestnut in the honey. "It's Beth in English."

She smiled again, patient and cheerless. "Yes, yes," she said. "And you have a family name?" I understood from her tone that this is what she'd meant by her initial question.

"Oh, yes, of course. DeLuca." My hands were making circles in the air, as if I were directing a choir.

"DeLuca. That's an Italian name. Though Southern, no?"

Now it was my turn to give her a cheerless smile. Florentines were not famous for accepting those from the south of Italy.

She set down her teacup, then rose and crossed the room to a fragile desk built with many tiny, brass-handled drawers. She opened one and pulled out a leather-bound appointment book, then changed her glasses, putting on a rimless pair with even thicker lenses. "You may come Tuesdays and Thursdays and Fridays," she said, opening the appointment book. "At precisely this time. Three o'clock." She wrote something, then looked up at me as two clocks chimed. "It will be a pleasure," she said, letting the book fall shut, and I understood the interview was over.

"And the charge for the lessons?" I said, rising and reaching for my tote bag.

She folded her hands around the book. "This I will decide at the end of each lesson, when we can see the value of what I have taught you."

And though this seemed all wrong—just the sort of arrangement that could lead to misunderstanding—I bowed my head in agreement and backed out of the room.

∽

At home, I found Giacomo waiting for me. He and my sister Cristina were in the kitchen cleaning strawberries at the sink, their fingertips stained red from the juice. Giacomo had tucked a towel into the waistband of his gray trousers to protect his clothing, and he turned toward me slowly, careful to keep his tie out of the strawberries. "Spring in the air, Giacomo," I said, and he jumped across the room to kiss me. Here's one Italian at least who understands me, I thought. He had left work early so that we could go to a dinner party in Chianti, about an hour away, but my strange day had made me forget the party, and I had to rush around to shower and change while he ran down to the corner cafe to buy a box of chocolates as our gift to the hostess.

In the car, I told him about Signora di Lando and my plans to take Italian lessons. "Good," he said. "This is a good idea. Three times a week, and soon you'll be fluent."

"Hah," I said. "I don't know. You Italians, you have a different word for everything."

"Elisabetta, c'mon, you already know a little Italian, a few lessons and you'll be perfect, a regular Florentine." Giacomo could sometimes make everything seem easy and sunny simply by gliding over the truth. "Just make sure you pay a fair price."

"I don't know, Giacomo, there's something about the Signora, something otherworldly. I mean, she lives in this former palace with all this stuff, stuff that needs more care than pets—clocks she has to wind, things she has to polish. And she's tiny, with this look on her face like she's keeping a secret."

Giacomo turned onto a busy road, honked his horn, and said, "Everybody has secrets."

"Do you think so?" I said, then crossed my arms and furrowed my brow, an emotion I couldn't translate cooling me.

"Do you know who I saw today?" I said. "Carlo. Can you believe it? He brushed right by me on his motorcycle. The weird thing is, I've been sensing for awhile now that he's been watching me. I wonder if he's following me." Giacomo tipped his head and made a skeptical face. Outside the car window, the city gave way to tapering cypresses and vineyards. "I just want him to go away. Though I suppose I should feel guilty about how things ended between us. I didn't ever even talk to him about you, though that wouldn't have helped much. His English was terrible." The truth was, even when Carlo had asked me if I was seeing someone else, I avoided a direct answer. I didn't want to hurt him, or get embroiled in an emotional confrontation, so I just let him think I was a capricious American.

"Feeling guilty doesn't prevent you from doing something wrong," Giacomo said. "It only prevents you from enjoying it." I rolled my eyes at him.

We turned onto a dirt road and pulled up next to a well-lit farmhouse. He yanked up the brake. "C'mon," he said, opening the door. "Let's just relax and have a nice time with some friends, huh?"

But the party was given by Giacomo's friends, none of whom spoke English, and I was seated between a man and a woman who both chatted with me politely, then turned to the person next to them and launched into involved conversations punctuated by laughter and the rapping of knuckles on the table. After the man to my left rearranged the silverware to explain the details of a funny story I couldn't follow, I looked across the wide table to Giacomo, who smiled at me, then plunged back into talking about rowing with our host. I stared into my wineglass until the pasta was served, sitting on my hands as if I were enduring a punishment I deserved.

～

On Tuesday, I rang Signora di Lando's bell again, ready for my Italian lesson. Valeria opened the door, hiding herself behind it, then led me into the salon, which smelled of sage and oranges, and left me to wait for the Signora.

I found the suede chair I'd used the last time, and as I sat in it, I let out a long breath, my shoulders relaxing. I was glad to be there, felt privileged, a novitiate ushered into a restricted sanctum.

The salon was high ceilinged and cool, though it was already warm outside. When I leaned back in the chair and looked up, I noticed a fresco in the vault of the ceiling ringed by a terra-cotta frieze. The fresco depicted a procession of women, one carrying an ointment jar, another a bunch of keys, another a palm, and one, a spoked wheel.

Valeria returned to set a tea tray on the grand piano in the corner. As she opened a section of each window shutter, I could see an emblem of lilies and skeins of wool painted on the wood.

"You are looking at my family crest," Signora declared, her English more heavily-accented than I recalled. I turned toward her, startled, as if I'd been caught in a forbidden act. She was wearing her tasseled shawl again and leaning forward so that a round gold saint's medal swung from a chain on her neck. "Michele di Lando built this house after he was the governor of Florence back in the fourteenth century," she said in an instructive tone. "He was a wool carder who came forward to create peace among the guilds in the city's dark days. A great man." She sat in her high-backed chair. "My brother too is in the wool business. I live here because of his generosity, being a spinster." She smiled as her dog trotted into the room, his paws clicking on the parquet floor. As Valeria set out tea and fruit on a glass-topped table, Signora reached down to pet the chow on its head.

"Well," she said in Italian, "let's begin by making conversation." The sound of the language in her mouth was beautiful, as melodic as a song. "Where have you traveled in Italy?"

"Where have I traveled in Italy?" I repeated in my hesitant Italian, not at all like making conversation. "Well, I've been to Rome, of course, and some, ah, little cities around here."

She leaned her head toward me, her gold and cabochon earrings gleaming against her neck.

"Little cities, that's not right," I said, "but I mean like San Gimignano and Siena."

"So you've been to Siena then?"

"Yes."

"Then you've seen the church of Catherine of Siena."

"Well, yes, I think so."

"You know," she said, switching to English, "Catherine was the youngest daughter of a Sienese man who dyed cloth, so he was prosperous, and wanted an advantageous marriage for Catherine. But because she had a dream of a shining path, she refused to marry and joined the Dominican order instead. She prayed and experienced raptures. She saw the true arrangement of the planets before Galileo. She spoke with angels and learned their language, which involved humming high tones for various durations. She kept this language a secret, even when she suffered the pain of the stigmata. She converted evil-doers by stepping into flames and emerging without burns. She received angelic intervention to return the church to Rome from France, and the pope named her a saint. She was a great woman who never faltered in her way." Signora stared at me, fierce and detached, like a wildcat.

"Well," I said, blinking, "I didn't know that."

She picked up a newspaper and handed it to me. "You have a lot to learn. Now, read the main story on the first page, and then we will discuss it."

I sat and read, listening to the clocks ticking, the dog sighing and grunting in his sleep, wondering if the Signora were mad. But when I looked up, she was polishing her glasses with a tissue, and began to ask me factual questions about what I'd read. The rest of the lesson continued this way until one clock chimed five times. Signora asked me for twenty thousand lire, about eighteen dollars, which I paid. Then I let myself out, noticing Valeria in a side room, dusting a tiny oil painting in an enormous carved frame.

∼

I was late for the next lesson. As I walked out the door on my way to the Signora's, I found a Botticelli calendar I had given to Carlo. Thick black X's were drawn through most of the days in September, days I figured we must have spent together. I waited until I heard my neighbors open their door, then I rode down in the elevator with them, hurried out the side exit, and caught a bus to Via Maggio.

When I arrived, Signora was seated at the piano, her tiny white hands with their double rows of rings poised over the keys. Boccaccio's *Decameron* was opened on the music stand in front of her.

"Good afternoon, Elisabetta," she said, and nodded to a chair next to the piano bench. "You will please sit and read."

I stashed my tote bag under the piano, then took off my wet jacket and held it out in front of me. "It's raining," I explained. "And cold for April."

"Yes, so it is," she said. "Would you hang it by the fireplace? It's Valeria's day off."

I found a hook in the concrete flue, and smelled some kind of fragrant wood, cedar perhaps, burning slowly in the fireplace. Then I sat next to Signora di Lando and began to read *The Decameron*.

As I read, Signora played a light arpeggio. "What you just read is the simple present," she said. I continued and in the middle of one sentence, she struck a minor chord, letting it reverberate. "The subjunctive." I read some more and she interrupted me by playing chords with her left hand and a melody with her right. "The gerund."

I read and she played until my mouth became dry. "Please," I said. "Could I have a drink of water?"

She smiled, her nose flaring, then rose and sat in her chair, filling a hand-painted bowl with steaming hot chocolate from a silver samovar. " Hot chocolate is more suitable for the day," she said, handing me the bowl. When I sipped, the chocolate tasted dense and bittersweet, and made me even thirstier.

Signora poured herself a bowl from the samovar, then watched me, her cheeks pinkening from the rising steam. She seemed to be waiting for me to say something, though I wasn't sure—I hadn't really learned to read her yet. "You play the piano well," I said, happy that sentence rolled out automatically in Italian.

She fingered the medal on the gold chain around her neck. "This is because I have Santa Cecilia with me, the patron saint of musicians." She set down her hot chocolate, then picked up the medal and pulled it away from her neck so that I could see it better. Its back was engraved with a picture of a pipe organ.

"Santa Cecilia," she began, setting her slippered feet on the footrest, "was a Christian girl in Rome in the early days of the church, betrothed to a pagan. On her wedding day, while the organ played, she heard God singing in her ear as she entered the temple, and she sang back, so powerfully the walls shook. She sang notes only dogs and martyrs could hear. She fell to her knees and told her betrothed that she could not marry him, that she had consecrated her virginity to God. Her hair turned white before his eyes, and she grew wings, tiny white wings on her shoulders. He converted instantly, and so did his brother. She went through Rome carrying palm leaves, knocking on the doors of pagans and converting them when the palms changed to crosses in her arms."

Signora turned the medal and rubbed the face of Saint Cecilia with her thumb. "She was sentenced to be stifled to death in the bathroom of her own house. But the steam they used didn't suffocate her, so a soldier tried to behead her, though he only succeeded in slashing her neck. Her blood flowed into a basin and changed into wine and holy water, which is still used in certain churches in Rome. Everyone who has blessed themselves with this holy water hears her singing to them in their sleep."

"Signora di Lando," I began, leaning forward. Her face was livid, and I was concerned that the stories she told excited her in a way that was not healthy.

She pulled an embroidered handkerchief from her sleeve and blew her nose elaborately, honking and wheezing. Her eyes watery, she looked at me, sneezed twice, then blew her nose again. Her sudden cold made her face look as puffy as a child's.

"Are you feeling all right?" I said in perfect colloquial Italian.

She pulled her tasseled shawl over her shoulders and hugged herself. "I have a great faith," she said, her congested voice resonating, then fading. Her frailty just then wounded me—whether she was crazy or merely too much alone, I worried about her, how she managed, bought groceries, paid the phone bill, negotiated her way around the city. Valeria, I supposed, was a great help. But what about tonight, Valeria's day off, what would Signora do for dinner?

"Shall we make conversation?" I said, pushing away my hot chocolate.

She nodded and dabbed at her nose with her handkerchief, clocks chiming around the room.

"What will you do tonight, after I leave?" I asked. "I mean, will you be all right without Valeria? Would you like me to stay and keep you company?"

She narrowed her eyes, recrossed her arms, then smiled her humorless smile. "I had always heard that Americans were brash, but they're not exactly brash, only lacking subtlety." She rose, picked up an iron poker, and pushed at the logs in the fireplace until they caught fire again. The flames were reflected in miniature in her glasses, hiding her eyes. "The hardest thing to find in Italy is simplicity—people saying what they think and feel, openly and directly. We think it's naive, childish to be so direct. We like finesse, cunning, cleverness." Her voice now was clear and low, nearly unaccented.

Then we both turned toward the noise of a door opening in the back of the apartment and watched the shadows in the hallway until someone appeared—a humming, middle-aged man who wore a thick gold chain around his neck, Signora's chow scurrying behind him.

"My nephew," she said after he kissed her cheek.

"Luisa is ready with dinner for you," he said, taking a fur-trimmed coat out of an oak wardrobe, and holding it out for her. "We can't be late again."

Signora put on her coat, then handed me my jacket and led me to the front hall. She watched me step out into the atrium and shake the rain from my umbrella, then she whispered, "Be true," before she closed and locked the door.

⁓

A few days later, Giacomo and I were heading for the central post office. I had received a notice that a package had arrived for me, and, typical of Italy, I had to fill out postal service forms in triplicate before I could retrieve something that was mine. We were walking along the river, moving faster than I wanted to. My idea of walking was to stroll, arm-in-arm preferably, slow enough to keep a conversation going. Giacomo, on the other hand, liked to stride, to work up a sweat and "catch two pigeons with one bean," as he said, a direct translation. When I started to lag behind, he stopped at a corner and waited, smiling.

"Don't you want to get some exercise," he said, swinging his arms over his head. The corners of his mouth were always perked up, making him look constantly pleased. "Keep your body in shape?"

"Giacomo, who needs exercise? Isn't it enough just getting your head from one place to another?"

When he shrugged, turned toward the traffic, and looked back over his shoulder to smile at me, I experienced something that could only happen with him: everything felt simplified, as if clothes were slipping off my body, leaving me cool and happy and unconstrained.

As I stepped toward him, light and unabashed, ready to continue our teasing,

I saw Carlo across the street, walking slowly along the river, looking down at the water. With his long wavy hair and unseasonal tan, he had about him a celebrity's air of arrogant self-absorption, and because of the way he held his head, staring out over the riverwall even as he walked, I knew he'd been watching me and Giacomo.

I took Giacomo's hand. "You see? What did I tell you? There's Carlo." My throat was squeezed tight, my voice breathy. I turned away from the river, toward the center of town. "Let's cut over to the post office from here." I was not going to let Carlo get to me, or infect my happiness with Giacomo. Perhaps what I'd done—started seeing Giacomo when I was still sleeping with Carlo—was capricious and even unscrupulous, but things with Carlo were clearly over now, and I just wanted him to go away and leave me alone.

The package the whistling clerk handed me was book-shaped and wrapped in brown paper, my name written in European script. There was no return address. I couldn't imagine what the package contained, or who had sent it, and even when I unwrapped it to reveal the red cover and black binding, I didn't recognize my college journal until I opened the first page. Then I saw my own handwriting, remembered the fountain pen I'd used with its peacock blue ink, how I recorded all my undergraduate ups and downs, the moodiness of those rainy springs, the dates I anticipated, even those for coffee on Sunday afternoons. Turning to the second page, I saw someone had used a thick black felt-tipped pen to scribble in the margins, write and circle numbers in the text. It was Carlo's handwriting, I knew. He must have found the journal when he helped me unpack a box of my things shortly after I met him. This is man number 5, he wrote on one page, Number 8, he wrote on another. Then later, in heavier, clumsier script, Putana, written five or six times. The word in his slanted and squared-off handwriting looked explosively obscene. Carlo had filled the first blank page with a long malediction, half in Italian and half in English, cursing me for promiscuity and callousness.

"There's something very wrong with the guy," Giacomo said, his face creased and dark. "I'm going to talk to him."

"No, no." I folded the wrapping around the journal, smoothed down the cellophane tape until it stuck again, annoyance as dull as a headache making me want to fling the journal into a nearby trash bin. "He's just making himself look ridiculous. He won't go any farther than this." I thought awhile about how far he'd already gone, nursed my annoyance until it opened out into anger, then self-righteousness. I was beyond him and his curses, wouldn't waste my time worrying about him. Then I pushed away a dark thought—I didn't want to understand that Carlo's obsessiveness was escalating, and the cumulative effect of his actions could be destructive for us both.

"Let's go to Gilli's for a lemonade," I said. "I want to relax before my Italian lesson."

Giacomo pushed open the heavy doors of the post office, looked up and down the block, then cocked his head for me to follow. I rolled my eyes. "Just because you're paranoid doesn't mean they're not out to get you," I said, then crossed over to Piazza Repubblica and its cafes.

⁓

At Signora di Lando's, Valeria seated me on a Savonarola chair in front of a painting of a robed woman brandishing a sword, and facing a painting of Signora's paternal grandmother, clad in a wool suit. I heard Signora's quick, light steps on the wooden floor, then stood when she entered in her velvet slippers.

She sat across from me and smiled—a genuinely pleased smile—at the white package and the copy of Dante's *Paradiso* I'd set on the table between us. Her face was lively and pink, her brown eyes watchful and alert behind her glasses. She seemed to get younger every time I saw her.

"Well," she said, folding her hands in her lap. "We're going to start with Dante today. And you've brought something from Gilli's, my favorite sweet shop. Very thoughtful of you, Elisabetta."

"Please," I said, sitting and looking down at the package, which suddenly seemed festive and perfect with its spiky little tiara of gold ribbon and its faint fragrance of chocolate.

Signora rang a cloisonné bell, and Valeria reappeared with a tray of tea and mineral water. She poured our tea, then pulled a pair of scissors from her apron pocket and snipped the ribbon from the package. When she parted the white paper, Signora clasped her hands together, then leaned forward, snatched up a hazelnut cookie dipped in chocolate, and ate it in three bites. Then she snatched up another and ate it just as quickly.

"So we're having a soirée here," I said and laughed, "reading Dante and eating chocolates."

"A soirée is a female invention, an opportunity for intellectual and physical sisterhood. Soirée, sorella, sisters. You see." She took a bite of a layered, frosted pastry. "Santa Marcella in Rome was the first to have one, when she organized her sisters at her mansion on the Aventine Hill to welcome Saint Jerome. Though he was no intellectual match for her."

Signora settled herself and brushed crumbs from the front of her angora sweater. I was impatient, eager to get on to Dante, but I knew her saint stories were inevitable, so I selected a cookie, sat back, and waited this one out.

"Marcella was a woman of great intellectual ability. In the fourth century, she proposed the existence of bacteria, made a map of the New World, and gave instructions on how to breed a winged lion, which Saint Mark raised in Venice. She invented gunpowder, saw its harm, and hid it in an urn in her mansion, telling everyone the urn contained the ashes of Pope Sixtus, her grandfather."

She removed her heavy glasses, rubbed her eyes, and stared up at the painting of the woman with the sword. "Santa Marcella is one of my particular heroes," she said. "Santa Marcella and Santa Margherita, the virgin martyr."

"Signora, please," I said. "Shall we begin our lesson?"

She blinked at me, her face soft. "Margherita was the daughter of a pagan priest, but she became a Christian and resisted the advances of men, including the town prefect, who denounced her and ordered fabulous ordeals. She was bled by snakes, and made to sleep with wolves and demons. She was swallowed by Satan in the form of a dragon, then emerged to behead him with a sword. Through this all, she remained true. She was inspired and resolute and finally true."

Signora's voice had made me dreamy, and with this last line I relaxed back into the chair and was struck by a wistfulness as heavy as honey. Listening to Signora, watching her smooth, untroubled face, I wished my path were as clear as hers.

I looked up to the painting of Saint Margherita with her sword, then beyond that to the ceiling and its fresco of saints I could now recognize and name. I scanned the salon that had come to seem like home to me, its smells and textures familiar and evocative, thought how entering it made me want to touch everything, open my pores to its sensations, and I felt calm and clean and full of anticipation, as if I'd just emerged from a hot bath, and were cleaning a fogged glass through which I was about to see something startling.

I remembered how I'd found Carlo earlier in the day, skulking along the riverwall, how I'd slipped away into the center of town, used my annoyance to fend him off, when I could have used swords, wings, angelic language, divine music. I was Italian and named after a saint; I could tap into that bloodline. Saint Elizabeth, after all, marched with the Portuguese army. I watched Signora sipping her tea and wondered if she were mad at all, but only cunning.

Then I began to rehearse the lines in Italian I would say to Carlo. He was going too far, that was true, but I had misinterpreted him from the first, and my inability to read him correctly and speak plainly prolonged the animosity between us. It may not have been heroic or angelic, but I knew what to do—my words would be inspired and resolute and finally true.

CYNTHIA MORGAN DALE

Ancient History

IT WAS THE THIRD morning in a row he'd noticed the woman. He was quite certain he knew her, from the rare book room at the library, perhaps. She looked so familiar. She was sitting alone, two tables over on the cobbled terrace, at the very edge of the verandah. It was not yet eight a.m. Theirs were the only two tables occupied. He nodded to his wife of three days and said, "The blonde. I know her. From Cambridge. I'm positive."

His wife broke off a piece of bread, unscrewed the top of a miniature jar of marmalade, and spooned out a generous dollop. Shading her eyes with her hand, she looked up and squinted against the white July morning. The sun rose early down on Italy's cragged coast this time of year. Neither of them had yet acclimated themselves to either the climate or the time zone.

"She looks lonely. She's been by herself every morning," the wife said, indicating that she, too, had noticed the woman. "Why don't you invite her to join us today?" Nonchalantly, she returned to the task at hand, the preparing of her bread.

The lone woman looked American. She had long dirty blonde hair and a bottled tan. She was wearing dark sunglasses and a sundress, that faded green color of a much-used American Express card, the waist of which was belted loosely with a drab mustard sash. There was a guidebook propped open at her bare, bangled elbow. The man noted that it was in English. A good 35mm camera rested in front of her, lens cap off, ready to shoot. But it was her feet that gave her away; her toes slid easily between the rubber thongs of a pair of cushiony Crayola-green flip-flops, the type sold for $1.99 at the checkout counter of every discount drugstore back home.

The man took a roll from the breadbasket, broke it, and buttered it slowly, turning his attention back to his wife. The couple ate lazily, smiling conspiratorially across their coffees as only lovers do.

"*Bon giorno.*" A waiter wearing a starched white jacket approached the woman. He was tall and dark with a chiseled chin, a long narrow nose, and deep-set eyes that soft welcoming color of melted chocolate. He set a basket of fruit down in front of her. Apricots. Pears. Plums. Then he poured coffee from a heavy ceramic pot into an oversized enameled saucer. Tangerine and turquoise patterned fish swam in circles around the saucer's brim, their mouths wide open, gaping, each one nearly catching the tail of the fish in front of it.

"*Grazie,*" the woman said, making it three long syllables. Her voice drifted lazily across the terrace. A man she'd met in Rome two days earlier had taught her to pronounce the word properly over Camparis one evening in a sprawling café in the Piazza Novona. As dusk settled on the city, he made her repeat the word over and over again until she had it right. Later, in a darkened doorway near her hotel, a stone's throw from the Spanish Steps, he had pressed her back against a cold stucco wall and kissed her suddenly, softly and expertly, in the warm summer rain. The first kiss since Charles. "*Grazie*," she had whispered afterwards, ducking under his arm, escaping into the tiled and potted palm foyer of her hotel. As his shadow, elongated by the evening hour, disappeared, she had hugged her bare arms tightly around her damp body and smiled for the first time in ten days.

She was a day's journey south of Rome now in a popular resort town along the Amalfi Drive. The pace of life lagged down here, for which she was grateful. She took an apricot from the bowl of fruit and bit into it. The fruit was deeply bruised and the juice dripped slowly down her chin.

From across the terrace, the husband, still trying to place her, watched as she flicked a bead of juice away from her chin with the tip of her finger.

Down below, the town stretched awake. The hotel sat high above the stiff cliffs. Terraced rows of pretty pastel houses rippled down to the black beach. The cabanas below were still closed, their striped umbrellas neatly folded, bound tight with thick canvas ties. Random sounds punctuated the early morning. A bird squawking. The dull buzz of a moped rounding the bend. Dishes clattering. The clip clop of the waiter's sandals clapping against the naked cobblestone. Twice, the impatient honking of a horn.

The woman gazed over the low stone wall. A thorny cluster of pale pink roses in full bloom framed her view. The sea below was flat and smooth. The tall masts of three wooden sloops pierced the cloudless sky. The glassy blues of the sky and sea were nearly indistinguishable. In the distance the woman could hear the rhythms of a steady, measured crawl stroke coming from the pool. An old man from the outskirts of Paris, staying at the hotel for the summer, swam sixty laps every morning. She'd had a faltering conversation with him, half in French and half in English, while sitting at the terrace bar the night before last. The old man was a painter. His wife had died of lung cancer six months ago. It was only when he was swimming, he had confided in her, that he was able to forget. As she listened to the old man's steady stroke, she imagined the cool water brushing his skin, salving his wounds.

She sipped her coffee, enjoying her solitude until, abruptly, the clear unmistakable Boston accent of the man two tables over broke her reverie.

"It's beautiful, isn't it?"

She looked up, momentarily shaken. He was standing over her, looking down. "Yes, it is nice, isn't it?" she answered. He was tall and lean with a thick head of wavy coal black hair. His eyes were the same color as the sea below, or nearly so. He hadn't shaved that morning and a bristly stubble darkened his narrow jaw. He was wearing running shorts and a faded Boston Red Sox T-shirt.

She'd noticed him watching her, of course. In fact, for a split second on first sighting him three days ago, she could have sworn she knew him. He was someone from her past possibly, a bit character only, one she could no longer quite place. Seeing him again that second morning though, sipping at her coffee, nibbling on a buttered roll, she was less certain, positive that she didn't know him, had, in fact, never seen him before in her life. But now, at close range like this, the prickly rash of recognition rose again. She'd noticed the woman with him, too. His wife, she'd correctly presumed. She looked to be her own age, early thirties, maybe a year or two older. She was petite, with pale porcelain skin, pretty in a plain, New England sort of way. By the way the couple looked at each other, how their knees touched lightly beneath the glass top of the wrought-iron table, she guessed they were newlyweds, most likely on their honeymoon. This place was a good choice for it.

She grimaced at the irony. It was to have been her honeymoon, too. Until Charles had jilted her two weeks earlier, six days shy of the altar, explaining in a short, terse note that he was in love with a marine biologist named Star whom he had met changing planes in San Francisco three weeks earlier. Star lived in a solar heated house on one of the San Juan islands off the coast of Seattle. He was going west, the inadequate note explained, moving in with Star and her two golden retrievers, Alpha and Omega, as soon as he could break his lease in New York and arrange a transfer to the west coast of the engineering firm he worked for. It was the first, and only, unpredictable thing he had done in the three and a half years she had known him.

He'd left her brokenhearted. He'd also left her with a paid-in-full wedding and honeymoon. Monogrammed matchbooks. One thousand dollars worth of lilies, orchids and gladiolas, primarily in pink and purple. A five-piece jazz band. This hotel. The place had been Charles' choice. Why not go anyway, she'd thought, still stunned by the sudden turn of events.

"You're from the States." It was a statement, not a question.

"New York. And you?"

"Cambridge." He moved closer.

"Ah—" There was a tiny gap between his two front teeth. She remembered it, but from where?

"I could have sworn I knew you. From Cambridge. I said to my wife—" He nodded at his wife who, her dark head bent, her hands cupped around the porcelain saucer, sipped coffee tentatively. "I know that woman."

She shook her head. At arm's length the initial flicker of recognition dissolved. Once again, she was certain that she didn't know him. A pale crescent scar marred his left cheek. She would have remembered that. Besides, this sort of thing happened to her often. She had a common look, features that were malleable, easily stretched this way or that by memory into someone else's.

"Joy," she offered. "Joy Barnes."

"Matt Green," he said. He nodded again at the woman. "And that's Andy, my wife. It's short for Andrea, after the Andrea Doria. She was born the day it went down." He grinned, a grin that was immediately infectious.

"You're on your honeymoon?"

"Yes. And you?"

"Holiday. Two weeks."

"You're alone?"

"Yes."

He nodded at the guidebook splayed open on the table beside her. The spine of the book was cracked. "A good guide?"

"It's okay."

"Where have you been? Capri? Down to Paestum?"

She shook her head. "Nowhere yet. I was thinking maybe Pompeii today, but

I'm not sure how to get there. Is there a bus? A guided tour?"

"None of the above." He smiled broadly, that winning grin again, a grin she could easily imagine falling for under different circumstances. "Come with us. We're going today. We've already rented a car, and are leaving in an hour."

She started to say no, not wanting to be a third wheel.

"Seriously, we'd like the company." He read her mind. "We've talked to no one but each other for three days now, and Andy's great. You'll like her. You'd be welcome."

"Okay," she agreed somewhat hesitantly. One of the things she'd always liked about traveling abroad was encounters like this, the spontaneity sparked among strangers. It was the sort of thing that never happened back home, except maybe at the San Francisco airport.

"We'll meet in the lobby in an hour." He touched her bare elbow lightly, eliciting a tiny tremor of electricity. "See you then."

Joy watched as Matt and his wife climbed the long marble staircase and headed toward the north wing of rooms. She imagined them making hurried after-breakfast love, simple sex on full stomachs and an unmade bed, quickly before the maid arrived, before the designated hour dissolved. Fleetingly, she thought how it could easily have been she and Charles dampening the same crisp cotton sheets.

For a moment, she allowed herself to think of Charles and the way he used to make love to her. How he would turn her softly in the early morning sunlight, untangling her from the sheets, reaching for her breasts from behind, moving gently against her curved back, whispering, quietly, endearments into her ear. She wondered if he made love to Star in the same manner, then stopped herself abruptly. It was no good to dwell on what was not to be. It was time to forget. Why, yesterday she had only thought of him every forty minutes or so! She was making progress.

⁓

"I'm an archæologist," Matt said, one hand on the steering wheel of the compact rent-a-car, the other stretched loosely across the back of the front seat. Joy watched as his fingers played softly with his wife's bare shoulder. The car zipped speedily around a second curve, far too sharply to be safe, Joy was sure. She closed her eyes to avoid looking down, vertigo descending.

"Pompeii and Herculaneum. I studied them both in grad school. Did you know that Pompeii was only accidentally discovered in 1748?" He paused. "There's a story, probably apocryphal, about a farmer working the land who discovered an enormous stone phallus. It was something like two feet long."

Joy noticed Matt and Andy exchange sly smiles.

"Exploration was interrupted for a while following the Napoleonic Wars," Matt continued. "It picked up again after the French occupation in 1799. Still, even today, there are whole sections yet to be excavated."

"You've been here before?" Joy asked, once again averting her eyes from the steep cliff they had just zoomed around. All she knew about Pompeii was what she'd read in her Michelin guide earlier that morning: that on the morning of August 24, A.D. 79, Mount Vesuvius erupted, completely burying the town of Pompeii before the day was done, preserving for all eternity the city and the remains of those who had not heeded earlier warnings.

"No, this is his first trip." Andy answered for him. "It was one of his stipulations for marrying me," she laughed. "That we honeymoon here."

It had been Charles' first choice, too. He'd been here once before, a back-packing undergraduate conquering the continent on five dollars a day. He'd camped on a pebbled beach south of here, in a cove that curved inward to a grotto that was, back then a least, undiscovered. One morning, he liked to tell her, he awoke to the most glorious sunrise he'd ever seen. He'd vowed then that this was where he would honeymoon. Flying solo to Rome at 45,000 feet above the Atlantic, Joy wondered if he would book the exact same trip if he married Star. Perhaps the trip was the thing and the brides were interchangeable.

Matt squeezed Andy's shoulder and gave her another of his smiles. "We wrote ahead," he continued. "We're getting a private tour. You'll come along, of course. There's this one house, the house of Marcus Flavius Rufus, that I particularly want to see. They're still excavating. It'll be years before it's open to the public. It was one of the largest houses in Pompeii. Very different, architecturally."

"He's been talking about that house for years." Andy looked up at her husband. Pride flushed her pale face. "We've even got a scale model of it, which Matt built as part of his thesis, on the dining room table back home."

"Took me ten months to build," Matt filled in.

"It took us months, getting permission. We wrote eleven letters in all, to government officials, local authorities. It was amazing. For awhile there, we never thought we'd hear. Even with Matt's Harvard connections and all—"

"Then one day, two weeks ago—"

"Ten days, really. There was a letter saying that a private tour had been arranged for today—"

Joy envied the way the two talked in terms of we and finished each other's sentences. She tried to remember if she and Charles had ever dovetailed quite so effortlessly.

"We're meeting a man who's conducting the excavation at one," Matt said. "He's agreed to give us an hour of his time. I still can't believe it."

"I tease him," Andy laughed, "that the tour will be the highlight of our honeymoon."

Matt grinned at Andy. "It'll be a hard act to follow." Impulsively, he leaned over and kissed her. Joy clenched her eyes closed, certain they were about to careen down the sharp embankment as a result of the couple's spontaneous tenderness.

"You've lucked out. Hooking up with us today," Matt said, his hand back on the steering wheel, certain death averted once again. "This is a once in a lifetime opportunity. You won't be sorry you came."

"Yes," Joy said distractedly. She was only half listening, and was, in fact, not thinking about Pompeii at all. What she was thinking about, against her will, was Charles. She wondered if he'd called her answering machine back in New York, checking to see where she was, if she'd gone anyway as she'd threatened to do in one of many teary telephone calls, taking their "honeymoon" trip alone.

"Enough on Pompeii," Andy said. "Tell us about you. You're from New York? Matt's family's from Brooklyn originally. What do you do there?"

"I'm a package designer at a design firm," Joy said. "We do mostly health and beauty products. You know, shampoos, soaps, toothpastes."

"Ah, an artist!" Matt eyed her narrowly in the rearview mirror. The way he squinted triggered something in the back of her brain.

"No, not really. I sold out." She gave them an apologetic shrug. "It's pure commerce, what I do."

"Oh, but it's still creative," Andy offered.

"It pays the rent," Joy said flatly. Matt was watching her in the mirror, his dark eyebrows furrowed together. It unsettled her.

"You're not married?" he asked abruptly.

"No," she said, offering no further explanation, not wanting to get into the whole Charles thing.

"Your day will come," Andy said. "Why, look at me!"

⌒

They were halfway to Naples, off the curving Amalfi Drive, on the wide Autostrada leading into town when she remembered how she knew him. It was a long time ago, in a small college town in upstate New York, on a cold November weekend just prior to Thanksgiving break. She, in fact, was already on break, visiting an old high school friend, a girl named Susan she had long since lost touch with. It was a Friday night and it was snowing hard. They had gone to a fraternity party on campus, at Phi Gamma Delta, she recalled dimly. There, across the proverbial crowded room, she'd seen that amazing grin of his. "Don't I know you?" he'd asked, just as he had this morning out on the terrace. "No, but I'd like to," she'd replied, so much braver back then.

Later, they'd walked across the campus through the swirling snow. She remembers how he had whirled her in wide circles down by the gazebo on the square, swinging her like a child in a game of statues, landing her softly on the deepening snow, pinning her flatly and kissing her long and hard against the frozen ground. The snow fell lightly, like volcanic ash, dusting them in white. They had flapped their arms, scissored their legs, and made matching snow angels. Much later, in a single bed on the third floor of his dorm, they had fallen asleep, spoonlike, beneath a heavy patchwork quilt, one that his grandmother from Brooklyn had made. They had not made love.

Somewhere in the middle of the night, they had awakened and talked until the sun rose. She had told him she was going to be a painter. Not abstract, but landscapes and pastorals. He said he was studying archæology. He had kissed her then, the snow still falling outside the window, and told her she had the shoulders of a Roman goddess.

In the morning, they had breakfast together in the school cafeteria. Bagels and cream cheese and cup after cup of watery coffee. Afterwards, he walked her to the parking lot where her friend was impatiently waiting, standing in the cold next to her packed Pinto, ready to go. He had kissed her good-bye in the gray, misty morning with a Bogart-like panache. At his request, she had written her name and address on the inside cover of his copy of Plato's *Republic*. He had promised to write.

He never did.

⌒

The road leading to Pompeii was flanked with kiosks selling all kinds of souvenirs, cold drinks, Italian ices.

"It's impossible to escape, isn't it?" Andy nodded at a man motioning tourists towards a table of miniature battery operated models of the volcano. "What will they think of next?"

Matt shook his head. "Who buys that stuff?"

Joy frowned. She was a saver. Back home she had T-shirts, coffee mugs, kitchy reminders from every trip she'd ever taken. She had ten albums full of photographs, too, the last three devoted exclusively to Charles. Impulsively, she lifted the camera from around her neck, popped off the lens cap and took two quick shots of the row of souvenir stands from her open window. The man behind the second kiosk waved as the shutter clicked.

"We'll park here." Matt pulled the car into a nearly empty lot. He handed the attendant a five thousand lira note. "*Grazia*," he said. The attendant, a scrawny fellow wearing a California Raisins T-shirt, deftly pocketed the bill. In the distance, Vesuvius rose majestically, cutting through the smoggy summer sky. The mountain looked so harmless. It was hard to imagine her angrily spewing out hot lava, pumice and mud, catching off guard all those nonbelievers who hadn't heeded the days of warnings, freezing them for all eternity.

Matt gazed up. He shielded his eyes with his left hand. A ray of sun caught his wedding band and sent out a splintering flash of light. "Wow!" he said, his wonderment unabashed.

Andy took his free hand in hers. "At long last," she said. Joy watched as the pleasure flushed her pale face.

It was only ten-thirty, but already the sun beat down relentlessly. The thermometer outside the entrance gate read ninety-five, and it was in the shade. The guidebook had strongly suggested bringing a hat. Joy was instantly sorry she hadn't heeded the advice. She tied her hair up on top of her head in a loose knot and was thankful, at least, that she had worn shorts and comfortable shoes.

Even before they were through the entrance gate, they were besieged by pith-hatted, mostly middle-aged men offering their services. The men's skins were creased leathery brown from days, weeks, years in the sun. "Guided tours, cheap! Very cheap!" they called out, fanning themselves lightly with brightly colored guidebooks for which they would surely charge extra.

Matt haggled in Italian with one, settling on a price. The guide told them his name was Romeo. He was tall and bony and had one gold front tooth. Romeo led them briskly through the dusty streets of Pompeii, rattling off a canned speech as they sped through forums, gardens, private houses. They paused briefly now and then at a painted fresco, a terra-cotta vase, a stone effigy. Joy had never been so close to death before, even to death so many times removed by geography and time. The frozen bodies of the long forgotten caused her breath to catch. She snapped picture after picture, changing film twice in under an hour.

Romeo hurried them on. They lingered in a tiny room filled with phallic symbols and watched a clutch of English schoolgirls giggle and point shyly at the oversize organs. Matt expanded on Romeo's cursory monologue, dispensing more details than Joy could ever hope to digest. Andy glowed brighter with every new piece of ancient history he imparted.

At a quarter to one the tour was over. They were back where they had started. Romeo, his palm plainly extended, thanked them very much. He pointed them in the general direction of the entrance where they were to meet their guide for their private tour. "That way," he said in his practiced English, his eyes already scanning the crowds in search of his next customer.

The three of them walked slowly through the dusty streets towards the information kiosk. The sun was now directly overhead, beating down. Matt glanced nervously at his watch, but there was really no rush. Italian time, Joy had learned, had its own clock. One o'clock didn't mean one o'clock, but more likely two or two-fifteen.

They sat on the stoop by the policia station to wait. Matt bought three ice cream bars which melted quickly under the midday sun. He drummed his fingers lightly against Andy's rapidly reddening thigh and checked his watch every few minutes. Joy could tell he was nervous. But then again, he had a right to be. He had waited so long for this moment. She understood.

"What if he doesn't come?" He took out the letter stating the date, time and place of the appointed tour and read it out loud again.

"He'll come. Don't worry," Andy said, lightly touching his bare knee in response.

"We've come four thousand miles for this. I've been waiting a lifetime for this. What if—"

Suddenly, a short stocky man in cool khaki-colored clothes approached them. "Mr. Green?" he asked. It was 2:27 digital watch time. Seven-thirty a.m. in New York, the middle of the night in Seattle, Joy thought, calculating the hour back through the time zones, as she'd been doing regularly since her arrival. She wondered idly if Charles and Star were making love. The narrow corridor of time just before dawn had always been his favorite hour. Often she would awaken from a dream to find him kissing her, pressed against her, already hard.

Matt leapt up. "Yes! I'm Mr. Green!"

"My name is Antonio. I am your guide." He eyed the women critically. "Who are these?"

"My wife and an old friend of ours." Matt reached for Andy's hand and gestured towards Joy with his free hand.

The "old" did not escape Joy.

"The letter does not say three—"

"But—" Matt's face fell.

"Go without us," Andy offered, disappointment clearly clouding her face. "It's okay. We'll wait here."

Antonio looked the women over again. "Never mind. Let's go. But you no touch, *capite?*"

Joy and Andy nodded solemnly in unison.

"And no photographs, *capite?*"

"Right, no photographs. We understand." Matt answered for all of them.

"What, no photographs?" Now it was Joy's disappointment that was transparent. She had been taking pictures non-stop since their arrival and had just loaded a new roll of film.

"No, no photographs," Antonio said gruffly. He narrowed his eyes and stared at the 35mm dangling between Joy's breasts. She lifted the camera over her head, screwed on the lens cap, and dropped it in her canvas tote. Antonio flashed a satisfied smile. Then, he was off, Matt fast at his heels, the two women scrambling to keep up five or six yards behind them.

From the outside, the house was nothing much to look at, just a low-slung wall with several evenly spaced windows, set behind a tall iron fence a good foot too high to scale. Antonio pulled a large loop of keys from his pocket, inserted one, and swung the gate open. He selected a second key and unlocked a heavy wooden door. "*Avanti,*" he called pushing the door open with the palm of his hand.

The three followed him as he briskly made his way through a maze of narrow corridors. They came to stop at last in a large, dark room. "Welcome to Casa di Marcus Flavius Rufus, once the house of a very rich and powerful man," he said in choppy English. A cool dampness surrounded them. There was little light and Joy had trouble adjusting her eyes. She took off her sunglasses, which were prescription, and blinked blindly. Slowly the room came into fuzzy focus. It was much larger than anything she had expected. Two tall stone columns flanked the back wall. A large picture window offered a sweeping panorama of what Antonio told them was once the sea. From the window, the people of the house must have seen everything. The ships coming into port with cargo or trade. The comings and goings of those from neighboring towns. And, on that fateful day, the slow but steady stream of citizens who had wisely heeded the early warnings, departing Pompeii. Finally, the flood of lava when it was already far too late.

"Oh my God!" Matt whispered. He circled the room, repeating the three words again and again, like a litany.

"*Avanti*," Antonio waved them on impatiently. They sped through two more rooms then descended, single file, down a narrow wooden staircase. It got even darker and Joy had to adjust her eyes again.

Matt repeated his three-word refrain at each turn, more reverently each time.

Joy started counting. By the time they got to the bottom of the stairs, he had said "Oh my God!" eleven times.

The house, it turned out, was very deceptive from the outside. There was room after room filled with mosaics, sculptures, ancient artifacts. One center room was blocked with scaffolding. Against the back wall, restoration on a mural was in progress. Joy studied the scene. It was a pastoral thick with birds, flowers and butterflies in a field of green, the kind of thing she had always imagined she would paint. "*Avanti*," Antonio called, impatient with their progress. They descended yet a second staircase to a lower level, what was once sea level.

It was there that they came unexpectedly upon the child. His body was crouched low, his elbow raised skyward, blocking his face. There was no encasement. For a moment, Joy was sorely tempted to reach out and touch the child's frozen elbow, as if by simply touching him she could bring him back to life. She leaned forward, her hand extended. Antonio cast her a dark glare and spat out a string of words in Italian. The words were foreign, but she understood their meaning. Joy stepped back and folded her arms squarely under her chest to dispel his concern.

"Oh my God!" Matt whispered for the twenty-third time. "Would you look at that?" He crouched in front of the child's body. Andy squatted beside him and took his hand.

The tour, true to the letter's word, lasted exactly one hour. As they emerged back into the sunlight, Joy looked at Matt. She was certain she had never before in her life seen anyone as happy as Matt was at that moment. Then she turned and saw Andy, and knew that she was wrong.

"Look at him," Andy beamed. "Have you ever seen anyone happier?"

Joy turned to her. "Yes, you."

Andy's face flushed. Her eyes sparkled. She knew how lucky she was, and she knew that Joy knew, too.

"He'll be talking about this forever," Andy said quietly. "On our golden anniversary, I'll still be hearing about today."

"You're very lucky. Both of you," Joy said.

"I know," Andy whispered. She looked Joy in the eye without blinking. "I never thought I would be lucky like this. I never thought someone else's happiness could matter more than my own But it does, and it's wonderful. The most wonderful thing."

Standing there on the dusty streets of Pompeii, under the blistering late afternoon sun, a shiver running down her spine, Joy knew as surely as she'd ever known anything before that she had never truly loved Charles. Oh sure, they got along well enough. They liked the same movies, read the same books, and were better than average in bed. But they'd never been happy, at least not happy like Andy and Matt were right then. The knowledge swept over her, catching her by surprise, in much the same way that she imagined that hot wave of lava caught that child at play nearly two centuries earlier.

Yes, Matt and Andy were lucky. She knew instinctively that the old man from Paris, the morning swimmer back at the hotel, and his dead wife had been, too. Perhaps Star and Charles were as well. Much to her surprise, she found herself hoping they were. She remembered in a flash the shiver that had shimmied down her spine four days ago when a near stranger had kissed her in the Rome rain. Why, love could tap her on the shoulder tomorrow, the day after, next week, or, she conceded grimly, not at all.

~

After Pompeii they headed for Herculaneum. It would be a sin not to go, Matt said. After all, they were so close. The short drive was clogged with traffic and took longer than expected. The whole way Matt talked nonstop about the house, as if verbally pinching himself to make sure it was real.

At Herculaneum, they paid their entrance fees and roamed the grassy, largely deserted streets. The town was smaller, and much greener, than Pompeii, but no less daunting. Joy snapped another complete roll of film.

By six o'clock they were all very tired, drained by the heat and the history of the day. "Let's go," Matt said. "We've had enough for one day. Hell, I've had enough for a lifetime. Today surpassed my wildest dreams." He put an arm around each of the girls' shoulders and guided them towards the car.

Surpassing dreams. Matt's words lingered. Joy thought of her own dreams. Marrying Charles, living happily ever after. Becoming a painter. What a hoax her entire life had been! She had been forever sidestepping happiness, settling for less, believing all those things the women's magazines would have you believe. That alone was not lonely. That you didn't need another. That happiness didn't require two. She watched Matt bend his head toward Andy's and thought, not morbidly at all, that should their car crash on the journey home, careen down one of the steep cliffs as Princess Grace's car had on that curving road to Monaco, this life would have been enough for them. A line from a song she couldn't quite place popped into her head. "If it suddenly ended tomorrow . . ." She thought of Pompeii and floods and major airplane crashes and earthquakes. She thought of random shootings and nuclear war and incurable diseases and the multitude of other dangers that lurked around every corner, things that you could never see, dangers like delayed planes at airports that changed your entire life, and she grew very scared. Why, she hadn't even scratched the surface yet!

Outside of town they stopped at a small *tabaccheria* for cold beers and pressed cheese sandwiches. Except for the ice cream bars, they hadn't eaten since breakfast at the hotel. Joy was hungry and very thirsty. The dark shop was long and narrow. An old woman, her ample chest drooped to her waist, her rounded back curved by time, pushed a wet mop across the floor, sweeping away at imaginary dirt. At the bar there were three worn stools with cracked leather seats. Matt selected the middle one. Overhead, a ceiling fan slowly circulated the thick summer air. Italian music played softly in the background. The barkeep was reading a newspaper, smoking a cigarette. Matt got his attention and ordered three Peronis. Joy sat to Matt's left. The two of them drank their beers quickly. Andy sipped at hers more slowly, then excused herself for the ladies' room. When she was gone, Matt ordered them two more beers. The barkeep slid the sweaty bottles across the bar. It was the first time they had been alone all day. Joy lifted her beer in a toast. "To you and Andy. Continued happiness," she said.

"1975. Union College," Matt replied, startling her.

"What?" She tried to mask her surprise, making her response confusion and not acknowledgment. "What are you taking about?" She could tell by his eyes that she had failed.

"We made snow angels on the square. You were going to be an artist." He was looking directly at her, his hands folded in his lap.

"You must have me confused with someone else," she replied steadily. "Lots of people do that. Confuse me with someone." She averted her eyes, lifted her beer again and took a long swallow. Her hand was shaking.

"I'm sorry I never wrote." He reached out with his left hand, the one with his wedding band, nearly touching her bare arm. Her arm was tinged red, burned from the day spent under the hot Italian sun, but goose bumps rose anyway, as if it were midwinter back home.

For a moment she thought to feign sudden memory, but stopped herself. It was ancient history. It was one night, a night long buried under layer upon layer of memory, and nothing more. Sure, there had been disappointment when he didn't write, but in the end it was only one disappointment in a long line of disappointments that life dealt you. It didn't matter now, if it ever had. What she had learned today, in the company of Matt and Andy in the long, cool corridors of the House of Marcus Flavius Rufus, was that it was not dreams dashed that mattered, only dreams realized.

"You're a lucky man," she said, looking him in the eye for the first time all day. "Your wife—"

"My wife is the best thing that's ever happened to me." He cut her off. "I never dreamed I'd be so lucky."

"Who does?" Unconsciously, she wrapped her arms protectively across her chest.

"Your turn will come," he said, finally touching her elbow, making her bare skin prickle.

"How'd you meet? I'm curious," Joy asked impulsively.

"Standing in line to buy beer at a Bob Dylan concert in Buffalo." Matt shrugged his shoulders at the ordinariness of it all.

Joy nodded. It was right.

Just then Andy rejoined them. "Your turn." She smiled at Joy. "But be forewarned. There's no toilet paper."

"Thanks." Joy grabbed a stack of coarse napkins from the bar. The soles of her feet squeaked against the newly mopped floor. She was still hugging her chest. Quietly, she thanked Charles, for leaving her. Tomorrow she would buy a postcard, one picturing Pompeii, and send it to him. She would say that she understood, and she would wish him well. She would say that she forgave him. As she closed the bathroom stall behind her, she began composing the postcard in her head.

Back at the bar, Matt kissed Andy. "I spoke to her," he said. "She pretended not to remember."

Andy nodded. "That's what I thought she'd do."

"Me, too." He gripped Andy's stool and turned it so she was facing him. Bending forward, he kissed her again. "I love you, Mrs. Green," he said.

Andy leaned into the kiss and their two heads became one.

"*Amore*," the old woman muttered. She turned her hunched back on the couple and pushed her mop brusquely across the same stretch of floor.

GRETCHEN GAD FOURNIER

Are There People . . .

I SNATCH MY GLASSES from the bureau, march over to the window, and fling open the two white wooden shutters. Their loud slam against the concrete apartment building echoes throughout the courtyard and sends a family of gray and white pigeons bobbing up onto the sheet-metal roof. Falling chips of white paint fade into the air as I look down and finally identify the peculiar noise that has persistently interrupted my sleep—explosive sprays of water are slapping the cement tiles five flights below me. Madame Carrasqueira, the building's concierge, is gripping a thick green waterhose, spraying off the tiles, and looking as if she is desperately extinguishing a fire rather than rinsing off the collected grime.

She is a stout, ordinary looking woman with dark hair and eyes. She emigrated from Portugal about ten years ago, although her accent as she greets the passersby sounds as if she arrived last week. She spends her days in slippers and an apron, and for a small fee does extra cleaning, washing, and ironing for some of the tenants. She must have heard the slamming shutters because she turns, looks up my way, and shouts, "*Bonjour mademoiselle, Ça va?*" I lean out over the wrought-iron ledge and answer with a simple, "*Bonjour!*" She hasn't changed a bit.

Paris. The sounds and smells of the city are exactly as I had left them. I stand by the window, breathing the cool air, comfortably recognizing everything around me. Emissions from some distant industrial smokestack abandon a stale burn in the air, honking cars blaze through the streets, and motorbikes shriek by.

Our secluded courtyard is charming. There are pale white concrete walls on all four connected sides and the white shutter-filled windows are stacked evenly atop one another—some open and some closed, some with red window-boxed geraniums, and some veiled with sheer white curtains; we are all acquainted.

This is my second summer in the apartment at 49 rue des Martyrs. François-Pierre and I have come a long way, in so many ways. Including the airplane's "routine" engine failure and waiting between flights, the trip from Fargo to Detroit to Paris topped seventeen hours. But from the time I fell in love with the handsome foreign exchange student in high school and the first time we flew to Paris together, three years had passed—two divided into a Christmas vacation here and a summer there, while astronomical telephone bills clogged all the lonely time inbetween. The third year François-Pierre returned to Fargo, settled in with me, and entered a university in western Minnesota. We indeed came a long way in both distance and persistence.

We arrived two days ago, but spent most of the first evening unpacking, eating, and talking with his mother, Ray-Christine, and her companion Emmanuel. Not much was new. Edith Cresson, the new prime minister of France, was the latest topic, and the last one I remember discussing. I think I've been sleeping ever since.

I turn from the window yawning and rub my eyes. I notice a note taped to the digital clock on the bureau. Lit up in green, the clock reads "13:21" and the note says: "Gretch—You were sleeping so well I just couldn't wake you. I went to get a haircut, check on my army obligations, make a dentist appointment, and take care of as much as I can right away. Help yourself to anything—I'll be home early evening. An extra key is on top of the TV and a *pain au chocolat* is on the table. I love you. *A plus tard*—Fp."

I flip on the stereo, pop in a Lloyd Cole cassette, and head straight for the table. The hardwood floor is cold under my bare feet and lets out a muffled cracking sound as I enter the living room. A voice screams from the apartment below, "*Oh ça suffit le haut! C'est pas fini oui!*" I squeeze my eyes closed, clench my fists, and stop dead in my tracks. "Oh the woman below," I murmur. She is hysterical. I once found it funny, at least amusing when she'd explode over the smallest of noises—a dropped fork, a chair edged against the floor, even laughter. But as I tiptoe the rest of the way to the table, I recall Emmanuel telling us late in the night of our last departure that he'd learned, via Madame Carrasqueira, that the woman, as well as being a high-school math teacher, is old, alone, viciously embittered, and presumably a bit off-balance. She is a virtual recluse who, I imagine, survives through these one-sided communications and false dramas. She's never really reacted beyond her infernal wails. I think she craves the noise; we may be the only people she talks to. A year later and she is still here.

Floating ghosts of cigarette smoke and traces of Christine's bitter Yves Saint Laurent perfume hang in the air. I hold my breath, open another window, and carefully sit down at the table to eat.

Christine has really cleaned the place and somehow made room for our three-months worth of clothes. The apartment is extremely small, but quaint. Basically two rooms, the living room, with a gold-striped couch that converts into her bed, and "the other room," where we stay, which is the closet space, the library, the music room, François-Pierre's bedroom, and anything else it needs to be. The kitchen is on the other side of the living room and is about the size of a roomy telephone booth. Otherwise, between the living room, our room, and the front door, the cramped bathroom holds a toilet, a sink, a shower, and a miniature washing machine.

The apartment has a great deal of character, regardless of size. Christine decorated the place in various shades of gold and blue. The top half of the walls is covered in gold burlap-like fabric and the bottom half is painted off-white. Across from the table a small fireplace bulges from the wall. Instead of ashes or wood, a tall blue-stucco vase pervades the hearth with bunches of white and yellow daisies, bright blue delphiniums, yellow gaillardia, and tall red lilies. Christine buys freshly-cut flowers in a small shop across the street to fill the cast-iron cavity.

While I sit back eating the last bite of pastry, I stare into a young man's cold marble eyes—a sculpture resting on the mantle's left end. The icy white piece is a smooth replica of the early Roman head effigies now housed a few miles away in the Louvre.

Between the fireplace and the couch stands a tall dark wood cabinet packed with leather-bound volumes of celebrated French literature—Moliére, Sand, Sartre, Voltaire—family photographs propped up in gold frames, and a delicate crystal clock.

Assorted hanging lithographs fill the walls with color, depth, and a certain mystery. I notice a new one near the fireplace—a limited scene of a simple open window with shadows in the foreground and a barely traceable city through its pane. I have seen all the others before, but they are rearranged. Christine likes change. I don't know her, mainly because she works most of the time (she is the director of Le Parc de Montfort, a highly posh retirement complex just west of Paris), but I know she likes change. In the short time I will see her, she might change her hair style and color two or three times. Sometimes long, straight, and dark brown; then shorter, curly, and auburn; and other times severely short with her natural brown and hints of gray. One day she'll wear a flowery silk dress and the next she'll be clad in black leather. And we constantly find variety in dinner—one night pizza, the next couscous, and the next quiche. I am anxious to know her, for him.

Since Christine works into the evening and François-Pierre will be out for a while, I decide to spend the afternoon outside. I shower, slip on my jeans and a white T-shirt, pull my hair back, and lock the door behind me.

I jog down the wood steps, turning at each flight until I come to the enormous mirror at the end of the staircase, where I fuss with my clothes a bit and then proceed through the courtyard. The cement tiles are still wet from the waterhosing, and small pools of water have formed in the crevices. As I slop across, Madame Carrasqueira taps her fingernail on her apartment window and waves out to me. She invariably greets me with a smile. It seems as though she always tries to help me feel more at home in this big city, a city where, other than the Fourniers, I know no one. I suppose she understands what it means to be a foreigner and thinks she can give me something she perhaps never had—a warm smile and an easy "*Bonjour!*" It is simple, but each time it actually makes me feel completely comfortable, like home, at least for a moment. I wave back, returning a smile, and go on my way.

I step up into the dark musty corridor that leads to the door on the street. I reach the massive brown door, press the lighted porte button, and with a click, I am out.

The street is busier than I remembered—people buzzing in and out of shops. Rue des Martyrs is a great street, not crazy like the Champs Elysèes, but alive. The sky is gray and the air is full with a million different smells—exhaust fumes from the cars, newly baked bread from the nearby boulangeries, lingering perfumes, the sweet smell of flowers from street vendors, and especially, the stench from the fresh fish market two doors down. All the smells inform me that this is a place I already know.

The buildings look alike. Every facade is ordered with shutter-filled windows identical to those on our apartment. Pressed one against another along both sides of the street, each building appears to be an extension of the next. The cement structures stretch up high with only subtle variations in color, alternating between brownish-gray and yellowish-white. The dull colors are not unattractive, though; they make a wonderful backdrop for all the bright red, green, and blue awnings hanging outside the shops. This section of Paris, the 9th *arrondissement*, is one of the oldest in the city and most of the same buildings have been standing since before the turn of the century—buildings where Baudelaire, Flaubert, Toulouse-Lautrec, Van Gogh, Picasso, and Hemingway once lived and worked. And here I am. The street got its name centuries ago from the execution of a Parisian bishop, St. Denis, who was martyred by beheading. The same event named the section Montmartre. With several other streets, rue des Martyrs climbs a hill that hosts a towering white basilica called Sacrè-Coeur—in my eyes, the most beautiful structure in the city and I can see it directly outside my front door. Three bright white mountainous domes peak over all the other buildings for anyone on the street to admire.

On my way to exchange money in the bank down the block, I decide to stay on the street today and stroll around. I hold my nose walking past the fish market, compelling the man behind the glass case to chuckle and extend a large smelly salmon out my way. The case displays piles of fiery red lobsters packed in ice; they are beautiful, and motionless. As I smile and hurry by, I notice two men in the back of the shop dressed in white lab coats splattered with blood. The table in front of them is crowded with bloody fish heads, tails, and other unidentifiable parts. I wonder how they can work in that smell and that blood every day. Just after the fish market, I come to a butcher shop. More blood. More smell. I cup my hand over my mouth and nose. Skinned pigs, chickens, and cows are strung up, hanging down from the ceiling as if it were a show. I ask myself if there are people in the market for an entire cow.

I continue walking down the wide sidewalk watching all the faces of the people I passed. I see every size, every shape, every color there. I am comfortable walking with such a brilliant patchwork of people. For me, each passing face holds an access to more of the world. I know I fit in somewhere.

When I arrive at the bank, a small branch of the Banque Nationale de Paris, I open the tall glass door and step over to a free space at the counter. On the floor, along the walls, and across the front of the counter, pallid brown carpet lines the interior. Smoke congests the room while both women behind the counter dangle cigarettes over an ashtray spilling with old cigarette butts. It takes a minute for someone to notice me and then the tall, pale, black-haired woman wearing black-rimmed glasses approaches and asks how she can help me—actually she just blurts, "*Oui?*" I am nervous. François-Pierre usually does most of the talking for me in public, so I memorized the one humble sentence I will have to use. I will say that I'd like to change two hundred American dollars into French francs and that will be it. I pull the money out from my jeans pocket and say, "*J'aimerais changer...*" when like a resounding buzzer the woman interrupts me, forcing from her lips, "What do you want?" I suppose that "rude French" stereotype started somewhere. I grab my francs and leave.

The sun is beaming down on the other side of the street leaving my side shady and cool. Wandering along, I peek in the shop windows filled with various displays of clothes, shoes, jewelry, watches, electronics, chocolates, cheeses, wines, and all sorts of knickknacks. I stop in front of a pastry shop's deliciously colorful display and gaze in at the rows of cream puffs, chocolate eclairs topped with nuts, pistachio custards, strawberry tarts, and chocolate cakes. I will definitely return another day for a tart and more importantly, the chic navy blue suede shoes in the window of a little shop called La Miranda.

I walk to the green kiosk on the corner to buy a newspaper, squeezing between the bumper-to-bumper cars parked along the curb. The old man working inside is sitting on a tall stool behind a hill of stacked newspapers reading a copy of *Paris-*

Match. The kiosk is framed with nude and semi-nude women frozen in glossy magazine cover photos. I stand staring, perhaps visibly blushing, and cough slightly to quicken this exchange. I must have surprised him because he falls forward on the stool, yanks down the magazine, and clears his throat with a startled *"Bonjour."* I politely smile, pick off an *International Herald Tribune*, and hand the man my coins. *"Merci,"* I whisper.

With the newspaper tucked under my arm, I wander back to the other side of the street. My eyes lock onto the face of a man sitting in the broad windowsill of a gift shop. It is the same homeless man I'd seen probably every week the last time I was in Paris. I had forgotten him. He is more the same than I could've imagined. Still wearing the same long dusty brown coat, no matter if it is hot or cold outside—I presume living without a home gives a new slant on protecting your worldly possessions. He wears the same Pan African red, black, green, and yellow bulging knit hat. His face is dark and his eyes darker—they still look sad, always watering. The first time I saw him, François-Pierre told me he couldn't remember a time when the man hadn't been roaming along rue des Martyrs. And François-Pierre came to the apartment when he was fourteen, seven years ago, after his parents separated. I wonder if the man has family? Do they know he is here? Is he alone? Probably. What is his past? I walk in front of him; my stomach aches; and we share a modest smile. For a moment I think he remembers me, but then I am sure not. I feel numb.

Ascending the street, I come to the Rex Café where I sit down before heading back to the apartment. I take a table in front of the café and motion to the waiter, *"S'il vous plait?"* He flashes by, drops a menu on my table, nearly over my head, and dashes off. He is dressed in a crisp white shirt, a tight black bow tie, black vest, and black pants and strikes me as very composed for a young man faced with serving, seemingly single-handedly, the entire café. I look over the menu and choose my usual—passion fruit sorbet. I can hardly wait to taste it again. I've not been able to find anything like it at home.

The waiter appears abruptly in front of me and says, *"Oui, qu'est-ce que vous prennez?"* I reply slowly, *"Je voudrais un sorbet."* *"Et le parfum?"* The flavor, he asks impatiently, surely detecting my American accent. My heart beating quickly, I manage a timid, *"Fruits de la passion."* *"Fruits de la passion, o.k., C'est tout?"* that's all, he asks. *"Oui,"* I say with a huge sigh. The bowl is in front of me even before my palms stop sweating. I can't wait for these moments to end, these minor linguistic panic attacks. I can understand what people are saying, generally, but unfortunately, my responses in French are choppy, slow, and evidently render people somewhat anxious, including me.

The sorbet is as tangy and wonderful as I remembered it. Barely aware of all the people passing my table, bustling along the sidewalk, I open my newspaper and begin to glance up and down for news from home. I am stunned, then embarrassed to read that President Bush is the only leader of an industrialized nation who refuses to sign a treaty protecting the Arctic from oil exploitation. Things haven't changed without me.

Inside the café is full with people, but there is only one other person outside with me; a stoic man dressed in a dark gray business suit and a bright red necktie. Punching the keys of the calculator on his lap, he sips a cup of coffee and is intensely writing on a pad of paper. My guess is he works with IBM—an office is in this part of Paris near the Opera.

"Oh-oh!" Our attention is interrupted by a young man's bellow. The business man and I look up, startled to see him shaking his head and shooting up the sidewalk, past the Rex, around the corner, and out of sight. We look at each other, in the young man's direction, and back at each other. Screaming down the block behind, a woman races to catch him. "*Tu n'y comprends rien. Tu n'y comprends jamais rien*," she yells, something about him not understanding her, but she is speaking so fast I can't follow. The whole street can hear her shouting for blocks. The scene is comical; I can hear pockets of laughter from all directions. I am laughing, the businessman next to me is laughing, our waiter is laughing — it's exciting to feel the capability of comfortably communicating with all these people. Laughter is a consolation. It can inevitably make things equal.

I finish reading the newspaper, leave some coins on the table, and continue walking. It's nearly four o'clock, so I make my way back up to the apartment. At the butcher shop, the shopkeeper is unstringing the skinned chickens; the cows and pigs are already down. Most of the other shops have closed and are covered with metal garage-door-like protection. The flower shop on the corner across the street is still open, so I cross over to buy Christine flowers.

Outside the shop window, big blue buckets of flowers stand inside a wide crate for people to arrange their own bouquets of single flowers. I shake off the water and pull out several blue irises, yellow and white daisies, a bunch of red lilies, and Black-eyed Susans. I wrap a piece of tissue paper around the long green stems and hand the vendor thirty francs.

Just next door, in front of a tiny bookstore, I spin a postcard rack and find an aerial photo of the street, including the apartment. How wonderful to send my family a whole image of my home here.

The sun is setting behind the buildings now, leaving streaks of pink and red in the sky. The street is quiet and nearly empty, probably following its daily cycle. From across the street, I catch another jovial wave from Madame Carrasqueira. She is still wearing her apron and slippers standing at the door in front of our building holding a long loaf of bread. She must have noticed me on her way home from the bakery up the street. I watch her punch in the apartment code and slip behind the big wooden door that soon clicks shut.

François-Pierre appears around the end of the block, calling my name and smiling, his black hair cleanly cut. I wave and smile, relieved to finally see that face again. He scoops the flowers from my arms and takes a long sniff. We grasp hands and jog across the street back to the apartment together.

⁓

It was a typical day on the rue des Martyrs. Nothing different or new happened and more days will come and pass just like it. With or without me.

Maxim's at the Revolution

THE LADIES from Maxim's came recruiting at Bryn Mawr, where I was a sophomore in 1966. They were looking for the "best girls" from the "best colleges," and
thus considered only the East Coast and the Seven Sisters (Bryn Mawr, Barnard,
Wellesley, Smith, Mt. Holyoke, Vassar, Radcliffe). They didn't realize they were
including me, a scholarship girl from a working-class family; I don't think the possibility of someone like me occurred to them. They took it on faith that Bryn Mawr
knew what a "best girl" was and left it to the college to determine our eligibility.
They were imagining long-rooted New England and New York families with old
money and genteel professions, some dim American version of an aristocracy. By
French standards, they were new money themselves, which probably accounted
for their snobbishness.

Their husbands owned Maxim's Restaurant in Paris and probably had other,
less showy but more profitable holdings as well; at any rate, there seemed to be
plenty of money for the peculiar, high-minded venture that the wives had embarked
on a couple of years earlier. They ran l'Academie, a high-powered Junior Year
Abroad program for smart girls from the right colleges. Elitist to the hilt, they
offered an intellectual finishing school of great rigor and enormous expense.
While other college students in Paris were herded by the hundreds into Sorbonne
amphitheaters to hear watered-down lectures on literature and art, the Academiciennes, no more than twelve per year, sat in plush conference rooms taking seminars from famous writers, art critics, philosophers, linguists—the best coaching
line-up Maxim's money could buy.

I was taken aback by the vehemence of my desire to go to Paris, and by my
certainty that this program and I were made for each other. Such directness and
optimism were—and mostly still are—foreign to my hesitant, excruciatingly
thoughtful character. Lack of money, lack of social polish, fears of loneliness or
of getting in over my head, all the buts that might ordinarily have encumbered me
and sapped my enthusiasm, couldn't make a dent in my joy. L'Academie seemed
so extravagant, so marvelous, that its very implausibility seemed to promise my
success. How could I shrink back when fate, clothed in Givenchy and Chanel,
offered to fulfull my fantasies? Although Bryn Mawr was a sedate, scholarly
place, I had somehow come to equate intellect and glamour, fed largely by a substantial diet of literary biographies and memoirs. Virginia Woolf, Mary McCarthy
and Simone de Beauvoir had formed my image and my expectations for myself.

I wanted my name to sound in concert with theirs, and to possess, as they did, a protean mind and a cosmopolitan ability to write imaginative literature in the morning and lapidary criticism or theory in the afternoon. The event-filled, climax-seeking structure of the biographies I read, with its highlighting of significant details that gradually revealed a life theme, had led me to confuse life with its written recomposition. The sign of my election (by whom or what I never analyzed) would be a serendipitous event, perhaps a crucial encounter that would galvanize me and transform me into my definitive self. In the future book of my life, the year in Paris would figure retrospectively as a crucial turning point in my intellectual development. In biographies, there were always such decisive moments that made the subject's career seem to recapitulate Darwinian evolution. Ordinary people might evolve randomly and modestly into mature accomplishments; extraordinary ones went through mutations that fit them for original exploits. Deep down, I was afraid that my shyness and self-doubt were signs of ordinariness. All the more reason, then, to leap at this glorious gift of chance that flattered my hope that I could become extraordinary.

Madame Vaudable and Madame Boyer were an unlikely pair to be running l'Academie; they were not academic or intellectual themselves. But they clearly enjoyed playing at the great-lady role. Madame Boyer was tall, slim, blond and charming. Her voice was a melodious drawing-room instrument. The words "*roucoulement*" and "*gazouiller*," evoking French songbird warblings and trills, always accompany my memories of her. Madame Vaudable, though equally elegant, was a different breed: compact and impatient, sharp-eyed and sharp-tongued with the show-me truculence of French farm women. Her gray hair wanted to be unruly, and makeup did nothing for her seamed, hard-bitten face. Her gaze was suspicious; it fingered us and bit into us, on the alert for counterfeit coins.

Once a week we were invited to lunch with them at the restaurant. Madame Boyer always smiled lovingly at no one in particular, offering more champagne, and asking, in that well-bred way so close to warmth that, in fact, it did the job for us as well as deep sincerity, how we were enjoying Paris and how the courses were going. Madame Vaudable, irritably snapping at the waiter about the dessert course, would turn her attention to us only to give another version of her lecture about how lucky we were to be exposed to the best and the brightest. I loathed and feared Vaudable; the only way to resist her efforts to maneuver me into the grateful-orphan position was to exercise my weak fledgling capacity for contempt. She was much better for me than the adorable Boyer, I realize now, because she forced me to try to articulate to myself my hazy daydreams of glory and in the process turn them into realizable ambitions. You just wait, I addressed her silently in the time-honored way of unsung heroines; I'm not just another smart girl like the others here; I'm the real thing. Outwardly, I tried to look pleasantly attentive, secretly titillated by my initiation into social hypocrisy. I would enjoy every sumptuous meal, and still reserve the right to patronize my hostesses.

Our ladies, we all saw quite early, were groupies. It was through us that they could treat anthropologist Claude Levi-Strauss and critic Roland Barthes as equals. Having hired them for us, they could escort them importantly into our classroom at the beginning of each seminar. *Les dames de Maxim* played the roles of heralds and ladies-in-waiting, trailing clouds of designer coat and designer perfume, settling themselves into the front row after intimate conferences with the professors about what else their lordships might require to bring them into full pedagogic bloom. Ask questions, Madame Vaudable would harangue us, impatient with our dullness. She and Boyer would leave after the teachers' introductory remarks. Only then did we struggle to remove our self-conscious good-girl masks and try to become real and curious people again. That was no easy task. I had constantly to keep at bay the unsettling feeling that I was impersonating myself, or borrowing confidence against the brilliantly honed, refined and decisive woman I expected to be, some vague day. I was desperate to be recognized as the self I yearned toward, but could only try to imitate, hoping to make it real.

We realized, after the first heady champagne buzz wore off, that our professors didn't know, or care, if we were the best, or the worst, or just girls out for a good Paris time. Intellectual stars, but not especially well off, most of them, they liked the salary and the teaching conditions. They were surprisingly good teachers, or do I mean we were such willing sponges? Most of them didn't really notice us, even as they appeared to weigh our haltingly expressed ideas about the relationship of Freud and Marx in Surrealism, or the philosophy of Teilhard de Chardin. Some of them gave lectures in the traditional French manner, dividing each topic into two parts, those again into two and so on. . . . But the working artists and critics simply talked about their current subjects of interest, working out in front of us the ideas they were writing about.

Jean-Louis Ferrier, the art critic for *L'Express*, was planning a book about the contemporary painter Dubuffet, whose cause he championed in the magazine. Dubuffet worked in a neo-primitive style, in rudimentary stick figures scratched into flat gray surfaces; his paintings looked like the work of a stone-age child. Dubuffet was the greatest living painter, Ferrier told us. The paintings I looked at were stark, uncommunicative. How had Ferrier made the blankness yield its mystery, its "greatness?" It was only when I lay Ferrier's complex analysis, his sophisticated words, over the incoherent marks that I "saw" and understood. I do not mean to debunk Ferrier's assessment; pictures do not speak for themselves, especially unfamiliar ones. What fascinated me most, however, was not Dubuffet's rank, but the shiftiness of his reality. His pictures looked different depending on which critical language I used and which art-historical context I stood in to gain perspective on my subject. Dubuffet was an existentialist whose stark palette testified to man's loneliness and "thrownness" into the modern world. He was a neo-primitive who cleared away the Doanier Rousseau's sentimental jungle colors to show the geologic bedrock of reality. He was a Klee disciple who tried to reconstruct through art how the untutored eye might begin to construct space and object relationships. He was a Surrealist latecomer diving into the murks of the unconscious. He was, was not, could be seen as all or none of these. It all depended on the critic's choices of example and method. It made me dizzy to realize that Dubuffet was just one case, that in fact this instability of meaning coursed through everything I thought and studied. Far from being disturbed about the ground of bedrock truth being swiped from under my feet like the magician's tablecloth, I was thrilled with the fluid complexity of the mind's way of inhabiting the world. All the world was a floating world, in metamorphosis.

I can still hear the slow, ironic, mesmerizing voice of Roland Barthes, who seemed to be dreaming aloud as he lead us through the work of Balzac and Flaubert. He meant "work" as labor. He seemed to brush aside the perfection of Flaubert's finished prose, the larger-than-life energy and exuberance of Balzac's monumental characters, to call our attention to the first, the third, the fifty-seventh drafts of their compositions. He showed us facsimiles of Flaubert's hesitations, cross-outs, indecisions over the placement and length of a dependent clause; Balzac's pages looking incongruously cheerful, as balloons with crabbed insertions blow off into all the margins. Those inevitable-seeming masterpieces had only just made it to completion, through perils, rages, agonies of self-doubt, and all manner of disheveled trial and error. These writers I'd been taught to revere as masters had never arrived at a finished state, of either self or work. They cast insubstantial words upon the page, never certain of what, if anything, they'd pinned down. The solidity and inevitability of their books was an illusion, the fond dream of beguiled readers and critics. My love of books underwent a complication; I was drawn increasingly to the "dark side" of writing, to the tensions and ambiguities lurking beneath clarity and simplicity. And since books were so deeply woven into my imagination, my sense of myself developed complications as well. I was still a naive aspirant to literary glory, to the finished state of artistic mastery, but an ironic spirit became increasingly audible in my internal dialogue. My biography, should such a book ever be written, might, I sensed but didn't fully avow to myself, be full of cross-outs, hesitations, meanderings, double meanings, and things that didn't add up.

Our class star was Jacques Filliolet, a linguist who taught us French grammar and rhetoric. But that's like saying of a skating coach that he taught his students to stay on their skates and do a figure eight. He looked like a shorter, slimmer Gerard Depardieu, and he tried to teach us how to do triple salchows in the sentence, and a dazzling short program in the paragraph. He used a lot of body English, a pun he would have liked about himself, I think. He'd race from one end of the room to the other, his gold glasses frames reflecting glints from the overhead chandelier. When we read off a graceless, lumpish paragraph, he'd shout "Charabia!" a word of his own invention that meant something like nonsense and garbage, then give one of those inimitably impatient-sounding French tongue clicks, and hop onto the conference table to demonstrate the Genius of the French language. To Barthes's philosopher, he played the technician. As I wrote and rewrote sentences, revising, backtracking, adding and deleting, I learned as painfully as Flaubert, as maddened by impatience as Balzac, that writing was not about expressing my thoughts or my personality, but the process of making, and remaking both. The grammatical strictures and idiosyncrasies of a language were at once obstacle and inspiration, just as the body both makes possible and limits the fulfillment of what our spirits desire.

Though I was almost crazily high on intellectual excitement, I wasn't about to cloister myself with Ideas, no matter how alarmingly seductive. I hadn't forgotten Paris, and the life of the appetites. My social experiences turned out to be just as unusual and extravagant as my academic ones. On the social side, the Maxim connection opened salons and chateaux to the *Academiciennes*, inhabited by their titled owners. We had cocktails with wealthy patrons of the arts, and spent a weekend in the country at Epernay at the Taittinger estate where M. Taittinger showed us the wine cellars and taught us to distinguish between his pink and his white champagne.

Once, Boyer and Vaudable arranged a formal dinner dance for us in one of Maxim's private dining rooms, whose black and red furnishings, set off by turn-of-the-century murals of *demi-mondaines*, (euphemistically called "grand horizontals") flirting with tuxedoed, cigar-hazed gentlemen, still had an unsettling brothel atmosphere. The room, like the event, like the restaurant itself, was like a slightly seedy museum installation of a bygone era, the period and the society chronicled by Proust and before him, Balzac. It was easy to imagine Proust's Charlus or Balzac's Rastignac slipping into one of Maxim's private rooms with a lover of uncertain lineage and ambiguous gender.

Here we were introduced to young men of "family." (old and titled; "good family" was a patronizing way of referring to the upper middle class.) None of us knew the first thing about playing the debutante role our worldly "mothers" were pushing us into. At least the other girls, though not wealthy, came from educated middle-class backgrounds and were somewhat accustomed to social gatherings. I'd landed here from a Levittown-style tract house on a street where people worked as bus drivers, policemen, maintenance workers. As I let myself be served raw oysters and "*queues de langoustines Orleannaise*," I observed the gliding swallow-tailed waiters and compared their technique with my father's, who was, perhaps at that moment, on duty at Westbury Manor on Long Island, and asking if "Madame" cared for another cocktail. What aplomb I had at the table, glittering with a bank of goblets and a raft of silverware, came from being at home not with the guests, but with the rituals of restaurant service from the waiter's point of view.

My date, a young baron, poured me a fine cognac at the end of the meal, and offered me a Moroccan cigarette. Lowering his voice so as not to be overheard, he tried to bait me with insinuating remarks about what women were really good for. I was flying so high, on good champagne as well as intellectual arrogance, that I couldn't be insulted, or intimidated. Deliciously intoxicated by the alcohol, the setting, the whole incongruous situation, I felt as if I were starring in a French drawing room comedy. Bantering replies were called for, as supple and witty, outrageous even, as I could manage. I was pleased with myself, with my French accent, my poise, made up of equal parts bravado and beginner's luck. If only the elegant, titled twit knew who I really was, I thought as I smiled at him; he thinks he's talking to an American princess, whereas I'm really the maid in disguise. I don't suppose I really fooled him, though my manners and my French could pass, because one look at my dress would have enlightened anyone with money, old or new. And it occurs to me now, my style wasn't off-hand enough either.

My clothes came from a tacky department store in Freeport, Long Island; my wardrobe was a symphony of cheap synthetic fibers masquerading as their betters. The best thing I owned was a jumper made of real virgin wool, and that was a hand-me-down from a family my mother cleaned for. Whenever I went to lunch at Maxim's, I watched the doorman's face as he took my plastic briefcase and my old blue pea jacket with the torn lining. I'd nod graciously at him, feeling wickedly like a gate crasher. I loved slumming among the upper classes. Fortified by heady academic adventures, I was unfazed. Playing out of my social league was an entertaining game, and I loved learning the rules, even though I couldn't afford the uniform. I belonged anywhere and everywhere, I thought with surges of powerful joy. Levittown and Paris, Westbury Manor and Maxim's, Bryn Mawr and l'Academie: I did not have to choose or define myself; I could be a subtle, rich, shimmering combination of these social classes and more. My linguistic make-up was already a complex stew. Since I was an immigrant to the U.S., my first language was German, my second English, and each of these fostered a different mode of thinking and feeling. Now, with French, I was creating a third self.

Everyday life was just as theatrical, unsettling and peculiar as the classes and the outings and parties. It was riddled with literary themes, and there was plenty of significant detail for my biographer (though what would he or she make of my odd year, which increasingly seemed to be not about finding or making myself, but losing fixed images and the stereotypical identities I'd sketched for myself in my adolescent daydreams). Through l'Academie, another student and I rented a room in the home of a well-off widow. Madame des Vaux had a large apartment on Rue Greuze, in the conservative 16th *arrondissement* where all the bankers and diplomats lived. We were a half block from Place Trocadero and the Eiffel Tower. To one side of our building we had the Japanese embassy, on the other the embassy of a former French colony, I think Cameroon. Margery and I shared a large bed-living room whose airiness was considerably subdued by the enormous marble and gilt and ebony Empire furnishings. The room was dominated by a huge, claw-footed table, suitable for signing peace treaties. We wrote our papers and letters there, and ate the sandwiches and pastries we picked up for dinner on our way home from classes.

We had contracted for breakfast only, served to us every morning by the Spanish maid or by the live-in companion, Mlle. de Montgazon. With Madame, we had as little to do as possible and were grateful she didn't try to monitor our comings and goings. She spent her days on her chaise longue, talking on the telephone, watching television, or giving, preparing to give, or holding voluble post-mortems on her card parties. Her sitting room adjoined ours so we heard the blow-by-blow, delivered in a yoo-hooing breathless voice that comes back to me now when I listen to Julia Child.

Sometimes we'd hear Madame and Mademoiselle arguing at a furious pace. Mademoiselle was a thin, dry, gray woman with thick glasses who looked and moved like a mouse, and chattered at us whenever she could get us to hold still for one of her excited litanies of complaint. She'd been a nanny in Uruguay, recently returned, and didn't like the way things were going in France. DeGaulle should really put his boot down on all those hippies and student agitators; that was the only subject on which she and Mme. des Vaux agreed, Madame's husband having been a Gaullist military man. Margery and I, though not hippies or agitators ourselves, were sympathizers, ready to fling our half-baked Marx and Marcuse at her. Our arguments with her enlivened breakfasts: always the same prissy meal of two *biscottes*, one cafe au lait, half a tiny crock of butter and another of jam. Mademoiselle's main job in the household, besides hectoring Madame to keep her from falling into terminal stupor, we surmised, was to weigh our food portions to the last milligram. When we asked for fresh bread as an occasional change of pace, she was almost beside herself, trying to explain to us the almost insuperable difficulties of rearranging our domestic universe in such radical fashion. She had a gift for bureaucracy, like many of her compatriots. (The French, after all, invented it.) We found Mademoiselle entertaining, unlike anybody we'd ever met before, and we felt sorry for her in a detached sort of way. She lived in a cell beyond the kitchen and seemed to have no possessions, not even a poster or a flowerpot. What was she doing here, we asked each other, and decided she must be a Poor Relation, living on Madame des Vaux's not very generous charity.

This was a different world from Maxim's glamour. The elegance, as well as the spirits of the household, were threadbare, meanly measured. In some ways it suited me, because I was threadbare too, and trying to put up a good front, financially. My Bryn Mawr scholarship covered l'Academie's tuition, and my room, but I had to be careful about what I spent for food and books and subways. There were the cold suppers and a little restaurant Margery and I often went to, in a working-class neighborhood south of the Eiffel Tower, just beyond the tourist district. Le Commerce was frequented by railroad workers, subway employees and African and Algerian students. To be accepted there, we had to go through a testing period of taunts and jokes, and not get insulted when customers, or waiters, tried to pick us up. Our line was to stay calm, say no but in a vague, pleasant sort of way, and keep eating our steak and *frites* with unperturbed satisfaction. They were superb and remain hot and delicious in my memory, as good in their way as the refined dishes we got at Maxim's.

Through winter and the early spring of 1968, I walked around in a state of euphoria, excited by my courses, thrilled by Paris, hardly noticing that there was a feverish instability to the general atmosphere, as of social storms gathering. But then, since my entire existence in France was anomalous, how could I have noticed anything? Everything that happened that year was extraordinary. Madame and Mademoiselle seemed always glued to the television now, where deGaulle and his ministers sounded graver and more pompous than ever, warning against agitators who were trying to bring down the glory that is France. I heard rumors about stirrings at the Sorbonne; the French students were demanding changes in the rigidly bureaucratized and centralized university system. The spirit of Berkeley and Columbia had come abroad, carried by American students and expatriates in Paris protesting the war in Vietnam. Now the French seemed to be catching the anti-authoritarian fever.

My spirit was blowing wildly all over the place. I couldn't sort out what I should do, where I should go. I'd sit in the early spring sun with new American friends I'd met through Margery, (many of them seasoned anti-Vietnam protesters), who were helping the French students plan meetings and marches and ominous-sounding "actions." I'd help distribute leaflets and then go home to work on my Max Ernst paper for Ferrier. I was planning a study of a central image in Ernst's work, the round eye of his surrealistic bird "Loplop" which metamophoses through painting after painting into knotholes, full moons, mysterious portholes to the infinite. Walking the streets of the Latin Quarter, I was often so deeply sunk in Ernst that I started hallucinating. That nothing in daily life was normal any more seemed entirely fitting to my state. Surrealism was the order of the day.

There was a social upheaval going on around me. Peugeot workers in the factories near Paris were having picnics and consciousness-raising sessions with students in the Sorbonne courtyards that seemed to consist mainly of ever-escalating rounds of mutually admiring speeches. The city's business was neglected as strikes shut down the subways, electricity, mail, even TV and radio. Spontaneous communes sprang up in factory yards and university halls. The walls bloomed with high-spirited slogans like "All power to the Imagination," "It is forbidden to forbid," and this one which summed up the mood: "We lead a marvelous life here. We sleep; we eat; we don't touch money; no one thinks of it. This is already the society we want to create."

All rules were suspended; all the world's adults seemed to have been banished while the young held perpetual carnival in the streets. Even our professors at l'Academie started holding bull sessions with us, sounding just as lyrical and loony as the students about the dawning of a new age, a total transformation of society.

In these weeks without newspapers or electronic media, rumors flew. We heard that the police were preparing an attack on the university and that de Gaulle was going to use the army to force Paris back to order. One afternoon while I wandered around the Left Bank, my attention divided between new graffiti and ideas for a paper on Flaubert, I heard a rumbling echoing through the narrow streets. It quickly came closer and suddenly I was surrounded by people, running and shouting. I turned in the direction they'd come from to see a phalanx of gendarmes, batons raised. I started running too and suddenly we were all aswirl and aswarm, formless, wild, running in all directions. This isn't real, I thought. This is literature or the movies. I kept running, darting down one street and another until, just as quickly as it had arisen, the hubbub was over. I came into streets that were calm, with the self-absorbed pleasures of people at café tables drinking espresso and basking in the late afternoon sun as if nothing had ever happened and nothing ever would. I went home and thought some more about Flaubert.

Margery was spending most of her time at political meetings now; she'd abandoned schoolwork for this chance to be involved in something "real," as she put it. Our treaty table was covered with tracts and underground newsletters. I couldn't decide, couldn't choose. Politics seemed immediate and alive in a way it had never been for me, but so was the realm of books and ideas. I couldn't give my soul to the revolution that Margery and many of our more radical friends were certain was occurring around us, about to transform French society, maybe all of Western society, irrevocably. (The following year, back in the States, I heard that Margery had joined SDS.) From what little I knew about how revolutions worked, I had trouble believing that spontaneous street festivals were going to lead to the fall of the government, or a more liberal university, or even the demise of Maxim's, which had temporarily closed. I was also conscious of a tension that Margery dismissed as my usual tendency to over-analyze. The wildly creative, metaphorical language of the streets, which took its inspiration from Dada and the Surrealists, was strongly at odds with the leaden abstractions of the tracts Margery brought home. Those were a mishmash of the terrible simplifications of Maoism and the turgid Marxist terminology of class relations. There was exploratory, humorous conversation in the cafés, but in small fourth-floor walkups there were the usual plottings and grim policy debates of the professional left-wing organizers. I saw no way of translating one language and mind-set into the other.

In the end, de Gaulle prevailed. Like the father of a contentious brood who is going to stand for just so much insubordination, he combined threats with bribes. He made deals, dividing allies against each other. Little by little, "the events of May" gave way to business back to usual by late June. There were, I heard later from French friends, a few changes in the way the university system was run, but not many.

Maxim's reopened, but l'Academie had already ended its school year prematurely at the end of May. Boyer and Vaudable, sure the end of civilization was at hand, packed us unceremoniously home on U.S. military transport planes.

This abrupt ending left me dangling and disoriented, still in the throes of some complex process of shape-shifting and border-crossing that couldn't be stopped. I wasn't myself, and I was no longer sure I ever would be. I became cynical about political change, and turned a newly wary mind to the roles of language in my life. I was sure only that in all the universe of speech and writing, there was not a simple, truthful, sentence possible anywhere. The world was a cubist construction of multiple points of view, never settling for long into the Renaissance single perspective I'd grown up thinking was the privileged one. I had wished for a protean mind, a rootless, cosmopolitan mind, and now I was underway. Since that unsettled and unsettling time in Paris, I have deliberately cultivated not only my tolerance, but my taste for ambiguities that never come clear. My way of being in the world has turned out to be much more difficult than I once dreamed. I suspect that Margery, with her forthright practicality, her confidence and firm beliefs—if she's still as she was then—is happier than I am. But I can no longer imagine a different life for myself; I'm playing out my themes. Still, I wonder sometimes, late at night, if I should have been more careful about what I wished for.

Red Geraniums

CHURCH BELLS were ringing close by in the village—twelve strokes skipped across the slate roofs. The mountains were misty, fading into purple in the distance. The haze was a good sign, the weather would remain warm and sunny.

Papa and Maman were waiting. Their children and grandchildren were gathering for family dinner, as we did each Sunday in summertime.

"Susie, come on," called Pierre.

"Go ahead, I'm coming." I looked out the window, over the flower boxes, down to the backyard and the swings, the tennis court and the little hay chalet, carried down from the mountains years ago, before I arrived in the family.

"The children have already gone."

"I know." Minutes earlier I watched them happily disappear down the path to their grandparents' chalet. They had grown up with Sunday dinners.

Pierre waited patiently. "Susie?"

Even after twenty years, I still wasn't used to the way he said my name. He drew out the vowels, saying something that sounded like *suu-zii*. I went down the steps. The sky was porcelain blue, almost cloudless. The copper beach trees, the hollyhocks, the cut grass, everything was shining in the sunlight. "Why don't we go for a picnic?" I suggested. "Just the two of us?"

"We can't, not today. You know that. Everyone is waiting for us." He turned as I caught up with him. "Whom do you want to sit next to this time?"

"You." I answered, thinking how nice it would be to sit together at Sunday dinner.

~

But at Sunday dinners Pierre, the oldest son, always sat at Maman's right, and Monique, the oldest daughter, always sat at Papa's right. The rest of us sat wherever we wished except next to our spouses.

All nine children—Monique, Pierre, and the seven younger brothers—were married. They were married in order, every two years, the way they were born. Now they were having children in order, every two years. Eventually the children would get married in order and then they would have children in order.

So it was and I was part of the pattern.

Red geraniums beckoned to us from the windowsills of the large chalet. The tables were set like flower beds on the green lawn under the trees. I wanted to sing a Sunday song, do a dance, clap my hands, but Pierre's family was not effusive. They approached one another. They did not hug one another.

"*Bonjour Papa.*" I curtsied slightly and kissed my father-in-law lightly on both cheeks.

He was dressed in knickers and a beige sweater with a matching golf hat, as if he were walking out of the 1920s. And he stood as always with his feet pointed straight sideways. Lucie, our young ballerina daughter, would be forever grateful to her French grandfather's nimble toes.

"*Bonjour Maman.*" I curtsied and kissed again.

My mother-in-law asked me if I slept well. At first when she used to ask me this, I thought she was being indiscreet. Then I learned that the French always ask one another if they slept well.

She soon excused herself to go see about Sunday dinner. I watched her walk up the little slope toward their new chalet, her chignon as white as the single cloud brushed across the middle of the blue sky.

∽

Papa rang the dinner bell, an old large cowbell like the ones still worn by the cows high up in the mountains. The family responded and slowly moved to take their places. Soft sunlight nudged through the branches of the trees, playing shadows on the tabletops.

"*Bonjour,* my prettiest sister-in-law," said Maurice, the older sister's husband, the one brother-in-law who didn't look like all the others.

I was surprised to see him. He and Monique weren't expected this Sunday. Maurice was more gallant than the others, always telling each of his eight sisters-in-law that she was the prettiest. I didn't mind. Pierre and his seven younger brothers never seemed to look at their sisters-in-law.

The adults sat down at the long table with the hand-embroidered green and white tablecloth. The older grandchildren took their places at the large round table with a flowered cloth. The younger grandchildren, matched in size, settled down at two little tables with pink paper cloths.

Today there were about thirty of us.

∽

Thierry, the youngest son of the family, carried in two bottles of iced champagne. He was our wine butler for the day. It was always the youngest brother present who took this role. With age, all the brothers looked more and more like Pierre—tall and slender, lots of curly dark brown hair, high foreheads, dark eyes, even a dimple or two.

"It's a special Sunday," said Papa, standing up and raising his glass. "We have our new grandson with us for the first time. Let us toast the proud parents, Thierry and Colette."

I looked over at the black baby carriage sitting under the white birch tree. The carriage had been in the family close to half a century, carrying close to fifty babies. It had held Pierre and all his younger brothers, and then each of ours. Now it held a new baby, a quiet baby, lulled by preceding generations.

"Let's also toast the proud grandparents," said Pierre, the oldest son, standing up, to the right of his mother and opposite his father.

"Hear ye, hear ye! *Le prince* has spoken." Maurice waved his champagne glass in front of my face. He knew how much I disliked the nickname—*le prince*—for my husband. It was not so much a nickname as a title, inherited like an old family heirloom and still more difficult to get rid of.

I pushed Maurice's hand away. "His name is Pierre." I said, repeating myself once again.

"But Susie, he'll always be *le prince*," said Thierry, coming up behind me with another bottle of champagne. "Nothing can be done about it. He was born that way."

"What way?" I asked.

Maurice leaned back out of the way and listened, visibly delighted with what he had provoked.

"The way every prince is born, first!" said Thierry. He refilled my glass. "He's always first and I'm always last. Even on the tennis court, he's first." Bubbles of champagne overflowed. "What can I do?" he asked. "I can't beat him!"

"It's true," said Colette, his pretty dark-haired wife. "Thierry always loses."

Thierry frowned and moved farther down the table with his bottle of champagne.

"Colette, is that really true?" I asked. "Does Thierry always lose?"

"Yes, but they haven't played for a long time. Maybe they could play together this afternoon."

I looked down the table. People had stopped talking and were listening. Pierre was staring at me. His eyes were suggesting I talk about something else, something less personal, less intimate, something more appropriate for Sunday dinner.

～

The older grandchildren were serving the adults and the middle grandchildren were serving the younger grandchildren. They rehearsed their roles, year after year, summer after summer.

I looked at the red geraniums in the flower boxes on the windowsills all around the chalet. They were especially lovely this summer. My mother-in-law kept the same ones year after year, putting them in the cellar in winter and then back on the windowsills in spring.

At the beginning of our marriage, I tried to do the same thing but the plants never blossomed properly the second year-round. And they barely grew leaves the third year. Then one spring I decided to leave them in the cellar and buy new ones. Finally I threw out the old ones and started buying new ones every spring.

It wasn't the only thing I tried to do in the beginning. I also tried to make yogurt. My mother-in-law initiated me, giving me lots of bottles and brushes, pots and pans. I remembered washing and rewashing the bottles, that's what the brushes were for, and the pots, and the pans. It all smelled awful. Only our first two children got to taste my homemade yogurt. It was never very firm, nor very smooth. The other children tasted store-bought yogurt, with different flavors and colors.

"Francoise, do you make your own yogurt?" I asked, trying to find a more neutral subject of table conversation. I addressed my innocent question to the sister-in-law who was closest to me, both in age and affinity. We both liked the same things, read the same books, went to the same movies. And neither of us liked yogurt, homemade or not.

"No, I don't really like yogurt," answered Francoise.

"What a pity!" chided Maurice. "There's nothing quite like homemade yogurt."

"Well, I make yogurt for Thierry," said Colette.

"Do you really?" I asked. I could picture myself twenty years back, with pots of yogurt germinating around the entire kitchen. I could almost smell it.

Pierre was looking at me again. Even yogurt was too intimate for Sunday dinner. I decided that perhaps I should talk about the red geraniums and tell my mother-in-law how lovely they were, especially this summer.

⌒

Just then Monique, the older and only sister, asked for the family's attention. Maurice stopped staring at his sisters-in-law and sat up straight. Everyone listened. Monique took a deep breath, smiled, and announced the forthcoming marriage of their third child. He was not with us today. Neither were his older brother and older sister.

There was startled silence. No one was expecting a wedding announcement. It had been several years since the last of the marriages. The whole family was out of practice. Besides Papa and Maman were still waiting for Monique's first son— their oldest grandson—to get married. Now instead number three was stepping out of line and getting married first.

No one spoke. A second cloud appeared in the blue sky, the trees whispered, the tablecloths rustled. Monique was waiting for her parents' approval. Maurice was looking around the table for support.

Even the grandchildren were standing speechless with their silver serving trays, so many statues in the sunlight.

"Here's to the future newlyweds," I said, raising my glass. "And here's to their parents and to their grandparents."

The family stirred. The ripple passed. Thierry went back for more champagne. Corks popped like fireworks. Papa and Maman congratulated Monique, their one daughter. Maurice sank back with relief into his chair. Conversation zigzagged down the long table under the trees.

Pierre was smiling at me, his dark eyes approving. Red geraniums, tennis matches, homemade yogurt, Sunday dinners. I smiled back. Another summer, maybe not too far away, it would be one of our children getting married, in or out of order. And the family would celebrate with champagne.

Maurice alone was quiet. I turned to see if he'd fallen asleep in the midst of all the excited anticipation. "Maurice, are you sleeping?" I asked, poking him gently.

"No, I'm recovering."

"Maurice," I continued, "did you and Monique come especially to announce the wedding?"

"Yes," he answered. "It was Monique's idea. Thirty years ago, almost to the day, we announced our own engagement right here at Sunday dinner."

I thought back. That was before I had come to France, before I had come to Sunday dinners. "And were there red geraniums then?"

"Susie, there were always red geraniums."

⌒

The mountains remained misty and the sun grew warmer. Our thirteen-year-old daughter Lucie arrived arm-in-arm with her favorite cousin Nicolas, carrying together the tray of ice cream cups for the younger grandchildren. The two cousins were the same age and looked surprisingly alike.

"Lucie, stand up straight," scolded gently Bonne Maman, their grandmother. "Nicolas, hold the tray with both hands, shoulders back!"

Lucie took back her arm and stood up straight. Nicolas lost hold of the tray, and the ice cream cups went rolling over the grass and under the tables. The younger grandchildren went tumbling after them, all too happy to have an excuse to roll on the ground. Lucie and Nicolas burst into fits of laughter.

Maman couldn't keep a stern face. She let the little ones leave the table, taking with them their ice cream cups and going to play on the swings near the tennis court.

Lucie went back inside to fetch the second dessert tray, the one with the traditional blueberry sorbet, from the berries that grew wild on the side of the nearby mountains and made in the local pastry shop. The sorbet was cool and refreshing and gave us all purple-colored lips, making us look theatrical.

～

Coffee was served with chocolates. The leaves fluttered lazily in the light afternoon breeze. The older grandchildren came to say thank you to Bonne Maman and Bon Papa and to be excused. Lucie and Nicolas were careful to walk in single file. Then they rushed off with the other cousins to warm up the tennis court for the match between Uncle Pierre and Uncle Thierry.

The red clay tennis court was part of the family setting. With eight boys in the family, it was the domain of the brothers. The sisters watched. It was the rule to play in white tennis shorts and white tennis shirts. Only when it was too hot to play or when the brothers were having coffee after Sunday dinner, did the younger generation have the court.

We sat quietly, enjoying the sunlight on our backs.

"Susie," said Francoise, my closest sister-in-law, "when is your next trip to America?" The question floated above the white coffee cups.

I looked about for an answer. "I don't know, maybe next summer." I was quiet for a moment and then tried to explain. "It seems very far away. I feel like there's here and there's there and I'm somewhere in the middle."

A red and white hang glider swooped down the mountainside and stayed suspended in the blue sky above our heads.

Next to me Maurice was napping. He had not heard my lofty statement.

～

We finished our coffee. Papa and Maman stood up. The dinner was ended. The sisters-in-law started to collect the empty cups and saucers.

Pierre came and gave me a kiss on the forehead. "We'll have our picnic tomorrow," he said, "just the two of us with the children." He looked at me, wanting me to smile. "And now, will you come and watch us play? I think I may need your support this time."

"Of course I'll come. The whole family will come and watch." I stood up and started to stretch in the afternoon sun. "Maybe this once you should lose."

His brothers were waiting for him. I watched them go off together to the tennis court. Pierre was the tallest of all of them. I wondered what Thierry would do about that.

Francoise and I folded the green and white embroidered tablecloth and went to thank Papa and Maman. They were standing by the baby carriage under the birch tree and looking at their newest grandson. Papa's hand was resting on Maman's shoulder.

The baby was still sleeping. We waited a moment and then thanked them for the Sunday dinner.

"It is our pleasure," replied Papa.

"The red geraniums," I said, "are especially lovely this summer."

Maman smiled. "Yes, they're lovely from one summer to the next."

SHELLEY ANDERSON

An Innocent in Amsterdam

"**D**O YOU MIND if I put the chocolate in the freezer?" I ask.

"Yes," she says, giving an indifferent shrug. She stares at the newspaper, intent on reading the article. She needs to concentrate. The article is in a foreign language, the language I just spoke: English.

Her body and tone of voice say go ahead. But her words say no.

It's not the first time. She's tried to explain it to me before. In French a positive answer to a positive statement means agreement; there is a special word form for disagreeing with a negative sentence. I wish I had paid more attention to grammar lessons in junior high.

"Does that mean yes, you mind, or yes, go ahead and put them in the freezer?"

This time, at least, we recognize there is a misunderstanding. There are times when hours have been spent in brittle silence, when tears and anger were caused by a misplaced nuance, an unknown connotation. We backtrack and reconstruct the argument, searching for the intended meaning.

Reconciliation is sweet. Our bodies have a common language. In bed, we have a mutual mother tongue. Every orgasm is a marvel, but I know she has been especially moved, the lovemaking particularly intense, when she cries out "oui!" instead of "yes!"

We dodge misunderstood metaphors, run across a minefield of slang and false cognates. We have built a home together, in a country neither of us called home. She has done most of the work, before she even met me. In her school near Paris, the children were reading Dickens before I discovered the Hardy Boys. Later, working in an international office near Amsterdam, she learned about American humor, television shows, books.

After five years of living together, we know morning is the trickiest, the time most ripe for misunderstandings. Still groggy from dreams mixed in English, Dutch, French, our speech is slurred, difficult to understand. The accents are boulders strewn on a trail marked communication. "Uh-huh" becomes indistinguishable from "Unh-unh" and I cannot tell if she wants the juice or the jam.

There are other tensions. It is a drag to speak slowly, deliberately, to avoid wonderfully creative slang, to have to constantly reduce ideas to the lowest common denominator. It is irritating when she doesn't use the correct plural form, talks of "deers" and "the poors" and "pass me a underpant." She is sad she can't share the beauty of Yourcenar's writing, impatient with the constant requests for

351

translation, angry at the expectation that everyone can speak English. Imperialism, I learn, means never having to learn another language.

There are other differences, too. Her family got their first television set when she was fifteen. I was breastfed "I Love Lucy" and weaned on the Saturday morning cartoons. Television is harmless fun to her; a capitalist conspiracy to me. I rejected television viewing as part of a rebellion against the worst in American culture. She finds American sitcoms exotic, hilarious; they set my teeth on edge.

Her parents went hungry during the Nazi occupation of France. Mine ran a cafeteria in a college town. She will eat the bruised bananas first, cook the beets that have been in the bin for a week; I throw them away. My family ate out twice, three times a week, either in the cafeteria or at a competitor's. She cannot remember ever going out to eat as a child. Restaurants are for the rich. She darns, makes soup from nettles, knits, clips coupons from the newspaper, dries the herbs she gathers on walks in the woods. She is surprised that her knowledge of how to treat wines impresses me. It is a normal food to her, something every housewife uses, not a symbol of yuppie indulgence.

I throw out socks that have holes in them, and anything else that has no immediate use. I'm an American: there will always be more. I am afraid to eat food that comes directly from the earth. It can't be safe if it's not from a can.

It is a relief, with so many differences, to have our bodies in common. It helps that we are both women, acculturated to bend, to listen in relationships. Lesbian relationships are always terra incognito, the boundaries blurred, undefined. The fact that we have no road map forces us to look at and negotiate things others may take for granted. We know that companionship is a gift, not a given. We have already risked much to love one another. Lesbians are outsiders in our own countries, so we are at home with one another.

But being permanent foreigners in another country sometimes taxes even our finely honed survival skills. When it comes time for my work contract to be renewed, I face the most difficult decision of my life: do I go back home, or do I stay? The things I miss from home (and home still means America) have changed, become harder to define. Two years ago I hungered for friends, cheap take-out Mexican food, free public libraries, decent ice cream. Now? Friends, still—but also something more intangible. It's that extravagant love of life, that exuberance that comes from having endless possibilities, that seems so American. The generosity, the optimism, the humor.

And the language. That awful feeling of forgetting words, getting slang phrases mixed up. That sickening feeling of being suspended over a void when you stare at a sentence and can't, for an eternal split second, remember if it's Dutch or English. Who are you if you forget your original language? Speaking to another American, hearing that accent again, feels like blood rushing back into a numb hand: the cadence picks up, synapses snap and crackle, you're off and running. You remember what it's like to laugh, to be excited, rather than intimidated, by words.

Most of the friends I've made have gone back to their own countries: an occupational hazard for the heart. They write: don't stay away too long or you'll never fit in again. But the home I remember is the America of five years ago. It no longer exists. Friends' letters are full of references—new books, television shows, political scandals—I don't understand.

It has been too long already. Whatever the choice, something will be lost. There are people I love on both sides of the Atlantic now, habits I've grown accustomed to. This realization brings a sense of irreparable loss. And then, unexpectedly, the prison door opens. The world has not shrunk, but rather expanded. I have not lost my home: I have built another one. My circle of friends has grown larger, and I will be welcomed wherever I go. The world is my home now.

The process was—and remains—painful. Yet what has been gained far outweighs what has been lost. I have a loving relationship and a new identity, grounded in the respect and clarity I've gained of my own culture. I have learned just how American I really am. Before moving here, I had little good to say about America. The friendly contempt most Dutch people have for things American produced a counter reaction: I could either be ashamed or proud. I choose the latter path. Both the lynch mob and the Underground Railroad are my heritage; the people who dreamed of a better world and the people who killed the dreamers. America produced Rosa Parks and Susan B. Anthony, and murdered innocent women and children in Iraq. The fact that I claim a kinship with the former means that I have a responsibility toward the latter. A sense of justice is not uniquely American; rather, our particular history gives us a special responsibility to stop future My Lais and Wounded Knees.

Europeans do have a peculiar love/hate relationship with America. So do Americans.

The glamour of an American living in Europe wears off quickly, replaced by reality. Reality, as in people laughing at clumsy attempts to speak their language, drifting off at parties after a certain conversational level is exceeded (i.e., your name, where you are from, isn't the weather nice today?). As in missing friends desperately and being ready to kill for take-out burritos, Dr. Pepper or Haagen-Daz ice cream. As in no one understands your jokes and you are no longer you, but the American.

So I struggle to learn Dutch, skip night class repeatedly, give up. It is frustrating to have the vocabulary of a five-year-old when you are thirty-five. I enter a women's bookshop and cry, because I do not have the key to unlock all the novels' hopes and dreams. For the first time in thirty years, I am illiterate.

My partner understands. She knows what it feels like to be ripped up by the roots and transplanted. She followed a lover to this flat land. She came out in this country, away from family and everything familiar. She says she has never met another French lesbian.

We bump up against different standards of courtesy and respect continuously. She argues a lot, gets visibly angry, contradicts openly. Anger to me means a loss of control, and it isn't expressed in public. To contradict someone to their face is an insult. It isn't only a question of not knowing the tactful words, words that act as oil for friction. She was educated to question, to look critically at ideas. I was educated to obey.

Still, it works between us. We skirt misunderstanding and discover some common values. It's like unwrapping a gift: the paper and ribbons may be pretty, but they are not the essence. It takes awhile to work your way through the packing, but you gradually learn what is of real value. We learn what we can share, how far we can bend. She explains why Simone Signoret is laughing in the film; I translate Shug's Black English from *The Color Purple* for her. Together, we complain about how rude the Dutch are. She makes cornbread and chocolate chip cookies now; I try once more to learn a language that twists my tongue into unfamiliar shapes. I know which cheeses never to put in the refrigerator, and how to make a proper salad dressing. We untangle strands of culture, language, class, looking for what can be discarded, what is essential to keep. It is uncomfortable to learn how culture-bound you are, how arrogant, ignorant. It is also liberating. The boundaries shift, the horizons expand. The world is bigger than I ever could have imagined it. It is also a far happier place because she is in it. Learning about her culture, and living in another country, have enriched my life. I marvel at the circumstances that brought us together, the fact that we had a language in common. I wonder at how much I miss because I do not know other languages, how much of the world is lost in translation. Home is no longer what it once was. It allows for much more possibilities now, demands much more humility and patience. Slowly, I come to learn a common language of simple human kindness, a language of the heart.

My Pseudonymous Life

I HAVE A RECURRING dream from which I wake feeling gloomy and fretful: An academic conference I am attending is just over and I am scheduled to leave for home immediately. Only now do I realize that the conference is in Sweden and I have missed the opportunity to visit old friends. Moreover, I have not spoken a word of Swedish, which looms large in the dream as a source of regret. Typically, my departure is complicated by wrong trains, forgotten luggage, missing passports, all the standard ingredients of the life-is-passing-you-by nightmare. But the dream has a literal meaning as well. I have left Sweden behind.

Between 1968 and 1982, I made seven trips to Sweden, varying in length from three weeks to six months. The first time, as a twenty-three-year-old graduate student hesitant to speak Swedish for fear of grammatical errors and mispronunciations, I took comfort in the solitude and anonymity that are the classic pleasures of foreign travel. By the time I turned twenty-seven, I was confident enough to tell people my age: "*tju'sju*," a tongue- and lip-twisting pair of sibilants that feel incompatible to a speaker of English. Soon I could obscure my American accent enough to pass as a Swede in brief conversations.

Along the way, my identity switched from anonymous to pseudonymous. I heard my name pronounced "Tjäri Re-YEE-ster" by strangers and "RET-chess-ter" by knowing friends. Once, sitting in an auditorium, I overheard myself referred to as "hon, Registern," literally "she, the index." My book on the uses of literature in the American and Swedish women's movements had made mine a voice to contend with in the world of Swedish literary feminism. No matter that it was an insular world. It was comfortable and manageable. I could publish, give lectures around the country, and be rewarded with grants doled out in checks bearing my *personnummer*, a registration number whose first digits, however, marked me as a foreigner.

The pseudonymous, Swedish-speaking Tjäri Reyeester was privileged to be my best self—innovative, analytical, independent, politically engaged. I could dial up famous people on the telephone, introduce myself, arrange interviews over coffee. At home, phone phobia often kept me from calling friends. It felt as if my failures and flaws were only operative in English, or in the presence of my husband, the source of the flat, blue aerograms that arrived once or twice a week.

Those fifteen years are rich in anecdotes. The ones recorded in my journals are flavored with the sardonic comments expected of the initiated foreigner. My relationship to Swedish culture was not entirely amorous. Its order and predictability put me, by the end of each trip, in want of chaos, which was, indeed, waiting to greet me on my layover in New York. The Swedish left's rituals of identification with the oppressed of the world brought to mind confirmation class recitations of Luther's Small Catechism, which Marx had barely replaced.

There is no cynicism, however, in my memory of the landscape: the blue haze rising from the rock-strewn forest floor in the fantastically abundant berry season, or the emerald green of midsummer's wheat setting off the intense yellow of an adjacent canola field. The mention of fond names makes me sentimental: Ann-Katrin, Ingeborg, Elisabet, Barbro, Maud and Ove, Bertil. Karin, however, is still a figure to reckon with. It was she who conferred my pseudonymous identity upon me and, I realized as time went on, determined how I experienced Sweden. The conference site in my dream is usually the slope of the hill below her apartment on Uppsala's dominant ridge, where she waits, between the contending powers of castle and cathedral, for my frantic, last-minute phone call.

~

I first heard Karin's name in a graduate seminar in Scandinavian Languages and Literatures at the University of Chicago in the spring of 1969. We four students, hyperconscious as the times warranted, saw no "relevance" in the course the visiting professor from Sweden had been enlisted to teach and persuaded him to arrange a seminar on women in Scandinavian literature. The newest publication on our reading list was a paperback anthology, in Swedish, called *Sex Roles in Literature from Antiquity to the 1960's*, edited by Docent Karin Westman Berg of the University of Uppsala. It was the first Women's Studies text in Sweden, and our seminar was among the first Women's Studies courses in the United States. "*Pionjärer*," Karin was later fond of calling us both. The image of covered wagons it conjured for me was decidedly un-Swedish.

The test of relevance also prompted me to begin a Ph.D. dissertation on Swedish women's literature. "How can you, a woman yourself, possibly be objective about such a topic?" the next year's visiting professor asked, in the pinched nasal tones of the Swedish academic elite. Just a little daunted, I set off, in May 1972, for a forty-five day research trip to Sweden, with two newly drafted chapters stuffed inside my shoulder bag.

I took the train up to Stockholm from Luxembourg, the destination of my cheap Icelandic Airlines flight, and sought out the city room-rental agency, where my illusions about Sweden as an egalitarian utopia were quickly shattered. Waiting behind two Asian men, I eavesdropped as the agent telephoned a prospective landlady. "Do you rent to foreigners?" he asked. "*Japaner*," he added, and then "*Jaha, jaså, jodå*," concurring with the presumably reluctant voice on the other end of the line. "I'm sorry, that one is no longer available," he informed the two men in polite English.

So I was the one dispatched to Fru Frank's apartment near the Odenplan subway stop. Fru Frank was washing her plastic flowers when I arrived and had just wiped down the plastic sheeting on the chair and dresser in anticipation of my arrival. When I set my suitcase on the clean bedspread, she shrieked. On trips to the bathroom, I caught her peering at me around the kitchen door. She rearranged my things while I was out, and stopped me frequently to offer her opinions. She didn't rent to Finns, she said, because they drank and fought. She didn't rent to

Arabs, because one of them, dirty black with big lips, had kissed her on both cheeks. When I moved out a few days later, frazzled by her constant surveillance, I imagined her scratching Americans off her list. "They put their filthy suitcases right on the bed," she would cluck.

I had seen a poster announcing a meeting of Grupp 8, the closest counterpart to my women's liberation group, and there I had blurted out my discomfort. A shy graduate student in history, Ann-Katrin, invited me to sleep on her couch. Fru Frank was to be my last uncongenial landlord. Wherever I went after that, I could count on friends or friends of friends to offer lodging. Trips to Stockholm always included a stay with Ann-Katrin.

I made daily bus trips from Ann-Katrin's to the Royal Library, where I compiled bibliographical data, my refuge in times of uncertainty, soothed pangs of homesickness in the basement cafe with rum-flavored chocolate rolled in marzipan, and dropped twenty-five *öre* pieces into the telephone to make appointments with writers and journalists and feminist activists. "Have you met Karin Westman Berg yet?" people asked when I told them what I was up to. "You must," they urged. "*Entusiasmerande*" was how one woman described her, a formulation not quite as awkward as "enthusiasmizing."

I finally reached her by telephone. "I am very busy," she said in precisely articulated English, "but I can give you one hour tomorrow afternoon." I was annoyed by her use of English, which I took as a comment on my Swedish proficiency, and I felt intimidated by her formality, which seemed stiff even by Swedish standards. Uppsala was only one hour north by train, so one night there would not delay my trip to Göteborg, where I planned to finish out my time at the new women's history archives.

Karin's apartment was three floors up by a wire cage elevator that banged to a stop as if to warn occupants of an intruder. The person who met me at the door was livelier and friendlier than I had imagined from the reception on the telephone. She was older, too—at least my mother's age—and her face was a splendid web of wrinkles, testimony to the Nordic ideal of invigorating exercise in winter cold and salt air. "Step in, step in," she invited in a voice so resonant that I rushed to comply. She led me down a darkened hall and through a curtained doorway to a large, sun-filled study with floors of polished parquet. She apologized for her lack of time, but she was caught up in the final details of a conference, for which participants would soon be arriving from all over Europe.

She installed me at a tea table, offered me Earl Grey tea, and sat down opposite me, hunching over the table as if to leap on any word that might flit by too fast. Her blue eyes—*kornblå*, cornflower blue, a description I had read in novels—were fixed on mine with intense interest. She was pleased to know that her book was read in America, and she tossed her head back in an open-mouthed laugh that rang like silver against crystal. Her English was carefully measured, but when she switched to Swedish, finally, the pace picked up. She spoke without pause, and prodded my responses along with vigorous nods of the head and frequent repetitions of a sound I never did master: the punctuating "*ja*" spoken on an intake of breath.

She was excited to hear about this new development I called "feminist literary criticism," and with each question she asked, I grew more convinced of the importance of my dissertation, which I had almost junked for its impracticality just months before. My allotted hour passed quickly, and then another. Her conversation was so animated that even the expected gestures of leaving would have been rude interruptions.

As it turned out, my hastily booked tourist room had fallen through, and Karin offered me a bed for the night. I had, I knew, passed preliminary inspection. I slept between starched, monogrammed linens in a room with its own sink and several pieces of original art depicting the local landscape. The bathroom across the hall offered me my first encounter with a bidet, not an ordinary Swedish plumbing fixture. *Borgerlig* was the word that came to me—"bourgeois," a term I heard often in my meetings with Stockholm's radical women.

～

An opaque blue window shade blocked out the sun so effectively that I wasn't startled by full daylight at four a.m. as I had been at Ann-Katrin's. Instead, a spirited *"Hallå!"* rang me awake. Karin was dressed in another blue pantsuit and her hair was freshly pinned back in the charge-ahead style that never changed in the next decade. "I must have more time with you," she announced. "I am going to hold you prisoner here until my conference is over." I had left my two barely drafted chapters in her study and she had looked them over at bedtime. She was full of superlatives: *"Utmärkt! Jätteduktig! Toppen bra!"* My perspective was fresh and exciting and needed to be heard. There was nothing like it in Sweden. In fact, I should take part in the conference, which was, after all, on the foreign reception of Sweden's first novelist, Fredrika Bremer. And so I appeared on the list of participants: "Cheri Register, Minneapolis USA," introduced as a clever young woman from America with such brilliant new ideas. In time, on Karin's many lists, I would become "Ass. prof. Cheri Register," a title that helped me keep Karin's enthusiasm in perspective.

From that morning on, Karin's labyrinthine apartment served as my primary Swedish home. On subsequent trips, I came and went as my schedule required, whether Karin was there or commuting by train to the family home she shared with her husband and an adult daughter up north in Härnösand. After a single night's stay, I folded my sheets, pinned my name on them, and stacked them in the linen closet among others marked with the names of passing guests. It took me several visits to figure out where Karin slept. She simply materialized each morning, fresh and energetic, sweeping into the study with a breakfast tray of tea, crisp bread, cheese, and cucumber and peppers. But one day a door in the pantry that I had taken for a closet was left standing open. Behind it was a tiny room, originally the maid's quarters, barely wide enough for a bed. She would do without sleep if she could, she sighed. There was so much work to be done.

Aspects of Swedish life opened to me on that first visit that I might never have explored on my own. We bicycled into the countryside with picnic basket and thermos, and I matched spring wildflowers with names I knew from novels while Karin exclaimed over their beauty. We visited an elderly suffragist who brought life to the history I had learned. A short-story writer I had been working up courage to call showed up at Karin's in a formal gown, accompanied by her notorious novelist-husband in tails. They were headed for the University's convocation, and they ushered me along, despite my unsuitable dress. I felt as though I'd walked into Ingmar Bergman's *Wild Strawberries* as I watched top hats being placed on the heads of the new doctors of philosophy. Each time a hat was settled into place, a cannon boomed. The hat, it seemed, had set off an explosion, as if the pressure of all that newly acquired knowledge could not be contained. Quaint academic customs, I thought, but as the *rector magnificus* spoke about the importance of keeping the University selective and isolated from worldly concerns, I realized these customs were deeply entrenched. The *docent* before Karin's name was, I gradually caught on, little more than a title. She held a position at the University but was seldom assigned courses to teach. A seminar she offered in her apartment drew participants from as far away as Stockholm, but was never given *legitimation*. Her colleagues failed to notify her of faculty symposia, and had never asked her to present her research. Doctoral candidates who wanted to work with her were discouraged from doing so. A dissertation in her area of expertise would render them *inkompetent*, the damning term used of those not chosen for an academic job.

I knew the risks of pursuing women's studies in the United States, and I gloried in the struggle. I was already an intruder, a small-town packinghouse worker's kid who had survived the snooty University of Chicago. Swedish academe, far more rigid and exclusionary, was, nevertheless, Karin's native environment, her birthright. Her father had been an esteemed professor of theology. The apartment, which she inherited, was a measure of his prestige. The study was her father's, the desk his, the lamp his. His spirit still inhabited the room, tempered by the female artifacts Karin had acquired: books and artwork that had belonged to earlier women writers, and the centerpiece: a mahogany sofa upholstered in pea-soup yellow where philosopher and theologian Emilia Fogelclou had instilled her young devotees, Karin included, with the spirit of perseverance. Nevertheless, for Karin to have the trappings of academic life without the institutional rewards was a humiliation that even media attention and a loyal community of women could never soothe.

～

I returned home with enough momentum to finish my dissertation, "Feminist Ideology and Literary Criticism in the United States and Sweden," by the following spring. Karin had already begun citing it in speeches, articles, radio interviews. Once, lacking a glossy photo of me to accompany a newspaper article, she sketched my portrait and submitted that. Under Karin's sponsorship, Tjäri Reyeester and her *feministisk litteraturforskning* were soon noteworthy enough to warrant invitations to conferences. Once, Karin wrangled honorary citizenship for me so that I could qualify for Swedish funds to attend a conference in the Netherlands. The letter in which she announced this good news was signed "*Din adoptivmoder.*" In fact, our relationship became more complex than that of mentor and protégée. She longed for colleagues with whom to exchange ideas and collaborate on research. I was thrilled with the opportunities she offered me, yet more wary than I dared admit of having my work misinterpreted or reduced to formulas. It was tempting to see her enthusiasm as the reflection of my youthful brilliance, but that would be naive. The unappreciated prophet in her own land, she saw in my work the possibility of validation for hers. Look! she could say, Scholarship on women's literature is honored at American universities.

Buoyed by the attention to my dissertation, I sent off query letters to Swedish publishers, hoping to turn it into a book. It wasn't until Karin called up the wife of a major publisher and waxed *entusiasmerande* about the innovative nature of my work that I got a positive response. So I left for Sweden in March of 1976 intending to delve deeper into the women's movement, both to update my view of the constantly changing situation and to make a bolder statement on issues that concerned me personally. Now that I was no longer bound by academic strictures, I looked forward to publishing the book I had wanted to write all along. Though I longed to settle in, to let Tjäri Reyeester become just another *syster* in the struggle, my trip had to be financed by a lecture tour, arranged through letters to people whom Karin had recommended. I spoke to university classes, women's organizations, literary societies, and study circles, a Swedish phenomenon I would eagerly have imported to the United States.

Only the literature department at the University of Uppsala turned me down. Their policy, they explained in highly bureaucratic syntax, was to engage only professors as guest lecturers. My temporary, unbudgeted "ass. prof." at the University of Minnesota was apparently not merit enough. I was staying with Ann-Katrin in Stockholm when Karin called in a panic. She had just returned from Italy and found a letter in her mailbox asking her to inform me that I would be speaking to the graduate collegium the next week. I had not been consulted, yet the notices had already gone out. The newly formed women's caucus of the writer's union was meeting the same night and had invited me to come. Karin pleaded. Never before had Uppsala's literature department taken up the topic of women and literature. The anger I felt at their presumptuousness should be set aside for this pathbreaking opportunity. My feelings were very confused. I didn't want to fail Karin after all she had done for me, but I was unwilling to give up the writers' meeting. Karin called back a few minutes later with a change of heart. Why should we curtsy to these haughty men? she fumed. It would be a humiliation. We decided that I would write them, in English just to be smug, and suggest that Karin speak in my place—her first appearance ever before the graduate collegium.

I was learning to walk cautiously, to steer clear of personal disputes and rivalries, and to avoid falling into the chasm that divided the Swedish women's movement in two: socialist, and independent or bourgeois, depending on who did the naming. It was hard to take this division seriously at times, because the two sides shared the same comforts and the same tendency to ensnarl their ideals in bureaucratic procedure. It seemed so easy to be radical in the wealthy, still quite homogeneous country that Sweden was in the 1970s. I learned to distinguish between the vulgar-Marxist youth, who kept splitting into ever more purist sects; the intellectuals who spoke in abstractions and analyses; and the gritty, devoted members of *vpK*, the Communist party, which took issue with Sweden's much vaunted classlessness. These people together made up the mere five percent of voters to the left of the Social Democrats, but they predominated in my life.

However I might characterize Sweden, it is, before all else, a small country. At times, impressed with how easy it was to have my work read and heard, I wished that Minnesota could secede from the union and become a cultural realm unto itself. As Tjäri became a more comfortable persona, I had fantasies of being a Swede. Where would I fit? I wondered, as a girl from a working-class family in a small food-processing city somewhere in the interior of the country. Would I have made it to the university? Maybe Lund or Umeå, but surely not Uppsala. An apartment like Karin's would be well beyond my reach. If, like most laborers' children, I followed the vocational track in school, where and how would I live?

Only a few of the people I knew came from backgrounds like mine, including Maud Hägg, a writer and musician whose father worked at an LM Ericsson factory. I had begun dividing my Stockholm time between Ann-Katrin's apartment, which she now shared with a husband equivalent and a toddler, and a large nineteenth-century house out in Lidingö where Maud and her family lived communally with other adults, kids, and cats. One Sunday Maud invited me along for an afternoon visit with her sister. We took the subway to Tennsta, a suburb of huge, new apartment complexes, and followed a walking path through a landscaped commons to an entrance I would never find on my own. Maud insisted on taking the stairs. The brother-in-law I was about to meet installed elevators for a living, so Maud knew too much about human fallibility to trust in their safety. Their apartment was small, unadorned, a little dreary. I felt claustrophobic imagining a frantic day of shift work and childcare played out in that monotonous housing, among other families with the same restraints. This was a side of life I rarely got to see as a foreigner, but I might have known it all too well as a Swede.

At first, the commune dwellers had treated me like a guest and even refused to let me cook, relenting only if I fixed something typically American. Tunafish hotdish was an easy choice, but not so easy to accomplish without Campbell's mushroom soup. I felt seditious mixing canned tuna from Taiwan, an expensive delicacy, with canned mushrooms from the People's Republic of China, which would have been contraband in the United States at the time. With everyday Findus peas, a box of noodles, and homemade white sauce, it added up to the costliest hotdish I've ever made. The diners took tiny forkfuls at first, smacking their tongues and grimacing slightly as I had once done with bloodpudding.

I could talk freely with Maud and Ove, vent my frustrations with academe, and ask probing questions about Swedish life. The commune began to feel like home. When one of the residents announced that she might be leaving, we had the same thought: I could take her place. Had I not had a husband waiting in Minneapolis USA, I might have moved right in. Maud and Ove, after all, had paid me a high compliment . . . I think. "We keep forgetting you're American," they said. "You're not loud and overbearing."

~

The first half of 1979 was my longest Swedish sojourn, interrupted only by an Easter rendezvous with my husband in Holland and England. Karin had persuaded a government agency to fund a group research effort called the Women's Literature Project. My book had come out two years before, in a red cover with the catchword *kvinnokamp*, "women's struggle," in the title and the ubiquitous female symbol with fist that I never cared for. It was too *subjektiv* to be accepted as course literature—a disappointment for Karin—but it established me as one likely to produce more work.

Karin found housing for me with an old friend from her undergraduate days who lived around the corner. Ingrid was calm and steady and offered just the right balance of company and solitude. I slept in the maid's room behind the kitchen and had sole use of an heirloom-filled study facing the cemetery where Dag Hammarskjöld and other Swedish notables are buried. With two suitcases, two rooms, and focused work to do, I was quite content. Karin had also gotten me an assigned desk at "Carolina," the University Library. Number A1, it sat in the back corner of the reading room, next to a large window. My days were spent compiling notes on female novelists from the 1910s who were both feminist and pacifist in their literary orientation and public activity. It was engrossing work, discovering recurring literary images and revealing passages and transferring them to index cards while my mind shuffled this new data into thrilling patterns. Yet I must have done some gazing out the window. The dominant image in my memory from that time is black tree trunks against an expanse of snow tinted blue by the long midwinter dawn.

No longer a guest, I assimilated quickly to ordinary life and made friends with my project colleagues, Åsa and Ingeborg. Most evenings, I watched the TV news with my landlady and grew fond of her standard response to violence, whether in Iran or Northern Ireland: "*Ojojojojoj.*" Åsa took me along to an exercise class designed for academics who spent their days hunched over books. The leader, a bubbly Chilean refugee, whooped and sang and cajoled us reserved Northerners into swinging our arms and hips. To keep my spirit in shape, I went to organ concerts at the cathedral and at small medieval churches and sometimes stayed through the formally delivered evening prayers, while the few locals in attendance made a quick getaway, their heels clicking on the stone floor. On Sundays, the loneliest time to be a foreigner in Sweden, I took long exploratory walks. I followed the main street down the hill and under the railroad tracks to Vaksala Square, where I saw Uppsala's other face, an industrial city oblivious to academic disputes. This was where I might have spent my childhood.

I had looked forward to extended time with Karin, whose passion for life was infectious. Beautiful sights, fragrant smells, pleasant tastes all elicited sighs of wonder. I remembered a trip to Härnösand one March, when Karin pulled a chaise lounge outside, tucked a blanket around her legs, and read all afternoon, as crocuses poked up through the snow. In the sauna, I heard an impassioned lecture about how glorious it must have been for preindustrial peasants to have this means of hygiene available. A questionnaire that one of the glossy women's magazines had sent to a number of celebrities asked, "What is your greatest fault?" and Karin had written, "Too much energy." I laughed, thinking she meant it as a joke. Now, with daily contact, I began to see its obverse side. Sometimes her enthusiasm could feel like domination, her excitement about new ideas a way to silence those with which she didn't agree. In exchange for praise, she expected unfailing loyalty. I sought advice from a friend who respected Karin and knew how to stay in her good graces. "A little flame is nice," Barbro said, "but a fire will burn you up." My challenge was to stay comfortably warm.

There were complicating changes in Karin's life that year. Her brother died, and her only acknowledgment of grief was a black Persian lamb coat that made her look like an elderly *dam* rather than the youthful iconoclast we knew her to be. She struggled to maintain her jolly demeanor and kept up a frenetic work pace that stressed the rest of us. This was not her only sorrow, we guessed. Her husband had just retired and moved to Uppsala with plans to renovate the apartment. The wall of the maid's room had been removed to enlarge the kitchen, and new cupboards and appliances were installed. Karin grew irritable, preoccupied and forgetful.

Adoptivmoder began to feel as weighty as truth. As a displaced intellectual teenager, I had wished for a mother who shared and encouraged my interests. Karin had played that role in my life, and now, at thirty-three, I began to feel adolescent again, intent on proclaiming my independence. When conflicts arose in the project, Karin looked to me to defend her position, though I was the most outspoken participant—a privilege I could afford as an outsider. I got impatient with people who humored her by paying reverence to the awesome historical figure. It seemed to me they dismissed her, as though she had nothing to offer the present.

I began to experience my work in Sweden as exile. Feeling stifled by the conformity and predictability of my beautiful new environment, I longed for the creative turbulence of American life and the infinite malleability of the English language. One day it occurred to me that I may well be the only person in the world reading Anna Lenah Elgström's ponderous short stories. It also occurred to me that I could write my own.

On the flight to Sweden, I had thumbed through a special issue of the journal *Feminist Studies* called "Toward a Feminist Theory of Motherhood," while a woman across the aisle fed pieces of apple to her baby out of a plastic bag. The absurdity of that scene stuck with me, and when I came across a statement of purpose by turn-of-the-century social reformer Ellen Key, I was provoked. "The meaning of life," she wrote, "is life itself." I left in June determined to do some living and to write about it in my own voice, my own language. Karin gave me a book as a farewell gift and thanked me for being a support to her in her "worst Uppsala spring ever." I felt like a hypocrite, about to betray her.

I came home that summer with three gray hairs, dysmenorrhea, and a frayed stomach lining, the consequence of drinking Swedish coffee in American quantities. My department at the University was in disarray and the yearly renewal of my job in jeopardy. I had little interest in fighting for it. My husband and I made the long delayed decision to adopt a child, and I began my new and scary life as a writer. I remember well how Karin responded when I wrote her: "We have plenty of literature already, and you are so skilled at literary research."

~

Tjäri Reyeester made one final appearance, three years later. I left my two-year-old daughter at home to attend a seminar on an island in Lake Mälaren for women writers from all the Scandinavian countries. With no lectures to give, no tasks to perform, no reputation to ruin, I was entirely free to enjoy myself. I avoided literary criticism altogether and confined my bedtime journal entries to character portraits and nature descriptions—material for essays and stories.

A petition drive on Karin's behalf had reached the ministry of education, and word came in the middle of the week that she had been named a professor-at-large—a little like the lifetime achievement awards given to beloved actors who have never quite won the Oscar. Karin radiated happiness as we toasted her and crowned her with an elaborate wreath of June wildflowers. Then she sang to us, in a haunting alto, a song about a widow burned as a witch for stealing food for her hungry children.

~

I had told myself that if my life ever fell apart, I could always pack up and move to Sweden. But when it happened, I didn't. I was alone with two preschool children, no paying job, an unfinished book manuscript, and a persistent illness. That same year, Karin's husband died unexpectedly, and we consoled each other by mail. Divorce was probably worse, Karin speculated, since death at least left happy memories. I pictured her dressed in mourning clothes, searching for those memories in her now needlessly remodeled apartment. Gradually, Karin's letters gave way to postcards and then to notes scrawled on photocopies and newspaper clippings. In time, friends reported that she was in poor health, withdrawing more and more.

~

In 1992, after an absence of ten years, I had an impulse to buy three charter flight tickets to Sweden. We took the airport bus directly to Uppsala, where Barbro welcomed us. My older daughter, on the ornery front edge of puberty, found no pleasure in the unfamiliar and was mollified only by the mini-malls that had taken over Uppsala's main square. My younger daughter, usually the shy one, was emboldened by the graphic signs and symbols that explain everything and make talking to strangers as unnecessary as it is unhabitual to Swedes. She, however, was frustratingly short-legged and we covered little ground.

"Karin would probably be happy to see you," Barbro said, "even if she doesn't know who you are." It was not Alzheimer's but a form of senile dementia that didn't affect her mood. "We bring her along sometimes to lectures and introduce her as the mother of women's studies and everyone applauds. She seems to like that, but we have to be careful that she doesn't wander away." She still lived in her apartment, alone except for a nursing assistant who came in to help her dress and to fix meals. "See her for your own sake," Barbro urged, but my phone calls to Karin's sister, now her guardian, went unanswered. I considered taking the elevator up and simply ringing the doorbell of the apartment, hoping I might stir a memory that had not yet hardened over. We never even made it up the hill.

After a pleasurable week with American friends on sabbatical in Göteborg, we took the train to Stockholm for our last day and a half in Sweden. Except for dinner with Maud and her daughter, the only ones home in the commune, we behaved like tourists. We walked around the Old Town, took the ferry out to Skansen, watched the life-sized chess game in the King's Park, and stopped at every phone booth to try Ann-Katrin's number once more. As the subway passed the Östermalmstorg station, I pointed out Siri Derkert's wall etching, where the name Karin Westman Berg is preserved beside Sappho, Virginia Woolf, and Simone de Beauvoir.

Back at the Hotell Gustav Vasa, around the corner from Fru Frank's apartment, I finally reached Ann-Katrin to say hello and good-bye—actually *hej* and *hej*. The girls stayed behind at the hotel while I took a solitary walk, feeling as frantic and unfulfilled as I do in my dream. Had I really been to Sweden, and without Karin? I passed the Hard Rock Cafe and the McDonald's where Corso, my favorite cheap cafeteria, used to be, then slowly began to hone in on the familiar. It was the paving blocks on the sidewalk that caught me first: small squares of mauvish gray interspersed with narrow troughs where the water runs off. How accustomed I had been once to those paving blocks, and to the sound of wooden clogs behind me, and the slowed-down pace of an evening near Midsummer. I stepped into a candy store, picked out an assortment of *godis*, and found comfort in simply knowing their names: *polkagrisar, kolabönor*.

~

Sweden comes back to me sometimes. Diesel fumes from a passing bus transport me to Fleminggatan in Stockholm, the bus stop nearest Ann-Katrin's. When I get out my frayed camel-hair coat on subzero days, I am walking alongside the cemetery in the midwinter dawn, on my way to the library. The fragrance of Earl Grey tea will always be Karin.

The last time I dreamed the passing-life dream, I was standing at the side of a narrow bed, where a single suitcase lay open. Piled all around it were clothes I had bought, unrolled posters of Swedish art, berry baskets and wooden kitchen utensils. I had an hour to get to the plane and my books were still on the shelves. As I climbed on a stool to take them down, I discovered uneaten food on the top shelf: a princess torte with its mound of green marzipan, a pan of meatballs, a half-eaten pancake with lingon. I climbed down with my arms full, stared into the open suitcase, and woke up with the problem unsolved: How will I ever bring it all home?

Lounge Girls

MY FACE IS COLD and, for no particular reason, I am late again. As I burst through the door, the pub feels warm, inviting. Fiona, the other waitress, passes me on my way to the kitchen, "Graham is on the warpath," she warns me.

I throw my coat in a heap on one of the stainless steel counters in the kitchen and keep my eyes averted as I almost run to the other side of the long bar, knowing full well that Graham's eyes follow me. He corrals me at the waitress station, blocking my escape with his body. His blue eyes glare at me, and I think how his face is the color of the inside of a conch, radiant coral.

"What's yer fuckin' story?" he demands.

I try to push by him mumbling something about a phone call from the States. A lie. I lingered too long over tea with my roommate, Niamh, and Paul, the man who lives upstairs. Because they are both actors, their lives seem to be an endless circle of low-paying minor roles and dole lines. They tell me how the dole employees treat them with disdain, think they are college students trying to collect or that they're lazy.

"They sneer at you," Niamh says, "'You have your PS2113 form, but you don't have your LG115 form. Come back next week.'" She perfectly imitates the demeanor and speech of the imaginary welfare employee. Paul jokingly tells me it is the place actors go to see theater friends that they "haven't seen in ages," to get caught up.

Finally, reluctantly, I had to leave them, had to leave the tiny Haddington Road basement flat that always smells of damp earth. Niamh, regal in her purple crushed velvet top, blows me a kiss. "Be brilliant tonight," I say. She smiles, lifts one perfectly arched eyebrow, "Always," she replies.

I rush away onto the busy street long after the latest I can leave and still be on time, but worried in only a distracted way.

Rush hour is kind to Dublin, electrifies it. Trench-coated people run for buses or taxis, thick traffic clogs the roads. I pass Merrion Square where prostitutes supposedly gather at night. On Nassau Street, I slow in front of Green's Bookstore, famous for its collection of used books, where T-shirts hanging in the window immortalize the faces and words of Joyce, Yeats and Beckett.

I remember. The only gift that John, the Irish man I loved, gave me was a Yeats T-shirt. I begin reciting to myself, "Come away, O human child. . . ." The words printed so clear on cotton. It is mostly because of him that I am here now. Two years before, I had studied at Maynooth College, just outside of Dublin. During that year, John and I had a tumultuous affair—a meeting of minds and bodies, that more often than not, ended in battle. Now, fittingly, a tall, sallow man is pulling down the shutter, over the books and the faces.

Next to Green's, two teenage boys recklessly grab crates of fruit and vegetables—the satsumas, apples and broccoli that until now had sat colorfully on the sidewalk, as a news agent closes down. On the next block is the Blarney Woolen Mills where reassuring sweaters hang in the darkened windows.

Trinity looms on my right, a sprawling gray scowl. The commuting students pour out now in a stream of black biker jackets, stopping to light cigarettes, their backs turned to the wind.

I pass a ragged woman, a carrot-top toddler cradled in her left arm. "Please miss." Her face freckled and smudged, a Styrofoam cup held out.

All around her, shutters slamming down with finality and relief. The darkness of early winter swathed in soft yellow light and the sheen of wet cobblestone. Dublin closing in on itself for the night. I am part of it all.

～

Graham claims my attention again. Bends down, shoves his face into mine, "You girls are doin' me fuckin' head in! Don't think I won't fire you, 'cause I will you know!"

I bite back a smile. It's an empty threat, I know. I had already been fired twice since starting work four months earlier. Once, they took me back as I was getting my coat on, and the second time, when I came to collect my final pay, I discovered my name on the schedule as though nothing had happened.

He stomps off. Fiona hands me a cappuccino and rolls her eyes, "He's still sober," she says. I smile gratefully. Fiona is nineteen, three years younger than I am, and a second-year law student at Trinity. My favorite. People mistake us for sisters because we both have long dark hair and blue eyes. She is more a study in contrasts with eggshell white skin and cerulean eyes, while my skin is freckled and darker and my eyes cloudy, almost gray. But we are both tall and strong through the shoulders; neither of us frail or terribly feminine. We both bite our fingernails.

The Brasserie is a restaurant during the day, a pretentious one, in an expensive courtyard behind Grafton Street, host to the "ladies who lunch and shop." At night it grows even more pretentious, home to Dublin's self-proclaimed yuppies, many of them without a dime to their name. They drink away daddy's money while wearing one of the two Hugo Boss suits they own. Most nights a couple of models sit, leggy and coifed at the bar, rarely buying their own drinks or lighting their own cigarettes.

Tonight is Friday. Later, the pub will be packed and it will take every ounce of willpower I have not to quit, to bear the condescension, to bear being called a "lounge girl"—a name that conjures images of red velvet and lingerie, a name I never imagined someone would use in reference to me. By the end of the night I will have been patted and pinched. My white shirt will be Guinness-stained, my fingernails circles of black from emptying ashtrays.

But now, it is only seven and there is a lull, the after-workers have gone home to change and the late-nighters are not yet out. Fiona and I wait for this moment of sanity to sneak a cigarette. Usually, Fiona is full of spunk with a smiling open face; but tonight she says little, seems far away. I pull myself up on the metal counter next to her and light my cigarette. Although we are friends, I don't know her well enough to know her darker moods, so I decide to wait her out.

"Did you see that bastard Rory in here earlier?" she finally blurts out. Rory was her old boyfriend and had lately been parading around town with a model.

I throw an arm around her, give her a squeeze, "Aw, Fiona, he's a wanker and you know it."

"Yeah, I know," she gives me a small smile, "but it's just not that simple."

True. I think again of John, how simple everything seems now, but how complicated it seemed once. I remember the contempt on his face when he asked me why I'd come back. For him, it was over shortly after I left. At first, there were a few letters and phone calls, but eventually, my letters went unanswered and I hesitated calling at all. But I was always looking over my shoulder, believing I had found a new life I never wanted to leave. Sometimes that happens. You try on a new personality that has lain dormant within you, fall in love with it, give credit for its discovery to the person whose touch or voice unearths it.

I want to tell Fiona this, hope it will make sense to her. But, I don't. Instead, I fall back on, "Love is the curse of the earth." Because I suspect even that is enough.

One of the first regulars to make an appearance tonight is Ken Kiernan, a married forty-something singer and songwriter. He sits down at the bar; his long blond hair and expensive leather coat stand out, and I recognize him immediately.

"Oh. I'm glad you're here," he says, "how've you been?"

"I could complain, but I won't. How's the music business?"

"Good. Good. I think I might be going to L.A. soon for a project I'm working on."

I have known Ken ever since I began working in the bar; I also know there's about a much truth as there are lies in anything he says. But, he tips well and once gave me a great Jennifer Warnes-Leonard Cohen tape. I like him, so I try to believe him.

He clears his throat, "Um, there's something I've been wanting to ask you."

Ken seems nervous, clears his throat a few times, but once he begins talking, I immediately wish he'd stop. I can feel the blush beginning to burn in my cheeks. He was asking to have an affair, no, a tryst with me. "I love my wife," he tells me, "and I don't ever want to screw that up, but it's just that I find you so sexy, so intriguing." He goes on to tell me that it would be just one night, curiosity, never done anything like this before.

I say very little. I watch his kind thin face, his round, blue eyes like dimes, the wrinkles on his forehead. I think he is attractive in a way, and flattered by the compliment. "I will think about it," I say, surprising myself. He is married, at least twenty years older than I am. It's crazy to even consider it, I never would at home —but that is also precisely why I will.

Around nine, people begin filing in, ruddy cheeked and high spirited. By nine-thirty it is difficult to move, hot and smoky. The owner, Jimmy, is there, chubby, short, apple-cheeked and good-natured with his sleeves rolled up and hard at work at the bar

A regular, Ben, sits at the other end of the bar. Night after night he comes in with the women he is having an affair with. As I look at them I think of all the loneliness, the indiscretions, the liaisons that are formed and broken, assuaged and inflamed in this bar. It is not the world I expected, but it is a world in which I have carved out a place for myself, creating myself along the way.

At ten-forty-five in Irish pubs the barmen line rows of half-poured Guinness on the tops of the taps. The proper way to pour Guinness is to pour two-thirds of it, let it settle five minutes and then pour the rest. By lining them up, they can grab them and top them in the general panic at last call a few minutes later. There are pools of beer on the tables and the floors and the ashtrays are spilling over. Drunks stand splay-legged or lean heavily on the railings with one pint half full, another one full and a cigarette clamped between the second and third fingers. One of them will decide I should come home with him, will get angry, tell me I'm not pretty enough to be so surly, or look me up and down and say "tis a pity" my legs are not longer. At this time of the night I wonder how this could be worth the twenty quid a night I make, thirty-five, if the tips are good.

"Give me a rum and diet, a Guinness and two pints of Fürstenburg and then I'm done." I yell to Smack, a ginger-headed brawler with a missing front tooth from a tough area called Ballymun.

"Any chance of a blow job?" He shouts from where he is pouring the beers. This begins the verbal sparring that has become routine between us. A kind of test to measure my toughness, to see if he can get me to blush. I smile indulgently but I feel like socking him.

"Give me a look at it first, who knows, you might get lucky?" Guys sitting at the bar smirk and by the scarlet I can see spreading across his neck and face, I can see I've won that round.

After last call I sneak into the kitchen for a smoke. Fiona is already there, sucking hard on a cigarette. "Thanks for taking that last order for me," she says.

"Hey, no prob."

I ask her if she wants to go dancing tonight after close. She shakes her head, "No, not tonight."

"Come on," I prod, "We'll find you a new man. Who needs Rory?"

She starts to cry and I feel a lurching in the pit of my stomach. Suddenly, I just know. "Oh God, Fiona. You're pregnant aren't you."

She nods her head. Through tears, she tells me it's Rory's, that she doesn't have the money to go to England, the Irish euphemism for having an abortion.

"And if you think I'm asking that bastard for it you're cracked."

I know what it means if Fiona has this baby. It means the end of law school, shame, probably many more years of jobs like this. As far as I'm concerned there's nothing to think about. If she wants to go, I promise to take her to England with my credit card, the one I keep for emergencies and occasional indulgences, promise to keep her company and won't take no for an answer.

I get her to calm down, stop crying. We have another cigarette. "Keep a bright face on, until we get the floors mopped luv. You have to go back out there." We collect ourselves, pour the mop water and head back out to survey the damage.

Later, after ties are loosened, shoes kicked off and pints poured I tell Graham and Jimmy that Fiona and I need two days off and before they have a chance to complain I tell them why. Honesty catches them off guard. They tell me they don't want to hear about it, they'd fend for themselves on Sunday and Monday.

One of the barmen puts on The Commitments soundtrack and the other starts doling out bags of salt and vinegar crisps. Fiona and I dance playfully in our nylons, cooling our swollen feet on the freshly mopped tile. We are suddenly exhilarated by the opportunity to go on a trip, distracting ourselves from our mission, trying instead to see it as a holiday. Before we leave, Jimmy slips a fifty-pound note into my hand.

Fiona and I walk part way home in a soft mist and I tell her that a girl only has to cross the Mississippi at the 46th St. bridge at home if she needs an abortion, not cross an entire sea. We walk arm in arm on Baggot Street as taxis, their windows fogged, roar by us full of people heading to the discos on Leeson Street. People stumble by, drunk and friendly, in groups of two or three, singing or laughing. We keep our heads down, hoping we won't see anyone we know, enjoying our solitude together.

After Fiona leaves me, I think of Niamh, hoping she'll still be awake when I get home. She is currently playing a slut who destroys the harmony of a women's commune by sleeping with the bishop's servant. Before that she played a shallow tart in "The Tender Trap." The light is on in the front room of our basement flat and she is there, just home, making tea. She tells me that she is such a good slut the play has been extended an extra month. One more month playing a slut means one less month on the dole. I am happy to see her, happy in that little kitchen where both of us cannot be without somehow being in the other's way.

"Digestives or Jaffa Cakes?" she asks. She stands with a package of biscuits in each hand, one hip jutted forward. Her legs are long and lean in the tight faded jeans. Her black hair is down now, held back by an Alice band, but still gleaming from the hairspray. There is never a shortage of cookies in our flat, and she always lets me choose, except when I make chocolate chip cookies, then there is no other choice in Niamh's mind.

"Both," I say. "I'm too tired to choose."

We go outside and sit in the back garden under the balcony, away from the damp air, and look out at our rectangle of sky. As I cup the steaming mug of tea in my hands I remember Ken. I know that I won't call him tomorrow or any day after and now it seems absurd that I even considered it. I can't help thinking too of Fiona. As Niamh's tape of Marilyn Monroe croons in the background, I tell her Fiona and I will be taking a trip to England on Sunday. "The poor thing," she says. "I did that with a friend once, it's not a good thing to do alone."

Paul's white cat, Joe-ninety, suddenly appears on the rounded top of our garden wall. He pauses for a moment, then jumps into the rakish skeleton of our winter-barren plum tree. He leaps lightly from one limb to another until he finds one that seems to suit him. He curls his tail around him and settles comfortably in, a lumpy white globe. Niamh points to the tree, "Look at Joe," she says. "That's all it's about. You find a branch you like, hunker down and call yourself the moon."

Ogoronwy

CULTIVATION

I SLEPT ALL NIGHT listening to the sound of the stream. Now I hear Irene calling David awake from the house. Light comes through me as I turn against the mattress. I smell the heat on wet leaves near the door. Soon I hear the crunch of gravel as David goes to let the chickens out.

I sleep and read in a small stone house in the north of Wales that David has reconstructed. It is, perhaps, three hundred years old. From my bed suspended above the main room on a loft, I look out across the room to a landscape of white, rounded walls that follow the contours of the stones. The wooden windows are open to the night air now that the weather has cleared.

Light comes to me often here, pure, a bit yellow, old light remembered from somewhere else. Beauty is commonplace each morning. Elements arranged like a gift for me on the stones outside the bothy. Air, water, light, sun, one bird dipping into the shallow pond that fronts the house. Her long yellow and gray tail flicking up and down.

How powerful I feel as I throw the covers off and climb down my ladder to the stone floor. The water in the basin is cold as I wash my face. I leave the door open when I walk toward the house for breakfast.

I sleep late here. It's nine o'clock as I walk around David's office which juts out along the little stream, to the table set on the east side of the main house. The stones of the house are not painted on the east side. Their rough gray glows in this light. David is pouring tea into pottery cups. Berries Irene picked yesterday are shining in blue bowls.

"Why aren't there any windows on this side of the house?" I ask David as I pour the warm sheep's milk onto my cereal and toss a few red currants into the bowl.

"They just didn't put them in," David says. "I like the simplicity but still it would have been nice to have some there."

He's working on drawings for a college housing project that take their heft and presence from this wall. I like David's view of things. His quietly cantankerous vision.

Irene comes around the corner of the house holding Teleri. She sits beside David on the wooden plank with a pillow propped behind her back against the stone wall. The baby cries and Irene suckles her. I have wanted a baby for some time now. In April it was four years since my husband's death.

~

Irene has been teaching me how to milk sheep. She has two sheep she milks in the shed northeast of the bothy where I sleep. I grab the teat too tightly and get only a small stream of warm milk, sticky on my hand. On the other side of the sheep, Irene squirts milk in a series of spurts into the plastic jug.

"Is it okay if I get junk in the milk?" I ask, as pieces of hay fall from my hand into my jug.

"Oh, I strain it anyway," she answers. Her container half filled. "It took me quite a while to learn how to do this," she says. I don't believe her.

The last time I tried milking an animal was in Norway years ago. I remember the hot teat of the cow, how soft and warm it felt in my hand and the light coming into the barn through spattered windows.

As we milk Enid, she butts her head against the wood of the stall. "It's okay, Enid," Irene croons, "we're almost finished."

~

When Irene finishes feeding Teleri she hands her to me and I hold her while Irene eats. I touch her small feet, I look into her eyes, and I follow the sun as it moves across her face. When she's hungry she nuzzles me until she's frustrated and either cries or stuffs her hand into her mouth. When I was last here Trystan was a tiny baby and I held him, too, bound in the crook of my arm.

Children have redefined the heft of things at Ogoronwy. Irene's day is split with the management of children. Always skilled at putting things together, she has organized a play group in the village that meets at the school hall two days a week. When Trystan is at play group, Irene drives a few miles to Croeser, a village over the hills from Ogoronwy, and has a massage.

David leaves most of the child care to Irene. He'll hold the baby until she cries and then pass her to me. "Take her, will you?" and strides off to his studio where his firm designs projects in England and Wales. Irene and David met at a meeting for nuclear disarmament in a village near Ogoronwy. Children complicate politics, the focus changes.

I see the compost heap here as political. The duck dead a month ago, tossed on the pile with the night soil from my toilet, garden weeds, kitchen garbage. There's an attempt here to circle back, make things whole. A line of movement that follows the action through to consequence. History takes on a new texture. The present responds to past and future, bends a certain way because of the press of time.

~

When we finish breakfast, Irene goes off to a picnic with the children, and David and I decide to work in the gardens. His series of beds is both beautiful and productive. The vegetable garden off to the left of the cottage where I sleep is thick now with lettuce and potatoes and broad beans. Off toward the front pasture there is an herb garden growing wild against a stone wall and below that, the orchard. East of the main house in a terrace are two wedge-shaped plots where we'll prepare the ground for planting.

"I thought you might use this tool and break up the weeds like this," he says. He jumps down and starts to chop and tug at the patch he cut yesterday, cleared of wheat.

The tool he uses looks easy to manuever. Until I too jump down and start to jab it into the soil and pull clumps of weeds toward me on the slope.

"Where'd you get this—mattock—is it?"

"Oh, Birmingham, I think, but a long time ago—you probably couldn't get one there now."

Suddenly I've got the hang of it. I lift the smooth carved wood up a bit and then bring the three-pronged iron down into the dark soil, loosen up the roots of pigweed and witch grass and pull. I don't have to stoop. I relax and work up a rhythm across the first row. Soon my hands are blistered. Sweat runs down between my breasts, my legs ache.

David is below me on another field, cutting the rough hay with a machine Trystan calls "the horrible machine." Its blades are tough enough to go through the rough grass and reeds, but the noise slashes through the silence broken only now and then by the boom of air force jets swooping in low.

I'm not thinking of anything for awhile. I want to finish the upper garden before lunch, so I keep moving from row to row producing long piles of weeds as I work. I wonder what it would be like to have a place like this. A small holding Irene calls Ogoronwy.

I concentrate on the dry, crumbly soil, the way I can switch hands to move from one row to another, how I brace my legs against the toughest weeds.

~

David has finished cutting the grass. I move to the last patch of the plot. He starts to rake and gather the weeds. I'm in a section now riddled with roses, the last roots of parsley. I can taste salt on my skin. Each pore of my body breathes. I can't remember who I am, where I came from, what my sorrows are. I keep thinking about water with a slice of lemon, a few ice cubes. I know David won't stop now until we're finished.

Work is part of the fabric of days at Ogoronwy. We are in the gardens today because it's Saturday. During the week there are other tasks to complete. David's office fills by ten—he's working by a few minutes after nine, sitting at his drafting table near the window. Last week I went in to ask about a reservation at a mountain hotel. He looked up. I knew it was dangerous to interrupt—he was in the middle of putting meticulous dots on a drawing for a project he's doing for Cambridge University.

"Can you do dots?" he asked.

David's one of the few people I know who moves through his days with a kind of fierce integrity for the whole. He hardly ever compromises. Now he finds that he's spending too much time at his work and wants to cut back to a thirty-hour week so he can spend more time with Irene and the children. And spend more time designing instead of implementing the work.

One night after we've eaten a dinner of omelettes—eggs from the chickens who live in the hut beyond the bothy, onions, broad beans, peas from the garden below—David asks Ben, a woman who has worked for him for about a year, if she would take charge of more of the projects.

Ben has been telling us about Malaysia where she grew up. "I don't understand the signs now," she says, "the language has changed so much."

~

When Irene and David were gone and I was alone at Ogoronwy, I spent some time sitting in the sun, reading. I found a plastic chair with a thick fiber-filled cushion in the closet near the bothy. It was a wonderful chair to read in and I sat there for hours watching Adrian, a man who was insulating the main house, move back and forth between the workroom and the stone house with pieces of wood. For awhile Adrian's dog, a border collie, would sit with me beside the cold little stream.

"That's a great chair," I said to Irene when she returned.

"Oh," she said, "that was my mother's chair. David doesn't like it, doesn't think it fits in with the rest of things at Ogoronwy so I've ordered a new chair for my birthday."

~

Irene's work starts early—sometimes she lets the chickens out and then, on alternate days, milks her two milking sheep. Then she strains the milk and brings a fresh jug into the house for breakfast. David's usually up in the garden, picking berries.

"My life is very different from what I thought it would be," she told me the other day, as we drove back from taking the children up the cog railway to the top of Snowden. The road twisted through the oak woods' spotted light.

"What did you think you'd be doing?"

"Oh, something in a city, some kind of social work like the community center for the church, not so isolated as what I do now."

She sees herself in a community and her fledgling sheep business as the kind of work that fits into that community. For awhile she commuted to Caernarfon, a town almost an hour away, and then she worked in the village store and post office. Now she's trying to figure out how she can get by without a car. But the walk into town is two miles and that would cut into other projects she has in mind.

I met Irene a long time ago in Oxford. I was there for my junior year of college and we met at Manchester College on the first day of term. Early October and I was nineteen. Once I got to know her better, I admired her knack for making do, transforming simplicity into elegance in the way she dressed, tied a scarf or entertained in her room above a garage that looked out on a garden where I would sleep out some nights, drinking in the smell of roses.

I visited Irene in Dominica several years later when she was working as a Volunteer Service Organisation volunteer. There, too, she managed to make small things seem perfect. We drank from calabashes and ate crawfish caught in the river near where we had lunch.

A few nights ago I stripped a chicken to make curry. Irene came in from shutting the chickens in their pen and examined the carcass.

"I'll see what else I can get off," she said and tore the bird apart, accumulating a pile of meat. "In Dominica," she said, "they boil the bones for two days, getting every last bit."

~

The garden at Ogoronwy is carefully tended. In the morning we eat the fresh-picked berries, sometimes strawberries a bit white, the shiny black and red currants, the raspberries, soft like the muzzle of a horse. At noon I watch David walk past the window of the bothy on his way to gather white radishes, lettuce and peas, and broad beans. He carries an oval basket.

In the evening we usually eat potatoes dug just an hour before, boiled with butter, lettuce unadorned, and the other vegetables stirred up in the wok with olive oil and herbs.

～

I have a notion that I want all this for myself so I try to pick up the methods. I wonder if I could do it alone. At home I garden, rent a small house, try to follow through—but I'm not all that successful. I don't preserve the vegetables. I have no compost heap. I watch the television. My sins are manifold. I forget what it's like to eat outside, how the potato tastes. I don't go camping anymore. I close myself off to a community. I become preoccupied with the animals who live near me— spiders in the house, hummingbirds in the garden, the woodchuck who eats ripe peaches in August.

I have a map of this hillside in Wales in the corner of my mind. It stays there, protected, a refuge, a sure thing. I rely on Irene and David to keep up the good work. I need to know that this kind of life can still be had.

～

I was at a meeting a few nights ago where the talk was all about cultivation. A different sort of work but the same kind of impulse—stirring up the ground to plant new seeds. Irene is involved in a movement started a few years ago to connect new immigrants to Wales, who, for the most part, don't speak Welsh with Welsh speakers.

The group I sat in on was made up of native Welsh speakers like Irene and a man who stepped down as chair, English immigrants who were Welsh learners, other immigrants who were fluent in the language, and a few people who knew a smattering of words.

The idea is to connect the groups of people to preserve the Welsh language and culture by education instead of confrontation. A gentle persuasion to change such things as the tourist pamphlets in Portmadoc now printed in English or the signs in the Welsh craft center, all in English, or the translations into Welsh in brochures and pamphlets often "atrocious," according to several committee members, all put out by the tourist industry. The group, which was searching for a name at this meeting, also wants to promote more Welsh speakers in establishments like Leo's, a slick, large new store in Portmadoc. Their manifesto is to foster a respect for Welsh culture, language, history, literature that goes beyond the familiar image of women in tall black hats.

The ten or so people at the meeting discuss ways to integrate the language, as well as ways to help learners feel more connected and thus more responsible for culture—keepers of the culture.

We sit around a rectangular table in the almost empty hall in Blaenau. White walls, wooden benches pushed against the walls. I take notes on the formica top of the table. There are several women—a doctor from Portmadoc who smiles at me as I write, the two English women who drove with us to the meeting, one who like me knows a few words in Welsh, a large woman from Australia.

"The Welsh are very good at discussing things," one man says.

And another of several older men says in Welsh that he would be happy to switch back and forth from one language to another. Irene translates for the three of us who have learned only a few words in Welsh. This gets to be too distracting at the small table. The speakers switch for the most part to English. This irks the woman from Australia and a younger man who leans over the table and speaks only in Welsh throughout the meeting.

"We want awareness to underlie what we do—the point is to get a groundswell going, till the fields, put the manure in," says the man they have chosen to be the next chair. He's a retired minister whose wife, he tells me later, is a paraplegic. "I didn't want to be chair you know. I think the young people should lead this."

"The point is," he says as we stand outside the church later, roses blooming along the fence, "that just by meeting like this we're doing something. We are making a community."

Irene disagrees and has offered to do two canvassing projects that will further cut into her day. "If the talk goes nowhere, nothing gets done," she says later. "The words must result in actions."

~

I'm on the second patch of knotty weeds by now. My arms ache. I've watched the sun swing through the trees, the sky scrubbed clear after weeks of rain.

Death has become as ordinary as work to me. Work is like death, turning the roots up, pulling the weeds across the soil to the pile. Ordinary death dispatching itself through the clods.

Everyone here has lost someone—a mother, a father, a husband, a child. A man calls whose wife committed suicide a year ago. "She went out," Irene tells me, "to the garden and hanged herself while her children were at school. She was in love with another man and couldn't face it."

"Couldn't she have done something else?" I ask. "I mean, have an affair or get divorced or something?"

I hear later of another mother who drowns herself in a hotel bathtub.

~

Drama makes its way to the house, shunting against us like waves. Irene's in the middle of some of it. The rest of us watch.

A man who runs the shop in town is in love with a woman who works at the shop. This woman has left her husband. The husband had threatened to shoot the shopkeeper and beats the wife up in the shop when he isn't there. Irene has invited the wife to live at Ogoronwy. David objects. "He doesn't like her perfume, he doesn't like her voice," Irene tells me.

~

I've come to a patch where the soil isn't worked as much. I bring the mattock down as hard as I can into the earth. Hacking away at the roots. I'm thinking about sex. I'm thirty-seven years old. I have six more years to have a baby.

Yesterday I hayed a field with Irene and her friend Nia. The children were playing in a pool near the bothy and the babies positioned in prams under a tree near the two ponies, Patch and Katie. We could hear the sheep calling to their lambs.

Patch was sick. He couldn't eat fresh grass so we scooped the fresh cut hay and tossed it over the fence where he couldn't reach it. My job was to rake the hay into piles with a hay rake—a large wooden rake with thick separate prongs. Nia forked the hay and tossed it over the fence neatly. She is slender, her hair pulled up on her head in a dark bun.

"You should just go ahead and have a child and then get married," she tells me.

"Nia doesn't have time to clean her ears," Irene says later. "Sometimes I worry if my ears are dirty too."

WALKING

I've been taking long walks from Ogoronwy in all directions. The first week I was here, I walked up to a ridge overlooking Blaenau Ffstiniog, a slate-mining village to the south. The dark shiny tailings of the mines spill out along the slopes above the town.

I was with a man from home who was spending a few days walking with me. As we hiked along the narrow shaley path that traversed the slope above a large reservoir, we talked about the precarious nature of love. "I am a bit dizzy on paths like this," I said to him.

He was telling me a story about friends of his who are burdened with a child. "He wanted to do the right thing so they got married, but I don't think things are that good."

The wind was so strong I was pushed flat onto bits of grass growing up in the tailings. We were on our way to a mountain hotel at a pass north of Ogoronwy in Snowdonia National Park.

We walked north to the ruins of a slate-mining village at the head of the valley above Croeser on Moelwyn Mawr. It was cold. Other hikers were huddled in the shelter of the dark, square stone buildings, polished with mist. The outline of the village was still intact after fifty years of ghosts.

In *A History of the North Wales Slate Industry* Jean Lindsay records the misery of the men who live in the barracks where we sheltered and sipped water from a plastic bottle.

The living quarters were often overcrowded and dank. She writes: "The clothing and habits of the quarrymen were often blamed for their poor health. They were accused of drinking too much stewed tea, and of not changing their underclothing often enough."

We hiked out on an abandoned railway incline at the very lip of the valley, an expanse softened by mist, rock hard under my feet, the delicate cropped edge of the cliff. We were lost and took photographs of each other against the distance that dropped off from where we stood into a series of landscapes to the sea.

My companion went through a painful divorce. He's only just now decided that he no longer loves his wife. He sees new involvements as the doors to pain. He went on a raft trip years ago, he tells me as we walk along one of the drover's roads, caught his foot in the lines along the side of the raft, and was dragged under the water for a long time. He almost drowned. He hasn't been on a raft since then.

I'm willing to consider the idea that I might love someone again. I've had to do some violent things to come to this thought.

The man is telling me about a barn, about the beauty of the barn, how it was made with local materials, how it was set on sand, how the beams worked, and roof, and the doors.

Later, we visit a quarrying museum at the foot of Snowden where two men are chipping out blue hearts from large slabs of slate.

~

When I visited Irene and David three years ago—a year after my husband's death—
David urged me to go to the Hebrides. I wanted to go somewhere wild. I remembered that coast of Scotland as windy and empty. I wanted to be scoured clean.

I took the train to Oban to discover I couldn't get to Harris from there and
ended up going across Skye on a bus. Once on Harris I couldn't get an answer at
the hotel David had suggested I call for a room. He described it as a true fisherman's hotel at the edge of the sea. I imagined Isaac Walton and his crew, drinking brandy, pulling their wet cloaks off. It had taken me three days of travel to get
to the island. I hadn't been alone for a long time.

After a long series of calls I scouted up a room in a bed and breakfast and was
told the hotel had been closed for years except for a bar that was open some nights.

I rented a bicycle and set off across the island to the bed and breakfast several
miles away. The land was just as I expected. Bare, shorn by sea wind and sun, the
yellow curves of sand set against a forest of trees planted by lairds who kept houses
on the island. I wanted to look at birds and biked out along a spit of land a man
in town had told me was a good place to see puffins.

I rode the bike as far as I could and then left it at a fence, climbed over, and
walked along a narrow path above the sea until I came to an old church. Sheep
were scattered around the open nave.

I sat outside on a stone, the yellow buttercups, the stiff grasses shining, and
that sea—open, wide, blue, clear expanse. I was perfectly alone. I had a sense that
I was safe there—that my quiet would go out like a prayer—that this pilgrimage
by train and bus and bike and foot was an act of faith.

~

One day I walk to the sea from Ogoronwy. I set off early so I can take a round-
about way across the hills to Penrhyn and then round the headland across the fields
to Portmadoc.

The lane that leads down to the village passes Francis's wood and then the
fields of Hendre where the black cows stand haunch to haunch in the heat, flicking off flies and the black-faced sheep crop the nubs of grass. Seagulls dip above
the heads of the animals. Sometimes a heron flaps up in her heavy grace and moves
across the green pastures.

The road passes through a farmyard, the house large and stone, set back, bordered by flowers. For several days I watched the farmers haying, rolling the cut
hay into long bundles or scooping it up for silage.

After the farm the lane is shady aand threads its way to the main road,
hedged with thick-leaved plants, holly, berry bushes, foxglove nodding with seed
pods, velvety rhododendron leaves that catch silvery light.

This small road comforts me in its particularity. I know at the end of the day
I can retrace my steps back to an order cultivated on the ridge above the flats that
stretch out to the embankment along the sea. This is a good lesson for me to
learn—the persistence of order, the ability to prune life to flower.

My walk is through reclaimed land. The embankment , a six-foot high bank,
stretches for half a mile along the sandy shore at Portmadoc. I learn the story of
the embankment from several people. David tells me the poet Shelley had a hand
in it.

William Alexander Madocks built the earthen dam in the early nineteenth century and was supported by Shelley who contributed one hundred pounds to repair the structure after a storm in 1812. Later, Madocks built the harbor at Portmadoc which handled the slate from the quarries in the mountains where I walk.

My route takes me past a church where the sea once touched the stones along the back in a long finger of estuary, almost two hundred years ago. I meet a man carrying a milk jug who lives in the house next to the stone church. His sweater is buttoned once. He wears rubber boots caked with mud.

"I was a pilot on the Mississippi," he says. "Come in for coffee."

Irene tells me later his wife is dead. I pass his pile of split wood on the slippery cow path.

A few miles closer to the sea I meet a man at a shed in a dirt farmyard, metal sheeting covering the barn, where he's been talking to a younger man. The farmer's dog jumps up on me, and I struggle to push her off from my face where she hits her nose again and again.

He gives me a ride to the place where he tells me the footpath to Minnforth starts. I remember this man from three years before.

"Some people," he says, "call it a footpath and others don't. Now the old ones, they've been using it as a footpath for years, but the council doesn't want to keep it up."

He's a small man and very old, his coat buttoned lightly across his narrow chest. I offer to open the cattle gates, but he says he's used to doing it. His white stone house is snugged low into the hillside. A tall hedge runs along the side near the footpath. He was cutting the hedge three years ago when I met him.

"The footpath," he says, "is marked on a map I have that was printed in 1800."

He mutters about the gates. "We've been here for forty years and had no trouble and now the man who lived in that farm has given it to his nephew who keeps all the gates shut to vex me. The Welsh are funny, they'll be nice to you and then they'll cut your throat."

An Englishman from the Midlands who worked in two mines, he came here as a farm bailiff. His wife made figurines. When I first met him, he had been retired for twelve years and complained that he couldn't keep his hedge in shape. It was too high for him to cut. When he moved up in 1947 everyone spoke Welsh, he told me.

I follow the footpath through waist high bracken, gold flies buzzing in a fist around my head.

When I reach the paved road to Portmadoc I see a man on the first bend shading his eyes. He's looking toward the bluff we can see from Ogoronwy that slopes down to the sea at Portmadoc.

"Did you hear a siren?" he asks. "Did you see someone on the side in orange?"

As we stand at the side of the road he tells me his history.

"There's more glare to the light now," he says. "It's much hotter than it used to be."

"You know that cottage on the slope below Cnict?"

I say yes.

"My mother lived there and my father used to walk from where you are at Ogoronwy just above there at Hendre Gilian to Croeser. When I came back from the army, my tenancy was up and even though the landlord, a lady, promised me a holding there was nothing."

"My regiment came over the pass there," he points. "They've been quarrying that mountain for one hundred years."

"I'm still not married," he grins. "The nurse was just here to look at my varicose veins," he says and slaps his leg.

~

Not long after I meet the pensioner in the road to Portmadoc, I go with Irene to Croeser, the village his father walked to over the cold hills to visit his mother on Christmas. We drive to a house that sits below Cnict in the place where his mother lived. The farmhouse is set against the hillside like the bothy where I'm staying. Jo, the woman who owns the house, has planted a garden on the side. The gate creaks as we open it.

Irene has her massage and I take care of Teleri. I wheel her carriage down the steep rough lanes to the town. When we come back the two women are still in the other room so I go into the kitchen where the stove is on and rock Teleri back and forth in my arms. She nuzzles my neck and starts to cry. She wants her mother.

When Irene and Jo come out, Irene suckles the baby and Jo tells me about the house. English, she's been here for over thirty years off and on, twenty with her parents, who owned several cottages in the valley. Her daughter lives in a house that was Jo's mother's after her father's death. "She's a hermit," she says simply. Her daughter's passion is to photograph an erratic boulder field near her cottage. She records the boulders in all kinds of light.

"The photographs are beautiful," her mother tells me.

TOLERATE CONTRADICTIONS

My sin is sometimes despair. Small movements, concentration on detail will fend this off. Thinning the carrots, sifting the soil through my hands to sort out rocks and weeds, holding the bottom of Teleri's feet, hearing Irene call the sheep across the fields: "Anharrod, Meriana, Enid. Anharrod, Meriana, Enid. . . ."

~

We don't swim in the sea on the Lleyn Peninsula. When we go there I walk down to the water's edge across the smooth stones in my bare feet and touch the water. It's tepid and very salty; I can't seem to get the feel of it off my hand.

This is probably the most polluted sea in the world, Irene tells me. But we spend a pleasant hour or so there, eating fish and chips, playing in the sand.

Like Wales, I feel as if I'm bordered by a radioactive sea, trouble on the shores, waves washing over the stones clear blue and beautifully dead.

~

I have a litany of events that clicks on and off. Most of these images are very clear but at the same time indistinct. Still photographs connected to my late husband, Steve.

~

There is no sadness in the touch of the horse's mouth on my hand. His warm breath, the soft velvet of his mouth. Or the tough wool of the sheep as she rubs her head back and forth under my hand. One day I hold Anharrod for Irene. We tip her up on her haunches and I rest her head in my arms. Irene struggles with her hooves, clipping them, scraping the foot rot out, spraying the tissue with medicine.

"They're quite docile," she says, "once you have them on their bottoms like this."

When she's finished, Irene sets Anharrod on her feet again, and we let her out of the pen to join the other sheep grazing the steep pasture. Trystan and Teleri are up on the hill. Trystan's taken Teleri's blanket and she's lying on the grass screaming, her head wobbling back and forth like a buoy. Trystan's built himself a fort above us in the crook of a small tree.

∽

We've finished preparing the plots.

David goes off for the mustard seed and I continue to comb the soil with the rake, pulling up patches of weeds I missed earlier. Now and then I look up to the buildings—the old farm on the left, whitewashed in front, bare stone on the side, the office—all glass where it fronts the stream and the garden where I work, and behind me Francis's wood, next to the office, Irene's work room, and then the bothy.

∽

The main house is torn up with reconstruction. Adrian comes at nine or so and makes himself some coffee and commences to pound away at the walls. He runs long miles on the old Roman roads in the hills and is a potter.

"They left the gates open during the run up Snowden," he tells me, "and seven hundred sheep got mixed up."

Right now a conflict has cropped up over the materials he's using to insulate the walls.

David, after many phone calls to the manufacturer, has discovered that the boards he ordered—expensive wall boards complete with a backing of orange insulation—contain formaldehyde. He's decided not to use them. There are two large stacks piled outside my bathroom window. I can smell the stuff as I bathe.

"All these things chip away at one," David says when I ask him about the materials. He's decided to use some other method and materials for the rest of the rooms. One is already completed.

"We're only holding on in this tiny niche," he once told me.

"I wouldn't have kept on with the job," Adrian tells me, "if they had told me to rip out the room I had finished."

∽

I'm reading a biography of Isak Dinesen. Her biographer Judith Thurman writes that the writer believed the key to life is to tolerate contradictions. It seems to me that this is good advice. A tolerance of contraries—Peter Elbow calls it embracing the contraries—and isn't that what Buddhism is all about?

Christianity, on the other hand, is always purifying the dross. Chopping the soul clean over and over, flushing out the sins with confession, making the mind new over and over, the body cleared out so it's scraped clear of those complications, those sinful thoughts.

But then again that's the draw, isn't it? At least for me growing up. I could purify myself with confession, get rid of all those bad thoughts and start all over again. There was still a chance that I could be good.

I've just started to realize that being good might not be the point—being happy might not be the point either.

～

David comes back with the seed in a paper sack, the edges rolled over so he can scoop the tiny mustard seeds up easily from the bottom.

"What's the method here?" I ask.

And he says, "Here, take some in your hand and walk there, right next to me and just do what I do."

He scoops a handful up from the bag and lets the gold seed fall between his fingers as he moves his arm back and forth in front and walks slowly down the patch we've prepared. I'm not as good at it, my hand smaller, less steady, so I go back over sections we've already walked through.

"There's enough there," David says. "You don't have to worry about it."

～

I am soothed by the simplicity of elements in Wales—sheep, bracken, foxglove, heron, child, mother, father.

The colors work on a palette of greens and pinks. Someone has made sure the hills correspond to the sea. Nothing jars from where I watch. I know there's a nuclear plant just about to come off-line after twenty years. The government wants to keep it on-line and the community wants to shut it down. I know the sea is radioactive, the worst sea in the world. But none of this touches me as I sit on the wooden bench in front of the house at Ogoronwy—a word Trystan says like an incantation. I'm not thinking of much of anything except how hungry I am and how sweet the air smells.

Sometimes I am perfectly happy in my portions of a life lived well. A long walk, fire on my face, cat in my lap, cheese under the knife, stone, heather, fern the size of my palm, sheep cropping the grass, sky, wind, smell of fire in my nose.

～

We sow the seed in the lower path first and then move to the plot set into the bank below David's office. We are moving in precise geographical territory here. I feel very safe.

Once we finish sowing, David picks up the rake and draws the soil lightly across the surface of the seeds.

By the time we finish, Irene has come back from her picnic with the children. I lean the mattock against a tree and walk to the bothy for a bath. It has started to rain. My legs ache from bracing against the pull of the weeds. I rub the blisters on my palms. All through me there's the steady tug of a day at work. My mind is clear. I walk across the gray pebbles to the wooden door, flip the latch, and walk inside.

Home / Heimat

SHUTTLING BACK and forth between my former home in Germany and my present home in the United States I am reminded of an old film in which Alec Guiness plays a bigamous sea captain who sails between Cairo and Southampton with a faithful wife in both ports. Their portraits hang, back to back within the same frame, on the paneled wall above his bunk. Each time his ship passes through the Strait of Gibraltar, the captain flips the frame over and smiles with anticipation at the image of the woman who will greet him in the next harbor.

I, too, know about loyalty to opposite shores, and like the captain, I make adjustments in preparation for each arrival. Flying eastbound across the Atlantic, halfway through the in-flight meal, I move my fork from my right hand to my left and my wedding band from my left hand to my right. Nodding to the passenger beside me, I wish her a good appetite, *Guten Appetit*. Soon I will make my way down the aisle to the magazine rack and exchange my copy of *Newsweek* for *Der Spiegel*.

At sixty-two comfort is essential, and I am wearing well-worn jeans and Birkenstocks for the flight. Mentally, however, I have already exchanged them for the worsted skirt and sturdy oxfords I keep in the closet of my mother's apartment. A subtle change comes over me. When I arrive in Stuttgart I will no longer be quite the same woman who left Portland, Oregon, just a few hours earlier. But I have not landed yet.

We are approaching, and the plane flies low enough for me to watch the fields below. They are not divided into large rectangles as they are in the Netherlands or the United States, but are oddly shaped pieces molded to a hilly landscape. Fields embrace villages and are separated from the next village by a dense fringe of forest. The center of each community is formed by a fountain surrounded by an open space for markets, bordered by a church and city hall. In summer there will be geraniums in all the window boxes. We are above *Wuerttemberg*, land of the *Suevi*, or Swabians, as the Romans called us. The map below is so familiar that for all I know, it may be imprinted in my genes. Is this what it means to come home?

But more than a familiar landscape, home is the sound of the mother tongue. To the fine-tuned ear, the Swabian spoken in Stuttgart is so distinct that it cannot be mistaken for the same dialect a mere fifty miles away. Outsiders rarely appreciate the sound; even many Swabians try their best to lose it, but it is music to my ears. I play with the phrases in my mind and on my tongue. Here harsh consonants are softened, and the diminutive 'le' is added in the most unlikely places. God himself is not exempt: among friends *Gruess Gott* may become *Gruess Gottle*, or—stranger yet—the sophisticated French import *adieu* a modest *adele*. Here, and only here, I am never asked where I come from.

Outside the terminal, a crowd has gathered. There are not enough taxis today due to an event in the Neckar Stadium. When there were shortages during World War II, Britons learned to queue, Germans learned to push. Old habits persist. I plant my feet firmly on the ground and mentally roll up my sleeves. When the next cab pulls up, I am ready. The fur-coated woman to my right pushes me aside to yank open the door of the taxi, but it takes one to know one, and I am prepared. Before she can squeeze past me I have thrown my backpack on the seat. The taxi is mine. I am home at last.

The recently expanded airport is located in what once was the center of a major cabbage growing region. While the taxi winds its way through construction detours my eyes search eagerly for the familiar. An ancient barn remains at the edge of the airfield, no doubt a historical landmark now rather than a home to livestock. We reach the open road where fields alternate with housing blocks. The sky is gray, and only a few leaves are still clinging to the oak trees dotting the landscape. Fall has advanced further here than in the Willamette Valley. Watching the scenery fly by I spot my mother's home at a distance. It looms incongruously above the suburban landscape but is welcomed by nearby communities for the business it brings.

This is the *Augustinum*, a retirement home enclosing individual apartments for seven hundred residents who are fortunate enough to have found a place there. Despite a facade of solid elegance, it is still an *Altenheim*, with bedridden nursing patients under the same roof as the recently retired, whose luxury cars are parked below. Lobbies and halls are marble, amplifying the sound of tapping canes, slow shuffling steps, and the quick patter of the feet of young helpers. I, too, find myself accelerating my pace, as if old age were infectious, and by moving fast, I could avoid catching it. Nervously I notice that the younger residents are not much older than I am. Here my mother lives, and although she has a daughter, she is cared for by strangers. Since my brother's death three years ago I am her only child.

Adjacent to the marble corridors there is an indoor swimming pool, a theater, music room, game room, a mini-golf course, and a giant chess set. My mother no longer avails herself of these amenities; she is barely mobile. Each time I see her I am shocked: This once formidable woman has shrunken to a tiny speck of white-haired energy. I hug her, and I am afraid she will crumble in my embrace. But she is not as fragile as she looks.

My mother welcomes me with my favorite food, the local pretzels, *Laugenbrezeln*, crisp at the twisted part, soft and salty on the wide part, split and spread with sweet butter. Coffee and hot milk, local apples, tough skinned and wrinkled. In my honor she is wearing a dress I bought for her in Portland, a necklace I sent from Mexico, a vest I once knit with filial devotion.

"You had to leave Portland so early in the morning—that was yesterday, wasn't it? That time business is so confusing," she says. "Did Marv take you to the airport?"

"Yes," I say, "he sends his love." I know how much she needs to hear this.

"And the children, are they all fine?"

"They are, and they always talk about how nice it used to be when you could still travel and visit us instead of me coming here. They really miss seeing you." She nods, looking satisfied.

"Are you very tired?" she now asks, anxious to make me comfortable, and, without waiting for an answer, "I hope you won't get one of your headaches; I need your help with so many things. If only you could come for longer visits!"

"I'm fine," I say, while I fish in my purse for some aspirin. "What's the first thing we need to do?"

"Frau Schleier will come tomorrow and bring *Spaetzle* and plum tart. You must be sure and eat all of it and tell her how good it is, or she will be offended. She makes the *Spaetzle* by hand, you know, just for you. She will also drive us to the cemetery. I know you don't like that, but she would take it badly if we didn't go. I have to be so careful about her feelings. She works for some other residents in this home, too, and I don't want to lose her." The phone rings before I have a chance to answer.

The telephone is my mother's lifeline. It is a special phone, with extra-large numbers that are easy to see and a long cord to carry it from the bedroom to the table where we are sitting. Although she keeps her conversations short (she is always the one to hang up), it is sometimes difficult for us to talk because of the telephone. It is either ringing and has to be answered, or she interrupts herself in mid-sentence, saying, "Excuse me just a moment, I have to make a call." As I get older, I better understand this need. A thought, once lodged in the mind, must be acted on quickly or it may be difficult to retrieve later on.

"Hello," I now hear her say, "not this week. You can't visit me this week. My daughter is here from America." She hangs up with an emphatic click and turns back to me.

"I am so lonesome," she tells me, "nobody ever calls or visits me. If only you weren't so far away." Yet there will be many of these calls, and each caller will be told to wait and come in two weeks after I am no longer here. There are many friends who look in, but they are not the person she most wants to see.

The phone rings again. "At ten tomorrow," my mother says, "and don't forget the *Spaetzle*." Click. She turns to me, then back to the phone, remembering something that needs attention. She is voicing numbers, while her fingers search for the large square push buttons. My mother knows dozens of phone numbers by heart; now she has reached the one she wants. "Frau Schleier, one more thing. Don't wait downstairs, come up. We have to put the *Spaetzle* in my refrigerator. Tomorrow, all right? Ten sharp. In my apartment." Click again. Frau Schleier will receive several more calls before ten o'clock tomorrow.

Unlike my mother, I prefer letters to the telephone. I scribble a quick note to my family in Portland, and head for the door to mail it downstairs. "Not in the house," my mother advises, "they don't empty the lobby mailbox till noon tomorrow. It's awful, just once a day. If you go outside, go straight for a block and then turn right, there is a mailbox. It gets emptied every two hours." Like telephone numbers, mail collection times are my mother's link to the outside world. Until she became too frail to travel, she also knew the streetcar schedule to the main station and train schedules, both on- and off-season, to all the places she might want to go.

Clad in my mother's Loden coat, scarf, leather gloves, I step outside. The sky is pink and purple, the fresh air feels good. Briskly I walk along the sidewalk toward town, turn a corner and another corner, searching for a mailbox. Streetlights come on. Suddenly I realize I have no idea what I am looking for; I have forgotten what German mailboxes look like. When I was a child they were red, curved on top, with slots on either side, and mounted on the walls of houses. I remember standing on tiptoe to mail letters to relatives abroad. But what do mailboxes look like now, in the last decade of the twentieth century? Are they freestanding and blue like the ones back in the States? Or red pillars like in England? I feel as if I am dreaming, finding myself in a world I thought was home yet unable to locate the most ordinary object. I spot a pedestrian hurrying along, briefcase in hand, and ask him where I can find a mailbox.

"Around the corner, one block," the middle-aged man with the Tyrolean hat says impatiently, pointing back in the direction from which I came.

I have to brace myself for the next question. "What color are they?"

"What color are what?"

"Mailboxes. What color are mailboxes?"

"Yellow, of course, what else?"

"They used to be red," I say defensively. That was a mistake. Here no disagreement is small enough to end in a draw; it must be settled firmly, once and for all.

"They were never red, always yellow," he says resolutely, starting to walk on. But I am not done with him yet.

"Just what do they look like?"

Now he leans close, inspecting my face. "What do you mean, what do they look like?"

"I mean do they stand on the sidewalk or hang on a wall?"

Now he smiles in recognition. The *Altenheim* is near; that explains this gray-haired woman who speaks like a local but has such odd questions. "They are square," he says with unexpected kindness, "and they stand against a wall." Before he can lead me home, I hurry back in the direction from which I came. Now I see the mailbox; it is shaped like a cigarette vending machine back in the States.

~

Frau Schleier is not much younger than my mother, but her eyesight is better. Stretching her neck to look over the wheel, she steers her Fiat expertly through traffic to the opposite end of town. Her family was among my father's patients, but I remember her best as a young woman who came to do our laundry. She still helps my mother now and then, by the hour.

Now she is encased in a brown fur coat that was my mother's long ago. My mother also is wearing fur. I am in Loden, hunched in the back seat, beside a large case of mineral water. Frau Schleier does not approve of my choice of clothes. In her view they are not appropriate for a lady. I should own a fur coat like my mother's. She has actually told me this. My mother is more generous in her judgment.

"We are almost at the Daimlerplatz." Frau Schleier now turns her head back to me, making me nervous; there is a pedestrian crossing just ahead. "This is where you used to live. I remember when my mother first brought me to see your father; I had a sore throat. His nurse, Gertrude was her name, gave me a candy. Must have been around 1932; you were just a toddler. Those were happy days for your parents." I have actually come to see the house each time I am in

Stuttgart, but now I have a lump in my throat and can't answer. The six-story golden sandstone building survived the war. Even the turrets on both ends are still intact. On the second floor I can see the windows of my room on the far right, and those of my father's office on the left. Nurse Gertrude gave me candy, too, whenever I came to see her in her domain, which I did often. The candy was in a tin can with pink roses, and was by no means the only attraction in the office. There were cubicles enclosed by white drapes behind which patients undressed for sun lamp treatments. I desperately wanted to know what naked grownups looked like and hoped to achieve my goal by crawling under one of the curtains. I still remember the linoleum cool under my knees, pebbled brown and gray. Nurse Gertrude was on guard, however, and invariably pulled me back by one leg, mission unaccomplished. She was with us from before I was born until she went off to serve the wounded in the war. I loved her almost as much as I loved my mother.

Frau Schleier continues talking about the old days, how my father first made house calls on a motorcycle, then in the little green Opel that I still remember. She is talking to my mother, but I feel as if the conversation were meant for me. "This is where you belong," she seems to say, "where you have your roots, way back, to the time before you were born. This is your real home, your *Heimat*, and I won't let you forget it."

Smartly she turns into the parking lot of the cemetery. A frequent visitor here, she is on familiar ground. Unlike me, she is a faithful daughter who comes every Sunday to water and weed her parents' graves, to see who else is there, and to be seen carrying on this tradition of service to the departed.

Enders' Nursery and Flower Shop is on the opposite side of the street. While Frau Schleier stays with my mother, I hurry across to buy a potted plant for my father's grave. I do this each time I am here; I know the routine. Frau Enders, too, tells me about my father, that he delivered her, which she does not claim to remember, and that he saved her life by diagnosing her appendicitis when she was twelve. I am not good with flowers and accept what she recommends, an orange begonia. I can imagine my father's amused grin if he could observe the charade in which I am trapped, yet my eyes are watering. I almost get run over hurrying back to the parking lot.

There a decision has been made while I was gone. My mother no longer feels up to walking the half mile from the lot to the grave, and I am to go with Frau Schleier and leave her alone in the car. I remonstrate; the main paths are paved and wide enough for vehicles; in fact, a cemetery truck is turning out into the street at this very moment. "That's no problem," I say. "Frau Schleier can drive closer to the grave. That's what these service roads are for."

"Cars are not allowed." Frau Schleier's face bears a look of resigned patience as if dealing with a slow-witted child who just does not understand rules.

"But surely an infirm widow can be driven closer to her husband's grave! I'll go inside and show them Mother's handicap I.D. and they will have to allow it." Certain of victory, I enter the little office by the gate. Bulletin boards are lined with announcements and schedules of services in the adjacent chapel. The guard, however, is not interested in the condition of my mother's legs, and points to a bold sign on the wall. "*Privatfahrzeugen ist die Einfahrt in den Friedhof nicht gestattet.*" Gratuitously he adds "Official vehicles only." Frau Schleier was right, it's not allowed. When I was young they would have said "*verboten,*" forbidden, instead of "not allowed." Such is the ameliorating influence of a democratic form of government.

My mother will stay in the car, alone. With her white hair above the gray fur coat she looks like some Arctic creature curled up in a cave. Solicitously, Frau Schleier lays a blanket over her lap. I wish I had thought of doing that myself, but I was too preoccupied with my frustration. Curiously, my mother does not seem to mind being left behind while I follow Frau Schleier along the neatly bordered paths.

Under the older woman's watchful eye, I plant the begonia on my father's grave. The headstone is simple: my grandparents' names, his name, room for my mother's when her time comes. My mother had the stone erected when my father died twenty-five years ago. At that time his parents' urns were moved into the new grave from a larger family grave where space was running out. My mother's family, too, has lived in Stuttgart for many generations, but most of her ancestors are buried in the Jewish cemetery. Of her own generation many have escaped before the war to South Africa, England, the United States, Argentina, and Switzerland. Two cousins died at Auschwitz. In 1941, while my father was hospitalized with a recurrence of throat cancer, my mother invented the clever and dangerous lie that she had been fathered by an Aryan. Records were changed making her into a *Mischling Ersten Grades*, a Half-Jew. She was thus spared wearing the yellow star and being deported. I became one-quarter Jewish, and could go to the same school as other children. What set me apart from them was not so much how I was treated, but the things I knew and feared and could not say. My mother will be the last of the Rosensteins to be buried in Stuttgart, but she has asked me to omit her maiden name from the headstone. I have argued with her, but she was firm. "All my life I have been set apart because of this," she said. "At least when I am dead no one will be able to read my name and to say that I have no right to lie here." I am deeply saddened by her defeat: having lived most of my life in the United States I have been spared the cold fear of discovery that she still carries in her bones.

I now press down the damp earth around the orange flower, tears blinding me. Though my grief is real, in Frau Schleier's presence I feel like a fraud, as if my muddy knees and tear-stained face were for her benefit. She has fetched a watering can and is dowsing the new plant. She is in her element. My mother can count on her to spread the news that with her help, the daughter from America has paid her tearful respects once more.

Back in the car I am fishing for my handkerchief. It is wet and useless. Over her shoulder my mother hands me a new pack of tissues. I blow my nose. Frau Schleier puts her Fiat in gear and we are on our way. I feel vaguely unwell; it must be jet lag. Closing my eyes, I try to relax, but am too curious about the conversation in the front seat to let myself drift off to sleep. Hard of hearing, both women speak loudly. They address each other by their last names and formally with "*Sie*," as they have for fifty or sixty years, but I sense a change in their relationship. This is no longer the dialogue between a servant and her mistress. "Which one do you think I should wear?" I hear my mother ask. Her voice sounds anxious.

"Your white one, it looks elegant with your gold necklace," Frau Schleier says, soothingly.

"I can't wear that. I wore it on my eighty-fifth. It's all I ever wear." Now my mother is a little miffed. Frau Schleier should have known that the white one was out.

"Your red one, then, the silk one, with the white stripes."

"That's not warm enough. You know how cold I get."

"But it's not until July, that's months from now. It will be warm, you'll see." They are talking about the party to be given to the original residents on the twentieth anniversary of the opening of the *Augustinum*. Only a handful are still alive. Now I realize what struck me about the tone of the conversation: Frau Schleier is filling a role that would have been mine if I had stayed in Germany. I resent her for it, but I am also grateful. Her presence will make my departure easier.

~

My mother takes her medicine and retires to her bedroom. Her light goes out, but I cannot sleep. Only a few days until I go back to the States, but I feel as if my life there is only an illusion. I take my passport from my purse and study it for reassurance. It is dark blue: American. America is where I love, work, drive my car, clip coupons. I may speak with a slight accent, but I know English well: I am able to converse as pompously as anyone on politics, art, philosophy. The United States is my home, although after forty-five years I am still asked where I come from.

Now I would like to use the telephone, to call home and hear my family's voices, but the phone is by my mother's bedside. I turn on the television, searching for an English-speaking channel. The presidential election campaign in the States is in its last days, a Clinton victory a distinct possibility. News from Germany, on the other hand, is disquieting: attacks on foreigners are more and more common, police response is often late and ineffectual. Demonstrations are planned for November 7th in Stuttgart and the following day in Berlin to protest the attacks and Bonn's indifference. Since my departure is not scheduled until November 10th I decide to go. I expect this demonstration to be similar to rallies I attended in Portland just before I left, protesting Measure 9, Oregon's anti-gay initiative.

In the morning I tell my mother of my plan while Frau Schleier is making coffee. I would have preferred to make breakfast without her help, but the women have decided that I needed a vacation. Frau Schleier is now clicking her tongue, and I sense disapproval. Not for political reasons—she was never a Nazi and I have heard her express sympathy for the foreigners—but because ladies do not demonstrate. My mother has other reasons for not wanting me to go. "It's dangerous," she says. "You don't know what it's like here, you are never here."

"Not as dangerous as driving a car," I give the standard reply, "and with all the guns in America it's not all that safe there, either."

"But what about me—you came for just twelve days and you want to spend one day in town. I need your help." The truth is out. She is not worried about my safety after all, just greedy with my time.

"Thirteen days," I can hear the irritation in my voice. "You know that I have to go to work again the day after I get back. But I promise I'll do all you ask before I leave." I, too, am a hypocrite. I want to participate in what I see as an anti-fascist demonstration, but it is also a good pretext for leaving the *Augustinum* for a few hours and going downtown, and I look forward to the event. Frau Schleier hovers silently.

By Saturday I have made good on my promise. I have searched every corner of my mother's small apartment for her missing rings, without success, and I have reported the apparent theft to the administrator. I have spoken to the kitchen about her diet, although my conversation with Frau Rumpf, the director of food services, took an unexpected turn. A woman in her forties and a head taller than I, Frau Rumpf barely listens when I tell her that my mother finds her soft diet so tasteless she is losing her appetite. "We do what we can, but your mother complains every day. She does not like noodles, nor rice, nor mashed potatoes, and she is tired of scrambled eggs. Your mother has lost her sense of taste and she cannot chew, but that is not our fault. But, please, do something about her dentures."

"She has already done everything. Three sets have been tried. She simply can't tolerate them when she is eating. The dentist has explained to me that many patients past eighty simply cannot adjust to new dentures."

"Then tell her to leave them in her apartment when she comes to dinner. There have been complaints, you know, from other residents."

"Complaints?"

"Yes. On several occasions. Your mother takes her dentures out during the meal and puts them on the table. It's not appetizing for the others. We try to have an orderly dining room, you know."

Feeling chastised, I return to the apartment. My mother is not amused when I tell her what I have heard. "Outrageous," she says, "I have never done that. Put my dentures on the table, indeed! You should have told her it's not true. You can't imagine what these people are like—they will say anything at all."

Without telling my mother, I decide to speak to the *Sozialreferendarin,* Frau Seehaus, a social worker like myself. She will arrange a meeting for my mother with the cook in charge of special diets in order to plan a more inviting menu. We both agree that the situation in the dining room might also be less stressful if my mother had more positive contacts with other residents, and more variety in her daily routine. She still has an active and curious mind, but her poor eyesight prevents her from reading the books she loves. I am impressed with Frau Seehaus's sensitivity and the thoughtful array of activities that have been planned for residents with a whole range of handicaps. There are not only talking books, but also regular gatherings for discussions and various games to enhance memory function. My mother does not like my suggestions. She already knows about the books and uses them when I am not there. As for the games, she is not interested. "I already live among old people, that's all I see. Why should I sit around and play guessing games with them? Besides, some of them are senile, you know."

"Alzheimer's," I correct her.

"It's the same thing. They don't remember. You wouldn't want to play with them, either." Clearly, she is more annoyed than comforted by my concern, as if in suggesting games with other seniors I was denying the depth of her loneliness. Perhaps I am.

～

Saturday, November 7th, is a beautiful day and I am still euphoric from Tuesday's election result. The weather is sunny and crisp, making the thirty-minute trip from the Augustinum to the Schlossplatz especially pleasant. The streetcar traverses the Silberwald, once a hunting forest of kings and now a public park, passes beneath the television tower, and winds its way slowly into the Neckar Valley, offering splendid views of the city, *die Stadt zwischen Wald und Reben*, "the city among forests and vineyards." Yet there is a touch of grief in seeing the town below: it is not the place of my childhood. By 1945 Stuttgart lay in ruins, seventy-five percent of its core destroyed. At the time of the bombing I was a young teenager, eager for the Allies to liberate us, and I remember thinking during an air raid that I was willing to die for their victory. Fifty years have passed, I am an American now, and I feel shame when I remember the bombing of civilians. It did not seem to speed the end of the war and only provided grist for Hitler's propaganda mill that painted the Allies as inhuman and cruel enemies. Meanwhile, big Nazis sat in safe shelters in the country, while ordinary people, among them many prisoners of war, were killed. By now, of course, most of the victims would be gone, but the city, with its historic center, its market square and city hall, the handiwork of generations of masons, carpenters, and artists, would still be there. All that remains now is the quaint layout of streets, lined with ugly buildings thrown up during the economic miracle of the fifties. Nor am I much comforted by the sight of the Stiftskirche, the new and old castles, or the Koenigsbau, which have been restored by using some of the original stones. Old buildings have a life of their own, with each step and door handle bearing the imprint of the past. These reconstructions have no more in common with the real thing than figures in a wax museum with the living originals.

Arriving downtown brings me back to the present. The Schlossplatz is already packed with a crowd of mostly German-speaking people under fifty. Many are there with their families, children riding on the shoulders of their fathers. The mood is one of earnest, almost passionate concern that history should not repeat itself, very different from "No on Nine" rallies in Portland which often took on the festive atmosphere of street parties with music and occasional humor. I buy a button for my lapel: *Gemeinsam miteinander leben—gegen Fremdenhass und Gewalt.* To live together—against hatred of foreigners and violence.

The crowd is too dense for me to see the stage, but I listen to speeches, the last one given by a Sindi. She reminds us that this is the fiftieth anniversary of Himmler's order to deport and exterminate all gypsies remaining in the Reich. A young man next to me comments that this is the first time he had heard a gypsy give a speech, and I realize that the same is true for me. Illogically, I am surprised that she speaks perfect, accent-free German. The demonstration ends. It has been peaceful and orderly, without counter demonstrations or violence.

I am still wearing my button when I go into my favorite cafe in the Koenigsbau overlooking the Schlossplatz. The crowd below is slowly dispersing, casting long shadows in the low November sun. The square is now a pedestrian zone, but was once busy with yellow streetcars going in all four directions. I imagine myself standing there, in 1946, changing trains, clustered with my girlfriends at one end of the traffic isle and pretending not to notice the gymnasium boys at the opposite end. We are surrounded by ruins, but I am happy. The war is over, I can speak without fear, and my application for emigration is being processed at the American Consulate. I wear a new dress made from curtains that used to be in our living room but were torn by splinters from the flak. The tallest boy smiles at me. I toss my head. Life is good.

I now share my table with a German gentleman old enough to have been an adult during the Third Reich. He does not notice my button, but encouraged perhaps by my gray hair complains about the youth of today. I volunteer that the demonstrators have behaved very well. He looks disgusted while he vigorously stirs his coffee. "When I was young we did not act like that. We knew what was proper."

~

On Sunday afternoon we have a visitor for tea, my second cousin Rolf. Although he is twelve years my senior, I fell in love with him when I was five. He has retained the gentle quality that allowed him at age seventeen to wander with me among the firs of the Black Forest in order to select the one perfect tree that we could carve out with his pocketknife and make into a canoe that would take us across the ocean. Although we never found our tree Rolf remains my favorite German cousin. On my father's side we share a set of great-grandparents. On his mother's side he also had a Jewish grandmother. Before the war when Rolf was old enough to enter university he was not allowed to choose his field because of his ancestry, yet as soon as war began he was drafted. He lost a lung while he was a soldier in Russia, and his only brother fell on the last day of the war on the Western front. Rolf practiced medicine in a nearby town until he retired last year. He traveled to Stuttgart by train today to see me on my last Sunday in Germany. My mother is not altogether pleased.

"I wish he wouldn't come today, when we have so little time left together," she confides in me before he arrives. "I don't need visitors now. He should come after you're gone." But Rolf brought just the thing to lift her spirits: a cheesecake made by his wife Marie especially suited to my mother's diet.

Unlike my brother and most of my friends and my father's relatives, Rolf understood why I jumped on the chance to emigrate when relatives in the U.S. offered me an affidavit after the war. Now I want him to help me understand the meaning of yesterday's demonstration.

"I was there at the Schlossplatz—it was packed," I tell him. "Twenty-five thousand people according to the paper this morning; that's a lot for this city of half a million. And three hundred and fifty thousand in Berlin! There is no way a fascist state can happen again here—you should have heard the speeches."

"I did, on the television. And don't forget, there were disruptions in Berlin from skinheads. You only saw one side. When you live here as I do you can hear an amount of anti-semitism expressed that's frightening. You may hear certain remarks, like test phrases, and if you give an encouraging response anti-semitic comments are expressed openly without embarrassment and by individuals from whom you would not expect it. It has not been like this since the end of the war."

I turn to my mother. "Is this true?"

"I wouldn't know, I don't get out among people the way Rolf does. But there has always been anti-semitism here— it was there when I was a child. When Hitler came racism became law. After Germany lost the war it wasn't fashionable to express it, but it was always there."

"What about America, is there no anti-semitism at all?" Rolf wants to know.

"Some, sure, but not much. When I first came in 1947 there were restricted areas around Chicago, but that's long ago."

"Maybe Americans have enough other minorities to pick on, so they don't need Jews."

I think of Measure 9 that almost passed, and I fall silent. My mother coughs, a dry hacking cough. Rolf tells me where I can get a humidifier tomorrow that would help her in the dry air. We share the cake he brought, and some chocolate my mother keeps in her bedside table. Dusk is falling outside, and I light a candle. I am content, among people who have known and loved me all my life.

~

The Augustinum restaurant is always closed on Mondays, hence residents may bring their guests to the common dining room. Only the noon meal is served, residents take breakfast and supper in their own apartments. Although tables are large enough for four, most have only two or three occupants, allowing for flexibility when guests are there or when conflicts arise among table partners. The diners who first shared my mother's table have all died; her present dinner partners are at least ten years younger than she. Herr Mueller is a retired banker and Frau Plessing a minister's widow.

The conversation centers on the news of today, November 9th. This is the anniversary of the 1938 *Kristallnacht*, when synagogues were burned and Jewish men were thrown in jail or taken to Dachau, my grandfather among them. On this day every year commemorative events are scheduled, and according to today's news this year's participation is expected to be larger than usual because of growing concerns about neo-Nazi activities. Moreover, photographs of pro-foreigner demonstrations over the weekend are in all the papers. Unlike Stuttgart, Berlin experienced disruptions, first from right-wing groups and then from anarchists.

Herr Mueller is eager to share his opinion of what he has heard. He speaks with authority, a man who is used to being listened to. "Young people are causing a lot of problems in Berlin. Those demonstrations ought to be forbidden" is his opening statement.

Heads are nodding at the table next to ours, but Frau Plessing offers a different view. "It's just the extremists from the Right with all their violence." There is an awkward silence. I want to support her, but feel oddly uneasy, an outsider. I look toward my mother. She is preoccupied with her dentures. Now she takes them out and lays them next to her plate. I cover them with my napkin. She looks at me, annoyed, and places her napkin above mine.

Herr Mueller is unwilling to surrender the last word. "It was the Left, it's always the Left that are causing problems. They are nothing but troublemakers, with no respect for law and order."

More nods all around, and a summing up by one of our neighbors, a woman who was brought in a wheelchair. "In our day young people would not have dared to behave like that." She does not specify whether she means the young people demonstrating or those disrupting the demonstration, but everyone looks pleased. At last there is agreement.

We are halfway to my mother's apartment when she remembers her dentures. I race back to the dining room, retrieving them just in time before tablecloths and napkins were gathered up for the laundry.

~

I can hardly swallow breakfast on Tuesday morning. We are alone. My mother is in her housecoat, slowly chewing a piece of toast, looking toward me. Her eyes used to be green, but now are almost without color. "We've done this so many times. We should know how to say good-bye," she says.

"And each time we are afraid that it's the last, and we always see each other again."

"Maybe you can come sooner next time, a year is a long time." I promise to try. She slowly gets up and goes into her bedroom, closing the door behind her. I hear her rummaging in her dresser.

When she comes back she hands me a small box, with the name of a jeweller in gold letters on the lid. I recognize the name; he was a patient. "Here, keep this. Father gave it to me on my fiftieth." It's her gold necklace, three strands, beautifully worked.

"I can't take this, it's yours."

"Take it. As long as it's here it will just get stolen, like the rings. I know you don't wear much jewelry, but maybe you will, some day. I want you to have it."

"What about the *Augustinum* anniversary? You will want to wear it for that."

"I'll wear the silver one you gave me."

I put the box in my purse. The taxi calls from downstairs. A few tears, mostly mine. One more gentle hug. I am on my way.

⁓

The plane takes off. No view this time; the cloud cover is dense and we are enveloped in white. I reflect back on my brief visit. There was not enough time to see more relatives and old friends—I have been gone too long to have made new ones here. Oddly, neither have they. In Germany, important relationships are always old and deep, a fact that may escape the casual visitor who mistakes the easy conviviality at restaurant tables and wine festivals for the beginning of friendship. It will last only for the duration of the evening and the effect of the wine. Where a longer relationship could develop Germans are more cautious. For instance, in the neighborhood in which I grew up no one ever moved. They might be gone during the bombing, but after the houses were rebuilt the same families returned. We knew their names. The children played together on the sidewalks. Women sat by their windows watching comings and goings on the street, but they never entered each others' homes or apartments. On the other hand, when we moved into a new house in Portland, neighbors came with coffee pots and muffins and we sat together on packing boxes before the furniture truck was completely unloaded. Friendships resulted, at least for the duration of living in the same neighborhood. How different it is here. Sometimes I feel as if my life in the United States had been like swimming easily on the surface of a river, but in Germany I am pulled here and there by deep and invisible currents. Is this what it means to be home, to see people who have known my parents, who tell me stories of my childhood, who speak that familiar dialect?

⁓

On my return flight I wearily move my wedding band back to my left hand. I realize it makes no difference to anyone whether I hold my fork in my right hand or my left, or whether I eat with chopsticks or forget about utensils altogether and use my fingers. Suddenly I remember the rest of *The Captain's Paradise*. The captain's system worked so well that he relaxed and forgot to flip the picture above his bunk. He made a mistake that ruined his scheme: He mixed up his wives' presents and brought the British wife lace underwear and the Cairo wife a flowered kitchen apron. Far from being annoyed, both women were delighted. At last their husband recognized their secret desires! The wife in Southampton rushed for the bedroom, the

Egyptian belly dancer headed straight for the kitchen. The wives had the same likes and dislikes; it was only the captain's fantasy that made them different.

~

We land in Atlanta. I am in the blue line, the line for U.S. citizens. The controller smiles at each passenger coming through the gate, "Welcome back." I return his smile. I am home at last.

Pilgrimage 1990

THE CHANGES WERE subtle, hardly noticeable, as the train headed east from Vienna. The land flattened and dried out. For a middle-class Western woman, crossing into the former Eastern Bloc only months after the Berlin wall fell was adventure enough. But I was the first in sixty-eight years to return to my family's native Hungary. I rattled away the hours to Budapest in a cramped compartment, my thoughts swirling above the odor of sausage and the unwashed, like smoke from my grandfather's fat cigars.

A passionate little man, he had raged through my childhood with chronicles of his country's misfortune, followed from afar.

"We have been ripped apart by cruelty and lies" came the angry voice across the years. "But this time, the Hungarian spirit has been strained too far." His eyes were veiled; I thought it was my fault.

My grandmother, whom I never met, had a crest embroidered on her linens—green stars above the points of a gold crown. She had danced away soft nights in Vienna, traveled to Paris, and vacationed on a lake in a house with servants.

"Your grandmother was a member of the Intelligentsia." My mother's eyes burned with pleasure.

But nothing was left. I hurtled into a mysterious present-day reality.

Adventure circled but didn't touch me at the border crossing where a U.S. passport was of no interest. I was treated to smiles while the middle-aged couple (with the offending sausage) was abruptly escorted off the train after an eternity of paper shuffling and unintelligible conversation. Two pale Rumanian girls filled their seats. The tyranny of one sense was immediately replaced by another: they cried all the way to Budapest.

Keleti Pu, one of Budapest's four railway stations, was as formidable as any in Europe with its nighttime population of bums and druggies. But the Magyar language was, by far, the bigger challenge. With none of the usual cross-language references and no recognizable rhythm it was a major accomplishment to find the station's main exit and a taxi.

Real, tangible fear accompanied my Formula One ride through Pest in a clap-trapper that could have been part of a Lego set. The driver raced across blinking neon avenues, downshifted in lung-blowing pollution, smoked, and talked non-stop, presumably about the possibility of my luggage falling off the roof.

At the pension, a beefy, chain-smoking character showed me to a comfortable, modern room, which I considered never leaving. But the smell of pork and paprika lured me down to the red-checkered ambiance of a restaurant next door where Marcus, former member of the Intelligentsia, now night watchman, introduced himself. After twenty-two years of exile in Canada he spoke perfect English, and told tales into the night of a Stalinist government that confiscated his family's five-thousand-acre farm with no compensation and thirty minutes to clear out, one suitcase each.

"This was a common experience," he assured me. "You can still see it in people's eyes."

Smoldering over these injustices and sobered with compassion I set off the next morning, on public transportation, to see for myself. I encountered a city where everything that moved did so, like the taxi, with gusto, in a cloud of smoke. I stood on street corners with a cloth over my nose and mouth, eyes burning, as little Trabants and ancient trucks belched soot and stink all over Pest. But beneath the blackened facades was a Parisian elegance—wide boulevards broken by neat little squares of pale grass, wistful trees, and grand old coffeehouses where my grandmother must have lingered over poppyseed *retes* and fine coffee. I found an empty cane-backed chair and installed myself in the smokey old world of Cafe Gerbaud to ponder it all.

It wasn't a beautiful city, but proud and handsome, full of contrasts, momentary joys, and startling disappointments, all of it gasping in the polluted air. The Danube River, which separates the cobbled calm of Buda from Pest and whose very name stirs up a waltz, visions of glamorous ferries or powerful barges, was a churning mud-brown without a boat in sight. Buda's medieval-looking Fisherman's Wharf towers are actually turn-of-the-century, their deception coldly reflected in the Hotel Hilton's glass facade.

My grandfather's fiery Magyar temperament was clearly evident in public sculpture. The monumental, impassioned figures reminded me of his heated exchanges with my mother over religion and politics, which sometimes found my quiet German father poised in the shadows, ready to run.

As I listened to Puccini in the gilded Italianate Opera House, I thought I saw my grandmother trailing her long dresses over its mosaic floor, settling into a luscious velvet-curtained box in crimson candlelight, or reflected, perhaps, in the golden mirror where I sipped champagne at the entr'acte.

"We have very deep pockets" whispered an intense, balding man who followed me from the Opera. "There is nothing wrong with our pockets, except that they are empty!" I thought he was after the contents of mine, but he wanted only to speak English.

Capitalism on a comically petty scale was alive and well. At busy intersections, oblivious to the exhaust, twelve-year-old boys smiled and hustled Pepsi and 7-Up; along pedestrian streets Rumanians sold wool-lined, embroidered leather vests and handwoven smocks; bargaining was the language of business and they spoke whatever was needed.

Most of these people sold illegally. They stood side by side, arms outstretched holding their goods looking like a washline with feet. Suddenly heads turned, goods crumpled into shopping bags and in an instant, line and vendors had vanished into the crowd. Two steps behind the knowing but indifferent police this wave action reversed itself, with vendors and goods wordlessly reconnecting in washline form, symbolic manifestation of a long history of ruptures. Everyone smiled, including the police, sharing the joke with a complicity unheard of in the not-so-distant past.

Some did have a sad aura about the eyes, but on its surface Budapest did not look strained or ripped apart. It pounded with enthusiasm and touched me as I wandered from museums to cemeteries. I felt suspended in time, wordlessly linked to these round-faced women who looked like my mother, spontaneously drawn to families clamoring onto buses.

I wanted to call out to the young girl who teased a university student selling obsolete busts of Lenin; her light hair and slight figure resembled my cousin's. A middle-aged businessman with my brother's eyes smiled at me in one of Buda's lively cellar restaurants as we downed hearty goulash doused with sour cream and wailing violins. . . . That old one who walked like my uncle stopped to wink, then swayed to an accordion, arm in arm with a teenage boy who snapped his gum. The dust and dirt settled unnoticed on our solidarity, our connection. My eyes filled with tears as I ached for something unexplainable, something lost in my modern linear world where the past is left behind. I wanted to know these people. . . .

On the Saturday of my departure, they melted away like "washline vendors" into the afternoon. That wordless complicity was nowhere in sight when my reserved couchette seat, or rather the entire Swiss car, was not on the train. I panicked, all alone, desperately trying to find help or at least an explanation. It was a Westerner who came to my aid.

Hours later a collective sigh echoed through the packed train as it settled into exhausted silence. Disorienting kilometers passed into deepening dusk. I woke to the dawn in a gently rocking train-car bed, breathed the fresh air of alpine villages and misty emerald hillsides. In the distance of twelve hours, Hungary had faded to black and white.

Margaret

Margaret and I had met once, by chance, in the cemetery of a small Hungarian town. Although we spoke no common language, she had understood, and marshalled me through a maze of neglected graves to the tomb of my great-grandfather. Later, with the help of a translator in Geneva, we began a correspondence. When she accepted my invitation to visit Switzerland I sent her a ticket. I remembered a warm, energetic person with snappy blue eyes, large hands. . . .

Now she stood beside the last passenger car at the end of the platform. Soldier straight in a black and white coat she clasped, with both hands, a gray plastic pocketbook. Two battered, boxy suitcases set squarely on the ground flanked her ample form.

Her train had come in early and was already humming an impending departure. Fellow passengers had disappeared into the station's moving mass, but Margaret followed instructions: "When you arrive in Zurich, stand beside your car. I will find you!" Except for an unseen passenger whose cigar smoke curled out over her white hair, she was alone.

As I swept toward her she began to fidget. She let go of the purse with one hand and shifted her weight from one brown pump to the other. She did not avert her gaze nor alter her fixed expression. I smiled and walked faster, but she allowed no sign of recognition until I waved. Then she bent with effort to pick up the suitcases and walked briskly toward me. We met in a wordless embrace, but our smiles spoke all languages.

Exchanging frequent reassuring glances, we marched down the long platform into the station and almost as far down another to board our train for Geneva. She seemed anxious about the gray purse and did not allow me to touch the heavy bags, thrusting a light canvas pack into my arms.

She again brushed aside my offer to help as she fumbled with the cases in a crowded second-class car. Finally installed, she unfastened her heavy wool coat and revealed the simple brown sweater and skirt in which I would see her every day of the next three weeks.

As the train silently slipped along its track, passengers settled into soft talk, morning papers, or sleep. Margaret decided it was time to eat. She tugged at the canvas bag producing a baked chicken with cold fat congealed on its yellow skin. My protestations were useless. Slices of coarse bread, paper napkins, two plastic cups and an unopened litre of water appeared.

It was 6:55 in the morning. The well-dressed businessmen opposite us watched over the tops of their newspapers as we silently pulled chicken off bones and chewed thick bread. Margaret clicked her tongue when I firmly refused the skin which she swallowed without a thought. She poured water on a napkin to clean our greasy fingers, then whipped out a green kitchen towel to finish off the damage. With a curt nod she accepted my contribution of tangerines.

The smell of chicken had piqued our fellow travelers' interest. They stared as soft laughter and strange sounds, but no words, accompanied our intense need to understand each other. Using body language and my written list of translated words and expressions, I learned that she was very tired but happy to be in Switzerland, her trip had been uneventful except she'd lost something and I couldn't understand what.

After a distressed sigh, Margaret stood up, suddenly animated, and hauled down one of the leaden suitcases. It was my turn to stare as she rummaged through corrugated boxes of jam-filled cookies and sugar-dusted pastries, a chocolate nut torte, one half litre of pale translucent honey, two liters of white wine and a sweater. Whatever she was looking for was not in that case. We wrestled it back up onto the rack and down came the second.

It was full of apples and jars of syrupy apricots! There was a change of underclothes, a striped housedress, and a pair of worn slippers under which was the coveted object—a blue pocket-sized Hungarian/English, English/Hungarian dictionary.

We moved miles ahead. Margaret looked up "kolbasz." She stretched her arm, then pulled her fist to her chest and eagerly pointed to the word. Long sausage? She made the same movement with her fist but scrunched up her brows and pursed her mouth. Something was wrong with the sausage. After a moment's reflection, she paged rapidly through the book to find "vam." Once again she yanked her fist and said kolbasz. Ah! Customs confiscated the sausage! That's what she'd lost! We laughed and patted hands to celebrate the comprehension. Then Margaret frowned, pounded her chest, and looked up "csinal." When she touched my arm I understood that she had made that sausage herself, for me. I found the word for "sorry."

Sometimes we drew pictures because half of the "Ls" in the dictionary were missing and the "Ts" were printed twice in Hungarian. Using our special brand of theatrics, we huddled together and "talked" for two hours.

I learned that she raised chickens and geese and, every year, a pig or two, plus her own bees, fruit, and vegetables. To make ends meet since her husband's death, she had been growing grapes to sell to a winery. She had traveled the three hours by bus to Budapest where her son's family waved her off on the 17:55 train to Zurich, the first and only such trip of her sixty-six years.

Margaret waved her arm across the window, then found the words for "green" and "winter." Her face showed surprise. And once she said "beautiful," "tidy," as we passed a Swiss village. She looked up "gazdag" and indicated everything around her, including me; "rich," with a no-question-about-it nod.

She slowed down but didn't fall asleep. Just before we reached Geneva, after we'd been "quiet" for several minutes, Margaret put away her dictionary. As she carefully opened the gray plastic pocketbook, I saw that it was empty.

No Way Out

The slaughtering team arrived at her gate as we left for the station. On the handlebars of her bicycle, which she pushed through the snow, Margaret carried both my bags. We were silent during the twenty-minute walk. She seemed nervous, her mouth pinched shut in a permanent pucker. I was confused—sad to leave her in her cold house in that shabby Hungarian town; glad to escape it and the scene about to unfold in her orchard.

I climbed onto the train and sat opposite a large man who snored softly. Below quivering lips, his tiny chin sank into a mass of flesh beneath his fat, deeply-creased face. He slept on, even as the train lurched forward. I waved good-bye to my dear friend but she was already hurrying home to the pigs.

She had been fattening them for months. Twice a day she filled a metal bucket with powdered grain, table scraps, and hot water, then set it in the kitchen corner to soak.

Margaret would march through the cold courtyard with the steaming pail as the pigs snorted and rummaged in the dark recesses of their pen. A foul cabbage stench permeated its wooden slats. Two flat snouts eagerly thrust toward her approach. Their crinkled beady eyes squinted in the daylight as Margaret raised a heavy plastic cover and opened the door. They squealed excitedly, then grunted satisfaction. Their immense pink bodies, covered with wispy greenish hairs and manure, strained for the slop she poured into the trough.

I had watched this grunt and slop routine and felt no affection for the pigs. I was struck by their innocence. They were eating and enjoying all they were given. They were getting fat, like me. Margaret, who lives alone with her chickens and geese, five cats and a dog, clearly enjoyed cooking for a guest. But I got out alive.

In less than an hour one of the pigs would be pulled from his dark house and stretched out under the fruit trees in great confusion and fear. Unaware that he is about to further the food chain but clear that something is terribly wrong, his screams will terrify the other. Their throats will be cut, their blood drained into a bowl.

As the train clacks peacefully through pristine fields of snow I sigh my relief that those cries cannot reach me. They are part of Margaret's life. For this woman of sixty-six years whose annual income hardly exceeds what I have in my pocket, slopping the pigs to gigantic proportions is an investment. She sells most of the slaughter and fills her own pantry. Even at the "empty" stage, that dirt-floored treasure house was stacked with jams and grapes, apples and dried peppers, pickled beets. . . .

My thoughts settle in Margaret's kitchen on a quiet afternoon. The cement floor has been scrubbed clean with used dishwater, and red-checked rags dry on a line above the spigot. An enormous pot of water ticks and pings as it cools on the wood/coal burning stove. The pig slop bubbles in its corner, and Margaret snores in the other room. I sit drowsy on a stool, elbows resting on the wooden table, and savor the "silence."

Suddenly, the door flies open. Margaret bustles past in blue apron and slop boots. She sets before me a cracked plate of greasy salami—homemade, she says—and black bread thick with butter. It is delicious and she gives me more. I say, "No thank you" but she is oblivious. From the pantry she produces sausage and insists I eat that too. All of it. I try to say "Koszonom szepen" but the words stick, like the sausage, in my throat. Margaret is in high gear. She has pulled back my head and is stuffing solid goose fat into my mouth, fried chicken, soft cheese, and noodles. "Csinal," she barks and pounds her chest. I don't care who made it, I cannot swallow, cannot even move. She laughs at my terror, leans into my bulging face with her steely gray eyes, stuffs down more salami and potato dumplings. I sputter, I choke. She has no pity, keeps coming with more. And more. We struggle. I push her away towards the plastic cabinet with the broken glass doors. She leers at me and picks up a gleaming cleaver. Finally I clear my throat and scream "Stop!"

The snoring stops. Stiffly picking chin off chest and breathing heavily, I open my eyes. In the rocking train compartment, the man riding across from me is also awake. From under greenish wisps of eyebrow, his beady eyes squint uncomprehendingly at me from the massive pink face.

The pigs' screams ring out across the kilometers. I press hands to my ears and try not to hold Margaret responsible.

Making Connections

I WENT BY RAIL from London to Vienna. I had visions of myself sitting in a dining car, drinking coffee, reading Rilke, Proust, and Kafka alternately, looking at
passing cathedrals, discussing the meaning of both World Wars meditatively with
foreigners who knew about World Wars. I had had good luck on trains in Europe
when I spent a semester abroad in college, and, more importantly, my mother took
a train when she and her mother left Vienna together in 1938 for the last time. If
it hadn't been for the trains back then, my mother might not have gotten out alive.
To Freud, trains were symbols of death, but for me, trains meant life—mine, in
particular. I changed trains outside of Zurich. There was a delay and outside my
open window I watched two little girls—one blond, the other brunette—playing
while their parents said good-bye on the platform. The girls were charming—
singing, skipping, doing pretend cartwheels and pseudo-pirouettes. They did not
seem to notice that the grownups were teary eyed. Then, rather abruptly, the little blond girl left the station with her parents. The little brunette girl stood watching them leave, her white knee socks fallen loosely around her ankles. The
brunette's father stood behind her and put his hands on her shoulders. For a
moment neither the father nor the daughter said anything. They just stood there
watching the other people walking down the platform, away from them. My train
began to move. The passenger across from me—a German wearing jeans—took
out a dog-eared copy of a German *Let's Go* from his backpack, and ignoring the
fields of sunflowers that now appeared outside our window, began to read.

When my mother left Vienna for the last time she never said good-bye to her
best friend, Inge. There was no time, she said, and there was hardly any opportunity. To tell anyone of their departure would have put her parents in jeopardy.
Indeed, her mother wouldn't even say when they were to leave until the night they
finally did. My mother's father left in March of 1938. My mother and her mother
left in April. They were to all meet up again in Zurich. My mother says she did
not know exactly why she and her parents were in danger—that it had something
to do with her father's job—he was a Professor of History at the University of
Vienna and every day at lunch the head of the department would call to complain.
He was not teaching the way he was supposed to be teaching according to new
German law. My grandfather was working on a book about the Vatican and the
Germans at that point were hardly interested in religion, let alone a foreign reli-
gion—the religion of Rome.

The atmosphere in Vienna had changed—even a ten-year-old would have noticed. On March 14, 1938, church bells rang and hundreds of thousands of people cheered while my mother stood at the window of her dentist's office high above the crowds, watching a motorcade drive through the streets of the old Habsburg city. It was Monday and there was still snow on the ground. My mother was getting a cavity filled and she was relieved, no, glad for the parade because for that moment, the dentist had stopped his drilling to have a look at the funny little man with the mustache standing upright in his Mercedes, his right hand raised in the salute that is reappearing in newspaper photographs yet again.

After the Anschluss my mother witnessed German soldiers dragging away the shoemaker up the street. They put him in a truck and she never saw him again. Every day at school the niece of Hermann Goering, who had one day suddenly become my mother's elementary schoolteacher, asked the class who their parents had dined with the night before. Students were rewarded when they supplied names and sometimes even addresses. During her ice-skating lessons after school my mother was not allowed hot chocolate because she did not wear high, white knee socks, and was, therefore, not a member of the Hitler Youth Group.

The night my mother left with her mother, my mother was not allowed to run up the street to the Karl-Marx-Hof to say good-bye to her best friend, Inge. And that night my mother simply said "*Gute Nacht*" to her grandmother whom she thought she would never see again. Her mother warned her not to cause a scene—they had just discovered that their maid, Agnes, who lived with them, was a Nazi spy.

My mother says she remembers watching her grandmother closing the door to her rooms and she remembers seeing the sliver of light leaking through from underneath.

Sometimes I imagine what my great-grandmother did that night in her room, knowing that she was now alone in the world. To calm herself, perhaps she took out her big red stamp book, opened it, and proceeded to arrange and organize the stamps she collected from all the different countries to which she had traveled by train with my mother. Meticulously, she used tweezers to lodge Germany, Hungary and, Austria into their correct slots. I imagine that she sat up late that night putting her countries in order and setting the world right again.

That spring my mother's grandmother decided not to leave, at least not that night. Not by train. Later though, less than a year later, she would flee with an orphan in a hay wagon into Czechoslovakia, a country already occupied by the Germans by that time, and which, she rightfully calculated, would be the last place they would look. In the spring of 1946, after the war had ended, she would get herself to an American army camp in Bremen, Germany, and write to my mother and her parents in Washington, D.C. They would send her a ticket, and there, in Washington, my great-grandmother would live to be 105 and she would have only one wish in her will—that her ashes be sent back to Dobling in Vienna. But that night, the night my mother and her mother left, my great-grandmother had no intention of ever leaving Vienna. She was in her seventies and she felt she was too old to become *eine Fluchtlinge*—a refugee.

"She didn't want to be a stranger in a strange country," my mother once explained to me.

The night my mother became a refugee she wore a dark blue coat and she carried a big doll with her. The doll was almost her size, the approximate size of her best friend, Inge, and for a long time afterwards, when my mother lived in three countries in which she did not know the language—France, England, and finally America—that doll and three imaginary friends would be her only friends and would take the place of Inge.

When I ask a lot of questions about her past, my mother sighs and says she wishes she remembers more. She wishes she looked closer at her room and outside the windows of their home on Hofzeile and down at the streets in Dobling. She wishes that she had tasted the Christmas food more carefully, seen the branches of the Linden trees more clearly. But of course you never think of missing your country until you leave it.

My mother has only two photographs from that period of her life. One of the photographs is a yellowing black and white of herself with her friend Inge. They are standing in front of a train station. They both have long dark braided pigtails and they are both wearing white peasant blouses and dirndls. The sides of their heads are touching as though they are siamese twins. The sun is in their faces.

The other picture is in my mother's passport, which lists her as a German citizen, not Austrian. My mother looks older and more serious even though it was taken in the same year that the picture with her and Inge was taken. She has long black braids and she is not smiling, though she looks beautiful. On her right cheekbone is the date—5 April 1938—and a black stamp of the German eagle that holds the Nazi Swastika in its claws as it flies and looks the other way. Someone has stamped this on my mother's cheek so hard it has left an indentation.

There are no other pictures of my mother's life before she was ten years old. According to her photo history, it is as though her life starts at age eleven in England.

When she was applying for her social security payment, my mother had trouble because she couldn't come up with a birth certificate or anything, for that matter, that said she was who she said she was. The woman at the social security office was very understanding. In fact, she cried on the phone when my mother explained how everything had been destroyed.

"It's not so bad," my mother said, trying to comfort the woman. "I was really very lucky. I mean, there's not a bit of shrapnel in my body and I never actually saw anyone die."

Sometimes I'll have these waking dreams—I'll hear a train whistle and suddenly I'll see that spongy Manet train smoke and everything around me is in black and white and gray and for a moment I feel as though I am living inside one of my mother's lost photographs. In these photographs I eat Sachertorte and play lawn tennis and walk arm in arm with friends and relatives from my mother's past—people whom I've never met nor seen. The sun is out, and though I am squinting at the camera, I look happy. I have found, it seems, my place.

My grandfather once wrote in a history book, "How well can we understand a foreign nation and especially that foreign nation's past? How well can we understand any past?"

～

Immediately, after the war was over, my grandfather went back to Vienna to live and to teach again at the University of Vienna. My mother could never understand why he wanted to do such a thing. That university, that city, and that country — their "motherland"—had betrayed them. Why go back? For her, Vienna was a past that no longer existed.

I met my grandfather once, briefly. He was in America on a speaking tour and my mother made him lamb stew, and over dinner he asked me what my favorite subject in school was.

"Anthropology," I said. "The study of man." I was sixteen years old and I had just learned the definition of anthropology and I had decided that I wanted to be Margaret Mead.

"And women," my mother added.

"Ah," my grandfather said, looking straight at me, his left eyebrow raised. "So."

I never got the chance to ask my grandfather about the past. The distances between us became too great.

My mother had the measles the night she left Vienna and she had an uncomfortable train ride to Zurich. But her measles prevented border guards from searching her and her mother because she was contagious. That night the measles spread into my mother's eyes and even though she insists she did not cry, there were tears running down her cheeks as she left Austria for the last time.

They traveled at night so she probably did not see the waterfalls and the mountains that I saw outside my train window when I made their same trip in reverse.

⁓

The week before I flew to England, I told my mother that I had finally accepted a marriage proposal from a man I had been seeing for three years. My mother—who had never met this man or his family—wanted to know who his people were. I didn't know what to say—he is Irish Catholic and "his people" were stone masons for all I knew. He had mentioned once that his mother was one quarter German, but I didn't tell my mother this.

"They're Irish," I said. There was a long silence and I could hear the hum over the telephone lines.

"We're getting farther and farther away, aren't we," my mother said, and she hung up before I could ask her where it was exactly we started from and why she felt our family history had to be linear.

My mother says that her mother never looked back that night they drove away in a cab—that she looked straight ahead. She told my mother never to go back to Hofzeile 12, the home they left behind, because it would depress her. My grandfather later wrote in his memoirs that he did look back when he left. He was, after all, a historian.

My mother has never described herself as a refugee. She says she doesn't like the sound of the word or the image it conjures up—a babushka huddled under a big blanket, walking against the wind carrying a bundle of all that she owns. I think this vision of the refugee, for my mother, is most certainly a woman, making her traveler even more the victim—still more in danger and in need.

My mother does not have my passion for trains. For her there is no cause to celebrate motion; trains simply remind her of leaving. She does not see a train and think: This is the vehicle that brought me to safety. She sees a train or a cattle car and can't help but think of Auschwitz, Theresienstadt, Buchenwald, Treblinka, Dachau and all the rest.

⁓

On that train trip through Austria, I wondered what my fellow train companions were hoping to see. I realized of course they didn't have to have a goal in their travels, just as some did not even have destinations. But I think in traveling, we all hope to find someone or something that will change us.

In Vienna I visited my step-grandmother and my godmother—all that is left of my mother's side of the family. Women who are not even related to me. Over *Leberknodlsuppe,* my step-grandmother chided me for my bad German and then she complained.

"But my darlink, vhy hasn't your mother taught you German? She knows it."

I considered explaining, but I did not. My mother tried to teach me German when I was ten, the same age she learned English. We never got beyond the present tense. She never said why she stopped the lessons, but I imagine, to her, after 1938 the German language sounded ugly.

My step-grandmother pushed more liver-dumpling soup on me and insisted on reserving me a couchette for the train ride back, because, she said, "there are so many different kinds of people traveling and you will be forced to sit next to them." My godmother, on the other hand, fed me *Apfelstrudel* and told me her plans for opening her apartment to a refugee family from Bosnia-Hercegovina.

While I was still in Vienna, I took yet another train out to Dobling and followed the notes my mother gave me. How to get back to Hofzeile 12, she wrote at the top of a lined sheet of paper. I am still moved by the word *back.*

I saw the yellow stone chapel where my mother was baptized and the brightly painted Karl-Marx-Hof where Inge had lived. And I walked the Grinzinger Allee which my mother had walked to go to her ice-skating classes. I hiked to the cemetery up the Allee where my mother's parents—my grandparents—are buried and where my great-grandmother's ashes are kept. And finally I sat at the steps of Hofzeile 12 which is now an apartment complex made of cement. Looking down the street, I noticed that all the other houses had either been perfectly restored or had never been destroyed in the first place. And there, on the steps of Hofzeile 12, I saw that of all the buildings on that street, only one had been bombed and completely done away with—my mother's childhood home.

Die with Me
at the Sovietskya

DANIEL AND I arrived this morning at Pulkavo Airport in Leningrad. I have come bearing a Samsonite filled with canned vegetables, soup, powdered mashed potatoes, panty hose, eye shadow, and eight cartons of Marlboro cigarettes. Having been warned of shortages, the food is for myself. The dry goods are for the Soviet film crew.

Daniel is our producer. As such it was his job to clear me through customs in Dublin. Daniel wined and dined me on Old Grofton Street and by the end of that first evening I had started to feel like a bonafide actress, rather than the substitute English teacher I had been back in Los Angeles up until forty-eight hours ago. In spite—or perhaps because—Daniel has a snaggle-toothed grin and prematurely graying hair, he is quite attractive. His sister dates a rock star, and his father is in advertising. *Die with Me* is the first film he's ever produced, but he's put on several plays in Dublin.

In baggage claims, at the metal and formica 1960s-style customs counter, I met Paddy for the second time. He had cast me for the role of Marta in New York three months ago. Before my arrival I had been paid eighty-seven-hundred American dollars and had been promised a daily per diem in rubles. My visa was in order and I was immediately allowed into the country.

The Arriflex camera Daniel had rented in Dublin was another story. Paddy had a permit to get through customs, but the Pulkavo guards were not impressed. One guard, who couldn't have been a day over eighteen, gingerly untied the string on the Arriflex camera box. It took him several minutes. With his rosy cheeks, blonde hair, and uniform oddly reminiscent of the American Civil War, he looked like something out of a Louisa May Alcott novel.

"I have a great idea," said Paddy of the camera. "Let's just leave it here!"

Gabhan, Paddy's Irish assistant, speaks nearly fluent Russian and translated Paddy's comment to the guard, who looked up at us with vague surprise. Then he looked back down at the camera and began methodically retying the string. We had inadvertently issued him a challenge; moments later, the Arriflex was permitted to join us in Mother Russia.

Yuri, butternut-colored, with a big, bushy mustache, piggybacked my suitcases up the cement steps to the lobby of the Ghastonitza Sovietskya. Hired by Lenfilm to be our first assistant director, he expounded dramatically in Russian on the heaviness of my bags. Embarrassed, I thanked him in English and followed Gabhan and Daniel inside.

407

The lobby of the Sovietskya was modern and not entirely unpleasant, though it lacked any color deviating from the photographic gray scale. Walls: medium gray. Counters: jet black. Floors: multi-colored gray. It was clean, though, and populous; and I was somehow reassured.

～

Gabhan settled me into my room, a five-star suite by Soviet standards. It has a lounge area with a sofa, stuffed chairs, coffee table, and small refrigerator (which will prove a godsend, I'm sure). The carpet throughout is a warm, indoor-outdoor gold, and the furniture and bed are covered in gold floral polyester.

I unlocked my Samsonite and was just settling down to a snack-pack of canned peaches when the phone rang. It was Gabhan, offering to take me on a sight-seeing tour. I accepted gladly.

Though only twenty-three, Gabhan has already crewed three other Irish-Russian films. He resembles some Gaelic hero with his long ringlets of hair, violet-blue eyes, and massive build.

Half the crew of *Die With Me* is Irish; some even grew up next to each other in Dublin. The camera, makeup and wardrobe people I have yet to meet; they are all native Soviets, employed by Lenfilm, our home studio for the duration of the film shoot.

Gabhan hailed a taxi in Russian and as we rode around, he pointed out various landmarks: the Hermitage, the "Red House," and a tiny chapel built by Czar Alexander, which reminded me of a recurrent dream from childhood about a surreal treehouse.

On the streets among the ever-present soldiers meandered people of races I'd never seen before: indigenous peoples from the Ukraine, the Urals, Lithuania; beautiful Arctic Indian faces . . . all going about the day's business.

The Baltiskya Hotel *barioshka* is the best in Leningrad and sells Russian-English dictionaries in exchange for foreign currencies. I put one on my American credit card. Gabhan sensed my enthusiasm for learning Russian and offered to tutor me. I accepted his offer gladly. By this evening, he had taught me how to count from one through ten, how to say "please," "thank you," "hello," and "good-bye," how to ask for a bathroom, and how to introduce myself.

I'm hungry—*Ya goden*. I like clocks—*Ya no buchasee. Ja nis nein*—I don't know. *Stoiy vosim*—Number 108 (my room number). I have pledged that by the end of my six-week stay here, I will be fluent.

～

I slept fine my first night in Leningrad. I bought a case of bottled water when I was with Gabhan at the *barioshka* and I brushed my teeth with some of it before bed, as the water is not potable. (During the revolution, there was a surplus of corpses that were not cured with lime, nor were they buried very deeply in the earth. Now the water table is falling, and bits of body are leeching into the water supply.) The water is cloudy, but no worse than the rusty water we would periodically get during the Hudson River winters of my childhood.

I memorized a few Russian words and tried to place a call with the operator. I was able to make my numbers understood and actually got through to L.A.—a good omen and a gift from providence which Amy, our film editor, says won't be repeated. Placing long-distance calls here normally takes days.

~

My first morning in Leningrad, after a breakfast of soft-boiled eggs, homemade brown bread and white cheese, Katarina, our script continuity girl; Amy, the editor; and Margie, the Irish film-crew nurse, escorted me to the Wardrobe Department at Lenfilm.

The buildings and people of Leningrad are European and sophisticated, but the poverty is inescapable. This is a country full of ironic passions: I arrived at Lenfilm to discover that a pair of leather loafers had been handmade for me, yet the wardrobe department was filthy and most of my costumes hadn't been cleaned after the last wearer. I was trying on sweaters when suddenly I felt sick. Thankfully, our nurse was there to take charge and demand a bathroom on my behalf.

Margie gave me a little pill meant to kill whatever bacteria had assaulted me and sent me home to the Sovietskya for some rest. After I'd slept for a few hours, I awoke feeling like a new person. The sun had come out and I could easily imagine being on the *Rive Gauche* of Paris rather than in the heart of the Soviet Union. Out the window and across the street from my hotel, I noticed an abandoned building with a collapsed roof, which I found strangely beautiful. I reminded myself to photograph it.

Paddy rang and asked if I felt up to shooting a brief scene later. I said yes. He gave me my "call time" and I got up to see about a bath.

I quickly learned that the hotel only has hot water part of the time, so I plugged in my portable plastic teapot and took a sponge bath instead. For a treat I used bottled water, and I felt cleaner afterwards than I had in days. Then Gabhan picked me up and took me to the train station, where I met Jill for the first time.

Norman Mailer's daughter has already been in the Soviet Union for a month, having toured here with a production of *Uncle Vanya*. She makes her living as a stage actress, resents her author-father, and is as different from me in temperament as a person can get. We will respect each other and work together without problems, but I doubt we will ever become friends.

Our first scene together was easy. I stood outside a train station, Jill walked up to me, backpack slung over her shoulder, and I gave her a hug. That was it. The whole exercise took less than an hour.

After the shoot, Nancy, our unit publicist, interviewed me about my life as an actress. Hah! I told her what film projects I aspired to work on, plugged my failed screenwriting career, and talked a bit about what it's like to work as an actress on low-budget independent films. Much to my dismay, I had to rehearse exactly what I would say in the event I were interviewed by the Russian press.

Rule number one: I must not say I don't know how I feel about perestroika. This was a tough one. I'm not exactly an expert on Soviet politics. We discussed the issue at some length, finally deciding on a "ten-year plan" opinion, i.e.: "If glasnost continues to change Soviet culture gradually, using a country like Sweden as a model, perhaps the crime and violence of the West will not flourish as they have in my country, the 'free-market,' free-for-all U.S.A."

Nancy stamped her "politically correct" seal of approval on our little diatribe and then we broke for dinner.

Later, I had my first and only story conference with Paddy. He was very defensive about the story problems in the *Die With Me* script and was dead-set against changes. I will do what he wants and hope for the best, but the script has major problems—including lengthy cryptic speeches, to be delivered by yours truly. Plus, there are symbolic acts which sail over the head of the average Westerner. For example, in two scenes I put my feet up on a table: this is meant to be ripe with subtext, as putting one's feet up on the table is considered incredibly rude in Russia. Hence my character does this not to relax, but to insult Asya (Jill's character) and to exert power over her. (My character, Marta, is working on a terrorist revolution here in Leningrad, with the reasoning that anarchy breeds on failed economies.)

~

Every night, Sue, our second assistant director, does up a call sheet for the scenes we're to shoot the following day and slides one under my door. Usually, this is enough to make me feel connected, but last night, a week and a half into my stay, this proved not to be the case.

With all the traveling I've done in my life I never thought I'd get culture shock, but in the wee hours of morning, I found myself taping snapshots to my walls in efforts to grab onto something familiar. When I ran out of photos, I taped up business letters and my film contract with Paddy. I even opened an American package of ribbon rosettes for sewing and put those up.

I feel like the edges of my psyche are being crushed in. The reality of six weeks here is daunting. The urge to pair up is enormous in this strange place. I don't have a lover; I would settle for a stuffed animal but I don't even have that. I have found, however, that a roll of toilet paper makes an adequate substitute for a teddy bear—sterile and soft. In the Soviet Union, you make do with what you've got. There's an immediacy to Russian life; if there's a tomato, you eat it.

Even though Russians are talented cooks, the meat, eggs, milk, ice cream, and mayonnaise continue to give me diarrhea. This leaves the ever-present tomato; cucumbers, potatoes, bread, smoked salmon and pâté, which I now consume in hefty quantities. Then there are the *barioshka* powdered soups and vegetables Margie says will eventually give me malnutrition if I keep planning my meals around them.

Paddy thinks prostitutes work out of the downstairs dining room at the Sovietskya. Tonight, after three helpings of tomatoes in garlic and oil, (the main course of fish had turned) I was drinking my usual wheatgrass *miniralnaya* when the young woman at the table next to us suddenly disappeared beneath the tablecloth. Meanwhile her companion sat there quietly with his drink. Paddy said the woman was giving him a blow job. *If there's a tomato, you eat it! If there's a paramour, you eat him!*

A band plays during dinner almost every night. It is nearly impossible to buy records or compact discs, so the musicians here play renditions of songs from the radio. If a sheet music version sells a lot, the song becomes a hit—just like in America fifty or sixty years ago. The Latin dance tune, the *Lambada*, is really big, as is a song called *Attas!*, which means "police" in Russian.

~

I turned twenty-eight today. I've been craving raisins all week and Gabhan left a paper bag full of them outside my door. I got a bracelet from Katarina and Margie, some flowers from Sue, and tonight, Daniel took me out for dinner at a hard-currency Finnish pizza place.

It was like walking into another world. Everything was new and Western and the food was fresh, abundant, varied and good. We were the only people there; Soviets rarely come to restaurants like this because Finnish restaurants won't accept rubles. The Finns also operate an ice cream parlor on this basis.

How terribly unfair to the people of Leningrad to be shut out of restaurants in their own city. I've come to believe that there is a system of neo-apartheid here—those with foreign cash can function and those without are desperate, though it is not true apartheid because the "oppressed," in this case, want to hook up with and emulate their oppressors (meaning foreigners or anyone else with access to hard currency).

The mayor of Leningrad resigned from the party two months ago along with the mayor of Moscow. They say this is March, 1917, all over again. There is talk that martial law will come in late October. The Soviets on our crew are not worried, however. They fear anti-semitism far more than they do the army, which has become a familiar and predictable feature of life here.

There is no way to gage Western reaction to the latest rumors because there continues to be a dearth of English-language newspapers. The only time we hear any world news at all is when an actor flies into town—and the last one arrived last week.

∽

I hate having to come back to my room at night. I watch Soviet television to feel some sense of contact with the outside world—black and white TV that starts with a white dot in the center and widens out into a picture after three minutes—and I fight like hell to hold onto any cultural anchor I can find. Along with everything else on my walls, I've taken to plastering up brand-name labels from my food cans, to assure myself I still exist.

I am sick of being by myself, of the boundaries of my body. At this time of night I find I have nothing to do but to ponder the tiny freckles on my arms.

As a child I had no marks on my skin. Then I moved to California, or the ozone layer started to go, or both. The freckles make me feel less pent up inside my olive skin than I did at six, or eight, or ten. They hint of American girls with dimples who drive convertibles and drink canned beer—the kind of girl I'll never be, no matter how hard I try.

By necessity I am more sociable than I've ever been, yet I feel profoundly isolated. I keep dreaming I'm paralyzed. Gabhan says paralysis dreams mean one subconsciously feels trapped. He has them every night.

The whole crew has nightmares for no particular reason—my theory is that communism really is evil.

∽

The apartment we're using as a set is within walking distance of the Sovietskya and is next to a bakery. Every morning as I walk to work, I pass a dozen or so housewives, often with toddlers in tow, waiting in line to purchase sweet-smelling loaves fresh from the oven. There is a wonderful normalcy to this daily activity, and the bread-dough scent drifts up into the windows of our building, neutralizing the ever-present smell of diesel from the Soviet tanks.

Our apartment building is actually an old mansion cut into fours. It has high ceilings, gingerbread moldings, and french windows with a good view of the city.

Looking down onto the street one can see that there are no parking laws here. Citizens park their few Volvos and Citroens wherever they please—this includes a portion of sidewalk.

In Leningrad, people still live for poetry, live for music, and live for art. The Russians on our crew are like Italians when it comes to cinema—they worship it. Though there are the occasional perks, for the most part the talented devotees of Soviet cinema work with empty pockets and perpetuate the film industry out of the kindness of their hearts.

This is certainly true of *Die With Me*. The Lenfilm art department has redecorated my character's digs down to the rose fleurette wallpaper and every prop is perfect. Oddly, I have been sucked into the unreality of the script and feel as though this were actually my apartment. I feel at home here. I feel safe.

Jill has some beautiful costumes. As the lead actress in *Die With Me* she plays a Russian country girl and gets to wear hand-embroidered traditional blouses. I was admiring them in our dressing room when the costume lady from Lenfilm pointed to a spare and said I could have it. I thanked her profusely and tried it on. The blouse is new, made from sheer cotton lawn, with yellow, orange and red flowers embroidered around a scalloped neckline. I removed it carefully and packed it in my bag to take back to the hotel.

My makeup man, Mik, is hilarious but intimidating. In his contract he requested a list of cosmetics three pages long from Dublin. Apparently Mik wants to be well-stocked for this film and many future films as well, at Daniel's expense. Before we left, I went with Daniel to the theatre store in Dublin to help fill the order. While there I paid for my own supply of corrective powder, to keep my skin from going sallow on camera.

Jill did not take to Mik; he is missing half a thumb, and the idea of his doing her makeup with his stub gave her the creeps. She requested a female makeup artist and got one. As for me, I got stuck with Mik, but we get along fine. He does rub in my greasepaint with his stub, but I am determined to be a trooper.

～

Tonight, Sue celebrated her thirtieth birthday by hosting a party. The entire crew met up in the private dining room at the Sovietskya, which is circular, like a tiny forum. Sue applied all of her production skills to pull off the near-impossible: the delivery of a chocolate mousse birthday cake.

She got lots of *barioshka* products, including a beautiful black wool scarf with flowers, books (written in English!), some Russian jewelry, and fresh flowers. Someone even managed to find us a few pounds of smoked Nova salmon which hadn't turned.

I had an OK time, but during dinner it dawned on me that Sue and Gabhan were involved. I know it's just a "shipboard" crush, possibly brought on by the fact that Gabhan's the only one around here who is bilingual, but I've grown fond of Gabhan, and I'm jealous.

Watching Nastia, a beautiful Russian girl of nineteen who assists in the make-up department, I realized that she, too, is interested in Gabhan. Frankly, the two of them would make a much more attractive and likely couple. Gabhan is, after all, only twenty-three—seven years Sue's junior.

After dinner we went up to Sue's room and danced to cassette tapes. There was lots of champagne, one bottle of which Susan poured over Gabhan's head. His long brown hair was down, his shirt tails out, and he was an epiphany to look at. I was bummed.

Susan and Gabhan kept giving each other drunken little kisses while they danced. As Sue waved her arms to the beat, she exposed her underarm hair, which looked obscene. I took pictures for awhile, then went into the bathroom and cried. One of the Russian ladies from the crew came in through the unlock-able door to check on me, telling me not to be homesick. *She thinks I am crying because I am in the Soviet Union,* I thought, *but I am crying because I want to have sex with Gabhan.*

My desire to be treated like a professional actress never stops me from having an affair, my shyness does. Whenever I feel lustful, I become inadvertently aloof and fail to make eye contact. I send out crossed signals and then curse myself.

~

This morning at breakfast I overheard Margie say to Sue, "Maybe he has another girlfriend," in reference to Sue's live-in boyfriend back in London. "I hope so," Sue said. "Maybe he'll still come and visit," Margie reassured her. "He needed to come two weeks ago," Sue replied.

I pretended not to hear, let alone to care.

~

Today Mik brought me the most thoughtful gift—two flawless, fresh, ripe bananas from Georgia. It's the first fresh fruit I've had in three weeks! The man is an angel— all because I didn't throw a fit over his thumb stub.

We shot this afternoon at the Literary Cafe, which dates back to before the revolution. Between the tables are bronze trees which explode with crystal leaves and little lights. Visions of *Dr. Zhivago* danced in my head. I don't think I've ever seen such a beautiful restaurant.

Later, we did a scene at the art college, where Yuri knew a few students. During a break he tried to persuade us to buy some student artwork in exchange for hard currency. I tried to fight it, but I felt used.

After I was done for the day I took the metro home. The *stantsiya mitro* (stations) in Leningrad are architectural masterpieces: elegant, lavish, impeccable. Despite shortages, the gold-leaf appointments stay fresh and shiny, the marble polished. The metro stations here could house black-tie dinner-dances or wedding receptions, they are that spectacular.

I arrived home and picked up my laundry from the Sovietskya housekeeper. The yellow ribbon rosettes I taped to my wall are gone. Those rosettes were a part of my plan for sanity. I confronted her with phrases from my Russian-English dictionary but got no action or reaction. As for the light bulb that just burned out above my bed, I'm told it could take months before a new one is found to replace it.

Tonight on television the regional delegates held court with Gorbachev, his dignitaries, and several old ladies in black whose presence in the cabinet was a mystery to me. The greatest applause came when one of the delegates said (screamed, rather) that he was all for privatization and enterprise but that if they weren't careful they would end up like Brazil; the most important thing was that the needs of the USSR come first.

Could it be that I'm finally beginning to understand some Russian?

~

Today is Sunday, our day off. Nancy and I hooked up with a group of Americans at Brezhnev's dacha. We arrived during brunch. They had ham, toast, jam, and oranges. I must say, Nancy is very well connected.

The board of directors of Ruskoevideo Residentia are putting together a cable station in Leningrad, which will be a Soviet/American venture. The funds are coming from a New Yorker named Larry, who invested in the Broadway play, *The Amazing Technicolor Dreamcoat*. Larry is here on his honeymoon with a pretty gold digger named Victoria. His partners include Anthony, a loud-mouthed producer from L.A.; and Dmitri, a Soviet on staff at Ruskoevideo in Leningrad.

After breakfast Anthony took Nancy and me on a tour of the dacha. In the billiard room, he told a story (which may or may not be an urban myth) about how Brezhnev's cabinet decided to go into Afghanistan. Legend has it the Premier had been partying all night, and during a game of early-morning pool he said: "What the hell; let's go into Afghanistan." Then one of his aides picked up the phone and called the Kremlin.

The directors asked Nancy and me if we wanted to join them for dinner that evening. We accepted and went back to the Sovietskya. Later, Anthony and his entourage picked us up outside the hotel and drove us to one of the better restaurants in Leningrad.

When we arrived at the dinner table Dmitri presented all of us ladies with single pink rosebuds. Dmitri's wife (his fourth, Anthony had informed us on the sly) seemed bored and unmoved.

During dessert Victoria announced that the *Master & Marguarita* was her favorite novel, no doubt trying to impress us with her eighth-grade knowledge of the classics. Meanwhile Anthony proposed a toast: "Dmitri's enemies are my enemies." The men then toasted the CIA, the KGB. . . "I can get these guys to do anything for a carton of cigarettes," Anthony tactfully declared . . . and they toasted Gabhan's house in Dublin, which had once belonged to James Joyce. I found this last *nostrovya* particularly odd, seeing as Gabhan wasn't present to hear his house so honored.

Once after-dinner liqueurs had been served, Anthony started coming on to Nancy and me, suggesting we come back to his hotel with him and try uncharted sexual positions. I politely said we had an early call in the morning. "You mean you would go if you didn't have to get to the set early?" Nancy asked me angrily.

Anthony took the hint and turned sensitive on us, saying he wanted to "share" about his life as a divorced parent. "I have a twelve-year-old who's gone a little Beverly Hills on me," he said gravely. I told him I hated Beverly Hills. There was never anywhere to park, unlike here.

~

Nastia phoned close to midnight to tell me what costume to wear for tomorrow's shoot. Her English gets better and better. "Gabhan must be tutoring you in English," I said, complimenting her. She giggled, then covered the phone and spoke to someone. Was Gabhan *there*? Never mind. It's none of my business.

At five this morning a trolley car broke down just outside the hotel, creating a terrible electric buzz which woke me. I looked out the window; the trolley sent up a veritable fountain of sparks. It took me a long time to get back to sleep.

Later, on set, Gabhan brought us a breakfast of cold boiled potatoes and cucumber strips. Sue plunked her Russian army hat on his head. I walked into the middle of a conversation between them. "I already have done that on you," I heard Gabhan say.

~

I caught a glimpse of Gabhan's back tonight in the upstairs dining room. Unconsciously, he pulled his shirttail out and scratched an itch while engaged in conversation.

Men with skin as translucent as Gabhan's often have shiny jellyfish bodies, but his skin is firm and white. Gabhan is still young enough to be both big and fit, but with age he will become stocky, portly, though probably not fat. He has eyes like a girl's, like a bluejay's belly—nature's equivalent of "derma-lens" blue.

Behind him, a man and woman in faux leopardskin costumes performed a modern dance on the dining room stage.

~

"I am an actress at Lenfilm." I have mastered that phrase in Russian and use it in every conceivable situation. I use it apologetically; I use it to describe my various moods; I use it to avoid paying hard currency in taxi cabs; I use it to get service in the hotel restaurant, to make new friends, and to get directions when I'm lost. "Ya actryssa a Lenfilma," I say with an endless number of inflections. That one short sentence allows me a narrow lifeline to all I need or desire in my new city.

Today is my day off and Leningrad is gloriously bright and sunny. Everyone is happy, including me. I feel like a Russian woman, out running my errands for the week, taking in the comforting familiarity of the sights around me: A roly-poly baby in a carriage puts his arms round a loaf of bread his mama has set in his lap. He is smiling and gurgling, like a happy little elf with a secret. Three boys not more than six pull up the anchor from a pleasure boat on the River Fontanka. Housewives huddle around a sidewalk entrepreneur, watching him demonstrate the pantyhose repair wand he's invented. I buy one for my grandmother.

The freesia and lilies at the flower market are surprisingly cheap. I buy a bouquet for my room. I then visit a ballroom that has been converted into a deli and pick up the first-ever Russian sandwich meat I've gotten on my own.

My per diem in rubles is very generous, and somewhere along the line I have become determined to live like the Soviets do. Somehow I got tired of falling back on hard currency, of only circulating in snobbish little crowds of foreigners—the kind who eat at private Finnish clubs and barioshka bars. If I were Russian, I would definitely resent someone like me.

After casually visiting the Hermitage Museum as if I lived here or something, I stumbled across a wide deserted boulevard that begged to be revived. I could just envision a Russian Champ d'Elysees with sidewalk cafes, musicians, boutiques and newsstands. I have no doubt this boulevard will live again one day, but how long and how many governments will it take?

If perestroika works, maybe when I return, Leningrad will have become the "Paris" it longs to become. The original Astoria Hotel, mother of all "Astoria Hotels" around the world, is being restored. I take that as a good omen.

~

Shopping at Leningrad's few department stores requires something along the lines of a lottery ticket. My Russian is still so scanty I have trouble understanding instructions, but somehow I managed to end up in the correct line for the sundries counter at the corner store.

I had entered without knowing what I wanted, and I was about to make an impulse purchase—something unheard of in this country of shortages. With funds from my obscenely high ruble per diem I purchased an orange faux chiffon scarf, some World War II-style brass bobby pins, a chocolate-brown coin purse (also of World War II workmanship), and a cheap metal ring, which makes my finger itch, so I think I'll have to give it away.

I was tired after shopping, so I hailed a taxi back to the Sovietskya. The driver heard my accent, saw my Western clothes and immediately demanded dollars. By now I was cranky and in a way, my feelings were hurt that I couldn't pass for a Soviet. "*Ya actryssa a Lenfilma!*" I announced angrily. The taxi driver backed down and I hopped in.

He was playing a *Pretenders* tape on his portable stereo. I commented on it in Russian patched together with French verbs. The driver was thrilled I knew who *The Pretenders* were and started expounding on a vacation he had taken to England and Europe the previous year.

"The mayor of Sheffield came to meet me and my wife at a party thrown in my honor, see?" He pointed to an engraved invitation written in English, which rested in a place of honor on his dash. I nodded enthusiastically.

A few minutes later he pulled up to the hotel. "Skolka?" I asked. "No charge," he replied in French. He explained that when he'd visited Paris, a shopkeeper had made a gift to his wife of a two hundred and ninety-nine-franc wooden box, after she'd purchased a figurine worth only ninety-nine-francs. "I love the French," the driver said, shaking my hand. I was too embarrassed to tell him I'm American.

～

Last night I dreamed I was in the upstairs dining room, watching a Soviet musical review about America. In front of a fifties diner setpiece, a dozen costumed Russians sang "Crocodile Rock" and the Carpenters' "Close To You." Corny, but I was moved to tears.

The next thing I knew, Paddy and I were back in New York, conducting film-related business with a man wearing overalls. I asked Paddy what street we were on. "West 23rd," he said.

Ah, the guy in the overalls is a downtowner, I thought to myself.

It then became clear that I shared office space with Paddy. Unable to settle down and write, I packed up all my supplies to leave. Paddy threw a fit, and I suddenly realized that I was in a romantic relationship with him.

I then discovered a Soviet woman had started making a wedding gown for me. I sought the woman out, and she assured me my romantic options were still open— she was making the dress "just in case." She had sewn a beige cotton-lace runner to the knee of the gown, and pointing to a white chiffon overlay, she explained the dress would come off looking ivory. I gave her the "thumbs up" sign and wondered if I would have enough per diem rubles to pay for the gown.

～

I've caught a cold from all the night shoots we've done outside. Katarina gave me some vitamin C drink which held it off for a few days, but I finally lost the battle. Jill is in much worse shape. Her asthma is chronic and today she had a panic attack at the apartment because she couldn't breathe. The set photographer got together with some of the other crew members and came to me, saying it was terrible Daniel hadn't stopped the film until Jill got better.

I passed on the crew's concerns to Daniel, who told me a doctor had already flown in from Helsinki to see Jill. His diagnosis was that she was addicted to her ventilator. She's used it so often, the bronchial dilator no longer works.

Daniel and Paddy are desperate. They are afraid Jill will jump ship, so they've paid for her boyfriend, Mark, to come and visit. In the meantime I gave Jill some Ensure, which I brought with me in case of emergency; Ensure is the liquid food doctors give to elderly people when they get malnourished. In return, Jill lent me her copy of Alice Walker's *The Temple of My Familiar*. With no movies in my language and a dearth of English-language reading material, I crave escape.

〜

Tonight our interpreter, Galina, threw a dinner party for us at her home. Daniel told me she would be spending a month's salary to feed the twenty of us, so instead of flowers or wine I brought some canned pineapple and deviled ham as a hostess gift.

During dinner we discussed the new rumor on the street—that the Union is going to fall within the next six months. No one at the table could quite bring themselves to identify this as a revolutionary dream . . . to say that it would never happen.

I have become quite close to Nastia, to our unit nurse, Margie. And now I have a new friend, Alexander, the son of one of the Russian producers. Alexander worships Nastia, but she won't have anything to do with him. He got onto our crew through his connections, and though this is the norm in Hollywood, in Russia pulling strings is considered vulgar.

Alexander draws well. He has a wonderfully dry sense of humor that he communicates through mime and our own brand of English-Russian pigeon. We have some ideas about doing a low-budget, bilingual art film and financing it with rubles. It makes some sense; after *Die With Me* is released in the Soviet Union, there will be opportunities for me here. I may well come back to the USSR, now that I've gone through my initiation and know the lay of the land.

I asked Alexander out of curiosity if he would ever consider moving to Los Angeles and pursuing film there. He said no, that he loved Leningrad too much to leave. What a gift—to love your home like that.

Tonight we stopped en route to our night shoot at an army barracks with a public cafeteria. The cooked vegetable plate looked promising, but as luck would have it, the vegetables were cooked in bacon fat and all of us got sick. I was glad that, for once, I didn't have to feel guilty about being the only victim.

Jill wasn't with us; she flew home to New York yesterday with Mark. Sue is standing in for her on camera and the remainder of Jill's dialogue will be voiced over in New York during post-production. I feel sad that Jill didn't make it to the end, but in truth, much tension has lifted with her departure.

〜

Today we shot at the Leningrad train station. I ate lunch at a restaurant with about half the crew because I was sick of eating out of my suitcase. I knew it might be a risky thing to do, and it was. I was pulling myself together in the bathroom after an attack of dysentery, with which I was becoming all too familiar, when someone knocked on the door. I opened it and was in the process of gathering my things, apologizing for monopolizing the room, when the short-haired woman standing on the threshold grabbed me.

I have never been mugged or molested before and I couldn't understand what the woman wanted. She did not rob me, but she would not let me go and she put a hand over my mouth to stifle my screams. Finally, I let out a guttural growl so deep and long I must have frightened her into loosening her grip.

I stumbled into the foyer of the restaurant, my knees wobbling, and through mime let the proprietor know what had happened.

After asking for a chair and a cigarette, I sat in the doorway of the restaurant waiting for crew members to pass by (I was too shaken to wander out into the train station and look for them). After a few minutes, Daniel and our bodyguard, Sasha, approached. I'd barely ever spoken to Sasha before, but he was the one I rushed to. As I threw my arms around him my legs collapsed, and I just barely managed to whisper, "I was attacked."

Meanwhile the woman from the ladies room came waltzing back into the restaurant as if nothing had happened. I pointed her out to the maître d and asked him to call the "attas" (police). He wouldn't.

Though I had completed my final scene in *Die With Me*, Paddy had planned one more shot with me, but I just couldn't work again that afternoon. As it was our final day of shooting, I felt guilty and worried, until Paddy assured me I had made it to the end of the film, and that the extra shot would have been just that—in other words, it wasn't very important.

Margie took me to the crew bus where somebody scrounged up a bottle of brandy. It worked so well on my frayed nerves that Daniel went to the Sovietskya *barioshka* and bought me a whole bottle. Back in my room, I curled up with that, a box of chocolates and a pack of cigarettes. I had visitors all afternoon—Margie had said it was important for me to talk about what had happened.

The others guessed I wouldn't attend our cast and crew party, but the brandy had done me good, and I decided I wanted more than anything to celebrate the completion of the film.

Our wrap party was held in a magnificent ballroom with frescos on the walls and those signature chandeliers with built-in themes one sees all over Leningrad: branches dripping with crystal icicles and snow. There were three kinds of smoked fish and the best quality food since our dinner at Galina's.

Earlier, I had decided that the drugstore trinkets I'd purchased in America for the purpose of this night were both contemptuous and simpleminded. How could a pair of sandalfoot pantyhose or a pack of Marlboros express my affection for these people? I started from scratch and went over to the Sovietskya *barioshka*, where I bought gifts for the complex individuals I'd come to know.

That night, when it came my turn to say "*nostrovya*," I said, "*Tavarishchi!*" ("comrades"—used in jest these days), when we first began filming with you, Galina had to translate every word spoken back and forth between us. Then, after about three weeks, the common language of film took over, and the only time we needed Galina was when we required a moderator to settle disputes. My hope for our respective countries is that the same thing happen on a larger scale—that we get to know each other well enough so that we no longer need translators, and then no longer need moderators either. Nostrovya!" Everyone clapped and cheered, and then I cried.

~

Today is our final day in Leningrad. I would stay and travel to Moscow but I have been denied an extension on my visa.

This morning I went to the park to sell the cartons of Marlboros everyone back home told me I would need for trading on the black market. Nobody wanted my cigarettes, and I felt like an ass trying to pawn them off on someone. How frustrating to arrive here with cold war travel advice twenty years out of date.

Finally I found a student willing to trade the cigarettes for a couple of faux military watches, which I've since learned are manufactured especially for tourists—tourists who think they have engaged in dangerous underworld trading when they go home with the ten-dollar plastic jobbies.

Soviets toy with capitalism like a violin—they pick it up, then set it down. Everyone does this. The catch is that Soviets daren't brag about their entrepreneurial experiments or preach capitalism's glory. Those who do can count on much the same condemnation as self-professed communists back in America. A society comfortable in its habits will quickly find some excuse to sweep dissidents under the rug. In this we are more the same than I ever would have imagined.

The real problem is the mass poverty, the shortages, the inability to come and go at will, the feeling of being trapped which makes so many of the women one sees in the churches rabid in their religiosity, so many of the men alcoholic. But curiously, desire for escape fuels the creative side of an already sophisticated and intelligent people. Discipline, spurred on by the rock-solid borders of a continent and a scanty selection of distractions has, I believe, inadvertently fostered a nurturing environment for the Soviet Union's many world-class dancers, athletes, filmmakers and musicians.

~

A few hours prior to our departure for the airport I suddenly kicked myself for not having purchased any original Soviet art. I dashed across the street to a gallery kitty-corner from the Sovietskya and found a beautiful painting by a local artist, but I couldn't figure out how I would transport it. Not only that, I had spent all of my rubles on amber necklaces. Defeated, I returned to the hotel, where all of us posed for a group picture in the lobby.

I felt I hadn't taken full advantage of my time in Leningrad. I'd measured out every ounce of my energy so prudently during shooting that I had turned down several social invitations, and I now regretted it.

After saying tearful good-byes to various members of our Soviet crew, we boarded the plane for Heathrow, where we passed a Walkman between us, listening to Billy Joel's "All the Friends We Had in Leningrad."

I vowed to make it back within the year. I vowed to try to get Nastia into the United States to visit Los Angeles. I vowed to hook up with Margie in Dublin. None of us could stop crying.

~

Postscript: In October, 1991, approximately three weeks after my return to Los Angeles, the Union of Soviet Socialist Republics fell. The plot of *Die With Me* became obsolete, and the film was never released.

Burr

ONE

IT'S LATE ON A November Sunday. The sun has long since set in the gritty Moscow sky. I am strolling along the Arbat with Michael, my Irish friend with whom I've shared a tiny Russian apartment for the last fifteen months of my three years living in Russia. We've spent this winter-gray afternoon wandering and watching the hustlers and the tourists try to beat each other.

The Arbat is the long pedestrian street that has become the center of Moscow's tourist trade. Here you can find crude copies of the famous *Palekh* lacquer boxes; watercolors of St. Basil's candyland domes; caricaturists who will sketch you in charcoal and silhouettists who will deftly snip your profile with scissors for only a few rubles; *matrioshka* dolls, traditional peasant-girl dolls, Gorby dolls, Yeltsin dolls; Soviet military badges and belt buckles; T-shirts with "Hard Rock Cafe, Moskva" printed on them in Cyrillic letters; and more.

The black-market money changers who have been swarming among the shoppers now retreat from the thinning crowd to gather in clumps in the darkened doorways. Fashionable in denim and leather, they huddle over their cigarettes and compare the successes of their day's work.

The outdoor vendors lazily close up shop as Michael and I drift by. They pack away their wares and exchange jokes and insults. A few hardy souls still call out to us in grotesque English as we pass. We smile and answer in Russian, which sends them into embarrassed silence. They know their crude hustling works only on the greenest of tourists, and Michael and I consider ourselves long-time residents, wise to the ways of the marketplace.

Michael usually looks in the cooperative kiosks along the Arbat for bargains on vodka; and I am drawn to the displays of handcrafted earrings. Seldom do we find anything we want to buy. This evening, however, as we near the end of the Arbat's pedestrian way, we come upon a street peddler with a tray full of primitive, brightly-painted clay figures, the charming little folk toys that have been made for centuries in the Duimka region of Russia.

Back in our apartment I have a small collection of these toys—a woman with milk pails slung over her shoulders, a scattering of colorful barnyard animals, a funny little chap in a boat serenading a bird. In this Arbat peddler's selection I see half a dozen examples of the same clay goats and ponies and whistles in the shape of roosters that I've seen in every tourist shop. But he also has a figure I haven't seen before, a brown bear with red ears and a row of blue buttons painted down its belly, standing on its hind legs and holding a sleepy-looking chicken. I am strongly tempted to buy the bear. It's only a hundred rubles, about a dollar. But something holds me back, maybe just the effort of digging my money out of my pocket and making the transaction, because it's getting late and I'm tired and cold and hungry. So I hesitate, and Michael looks at me with a question on his face as I start to walk away. "No," I say, "that wouldn't be a good bear to have—can't you see, he's going to eat that poor chicken?"

Michael stops me and puts his hands on my shoulders. "Oh, no," he says seriously. That's not what's happening. That's a *good* bear." Only with his thick Northern Irish accent it comes out "burr."

"What do you mean?" I play along, skeptical.

"Just take a look," Michael says. "The burr has just found that poor chicken in the forest and, carefully and gently, he's bringing it home."

Already convinced, I want to stretch out this moment. "Are you sure?"

"Yes," he says solemnly. "The kind burr is coming into the village, and he's saying, 'Excuse me, please. I found this poor sad chicken in the forest, and I'm bringing it home. Please, who has lost this chicken?'"

Michael's Irish rolls like brook water, soothing, laughing behind his straight-faced recounting of this impromptu fairy tale.

By now, we've turned back to the toy vendor, who smiles and bobs because obviously we—carefree tourists, he must think—are about to make a purchase. Together Michael and I continue to examine the "burr," ignoring the chatter of the seller.

I pretend to worry. "So he's not going to eat the chicken?"

"No," chuckles Michael. "Just look at him. He's looking at all the village people and saying, very hopefully, 'Please, who owns this poor lost chicken I found in the forest and brought home?' And then the woman who owns the chicken comes out, and she is ever so grateful to the burr for finding the chicken. She takes the chicken and hugs it and puts it to bed."

"And what happens to the bear?" I ask. By this time Michael has his wallet out and is counting a hundred rubles into the palm of the pleased toy seller. Affectionately, I stroke the little clay bear.

"Oh, the villagers are so grateful to him that they give him some cakes," says Michael. "And buns," he adds. "They give him cakes and buns."

I feel like a child trying to prolong a bedtime story. "Does the bear like cakes and buns?"

"Oh, yes," replies Michael. "He loves cakes and buns, and he gobbles them right up. Then he's so happy that he begins to dance."

I gaze fondly at the little bear in my hands, who now radiates precisely the personality Michael had given him. How could I ever have imagined that this sweet creature with his round eyes and open, hopeful face wanted to *eat* the trusting little chicken?

When we get home, I place the "burr" on the windowsill and make Michael tell me the story one more time.

Two

On a freezing Tuesday evening a few weeks later, Michael comes home from work with a surprise. The black canvas bag he takes with him whenever he goes out—the "perhaps bag" that everyone in Moscow carries on the off-chance of coming across an unexpected something to buy in the barren shops or on the streets—is awkward and lumpy in his arms.

"Look what this good Russian burr found in the woods," he grins. With his beard spilling over the collar of his bulky parka and his wide eyes twinkling beneath his Russian fur hat, he does look a lot like the clay bear on the windowsill. "I found these poor bottles lost in the forest. Does anybody have a home to give them?"

He opens his bag and pulls out, one by one, five gleaming bottles of *Soviet-skoye Champanskoya*. Like Russian caviar, Russian champagne is still a rare and exquisite treat, and almost impossible to find in these difficult times. Michael has found these five bottles at a kiosk in an out-of-the-way Metro station, priced— at two hundred rubles each, or two dollars—way beyond the means of the ordinary Russian.

I am delighted. The evening becomes a celebration. We have champagne with our supper and continue drinking it late into the night.

The surprises become a regular feature in our life. Every week or so Michael comes home with a special find and announces at the door, "Look what the burr found in the forest today." One time it is a chunk of real cheese, good cheese, that a toothless old woman was selling right out of her bag on the street. There has been no cheese in Moscow for many months, and we wonder where she got it. Another time it is candles, good wax candles, made in Czechoslovakia. And another time it is a current copy, in English, of *Time* magazine that Michael found on sale at the corner newsstand for the equivalent of a quarter. I tease him so often about being such a fine Russian bear that "Burr" verges on becoming his nickname.

One evening in January, Michael arrives home from work bearing in his arms, of all things, chicken. It's nothing like the bony, incompletely-plucked chickens sometimes available in the farmers' market for a hefty price. This is plump, packaged, frozen leg-quarters from America, part of a food-aid shipment that actually made it past the black market and into the Russian shops. We've heard the Muskovites wryly call these chicken quarters *nozhki Busha*—"legs of Bush"—but our friends report that they haven't yet seen any on their tedious daily rounds of grocery hunting. Michael sings out, in his best "burr" voice, "Whose chicken is this? I found this poor lost chicken in the forest. Does anyone want this chicken?"

We are equally pleased—I with Michael's good fortune, he with my obvious pleasure. Briefly we wonder if it was wrong for him to buy the chicken: after all, we can shop in the pricey hard-currency shops for foreigners that are off-limits to the Russians. Every bite of Russian food that we purchase with our cheap rubles is a bite of food that doesn't go into a Russian mouth. We worry about the ethics of our lifestyle and try to even things out by the elaborate meals we serve our friends, the gifts of food we bring them when we visit.

But on this January night, with fresh snowflakes dancing outside the window, there are no pangs of conscience as we feast by candlelight on broiled American chicken and drink the last of our Russian champagne. We punctuate our lazy conversation with frequent clinks of our wine glasses. Somewhere in the wintry evening we even offer a toast to the little clay bear who looks sweetly down from the windowsill.

THREE

Eating out in Russian restaurants is another one of our bright pleasures in this bleak country. Our Russian friends find this habit hard to understand. Restaurant food is often of very poor quality—as are most products and services offered in the Soviet command economy. Russians prefer to eat at home, with guests crowded around the tiny table that seems to expand indefinitely as more people join the group. The home-cooked food, though often simple, is always lovingly and lavishly prepared. In these difficult times when the shelves in the food shops are usually bare, we are mystified by the abundance that appears from our friends' kitchens whenever we visit.

As we walk through the snowy streets to the Hotel Dom Turista where one of our favorite restaurants is located, I comment to Michael on the paradox of the generous Russian hospitality in the midst of such scarcity. "Paradox," he muses. "That reminds me of something I heard at work today: 'The Six Paradoxes of Socialism.'"

"A joke?" I ask hopefully. "Tell me."

Michael's eyes twinkle. "The six paradoxes of socialism, here they are: In the Soviet Union, there is full employment—but nobody works. Nobody works—but the five-year-plan is always fulfilled. The five-year-plan is always fulfilled—but there is nothing in the shops. There is nothing in the shops—but there's everything on the table. There's everything on the table—but no one is satisfied. No one is satisfied. . . ." Michael pauses at the door of the Dom Turista. "No one is satisfied—but everyone always votes yes."

We check our coats and a waitress, unsmiling, leads us to our table. The tiny table is already spread with *zakouski*—a plate of smoked fish, a plate of sliced ham, cucumbers, tomatoes, potato salad, and caviar. Two kinds of bread, white and Borodinskii rye. The tablecloth is patched in several places, but it looks clean. Sardonically the waitress opens two bottles of Pepsi for us as we sit down. The band is tuning up, and we can glimpse a sequined showgirl behind the stage. It looks as though it's going to be a nice evening.

"*Moshno champanskoye? I tozha maslo d'lya khleb?*" Michael asks politely before the waitress disappears. "May we have some champagne? And some butter for the bread?"

"*Konyeshno,*" she replies. By the time we have served our plates with a dab each of the appetizers, she is back with a saucer of butter, a bottle, and two glasses. As she wraps the neck of the bottle in a napkin and starts to work loose the plastic cork, Michael puts out a hand to stop her. "I'm sorry," he says. "We want champagne."

"This is champagne," the waitress responds curtly.

Michael points to the label on the bottle. In ornate Cyrillic script it reads, not "*Champanskoye,*" but "*Salyut.*" Although the bottle looks like a champagne bottle, *Salyut* is in fact a dreadful, cheap imitation, considered potable by no one we know. Michael and I tried it once, then poured it out in disgust after one taste. "This isn't champagne," he tells the waitress.

"Well, it's all we have," she sniffs and takes the bottle away.

"She figured we wouldn't know the difference," Michael says. "She was probably going to charge us champagne prices, too."

A group of well-dressed gentlemen seated at the next table holds a spirited conversation with their waiter. In a few minutes the waiter returns bearing several bottles and wine glasses. "Look at that," Michael whispers to me. I follow his gaze. The labels on the bottles on the next table clearly say "*Champanskoye.*"

"Maybe their waiter had some put aside for them," I say. "Maybe our waitress ran out of her supply of champagne."

Michael gets up and walks to the serving stand just beyond the nearest post. When he comes back, he wears the smile of a practical joker. "There are a couple dozen bottles on the shelf under the table," he says. "Not *Salyut*. All of them are champagne."

He motions to the waiter at the next table. "Excuse me," he says graciously, "could you get us some champagne? Our waitress only has *Salyut*, and we want champagne."

"I can't help you," says the waiter stiffly. "You'll have to talk to your waitress."

Suddenly Michael is on his feet. "I'll be right back," he winks, and he is gone.

Our waitress passes by and looks curiously at me. "He'll be right back," I murmur. I occupy myself slicing the fat from the ham on my plate and wonder if Michael is off haranguing the maître d over the champagne that we aren't being served.

A few moments later I notice our waitress seating two couples at a table against the wall. Idly I watch them settling in, ordering. To my astonishment, the waitress brings them champagne, opens it, pours. Even at this distance, the label is unmistakable. It isn't *Salyut*.

Then Michael returns, just as suddenly as he departed. Triumphantly, he sets two bottles of champagne down on the table and deftly pops one of the corks.

"Where'd you get that?" I ask in surprise.

"I have ways," he grins. I suddenly visualize the little clay bear that sits on our apartment windowsill, the Russian "burr" who finds lost chickens and bottles of champagne to bring home. Michael reads my mind. "I did what any good burr would do at the Hotel Dom Turista. I went upstairs to the hotel snack bar. I figured if they had champagne here in the restaurant, they'd probably have it up there too."

He fills both our glasses and raises his in a toast. "To the luck of the Irish and the Russian burrs," he says and drains his glass. "It was only forty-six rubles a bottle, too." We're both aware of the high markup on champagne served in the better restaurants. No doubt it would have cost us two- or three-hundred rubles if we'd been able to command it at our table.

Our waitress comes to take our orders. When she catches sight of the bottles on the table, she moves on. Out of the corners of our eyes we watch her stalk down the waiter from the table next to ours. "Probably asking him how he dare serve champagne to her customers," Michael laughs. He is right. We can see the waiter wave his arms in protest, gesturing toward us and toward the door.

Back at our table, the waitress is suddenly very friendly. Cheerfully she explains the entrées and recommends the chicken. "The beef is very tough," she says. She brings more bread and butter without being asked, and smiles as she serves our chicken.

"Will you have coffee or ice cream?" she asks as she clears away our plates.

"No, thank you," we reply. We are still working our way slowly through the second bottle of champagne and enjoying the stage show.

When she brings us our check, the waitress gives us a slip of paper with her name, Lyudmilla, and her home telephone number on it. "I'm working here every other evening," she says. "On all the odd days. The next time you come, call me beforehand. I'll have your table all set up, closer to the stage."

Even after years in this enigmatic country, I am still caught off guard by the mysterious behavior of its people. "So why has she suddenly gotten so friendly?" I wonder aloud.

"She respects us now," says Michael. "At first she took us for chumps. But we showed her we could beat her at her game. So now she wants to please us." He is right, of course. Often I've found that politeness elicits only scorn in strangers; expressions of power are more likely to bring out cooperation.

Michael leaves Lyudmilla a large tip, and I give her one of the small perfume samples I have on hand to present to people whose goodwill I wish to cultivate. It's a form of bribery, but a necessary fact of life if a foreigner hopes to survive the hardships of Russia. Lyudmilla is clearly pleased.

We linger till the band puts away their instruments and the overhead lights come on. We toast the spirit of the Russian "burr" once more, but we aren't quite able to finish the last of our champagne before we finally leave to go home to our apartment.

FOUR

Six weeks later I am alone in the tiny two-room Russian apartment washing splatters of crusted spring mud off my winter boots, when the doorbell rings. Who can it be at three in the afternoon? My friends always call before they come over. No one makes a visit unannounced.

I release the three locks on the door and open it a crack. The sturdy, ursine bulk of the mail carrier looms before me in the dim light of the landing. She is bundled up against the cold, and I mistake her for a young man until she speaks. Her voice is strangely musical as she greets me and offers me a telegram. A telegram? I am confused. Yes, a telegram. Is this my name on the envelope? Will I please sign the slip of paper?

I retreat back into the apartment gripping the flimsy tan envelope. Some part of me thinks it must be a mistake: if someone had actually sent me a telegram, then Russian inefficiency would see to it that it was never delivered; and if a telegram is indeed delivered to me in midafternoon, then by the same logic it must belong to someone else. Thus have we learned to doubt and reason, we foreigners who have adjusted to the haunting dissonance of Russian life but who still have one foot solidly planted elsewhere.

I sink down into the chair by the window. The fading afternoon light over my shoulder barely permits me to read. At first I think the telegram is from Michael, who has gone back to Ireland for a week's vacation. There he's having his teeth cleaned, visiting his son, and buying fresh broccoli to bring back, the present I requested from the great shopping-mall world of the West.

The telegram is not from Michael. But it is from Ireland. It's from Kieran, Michael's friend in Shannon who once worked with him here in Moscow. Kieran used to go out with us on weekends when I was first showing Michael the city. I like Kieran; I've missed him since he went back home to Ireland.

I stare at the telegram. I start to open it, but I find I can't move. It is like the infrequent but terrifying nights in the past when I woke in a panic, paralyzed, unable to call out for help. Now I simply stare at the folded paper, almost forgetting what it is.

A strong memory of Kieran comes back in a rush, keeping me from focusing on the paper in my hands. Kieran is with Michael and me at the Dom Turista. An earnest band is pumping out imitation Beatles. Kieran has just finished dancing with a dark-eyed, gold-toothed maiden who tells him she is a gynecologist from Kirghizia. As he returns her to her companions at a nearby table, everyone applauds. Michael picks up Kieran's camera and takes a picture of him in the midst of the gold-toothed young woman's friends and family. All the faces are flushed, from the vodka and the dancing and the heat of that long-ago August night. Then, to the wail of a central-African folk song, Kieran and Michael perform a drunken Irish *Ceilidh* dance. More robust applause.

I shake the memory away and look back at my hands, at Kieran's telegram in my hands. I notice that my hands are shaking.

I read it once, twice, and then again.

I don't understand.

Then I do understand, but I don't accept it.

No, it has to be a mistake.

Oh, God, it's not a mistake.

An accident. Michael has been killed in a "road accident," Kieran writes. He has tried to "ring" me, but the long-distance phone lines into Moscow have been continually busy. Will I please "ring" him in Shannon? He will then tell me the details of what happened.

For a long time I can't move. I read the words over and over.

I feel sick, I feel like going to sleep, I don't feel like crying, don't cry, won't cry: Is this shock?

Then I cry. For days I cry. And sleep. My Russian friends help me pack, feed me, never leave me alone. I let them make all my decisions. I dream that Michael is at the door: again and again, Michael is at the door.

Most of my belongings I leave behind: they will be put to good use. I come home to the States with only one suitcase and one cardboard box. The suitcase I unpack right away. It takes five weeks for me to get around to unpacking the box.

My little clay "burr" is the first thing out of the box. With big wide eyes he looks at me in mid-question: ". . . your lost chicken?"

Yes, I say, and I'm so grateful to you for bringing it home, for bringing it all back home to me here in America.

Burr sits on my windowsill eleven time zones distant from Moscow. We begin to piece together a new life.

Contributors

FAITH ADIELE
is the daughter of African and Scandinavian immigrants. She grew up on a farm in Washington State and began living and traveling alone at age fifteen. She studied anthropology, was ordained as a Buddhist nun, learned several languages, and has lived with artists, prostitutes, monks, drug smugglers, and political activists in Asia, Africa, Europe, and the Americas. She has been a fellow at the MacDowell Colony and the Ragdale Foundation and has been published in a variety of literary magazines such as *Ploughshares*, *Sage*, and *Ms*. She has also had work in several anthologies including *Names We Call Home: Autobiography on Racial Identity*; *Life Notes: Personal Writing by Contemporary Black Women*; *Testimony: Young African-Americans on Self-Discovery and Black Identity*; and *Miscegenation Blues*. Her work will appear in *Go Girl Guide: A Travel Guide for African American Women* and *Men We Cherish*. She is currently Crista McAuliffe Chair/Visiting Professor in English at Framingham State College and is working on a memoir about traveling to Africa at age twenty-six to meet her father for the first time.

ANDREA WRIGHT ALEMAZKOOR
was married in a Muslim wedding ceremony in Tehran in 1964 and spent eight years living and traveling in Iran. Her first newspaper job was with *The Tehran Journal*. Living in the Islamic country under the reign of Shah Mohammed Reza Pahlavi, Wright Alemazkoor was present at the outset of the Iranian Revolution and left the country just weeks before the return of Ayatollah Ruhollah Khomeini. She is currently a freelance writer based in San Antonio, Texas.

SHELLEY ANDERSON
has lived half her adult life in different countries, working for various international organizations. She feels more American every day, and bitterly resents the monopolization of that word by the U.S. right wing. Her nonfiction articles and short stories have appeared in over a dozen anthologies and have been translated into several languages. She is working on her first novel.

MELANIE BRAVERMAN
is a poet and fiction writer whose work has appeared in various journals including *The American Voice* and *American Poetry Review*. She is a 1996 recipient of

427

grants for both poetry and fiction from the Massachusetts Cultural Council. She is the author of the novel *East Justice* (Permanent Press, 1996).

Teresa Buerkle

lives in New York City, where she works as a writer and editor. She received a B.A. from New York University and an M.A. from the Writing Seminars at Johns Hopkins University. She is currently at work on a collection of stories set in Africa. "The Feast of Abraham" was inspired by an encounter with a young Moroccan boy living on the streets of Tangier. Worldwide an estimated one hundred million children live or work on the streets—the majority in hazardous or exploitive conditions. This story is dedicated to them.

Naomi Feigelson Chase

is the author of *Waiting for the Messiah in Somerville, Mass.* (poetry) and two poetry chapbooks, *The Judge's Daughter* and *Listening for Water*. She has also written books on child abuse and the sixties and many short stories, one of which was nominated for a Pushcart. She won the 1996 Hackney Literary Award for Fiction.

Jacqueline Cooper

was born in Alexandria, Egypt, and spent much of her adult life in Washington, D.C. She is the author of *Cocktails and Camels, Tales from Alexandria*, and author illustrator of *Angus and the Mona Lisa*. She was well known in the Washington area for her humorous watercolor paintings of cats who spoke "franglais" and had much in common with people. She is a member of P.E.N. International and now lives in Geneva, Switzerland.

Kathleen Coskran—see editors

Cynthia Morgan Dale's

short stories have appeared in *The South Carolina Review, The Bridge, The Amherst Review, The Potomac Review, Turnstile*, and other literary journals. She was the recipient of a Fiction Fellowship from the Edward F. Albee Foundation. She lives in New York City with her husband and twin children.

Margaret D. Datz

grew up as a Navy brat all over the United States, including Hawaii and American Samoa. She earned an M.A. in English literature from the University of Michigan; then married and raised a son and daughter while teaching writing and literature—and continuing to move every few years. After her divorce, she earned a Ph.D. in linguistics from the University of Colorado. She has taught and done linguistic research in Guatemala, China, and Costa Rica; she has traveled in Thailand, Hong Kong, Morocco, Egypt, Greece, Italy, Spain, Mexico, and Peru. She usually travels alone, preferring encounters with local people to monuments, and the questioning of one's own assumptions such encounters can cause. She has finished a book on her third stay in China and is now working on accounts of two other cross-cultural experiences: adoption in Guatemala and building a house in Costa Rica, where she is trying to learn to live in one place—a foreign place.

JEANNE D'HAEM

has a Ph.D. from New York University and is currently a public school administrator for the Roselle Park Public Schools in New Jersey. She has traveled extensively throughout the world and writes and lectures frequently about her adventures. She was a Peace Corps Volunteer in Northern Somaliland in 1968. Her book, *The Last Camel*, is about village life in Somalia and will be published in 1997 by Africa World Press of Lawrenceville, New Jersey. A short story, "Shifta," was published in *Going Upcountry*, an anthology edited by John Coyne and published by Scribners.

NICOLE DILLENBERG

is a Los Angeles writer and an underground actress who has appeared in several independent films. Her poetry has been published in the *Southern California Anthology*, *Poetsfeet*, and *Anabasis*, among others. Currently, she abridges audiobook manuscripts for Harper Collins, Bantam Doubleday Dell, and Time Warner Books.

ANITA FENG

received the Pablo Neruda Prize and grants from the National Endowment for the Arts and the Illinois Arts Council. Her book of poems, *Internal Strategies*, is available from the University of Akron Press. She works as a potter in the Seattle area specializing in musical instruments.

BRIGITTE FRASE

is Critic at Large for the *Hungry Mind Review* and is an editor at Milkweed Editions. She writes book reviews for national publications and has published poems and essays. She lives in Minneapolis with her husband and two sons, and is working on a book of personal essays about emigrating from Germany to the U.S. An essay about her father was a Notable Essay in the 1993 edition of *Best American Essays*. In 1994 she won the Nona Balakian Citation for distinguished reviewing from the National Book Critics Circle.

GRETCHEN GAD FOURNIER

works in Moorhead, Minnesota, for the Lake Agassiz Regional Library, managing public relations for the library system's thirteen branches across Minnesota. She writes mainly nonfiction, often influenced by her observations, perceptions, and impressions of France and its culture. Gad Fournier and her husband, François-Pierre Fournier, recently returned to the U.S. after living for a year in Paris. The couple resides in Fargo, North Dakota.

THEODOSIA T. GREENE

has written many travel pieces for the *Los Angeles Times*, *Travel*, *Boating*, *Ford Times*, *San Francisco Magazine*, and *In Britain*. She is working on two novels and an illustrated cat book, *A Flee in Your Ear*. When not traveling—which she loves to do—she teaches watercolor painting to ElderHostel students at the Grand Canyon and in Sedona, Arizona, where she lives.

Rachel Hall

lives in Rochester, New York, and teaches Creative Writing and literature at SUNY-Geneseo. Her writing has appeared in the *New Virginia Review*, *Black Warrior Review*, and *Crab Orchard Review*.

Elizabeth Ann Haugen

lives in Minneapolis by a park and works in an office downtown. She does most of her traveling these days by foot, though sometimes she takes her car to St. Paul, Minnesota, or North Dakota. It seems easier to get lost at home.

Lynne Hugo

is the author of two volumes of poetry, *The Time Change* and *A Progress of Miracles*, and forthcoming novels entitled *An Endurable World* and *Graceland*. The recipient of grants from the National Endowment for the Arts, the Ohio Arts Council, and the Kentucky Foundation for Women, she serves as Writer in Residence for various school districts in Ohio through the Artists in Education Program there. She is married to Alan deCourcy and has two children.

Christine Japely

has lived and worked in Spain, Saudi Arabia, Oregon, Massachusetts, and New York. She received an M.F.A. from the writing program at Columbia University. Her fiction, poetry, and essays have appeared in *The Florida Review*, *Global City Review*, *Kinesis*, *The Sun*, *Fine Print*, and other magazines. She has been a recipient of a *Florida Review* fiction prize, an Authors-in-the-Park award, and a Pushcart nomination.

Susan Jones

is a freelance writer in Portland, Oregon. She worked as a teacher in the former Soviet Union from 1988 to 1992. She intends to resume traveling in 1998 as soon as her son Adam graduates from high school and goes off to college.

Nancy T. Kelly

has traveled via bus, car, and train in Central America, Mexico, and parts of Europe, bicycled through southern France, hiked the Grand Canyon, and driven the Pacific Coast Highway from California to Seattle. Her favorite place to visit remains Minnesota's North Shore (of Lake Superior). In 1987 and 1988 she and her partner lived in Panamá. This was before the U.S. invasion, before she'd heard of Manuel Noriega or knew much about that narrow strip of land that divides two oceans. "*Sal Si Puedes*," a work of fiction, is her first published story. Currently she lives in Minneapolis and is working on a novel.

Ruth Moon Kempher

retired after twenty-one years of teaching at the St. Johns River Community College in St. Augustine, Florida, "in order to have more time to (supposedly) devote to writing, travel, and her small press." She has five acres out in the woods west of town, with two dogs. Her father lives next door by her creek. She makes yearly trips to England, Kansas (The Great Bend Poetry Rendezvous), Rochester, New York (for family reunions), and anywhere else she can tuck in. Her eighteenth book of poetry, *The Recycled Sonnets*, came out from Mellen Press in 1995. Her short story, "The Scrabble Game," won the 1995 Pirate's Alley William Faulkner Society's first prize. It will be published in a book by Kings Estate Press in 1996.

GERALDINE KENNEDY

is a graduate in political science and English of Pennsylvania State University and has an M.A. in urban planning from the University of California, Los Angeles. She served with the first Peace Corps Volunteers in Liberia. She edited the 1991 best-selling *From the Center of the Earth: Stories out of the Peace Corps*, an anthology of memoir and fiction set in the Third World and addressing the personal touchpoints of culture. Her travel adventure, *Harmattan: A Journey Across the Sahara* (in which "A Grain of Sand" was published) won the Paul Cowan Non-Fiction Award in 1995. Kennedy is currently publisher of Clover Park Press, a small press devoted to books about life's wonders and wanderings. She is the mother of three young adults and lives in California.

LINDA LAPPIN

is originally from Tennessee. She received her M.F.A. from the University of Iowa in 1978. Since that time she has lived in Italy where she teaches translation at the University of Viterbo. She has been the recipient of several prizes and fellowships in translation (including two from the National Endowment for the Arts) and has published numerous poems and stories in various U.S. literary magazines. She has just finished a novel, *Prisoner of Palmary*, set in the eighteenth century on an island near Naples.

BEA EXNER LIU

was born in 1907 in Northfield, Minnesota, and has had a career as varied as the crazy century through which she has lived. Daughter of an impecunious professor, she married an impecunious professor, and has been impecunious ever since. After graduating from Carleton College, she lived in inter-war Europe, Depression America, and war-torn China. She brought up her children in Minnesota and now lives in seniors housing in Minneapolis. Her memoir, *Remembering China, 1935–1945*, was a 1994 Minnesota Voices Project winner and was published by New Rivers Press in 1996. She also has stories, poems, and a novel, published and unpublished.

MARGARET TODD MAITLAND

is working on a book of essays called *The Dome of Creation*. She lives in St. Paul, Minnesota, with her husband and son and works as the managing editor of the *Hungry Mind Review*.

ANITA MATHIAS

was born in India. She has a B.A. (Honors) and an M.A. in English from Oxford University and an M.A. in Creative Writing and English from Ohio State University. Her essays have appeared in *The London Magazine*, *New Letters*, *America*, *The Journal*, and *The Best of Writers at Work* (1994). She won a Minnesota State Arts Board Fellowship for Prose in 1992, a Jerome Travel Grant in 1993, a Jacobsen Scholarship to the Wesleyan Writers Conference in 1994, and a full fellowship in Creative Nonfiction at the Vermont Studio Center in 1997. She lives in Williamsburg, Virginia.

SHARON MAYES
lives in Menlo Park, California. New Rivers Press published her novel, *Immune*, in 1987.

KAREN LAUDENSLAGER MCDERMOTT
is a visual artist (sculpture and works on paper) recently writing short stories, essays, and prose poems freelance in Geneva, Switzerland. She is a contributor to the *Courier* and the *Geneva Post*, local English-language publications, and is included in *Offshoots III*. She is a member of the Geneva Writers' Workshop. She directs an ensemble theater troupe for adolescents in which new work is created from original material.

LISA MCKHANN
lives in Bellingham, Washington.

MARGARET MCMULLAN'S
first novel, *When Warhol Was Still Alive* came out in 1994 and she has recently completed her second, *In My Mother's House,* which has its roots in "Making Connections" (the story in this anthology). Her work has appeared in *Glamour,* the Chicago *Tribune, Southern Accents,* and in several anthologies. She is twice the recipient of an Individual Artist Fellowship from the Indiana Arts Commission and the National Endowment for the Arts. She is currently an Associate Professor of English at the University of Evansville in Evansville, Indiana.

LAVONNE MUELLER
is currently New Plays editor of Applause Books. Her play, *Letters to a Daughter from Prison*—about Nehru and his daughter, Indira Ghandi, was produced at the First International Festival of the Arts in New York City and went on tour in India. Her play, *Violent Peace*, was produced in London in 1992 and was the "Critics Choice" in *Time Out* magazine. Her play, *Little Victories*, was produced in Tokyo, and *The Only Woman General* was produced in New York City and went on to the Edinburgh Festival where it was "Pick of the Fringe" by Scottish critics. She received the Roger Stevens Playwriting Award, is a Woodrow Wilson Scholar, a Lila Wallace Reader's Digest Writing Fellow, and has received a Guggenheim Grant, a Rockefeller Grand, three National Endowment for the Arts grants, a Fulbright to Argentina, an Asian Culture Council Grant to Calcutta, India, and a U.S. Friendship Commision Grant to Japan. Her plays have been produced by Dramatist Play Service, Samuel French, Applause Books, and Baker's Plays. Her textbook, *Creative Writing*, is used by students around the world. She taught at Columbia University for five years. As a Woodrow Wilson Visiting Scholar she has helped colleges around the U.S. set up writing programs. She has been an Arts America speaker for the United States Information Service in India, Finland, Romania, Japan, the former Yugoslavia, and Norway. She was recently a Fulbright Fellow to Jordan and received a National Endowment for the Humanities grant to do research in Paris during the summer of 1995. Her play, *American Dreamers*, was selected for the book *Best Short Plays, 1995–96.*

JAIDA N'HA SANDRA

is a graduate student in the Anthropology Department of the University of Hawaii. She is also a grantee fellow at the East-West Center. Her area focus is Indonesia, with research interests in identity issues in ethnically heterogenous communities. Her first book—*The Joy of Conversation: A Complete Guide to Salons*—will be published by the *Utne Reader* in April 1997. It is a manual for building community through neighborhood conversation. Her real joy, however, is philosophical travel writing. She is working on a trilogy set in Indonesia, Japan, and Tibet. She is seeking publication for her second book, *Gut Reactions*, from which the story in this anthology was extracted.

ANNE PANNING

is a Bowling Green State University M.F.A. graduate and a Ph.D. candidate in English at the University of Hawaii. She has published a collection of short fiction, *The Price of Eggs* (Coffeehouse Press), as well as short stories and creative nonfiction pieces in places such as the *South Dakota Review, Black Warrior Review, Ambergris*, and in the anthology *Writing for Our Lives: Writing By, For, and About Women*. Her story "What Happened" recently placed in the Authors in the Park short story contest. Her story "Pigs" was anthologized in *Stiller's Pond: New Fiction from the Upper Midwest* (New Rivers Press). In June 1995 she was awarded a fiction-writing fellowship at the Millay Colony for the Arts in upstate New York. She is now at work on a novel, *Butter*.

JOAN K. PETERS

is the author of *Manny and Rose*, a novel, and short fiction that has appeared in *The Female Body, Michigan Review*, and *Global City Review*. "Foreign Exchange" is part of a collection of travel stories she hopes to complete between raising her five-year-old daughter and finishing *Breaking All the Rules*, a book on mothering to be published by Addison Wesley in 1997. She and her family live in New York City.

NANCY RAEBURN

is a native of the Twin Cities area. *Mykonos: A Memoir*, her account of the ten years she lived and painted on a Greek island, was a 1990 Minnesota Voices Project winner and was published by New Rivers Press in 1992. She has also received the Academy of American Poets College Prize and the Wendy Parrish Prize for Poetry from Macalester College in St. Paul, Minnesota. Currently, she is teaching composition at the University of Minnesota while working toward an M.F.A. degree in creative writing and finishing the first draft of a new memoir about her family.

JUDY RAY

grew up on a farm in the south of England and graduated from the University of Southampton. She lived in Uganda for five years and has also spent time in India, New Zealand, and Australia. She has made her home—together with her poet-husband David Ray—in Kansas City, Missouri, since 1971 but she now lives in Tucson, Arizona. She has published three books of poetry—*Pebble Rings, Pigeons in the Chandeliers*, and *Tokens*—and is the author of a memoir, *Jaipur Sketchbook: Impressions of India*. She is co-editor, with David Ray, of *Fathers: A Collection of Poems*, forthcoming in June 1997 from St. Martin's Press.

CHERI REGISTER

writes and teaches the personal essay and memoir. She is the author of *Living with Chronic Illness: Days of Patience and Passion* and *"Are Those Kids Yours?" American Families with Children Adopted from Other Countries*, plus academic work published in the U.S. and Scandinavia. Her essay, "The Blue Workshirt," is listed as a Notable Essay in *Best American Essays 1996*. She is currently at work on a documentary memoir of the infamous 1959 meatpackers' strike at the Wilson Company in Albert Lea, Minnesota. She lives in Minneapolis with her two teenage daughters.

LISA RUFFOLO

lives in Madison, Wisconsin, with her husband and daughter. She received a B.A. from the University of Wisconsin-Madison and an M.A. from Johns Hopkins University. Her fiction has appeared in *Cosmopolitan, Mademoiselle, Shenandoah, The Voices We Carry: An Anthology of Writing by Italian-American Women,* and *From the Margin: Writings in Italian-Americana. Holidays,* her first collection of stories, was published by New Rivers Press.

GRETCHEN SCHERER

first began traveling because her parents were paying for it but was amazed by how addictive and illuminating it was. Now, even though she has to pay for it herself, she gets a fix whenever she can. When not traveling, she lives in Minneapolis where she teaches writing and composition, and spends a lot of time staring at a computer screen. She also writes occasional travel articles for the St. Paul *Pioneer Press.* "Lounge Girls" is part of a collection of sketches about travel and identity.

BÁRBARA SELFRIDGE

began accenting the first syllable of her first name in eighth grade, after a visit to Puerto Rico. She began pronouncing it with the accent in 1978–79 when she taught high school English in Puerto Rico. *Surrounded by Water,* her collection of short stories about that time, is looking for a publisher.

SUSAN M. TIBERGHIEN

is an American-born writer living in Geneva, Switzerland. Her narrative essays and short stories, widely published in the U.S. and Europe, have appeared in many anthologies, most recently in *Two Worlds Walking* (New Rivers Press, 1995), *Breaking Convention* (Crossing Press, 1995), and *Swaying* (University of Iowa Press, 1996). She is the author of *Looking for Gold* (Daimon Verlag, 1995). An active member of International PEN, she directs writers workshops in New York and Geneva, where she edits the literary review *Offshoots.*

KAREN WALSH

was born and raised in St. Paul, Minnesota. She has had several careers, including teaching in the Ivory Coast (West Africa), Turkey, and on the Navajo Reservation in the Southwest. She has also conducted management analysis for several federal agencies. She lives in Burke, Virginia, and teaches English as a Second Language at Northern Virginia Community College in Alexandria, Virginia. Ms. Walsh earned her undergraduate degree at the University of Minnesota and her master's at the University of New Orleans.

CATHERINE WATSON

is award-winning travel editor of the Minneapolis *Star Tribune*. She a Minnesota native who has been with the newspaper since 1966. She was named Lowell Thomas Travel Journalist of the Year in 1990 for a series on Eastern Europe. Also in 1990, she won the Society of American Travel Writers Photographer of the Year Award. No other travel journalist has won both of these national awards. She placed in the Lowell Thomas competition every year since 1985. After a five-year stint as editor of *Picture Magazine,* the *Tribune*'s Sunday supplement, she became travel editor in 1978 when the *Tribune* began its travel section. She shaped its format from the beginning and has written about topics as diverse as the Trans-Siberian Railway and St. Catherine's Monastery in the Sinai, about the mini-countries of Europe and the polar bears of Churchill, Manitoba. Her book, *Travel Basics,* a collection of travel advice published by the *Star Tribune* in 1984, was named Best Book for that year by the Central States Chapter of the Society of American Travel Writers and received the silver award for books in the Lowell Thomas Travel Journalism competition. In 1994 she won the the Minnesota Associated Press Sweepstakes Award for her first-person account of sexual assault. Headlined "Attack," the article appeared in the *Star Tribune* in March 1993. She has a B.A. from the University of Minnesota and an M.A. in Teaching from the College (now University) of St. Thomas in St. Paul, Minnesota.

SHARON WHITE

is an associate professor of English at Springfield College in Springfield, Massachusetts. Recent work of hers appears in *The Writing Path*, *Yankee Magazine*, and *Appalachia.*

ANITA WITT

is a native of Germany who emigrated to the United States in 1947. She now lives with her family in Portland, Oregon, where she divides her time between her practice of clinical social work and writing a memoir. Her stories have appeared in *Other Voices* and *Tamaqua.*

THE EDITORS

KATHLEEN COSKRAN

(co-editor and contributor) is the principal of Lake Country School in south Minneapolis. Her short fiction and essays have appeared in numerous publications and anthologies. Her collection of short stories, *The High Price of Everything*, published by New Rivers Press, won a Minnesota Book Award. She has also been the recipient of artist fellowships from the Bush Foundation and the National Endowment for the Arts.

C. W. TRUESDALE

was also the co-editor of *The House on Via Gombito* (with Madelon Sprengnether). He holds a Ph.D. in English and Comparative Literature from the University of Washington (Seattle) and is the publisher of New Rivers Press. He is a poet, short story writer, and essayist who lives in Minneapolis with his wife Vivian Vie Balfour.